INTELLECTUAL PROPERTY, TRADE AND DEVELOPMENT

Strategies to Optimize Economic Development in a TRIPS-Plus Era

INTELLECTUAL PROPERTY, TRADE AND DEVELOPMENT

Strategies to Optimize Economic Development in a TRIPS-Plus Era

Edited by

DANIEL J GERVAIS

University Research Chair in Intellectual Property and Osler Professor of Law, University of Ottawa

OXFORD
UNIVERSITY PRESS

OXFORD
UNIVERSITY PRESS

Great Clarendon Street, Oxford OX2 6DP

Oxford University Press is a department of the University of Oxford.
It furthers the University's objective of excellence in research, scholarship,
and education by publishing worldwide in

Oxford New York

Auckland Cape Town Dar es Salaam Hong Kong Karachi
Kuala Lumpur Madrid Melbourne Mexico City Nairobi
New Delhi Shanghai Taipei Toronto

With offices in

Argentina Austria Brazil Chile Czech Republic France Greece
Guatemala Hungary Italy Japan Poland Portugal Singapore
South Korea Switzerland Thailand Turkey Ukraine Vietnam

Oxford is a registered trade mark of Oxford University Press
in the UK and in certain other countries

Published in the United States
by Oxford University Press Inc., New York

First published 2007

British Library Cataloguing in Publication Data
Data available

Library of Congress Cataloging in Publication Data
Intellectual property, trade & development : strategies to optimize
economic development in a TRIPS plus era / edited by Daniel J. Gervais.
p. cm.
Includes index.
ISBN 978-0-19-921675-8
1. Intellectual property—Economic aspects. 2. Foreign trade regulation—Economic aspects. 3. Economic development. 4. Agreement on Trade-Related Aspects of Intellectual Property Rights (1994) I. Gervais, Daniel J., 1963- II. Title: Intellectual property, trade, and development.
K1401 . I5775 2007
346 . 04'8—dc22

2007036869

Typeset by Cepha Imaging Private Ltd., Bangalore, India
Printed in Great Britain
on acid-free paper by
Biddles Ltd, King's Lynn

ISBN 978–0–19–921675–8

1 3 5 7 9 10 8 6 4 2

CONTENTS—SUMMARY

CONTENTS

III OPTIMIZING DEVELOPMENT WITHIN AND OUTSIDE INTELLECTUAL PROPERTY NORMS

INTRODUCTION

The World Trade Organization's Agreement on Trade-Related Intellectual Property Rights (TRIPS Agreement) is now entering its third phase. The first phase began with a well-documented push by the United States government, later supported by the European Commission and the Japanese government, to link intellectual property and trade rules in the WTO as part of the Uruguay Round of Multilateral Trade Negotiations, which ended in Marrakech in April 1994. Phase One did not end with the Round, however. It continued for a few years after the establishment of the WTO, while most developing countries (very few of whom had been active participants in the negotiations)[1] fully grasped the detailed scope of their TRIPS commitments. That Phase was informed from the demanders' perspective by *addition narratives* according to which adding high levels of intellectual property to the laws of developing and least-developed nations (a) would protect the property of intellectual property holders in both rich and poorer countries (and, by generating additional profits, would in turn lead to more research and development); and (b) was necessary to jump-start economic growth in those countries (intellectual property seen as a necessary ingredient of development).

Phase Two began just before the new millennium. It was characterized initially by highly critical analyses of the TRIPS negotiation process, which was said to have been based on coercion of and/or ignorance by and/or a very bad 'bargain' for the developing world. Some critics also underscored the absence of empirical data to justify the addition narratives (or the export of partly empirically based justificatory theories from industrialized to developing nations) while others tried to demonstrate the inadequacy of 'Western' intellectual property norms to protect certain forms of traditional medicinal knowledge or traditional cultural expressions (sometimes referred to jointly as 'traditional knowledge'). This discourse went much further than the casuistry and polite obfuscation so prevalent in international diplomacy. A sense of outrage pervaded many of the discussions. Not surprisingly, it led to a recommendation that TRIPS should be resisted and new norms developed. Phase Two was thus informed by *subtraction*

[1] Daniel J Gervais, *The TRIPS Agreement: Drafting History and Analysis* (Sweet & Maxwell, 2003), 12–26.

narratives: the lesser the impact of TRIPS, the better the situation of developing countries would be. Several books, articles and reports were published to explain how TRIPS could be fought both within the WTO (for example by coalescing or insisting on technology transfers) and outside it (for example by fostering the emergence of alternative norms in other fora, such as the Convention on Biological Diversity—CBD).

In the meantime, multilateral norm-making designed to increase protection levels (and reduce some of the flexibilities that remain within TRIPS) became increasingly difficult. After the outbreak of the debate between several African and Latin American countries, on the one hand, and pharmaceutical companies, on the other, and the companies' ill-advised attempt to enforce patent rights in the face of thousands of patients unable to afford antiretroviral therapies, increasing multilateral levels of patent protection became practically impossible, at least for the predictable future. In the Doha Round initial suggestions to strengthen the enforcement section of TRIPS, or incorporate two 1996 treaties negotiated under the auspices of the World Intellectual Property Organization (WIPO) dealing with copyright on the internet, were all but abandoned. In addition, recent efforts in WIPO to negotiate new treaties (e.g. on database protection, harmonization of substantive patent law, rights of broadcasters and webcasters) have met with strong opposition, in particular from developing countries. Also, while the WTO attempted to address some of the concerns raised by the developing world (e.g. by allowing the TRIPS Council to work on the relationship between TRIPS and the CBD and insisting on documenting compliance with the industrialized countries' technology transfer obligations), WIPO started work on a Development Agenda designed to align the Organization's work with the interests of the developing world. As of this writing, work on the Agenda was accelerating but its fate remained uncertain.

Yet the TRIPS demanders did not abandon their efforts. They began using their political ammunition in bilateral negotiations to negotiate trade and investment treaties. Recent bilateral agreements signed by the European Union and the United States almost always contain 'TRIPS-Plus' norms, including undertakings by developing countries not to use specific TRIPS flexibilities.

TRIPS has now entered a third phase, one that is informed by *calibration narratives*. TRIPS are no longer seen as the enemy of the developing world. The elements of the calibration process are many: (a) the recognition that developing countries are very different, from Chile to China, from Bolivia to Burkina Faso or from Egypt to India, and consequently may need different implementations of TRIPS, instead of 'cookie cutter' norm implants; (b) the recognition that below certain developmental thresholds, the introduction of high levels of intellectual property protection will not generate positive impacts (as was evinced by the extension of transitional periods available for least-developed WTO members); (c) the recognition that intellectual property protection is necessary to develop innovation and foreign direct investment (including technology transfers) but in itself is insufficient to achieve developmental objectives; (d) consequently, the recognition that any complete TRIPS implementation must form part of a broader strategic initiative; and finally (e) the recognition that the sudden introduction of high levels of protection and enforcement may induce significant welfare impacts, which must also be managed. This book is about the various facets of this third phase. Its aims are, first, to allow the reader to understand the three phases of TRIPS by presenting the salient findings of Phases One and Two and, second, to offer concrete analyses and policy suggestions to move Phase Three forward.

A number of analyses conducted during Phase Two confronted a fundamental two-prong query, namely (a) what is the causal relationship between intellectual property protection and foreign direct investment (FDI), and (b) does increased FDI necessarily lead to growth in the recipient economy's innovation? Because that query is at the heart of several empirical analyses of the impact of the internationalization of intellectual property protection and informs many of the policy outcomes suggested in Phase Three, it is visible in many chapters of this book.

The book intentionally presents different perspectives. The purpose is not to convince readers that there is a single best solution to TRIPS implementation and innovation policy development, because there isn't. Rather, the book presents a thorough analysis and a number of alternative options, a reflection of the myriad domestic policy configurations that should emerge from proper innovation policy analyses in each WTO member country.

The book is divided into three parts. Part I offers four complementary perspectives on the policy and theoretical levers necessary to understand how TRIPS impacts economic development and the challenges of its implementation. These include analyses of the emergence of the TRIPS Agreement as part of the Uruguay Round, and its interface with other international norms. A significant portion of Part I is devoted to recent empirical analyses of the impact of the TRIPS Agreement and, more broadly, of intellectual protection in all parts of the world, with particular emphasis on differences among impacts in various countries based on factors such as level of development, infrastructure, political systems, and education. Reflecting the underlying hypothesis that each country and region may face different challenges in implementing TRIPS and developing an innovation strategy, Part II offers various national or regional perspectives. From Africa to

Latin America, from the Arab World to the demander's perspective (in this case the United States), there is much to be said for regional analyses to complement global ones. Part III presents ways to develop and (re)structure international intellectual property regulation from within and also from without. The Part examines normative intersections that are likely to reshape the realm of international intellectual property. Some of those intersections are with other bodies of law, including international human rights and the related notion of substantive equality. They are not entirely new, but they are on the increase in both scope and depth. Other intersections are newer, such as with labour laws and standards. Intellectual property is intersecting with and readjusting to a better and less Eurocentric understanding of 'culture' and scientifically useable knowledge, in particular in the field of what is commonly referred to as traditional knowledge. There are several efforts afoot to reshape intellectual property norms. A concrete example that probably best illustrates those endeavours is WIPO's work towards a new treaty on *substantive* patent law (the Patent Law Treaty of 1 June 2000 deals essentially with more administrative issues) which would harmonize national laws to a much higher degree than the TRIPS Agreement, most notably perhaps in curtailing definitional flexibilities with respect to fundamental notions of inventiveness (non-obviousness), applicability (utility) and novelty. An epilogue offers concrete and often novel suggestions on various facets of the TRIPS implementation equation, viewed as a part of a broader context consisting of trade rules, and the need to protect biodiversity, protect traditional knowledge and develop effective domestic innovation policy, while limiting undue social welfare costs.

The following pages of this Introduction highlight the unifying threads of this book but are also designed to assist the reader who wishes to focus her reading on specific issues by pointing out the main topics covered in each of the 15 chapters.

Part I begins with a chapter penned by the editor entitled simply 'TRIPS and Development'. It presents an overview of policy-related developments concerning the TRIPS Agreement in Phases One and Two; a distillation of some of the lessons learned (mostly during Phase Two), many individual aspects of which are developed in detail in other chapters; an overview of the most recent policy developments; and concrete steps to understand how a national innovation policy including the implementation of TRIPS obligations, (or the revision of an existing one), should be optimized. It also offers thoughts on the displacement of the 'business of innovation' to developing countries where innovation policies apparently are working. The chapter weaves the canvas on which the other chapters will be painted.

Chapter 2, 'The International Intellectual Property System: Treaties, Norms, National Courts, and Private Ordering', was authored by one of the foremost international intellectual property scholars in the United States, Professor Graeme Dinwoodie. It begins with the completely accurate observation 'that viewing intellectual property through the prism of trade itself offers an incomplete explanation of the changes that have occurred in international intellectual property lawmaking', and presents the 'role of both litigation in national courts and private ordering by commercial actors in establishing international intellectual property norms'. Indeed, national courts are increasingly called upon to interpret international norms, some of which are transposed directly in regional or national laws and regulations (an obvious example is the 'three-step test' to measure the TRIPS-conformity of exceptions to copyright, design and patent rights, which was included in European Union legislation and recently applied by the French Supreme Court (*cour de cassation*)). Any complete implementation of TRIPS must take account, therefore, of the role played by courts in applying and, to a certain extent at least, defining intellectual property norms. Professor Dinwoodie considers the impact of private ordering on the development and application of intellectual property norms, including the use of technology known as Digital Rights Management to limit access to and/or use of copyright content. The chapter also discusses the somewhat hackneyed notion of 'balance', observing that 'the assessment of "balance" operates almost as a Rorschach test. The balance (let alone the oft-cited "delicate balance") that intellectual property strives to achieve is a rather protean concept. Yet it is now increasingly common to hear international instruments decried or celebrated depending upon their concern for balance. Every side claims the mantle of balance.'

Chapter 3, entitled 'Economic Growth and Intellectual Property Rights Protection: A Reassessment of the Conventional Wisdom' by Professor Robert Ostergard Jr presents a thorough, up-to-date economic analysis both of the economic growth perspective and its link with intellectual property protection, and of the determinants of IPR protection in developing nations. Using economic data is essential to understand the impacts of intellectual property protection and the factors that influence the diversity of those impacts in different national economic systems. This chapter is testament to the growing importance of economic analysis in intellectual property policy making and the search for evidence-based solutions—which also explains why economic analytical tools are used in other chapters as well. Professor Ostergard opens the chapter with a rather blunt assessment: 'In the conventional literature on the relationship between IPR and economic growth, the argument for strong IPR protection is predicated on the assumption that a positive relationship exists between strong IPR protection and economic growth (and development). This chapter is dedicated to the task of providing an empirical reassessment of the economic growth and IPR protection relationships. The research presented here indicates that there is reason to question at least part of the assumed relationship between IPR and economic growth. Moreover, with this relationship in question, additional evidence suggests that IPR protection is not always enacted as part of sound economic policy, but rather as a result of political pressure.' After a thorough review of available data and measurements (and of the concerns about such measurements), Professor Ostergard presents an empirical model of the determinants of IPR protection and ends with a discussion of the dilemma of developing countries which, at least in the initial stages following the introduction of high levels of protection, often finance growth in intellectual property exporting markets (mostly industrialized nations) at the expense of their own growth and development.

Chapter 4, by Professor Anselm Kamperman Sanders of Maastricht University, continues the analysis in Chapter 3. It adds an essential facet to the picture, namely the interaction between multilateral and bilateral norm-making efforts. In recent years, there has been a major push by a number of key players, in particular Europe and the United States, to enter into bilateral trade and/or investment treaties that almost always contain 'TRIPS-Plus' intellectual property provisions. The purpose of these provisions seems to be two-fold: first, to 'rectify' the legislative framework of the signatory country (which agrees to this because of perceived benefits of freer trade with the United States or Europe). This explains the number of very specific provisions contained in each agreement. Second, these provisions establish a new normative international baseline, for example on anti-circumvention of Digital Rights Management technology. Professor Kamperman Sanders begins with an assessment of the proper role of the State in the traditional policy tug-of-war between *laissez-faire* and interventionism, underlining the differences among the various intellectual property rights. Noting the rapid increase in bilateral treaties with an intellectual property component, he criticizes the 'one size fits all' approach which may clash with the need to take account of the special circumstances of developing countries generally, and each country or region in particular. Questioning the simple assumption that high intellectual property standards lead to higher FDI, he notes accurately that it is the 'ability to absorb knowledge and human capital [that] drives the capacity to innovate'. He concludes that 'for IPRs, capacity building, with an emphasis on effective and transparent enforcement mechanisms, may be much more useful than efforts to harmonize and increase substantive rights according to a "one-size-fits-all" philosophy.'

Part II offers regional perspectives on the impact of TRIPS. It seemed natural to begin the global *tour d'horizon* in China, where paradoxically innovation has grown at a rapid pace amid serious concerns about piracy and counterfeiting.

Professor Peter Yu seemed an ideal candidate to help us understand the Chinese picture. Like other contributors to this volume, Professor Yu questions the simplistic link between intellectual property protection and FDI growth. His analysis of developments in China point to at least two additional factors: 'First, the country needs to have a strong capacity to imitate foreign products and technologies. [. . .] Second, the country needs to have a sufficiently large market to enable foreign firms to capture economies of scale or scope.' Yet he embraces the exceptionalist approach: 'Commentators often consider China as an exception to the causal relationship between intellectual property protection and economic development. However, China is not the exception they suggested. Rather, it reflects the ambiguous relationship between intellectual property protection and economic development and the complex interplay of the different location advantages that can affect private investment decisions.' The chapter then offers a vivid and very complete picture of factors, both external (including pressure by the United States) and internal, that led China to adopt higher intellectual property standards—some of which are still deficient in their practical application—against the backdrop of the progressive opening of the Chinese market, occasional political unrest and technological change. Professor Yu suggests that the situation in China should change in parallel with economic growth: 'Although piracy and counterfeiting problems remain widespread in China, history suggests that intellectual property protection will vastly improve when the overall benefits of such protection begin to outweigh its costs. After all, a similar change occurred in Japan in the 1970s and in Hong Kong, Singapore, South Korea and Taiwan in the 1980s.'

The well-known TRIPS expert and critic Carlos Correa from the University of Buenos Aires in Argentina is ideally placed to present the impact of TRIPS in Latin America. In a well-documented chapter, Professor Correa notes that TRIPS was implemented in that region (as in many others) despite 'the paucity of evidence on the impact of intellectual property rights'. He notes, however, that over the last ten to fifteen years, a number of studies have been published in Latin America to assess the impact of TRIPS, beginning with analyses of the welfare costs of pharmaceutical patents but extending to studies dealing with the growth of copyright-based industries and risks to biodiversity and germplasm. The chapter then offers an excellent overview of legislative changes in various sectors and countries as a result of TRIPS implementation and bilateral negotiations. In Part III of his chapter, Dr. Correa describes efforts to protect traditional knowledge in Latin America. That region, one of the richest in the world in TK, has taken concrete legislative and administrative measures to document and protect many forms of traditional knowledge in keeping with the CBD. A good example is the Andean Community of Nations Common Regime on Access to Genetic

Resources (Decision 391) adopted in 1996. In his concluding thoughts, Professor Correa notes that after the initial, rather mechanical implementation of TRIPS (TRIPS Phase One), and following the availability of studies on the impact of TRIPS (TRIPS Phase Two), Latin America is now in a third phase fuelled by their better understanding of the intellectual property policy equations, a desire to adapt the international framework to meet their needs, but also regional and bilateral trade discussions. He notes this 'new wave of changes [. . .] triggered in some countries by the signature of FTAs with the USA. Chile, Colombia, Peru, Dominican Republic and the Central American countries have already undertaken that process, which implies, *inter alia*, the extension under certain circumstances of the patent term, exclusivity for test data and the patent–registration linkage for pharmaceutical products. [. . .] In addition to joining the WCT and WPPT, many Latin American countries have introduced the protection of utility models, as a means to promote minor or incremental innovations that characterize the innovation path in countries without a sophisticated scientific and technological infrastructure. Some countries have also been active in developing *sui generis* regimes for the protection of TK, in some cases based on intellectual property concepts.'

The following chapter by Professor Ikechi Mgbeoji considers the impacts of TRIPS in Africa in the wake of the public health crises caused by the proliferation of HIV, malaria and other tropical diseases. He begins his analysis by noting the diversity of the African continent and the 'foreign' nature of intellectual property: '[The] specific forms of IPRs recognised by TRIPs have their origins in the cultural, legal, and economic traditions of continental Europe and of western jurisprudence and economic tradition. The prevalent notion that TRIPS-compatible IPRs are universal truths distanced from the cultural and genetic fingerprints of their European origins and unmediated by economic impulses is simply false.' Noting the existence of divergent studies and narratives, he attributes the 'scepticism towards levels of IPR protection' to 'economic and political realities on the ground and the general perception that the benefits from such strong IPR enforcement are unidirectional and a drain of scarce resources from the continent'. Professor Mgbeoji suggests that African countries should be allowed to tweak and adapt their domestic IPR policies to suit their perceived industrial and economic needs, like the industrialized economies of today did yesterday. He then paints a very helpful sub-regional picture of efforts to implement TRIPS and TRIPS-Plus norms in Africa, explaining the economic, health-related and cultural factors that have influenced policy making and its practical application. In a part entitled 'The Paths Not Taken', he looks at various initiatives questioning the benefits of patents on life forms and biological resources, or the protection of geographical indications. He also questions whether Africa can reap the promised benefits of

TRIPS without adequate training in intellectual property law (and relevant institutions), and world-class scientists. Without proper resources, Africa may not be able to benefit from TRIPS to compensate for the welfare costs of higher protection, and needs to develop adequate local policies as it moves to implement or revisit existing implementations of TRIPS and TRIPS-Plus norms.

Chapter 8, entitled 'Trademark Policy: The Case of Arab Countries', by Professor Amir Khoury, presents the findings of the author's unprecedented empirical analysis of the impacts of the post-TRIPS introduction of trademark protection in Arab countries. Given that many of these countries went from a very low level of protection to TRIPS-compliant norms very rapidly, they offer a unique laboratory to measure those impacts. Two inescapable sources of tension are the closing down of counterfeiting-based businesses, on the one hand, and the less rapid movement from intellectual property consumer status to producer status, on the other. That is, in fact, one of the principal sources of tension observed in Phase Two of TRIPS: developing countries were asked to make the transition to higher intellectual property norms as a precondition for receiving FDI and technology transfers, which, in turn, were supposed to accelerate economic growth. However, the negative impacts of the new norms were necessarily felt first, ie before any IPR-induced growth became measurable, and certainly well before any benefits of noticeable growth became visible from the average citizen's perspective. In his chapter, Professor Khoury examines the role of the development and dependency theories, 'poster children' of Phases One and Two of TRIPS respectively. He then turns to a careful examination of the trademark policy of Arab countries and presents the findings of an empirical analysis of the impact of TRIPS on trademark use, including the number of trademark registrations. In keeping with the exposition of the lessons from TRIPS Phase Two and the emerging tenets of Phase Three, he concludes that the 'conduct of Arab countries appears to be driven by two primary concerns: namely, the possibility of losing foreign investments, and the worry about economic sanctions that might be imposed due to the lack of protection for intellectual property rights', and adds that, while his analysis supports trademark protection based on moral and economic rationales, 'the law should also be formulated in accordance with the needs of developing countries, namely by ensuring that they are able to secure a competitive edge in the world economy'.

It would not have been particularly productive in the context of this book on the intellectual property and development nexus to analyze the impact of TRIPS in demander countries such as the United States or Western Europe. Very few significant changes were made to national legislation in those countries as a result of the TRIPS Agreement. However, their perspective provides essential contextual ingredients to understanding TRIPS. Chapter 9, entitled 'Intellectual Property, Trade and Development: A View from the United States', offers a unique perspective, one that is useful for understanding both the demanders' perspective and the interface between Phases One and Two of TRIPS. Its author, the Hon. Jean R Homere, works at the United States Patent and Trademark Office (USPTO) but is also the founder of the Haitian–American Intellectual Property Association. Mr Homere is an advocate for the introduction of intellectual property in the developing world, suggesting that 'only technical progress can help stimulate their economies'. Yet while Mr Homere argues that there are significant advantages to adopting high intellectual property protection (especially as a precondition for increased FDI and technology transfers), he acknowledges the significant costs (and costs which were not fully understood and perhaps underestimated during TRIPS discussions), in particular for least-developed economies. In that respect, he concludes that, in least-developed countries, 'traditional implementations of intellectual property are not too cost-effective and pragmatic. For such countries, it appears that a more suitable approach should involve the protection of traditional knowledge as part of their intellectual property systems. This approach would stimulate the interests of such countries by allowing them to participate in the intellectual property process in more active manner as well as to fully derive the economic benefits that intellectual property has to offer.'

Part III presents a number of key intersections between intellectual property and other policy priorities and bodies of law and suggests policy options to optimize development within and outside intellectual property norms. The first chapter of Part III, by Professor Ruth Okediji, focuses on the intersection of international intellectual property and human rights. This area—and more generally the interface between intellectual property and other rights—is one of the fastest growing areas of study in intellectual property scholarship. While it was generally assumed until recently that, beyond occasional skirmishes with the right to free expression or competition law, intellectual property norms had sufficient intrinsic checks and balances (including exceptions such as fair use of material protected by copyright and trademark, or experimental use of patented products and processes), the increasing importance of individual users in copyright enforcement proceedings (caused in particular by the emergence of peer-to-peer technology), and the conflict between patents on pharmaceuticals and the right to life, have shown that new *extrinsic* equilibria must now be found.

The chapter begins with the assertion that the TRIPS Agreement 'advances a historical agenda for a truly transnational law of intellectual property by requiring incorporation of globally negotiated standards into each member country's domestic system. Unlike previous multilateral treaties, which established a framework for cooperation within which shared national interests could be pursued in coordinate fashion, the TRIPS Agreement articulates the bare elements of an international public policy.' There are, in other words, several policy and discursive gaps that need to be filled before a complete TRIPS implementation is possible (one that will effect an increase in domestic innovation and creativity). Instead of limiting her analysis to the potential conflicts between human rights and intellectual property, Professor Okediji offers a more synergistic perspective of the 'efforts to use human rights law [e.g. the rights to development and self-determination] as a source of norms capable of transforming the international intellectual property into an instrument of development'. In Part II of her chapter, Professor Okediji asks whether cultural claims are tenable and, concluding in the affirmative (within certain parameters), she suggests inventing a 'cultural intellectual property law'. In Part III, she takes a fresh look at international property doctrine and notably utilitarianism, and questions whether the dominant trends in TRIPS implementation are achieving the goals of promoting innovation and creativity in many developing countries. In that respect, she notes that 'the deeper question for developing countries is whether and how intellectual property rights make sense given the present realities of life in these regions. Doctrinal narratives are vitally important in resisting the wholesale propertization of knowledge goods. However, they cannot replace the fundamental need of developing countries to determine how to stimulate innovation domestically, or whether intellectual property rights as constructed can viably contribute towards long-term economic development.'

Chapter 11 by Professor Peter Drahos of Australia National University, one of the world's foremost experts on traditional knowledge (TK) protection, presents 'A Networked Responsive Regulatory Approach to Protecting Traditional Knowledge'. Reflecting the complexity of traditional knowledge forms of expression, Professor Drahos begins his analysis by noting that an optimal regulatory approach to TK protection should involve hard law and soft law, but also 'non-law forms (for example, codes of ethics and protocols)'. He suggests that responsive regulation in this area makes sense (which would seem to be true for intellectual property policy writ large). His approach is 'based on the idea that regulatory responses must take into account the motivations and conduct of those being regulated and these must guide the degree of intervention by the regulator. Its most distinctive idea is that the tools of regulation can be ordered in a way that enhances self-regulation, thereby reducing the actual need for governmental coercion while at the same time retaining it as an answer for some kinds of regulatory problems.' For example, he describes an adequate 'enforcement pyramid' enforcement which begins with persuasion and dialogue and moves up the pyramid using responses that are increasingly severe. Such a pyramid is described in detail in the second half of the chapter. In proposing a new international framework for TK, he concludes, first, that a treaty would be helpful not just because it would bind signatory governments but because a 'treaty that articulates general principles may over time evolve into a powerful international regime with a high rate of compliance'. In examining the potential contents of such a treaty, he discusses the challenges in the application of national treatment and most-favoured nation treatment and suggests that mutual recognition might be more relevant. The principle is applied to services such as banking and insurance. The normative heart of the treaty would be misappropriation of TK, a concept which has 'fertile vagueness', thus allowing for different possible statutory and non-statutory actions. This also seems to be the approach of WIPO's recent set of proposed TK Provisions. The chapter then considers the impact of fair trade and disclosure of origins rules. On the latter issue, he notes that 'probably the best chance that developing countries have of obtaining a disclosure standard is in the WTO, where the politics of complex linkages across the many sectors of the WTO may work in their favour. A disclosure standard in a treaty on TK would almost certainly consign that treaty to the waste paper basket.'

In Chapter 12 by Professor Chantal Thomas, the intersection of labour rules and intellectual property is discussed. Relatively little has been published on this issue, which is of fundamental importance for countries developing an innovation strategy within global trade and intellectual property rules. As the author notes in her introduction, '[t]he chapter relates the NAFTA Corn Case to prevailing discourses on trade, labour and intellectual property, showing that these discourses have not yet satisfactorily incorporated important lessons from each other'. For example, what is the impact of labour migration, or of economic industrialization and globalization, which rely on the technology yielded by biodiversity and may threaten physical environments and social practices? Is development (defined mostly as economic growth) compatible with environmental concerns and the protection of biodiversity? Up to now, labour rules and labour flows were seen as an (*ex post*) *result* of trade flows and economic growth, not an (*ex ante*) part of the development policy equation. However, as 'the NAFTA corn example demonstrates, [. . .] labour flows may actually catalyze a particular interaction between trade policy and biodiversity' and (in the corn case because it dealt with a resource so important economically and culturally in Mexico) increase local resistance to higher intellectual property protection. The chapter discusses TRIPS Article 27.3, the Convention on the Protection of New Varieties of Plants (UPOV), and private sector efforts to maintain and protect biodiversity against the normative backdrop of the CBD. The relationship between the CBD and TRIPS has been the subject of heated debates both in the TRIPS Council and among non-governmental observers over the past few years.

The following chapter, co-authored by Professors Jerome Reichman of Duke University and Rochelle Dreyfuss of New York University, examines WIPO's efforts on the Substantive Patent Law Treaty (SPLT), which aims to reduce distortions of litigation outcomes ('different applications of domestic and international patent norms to the same set of facts [leading] to conflicting judgments') in an integrated world marketplace. The chapter argues that deeper harmonization of substantive patent law is unwise at this juncture for several reasons. It would aggravate the distributional impacts of TRIPS in several developing nations, which are unable to benefit fully from increases in FDI owing to 'their different national and regional capabilities, institutions, and endowments [which] limit the developing countries' absorptive capacities and reduce the potential benefits of open markets for knowledge goods'. They also note that while a number of bilateral agreements have reduced the definitional flexibilities contained in the TRIPS Agreement, those were bargained for, that is, exchanged for trade liberalization measures. The authors also note that a 'freeze' on the development of patent law would have potentially deleterious consequences for patent holders in industrialized nations. As illustrated by ongoing work in the US Congress and in Europe, many legislators believe that patent law 'badly needs reform'. It hardly seems appropriate, then, to crystallize multilaterally standards that are often viewed as inadequate, in particular those dealing with software, business model or biotechnological inventions. The authors also question whether it is possible to achieve the stated aims of the negotiation: is it possible to agree a single standard for the 'height' of the inventive step that 'would suit countries at different levels of technological sophistication and for all kinds of intellectual advances'? Instead, Professors Dreyfuss and Reichman suggest 'a method for lowering the costs that discrepancies in national laws impose on international actors and a system that will gradually enable innovators in all countries to reach the world market by means that are geared to their different national and regional capabilities and endowments.'

In Chapter 14, Professor Margaret Chon presents the case for the inclusion of a substantive equality principle at the intersection of intellectual property, trade and development. The goal of this inclusion would be 'the enhancement of human freedom and capabilities through knowledge goods'. She discusses two paradigms for development, namely growth and freedom. The latter, she notes, 'emphasizes its multi-dimensional aspects . . . intellectual property not only stimulates innovation but also protects knowledge goods that enhance human capabilities, which in turn build national capacity for innovation.' As was illustrated in several other chapters in the book, different solutions are required for 'countries placed along various points of the development and trade spectrum'. She adds that '[g]lobal consumers, whether situated in developed or developing countries, simply do not benefit from the global trade in knowledge goods in the same way that they do from the reduction in tariffs on tangible goods.' Hence, the 'recipes' developed in the trade realm may not apply as easily to ideational goods. It is not entirely surprising, therefore, to see that a number of well-known economists, including Joseph Stiglitz and Jagdish Bhagwati, have lamented the inclusion of intellectual property standards in the WTO framework. Professor Chon's analysis is an essential part of the picture, but it also forms part of a broader context. She notes that the 'current *aporias* about the role of intellectual property law in development reflect ongoing perplexities about the overall project of law and development . . . Very little explicit reflection takes place within intellectual property about its relationship to development law, much less to development itself.' Her chapter, and this book as a whole, are a contribution to that debate.

The Epilogue is a 'non-scholarly' endeavour, the principal aim of which is to present possible answers to some of the questions that the editor encountered while assisting with the implementation of TRIPS in over 40 countries. Because dozens of countries implemented TRIPS mechanically (by implanting norms in their legal system) with few if any of the other essential measures required to maximize the benefits of TRIPS while minimizing its negative impacts, several developing economies are not able to take advantage of intellectual property protection, while trying to weather welfare costs resulting from such protection. The chapter, entitled 'TRIPS—An Implementation Toolbox', builds on the analyses contained in the first chapters and offers policy makers practical (though by no means exhaustive) advice that may be useful when implementing TRIPS and/or revising an existing implementation to optimize their innovation policy. It shows that intellectual property policy is inextricably linked to economic growth in a knowledge-based economy and that a successful innovation policy should also weave sometimes complex relations with trade and investment rules, administrative and judicial systems, education, labour, and human rights. This may very well be the most important challenge facing policy makers in this century.

Ottawa
April 2007

LIST OF CONTRIBUTORS

The Editor

Daniel J Gervais is University Research Chair in Intellectual Property and Osler Professor of Law at the Faculty of Law of the University of Ottawa (Common Law Section). He was Acting Dean of the Section. Prior to his teaching career, Professor Gervais was successively Legal Officer at the GATT (now WTO); Head of Section at the World Intellectual Property Organization (WIPO); Deputy Secretary General of the International Confederation of Societies of Authors and Composers (CISAC); and Vice-President, International of Massachusetts-based Copyright Clearance Center, Inc. (CCC).

The Contributing Authors

Margaret Chon is a Professor at Seattle University School of Law and the current Director of the Center for the Study of Justice in Society at Seattle University. Her scholarly interests include technology, law and critical theory. Author of over 40 articles, book chapters and essays, including recent works about global intellectual property and development, she is also a co-author of *Race, Rights and Reparation: Law and the Japanese American Internment* (Aspen, 2001). She is a graduate of Cornell University College of Arts and Science (AB, 1979), the University of Michigan School of Public Health (MHSA, 1981) and the University of Michigan Law School (JD *cum laude* 1986).

Carlos Correa is Director of the Center for Interdisciplinary Studies on Industrial Property and Economics, and of the Postgraduate Course on Intellectual Property at the Law Faculty, University of Buenos Aires. He has been a visiting professor in postgraduate courses at several universities, and consultant to UNCTAD, UNIDO, UNDP, WHO, FAO, IDB, INTAL, World Bank, SELA, ECLA, UNDP, South Centre, and other regional and international organizations. He has advised several governments on intellectual property and innovation policy. He was a member of the UK Commission on Intellectual Property and of the Commission on Intellectual Property, Innovation and Public Health established by the World Health Assembly. He is the author of several books and numerous articles.

Graeme B Dinwoodie is Professor of Law, Associate Dean, and Director of the Program in Intellectual Property Law, at Chicago–Kent College of Law. He also holds a Chair in Intellectual Property Law at Queen Mary College, University of London. Professor Dinwoodie has authored numerous articles on intellectual property law. He holds a First Class Honours LLB degree from the University of Glasgow, an LLM from Harvard Law School (where he was a John F Kennedy Scholar), and a JSD from Columbia Law School (where he was a Burton Fellow). He was elected to membership in the American Law Institute in 2003.

Peter Drahos is a Professor in Law and the Director of the Centre for the Governance of Knowledge and Development in the Regulatory Institutions Network at the Australian National University. He holds a Chair in Intellectual Property at Queen Mary College, University of London. His publications include *A Philosophy of Intellectual Property* (Dartmouth, 1996), and *Information Feudalism: Who Controls the Knowledge Economy?* (with John Braithwaite) (Earthscan, 2002).

Rochelle Cooper Dreyfuss is the Pauline Newman Professor of Law at NYU School of Law, and Director of its Engelberg Center on Innovation Law and Policy. She holds BA and MS degrees in Chemistry and served as Articles and Book Review Editor of the *Law Review* at Columbia University, where she was awarded her JD. She clerked for Chief Judge Wilfred Feinberg (Second Circuit) and Chief Justice Warren E Burger (Supreme Court). She serves on the National Academy of Sciences Committee on Science, Technology and Law, as co-Reporter for the American Law Institute Project on Intellectual Property: Principles Governing Jurisdiction, Choice of Law, and Judgments in Transnational Disputes, and was a consultant to the Federal Trade Commission. She writes on issues in intellectual property and civil procedure and has edited books in both fields.

Hon. Jean R Homere is Administrative Patent Judge at the USPTO Board of Patent Appeals and Interferences. He previously held the positions of Legal Advisor, Supervisory Patent Examiner and Primary Examiner at the USPTO. He taught *Introduction to Patent Procedure and Practice, Patent Law and Evidence* at the USPTO Patent Academy. He is a co-founder of the Haitian–American Intellectual Property Association. He holds a BSEE from University of Connecticut, MSIS from George Washington University, Master of Legal Administration from Marymount University and a JD from George Mason Law School.

Amir H Khoury is a lecturer at the Faculty of Law in Tel Aviv University. He was awarded a PhD in Intellectual Property Law (Haifa University, 2004) and holds an LLM in International Business & Trade Law (Fordham University, New York, 1998). Dr Khoury specializes in Intellectual Property Law and international trade as well as civil procedure. He has published a number of research papers and has presented his works around the world, namely in the United States, Jordan, Israel, Germany, Belgium, Italy, and Oman.

Ikechi Mgbeoji is Associate Professor at Osgoode Hall Law School of York University, Toronto. Educated in Nigeria, Canada, and Germany, his main research and teaching interests are in the areas of international, comparative and transnational law; international intellectual property law; and environmental law. His recent books include *Collective Insecurity: The Liberian Crisis, Unilateralism, and Global Order* (UBC Press, 2004) and *Global Biopiracy* (UBC Press, 2006).

Ruth Okediji is the William L Prosser Professor of Law, and Solly Robins Distinguished Research Fellow at the University of Minnesota Law School. Professor Okediji's scholarship focuses primarily on the development and welfare implications of the international intellectual property system. She has written, lectured and published extensively in the area of intellectual property globalization and its impact on developing countries; the role of intellectual property in the multilateral trade system; copyright law and the digital divide; and the protection of traditional knowledge. Professor Okediji has worked with several international programs including the United Nations Development Program's (UNDP) flagship project on Innovation, Culture, Biogenetic Resources, and Traditional Knowledge, and the United Nations Conference on Trade and Development (UNCTAD)–ICTSD Capacity Building Project on Intellectual Property Rights and Sustainable Development.

Robert L Ostergard Jr is Assistant Professor of Political Science at the University of Nevada, Reno. He previously served as the Associate Director of the Institute of Global Cultural Studies, and Assistant Professor of Political Science at the State University of New York, Binghamton. He currently serves as series co-editor of the Ashgate book series *Global Health* and is the author or editor of several books on intellectual property rights and on HIV/AIDS in Africa. His most recent book is entitled *HIV/AIDS and the Threat to National and International Security* (Palgrave, 2007).

Jerome Reichman is Bunyan S Womble Professor of Law at Duke Law School. He has written and lectured widely on diverse aspects of intellectual property law, including comparative and international intellectual property law, and the connections between intellectual property and international trade law. His articles in this area have particularly addressed the problems that developing countries face in implementing the World Trade Organization's Agreement on Trade-Related Aspects of Intellectual Property Rights (TRIPS Agreement). On this and related themes, he and Keith Maskus have recently edited a book entitled *International Public Goods and Transfer of Technology under a Globalized Intellectual Property Regime* (Cambridge University Press, 2005).

Anselm Kamperman Sanders is Professor in European and International Intellectual Property Law at Maastricht University, The Netherlands, and Academic Director of the IEEM Intellectual Property Programmes, Macau SAR, China. He was Marie Curie Research Fellow at Queen Mary and Westfield College, University of London. Anselm has worked in developing countries on WTO accession assistance projects for the EC/GTZ. His editorial and advisory board memberships comprise the *Maastricht Journal of European and Comparative Law, Intellectuele Eigendom en Reclamerecht,* the *International Journal of Intellectual Property Management,* and the *Intellectual Property Quarterly.*

Chantal Thomas studies the relationship between international law, political economy and social justice, with a focus on the areas of international trade and international development. Professor Thomas recently joined the University of Minnesota as a Professor of Law; previously, she taught at Fordham University School of Law in New York City. Professor Thomas has served on the Executive Council of the American Society of International Law, and on the Board of Directors of the American Foreign Law Association, and has consulted to the American Bar Association, the Association of the Bar of the City of New York, and private sector clients on international trade issues.

Peter K Yu is Kern Family Chair in Intellectual Property Law and the founding director of the Intellectual Property Law Center at Drake University Law School. He is also a research fellow of the Center for Studies of Intellectual Property Rights at Zhongnan University of Economics and Law in Wuhan, China. Before joining Drake University, he taught at Michigan State University College of Law and founded its nationally-renowned Intellectual Property and Communications Law Program. He held appointments in the Asian Studies Center and the Department of Telecommunication, Information Studies and Media at Michigan State University. Born and raised in Hong Kong, Professor Yu is a leading expert in international intellectual property and communications law. His publications are available on his website at <http://www.peteryu.com>.

TABLE OF CASES

ANDEAN COMMUNITY

Proceso No 34-Ai-2001 Sumario por Incumplimiento de Sentencia (2003) 228
Proceso No 114-AI-2004 (2005) 248

Australia

National Research Development Corp v Commissioner of Patents (1959) 102 CLR 252 396

Brazil

El Dupont de Nemours and Co v INPI (Superior Court of Justice – STJ), Third Jurisdiction no: 2004/0048736-1, Appellate Review no 652172/RJ, original case no 98.0001955-3 (Origin: 14th Federal District) Patent no 8401507-1 229

Canada

Bristol-Myers Squibb Co v Canada (Attorney General) 2005 SCC 26 22
Harvard Coll v Canada (Comm'r of Patents) [2002] 4 SCR 45. 467
Pro Swing Inc v ELTA Golf Inc 2006 Carswell Ont 7203; 2006 SCC 52 (2006) 70
SOCAN v Canadian Assoc'n of Internet Providers 2004 SCC 45, 32 CPR (4th) 1, 240 DLR (4th) 193 (SC June 2004) 470
Society of Composers, Authors & Music Publishers of Canada v Canadian Assn of Internet Providers ('Tariff 22') 2004 SCC 45, 32 CPR (4th) 1 (SC 2004) 97
Théberge v Galerie d'Art du Petit Champlain Inc [2002] 2 SCR 336 20

EUROPEAN COURT OF HUMAN RIGHTS

Anheuser-Busch, Inc v Portugal, App No 73049/01, Judgment of 11 January 2007 87

EUROPEAN COURT OF JUSTICE

Gesellschaft für Antriebstechnik mbH & Co KG (GAT) v Lamell und Kupplungsbau Beteiligungs KG (LUK) (Case C-4/03) (2006) 37 IIC 742 . . . . 96, 471
Roche Nederland BV v Primus (Case C-593/03) (2006) 37 IIC 865 . . . . 96, 471

Germany

Improver Corp and Sicommerce v Remington Prods 24 IIC 838 (Dusseldorf Ct App 1991) 70

Japan

Nigeria

United Kingdom

United States

WTO APPELLATE BODY

WTO PANEL REPORTS

TABLE OF LEGISLATION, TREATIES, AND CONVENTIONS

LIST OF ABBREVIATIONS

A2K	Access to Knowledge users' rights movement
ARIPO	African Regional Industrial Property Organization
BIT	bilateral investment treaty
CAFTA	Central American Free Trade Agreement (parties: Costa Rica, Dominican Republic, El Salvador, Guatemala, Honduras, Nicaragua and the USA)
CBD	Convention on Biological Diversity
CIPR	Commission on Intellectual Property Rights
CLIP	conflict of laws in intellectual property
DMCA	Digital Millennium Copyright Act
DR–CAFTA	Dominican Republic–Central American Free Trade Agreement
DRM	digital rights management systems
FDI	foreign direct investment
FLO	Fairtrade Labelling Organizations International
FTA	free trade agreement
GURT	genetic use restriction technologies
ICANN	Internet Corporation for Assigned Names and Numbers
ICESCR	International Covenant on Economic, Social and Cultural Rights
IGC	Inter-Governmental Committee; specifically, the WIPO IGC on Intellectual Property and Genetic Resources, Traditional Knowledge and Folklore (in Chapter 11)
IIC	International Review of Industrial Property & Copyright Law
IIPA	International Intellectual Property Alliance
INDECOPI	National Institute for the Defense of Competition and the Protection of Intellectual Property
IP(R)	intellectual property (right)
MFN	most favoured nation
MERCOSUR	Southern Common Market: Regional Trade Agreement between Argentina, Brazil, Paraguay, Uruguay, and Venezuela
NAALC	North American Agreement on Labour Cooperation
OAPI	Organisation Africaine de la Propriété Intellectuelle
PCDA	WIPO Provisional Committee, Development Agenda
S&D	special and differential treatment (in trade)
SCCR	WIPO Standing Committee on Copyright and Related Rights
SCP	WIPO Standing Committee on the Law of Patents

SPLT	WIPO's Substantive Patent Law Treaty
SPS Agreement	WTO Agreement on the Application of Sanitary and Phytosanitary Measures
TBT Agreement	WTO Agreement on Technical Barriers to Trade
TK	traditional knowledge
TNC	transnational corporation
TPM	technological protection measures
TRIPS	trade-related intellectual property rights
TRIPS Agreement	WTO Agreement on Trade-Related Intellectual Property Rights, 15 April 1994
UDRP	Uniform Domain Name Dispute Resolution Policy
UNCTAD	United Nations Conference on Trade and Development
UNDP	United Nations Development Programme
UNIDO	United Nations Industrial Development Organization
UNMDG	United Nations Millennium Development Goals
UPOV	International Convention for the Protection of New Varieties of Plants; also the International Union for the Protection of New Varieties of Plants
USTR	United States Trade Representative in bilateral agreements
WIPO	World Intellectual Property Organization
WTO	World Trade Organization

Part I

INTELLECTUAL PROPERTY, TRADE AND DEVELOPMENT: THE GLOBAL LINKAGES

1

TRIPS AND DEVELOPMENT

Daniel J Gervais

Introduction

As noted in the Introduction, the TRIPS Agreement[1] is now entering its third phase. This phase, which emerges against a backdrop of 'TRIPS-Plus commitments' in bilateral trade and investment treaties, focuses on the differences among developing countries and the *calibration* of their TRIPS implementations with their national innovation policies.

Developing or ameliorating an innovation policy is not a simple task. Any such policy has economic, cultural and social ramifications. An intellectual property regime must thus be viewed as forming part of a broader set of measures designed to optimize knowledge development and utilization. That optimization, in turn, should aim to enhance economic growth, cultural prosperity and human development.

The policy dilemma may be summarized as follows: while importing 'foreign' intellectual property rules wholesale into the legislative and industrial fabric of a developing economy is insufficient to succeed, it is fair to assume that a country's technology imports and foreign investment are unlikely to grow without adequate intellectual property rules. In other words, intellectual property rules are necessary to develop world-class innovation and creativity. At the international level, these rules are now essentially enshrined in the TRIPS Agreement.

This first chapter revolves around the idea that TRIPS norms should be integrated in a broader strategy designed to optimize innovation and access to knowledge. Viewed pragmatically, a part of any short- or medium-term strategy should include working with TRIPS as a given and, perhaps, even as a common reference point against TRIPS-Plus demands in bilateral discussions. TRIPS is not perfect, of course, but there is a significant degree of built-in policy flexibility that developing economies can use. More importantly, by developing a comprehensive innovation strategy, a country can limit the negative impact of moving to higher intellectual property protection and increase its chances of reaping the benefits thereof, including technology-related foreign direct investment (FDI) and growing domestic internet-based, pharmaceutical or other high-technology industries.

---

[1] World Trade Organization Agreement on Trade-Related Aspects of Intellectual Property Rights, 15 April 1994, Marrakech Agreement Establishing the World Trade Organization, Annex 1C, Legal Instruments–Results of the Uruguay Round Vol. 31; 33 ILM 1197 [hereinafter referred to as 'TRIPS Agreement' or 'TRIPS'].

Against this backdrop, Part I of this chapter examines the various narratives that have tried to explain the emergence of the TRIPS Agreement and considers political, economic and cultural factors influencing the profound changes concerning TRIPS-related policy discussions, including the growing importance of traditional knowledge and genetic resources and the relationship between TRIPS and Public Health.

In Part II, the chapter discusses recent economic analyses of the impact of intellectual property protection on bilateral trade flows and FDI. Appropriate distinctions are made between trade and FDI. Wherever possible, lessons about the 'right' level of intellectual protection are drawn. Recent efforts in the World Intellectual Property Organization (WIPO) and World Trade Organization (WTO) are also discussed and views concerning the future of TRIPS and its impact on global innovation are expressed.

In the third and final Part, the chapter suggests an analytical model based on a new narrative concerning the place of TRIPS implementation, as part of a broad knowledge-oriented economic strategy.

Part I Understanding TRIPS

A. TRIPS Negotiation Narratives

As Peter Yu's work has shown,[2] accounts and analyses of the history of TRIPS revolve around one of four narratives: (a) a bargain narrative 'in which the Agreement was considered the product of a compromise between developed and less developed countries';[3] (b) a 'coercion' or 'imperialistic' narrative, which is common among scholars who originate from, or who are sympathetic to, developing countries.[4] According to this narrative, 'the TRIPs Agreement is considered an unfair trade document that developed countries imposed on their less developed counterparts'[5] by threatening to isolate them from the global trading system if they did not accede to the demands of the West[6] and/or to impose

2 Peter K Yu, 'TRIPs and Its Discontents' (2005) 10 *Marq Intell Prop L Rev* 369.

3 Ibid, 371.

4 For example B I Abdelgafar, *The Illusive Trade-Off: Intellectual Property Rights, Innovations Systems and Egypt's Pharmaceutical Industry* (University of Toronto Press, 2006), 15–23.

5 Peter K Yu, note above, 371.

6 In a similar vein, it has been suggested that TRIPS was perceived by a number of developing nations as a lesser evil than isolation and loss of MFN status. See B Hoekman, 'Services and intellectual property rights', in S M Collins and B Bosworth (eds), *The New GATT: Implications for the United States* (Brookings Institution, 1994), 113.

punitive unilateral sanctions;[7] (c) an 'ignorance' narrative, in which 'less developed countries are portrayed as countries that did not understand the importance of intellectual property protection during the TRIPs negotiations', in part for many of them this was a first complete multilateral trade negotiation, a difficulty compounded by the lack of intellectual property experts;[8] and (d) a fourth narrative, which Professor Yu refers to as based on 'self-interest' and defended *inter alia* by Alan Sykes[9] and Edmund Kitch,[10] according to which less developed countries agreed to and/or benefit from stronger intellectual property protection because they found such protection necessary for knowledge development. As Professor Yu rightly noted, these narratives are not mutually exclusive and, as often happens, their proponents were all partly right and partly wrong. In fact, the history of TRIPS may not be the best candidate for Occam's razor. Let us examine each of these negotiation narratives in greater detail.

The Coercion Narrative

Beginning with the coercion narrative, it is true that a major concerted lobbying effort led by the United States, with strong support from the European

7 Peter K Yu, note above, 373.

8 Ibid, 375.

9 Alan O Sykes, 'TRIPS, Pharmaceuticals, Developing Countries, and the Doha "Solution"' (2002) 3 *Chicago J Int'l L* 47. Professor Sykes suggests that introducing high levels of IP protection in developing countries induces firms to invent products of particular interest to the developing countries (e.g. anti-malaria drugs) and to engage in technology transfer. Without uniform rules, there might be a 'collective action' problem. The problem arises because an individual developing country may benefit more if it chooses to have weak patent laws while the other developing countries have strong patent laws; that way, an individual country can obtain the benefits of inducing the invention of products of particular interest to developing countries without having to pay the costs. TRIPS solves the collective action problem by requiring all member nations to have strong IP protection. Sykes further argues that compulsory licensing reduces the pharmaceutical industry's incentive to undertake research into diseases that are endemic principally to the developing world. *Contra*, TF Cotter, 'Market Fundamentalism and the TRIPS Agreement' (2004) 22 *Cardozo Arts & Ent LJ* 307, 335–36. Prof. Cotter argues that even in the presence of strong patent rights, the developing nations' willingness to pay might be so constrained that little incentive will exist anyway for the pharmaceutical companies to engage in much of this type of research and development. Indeed, several observers who have considered this issue have concluded that it will take much more than strong patent rights to induce this type of research. In the United States, they point to the Orphan Drug Act (21 USC §§360aa–360ee (2000)). Under this act, the United States government provides funding, tax benefits, and exclusive marketing rights to drug companies undertaking research into diseases affecting relatively small numbers of people. See K Outterson, 'Pharmaceutical Arbitrage: Balancing Access and Innovation in International Prescription Drug Markets' (2003) 5 *Yale J Health Policy L & Ethics* 193, 215–16.

10 Edmund W Kitch, 'The Patent Policy of Developing Countries'(1994) 13 *UCLA Pac Basin LJ* 166, 171: '. . . the technology needed by the developing countries is not the same as the technology that is needed by the developed countries. The developing countries have their own, unique needs. The incentive to invent, commercialize and market technologies which address their needs will only exist if there are patents available to protect successful innovators in those markets.'

Commission and Japan, and research-based pharmaceutical companies, the entertainment and software industries, was a causal factor in the emergence of TRIPS within the WTO (i.e. trade) framework—client politics at its best, some might say.[11] Respected economists, such as Jagdish Bhagwati and Joseph Stiglitz, were critical of this effort, though for very different reasons, to which they referred as pure rent-seeking[12] on the part of these companies.[13] The move to the trade arena, while it may have generated substantial benefits for rights holders in terms of enforcement options, has also made it harder to use absolute, property-based justificatory theories for their intellectual property in the pragmatic, utilitarian/consequentialist world of trade regulation.[14] Some might also see some irony in the fact that TRIPS obliges developing countries to document and enforce (private) property rights in intangibles such as copyrights, trademarks and patents, a majority of which are foreign-owned, while approximately 80 per cent of real estate assets in developing countries are 'extralegal' and thus not documented in ways that would allow using such assets as collateral.[15]

The Ignorance and Bargaining Narratives

There is some factual basis for the ignorance and bargaining narratives. Developing countries accepted the Agreement in many, if not most, cases because of significant political concessions[16] in other sectors of the Round, such as tariffs on tropical fruit or textiles.[17] They may not have grasped at the time the full

[11] Which leads to highly concentrated benefits but highly distributed costs. See JQ Wilson, *Politics of Regulation* (Basic Books/Harper Collins, 1980) 369–72.

[12] See, e.g. Jagdish Bhagwati, *In Defense of Globalization* (Oxford University Press, 2004) 182–85. Dr. Bhagwati's criticism seems to insist mostly on the fact that TRIPS is not proper subject matter for the WTO.

[13] See Joseph Stiglitz, *Making Globalization Work* (Norton, 2006), at 116–7.

[14] A good example of this is the extension of the 'three-step test', a test originally designed to limit exceptions to the copyright right of reproduction in the Berne Convention (Art 9(2) of the Paris Act of 1971), to a test that in TRIPS is used to measure the legality of exceptions to all copyright rights (Art 13), design rights (Art 26) and patents (Art 30—in this case exceptions other than compulsory licensing). The test focuses on the economic impact on and interference with 'normal commercial exploitation' of an exception to exclusive rights, a staunchly utilitarian test far removed from traditional property-based or natural rights justifications. Berne Convention for the Protection of Literary and Artistic Works, 9 September 1886, 25 UST 1341, 828 UNTS 221 [hereinafter 'Berne Convention'].

[15] See Hernando de Soto, *The Mystery of Capital: Why Capitalism Triumphs in the West and Fails Everywhere Else* (Basic Books, 2006).

[16] For an interesting empirical analysis of how and why developing countries adopt higher intellectual property norms (in many cases not because they believe they need or will benefit from them), see Chapter 3 below (Professor Ostergard).

[17] A key difference between the WTO and organizations such as WIPO is that concessions are made in WTO negotiations across negotiating sectors. IP policy issues may be 'abandoned' for lower tariffs of cotton or coffee, for example. Interestingly, these issues are sometimes linked. The protection of intellectual property rights in agricultural products, such as seeds, is becoming an increasingly

extent of their TRIPS commitments.[18] At the time, there were very few people arguing that TRIPS *qua* TRIPS was good in the short term for all developing countries. Developing countries accepted it as part of a package. In fact, all GATT multilateral rounds were ultimately 'bargains', though obviously the bargaining power of each participant was very uneven.[19] Still, the story might be written differently today. As the Doha Round discussions have shown, when a group of developing countries do not feel that their end of the bargain justifies the concessions asked of them, which may include higher levels of intellectual property protection and enforcement, the bargain may not be struck—especially when industrialized nations refuse to reduce trade, significantly distorting agricultural subsidies and their egregious export subsidies. But the political economic landscape has changed significantly since 1994.

The Doha Development Round, which started in Qatar in November 2001—and independently of its ultimate fate—can serve as a reflection of the political changes since 1994 (at the multilateral level at least) in the world of intellectual property, which resulted from alliances among developing nations informed by better data and analyses on the benefits and costs of intellectual property protection. In the three paragraphs concerning TRIPS in the Doha Ministerial Declaration, there are very few hooks on which to hang demands to increase IP protection.[20]

---

important issue. U Lele *et al, Intellectual Property Rights in Agriculture: The World Bank's Possible Future Role in Assisting Borrower and Member Countries* (World Bank, Environmentally and Socially Sustainable Development Series: Rural Development, 1999). Stiglitz argues that 'while TRIPs would reduce developing countries' access to knowledge and force them to pay billions in royalties, it was meant to be part of the "Great Bargain". . .in which the developing countries would get greater access in agriculture and reduced agricultural subsidies by the advanced industrial countries. The developed countries did not keep their side of the bargain.' Stiglitz (note 13 above) 311 n 7.

18 A point made in rather dramatic fashion by the same author: '[a]s they signed TRIPs [in Marrakech], the trade ministers were so pleased that they had finally reached an agreement that they didn't notice they were signing a death warrant for thousands of people in the poorest countries around the world.' Stiglitz (note 13 above) 105.

19 Namely the 'founding' GATT (Havana) Round of 1947—though it never led to the formation of the International Trade Organization as originally planned; the Annecy Round of 1949; the Torquay Round of 1950; the Geneva (Fourth) Round of 1956; the Dillon Round of 1960–61; (named after C Douglas Dillon, then US Under-Secretary of State); the Kennedy Round of 1962–7; the Tokyo Round which lasted from 1973–9, where participation increased dramatically from 47 initial participants to 99; and the Uruguay Round which was launched in Punta del Este in 1986 and ended in Marrakech in 1994 with 125 participants, and which established the World Trade Organization to replace the 'contractual' GATT. The current Round started in Doha (Qatar) in 2001. As of this writing its future is uncertain. See generally JJ Jackson, *The World Trading System* (2nd ed, MIT Press, 1997).

20 World Trade Organization, Ministerial Declaration of 14 November 2001, WT/MIN(01)/DEC/1, 41 ILM 746 (2002), available at <http://www.wto.org/english/thewto_e/minist_e/min01_e/mindecl_e.htm> [hereinafter Doha Declaration]. On the Doha process generally, see Daniel J Gervais, *The TRIPS Agreement: Drafting History and Analysis* (Sweet & Maxwell, 2003) 43–51.

First, paragraph 17 states that TRIPS should be implemented 'in a manner supportive of public health, by promoting both access to existing medicines and research and development into new medicines . . .'. In the following paragraph, the Declaration addresses a mostly North–North issue, the completion of the negotiations over geographical indications on wines and spirits. The third and perhaps most well-known of the paragraphs instructs the TRIPS Council to 'examine, *inter alia,* the relationship between the TRIPS Agreement and the Convention on Biological Diversity, the protection of traditional knowledge and folklore', and other new developments. In undertaking this work, the Declaration says, 'the TRIPS Council shall be guided by the objectives and principles set out in Articles 7 and 8 of the TRIPS Agreement and shall take fully into account the development dimension'. In other words, apart from the possible increase in protection for the names of wines and spirits, the Doha Declaration essentially reflects the concerns of developing countries. The first paragraph insists on the balance between the need for access to IP and its protection.[21]

The separate Declaration on the TRIPS Agreement and Public Health, also adopted at Doha, emphasizes what had already been said in the Declaration itself—that the TRIPS Agreement should not prevent WTO members from taking measures to protect public health.[22] Such an interpretation means that the TRIPS Agreement should be interpreted in light of its objective and purpose, as expressed in the Agreement itself: '[e]ach Member has the right to grant compulsory licenses and the freedom to determine the grounds upon which such licenses are granted'; '[e]ach member has the right to determine what constitutes a national emergency or other circumstances of extreme urgency' (where public health crises may represent national emergency); and '[t]he effect of the provisions in the TRIPS Agreement that are relevant to the exhaustion of intellectual property rights is to leave each Member free to establish its own regime for such exhaustion without challenge, subject to the [Most Favored Nation] and national treatment provisions of Articles 3 and 4'.[23]

After intensive, and difficult, negotiations, the WTO General Council adopted an Implementation of Paragraph 6 of the Doha Declaration on the TRIPS Agreement and Public Health in 2003.[24] It allows WTO members, under certain

---

21 See LD Tully, 'Note, Prospects for Progress: The TRIPS Agreement and Developing Countries After the Doha Conference' (2003) 26 *BC Int'l & Comp L Rev* 129.

22 World Trade Organization, 'Ministerial Declaration on the TRIPS Agreement and Public Health of 14 November 2001,' WT/MIN(01)/DEC/2, 41 ILM 755 (2001), available at <http://www.wto.org/english/thewto_e/minist_e/min01_e/mindecl_trips_e.htm>.

23 Ibid, paras 5(b), (c) and (d).

24 World Trade Organization, 'Decision of the General Council of 30 August 2003,' WT/L/540 (2003), available at <http://www.wto.org/english/tratop_e/trips_e/implem_para6_e.htm>. It will

conditions, to export generic versions of drugs used to treat diseases, such as HIV/AIDS, to countries that can neither afford nor manufacture these pharmaceuticals. While a compulsory license may reduce the patent (royalty) cost, it does not eliminate the production costs, nor the problems associated with the distribution and timely administration of the medicines.[25] However, if patents are indeed more a part of the problem than of the solution for certain developing countries living with HIV/AIDS or other epidemics, then the Decision may help them overcome that obstacle. Be that as it may, even if the Declaration is imperfect, it unquestionably draws attention to a process essentially designed to take the needs of developing countries into account.[26]

Yet, it remains true to say that the Uruguay Round bargain was based on incomplete information and was an 'imperfect bargain' as a result of three main causes. First, most developing countries participating in the negotiation had no experts in international intellectual property norms. The few available experts (from countries such as Egypt, India and Brazil) had to carry a heavy burden. This expertise and resource asymmetry put them at a disadvantage when discussing detailed and arcane drafting points, especially those linked to the specific history of existing treaties such as the Berne and Paris Conventions.[27] Second, developing countries in most cases could not know what effects TRIPS implementation would have because of a dearth of empirical evidence. Third, the TRIPS text was essentially based on Western norms. In fact, by and large, the 'North' imposed its, then most advanced, set of norms on the 'South', and major industrialized countries made relatively few concessions, despite their disagreements on some issues,

be added as an Article 31*bis*, together with an Annex and an Appendix, thus preserving the format of the 2003 Decision.

25 See A Attaran and L Gillespie-White, 'Do Patents for Antiretroviral Drugs Constrain Access to AIDS Treatment in Africa?' (2001) *J of the Amer Med Assoc* 286, 15, 1886–1906.

26 See Carlos M Correa, 'Supplying Pharmaceuticals to Countries Without Manufacturing Capacity: Examining the Solution Agreed Upon by the WTO on 30th August, 2003' (2004) 1*J Generic Meds* 105–19; BC Mercurio, 'TRIPS, Patents, and Access to Life-Saving Drugs in the Developing World' (2004) 8 *Marq Intell Prop LR* 211, 236–37. As of April 2007, no country had made the necessary notification to the WTO Secretariat to be able to invoke the Decision. See Cotter (note 9 above), 310-19; KM Gopakumar, 'The WTO Deal on Cheap Drugs: A Critique' (2004) 7 *J World Intell Prop* 99; D Matthews, 'WTO Decision on Implementation of Paragraph 6 of the Doha Declaration on the TRIPS Agreement and Public Health: A Solution to the Access to Essential Medicines Problem?' (2004) 7 *J Int'l Econ L* 73. For a view saying that the Declaration goes too far in favour of developing countries and acts as a disincentive to research, see Sykes (note 9 above).

27 Berne Convention (note 14 above); Paris Convention for the Protection of Industrial Property, 20 March 1883, 21 UST 1583, 828 UNTS 305 [hereinafter 'Paris Convention']; see also PJ Heald, 'Mowing the Playing Field: Addressing Information Distortion and Asymmetry in the TRIPS Game' (2003) 88 *Minn LR* 249.

except in relation to the need to submit their intellectual property compliance level to the scrutiny of a new, binding dispute settlement.[28]

The Self-interest Narrative

The self-interest narrative offers an interesting viewpoint and has been discussed by a minority of scholars. Their analysis points to the benefits of (localized)[29] innovation for developing nations. Innovation (the generation and application of new ideas) is one of the five main drivers of economic development, and in the longer term perhaps the strongest one.[30] The proponents of this view assume, not only (as the Uruguay Round negotiators from major trading powers did) that TRIPS was necessary to maximize the rent that could be extracted from emerging foreign markets, and a difficult yet essential measure to jump-start global economic development;[31] but more importantly, that the intellectual property rules that had worked over decades or centuries of normative escalation towards

---

[28] The United States could not accept the Rome Convention for the Protection of Performers, Producers of Phonograms and Broadcasting Organizations, which protects neighbouring (related) rights. Therefore, the wording of TRIPS only refers to Rome with respect to exceptions. TRIPS Art 14; see also Gervais (note 20 above), 99–100. Also on this list are moral rights, the protection of biotechnological inventions (which was not settled in Europe at the time), plant varieties, and geographical indications. Given the comparable clout of the industrialized countries involved in discussions of these issues, they were solved either by introducing exceptions (as in Art 9 on moral rights or Art 27 for biotechnology) or by rather vague undertakings to negotiate further (as in Art 24 concerning geographical indications).

[29] For example, MA Lemley, 'The Economics of Improvement in Intellectual Property Law' (1997) 75 *Tex LR* 989, 1008–13 (discussing the reverse doctrine of equivalents which may apply to certain improvements).

[30] The other drivers are trade, finance, migration and aid. See I Goldin and K Reinert. *Globalization for Development, Revised Edition: Trade, Finance, Aid, Migration, and Policy* (World Bank/ Palgrave Macmillan, 2007).

[31] This debate was present in China when it was first considering the adoption of a 'Western-style' patent law. As Professor Alford explains:

> Proponents of a patent law placed primarily emphasis on its likely salutary economic effects, arguing that China needed to smash the [. . .] mentality of the Cultural Revolution that rewarded all equally, irrespective of the quality of their work [. . .]. This could only be accomplished, they contended, by adopting a patent system that provided meaningful material incentives. By permitting those who had so contributed to reap the fruits of their labours, a patent law would also, it was suggested, allow China's most innovative organizations to accumulate additional capital and strengthen their management, which would spur further inventive activity [. . .]
>
> Opponents of a patent system [. . .] expressed concern about Western 'literary-industrial complex,' which some believed might patent so broadly in China as to stifle the development of indigenous science and so leave the nation dependent on the outside world economically, scientifically, and militarily. It would be foolhardy, they argued, to risk draining China's limited foreign exchange reserves to pay royalties—especially when the same technology could be acquired at no cost, albeit without authorization.

WP Alford, *To Steal a Book Is an Elegant Offence: Intellectual Property Law in Chinese Civilization* (Stanford University Press, 1995) 67–8.

high levels of intangible property protection would work if parachuted into emerging economies. IP as policy 'castor oil', in other words: developing countries should overlook the distasteful aspects of introducing or increasing IP protection and enforcement in exchange for longer-term economic health. As I shall attempt to show, this narrative was partly correct, but also partly misinformed and woefully incomplete.

The TRIPS Agreement is indeed the poster child for the so-called Development Theory, according to which developing economies should import the normative, judicial and administrative infrastructure of more industrialized nations to achieve a similar level of economic development. According to this theory, copying the infrastructure will lead to increased foreign investment, availability of capital and economic growth.[32] However, Development theorists cannot fully prove their point now and were even less able to do so during the Uruguay Round. The data suggesting that developing countries may benefit from properly calibrated intellectual property norms was published *after* the end of the Round and thus, as an explanatory tool for the Uruguay Round this narrative is anachronistic and skips the logical step of demonstrating that the TRIPS regime is optimally calibrated.[33]

One should also mention, in this context, the related beliefs that the misuse of intellectual property was comparable to theft (or 'piracy'). The piracy discourse cannot be elevated to the level of a theory, however, and is more properly viewed as a lobbying tool, one especially powerful in the US Congress where private property has sacrosanct status. Yet, despite its shortcomings the self-interest narrative points to something exceedingly important by asking how developing economies can take advantage of intellectual property norms. I shall come back to this point later.

---

32 The intellectual backdrop for this theory is the Washington Consensus, according to which the recipe for economic development is to reduce the role of government, emphasize privatization, trade and capital market liberalization, and deregulation. According to this view, governments must mostly protect property rights and avoid corruption. While acknowledging that there is no guarantee of fairness in wealth distribution that comes with this world view, Washington Consensus advocates generally believe in trickle-down economics, i.e. that all or most citizens will benefit from GDP growth. Some commentators, including Joseph Stiglitz (Nobel Prize winner in economics) have questioned the evidence to support this view. Stiglitz (note 13 above) 27.

33 Stiglitz is critical of 'one size fits all' development strategies and intellectual property regimes (ibid, at 119). While TRIPS does contain Western norms (those that the industrialized nations could agree among themselves) as of 1990, as this chapter and Chapter 15 (Epilogue) will attempt to demonstrate, there are flexibilities in TRIPS and ways to optimize its implementation in developing countries.

B. TRIPS Implementation Narratives

The Polarized Narratives

The four negotiation narratives examined above, which try to explain the history of TRIPS, can be followed to the implementation phase. The TRIPS demanders believed that adding high intellectual property norms and enforcement measures in developing countries would not only generate higher rents for them but eventually for industries in developing countries as well, notably by increasing inward FDI. At the implementation level, one could label this approach an *addition narrative*. The demanders' decision to use the multilateral forum may be explained by the lack of alternatives: they could not easily lobby developing countries individually (having, in most cases, little to offer in exchange for higher intellectual property protection).

Not surprisingly, those who support the coercion and ignorance negotiation narratives, or consider that TRIPS was a misinformed, uneven bargain for developing nations because of TRIPS costs in comparison to the meagre benefits stemming from other negotiation areas of the Uruguay Round, have 'fought' TRIPS and recommended maximum flexibility leading to minimalist implementations of the Agreement (to the extent that this is possible).[34] In short, at the implementation level, the idea was to obliterate as much of TRIPS as possible both as an international normative vector and in its country-by-country implementation, hence the label *subtraction narrative* used in the Introduction. Proponents of this approach often support alternative norm-making efforts in other fora[35] that may be used to

---

[34] See generally the recommendations outlined in the UNCTAD–ICTSD Resource Book on TRIPS and Development (Cambridge University Press, 2005), which notes (at p 21) that '[o]n the whole, the TRIPS Agreement that was concluded allows substantial flexibility in the specific implementation of IPR rules'. The report suggests, for instance, that bilateral negotiations aimed at securing 'TRIPS-Plus' norms may contravene TRIPS:

> An important interpretative question is whether a Member that *demands* the adoption of TRIPS-plus standards in the bilateral or regional context might be failing to perform its TRIPS Agreement obligations in good faith. The argument on behalf of a Member's being subjected to such demands would be that it accepted its TRIPS obligations as part of a set of reciprocally negotiated commitments that represent a balance of rights and obligations on which that Member is entitled to rely. Bilateral pressure to exceed the agreed upon commitments is contrary to the object and purpose of the WTO Agreement and TRIPS Agreement to provide a secure framework for the conduct of international trade relations.

[35] Graeme B Dinwoodie & Rochelle C Dreyfuss, 'TRIPS and the Dynamics of Intellectual Property Lawmaking' (2004) 36 *Case W Res J Int'l L* 95, 121. ('[D]eveloping countries have recently seen regime-shifting as a bulwark against the established power balance in international lawmaking, and over time user groups might likewise view the ability to shift forum as a valuable defensive technique.').

interpret TRIPS (notably in a dispute-settlement context) in a way that is perceived to be more favourable to developing countries.[36] The value of these exercises as potentially relevant norms of public international law has not been fully tested before WTO dispute-settlement panels.[37] However, one may legitimately consider, in the longer term, that TRIPS is not static. TRIPS will evolve, and the exact scope of its provisions will become clearer with each panel and Appellate Body interpretation. The Appellate Body has indicated, for instance, that TRIPS should not be read in 'clinical isolation' from public international law.[38] Norms negotiated elsewhere may be used to try to interpret TRIPS as forming part of a broader normative regime.[39] Developing and other countries can coalesce to develop alternative sets of norms and the inclusion of TRIPS and WTO rules in the broader framework of public international law. The potential role of national courts in shaping the interpretation of international intellectual property norms should not be underestimated. Based on the old principle of ensuring domestic laws comply with international norms by which a state is bound, national courts are called upon to interpret TRIPS and other instruments, and their exegesis may, in turn, influence the approach taken by international tribunals and WTO

---

36 Examples include the Convention on Biological Diversity (UN Conference on Environment and Development: Convention on Biological Diversity (5 June 1992) 31 ILM 818)(see Gervais (note 20 above) 228–232); and the International Treaty on Plant Genetic Resources in Food and Agriculture (ITPGRFA), 3 November 2001, available from <ftp://ftp.fao.org/ag/cgrfa/it/ITPGRe.pdf>, Arts 6.2 and 12.3(d) of which may be interpreted as prohibiting the patenting of genes in certain cases. See *Impacts of the IPR Rules on Sustainable Development* (November, 2006) Queen Mary University, 72–74, available at: <http://www.ip4development.org>.

37 Indeed, in interpreting WTO Agreements, including the TRIPS Agreement, the Appellate Body repeatedly relied on the provisions of the Vienna Convention of the Law of Treaties as a primary source for interpretative guidance. In *India – Patent Protection for Pharmaceutical and Agricultural Products*, doc WT/DS50/AB/R, para 46, the Appellate Body confirmed the general principle of applicability of Art 31 of the Vienna Convention on the Law of Treaties in interpreting the WTO Agreement, including the TRIPS Agreement, as established in *United States – Standard for Reformulated and Conventional Gasoline*, doc WT/DS2/AB/R.

38 *US – Standards for Reformulated and Conventional Gasoline*, Report of the Appellate Body, doc WT/DS2/AB/R, para III. B. This principle was reflected in this and the subsequent decision, which relied on the case law of other international tribunals, namely the International Court of Justice, the European Court of Human Rights and the Inter-American Court of Human Rights, in interpreting the provisions of the WTO Agreement (*US – Gasoline*, ibid, para III.B, fn 36; *Japan – Taxes on Alcoholic Beverages*, doc WT/DS8/AB/R, part D, fn 19).

39 See Dinwoodie and Dreyfuss, note 35 above.

dispute-settlement panels.[40] The self-interest theorists have challenged the subtraction narrative head on.[41]

Subtraction and the Dependency Theory

A group of theories linked to the subtraction narratives is generally referred to as the Dependency theory, which, in response to the demanders' Development Theory, argues that adopting an advanced intellectual property regime and a related Western-style infrastructure, while this may produce growth, in fact leads to greater economic dependency by making it easier for foreign companies to invest in, and take control of, the fledgling economies of developing nations. Proponents of the Dependency theory argue that high trademark protection, for example, creates mostly low-paying jobs in franchises or retail outlets and does not contribute to innovation. Some have called it the Americanization (or more colourfully, if not tastefully, the 'McDonaldization') of the economy in developing countries.[42] They point out, in that connection, that of the 100 top global

---

40 Graeme B Dinwoodie, 'The International Property Law System: New Actors, New Institutions, New Sources' in *Proceedings of the 98th Annual Meeting of the American Society of International Law* (2004); Daniel Gervais, 'The Role of International Treaties in the Interpretation of Canadian Intellectual Property Statutes' in O Fitzgerald (ed), *The Globalized Rule of Law: Relationships Between International and Domestic Law* (Irwin Law, 2006), 549–572; and R Slate, 'Judicial Copyright Enforcement in China: Shaping World Opinion on TRIPS Compliance' (2006) 31 *NC J Int'l L & Com Reg* 665.

41 As Edmund Kitch notes:

> There are three reasons why the no patent strategy does not in fact benefit the country that adopts it. The first reason is that the argument that a no or anti-patent strategy benefits the country that adopts it depends upon particular views of technology and of the patent system that are inconsistent with reality. The argument implicitly likens technology to a collection of food recipes and the patent system to a cookbook. Neither metaphor is right. Technology does not simply consist of a collection of instructions as to how to proceed, and patents do not, standing alone, contain the necessary information.
>
> The second reason is that the technology needed by the developing countries is not the same as the technology that is needed by the developed countries. The developing countries have their own, unique needs. The incentive to invent, commercialize and market technologies which address their needs will only exist if there are patents available to protect successful innovators in those markets.
>
> The third reason is that the ability of patent owners to charge for the use of their patent rights, either in the form of royalties or through end product prices is constrained by the ability of the country granting the patent rights to pay. Poor countries will inevitably pay proportionately less than wealthy countries for the use of patent rights.
>
> Kitch, (note 10 above) 171; see also Walter G Park and Douglas Lippoldt, 'International Licensing and the Strengthening of Intellectual Property Rights in Developing Countries' (2005) *OECD Economics Studies*.

42 See Chapter 8 below (Professor Khoury). Hernando de Soto notes that franchising in itself is not productive:

> Widely accessible legal property systems are the silt from upriver that permits modern capital to flourish. This is one of the principal reasons macroeconomic reforms are not working. Imitating

marks, 64 are American and 34 more are from Western Europe or Japan. In other words, 98 of the world's top 100 marks are all based, and profits repatriated to, a very small group of heavily industrialized countries. They also argue that the positive impact on economic growth generated by higher IP protection is greatly reduced by repatriation of profits and huge inequalities in the distribution of the new riches.

Dependency theorists propose a number of alternative world views, including at one end of the spectrum Marxist-leaning authors rejecting capitalist and existing IP and economic models entirely, but also several others one could call 'proportionalists', who argue that developing countries should adapt the intellectual property models of industrialized nations to their own needs and circumstances. Advocates of an IP model adapted to the specific needs of developing countries point out that none of the industrialized nations had intellectual property rules, at their current high level of protection, when their per capita GDP was comparable to that of a developing economy. We could call this the 'parallelism argument'.[43] Those who hold this view favour the adoption of a variety of measures, such as the protection of indigenous intellectual property on the same level as 'Western' IP; price controls in appropriate cases; rules on franchises and profit repatriation. They also suggest counteracting the negative impact of high protection of foreign IP with subsidized import substitutions and local manufacture.

> capitalism at the level of the [river] delta, by importing McDonald's and Blockbuster franchises, is not enough to create wealth. What is needed is capital, and this requires a complex and mighty system of legal property that we [in the West] have all taken for granted.

de Soto, note 15 above, at 66. That said, in the Middle East alone, the international franchise industry reached US$14 billion in 2006 and was growing at more than 25 per cent annually. R Ditcham, 'Mideast Franchise Industry Touches $14b' *Gulf News*, March 31 2007, 29.

[43] D Drache, 'Trade, Development and the Doha Round: A Sure Bet or a Train Wreck?' (March 2006) Centre for Intenational Governance Innovation Working Paper No 5, 25, available at <http://www.igloo.org/community.igloo?r0=community&r0_script=/scripts/folder/view.script&r0_pathinfo=%2F%7B7caf3d23-023d-494b-865b-84d143de9968%7D%2FPublications%2Fworkingp%2Ftradedev&r0_output=xml&s=cc>:

> The current intellectual property regime suffers from patents of poor quality and overly restricted access to copyrighted materials that are critical for innovation and economic growth. In the US the Federal Trade Commission has concluded that a wholesale revision of the patent system's impact on innovation is needed. In the pharmaceutical area, patent challenges involving many important drugs and the challenger has won more than 70 percent of the cases according to a prominent US intellectual property lawyer. In the nineteenth century in the US and on the continent, infringement and unauthorized borrowing were an important part of American industrial development. [. . .] US entrepreneurs borrowed, adapted and stole British patented processes whenever they could.

The Calibration Narrative

It may be time to move beyond simplistic narratives and leave the sycophantic echo chambers. Recent efforts suggest that a *calibration narrative* is a better approach. Drawing from previous narratives, it recognizes that the introduction of TRIPS-compatible norms in the legal system of a developing country will not in and by itself generate massive developmental gains and may indeed entail substantial welfare costs. I will suggest the contours of this narrative in Part III of this chapter. Before doing so, let us continue our tour of the changing landscape by looking at traditional knowledge and other factors influencing the current changes.

C. TRIPS and Traditional Knowledge

Not much need be said here on traditional knowledge (TK),[44] particularly in light of detailed contributions on this topic in this book.[45] Nevertheless, the issue should be mentioned here. It necessarily forms part of the global intellectual property policy picture.

The protection of traditional knowledge has been discussed in international fora over the last few years[46] and the Doha Declaration put it at centre stage.[47] There are several reasons for the issue's sudden move to the forefront. First, a large number of countries believe that up to now they have not derived great benefits from 'traditional' forms of intellectual property, yet find themselves rich with

---

44 Traditional knowledge is a shorter form of 'traditional knowledge, innovations and practices'. See, e.g. the Convention on Biological Diversity, 5 June 1992, Art 8(j). The Draft UN Declaration on the Rights of Indigenous Peoples, UN Doc E/CN.4/1995/, uses the expression 'indigenous knowledge, cultures and traditional practices'. In its more recent documents, WIPO uses the expression 'traditional knowledge, innovations and creativity'. See *Intellectual Property Needs and Expectations of Traditional Knowledge Holders (1998–1999)* WIPO Report on Fact-finding Missions on Intellectual Property and Traditional Knowledge (Geneva: WIPO, 2000) 21–22. Traditional knowledge includes a broad range of subject matters, for example traditional agricultural, biodiversity-related, and medicinal knowledge and folklore. Daniel Gervais, 'Traditional Knowledge and Intellectual Property: A TRIPS-Compatible Approach'(2005) *Mich St LR* 137.

45 See especially Chapter 11 below (Professor Drahos), as well as the relevant section of Chapter 9 below (Hon. Jean R Homere).

46 For WIPO activities in this area, see: <http://www.wipo.int/tk/en/>. See also Chakravarthi Raghavan, 'ASEAN for Protecting Indigenous/Traditional Knowledge' (5 May 2000) *Third World Network*; and A Cosbey, 'The Sustainable Development Effects of the WTO TRIPS Agreement: A Focus on Developing Countries' (March 1999) available at <http://www.tradeobservatory.org/library.cfm?filename=Sustainable_Development_Effects_of_the_WTO_TRI.htm>.

47 Paragraph 19 reads in part as follows: '[ministers] instruct the Council for TRIPS, in pursuing its work programme [. . .] to examine, *inter alia*, the relationship between the TRIPS Agreement and the Convention on Biological Diversity, the protection of traditional knowledge and folklore, and other relevant new developments raised by members pursuant to Article 71.1'.

traditional knowledge, especially genetic resources and folklore. They would like to exploit these resources and several major companies share this interest. The second reason is the growing political importance of Aboriginal communities in several countries. While pharmaceutical and biotechnological companies are looking at ways to exploit indigenous medicinal knowledge, plants and other resources that are often found in developing countries, the internet is progressively allowing creators of folklore or folklore-based copyrighted material to disseminate their material worldwide at very low cost.

In addition to the development of treaty provisions under the aegis of WIPO, which could serve, at least initially, to produce norms on a regional basis, work in the Doha Round might lead to political recognition of the validity of some of the demands made by TK-rich developing countries.[48]

One question that is necessarily posed by the introduction of TRIPS-compliant intellectual property norms in environments rich in traditional knowledge and genetic resources, is whether these norms are adequate to deal with communally-held knowledge or genetic resources usually protected only once exploited by 'Western' scientific and industrial entities.[49] There was little attention paid to traditional knowledge and, more broadly, little in terms of economic analysis at the time those norms were developed, and there was hardly any hard evidence until at least the 1970s to justify their expansion and revision. Yet the last revision of the two major intellectual property treaties dates back to 1967–8.[50] The somewhat adventitious nature of intellectual property norms makes justification for such introduction (in its detailed characteristics at least) more difficult, and ultimately dependent either on political arguments or, where available, emerging empirical data (which may offer at best a blurred picture and not a precise set of justifications). It also tends to obscure problems, often considered very lightly in the West, that result from the fact that law and legal ideologies are a facet of culture, especially if culture is defined as the 'interactive aggregate of common

48 WIPO Draft Provisions on the Protection of Traditional Knowledge (TK) and Draft Provisions on the Protection of Traditional Cultural Expressions/Expressions of Folklore (TCEs). Available at: <http://www.wipo.int/tk/en/consultations/draft_provisions/draft_provisions.html>. At its tenth session (held from 30 November to 8 December 2006), the Intergovernmental Committee Intellectual Property and Genetic Resources, Traditional Knowledge and Folklore was still looking for ways to move the debate forward on both TK protection, and access to and protection of genetic resources.

49 Gervais, 'Traditional Knowledge & Intellectual Property' (note 44 above).

50 The Berne Convention (see note 14) was last revised in substance at the Stockholm conference of 1967, together with the Paris Convention (see note 27). In Paris in 1971 an Appendix was added to the Stockholm text to allow developing countries to issue compulsory reproduction and translation licenses (under certain conditions). The last Act of the Berne Convention is thus the Paris Act (1971).

characteristics that influence a human group's response to its environment'.[51] Creativity and innovation are so interwoven into the social and cultural fabric that it is fair to ask whether they can easily all be regulated by a single set of norms developed in eighteenth century Europe and then amplified in negotiations between Western nations until 1989, when a photograph of all such norms that industrialized nations could agree upon was included in the WTO framework as the TRIPS Agreement, giving developing countries little other than a few additional years to comply.[52]

D. Other Factors Affecting the TRIPS Policy Landscape

Changes Reflected in the Doha Texts

The changing landscape of international intellectual property, in respect of traditional knowledge, is also visible in *inter alia* the reference in the Doha Declaration to Articles 7 and 8 of TRIPS, i.e. the two provisions inserted originally to reflect the concerns of developing countries. Though they have been given little regard up to now in dispute-settlement proceedings in the WTO, these two provisions could be given a somewhat higher normative profile in future disputes because of what is a possible 'special status' in the Doha text.

TRIPS Article 7 is cut from the same tree as paragraph 17 of the Doha Declaration embodying the idea of balance between protection and access. This need for balance is voiced, of course, by many people in industrialized countries, which is another factor contributing to the fundamental change of the intellectual property landscape. There is increasing recognition that, while intellectual property regulation is necessary in certain areas to justify research and development expenditure, the optimal configuration of intellectual property norms cannot be

[51] G Hofstede, 'Culture's Consequences: International Differences in Work-Related Values 25' (1980) quoted in N V Demleitner, 'Combating Legal Ethnocentrism' (1999) 31 *Ariz St LJ* 737, 739. See also L Ross Meyer, 'Unruly Rights' (2000) 22 *Cardozo LR* 1, 49–50. The difficulty was the focus of the so-called Bellagio declaration, which argues that intellectual property, and copyright law especially, 'unduly emphasizes the role of individuals in knowledge creation. Consequently, intellectual property laws fail to reward those knowledgeable communities and collaborators that provided the raw intellectual material that formed the true basis for the copyrighted work or patented invention.' See <http://college.hmco.com/english/amore/demo/ch5_r2.html>.

[52] See also K McLeod, *Owning Culture: Authorship, Ownership, and Intellectual Property Law* (Peter Lang Publishing, 2001) Vol 1; R.J Coombe, 'Critical Cultural Legal Studies' (1990) 10 *Yale J of L & the Humanities* 463. Also consider economist Max Wirth's objection to the ownership of patents: '[i]nventions do not belong in the category of intellectual property, because inventions are emanations of the current state of civilization and, thus, common property... inventions are merely blossoms on the tree of civilization'. Wirth is quoted in R E Meiners, 'Patents, copyrights, and trademarks: property or monopoly?'(1990) 13 *Harv JL & Pub Pol'y 911*, 919; and Christopher May and Susan Sell, *Intellectual Property Rights: A Critical History* (Lynne Rienner Publishers, 2005), 43.

readily ascertained on the basis of available empirical data, as is discussed below in Part II of this chapter. Any *ex ante* analysis of the 'optimal system' is problematic and even *ex post* adjustments to the system are often difficult to justify conclusively based on available data. There is, in other words, an unavoidable element of (hopefully somewhat educated) guesswork in making intellectual property policy.

The Role of New Stakeholders

The international intellectual property landscape was altered radically over the last few years. This change was ostensibly driven by three main factors. First, many newcomers at the intellectual property table, those who might not have fully grasped the scope and depth of TRIPS obligations when they signed up to it in 1994 (the ignorance narrative discussed above), now possess much more sophisticated knowledge in the area of intellectual property norms. That knowledge is provided in part by movements in 'civil society' against intellectual property regulation, or at least against higher IP norms, which have led to a number of studies and alternative proposals.[53] Better knowledge about intellectual property has also prompted the development of research into the second factor, namely, a more complete recognition that theoretically, at least, intellectual property has an optimal protection point.

The Need to Avoid Overprotection

Empirically, intellectual property does not necessarily work better when measured in terms of the effectiveness of implementing the policy objective of incentivizing (*ex ante*) or rewarding (*ex post*) innovation.[54]

Falvey, Foster and Greenaway explain the balancing act as follows:

> A role for IPR protection arises because intellectual property displays many of the characteristics of a public good. It is typically non-rival and can be non-excludable. In the extreme these characteristics could remove the incentive to invest in R&D, and IPR protection can therefore restore that incentive. The importance of R&D and innovation has been emphasised by new growth theory [. . .]. In these models entrepreneurs invest in R&D in the expectation of profiting from their inventions. In addition to new products, innovation adds to a public stock of knowledge which

---

53 For a fairly comprehensive view, see A K Sanders, 'The Development Agenda for Intellectual Property', Inaugural Lecture, Universiteit Maastricht, May 2005. Scholarly work on the impact and optimal structure of intellectual property regulation did not start with TRIPS, but with the clash between copyright and privacy on the internet (see Daniel Gervais, 'Use of Copyright Content on the Internet: Considerations on Excludability and Collective Licensing', in M Geist (ed) *Copyright Reform in Canada* (Irwin Law, 2005), and the very public debacle over pharmaceutical patents on HIV and malarial drugs in Brazil and South Africa have taken the issue out of (only) specialized circles and into the public spotlight.

54 *Théberge v Galerie d'Art du Petit Champlain Inc* [2002] 2 SCR 336, para 32.

lowers the cost of future innovation. Besides rewarding innovation, IPR protection stimulates the acquisition and dissemination of knowledge, since the information in patent claims is then available to other potential inventors. The rate of growth depends upon the rate of innovation and the stock of knowledge. Strong IPR protection need not always yield higher innovation and growth, however. Giving innovators too much protection may limit the spread of new ideas and lead to monopoly. Entry by rivals may be impeded, and successful innovators may have reduced incentives for developing and exploiting subsequent innovations.[55]

The Search for Policy Equilibria

The analysis above allows us to posit that there must be both an *intrinsic* and an *extrinsic equilibrium* in intellectual property policies. Ideally, given the broader societal interests at play, one should protect adequately but not protect beyond what is necessary to achieve the policy objective(s) because the risk of negative welfare impacts is too high. However, as we will see below, it is extremely difficult to pinpoint that exact level, and thus governments have to make rules based on other criteria. One must also consider that many developing countries no longer agree that TRIPS is a negative that must be accepted because of cross-sectoral concessions in the Uruguay Round. They want to learn how to benefit from intellectual property, maximizing the positives while minimizing the negatives in terms of higher consumer prices, job losses, and other welfare costs.[56] They also have a better understanding of the trade-strategic game in which they are necessarily players.[57]

Externally, the increasingly visible intersection between intellectual property and other rights broadens the base of the search for balance. The search for such an *extrinsic equilibrium* then becomes unavoidable. The interplay between the intrinsic and extrinsic equilibria is apparent in a recent Canadian Supreme Court decision:

> Our Court has often spoken of 'the balance struck under the Patent Act' in which the public gives an inventor the right to prevent anybody else from using his or her

55 R Falvey, N Foster and D Greenaway, 'Intellectual Property Rights and Economic Growth' (2004). Internationalisation of Economic Policy Research Paper No 2004/12, available at: <http://ssrn.com/abstract=715982>, at 2.

56 Professor Yu explains that intellectual property may appeal to leaders in developing countries because it holds out the promise of new jobs, FDI, tax revenues, technology transfer and the development of local artists, inventors and indigenous industries. Peter K Yu, 'From Pirates to Partners: Protecting Intellectual property in China in the Twenty-First Century' (2000) 50 *Am ULR* 131, 192–3.

57 S Scotchmer, *Innovation and Incentives* (MIT Press, 2004), 329:

> . . . intellectual property rights are no longer a way to encourage domestic innovation. They also become a strategic instrument to affect profit flows among nations. To affect profit flows favorably, each country wants the strongest possible protections in foreign countries, and the weakest possible protections for foreigners in its own domestic market.

> invention for a period of 20 years in exchange for disclosure of what has been invented. As a general rule, if the patent holder obtains a monopoly for something which does not fulfil the statutory requirements of novelty, ingenuity and utility, then the public is short-changed. [. . .]
>
> In the present appeal, the Court is required to consider this 'balance' in the much-litigated field of patented medicines, where Parliament is concerned not only with the balance between inventors and potential users, but between the protection of intellectual property on the one hand and, on the other hand, the desire to reduce health care costs while being fair to those whose ingenuity brought the drugs into existence in the first place.[58]

Indeed, it seems difficult to contradict the position that intellectual property policy should be solidly based on economic grounds. It would seem almost absurd to limit the analysis of intellectual property to the traditional natural right theories, such as the Lockean view of a right in one's labour, or a Kantian/Hegelian view of (mostly copyright) creations being imbued with their author's personality (creating an inextinguishable link between the creator and the creation).[59] Once the societal impacts of intellectual property are factored into the policy equation, those philosophical views seem to provide insufficient justifications when the debates focus not on whether intellectual property should exist[60] but on exactly what it should protect, in what circumstances and for what period of time. That debate tends to be more productive when participants accept an instrumentalist version of utilitarianism as the proper starting point. This foundation recognizes that intellectual property regulation is essential to avoid certain market failures, because (without legal protection) ideas, creations and inventions are non-exclusive and non-rivalrous—not the case with profits. In other words, while many people can share an idea, in many cases the same cannot be said of companies seeking to profit from the making and selling of creations or inventions embodying the same idea. By the same token, however, intellectual property rules should aim to improve general welfare and be fair to social interests at play even if this cannot be or is not measured at the level of individuals. That

58 *Bristol-Myers Squibb Co v Canada (Attorney General)*, 2005 SCC 26, paras 1–2.

59 'Natural rights are those which always appertain to [human beings] in right of [their] existence. Of this kind are all the intellectual rights, rights of the mind, and also all those rights of acting as individuals of [their] own comfort and happiness, which are not injurious to the rights of others.' (Thomas Paine, *The Rights of Man*). For a general overview of the various theories, see WT Fisher, 'Theories of Intellectual Property' in S Munzer, ed., *New Essays in the Legal and Political Theory of Property* (Cambridge University Press, 2001).

60 A debate at that level is not altogether helpful. It often rests on a rejection of the dominant neoliberal model and/or emphasizes the fact that corporations are only thinking of profits and those who manage them are only driven by greed and power. That said, the higher-level critiques of the 'system' may lead to better 'corporate citizenship'. Cynics are quick to argue that those efforts are themselves usually marketing-driven, so as to allow the corporation to make more profit (and hence tending to demonstrate that profit and good 'corporate citizenship' are not incompatible).

is, in fact, the apparent paradox of intellectual property: the law grants a monopoly to allow society to gain access to new creations and inventions: to ensure that we can gain access, we limit access.

The Impact on TRIPS

I suggest that the two results of the above analysis, namely the recognition of the two equilibria (intrinsic/extrinsic) and the adoption of an instrumentalist view of intellectual property, are here to stay for the predictable future. Future multilateral discussions will necessarily have to take that into account. That may explain why, as other chapters of this book demonstrate, the best escape for those who do not want to explore this new policy terrain is quickly to move their ammunition to the bilateral field.[61]

Perhaps efforts to dilute intellectual property norms may succeed in part, but the bilateral tightening towards TRIPS-Plus is more likely to have significant normative impacts.[62] Besides, there can be no definitive answers given to questions such as whether the optimal term for a patent is 20, 18, or 22 years. Or is it 5 or 35? For copyright, is it 10 years, or life of the author plus 50 or 70 years?[63] What rights would achieve the policy purposes better than those now in place?[64] One would probably conclude that, for certain forms of invention or

---

[61] See Ruth L Okediji, 'Back to Bilateralism? Pendulum Swings in International Intellectual Property Protection' (2003–2004) 1 *Univ Ottawa L & Tech J* 125, available at: <http://www.uoltj.ca/articles/vol1.1-2/2003-2004.1.1-2.uoltj.Okediji.125-147.pdf>.

[62] See Part 1.E below.

[63] See *Eldred v Ashcroft*, 537 US 186, 193 (2003). It has been argued that the current US and European term of 'life plus 70 years' is the economic equivalent of perpetual protection. See Ch Sprigman, 'Reform(aliz)ing Copyright' (2004) 57 *Stan LR* 485, 522. Sprigman writes:

> The copyright term is now sufficiently long that the net present value to the rightsholder of a copyright is practically indistinguishable from what it would be under a perpetual term. In an *amicus curiae* brief submitted to the Supreme Court in support of the petitioners in *Eldred v Ashcroft*, a group of economists that included Nobel Prize winners George Akerlof, Kenneth Arrow, James Buchanan, Ronald Coase, and Milton Friedman argued that the current, post-CTEA copyright term of life plus seventy years has a net present value that is 99.88% of the value of a perpetual term.

[64] By which I mean copyright (and the bundle of rights it contains, together with exceptions and a long term of protection) for literary and artistic works; a 20-year patent for new, useful and non-obvious inventions (to use North American terminology, reflected in the footnote to Art 27 in TRIPS), etc.

> One could in theory devise a different system from scratch but the global spreading of any such new system would not be without very significant transition costs, and there is no guarantee that one could do better on the basis of available 'performance indicators' for the various types of IP protection. The temptation to build *sui generis* systems thus far has not met with complete success, as the database and computer chip examples demonstrate. That being said, the existing traditional structures of protection are far from perfect and can be improved upon, but most likely only in an incremental fashion. See Daniel Gervais, 'The Internationalization of Intellectual

creation—indeed for specific inventions or works—a certain term is optimal, while a different one is more adequate in a different context.[65] This analysis could depend, for example, on the added value of the invention, which depends in turn on the size of its inventive step and the degree to which this step overlaps the predictable industrial or commercial applicability of the invention.[66] One could add to the equation the degree of true competition in the industrial or economic sector impacted by the invention and, correlatively, whether there are dominant players by market share. This interesting theoretical discussion led one Canadian economist to suggest a protection term based on the social value of non-lifestyle pharmaceutical inventions.[67] However, even if such a proposal could pass the test of transaction costs, experts could only guess the future utility of the invention. In terms of predictability, time, and transition/protection costs, a single term may be a better, if theoretically less refined solution. It is certainly simpler.

The question here is not whether rights holder organizations will continue to push national and regional governments to adopt higher levels and longer terms for protection of intellectual property rights—they will. Not indefinitely, because most creators and inventors are also ultimately users of the intellectual property of others, but, when facing a policy doubt, they tend to err on the side of (and lobby for) more protection. The size of their effort will depend on the perceived benefit of better and/or longer protection. Conversely, user groups (with their myriad forms and mandates) will no doubt continue to argue for less protection or broader exceptions. Thus, the question for policy makers here is what precise level of rights within the range of TRIPS-compatible implementations would achieve the policy purposes (better than those now in place).[68]

Property: New Challenges from the Very Old and the Very New' (2002), 12:4 *Fordham IP, Media & Ent LJ* 929–990.

65 One *ex post* sign would be whether the invention is still actively being exploited at the expiry of the patent. However, if only inventions whose value had lapsed fell into the public domain, the societal value of granting a 20-year monopoly would come into question. In the United States, there is a long history of extending the term of specific patents by private bills. CL Stanley, 'A Dangerous Step Toward the Over Protection of Intellectual Property: Rethinking *Eldred v Ashcroft*' (2003) 26 *Hamline LR* 679, 694–5. Historically, the term of a patent was set by private bill until a standard term was introduced into federal law. See ThB Nachbar, 'Intellectual Property and Constitutional Norms' (2004) 104 *Colum LR* 272, 338–39.

66 In the area of pharmaceuticals, a difference is often made between pioneer drugs and so-called 'me-too' drugs. The latter are variations on a molecule developed by another laboratory which tend to have the same physiological/therapeutic effect, but without infringing the 'pioneer's' patent. See *US v Generix Drug Corp*, 460 US 453 (1983).

67 See A Hollis, 'An Efficient Reward System for Pharmaceutical Innovation' (2004), available at <http://econ.ucalgary.ca/fac-files/ah/drugprizes.pdf>.

68 See Chapter 15 (Epilogue) below.

Indeed, while TRIPS is undeniably here to stay, it only harmonizes national laws to a degree.[69] This is not the place for a summary of the content of TRIPS.[70] Evidently, it contains more than simple 'wishes', in contrast to many provisions of the Paris Convention.[71] A country must provide protection of copyrights, certain related rights, trademarks (as defined), industrial designs, certain geographical indications, patents on most classes of inventions, certain forms of confidential information, and, last—and in this case least—topographies of integrated circuits, in each case for a specified period of time. On the other hand, however, there is some measure of flexibility in how some of the protected subject matter is defined,[72] owned,[73] managed,[74] or subject to exceptions.[75] In the area of enforcement, the Agreement recognizes that the implementation in a given WTO member may be impacted by the availability of resources.[76] In 2005 the United Nations Conference on Trade and Development ('UNCTAD') published a detailed document on the flexibility of TRIPS.[77]

Admittedly, developing economies may need a partly different set of rules, depending on their level of development. As UNCTAD put it,

> experience shows that there is a need for policy instruments specifically designed with the aim of helping countries at lower stages of development to converge on the levels of efficiency and affluence achieved by the more advanced economies, and to improve the welfare of all groups of the population. Making this the principle for policy design at both the domestic and the international level requires recognition of the fact that successful development and integration of the developing countries is in the mutual interest of all countries, as longer-term growth and trading

[69] See Jerome H Reichman, 'The TRIPS Agreement Comes of Age: Conflicts or Cooperation with the Developing Countries?' (2000) 32 *Case W Res J Int'l L* 441.

[70] See generally Gervais, *The TRIPS Agreement* (note 20 above).

[71] For a trademark-related example, see the Paris Convention (note 27 above), Art 6(1) ('[t]he conditions for the filing and registration of trademarks shall be determined in each country of the Union by its domestic legislation').

[72] For example, while Art 27 states that WTO members must protect 'inventions, whether products or processes, in all fields of technology, provided that they are new, involve an inventive step and are capable of industrial application', the terms 'new', 'inventive step', and 'capable of industrial application' are not defined.

[73] See Appellate Body Report, *United States – Section 211 Omnibus Appropriation Act of 1998*, paras 215–21, WT/DS176/AB/R (2 January 2002), available at <http://www.tripsagreement.net>.

[74] For instance, rules as to the ownership of collective marks, or whether and how copyright and related rights are to be managed (collectively or otherwise), are not explicitly mentioned in the Agreement.

[75] Many exceptions are only limited by the 'three-step test' contained in TRIPS Arts 13, 26(2), and 30. See Daniel Gervais, 'Towards a New Core International Copyright Norm: The Reverse Three-Step Test' (2005) 9 *Marq Intell Prop LR* 1.

[76] TRIPS, Art 41(5).

[77] UNCTAD–ICTSD Resource Book, note 33 above.

opportunities of the more advanced economies also depend on the expansion of industrial capacity and markets in the poorer economies.[78]

There is a degree of normative elasticity within TRIPS that allows for several different types of implementation, even though the major concession to developing countries other than least-developed ones was a set of transitional periods. For such countries, these transitional periods expired in January 2000, and in January 2005 for pharmaceutical patents.[79] The real question is how these flexibilities should be used. I return to this point when discussing the various implementation narratives in Part II of this chapter.

E. Bilateral Treaties

Despite UNCTAD's suggestion that insofar as countries negotiating trade or investment treaties demand TRIPS-Plus norms they may violate TRIPS, it seems unlikely that a WTO panel would arrive at such a conclusion.[80] WTO and GATT law have always allowed for 'plus' agreements to be negotiated. Often, a 'new baseline' is established on the basis of those discussions. It is true, however, that post-TRIPS development has been going in two (arguably diverging) ways. TRIPS-related developments within WTO, as well as the recent developments in WIPO, have tried to be more responsive to the perceived needs of developing countries and the interests of users in securing access to protected content and material on terms they consider reasonable, including broad exceptions to obligations to obtain permissions and licenses. On the other hand, intellectual property developments in recent bilateral and regional trade agreements mirror the so-called maximalist approach.[81]

78 UNCTAD, Trade and Development Report 96 (2004), available at <http://www.unctad.org/en/docs/tdr2004_en.pdf> [hereinafter 'Trade and Development Report'].

79 TRIPS, Art 65(2), (4). A TRIPS Council decision of 29 November 2005 gives the WTO's 32 least-developed countries until July 2013 to implement TRIPS and, in the case of pharmaceutical patents, least-developed countries now have until 2016. See note 115 below and Reichman (note 69 above) 442 n 3.

80 UNCTAD–ICTSD Resource Book, note 33 above.

81 For example, recent US Trade Agreements 'export' the Digital Millennium Copyright Act, Pub L No 105–304, 112 Stat 2860 (1998), a specific piece of legislation concerning the protection and circumvention of technological protection measures (TPMs) that fits into the whole of the US Copyright Act, with its various safeguards, including constitutional protections stemming from the Bill of Rights. DMCA-like provisions are or will soon be part of national legislations in Central America and Asia as something of a stand-alone legislative instrument. See United States Bilateral Trade Agreements with Morocco, Chile, Bahrain, Australia and Central American Free Trade Agreement, available at <http://www.ustr.gov/Trade_Agreements/Section_Index.html>. These provisions are also being negotiated in a number of other agreements as well as within the Free Trade Area of the Americas. See Susan Sell, *Private Power, Public Law: The Globalization of Intellectual Property Rights* (Cambridge University Press, 2003), 121–162. Joseph Stiglitz notes that in preparing the bilateral agreement between the United States and Morocco, 'there wasn't much negotiations

The latter trend to regulate intellectual property rights through bilateral regimes may not be immediately threatening to the approach of the WTO and the WIPO, but these bilateral initiatives likely will have a significant impact in the long run.[82]

Part II Measuring the Impacts of TRIPS on Development[83]

The introduction, or updating, of intellectual property norms in all member countries and territories of the World Trade Organization (WTO), as a result of the Uruguay Round's TRIPS Agreement, sparked a relatively new field of study, namely the impact of the introduction of intellectual property norms on the social, cultural and economic development of developing and least-developed countries. Two notable institutional efforts include the World Bank's report on the impact of intellectual property on economic development,[84] and a report published by the UK Commission on Intellectual Property Rights.[85] There have also been initiatives concerning the origins of the push to have intellectual property included as part of the Uruguay Round package[86] and to provide a deeper understanding of the impact of intellectual property on developing and emerging economies.[87]

The purpose of this Part is to examine insights offered by economic analysis and to understand the impact of introducing TRIPS-compliant norms.

involved', and that 'the US negotiators were mostly interested in having their way—and they wanted the new agreement to protect US drug companies'. Stiglitz, note 13 above, 104.

82 Professor Yu labels this approach 'the double backdoors in international intellectual property lawmaking'. If a number of countries import higher level of intellectual property protection, it is likely that that high level will be codified as the existing norm in any revision of TRIPS. Peter K Yu, 'Anticircumvention and Anti-Anticircumvention', (2006) 84 Denver U LR 13, 55. See also Gervais, *The TRIPS Agreeement* (note 20 above) 68.

83 A full economic analysis is contained in Chapter 3 below (Professor Ostergard). This Part of this chapter is based on a paper by the author published at (2005) 74 *Fordham LR* 505 and republished at (2006) 5:4 *ICFAI J of IP Rights* 39–61. The Part focuses on policy impacts, though it uses some economic tools to do so.

84 *Intellectual Property and Development*, C Fink & KE Maskus (eds), (World Bank, 2004).

85 Commission on Intellectual Property Rights, *Integrating Intellectual Property Rights and Development Policy* (2002), available at <http://www.iprcommission.org/papers/pdfs/final_report/CIPRfullfinal.pdf> [hereinafter 'UK IPR Commission Report'].

86 See Gervais, *The TRIPS Agreement* (note 20 above); Sell (note 81 above) 96–120; C May, *A Global Political Economy of Intellectual Property Rights: The New Enclosures?* (Routledge, 2000); Peter Drahos and J Braithwaite, *Information Feudalism: Who Owns the Knowledge Economy?* (New Press, 2003); and A Koury Menescal, 'Those Behind the TRIPS Agreement: The Influence of the ICC and the AIPPI on International Property Decisions' (2005) 2 *Intell Prop Q*,155.

87 Many of the contributors to this book have published extensively on this topic. One could also mention S Scotchmer, 'The Political Economy of Intellectual Property Treaties' (2004) 20 *J L Econ & Org* 415, 435–36.

A. Overview of Recent Analyses

A number of recent studies offer a blurred and complex picture of the advantages of (high) IP protection in developing economies.[88] It now seems clear that since TRIPS was informed more by the belief that introducing 'Western' IP norms would induce development than by actual supporting analyses and data, TRIPS put the policy cart before the empirical horse.[89] We now know that a simple equation cannot be drawn between an increase in trade following the introduction of TRIPS-compatible IP protection, on the one hand, and economic development on the other, especially when measured in terms of welfare increases.[90]

Selecting Proper Indicators

There are (at least) two principal indicators that are helpful to analyze the impact of increasing protection, namely (a) the increase of trade flows in goods that include a significant IP component (as compared to the physical value of the material and components—for example, a music CD or a patented pharmaceutical molecule; such areas may be referred to as 'intellectual property-sensitive'); and (b) the increase in FDI in goods or services that require a high level of IP protection. It is essential to measure both because, to a certain extent, they cancel each other out: a company in country A (export) may have the ability to send goods to country B, but instead opt for local production (under license) in country B. The analysis of Maskus and Fink is based on data available from 89 countries.

[88] 'The Impact of Trade-Related Intellectual Property Rights on Trade and Foreign Direct Investment in Developing Countries', OECD Working Party of the Trade Committee, Document TD/TC/WP(2002)42/FINAL, 28 May 2003, available at <http://www.oecd.org/dataoecd/59/46/2960051.pdf>; Park and Lippoldt, note 41 above; UK IPR Commission Report, note 85 above; Fink and Maskus, note 84 above; *The Uruguay Round and the Developing Economies*, W Martin and LA Winters (eds) (World Bank, 1995), available at <http://econ.worldbank.org>; Scotchmer, 'Political Economy of IP Treaties' (note 87 above), 435–36. OECD Science, Technology and Industry Outlook 2004 (2004); OECD, 'Patents, Innovation and Economic Performance: OECD Conference Proceedings (2004)'; C Brenner, 'Intellectual Property Rights and Technology Transfer in Developing Country Agriculture: Rhetoric and Reality' (March 1998) OECD Development Centre Working Paper 133, CD/DOC(98)3.

[89] As Park and Lippoldt noted (in ibid, Executive Summary, page 1):

> Reform of the global IPR framework over the last decade has been at least partly motivated by the premise that developing economies will benefit from increased technological inflows as a consequence. However, the theoretical literature does not provide unambiguous predictions about this premise and the empirical evidence is scant, particularly at the firm or enterprise level.

[90] C Fink & CA Primo Braga, 'How Stronger Protection of Intellectual Property Rights Affects International Trade Flows' in Fink and Maskus, (note 84 above) 21. ('The implications of IPR0s for economic welfare are complex. The simple fact that trade flows rise or fall in response to tighter IPRs is not sufficient for drawing conclusions regarding economic welfare. Both static and dynamic effects need to be considered.') Obviously, an increase in overall economic development may not translate into a reduction of poverty. Other factors, such as wealth distribution and corruption, are relevant.

Their main conclusion is that higher levels of IP protection are useful in areas other than fuel (and, presumably, raw resources pre-value-added transformation) and, perhaps surprisingly, high technology.[91]

Maskus and Fink suggest[92] five possible explanations as to why there is no measurable positive impact in the case of high technology goods:

(1) strong market power may offset the positive market expansion effects of higher protection;
(2) higher FDI may lower international trade (as discussed above);
(3) it is possible that the impact of intellectual property protection was not accurately measured;
(4) factors in the destination country (country of export) may matter more than intellectual property (including first mover advantage); and
(5) finally, tariff and non-tariff barriers may impede trade flows.

It may also, perhaps mainly, be because intellectual property and especially patents are not a dominant consideration in many high technology industries. Waiting three years or more for a patent to be issued may not be a major consideration in deciding whether to develop new software, for instance.[93] Other factors may include the nature of the innovation process in that industry.[94]

---

91 Maskus and Fink, see note 84 above. In fact, those results seem at odds with Professor Mansfield's 1994 study of US business executives (E Mansfield, 'Intellectual Property Protection, Foreign Direct Investment, and Technology Transfer', Int'l Fin Corp Discussion Paper No 19 (1994)), which found that IP protection influenced mostly executives in high tech industries. For a discussion, see PJ Heald, 'Misreading a Canonical Work: An Analysis of Mansfield's 1994 Study' (2003) 10 *J Intell Prop L* 309.

92 See note 84 above, 28.

93 And in fact has given rise to the anti-innovative creatures known as patent trolls. See RE Thomas, 'Vanquishing Copyright Pirates and Patent Trolls: The Divergent Evolution of Copyright and Patent Laws' (2006) 43 *Am Bus LJ* 689. Professor Thomas notes (at 730–31):

> The negative impact on small-entity inventors and patent consolidators is why restrictions on a court's ability to grant injunctions are attractive to info-tech companies. Info-tech and other companies that employ low development costs and fast-depreciating patents are strong supporters of this provision because the number of potential patent infringement claims they face is high. In many cases the only requirements for developing info-tech patents are programming knowledge, access to a computer, and time. [. . .]
>
> The reasons that info-tech companies wish to restrict injunctive relief are the same reasons that biotech/pharma oppose such restrictions. Biotech/pharma's interests tend to be closer to those of copyright content holders in that their business model is based on selling products to end users that embody one or a very limited number of patents, whereas info-tech companies are more likely to use their intellectual property as production inputs. (footnotes omitted)

94 'ICTs and Economic Growth in Developing Countries', OECD Development Assistance Committee, DCD/DAC/POVNET(2004)6/REV1, 10 December 2004. Park and Lippoldt (note 41 above) suggest that in the biotech and electronics groups, stronger patent reform has generally led to greater increases (or fewer decreases) in licensing deals. However, in the computer group,

The Link Between IP and FDI

The traditional view on the effect of intellectual property, supported by case studies in countries such as postwar Japan, is that higher IP protection, especially of patent rights, will lead to higher inward FDI, which often has a significant technology transfer/intellectual property component.[95] However, in a recent analysis of the FDI component and its relation to IP, Professor Maskus concluded that many other factors influence FDI and technology transfer decisions, including market liberalization and deregulation, technology development policies and competition regimes, and a low level of corruption.[96] That said, as is shown by Professor Yu in Chapter 5, as regards China, the growth of FDI does not seem to be correlated to increases in the level of intellectual property protection or political reforms, suggesting that in some cases at least, there are considerations

---

the 'medium' reformers attracted the greatest increase in deals, whereas in the communications group, both the high and low reformers had the most gains in deals. Modest patent reform may be of some benefit to licensing activities in technological fields, such as computers and communications, where the innovation process is cumulative and sequential. Modest patent strength may better enable opportunities for knowledge diffusion and sharing of common pool resources (such as internet tools and data networks). Agreeing with Tim Berners-Lee, Stiglitz notes that in the software field, 'patents stifle innovation', adding that Amazon.com's patent on one-click online purchases is 'not the kind of major intellectual breakthrough that deserve[s] patenting'. (Stiglitz, note 13 above) 113–5.

95 Park and Lippoldt explain that licensing transactions are a means by which technology can be transferred from one party to another. Although the details of individual licensing agreements vary, they can include terms referring to technical support, training and other assistance to be provided by the licensor to the licensee. They can enable the licensee to acquire the right to use new technology (subject to specific conditions) without having to undertake costly research and development (R&D), and to capitalize on the licensor's reputation and expertise. In exchange, the licensor derives fees and royalties, can capitalize on the licensee's local reputation and knowledge, and may obtain reciprocal licenses to any technical improvements made by the licensee (e.g. grant-backs). Thus, licensing transactions can provide for technology transfer to developing countries, while yielding mutual benefits to both parties. (See note 41 above, Executive Summary, page 2) See also KE Maskus, 'Intellectual Property Rights and Economic Development' (2000) 32 *Case W Res J Int'l L* 471, 481–85; and KE Maskus and C McDaniel, 'Impacts of the Japanese Patent System on Productivity Growth' (1999) 11 *Japan & World Econ* 557.

96 KE Maskus, 'Intellectual Property Rights in Encouraging FDI and Technology Transfer', in Fink and Maskus (note 84 above), 70–71; see also C Fink, 'Patent Protection, Transnational Corporations, and Market Structure: A Simulation Study of the Indian Pharmaceutical Industry' in ibid, 250–51. In his summary of a study by Ginarte and Park (JC Ginarte and WG Park, 'Determinants of Patent Rights: A Cross-National Study' (1997) 26 *Res Pol'y* 283, 285–86) Professor Maskus notes that those authors found that the strength of patent rights across countries and over time depended positively on real GDP per capita, the share of R&D in GDP, openness to international trade, and a measure of the freedom of markets from arbitrary and non-transparent government regulation. Human capital, measured by the secondary school enrolment ratio in an earlier period, was a positive and marginally significant contributor to patent rights. (Maskus, 'IPR and Economic Development', note 96 above, 477).

of geopolitical or 'geocommercial' realities that trump intellectual property concerns.[97]

The received wisdom is that foreign firms invest internationally if there are location advantages and if it is more profitable for them to produce in that country rather than licensing their IP. Firms are more apt to invest in countries that implement strong IP protections (and to bring their IP or allow for licenses in such countries). Transnational firms may also choose to invest in vertical FDI (where different plants produce products that can be used by the plant 'above' it as an input to their product).[98] Yet the IP/FDI correlation is not universally supported by available data, probably because there are several other key factors at play.

The conclusions of Professor Maskus' above-mentioned study are based on data from the International Monetary Fund showing increases in inward and outward FDI between the years 1987 and 1995. Pre-2000 data may not offer ideal parameters to do a full analysis of the current situation. In many cases, IPR protection increased sharply after the TRIPS Agreement entered into force in developing countries, which, except for the least-developed ones, had until January 2000 to comply.[99] Interestingly, in China's case, the date of TRIPS compliance coincided with its becoming a WTO member: on 11 December 2001. Another developing country-specific study that compared African countries to India and China found significantly lower FDI numbers in Africa despite higher levels of IP protection.[100]

The *World Investment Report 2005* prepared by UNCTAD shows that FDI peaked in 1999–2000 (before or coterminous with the TRIPS implementation deadline) and then actually declined significantly in 2001, 2002 and 2003 (by

---

[97] See also Y Li, 'Pushing For Greater Protection: The Trend Toward Greater Protection of Intellectual Property in the Chinese Software Industry and the Implications for Rule of Law in China' (2002) 23 *U Pa J Int'l Econ L* 637, 638–41; KE Maskus, 'The Role of Intellectual Property Rights in Encouraging Foreign Direct Investment and Technology Transfer' (1998) 9 *Duke J Comp & Int'l L* 109, 115–19 (noting that FDI increased tenfold in China prior to the introduction of TRIPS-compatible norms); M Schiappacasse, 'Intellectual Property Rights in China: Technology Transfers and Economic Development' (2004) 2 *Buff IP LJ* 164; Peter K Yu *et al*, 'China and the WTO: Progress, Perils, and Prospects' (2003) 17 *Colum J Asian L* 1.

[98] See CA Primo Braga and C Fink, 'The Relationship Between Intellectual Property Rights and Foreign Direct Investment' (1998) 9 *Duke J Comp & Int'l L* 163, 172–73.

[99] TRIPS, Art 65. For patents on pharmaceuticals in countries where patents were previously unavailable for inventions of that type, the transitional period ended on 1 January 2005 (TRIPS Art 65(4)).

[100] Srividhya Ragavan, 'The Jekyll and Hyde Story of International Trade: The Supreme Court in *PhRMA v Walsh* and the TRIPS Agreement' (2004) 38 *U Rich LR* 777, 789; and RM Sherwood, 'Global Prospects for the Role of Intellectual Property in Technology Transfer' (2002) 42 *IDEA* 27, 33–34 (emphasizing the need for proper enforcement mechanisms).

41 per cent, 13 per cent and 12 per cent respectively, before increasing by 2 per cent in 2004).[101] However, UNCTAD also note that '[t]he difference between inflows to developed countries and developing countries shrank to $147 billion—a significant narrowing of the gap compared with previous years'.[102]

Another study, this one concerning the situation of FDI in so-called 'transition economies',[103] is perhaps more illuminating because those countries were, for the most part, closed to FDI until approximately 1990. The study confirmed intuitive conclusions, in particular that in IP-sensitive areas FDI is discouraged when IP protection is weak, and that, across all sectors, low IPR protection encourages foreign firms to focus on distribution rather than local production.[104]

In the specific area of pharmaceuticals, available data analyzed in another study illustrates that, at least for the large Indian market, the introduction of patent protection is likely to lead to increased R&D, price increases, and related welfare effects. However, research also shows that only 10.9 per cent of the top five hundred pharmaceuticals in this market are patented. Additionally, the government retained certain tools including price controls and, in cases where Article 31 of TRIPS allows, compulsory licenses.[105]

The UK IPR Commission Report[106] presents a picture consistent with the above findings but also stresses that it is important not to consider developing countries as a homogeneous group.[107] In fact, a fairly well-developed sequencing phenomenon exists. In an impoverished country, there is little rent that foreign firms can extract and limited innovation potential—with the possible exception of the exploitation of genetic resources or traditional knowledge, a topic to which I shall return below. Furthermore, technology to copy or improve on high technology goods is scarce, and it is unlikely that the country in question can benefit as an innovator from technology transfer. FDI is unlikely because of factors unrelated to IP, such as infrastructure, or absence of a viable domestic market. International firms take notice when a country becomes both a piracy threat and a potential market, even if the threat is limited to a fairly small

101 Available at <http://www.unctad.org/en/docs/wir2005_en.pdf>.

102 Ibid, at 3.

103 Essentially, these are countries in Central and Eastern Europe that formed part of the former Soviet bloc. Art 65(3) of the TRIPS Agreement refers to them as '[m]ember[s] which [are] in the process of transformation from a centrally-planned [economy] into a market, free-enterprise economy and which [are] undertaking structural reform of [their] intellectual property system[s] . . . .'

104 B Smarzynska Javorcik, 'The Composition of Foreign Direct Investment and Protection of Intellectual Property Rights: Evidence from Transition Economies' (2004) 48 *Eur Econ Rev* 39.

105 Fink (note 96 above) 250–51.

106 Note 85 above.

107 Ibid, 2–3.

percentage of the population.[108] While countries that implement IP norms may benefit from increased local development and inward FDI, they may also incur job losses in established copycat industries and welfare costs associated with higher local prices. However, consumers benefit from knowing they are purchasing the genuine product, especially in areas where the quality of the goods is essential.

In sum, economic analysis tends to demonstrate that sufficient IP protection is an essential component of increased inward FDI and trade flows in IP-sensitive goods for countries above a certain economic development threshold.[109] The trade regime (especially tariffs and non-tariff barriers), tax, and competition laws are also potent influences.

B. Policy Lessons of Recent Analyses

When higher IP rules allow foreign firms to begin exporting IP-sensitive goods and services to a country, local consumers and industries gain lawful access to those products and services. This may result in welfare gains. It may also, however, lead to price increases, especially when goods whose status changes to 'pirate' or 'counterfeit' after the introduction of IPR protection are displaced by genuine goods sold at a higher price. Increased trade flows may lead to new jobs in distributorships and the retail sector, but these are likely to be low-skilled, low-paying positions. There may also be significant gains in terms of product quality and reliability, most notably in the area of pharmaceuticals.

Inward FDI is a more powerful development lever than trade. It transfers technology and usually creates jobs requiring a higher skill level. This may be the case for the manufacturing of technology-intensive goods, which requires

---

108 For a discussion on the situation in Kenya, see JM Migai Akech, 'The African Growth Opportunity Act: Implications for Kenya's Trade and Development' (2001) 33 *NYU J Int'l L & Pol* 651.

109 A point made by Professor Cottier:

> [TRIPS] rules apply (subject to extended time periods for implementation) across the board and irrespective of real competitive relations. In reality, lack of protection, or inadequate protection, is mainly felt in relation to highly competitive economies and sectors, while it remains without much impact in relation to non-competitive products. Despite lack of protection, they are not in a position to harm and displace competitive products. Intellectual property does not really matter in such constellations that may frequently be found in DCs, in particular LDCs. On the one hand, the matter could therefore be left to benign neglect of failure to fully comply with obligations. Reality largely follows this model. It is not an accident that WTO disputes on IPRs mainly exist between developed countries.

T Cottier, 'From Progressive Liberalization to Progressive Regulation in WTO Law' (2006) 9 *J Int'l Econ L* 779, 802.

engineering and quality-control positions, as well as management and other softer skill sets. In the best-case scenario, some research and development jobs are created, which might have spill-over effects in areas such as higher education, or local laboratories.

Copyright

In the absence of sufficient rights and enforcement options in the copyright arena, one may reasonably conclude that music, films, and books are unlikely to be distributed and national cultural industries are unlikely to develop. In these areas, the gains generated by establishing sufficient protection are 'unambiguous'.[110] However, the introduction or beginning of enforcement of copyrights may also lead to the closure of businesses that rely on copying, thus displacing (mostly unskilled) workers. Ideally, some of these workers will be able to find work in the new, creative industry jobs made possible by the adequate protection of copyrights. There is little economic benefit to be derived from selling counterfeit luxury goods (whether in terms of jobs or income or sales taxes, which might not be paid) but there are clear risks in selling counterfeit pharmaceuticals or spare parts for automobiles. In addition, new jobs created by new IP-based industries are likely to pay higher wages and stimulate creativity and reduce the need felt by local creators to live in higher protection countries as exiles.[111]

Trademarks

Trademark protection is an essential ingredient for generating higher inward FDI. The purpose of trademarks is manifold. Trademarks protect the public by indicating the source of goods and services so that purchasers can identify the desired level of quality and receive a similar product or consistent service over time. Trademarks protect the trademark owner against commercial misappropriation of the mark and/or the goodwill associated with the mark. The value of a mark stems from the mental link between particular goods or services and a particular source that is created over time in the minds of prospective buyers. Many people will buy a product or service because, consciously or unconsciously, they associate qualities such as value, excellence, or efficiency with the trademark. A strong trademark is invaluable because the ability of a mark to raise these associations directs a potential buyer towards a company's own product

---

110 KE Maskus, 'Strengthening Intellectual Property Rights in Lebanon', in Fink and Maskus (note 84 above) 286–289.

111 If not physically, at least industrially. For example a book published by an author who is not a national of a Berne (or WTO) member country may still be protected if the book is first published in a member country, thus benefiting the industry of the country of publication.

or service rather than those of a competitor. Trademarks are influenced both by sellers' perceptions about buyers' psychology and the public's marketing-influenced perceptions of how goods and services are differentiated. Trademarks also serve an informational purpose: the legal protection of marks gives companies an incentive to invest in making their marks more recognizable and easier to remember so consumers can more easily identify which particular good or service they want.

As in the case of copyrights, introducing trademark protection will lead to the closure of businesses producing counterfeit goods. Some of the higher-end former counterfeiters may be able to produce non-counterfeit goods (either legal goods of the same class or licensed goods legally bearing the trademark). Counterfeit economic activity may thus be replaced by jobs in distribution, retail, and franchises.[112] These are, however, often low-level, low-skilled jobs. Trademark protection will also benefit consumers who will have access to 'genuine' goods, i.e. goods that come with the perceived assurance of quality associated with the mark via domestic or international advertising and reputation. Over time, the experience in product assembly, delivery, servicing, and management acquired through franchise and distributorship arrangements may be transferred to new, local businesses.

Patents

Patents do not ensure that new products will be supplied in the short term. When patent protection is unavailable, products that would otherwise infringe a patent could be made available legally for the domestic market. In terms of FDI, however, the impact is exactly the opposite, because global firms relying on patent protection need assurances about the level of protection and enforcement before considering any significant technology transfer. Fully exploiting a patent often requires expertise that is not completely disclosed in the published patent or patent application. Ongoing research and variants of the patented inventions may also exist. For this reason, firms also consider the level of trade secret protection in relation to information that, for strategic or other reasons, is not disclosed in a patent. In fact, for certain process patents, even in the presence of a presumption that a product not previously available results from a new patented process, many companies prefer not to disclose new processes in patent applications.[113]

---

112 See Chapter 8 below (Professor Khoury).

113 Art 34(1) of the TRIPS Agreement reads in relevant part: 'if the subject matter of a patent is a process for obtaining a product, the judicial authorities shall have the authority to order the defendant to prove that the process to obtain an identical product is different from the patented process'. See *A Patent System for the 21st Century*, SA Merrill *et al* (eds) (Joseph Henry Press, 2005) 20,23, available at <http://www.nap.edu/html/patentsystem/0309089107.pdf>.

Direct patent-related inward FDI is often the best way to create high-paying, highly skilled jobs, and it is therefore highly sought-after by many governments willing to go to great lengths to attract foreign firms.[114]

Introducing patent protection produces a shock to the economy. Like trademark protection, it will lead to closures of businesses that (legally before patents were issued) were copying products or using processes developed by foreign inventors. In certain cases, as in the area of trademarks, these businesses may become legal manufacturers. In other cases, it may lead economic players to move from imitation-based models to innovation-based models, thus adding to the TRIPS Displacement Effect.[115]

C. The Displacement Effect of TRIPS

The Role of the Demanders

The multinational companies that successfully lobbied to establish a linkage between IP and trade, first in the domestic US context and then in the WTO, did so because of their desire to increase profit and markets or, to put it differently, to maximize rent extraction and increase the number of foreign territories into which they could consider expanding their commercial or industrial activities. Imposing this harsh medicine on developing countries created difficult situations, especially in less industrialized nations.[116] However, it also created, or is leading to the emergence of, new competitors for the same companies that lobbied for TRIPS, as more developing nations at the receiving end of technology transfers and inward FDI develop the ability to innovate and compete. Combined with a healthy dose of economic nationalism, the medium-term impacts of TRIPS, and related measures such as free trade agreements and bilateral investment treaties, the purpose of which is to bring developing countries into the

[114] Javorcik (note 104 above) 60.

[115] Introducing patents may not help R&D efforts based on imitation, because it means in many cases that exploitation of the results of imitation (at least beyond experimental use) would require a license. Moving from a lax indigenous imitative base to a 'foreign seed' base model thus arguably favours countries (mostly in the West) that currently own the bulk of global patented knowledge. But shifts remain possible as innovation grey matter builds up faster in some parts of the developing world, where in addition research costs are lower.

[116] Now subject, however, to the postponement until July 2013 of the deadline to implement TRIPS accorded least-developed nations (TRIPS Council Decision of 29 November 2005, Extension of the Transition Period Under Article 66.1. For Least-Developed Country Members, doc IP/C/40.)

Western IP system, are certainly worth pondering.[117] Compare Japan after World War II and now, or China in 2000 and China circa 2025.[118]

Then again, under pressure to increase profits and shareholder value, the multinational companies that sowed the TRIPS and TRIPS-Plus seeds probably had no choice but to pursue this course of action.[119] A cynic might add that this also explains a possible tendency on the part of some of those companies—and the United States Trade Representative ('USTR') in bilateral agreements—not to accompany TRIPS implementation with strong measures destined to optimize local research, development, and innovation in developing countries, and thereby support the argument that patents in developing countries are best viewed as market creation tools rather than as innovation incentives (in those countries). In other words, with high intellectual property regulation in place, those companies consider these countries first and foremost as new export markets, and possibly lower-cost production centers, while maintaining the technological superiority of the West (where R&D is based), and hence, continued economic dominance. According to this view, as Professor Scotchmer noted, 'intellectual property rights are no longer a way to encourage domestic innovation. They also become a strategic instrument to affect profit flows among nations. To affect profit flows favourably, each country wants the strongest possible protections in foreign countries, and the weakest possible protections for foreigners in its own domestic market.'[120]

It should also be said that the displacement of innovation when it does happen is not a zero-sum game. In other words, it is not possible to say that for every new research dollar in the developing world, a dollar of research will leave the West. Measured on the global scale, innovation may accelerate and cross-fertilization between industrialized and developing nations will occur. The transfer of research and development to developing countries, where costs are lower and skilled and innovative labour abundant, should cause a tectonic shift in the geopolitical plates of intellectual property policy.

---

117 KJ Vandevelde, 'The Political Economy of a Bilateral Investment Treaty' (1998) 92 *Am J Int'l L* 621, 621–23.

118 J Straus, 'The Impact of the New World Order on Economic Development: The Role of the Intellectual Property Rights System', (2006) 6 *J Marshall Rev IP L* 1, 5–9, where Professor Straus describes 'China's commanding, complex, and almost scary development'.

119 Multinational (or perhaps more accurately transnational) corporations 'account for a major share of global R&D. Indeed, with $310 billion spent in 2002 (United Kingdom, DTI 2004), the 700 largest R&D spending firms of the world—of which at least 98% are TNCs—accounted for close to half (46%) of the world's total R&D expenditure and more than two-thirds (69%) of the world's business R&D.' UNCTAD, *World Investment Report 2005* (note 101 above) 119.

120 Scotchmer, *Innovation and Incentives*, note 57 above, 329.

The Transfer of R&D to Developing Countries

The TRIPS demanders' plan was totally understandable from a business standpoint.[121] Yet, it may very well be that the powers of innovation, once unleashed and properly supported, may cut Western dominance short. From this perspective, the end result of TRIPS for many developing countries, and global welfare, would be very positive overall, especially compared with otherwise bleak economic outlooks. As Michael Ryan noted:

> In the foreword to the 1998/99 World Development Report: *Knowledge for Development*, [then]World Bank president James Wolfensohn states that 'economies are built not merely through the accumulation of physical capital and human skill, but on a foundation of information, learning, and adaptation' and declares that in this new world economy . . . the 'globalization of trade, finance, and information flows is intensifying competition, raising the danger that the poorest countries and communities will fall behind more rapidly than ever before'. . . . The WDR recommends that closing knowledge gaps depend upon (1) the acquisition of knowledge through trade, foreign direct investment, and licensing, (2) the absorption of knowledge through education,[122] and (3) the communication of knowledge through advanced information technologies. Developing countries intent upon closing knowledge gaps and reducing information problems will do so with the help [of] intellectual property institutions—trademark to facilitate consumer knowledge, patent to facilitate technology transfer, copyright to facilitate literary, artistic, and informational expression.[123]

In other words, and as India's 'silicon valley' centered around Bangalore and Beijing's 'Z-Park' have begun to demonstrate, the appropriation process that began by the limited outsourcing of low innovation coding or other functions (e.g. 'customer care' call centers) tends to evolve to progressively more complex coding tasks and higher innovation activities, leading to significant innovations

---

121 RM Sherwood, 'Some Things Cannot Be Legislated' (2002) 10 *Cardozo J Int'l & Comp L* 37, 39–40. Sherwood explains that:

> a robust intellectual property regime may indeed not be the objective sought for developing countries by some global elites. The TRIPS level of protection may serve their interests enough to protect their sales into those countries without requiring a level of protection sufficiently robust to encourage local firms and individuals to conduct research and make inventions. In other words, from their perspective, half a loaf for developing countries is just fine. Another way of putting this is to suggest that developing countries are asked by TRIPS to go only half way in protecting intellectual property (primarily the intellectual property of others) without going far enough to fully encourage their own inventors and investors to build national intellectual property prowess.

> See also by the same author 'Global Prospects', note 100 above, 34 ('robust protection will release a great deal of energy into the economies of many of these countries').

122 Learning to learn, learning to imitate, and then to adapt and innovate.

123 MP Ryan, 'Knowledge-Economy Elites, the International Law of Intellectual Property and Trade, and Economic Development' (2002) 10 *Cardozo J Int'l & Comp L* 271, 303.

in the recipient (outsourced-to) country.[124] The outsourced low innovation becomes a form of technology transfer and serves as a stepping stone to higher innovation functions and eventually to world-class competitiveness.[125] Also, while a majority of the initial client base of India's programming powerhouse may have been foreign (most US and European) entities, the potential for home-grown innovation-based industries has now risen very significantly. The same could be said of China's manufacturing industries and more recently of the exponential growth of its information technology and telecommunications sectors.[126]

China's R&D efforts are increasingly rapidly, and it plans to match the US innovation levels (relative to GDP) by 2020,[127] and should have the largest number of researchers of any country by that date.[128]

The possibility of very rapid growth of a country to the top of the global innovation scale is perhaps best exemplified by Israel. As Professor Trajtenberg has shown, Israelis filed less than 100 patent applications per year in the United States Patent and Trademark Office (USPTO) before 1970. That number now

---

124 According to one well-known commentator, the acceleration of outsourcing to India is due to the need of Western companies to deal with the Y2K 'bug', which required extensive but fairly straightforward coding. In that case, the deadline was self-evidently immoveable. See TL Friedman, *The World Is Flat: The Globalized World in the Twenty-First Century* (Penguin Books, 2005), 131–7.

125 As UNCTAD's *World Investment Report 2005* notes (note 101 above), 102:

> Research and development (R&D) is one source of innovation. In the early stages of technological activity, enterprises need not set up formal R&D departments. As they mature, however, it becomes increasingly desirable to monitor, import and implement technologies. R&D as a distinct activity may appear as early as the second level of complexity, where multifaceted technologies are involved or if local conditions demand significant adaptation. In a developing country, such R&D is feasible once the operation is fairly large scale and the necessary technical skills are available. The role of formal R&D then grows as the firm attempts significant technological improvements to introduce new products or processes.

126 Christine Zhen-Wei Qiang, *China's Information Revolution: Managing the Economic and Social Transformation* (World Bank, 2007).

127 According to the China Blawg, 'The OECD (see <http://www.oecd.org/document/26/0,2340,en_2649_201185_37770522_1_1_1_1,00.html>) recently announced that this year, China's R&D spending will surpass that of Japan. Estimates have China's 2006 spending of US$136 billion edging out Japan's US$130 billion investment. . . .The rapid increase in R&D spending in China is one aspect of its current economic development policy that is designed to make China a major innovative force in the near future. The government announced a 15-year plan last February that has R&D spending rising to 2% of GDP by 2010 and 2.5% of GDP by 2020. This would put China's R&D spending as a percentage of GDP at U.S. levels by 2020.' Available at <http://blawg.lehmanlaw.com/english/archives/2006/12/05/199.html>.

128 According to the same OECD report, 'China, the number of researchers increased by 77% between 1995 and 2004. China now ranks second worldwide with 926,000 researchers, just behind the United States (more than 1.3 million)'. The Gartner Group recently ranked India's Infosys as the most innovative software company worldwide.

surpasses 1,200.[129] In terms of patents issued per year by the USPTO to foreign nationals, Israel's rate of growth between 1968 and 1997 was 13.3 per cent, compared to 5.5 per cent for Canada and Ireland, 2.4 per cent for Germany, and 3.1 per cent for the UK. Among the few countries that did better than Israel over this period are New Zealand (16.9 per cent); South Korea (27.9 per cent) and Taiwan (15.7 per cent). More importantly perhaps, Israel has the fourth largest number of patents per capita (after the United States, Japan and Taiwan).[130] A reason for the success of the Israeli innovation strategy is its focus, with 20 per cent or more of all patents issued in only three areas: electronics, computers & communications, and pharmaceuticals.[131]

Developing Countries as Global Competitors

It is not unrealistic to see a future where Indian, Chinese and other companies compete head-to-head with innovation-based Western enterprises (in fact, in certain industries, this process has begun). This innovation displacement effect of TRIPS and TRIPS-Plus agreements may be accelerated when considering that a very significant proportion of researchers in Western laboratories are nationals of developing countries (such as China and India).[132] Since the West cannot compete on manufacturing costs and less so on productivity than before, if (when) it loses its competitive innovation advantage, the picture of the global economy may be profoundly altered, with a shift of the gravity centre. To a certain extent that would prove that those who pushed for the application of TRIPS-compliant norms to the developing world were right (at least for countries counted as success stories). As we have seen, those demanders were largely US- and Europe-based multinationals. It would amount to historical irony if they should end up losing their economic dominance as a result.[133]

---

129 M Trajtenberg, 'Innovation in Israel 1968–1997', in AB Jaffe and M Trajtenberg, *Patents, Citations and Innovations: A Window on the Knowledge Economy* (MIT Press, 2002), 337–376.

130 Ibid, 347–8. Taiwan's per capita number surpassed Israel in 1996. Taiwan would be another interesting case study.

131 Ibid, 353. Mechanical and chemical patents constitute approximately 10 per cent (each) of the total. As of 1994, mechanical patents were still the largest category overall in the USPTO filings, with electronics, computers & communications, and pharmaceuticals standing at 15 per less or less.

132 The *Financial Times* reports that in order to compensate for the shortage of first-rate talent, the 'clamour for brains is driving elite employers in the UK to behave like football talent scouts in India and elsewhere'. A Clegg, 'In Hot Pursuit of the Best Brains,' *Financial Times*, 14 March 2007.

133 Joseph Stiglitz reports that both the Council of Economic Advisers and the Office of Science and Technology Policy in the White House had deep reservations about TRIPS, and that he believes that 'the way the intellectual property regime has evolved is not good for the United States and the EU; but even more, I believe it is not in the interests of the developing countries'. (Stiglitz, note 13 above, 116–7).

Perhaps the plan is that, through investment and acquisition, the same capital will remain dominant in most industries, though geographically reconfigured (an issue for Western tax authorities—who may have to move massively to sales-based taxes to replace income-based revenues—but not for the companies involved).[134] That would explain why, both in bilateral discussions and multilaterally (to the extent that the WTO remains a viable negotiation forum for new areas), there is such an emphasis on investment liberalization.[135] However, it may call into question the assumption that governs US bilateral and multinational intellectual property negotiations, that US domestic interests are co-extensive with those of multinational corporations[136] even though multinational corporations that label themselves as American companies, rightly or not, still need the US government (and occasionally, it seems, also its military arm) to spur growth of new markets.

In light of the high mobility of capital and innovation, the relative lack of scientists (especially compared to very high enrollment in science and engineering programs in a number of developing countries including China),[137] and the higher level of business regulation in the United States and associated compliance costs,[138] is it fair to ask whether US prominence in innovation (and its

134 One author argues that, once the proper legal system and protection is in place—and especially what he refers to as the invisible infrastructure of 'asset management'—the conditions required for the 'Western' capitalist model to be moveable and innovation fully to emerge will be present. See de Soto, note 15 above.

135 UNCTAD maintains a database of bilateral investment treaties. The list is impressive. As of June 1 2006 it listed 48 bilateral treaties involving the United States alone. Available at <http://www.unctadxi.org/templates/DocSearch____779.aspx>.

136 CJ Forster, *China's Secret Weapon: Science Policy and Global Power* (The Foreign Policy Center, London, 2006) 29–30: '[w]hile policymakers regard S&T [science and technology] as a race between nations in a zero-sum game, businesses see themselves as part of a global information network . . . Government officials are more concerned about stemming the flow of technologies to competitors and possible rivals who might use it for military objectives . . . However, firms and businesses prefer a system that leads to the dissemination of knowledge, including to political rivals.'

137 *World Investment Report 2005* (note 97 above) 159ff. One should also consider the number of students from developing countries enrolled in programs in industrialized countries. The *World Investment Report* notes annual growth of employment in R&D in developing countries (by local and foreign entities) of 20 per cent compared to approximately 2 per cent in the West. The cumulative effect of this growth over 20 years seems to support the displacement effect theory.

138 One well-known example would be the Public Company Accounting Reform and Investor Protection Act of 2002 (Pub L No 107–204, 116 Stat 745—also known as 'Sarbanes–Oxley'). According to the *Financial Times*, the severe restrictions on immigration after the 11 September attacks, including the major cuts in student and H1-B visas, are contributing to the shifting of research and development overseas. (This trend is also affected by the extremely unfriendly attitude of immigration officers and excessive, arbitrary deportations—their poll shows that 66 per cent of foreign travellers agreed with the statement that a simple mistake or single wrong thing could lead to detention or deportation.) The newspaper notes that 'presenting an unwelcoming face to the world has political as well as economic implications'. G Rachman, 'How to help the huddled masses through immigration,' *Financial Times* blog entry, 13 March 2007. Available at <http://blogs.ft.

insistence that other countries continually increase their levels of IP protection) will endure?[139] Is it clear that the pharmaceutical companies that drive US foreign intellectual property policy will forever remain 'US companies'? As Chris Patten, former Governor of Hong Kong and European Commissioner for External Relations noted recently, '[i]f the Western front has fundamentally changed, or been broken by events and cultural disjuncture, what international configuration will emerge during the short interval of years before the rise of China and India reshapes the world's power politics?'[140]

D. Intellectual Property in the Future World Economy

The latest developments in China, India and others such as Brazil and perhaps Russia[141] beg the question whether imitation is a necessary phase of industrial development (defined here as a movement towards Western-style capitalism with

com/rachmanblog/2007/03/how_to_help_the.html#more>. Rachman notes: 'A McKinsey report into America's financial services industry, also published in January, warned that New York risks losing its status as the "financial capital of the world" within 10 years. The first two problems it cited were over-regulation and fear of litigation. But problem three was US immigration restrictions which are shutting out highly skilled workers.'

139 As of 2003, United States was (still) home for 42.3 per cent of the top 700 R&D firms worldwide (*World Investment Report 2005*, note 101 above, 121). But the figure is based on dollars spent, which obscures two key factors: how efficiently the research dollars are spent, and how far can a research dollar be stretched in one country compared to another—per-employee expenditures of US firms are significantly lower in their overseas laboratories (ibid, at 122), and recent surveys show that cost and lack of manpower in industrialized nations (which slows time to market) have become major drivers of decisions about the location of R&D (ibid, 159). The recent announcement by Intel that it was moving design and manufacturing operations to Dalian (China) at a cost of $2.5 billion (though at this stage at least, not for the most advanced chips) is yet another example of a trend that is likely to accelerate. See 'Intel given green light for 2.5-billion-U.S.-dollar wafer facility in NE China', *People's Daily*, 15 March 2007 (available at <http://english.people.com.cn/200703/15/eng20070315_358013.html>). Intel set up Intel China Labs in 2000 and in April 2006 also formed an alliance with Baidu.com, a major Chinese search engine, to develop search applications for laptops, mobile phones, and home PCs. See 'Intel, Baidu to jointly develop search apps', *InfoWorld*, 13 April 2006 (available at <http://www.infoworld.com/article/06/04/13/77407_HNintelbaidusearch_1.html>).

140 Chris Patten, *Not Quite the Diplomat* (Penguin, 2006), 2. Mr Patten also questions the recent move by the United States government away from multilateral forums: '[t]here are other and better ways of asserting the primacy of values in which America has always believed than ultimate dependence on exceptionalism: doing whatever America wishes to do because she can get away with it. . . . international agreements and the rule of law offer more effective ways of guiding the international community and protecting America's interest' (ibid, at 307).

141 The four so-called BRIC countries. It seems the term was first prominently used by Goldman Sachs investment bank in 2001 in Global Economics Paper No. 99: 'Dreaming with BRICs: The Path to 2050', available at: <http://www2.goldmansachs.com/insight/research/reports/99.pdf>. See also 'The BRICs Dream: Web Tour', July 2006, available at: <http://www2.goldmansachs.com/insight/research/reports/report32.html>. See also RC Bird, 'Defending Intellectual Property Rights in the BRIC Economies' (2006)43 *Am Bus LJ* 317, 347.

a strong emphasis on innovation).[142] It could be argued that the imitation phase is essential to internalize the 'global' state of the art in any given field. In other words, before one can begin to innovate, one must know what the most advanced thinking is around the world.[143] Then, perhaps, one can invent improvements and obtain intellectual property protection. Naturally, one must have the intellectual, technical and material tools to access and process this global state of the art before improvements or adaptations can be envisaged. This explains the heavy emphasis on education in technical assistance analyses and in the last part of this chapter.

To take an example, the notion of novelty in patent law is generally defined as worldwide novelty, meaning that any element of prior art anticipating the invention claimed anywhere in the world will be sufficient cause to refuse the application. As a result, and also owing to the global nature of trade flows (especially in ideational goods and services), innovation is necessarily a global business and a huge step up for most developing countries. A possible exception are products and services, including variants of existing ones, developed to cater to the needs of consumers in a specific developing country or region. If that is correct, then those countries that had begun their growth and the imitation phase prior to TRIPS implementation may have benefited from a head start. For now, however, large exporting firms are the clearest winners.[144]

Another, related question worth asking is whether the Western economic institutions and capitalism are coterminous, or whether they are just an instantiation of a (somewhat 'free') market economy. Perhaps technological innovation can be woven into different social and economic fabrics, thus creating what Charles Taylor refers to as 'multifaceted' capitalism—the South may be redefining capitalism, and the broadly-held assumption that a free market may not exist without certain rights and freedoms (e.g. freedom of expression) may very well be proven wrong. Arguably, China, which is much less free than India, for instance, has been doing better over the past ten years.

---

142 Imitation is still widely practiced in the West, as part of the innovation process, notably in the form of reverse engineering.

143 To benefit from the patent system, innovators must be aware of the global state of the art. To become so, they should familiarize themselves with published patents and applications (most of which are published 18 months after filing). As Jaffe and Trajtenberg's research has shown (see note 127 above), patents are a window on the process of technological change and a powerful tool for research on the economics of innovation. Patent records contain a wealth of information, including the inventors' identity, location, and employer, as well as the technological field of the invention. Patents also contain citation references to previous patents, which allow one to trace links across inventions. On the impact on national innovation policy, see D Archibugi and S Iammarino. 'The Globalization of Technology and National Policies', in D Archibugi and B-A Lundvall (eds). *The Globalizing Learning Economy* (Oxford, 2002).

144 E Su, 'The Winners and the Losers: The Agreement on the Trade-Related Aspects of Intellectual Property Rights and Its Effects on Developing Countries' (2000) 23 *Hous J Int'l L* 169, 214.

What seems inescapable, however, is the move towards modernity, which I would define for the purposes of this chapter, and using Taylorian terminology again, as moving to a rational moral order in which, following neo-Stoic teachings (Grotius) and Locke, 'economic (i.e. ordered, peaceful, productive) activity has become the model for human behaviour and the key to harmonious existence'.[145] Ideology- or religion-based social orders, including those interpreted as excluding women or social classes or fearing innovation and change, will find it much harder, and it may be that to succeed in this scenario[146] this child of the Enlightenment we call modernity is not something that innovative societies can easily avoid inviting to their economic dinner table. 'The Eighteenth-century transition is in a sense a crucial one in the development of Western modernity . . . [it] generated new, stadial theories of history, which saw human societies developing through a series of stages, defined by the form of their economy (e.g. hunter–gatherer, agricultural), culminating in the contemporary commercial society.'[147]

The globalization of media, in particular the internet, feeds the social imaginaries. For one thing, it provides new images of what is, and of what is possible. This is crucial because, as Taylor's insightful analyses have shown, a perception of what is possible widens the array of norms that are realizable. In other words, people don't fight for utopia, but can move into action for something they know they can achieve.

The passage of time likely will show that some of the (Western) institutions we associate with an innovation-based capitalist economy are not in fact a necessary ingredient of a society that is able to compete (using the same science of course) with the West. It will be interesting to see whether Western-style democracy is but an idiosyncratic variant of modernity. Put differently, while stadial analysis is indeed inexorable, there may not be a single path forward and the very direction of technological progress may be altered as a result.

Part III Towards a Comprehensive Knowledge and Innovation Strategy

> Wealth in the age of flatness will increasingly gravitate to those countries who get three basic things right: the infrastructure to connect as efficiently and speedily as possible with the flat world platform, the right education programs and knowledge

[145] Charles Taylor, *Modern Social Imaginaries* (Duke University Press, 2005), 15.

[146] To quote Taylor again, '[i]ndividualism and mutual benefit are the evident residual ideas that remain after you have sloughed off the older religions and metaphysics' (ibid, 18).

[147] Ibid., 48.

skills to empower more of their people to innovate and do value-added work on that platform, and, finally, the right governance—that is, the right tax policies, the right investment and trade laws, the right support for research, the right intellectual property laws, and, most of all, the right inspirational leadership.[148]

A. Developing a Calibrated Innovation Policy

Many of the studies cited in Part II of this chapter insist on the fact that sufficient and adequate intellectual property protection is but one ingredient in a complex recipe to achieve innovation-based economic development. IPR protection is essential, but in itself insufficient to ensure growth. As Hernando de Soto noted in that respect:

> By stabilizing and adjusting 'the book,' the globalizers' macroeconomic programs have dramatically rationalized the economic management of developing countries. But because their book does not address the fact that most people do not have property rights, they have done only a fraction of the work required to create a comprehensive capitalist system . . . Because they concentrated only on policies dealing with the aggregates, they did not inquire whether people had the means to participate in an expanded market system.[149]

Refocusing the Policy Lens

Every developing country (or perhaps in some cases, region) wishing to succeed in a global knowledge-based economy should aim to develop a national innovation (eco)system,[150] which is 'constituted by elements which interact in the production, diffusion and use of new, and economically useful, knowledge'.[151] Unfortunately, there has been a myopic focus on the IP norms themselves which resulted in narratives being devised to justify minimalist or maximalist interpretations of TRIPS and related implementations and technical assistance initiatives. Yet intellectual property is but one train in a comprehensive knowledge and

[148] Friedman, note 124 above, 329.

[149] de Soto, note 15 above, 211.

[150] A term popularised by Bengt-Åke Lundvall. B-Å Lundvall (ed.) *National Innovation Systems: Towards a Theory of Innovation and Interactive Learning,* (Pinter, 1992).

[151] Ibid, at 2. Stan Metcalfe provides a more complete definition: 'set of distinct institutions which jointly and individually contribute to the development and diffusion of new technologies and which provides the framework within which governments form and implement policies to influence the innovation process. As such it is a system of interconnected institutions to create, store and transfer the knowledge, skills and artefacts which define new technologies.' JS Metcalfe 'The Economic Foundations of Technology Policy: Equilibrium and Evolutionary Perspectives', in P Stoneman (ed), *Handbook of the Economics of Innovation and Technological Change* (Blackwell, 1995). See also Organisation for Economic Co-operation and Development. *National Innovations Systems* (OECD, 1997), available at <http://www.oecd.org/dataoecd/35/56/2101733.pdf>.

innovation policy, and the trains of surrounding norms and policies must also make it to the station if the objective is to be attained. By themselves, intellectual property rules arguably benefit mostly major owners of intellectual property, who are largely concentrated in a few highly industrialized countries.[152]

Most of the narratives that try to explain the emergence of TRIPS (discussed in Part I.A of this chapter) often focus on the negative context for developing countries. Not surprisingly, they gave birth to implementation narratives I categorized as 'subtractive' because of their insistence on minimalist TRIPS implementation. In the meantime, certain lobbies, with the support of key players, insist on increasing the protection to TRIPS-Plus levels in bilateral and regional discussions. Both approaches are flawed. To successfully exploit intellectual property, to maximize its economic growth in areas that are information- and intellectual property-intensive, and to be able to produce goods and services with a higher ideational content (which is what intellectual property rules tends to protect), each country needs a comprehensive knowledge optimization strategy. This may include using to the maximum extent TRIPS flexibilities in certain areas, but not in others.

Innovation often proceeds along the following sequence: first a country imitates foreign technology (the *imitation* phase, which itself requires some technical skills); then it modifies the foreign technology to suit domestic needs and markets (the *local innovation* phase); then it produces innovations (whether new products or processes or improvements of existing ones) which are globally competitive (the *global innovation* phase). A strong intellectual property system will be required to support phase III. It will also be particularly helpful in phase II. Conflicts which may arise due to the need to license the foreign technology to which an improvement is made or applied often can be solved through licencing (market forces) or if that fails, by the issuance of a dependent patent compulsory licence (as allowed under TRIPS Article 31(l)).

Policy makers, especially those from more advanced developing and merging economies, may be well advised to focus more on developing domestic innovation than to limit rent-seeking efforts by foreign multinationals.[153] The latter is

152 According to UNIDO, 94 per cent of all privately-funded research and development was located in those countries during the 1990s. See UNIDO, *Industrial Development Report 2002/03* (Vienna: UNIDO, 2002).

153 Shari L Boyd *et al*, 'Agricultural Biotechnology Innovations *Versus* Intellectual Property Rights: Are Developing Countries at the Mercy of Multinationals?', (2003) 4 *J World Inv* 211, 212, where the authors note:

> . . . the real question is not how to prevent multinational biotechnology firms from exploiting developing countries, but rather, how to induce them to want to exploit developing countries.

a short-term fix in a much more complex, longer-term effort to establish, maintain or enhance competitiveness in an increasingly intangible world trading system. In other words, the *adequate* (not minimal) protection of commercially or industrially relevant knowledge forms part of an optimal strategy.

If the above seems a fair conclusion in light of the studies discussed in Part II of this chapter, then those studies are also illuminating by what they do not and perhaps cannot show. It is extremely difficult to isolate the importance of the intellectual property factor in the growth of bilateral trade flows and FDI. It is even more difficult to determine *ex ante* what the optimal level of protection is. This is partly due to the fact that the TRIPS Agreement imposes global minimum standards, and there remain very few statistically significant options to compare various levels of protection below that floor. *Ex post* analysis is not a policy panacea either due to the uneven quality of econometric studies, in turn due to the quality of available (*versus* ideal) field of empirical data. However, I suggest that what is a problem in theory actually forms part of the solution once we shift to policy setting.

The Future of TRIPS

The TRIPS Agreement is the strongest normative vector in setting intellectual property policy. In other words, because WTO members cannot legislate below the TRIPS levels without incurring the risk of dispute-settlement proceedings under the Dispute-Settlement Understanding,[154] and because it is unlikely that TRIPS norms will be diluted in the Doha Round,[155] it would seem to be pragmatically justified to take TRIPS as a given quantity in the policy equation. The remaining parts of the equation are to determine how the reasonably available flexibility in implementing the Agreement should be used, which should only be done, I would submit, as part of a comprehensive domestic strategy. I argue that integrating TRIPS norms into such a strategy is tactically sound

Multinationals lining up to extract monopoly rents from developing countries would be the surest sign that investments in the desired innovations are taking place. Unless developing countries or aid-givers are willing to subsidize biotechnology tailored to developing countries—and there is no evidence to suggest they will—the investment will simply not take place.

154 WTO Agreement, Annex 2, Understanding on Rules and Procedures Governing the Settlement of Disputes, Annex 2, Legal Instruments–Results of the Uruguay Round, Vol 31, 33 ILM 112 (1994). See also Gervais, *The TRIPS Agreement*, note 20 above, 340–44. One should note that not all countries are equal when it comes to the DSU. The EU and US have resisted applying decisions of the DSU that found their legislation incompatible with their WTO obligations. The long-standing dispute between the EU and the so-called 'dollar banana' countries (Conditions for the Granting of Tariff Preferences to Developing Countries, doc WT/DS246/AB/R) is an example, while in the United States a panel decision concerning the incompatibility of exceptions contained in s. 110(5)(b) of the Copyright Act rendered in 2000 remains unimplemented as of this writing (May 2007).

155 Gervais ibid, 43–51.

because (a) by and large TRIPS strikes an adequate balance if properly implemented and (b) TRIPS is here to stay.

And TRIPS is working in a number of emerging economies, to the extent that it has brought innovators based in those countries to the global IP table.[156] For example, in Korea PCT applications have jumped from 196 in 1995 to 4,422 in 2005;[157] in China, from 103 to 2,501 over the same period; in Brazil, from 67 to 275; and in India, from 0 to 675.[158] Trademark applications have also shown significant increases.[159]

What emerges below as a strategy is not a series of measures designed to nominally implement TRIPS rules and find loopholes that essentially shrink the protection away. Certain proposed interpretations of Articles 27 and 30 of TRIPS,[160] or the fact that the Agreement in many cases imposes no clear rules as to the ownership of IPRs, may mean that a country can formally implement TRIPS while systematically disempowering parts of it through legal 'gimmickry', while 'getting away with it' as far as the WTO dispute-settlement system is concerned. The objective of this chapter is not to suggest ways to avoid being found 'guilty' by a WTO panel. Rather, it is to optimize knowledge and economic development using TRIPS rules as an ingredient. This may involve some flexibility in the TRIPS implementation process but as part of a comprehensive strategy.

---

156 Owing to the postponement until 2013 of the implementation deadline, the discussion really should focus on developing, not least-developed countries. See note 79 above.

157 WIPO Statistics. Available at <http://www.wipo.int/ipstats/en/statistics/pct/index.html>.

158 Ibid.

159 WIPO Statistics. Source: <http://www.wipo.int/ipstats/en/statistics/marks/>.

160 For example, UNCTAD recently suggested that

> The exclusions in Article 27:3 are framed more narrowly, yet again leave substantial room for interpretation. For example, Article 27:3(a) permits the exclusion of 'therapeutic methods' for the treatment of humans. The use of pharmaceuticals is a method of therapy for treating human health conditions, and so arguably . . . a Member could exclude the use of drugs for medical treatment from patent protection.

UNCTAD. Course on Dispute Settlement: WTO: Module 3.14 TRIPS, UNCTAD/EDM/Misc.232/Add.18, <http://www.unctad.org/en/docs/edmmisc232add18_en.pdf> (2003), 20.

I do not believe that a WTO DS panel would agree with this interpretation. On Art 30, the same report indicates that '[t]he ordinary meaning of the terms in Article 30 would appear to allow considerable flexibility to Members in adopting exceptions to the rights of patent holders' (ibid, 22) which may create a sense of 'flexibility' that many a panel might not necessarily agree with.

B. Striking the Right Balance

> . . . our goal, which we hope is one that can be shared by all Member States, of ensuring that the international IP system functions for the good of all, with benefits outweighing any costs and in a way which encourages, and does not hinder, sustainable economic, social and cultural development.[161]

Defining Balance

Balance is ostensibly what every policy maker is striving towards.[162] But what is it? It is not, contrary to what one often reads or hears in policy debates concerning intellectual property, a simple axis with rights holders at one end and users of intellectual property on the other. For one thing, there is no uniform categorization that holds up to serious scrutiny. All rights holders have to get their 'inspiration' from somewhere or someone.

How can a government who wishes to do so adopt a 'balanced' innovation policy? Should that government err on the side of high protection or rather protect the 'public domain' and limit protection until a need for protection is shown? Should it take the policy gamble of increasing protection to see if it produces positive results without major or even overwhelming negative externalities? Clearly, it seems easier to make intellectual property *ex post facto* and adjust the framework, rather than wait for a perfect model to emerge from theoretical analyses.

---

161 Proposal by the United Kingdom to the Inter-Sessional Intergovernmental Meeting on a Development Agenda for WIPO (Annex), WIPO Document IIM/2/3, 14 June 2005.

162 Examples include: Federal Trade Commission, 'To Promote Innovation: The Proper Balance of Competition and Patent Law and Policy Executive Summary' (2004) 19 *Berkeley Tech LJ* 861; S Rodriguez Hurley, 'Failing to Balance Patent Rights and Antitrust Concerns: The Federal Circuit's Holding in *In Re Independent Service Organizations* Antitrust Litigation' (2003–4), 13 *Fed Circuit BJ* 475; PJ Gardner, 'US Intellectual Property Law and the Biotech Challenge: Searching for an Elusive Balance.' [2003] *BJ* 28; H Soehnge, 'The Drug Price Competition and Patent Term Restoration Act of 1984: Fine-Tuning the Balance Between the Interests of Pioneer and Generic Drug Manufacturers' (2003) 58 *Food & Drug LJ* 51; KE Maskus and EV Wong, 'Searching for Economic Balance in Business Method Patents' (2002) 8 *Wash UJL & Pol'y* 289; A Lacayo, 'Seeking A Balance: International Pharmaceutical Patent Protection, Public Health Crises, and the Emerging Threat of Bio-Terrorism' (2002) 33 *U Miami Inter-Am LR* 295; JS Golian, 'Without a Net: The Supreme Court Attempts to Balance Patent Protection and Public Notice in *Festo Corp v Shoketsu Kinzoku Kogyo Kabushiki Co*' (2003) 36 *Creighton LR* 541; J Langenfeld, 'Intellectual Property and Antitrust: Steps Toward Striking a Balance' (2001) 52 *Case W Res LR* 91; JA Harrelson, 'TRIPS, Pharmaceutical Patents, and the HIV/AIDS Crisis: Finding the Proper Balance Between Intellectual Property Rights and Compassion' (2001) 7 *Widener L Symp J* 175; T Klein, 'The Uncertain Balance Between Parody and Trademark Rights' (2001) 12 *J Contemp L Issues* 356; RG Frenkel, 'Intellectual Property in the Balance: Proposals for Improving Industrial Design Protection in the Post-TRIPS Era' (1999) 32 *Loy LA LR* 531; AN Littman, 'Restoring the Balance of Our Patent System' (1997) 37 *IDEA* 545; JC Yates and MR Greenlee 'Intellectual Property on the Internet: Balance of Interests Between the Cybernauts and the Bureaucrats'(1996) 8:7 *J Proprietary Rights* 8.

That analysis is complex, *inter alia*, because of the many sectors of intellectual property (and sub-sectors: should industrial machines, business models, biotechnology, HIV drugs and chemical agricultural products be treated the same because they are protected by patents?). I suggest that not only should a government favour a 'balanced' approach, it must also decide where to intervene and when.[163]

Balance, then, is far from being a simple game of 'pulling covers' and trying to please the often short-sighted demands of lobbies representing rights holders or various users or public interest groups. Balance means achieving an optimal degree of protection, which appropriately protects and rewards creativity and ingenuity, thus providing a good incentive to continue, while not deterring others' creativity and inventiveness. That optimal point is hard to define, and in fact will likely vary from country to country based on socio-economic, industrial and even cultural factors.

A Balanced TRIPS Implementation

Because TRIPS establishes a 'common denominator', its implementation should be a combination of a careful analysis of the proper intellectual property policy of a country or region, and use of flexibility left in TRIPS to achieve this policy objective. That determination of the most appropriate TRIPS-compatible legal framework must then be combined with corresponding policies in relevant sectors, use of systems such as compulsory licensing but only where appropriate, etc, as well as training of government and private sector players. Developing countries gain more by integrating TRIPS norms in a broader innovation and knowledge optimization strategy. As with market openness, intellectual property rules *per se* are at best a catalyst.

The suggested approach is not incompatible with the views of, e.g. UNCTAD, which wrote in its 2004 Trade & Development Report:[164]

> . . . most of the evidence suggests that the impact of trade openness has been highly uneven, and contingent on a variety of institutional factors, and that there is room for discretionary policy measures at the micro and macro level.

163 Stiglitz suggests that in developing countries he sees 'government having a more active role, in both promoting development and protecting the poor . . . While markets are at the center of any successful economy, government has to create a climate that allows business to thrive and create jobs. It has to construct physical and institutional infra structure—laws ensuring, for instance, a sound banking system and securities markets in which investors can have confidence . . .' (note 13 above, 27).

164 UNCTAD (note 78 above).

> A more balanced perspective, also taking its cue from Adam Smith, links a process of successful integration back to productivity gains from specialization, gains that are amplified through innovation, the use of better equipment, scale economies at the firm level and by 'externalities' such as learning and improvements in human capital. This ties economic success to a heightened degree of economic interdependence through the mutually reinforcing interactions between expanding markets and an increasingly complex division of labour. Extending and deepening such interactions depends on new investments under conditions of objective uncertainty. To improve and expand existing capacity as well as to introduce new products and processes, a 'profit-investment nexus' is needed that requires supporting financial arrangements, including accommodative monetary policy and relatively stable legal institutions.[165]

And further:

> . . . the openness agenda has perpetuated a lopsided view of the forces driving economic integration. It stresses the potential gains from participation in international markets while downplaying adjustment costs, and it stresses convergence tendencies while ignoring potential sources of cumulative divergence. As the previous sections have suggested, this approach has its limitations. Trade is just one among several interrelated factors shaping integration. Its impact is largely contingent on the presence of dynamic forces—specialization, learning and innovation, scale economies and capital formation—that do not respond in a simple or predictable way to the incentives generated from rapid opening up. Strengthening these forces requires a series of complementary institutional reforms and discretionary macroeconomic, industrial and social policy measures. This implies considerable diversity in the pattern of integration, even among countries at similar levels of economic development.[166]

True, importing intellectual property rules wholesale into the legislative and industrial fabric of a developing economy is insufficient for that country to succeed.[167] However, it is fair to assume that a country's technology imports and inward FDI are unlikely to grow without intellectual property rules. We can conclude that (a) intellectual property rules are required but insufficient; (b) it is more pragmatic to accept TRIPS (which does not mean that efforts to develop alternative sets of norms are ill-founded); and (c) intellectual property rules must

---

165 Ibid, 79.

166 Ibid, 95.

167 That point was well articulated in the Report of the UK Commission on Intellectual Property Rights, note 85 above, Executive Summary, 5:

> . . . it may be unwise to focus on TRIPS as a principal means of facilitating technology transfer. A wider agenda needs to be pursued, as is currently being done in the WTO. Developed countries need to give serious consideration to their policies for encouraging technology transfer. In addition, they should promote more effective research and cooperation with and among developing countries to strengthen their scientific and technological capabilities.

be properly calibrated as part of a broader domestic innovation and knowledge optimization strategy.

Except perhaps in specific areas such as traditional knowledge protection, it would be counterproductive to focus all efforts on the development of new and independent rules, for at least two reasons. First, there is little if any evidence that a new form of intellectual property or even variations on known themes would work better. Second, there would be huge transition costs and friction in convincing foreign partners of the validity of such new or customized rules. For multinational corporate investors, there is value in predictability and dealing with a known set of regulatory parameters.

The policy flexibility needed by developing economies is partly there in TRIPS. More importantly, by developing a comprehensive strategy, a country can limit the negative impact of moving to higher intellectual property protection and increase its chances of reaping the benefits thereof, including technology-related FDI and growing domestic internet, pharmaceutical or other technology-based industries.

C. Towards a National Knowledge and Innovation Strategy

Intellectual property rules *per se* do not automatically lead to better or more innovation and (commercially exploited) creativity. By themselves, they do not even achieve the limited purpose of increasing inward FDI. This is what has prompted many developing countries to insist on the technology transfer part of the TRIPS bargain, which is enshrined in Article 66.2,[168] as well as capacity building under Article 67. This is linked to the quest for an intrinsic equilibrium in the way intellectual property protection is implemented, measured country by country (even in the face of uniform multilateral rules).[169]

Granted, the task at hand is not a simple one. Yet, instead of devoting major efforts to turning back the clock on extant liberalization and intellectual property

[168] Which reads as follows: 'Developed country Members shall provide incentives to enterprises and institutions in their territories for the purpose of promoting and encouraging technology transfer to least-developed country Members in order to enable them to create a sound and viable technological base.'

The Council for TRIPS is actively following the implementation of this provision, notably by requiring reports on technology transfer initiatives taken by developed countries. See the WTO Annual Report 2005, 13 (available at <http://www.wto.org/english/res_e/booksp_e/anrep_e/anrep05_e.pdf>). See also WTO document IP/C/W/431 and addenda for a summary of the information provided.

[169] Note 57 above and accompanying text.

rules, I suggest that they can be put to good use. There is no room in this chapter to cover all aspects of a comprehensive knowledge optimization strategy, the primary purpose of which would be to strengthen a country's economy and its growth. Indeed, each one of the headings below could be the topic of a entire book (and some in fact have been). However, the following paths are probably some of those that could be followed.

Priority setting and Enhancing Domestic Innovative Capabilities

'IPRs without technology capacity building can do little.'[170]

Based on existing industrial infrastructures, successes, education programs, available natural and human resources, and potential domestic and regional markets, what are the realistic areas that a country should prioritize?[171] The primary target of a National Knowledge and Innovation Strategy should not be to obtain new imports, though they may be useful, but rather to build domestic intellectual property generating activities, in part through FDI (which almost always includes a knowledge and technology transfer component) and technology transfer and acquisition.[172]

Developing WTO members who want to maximize the benefits of TRIPS (while minimizing negative effects and associated welfare costs) should apply outcomes

170 H Salar Amoli and A Shamsavari, 'Modernisation of national Intellectual Property legislation in IR Iran and its effect on technology transfer through Foreign Direct Investment' (2006) 3:3 *World Review of Science, Technology, and Sustainable Development* 223.

171 Some scholars (e.g. H Ergas, 'The Importance of Technology Policy', in P Dasgupta and P Stoneman (eds), *Economic Policy and Technological Performance* (Cambridge University Press, 1987) have used a taxonomy which 'distinguishes *mission-* and *diffusion-oriented policy designs* to classify and analyse national systems of innovation. Mission-oriented systems are characterised by centralisation and the concentration of policy support on a small number of technologies and larger firms, unlike diffusion-oriented systems which concentrate their policy efforts on increasing an economy's capacity of innovating by concentrating on the scientific infrastructure, technology transfer and cooperation, i.e. formal and informal relationships between different actors etc.', U Cantner and A Pyka, 'Classifying Technology Policy from an Evolutionary Perspective' (Thesis, Augsburg Economics Institute, 1999). Available at <http://www.wiwi.uni-augsburg.de/vwl/institut/paper/84.pdf>. The taxonomy is useful, but for most developing countries, I suggest that concentrating on specific sectors may be required to optimize the use of available resources.

172 The Arab countries' proposal to WIPO on its Development Agenda (Proposal by the Kingdom of Bahrain on the Importance of Intellectual Property in Social and Economic Development and National Development Programs, WIPO doc IIM/2/2, 14 June 2005, Annex, at p 6 of Annex) contained the following:

> As a first step, Member States should be encouraged to and assisted in setting up national strategies on intellectual property, which identify areas of strength and weakness in dealing with intellectual property systems. Remedies should be found for weak areas and areas of strength should be further enhanced with a view to attaining a successful and efficient functioning of the intellectual property system.

of priority-setting exercises to idea-management strategies and help provide their domestic enterprises with idea management tools. As Professor Hargadon noted, the purpose of idea-management strategies is to 'link people, ideas, and objects together in ways that form effective and lasting communities and technologies'.[173] Another commentator suggested that 'a network-based idea management tool can be understood as a mechanism for transforming tacit, intangible human capital into explicit, tangible structural capital. Intellectual capital in explicit form can be managed, manipulated, exposed to and combined with other tangible and intangible resources and objects—people, funds and other ideas, for example. This is the intended function of idea management . . .'[174]

A strategy should include ways to develop the ability of the local economy to network private and public sector stakeholders, thereby increasing its ability to integrate and internalize innovative processes. As the OECD noted in its well-known report on national innovation systems:

> New types of policies are needed to address systemic failures, particularly policies directed to networking and improving firm absorptive capacities. Networking schemes put emphasis on improving the interaction of actors and the interplay of institutions within national innovation systems. Such policies stress the role of joint research activities and other technical collaboration among enterprises and with public sector institutions.[175]

Technology transfers can and should be part of this type of strategy. Technology transfers related to FDI are subject to appropriation, within the boundaries of applicable contracts and intellectual property rights. In certain countries they have become major stepping stones for domestic innovation. In order to compete in a knowledge-based global economy, emerging and developing countries must be able to innovate by improving on the worldwide state of the art and/or adjusting existing products and processes to local and regional preferences. The notion of novelty in patent law is a global one and presents no less of a challenge to policy makers. Innovators must be able to go forward and not forced to reinvent the wheel.[176] According to economic theory, innovation policies should be designed to balance the incentives to invest in innovative activity with the

---

173 A Hargadon, *How Breakthroughs Happen: The Surprising Truth about How Companies Innovate* (Harvard Business School Press, 2003).

174 JC Stratton, 'Idea Work Style—A Hypothetical Web-Based Approach to Monitoring the Innovative Health of Organizations' in J T Yao and P Lingras (eds). *WSS 2003: WI/IAT 2003 Workshop on Applications, Products and Services of Web-based Support Systems* (Halifax, 2003), 69, 70.

175 OECD. *National Innovation Systems*, note 151, at 41.

176 AJ Glass, 'Costly R&D and Intellectual Property Rights Protection' (2000) 19:1–2 *International J of Technology Management.*

promotion of technology transfer.[177] An appropriate research exemption should thus be considered.[178] However, innovation should also be encouraged by providing venture capital and seed investments funnelled through innovation incubators. This type of early capital to bring innovation to the marketplace is often the most difficult step for innovators, and appropriate assistance is generally required.[179]

Education and Institutional Capacity Building

This is probably the most important aspect. Education, both in the country and abroad, is the cornerstone of a viable, long-term knowledge strategy and economic growth in the information society. Technical education is necessary to understand the state of the art in any technological field. Training is also required to understand how to use patent search and other intellectual property-related tools.[180]

Universities play a crucial role in the development of a national innovation system, and in any innovation infrastructure. Universities are 'relied on for the training and retraining of scientists, engineers, and technically qualified personnel. [. . .] Universities and public laboratories are relied on for undertaking basic research. [. . .] In the early stages of technological development, public R&D institutions play a particularly critical role by assimilating and diffusing foreign technologies at a time when dependence on such technologies is strongest. [. . .] Finally, public research institutes and university laboratories affect innovation through their interaction with industry and society at large.'[181]

---

177 C Dent, P Jensen, S Waller & B Webster, 'Research Use of Patented Knowledge: A Review', OECD Directorate for Science, Technology and Industry (STI), STI Working Paper 2006/2.

178 See Chapter 15 (Epilogue) below.

179 In fact, Hernando de Soto argues that the ability to leverage assets to raise capital, in particular through efficient property documentation (which allows assets to acquire a financially fungible nature using a representational system not functionally limited to identifying ownership), linked to a reasonably transparent and enforceable securitization process, is what differentiates the Western economies from most developing countries (note 15 above). He also notes that many developing countries are 'very much like the United States of a century ago' (ibid, 9).

180 Patent databases are publicly available. By mining recent patents and published applications (which typically implies an 18-month delay after the initial filing—unfortunately, in certain industries, much can happen in 18 months) and providing copies to local companies with product development abilities, a number of upward technological steps may be taken fairly rapidly. Of course the obligation to comply with TRIPS means that if the patent is granted in the developing country in question, the technology cannot be used directly, but even a reasonable license cannot be obtained, the knowledge could be used, e.g. for non-commercial research. As was noted by the UK Commission on Intellectual Property Rights, TRIPS allows a WTO Member to determine an appropriate interface between intellectual property and competition law (Arts 8 and 40). However, many countries that implemented TRIPS recently did not and still do not have competition legislation.

181 Abdelgafar, note 4 above, 68-9.

Initially, a country could send some of the best students to the top foreign universities, especially in fields where the knowledge brought back can directly contribute to the innovation strategy in light of priorities set. This could include engineering, biology, chemistry, physics, and all other sciences, but also management and law. In science, engineers, scientists, and technicians are equally important.[182] Financial mechanisms might be used to ensure that trained graduates will return to their country of origin—if a country does not have patent protection, it will have a hard time attracting technology-oriented employers and will have a hard time retaining nationals that have studied in this area.[183] As a second step, world-class universities and research centers may then be established in the country, directly or in partnership with major foreign institutions.[184] In short, a country cannot invest too much in (good) education.

In the past, technological innovation and artistic creativity were separate fields of endeavour. Scientists and artists used different tools and generally found it difficult to communicate, let alone work together. Parallels were sometimes mentioned (between mathematics and music, for example), and sometimes realized by geniuses (Leonardo da Vinci), but those were rare, mostly theoretical discussions. This has now changed dramatically. The focus of education should be heavily biased towards computer technology, because code and computers have become a horizontal link between art and science.[185] To take a simple example, both artists and scientists (engineers) use three-dimensional design software. The future of innovation and creativity should bring art and science closer together and this should inform the design of any forward-looking educational policy.

At a more technical level, training for policy makers, judges, high officials and other persons involved in economic development projects should similarly be organized. It cannot be stressed enough that successful education program

[182] See JH Barton, 'New Trends in Technology Transfer (ICTSD Issue Paper No 18)' (ICTSD, 2006), at viii: 'The reduction of inventions to commercial application usually also requires skilled entrepreneurs and, depending on the particular field, skilled mechanics, lab technicians, or software writers. Many of the same skills are needed for the thoughtful adoption and application of a technology developed elsewhere. Hence, a broad range of scientific and technological skills is absolutely crucial for a nation to participate effectively in the international technological economy.'

[183] Kitch, note 10 above, 166.

[184] The higher education system in India, which attributes the necessary resources to elite home-grown institutions, attract the best students and soon will rival the intellectual output and level of their Western counterparts.

[185] A good example is the Montreal-based Society for Art and Technology. Using the design of artist Luc Courchesne's 'Panoscope', a three-dimensional spherical installation, the Canadian Space Agency was able to solve an issue concerning the robotized arm of the US Space Shuttle (often referred to as the 'Canada arm'). See <http://www.sat.qc.ca/article.php?lang=en&id_article=479>.

outcomes will depend on selecting the best candidates for each program, and not basing decisions solely or mainly on other factors.

Developing educational institutions and services is naturally very costly. Developing intellectual property institutions such as patent and trademark offices is perhaps even more so, but it is essential to be able to benefit from the international IP regime.[186] Yet developing countries can either delegate these roles to foreign institutions, a majority of which are located in the 'First World', thereby losing the some of their ability to customize the services; or take the policy bull by the horns and pay the price. Ideally, more industrialized nations should fund training and establishment of local patent and trademark offices, also because of their educational role with local businesses and research facilities. Absent this kind of funding, another option, used in part of Africa for example, is to build regional offices.[187]

Building intellectual offices is a complex task. As discussed as part of the Development Agenda process, WIPO may assist in providing technical knowledge. Developing countries should also consider regionalizing certain operations where appropriate, and working with offices in industrialized countries. Here, working with countries that do not necessarily have a leaning towards maximum intellectual protection may make it easier to separate the policy issues from the actual functioning of the office to be set up in or for each WTO Member.

The capacity-building effort should not be limited to officials working in the intellectual property office. Typically, intellectual property is also of direct relevance to the work of ministries such as agriculture, education, health, and international trade. In addition to training and capacity building within those ministries, countries should consider establishing a governance structure that coordinates intellectual property discussions among the various stakeholders, and ensures that policy making is based on as broad a consensus as possible, which also allows countries to speak with a single voice in international and bilateral negotiations.

186 As noted in a study published recently by Queen Mary University; 'The implementation of international agreements is often hindered through a lack of institutional structures that would serve as a basis for or facilitate the implementation of new legislation. In many cases this leads to incomplete implementation or adverse effects . . .', *The Impact of IPR Rules on Sustainable Development* (note 36 above) 3.

187 For example, the African Regional Industrial Property Organization, available at: <http://www.aripo.wipo.net/index.html>.

Research Subsidies and Innovation (Venture) Capital

Innovation requires funding, though not all types of innovation will require funding of the same magnitude (compare, say, computer programming and biotechnological research). To obtain the necessary 'venture' or development funding, innovators may rely on public funds, private funds, or both. It has even been argued that the ability to document the ownership of assets (tangible and intangible) and to use them as security to obtain financing is a key to economic growth in the West, rather than cultural or other factors.[188] What is certain is that mechanisms must be in place to allow innovators to obtain appropriate funds to prototype, develop and market new technologies and ideas.

Within WTO and other applicable rules, there is room for subsidies in the form of tax breaks or otherwise. Subsidies and publicly-funded and/or supported training, research, and development are an essential ingredient in any successful innovation policy.[189] Subsidies may also be used to attract FDI. By granting merit-based research subsidies or grants to local creators, especially in universities and public research institutes, an incentive is given to local innovators and creators.[190] By rewarding significant achievements at, e.g. an annual award ceremony, successful innovators and creators are recompensed and also a strong social signal is sent about the value of creation and innovation, which then functions as an additional incentive for others.

FDI Promotion

FDI is not an economic panacea, but in the game of economic growth and development it seems a better solution than a simple increase in imports. FDI generally comes with formal or informal knowledge and technology transfer creating more, and better, local jobs than simple distributorships. Each country (and may are doing it aggressively already) should thus market its advantages bilaterally, at international fairs, through graduate students, etc. It could survey multinational companies operating in its priority areas to determiner their perception of the

---

188 de Soto (notes 15 and 177 above).

189 Barton, note 179 above, 32: 'the subsidy criterion described previously must be the basis for all national technology policy. It clearly favors strong support for scientific education and for basic research in areas that are important to the particular nation and neglected by world technological research. The criterion favors academic research in areas of local interest, and, where the nation has specific capability, of global interest.'

190 Many economists believe that matching loans, or loans to be repaid only if a project succeeds, are inefficient and undesirable and may run foul of WTO rules, including national treatment. S Ostry and R Nelson, *Techno-Nationalism and Techno-Globalism: Conflict and Cooperation* (Brookings Institution, 1995), 30.

country's strengths and weaknesses, address shortcomings identified in the survey and provide information on positive aspects that are simply not known in interested circles.

Non-IP-Regulatory Adaptation

Based on WTO and other rules and surveys, regulatory shortcomings should be addressed. 'Political stability, desirable geographic location, adequate infrastructure, human capacity, functioning legal institutions, enforceable contract rights, open trade policies, [. . .] intellectual property protection',[191] a competitive tax system and access to a qualified workforce will rate fairly high in the list of FDI preconditions, as will a low level of corruption.

These are, of course, only examples of the components of a full strategy.

Conclusion

Without adequate intellectual property protection, economic development beyond an initial phase will not happen. We now know that while intellectual property regulation is an essential ingredient, it does not an economic plan make—many more elements are needed. Both for practical reasons, and on the basis of available empirical data, TRIPS should be seen, and fully accepted, as a given in the intellectual property policy portfolio, in spite of its dynamic nature. It may also be defended as an appropriate reference point for developing nations in the context of TRIPS-Plus bilateral trade discussions.

TRIPS contains a number of rules that WTO members must implement, but it also affords a fair margin of 'policy flexibility'. Implementing TRIPS should be viewed as part of a broader knowledge and innovation strategy resting initially on priority setting, but then mostly on education and institutional capacity building and, to a certain extent, also on regulatory adaptation and FDI promotion.

[191] K Kennedy, 'The 2005 TRIPS Extension for the Least-Developed Countries: A Failure of the Single Undertaking Approach?'(2006) 40 *Int'l Law* 683, 699.

2

THE INTERNATIONAL INTELLECTUAL PROPERTY SYSTEM: TREATIES, NORMS, NATIONAL COURTS, AND PRIVATE ORDERING

*Graeme B Dinwoodie**

* Thanks to Daniel Gervais and Tim Holbrook for comments on a draft of this chapter, which brings together, and elaborates on, two of my earlier publications: 'The Architecture of the International Intellectual Property System' (2002) 77 *Chi-Kent LR* 993 and 'Private Ordering and the Creation of International Copyright Norms' (2003) 160 *J. Instit. & Theor. Econ.* 161.

Introduction

International intellectual property law has become an integral component of trade and development policy. Likewise, trade and development concerns now frame much of the debate occurring within the international intellectual property system. Although part of the political impetus for international intellectual property law making has long come from the economic gains that particular countries could secure in the global market, the recent situation of intellectual property within the institutional apparatus of the trade regime has been an important factor in the transformation of the classical system of international intellectual property law.

This chapter analyses various aspects of this transformation, and suggests that viewing intellectual property through the prism of trade alone offers an incomplete explanation of the changes that have occurred in international intellectual property law making. Rather, it is the particular character of the World Trade Organization (WTO) and the dominant theoretical justification for contemporary trade policy (the theory of comparative advantage) that have magnified the transformative force of the shift to the trade regime. And, a full account of the contemporary system must reflect the role of both litigation in national courts and private ordering by commercial actors in establishing international intellectual property norms. This chapter stresses that these new contributors to the international system must be subject to no lesser scrutiny than traditional public international instruments such as treaties. Scholars should review national court decisions and private ordering for their effect on the balance of rights between owners and users of intellectual property. Moreover, such scrutiny must include an assessment of whether these new forms of law making take into account the appropriate allocation of regulation between national and international institutions.

Part I of this chapter describes the classical architecture of the international intellectual property system, and the basic conceptual and institutional pillars on which that system was built. In particular, I emphasize that the classical system formed around treaties concluded by nation states and effectively preserved substantial autonomy for states crafting domestic intellectual property policy. The system recognized that the promulgation of international norms affected not only the balance of rights between owners and users but also the balance of national and international regulation, the latter balance being a concern of public international law generally.

Part II discusses some of the ways in which that system is changing. For example, there is increasing pressure to find international solutions to intellectual property policy dilemmas without the period of domestic experimentation with alternative models that was emblematic of the classical system. This contemporary approach has costs. To ameliorate the costs associated with the speedy development of international rules, and perhaps to ensure that *some* international solution is adopted, policy makers have begun more overtly to support the adoption of soft law norms rather than hard law treaty obligations. In response, those sceptical of these trends in international intellectual property law making have sought to slow down the process or bring it to a complete halt. In order to achieve a political climate where public international law imposes fewer constraints on national law makers (particularly law makers in developing countries), sceptics have adopted a number of strategies, including the multiplication of international institutions in which intellectual property is considered, and the concomitant development of a range of rival norms that have massively complicated the political economy of public international intellectual property law.

Using examples drawn primarily from copyright and trademark law, I illustrate the pressure to accelerate internationalization, the varying strength of adopted norms, and the changes to the political climate in which public international law making is occurring. To some extent, these changes reflect increased political and popular attention to trade and development. However, regardless of the catalyst, these systemic changes remain crucially important to trade and development because of the entanglement of intellectual property with trade and development policy.

Part III focuses, in greater detail, on two further changes in the international intellectual property system, namely, the increased role of both national courts and private ordering in developing international norms. In the classical international intellectual property system, national courts played a relatively limited role in developing, interpreting or implementing international norms. However, in recent years national courts have become more involved in the construction of international intellectual property law. Part III.A discusses both those judicial developments and pending projects that might further enhance the emerging role of national courts in the development of the system of international intellectual property law. For some time, these projects included the development of a treaty addressing transborder intellectual property disputes. Thus, the draft Hague Convention on Jurisdiction and Foreign Judgments in Civil and Commercial Matters (the 'Draft Hague Convention'),[1] a proposed general treaty

[1] See 'Hague Conference on Private International Law, Summary of the Outcome of Discussions' in Commission II of the First Part of the Diplomatic Conference, 6–20 June, 2001, reprinted in (2002) 77 *Chi–Kent LR* 1015. The (June 2001) version of the 'Draft Hague Convention' is referred

addressing multinational civil and commercial litigation, included important provisions addressing intellectual property. Similar (and in many respects more ambitious) efforts were undertaken in a more academic setting by Professors Rochelle Dreyfuss and Jane Ginsburg, who authored a Draft Convention on Jurisdiction and Recognition of Judgments in Intellectual Property Matters (the 'Dreyfuss–Ginsburg proposal').[2] However, the consensus necessary to adopt a treaty, either with respect to civil litigation generally or dedicated to intellectual property disputes, never emerged. The Hague proposal was substantially narrowed, resulting ultimately in the conclusion of a convention validating exclusive choice of court clauses in business to business contracts. The Dreyfuss–Ginsburg proposal, however, was embraced by the American Law Institute as the basis for the development of a soft law instrument entitled 'Intellectual Property: Principles Governing Jurisdiction, Choice of Law, and Judgments in Transnational Disputes' ('ALI Principles'). After several revisions, that document was adopted by the membership of the American Law Institute at its annual meeting in San Francisco in May 2007.

The role of national courts in the development of international intellectual property law is not going to diminish. National court decisions may of themselves construct (or at least contribute to) international intellectual property law through the sheer fact of their geographical reach; and this contribution may occur whether effectuated through the ad hoc application and extension of existing doctrinal devices by national courts, or through the development and application of a treaty under which such developments are consciously encouraged or appropriately limited.[3] In Part III.A of this chapter, I sketch a vision of the contemporary international intellectual property system that accommodates (and actively seeks to incorporate) national judicial activity, and I situate the different proposals within that environment.

In Part III.B, I analyse another change to the classical model. Consistent perhaps with an evolution in international law generally, international intellectual property

---

to where necessary as the 'June 2001' draft Hague Convention in order to distinguish this text from the draft proposal published in October 1999. See 'Preliminary Draft Convention on Jurisdiction and Foreign Judgments in Civil and Commercial Matters' (adopted 30 October 1999), available at <http://www.hcch.net>.

2 Rochelle C Dreyfuss and Jane C Ginsburg, 'Draft Convention on Jurisdiction and Recognition of Judgments in Intellectual Property Matters' (2002) 77 *Chi–Kent LR* 1065.

3 Indeed, those critics who wish to reserve intellectual property issues to the control of local courts might wish to ensure that any treaty governing transborder civil litigation includes a broad exclusive jurisdiction provision rather than (as many do) advocating that intellectual property be wholly excluded from the scope of any such convention.

norms are increasingly established and developed through private ordering.[4] In this chapter, I focus on two examples of international copyright norm formation that would fall outside a classical understanding of international intellectual property law: (1) norms generated by the commercial practices of information intermediaries, internet service providers (ISPs) in responding to claims of alleged copyright infringement by their subscribers, and (2) norms arising from digital rights management systems (DRMs) employed by copyright owners to limit the ability of users of copyrighted works to engage in activity previously authorized by public copyright laws (e.g. fair use copying, or private copying where permitted by national legislation). While conventional international copyright law has left much law making in these areas to national law, in both contexts, international norms may be evolving with insufficient public scrutiny (as regards both substantive rules and structural allocation of norm making between national and international levels). Particularly in the online context, private ordering has been hailed by some as an elixir to cure the inefficiencies of the offline world and to enhance the political legitimacy of governing rules and institutions. Yet, although private ordering has largely been validated in several areas of intellectual property law, its efficiency and legitimacy has been questioned in several domestic contexts, and the same questioning will (and should) occur in the context of international copyright law.

Moreover, as in the domestic context, the legitimacy and success of private ordering will depend upon the legal underpinning of these nominally private transactions. These legal underpinnings, what I have called the public structuring of private ordering, provide the points at which public values can most easily inform and shape the regulation that private ordering effects.[5] Moreover, as copyright owners over-reach, or imbalances favouring copyright owners arise, political pressure will increase to subject private ordering to greater public oversight. The two examples I discuss illustrate some of the possible mixes of private ordering and public structuring that we might consider. No single combination of private ordering and public regulation will be appropriate in all cases. However, to the extent that private ordering is effecting the creation of international copyright

4 For a discussion of the different meanings of 'private ordering', see Niva Elkin-Koren, 'Copyrights in Cyberspace—Rights Without Laws?' (1998) 73 *Chi–Kent LR* 1155, 1160.

5 Justification for the elevation of public values may lie in the realist critique that public and private is an illusory divide. But it is at these points, where there is incontrovertible public structuring of the environment in which private ordering occurs, that the claim is easiest to sustain. The efficiency and the legitimacy of private ordering, and thus its ability to contribute to the development of international copyright norms, are intertwined with the public structuring.

norms, public regulation must also be constructed with an eye to the issues and basic premises of international copyright law.[6]

Part I The Classical System of International Intellectual Property Law

A. Public International Law

The beginnings of a developed system of international intellectual property law can be traced back to the 1880s, with the conclusion by nation states of the Paris[7] and Berne Conventions.[8] These treaties were built around two basic propositions.[9] First, signatory states had to provide in their domestic law certain minimum levels of intellectual property protection that met so-called substantive minima found in the international agreements. Second, as a general rule, signatory states were obliged to offer to nationals of other signatory states protection which matched that afforded to their own nationals. This is the principle of national treatment.[10]

This basic structure—national treatment plus substantive minima—persisted throughout the twentieth century. Although the substantive minima obligations

---

[6] The use of norms developed through DRMs might fit more easily within most notions of private ordering than norms developed through the practices of ISPs. The specific nature of ISP norm-generating practice is 'incentivized' by legislation that grants immunity in advance to certain practices; the ability of DRM systems to create copyright-inconsistent norms is ensured by legislation that, in response to the onset of DRMs, generally immunized the private acts of the content owner from being overridden by public values enshrined in the copyright law without reference to the content of any particular digital rights management. But both raise the question of the extent to which, and means by which, norms generated through the practices of private actors and enforced by contract and technology should be subject to ongoing supervision in order to ensure that in certain circumstances publicly developed norms trump inconsistent privately generated arrangements. So I treat them together in this chapter. Indeed, the ambiguities of the term merely highlight its truly mythical nature. See Margaret J Radin and Robert P Wagner, 'The Myth of Private Ordering: Rediscovering Legal Realism in Cyberspace' (1998) 73 *Chi–Kent LR* 1295.

[7] Paris Convention for the Protection of Industrial Property, 20 March 1883, as last revised at Stockholm, 14 July 1967, Art 28, 21 UST 1583, 828 UNTS 305 [hereinafter Paris Convention].

[8] See Berne Convention for the Protection of Literary and Artistic Works (1971 Paris text), 24 July 1971, 1161 UNTS 3 [hereinafter Berne Convention]; see generally Sam Ricketson and Jane C Ginsburg, *International Copyright and Neighbouring Rights: The Berne Convention and Beyond* (Oxford University Press, 2006). The first version of the Berne Convention was concluded in 1886.

[9] The Paris Convention also contained provisions designed to facilitate the acquisition of national registered rights on a multinational basis. See note 7 above, Art 4.

[10] See Paris Convention, note 7 above, Art 2; Berne Convention, note 8 above, Art 5.

were periodically revised to require greater and different protection, the conceptual approach has endured. Indeed, it remains the dominant approach in current intellectual property treaties.[11] Some essential characteristics of this system are worth noting. In particular, this approach only barely intruded upon the national sovereignty of signatory states. It left states with substantial latitude in crafting their domestic laws. Different countries, situated in different social and economic conditions, might optimize the production of knowledge through different calibration of various doctrinal devices of national intellectual property law.

This latitude was achieved through several features. First, the substantive minima were initially quite undemanding.[12] They were in most cases meant to reflect a consensus position, as codifications of existing state practice.[13] Second, many central concepts (such as who is an 'author' of a copyrighted work) were left open for signatory states to develop in accordance with their own national policies and values. And, this latitude was affirmed in practical terms by the fact that the obligations undertaken by states were not backed up with effective enforcement mechanisms. Although in later revisions of the Berne and Paris Conventions provision was made to refer disputes between states regarding the meaning of those conventions to the International Court of Justice,[14] this was never done.[15]

The international intellectual property system need not have developed in this manner. In the debates leading up to the adoption of the Berne Convention, some delegations advanced the alternative notion of a universal copyright law. But these attempts were defeated by the pragmatic demands of greater national

[11] See Agreement on Trade-Related Aspects of Intellectual Property Rights, 15 April 1994 [hereinafter the TRIPs Agreement or TRIPs], Marrakech Agreement Establishing the World Trade Organization [hereinafter WTO Agreement], Annex 1C, Legal Instruments–Results of the Uruguay Round, Vol 31, 33 ILM 81 (1994).

[12] See Graeme B. Dinwoodie, 'A New Copyright Order: Why National Courts Should Create Global Norms' (2000) 149 *U Pa LR* 469, 491 (discussing the Berne Convention and describing initial standards as 'hardly exacting'); Graeme B. Dinwoodie *et al*, 'International Intellectual Property Law and Policy 140' (Lexis–Nexis, 2001) (describing trademark-related obligations in the Paris Convention as 'relatively low-level'); Joanna Schmidt-Szalewski, 'The International Protection of Trademarks After the TRIPs Agreement' (1998) 9 *Duke J Comp & Int'l L* 189, 199–201 (discussing the 'few trademark rules' provided by the Paris Convention).

[13] See Dinwoodie, 'A New Copyright Order', note 12 above, 493 (noting that the traditional Berne Convention revisions 'constituted the received wisdom of the participating countries rather than prospective solutions to new problems').

[14] See Berne Convention, note 8 above, Art 33; Paris Convention, note 7 above, Art 28.

[15] See Jerome H Reichman, 'Enforcing the Enforcement Procedures of the TRIPs Agreement' (1997) 37 *Va J Int'l L* 335, 339 n.17.

control over the course of copyright law.[16] Similar tensions, though less starkly presented, can be found in the development of the Paris Convention.[17] International intellectual property norms were to be developed and enforced with important regard for the autonomy of nation states.

B. Private International Law

In this scheme, national courts had very little role to play in the construction of international intellectual property law. Public international standards in the treaties found their way into national law largely through legislative implementation in domestic law.[18] This was particularly true in the United States (where many, if not all, of the primary intellectual property treaties are not self-executing).[19] The treaties did not, in any event, contain a comprehensive code that could substitute for general domestic legislation. National courts thus interpreted local intellectual property law, even if the content of that law had, in part, been influenced by international obligations.[20]

Moreover, the causes of action which courts were called upon to adjudicate principally involved national rights. Even if international intellectual property treaties were self-executing, intellectual property rights remained national in scope. Territoriality of rights is a fundamental premise of classical international

---

16 See Jane C Ginsburg, 'The Role of National Copyright in an Era of International Copyright Norms', in Adolf Deitz (ed), *The Role of National Legislation in Copyright Law* (ALAI, 2000), 211, 213.

17 See *Crocker Nat'l Bank v Canadian Imperial Bank of Commerce*, 223 USPQ 909, 918–21 (TTAB *en banc* 1984) (discussing negotiation of Art 6 of the Paris Convention); United States–Section 211 Omnibus Appropriations Act of 1998, Report of the Appellate Body, WT/DS176/AB/R (WTO 2 January 2002) [hereinafter United States–Section 211], (noting the legislative discretion retained by national governments under the Paris Convention), available at <http://www.worldtradelaw.net/reports/wtoab/us-section211(ab).pdf> (last visited 7 June 2002).

18 See Graeme B. Dinwoodie, 'The Development and Incorporation of International Norms in the Formation of Copyright Law' (2001) 62 *Ohio St LJ* 733, 739 (discussing copyright law).

19 See Berne Convention Implementation Act of 1988, Pub L No 100–568, §2, 102 Stat 2853 (Berne Convention not self-executing); *Mannington Mills, Inc v Congoleum Corp*, 595 F2d 1287, 1299 (3d Cir 1979) (treating the Paris Convention as not self-executing); see also *Vanity Fair Mills, Inc v T Eaton Co*, 234 F2d 633, 640–44 (2d Cir 1956) (suggesting that the Paris Convention is self-executing, but finding no enlargement of substantive rights under US trademark law). But see *Laboratorios Roldan v Tex Int'l, Inc*, 902 F Supp 1555, 1568 (SD Fla, 1995) (recognizing claim under Art 10*bis* of the Paris Convention).

20 To the extent that domestic law was understood as implementation of international obligations, national courts would typically interpret any ambiguity in the domestic rule in accordance with the international norm. But this is only a canon of interpretation. The reference to the underlying international norm depended upon the existence of an ambiguity in the domestic provision. See *In re Rath*, 402 F3d 1207 (Fed Cir 2005).

intellectual property law. There is no such thing as a global copyright or trademark, or global patent, with a unitary set of rights conferred and governed by a single, substantive international law.[21] The creation of a fixed, original work of authorship, for example, gives rise to separate national copyrights in all countries affording copyright protection according to the different national laws of each of those countries.

Finally, the disputes that confronted courts were largely national in nature. National courts did, of course, have some occasion to address issues of private international law where cross-border effects occurred.[22] But such events were rarer than today. And matters of private international law were left largely untouched by the intellectual property conventions.[23]

Indeed, in the United States, courts generally have substantial discretion regarding the rules of private international law (such as jurisdiction to adjudicate, choice of law or applicable law, and recognition and enforcement of judgments).[24] Domestically, the United States Constitution, at least as interpreted, imposes greater restraints on the exercise by courts of personal jurisdiction than on the assertion of prescriptive jurisdiction (i.e. the Constitution contributes to the rules of personal jurisdiction but leaves choice of law rules largely unregulated).[25] And although recognition of foreign judgments is the norm in US law, this flows neither from constitutional mandate—the Full Faith and Credit Clause

---

21 See Dinwoodie *et al*, note 12 above, 1.

22 See, e.g. *Vanity Fair Mills*, note 19 above, 641 (US–Canadian trademark infringement); *Sheldon v Metro-Goldwyn Pictures Corp*, 106 F2d 45, 52 (2d Cir 1939) (awarding plaintiff profits from both US and Canadian exhibition of infringing motion picture where a copy of the motion picture had been made in the United States and then shipped to Canada for exhibition), aff'd, 309 US 390 (1940).

23 See *Itar-Tass Russian News Agency v Russian Kurier, Inc*, 153 F3d 82, 90–91 (2d Cir 1998) (noting lack of guidance regarding choice of law issues in the Berne Convention); Jane C. Ginsburg, 'Private International Law Aspects of the Protection of Works and Objects of Related Rights Transmitted Through Digital Networks', WIPO Doc GCPIC/2, 22 and 34 (30 November 1998) (discussing the extent to which the Berne Convention determines the law applicable to issues of copyright ownership and infringement), at <http://www.wipo.int/eng/meetings/1998/gcpic/pdf/gcpic_2.pdf> (last visited 7 June 2002); Graeme B. Dinwoodie, 'Private International Aspects of the Protection of Trademarks' (January 2001) WIPO Doc No WIPO/PIL/01/4, ¶ 14 (discussing the minimal influence of international trademark treaties on choice of law), available at <http://www.wipo.int/edocs/mdocs/mdocs/en/wipo_pil_01/wipo_pil_01_4.doc> (last visited 11 May 2007); see also Fritz Blumer, 'Patent Law and International Private Law on Both Sides of the Atlantic' (January 2001) WIPO Doc No WIPO/PIL/01/3, ¶ 2.1 (discussing how far the territoriality principle affects matters of private international law in patent cases), available at <http://www.wipo.int/edocs/mdocs/mdocs/en/wipo_pil_01/wipo_pil_01_3.doc> (last visited 11 May 2007).

24 See Eugene F. Scoles *et al*, *Conflict of Laws 2*, 3d ed, (West Publishing, 2000).

25 Compare *Allstate Insurance Co v Hague*, 449 US 302, 308 (1981) (choice of law) with *Asahi Metal Indus Co v Superior Court*, 480 US 102, 113 (1987) (personal jurisdiction).

does not extend to the international context[26]—nor from any international treaty obligations assumed by the United States.[27]

Of course, some private international law rules developed from those international intellectual property disputes that did arise.[28] Flowing from the premise that all rights were national, and from the mindset that regarded intellectual property laws as public in nature, courts were reluctant to adjudicate disputes involving foreign intellectual property rights. Thus, although there is an important difference between having jurisdiction to adjudicate a case and the choice of law or law applicable to the case, courts—both in the United States and elsewhere—would decline to hear a case if their own law was not being applied.[29] The question of applicable law drove the exercise of power to adjudicate.[30]

As a consequence, where infringement did occur in several states, suits typically had to be filed in separate national courts seeking relief for each national infringement.[31] Determining the applicable law was thought to be quite easy: where did the reproduction, the use, the publication, or the sale

---

26 See US Constitution Art IV, § 1.

27 See *Hilton v Guyot*, 159 US 113, 163–64 (1895) (resting recognition of foreign judgments on comity); *SARL Louis Feraud Intern v Viewfinder Inc*, 406 F Supp 2d 274 (SDNY 2005) rev'd F3d, 2007 WL 1598057 (2d Cir June 5, 2007). For a recent indication by the Canadian Supreme Court that internationalization of the exploitation of intellectual property requires reconsideration of traditional principles of recognition of judgments, see *Pro Swing Inc v ELTA Golf Inc*, 2006 Carswell Ont 7203; 2006 SCC 52 (2006).

28 See note 22 above (listing illustrative cases); see also *Steele v Bulova Watch Co*, 344 US 280, 283–84 (1952) (extraterritorial application of Lanham Act to activities in Mexico with effects on US commerce); *Robert Stigwood Group Ltd v O'Reilly*, 530 F2d 1096, 1101 (2d Cir 1976) (declining to apply US copyright law extraterritorially to performances in Canada).

29 See, e.g. *Vanity Fair Mills*, note 19 above (trademark); *ITSI TV Prods, Inc v Cal Auth of Racing Fairs Agric*, 785 F Supp 854, 866 (ED Cal 1992) (copyright), rev'd on other grounds, 3 F3d 1289 (9th Cir 1993); see also *Deepsouth Packing Co v Laitram Corp*, 406 US 518, 537 (1972) (suggesting that a US patent holder seeking protection in foreign markets should avail itself of its foreign patents); *Rectifier Corp v Samsung Elecs*, 361 F3d 1355 (Fed Cir 2004)

30 In practice, the cause and effect of this relationship might not have been so clear. That is, one could interpret judicial practice as reflecting the sentiment that, if the court found jurisdiction to adjudicate, it applied its own law.

31 This remains the norm. See *Computer Assocs Int'l, Inc v Altai, Inc*, 126 F3d 365, 371–72 (2d Cir 1997) (refusing to grant antisuit injunction against pursuit of French copyright infringement action notwithstanding that the defendant's program had been held to be non-infringing in parallel US proceedings between the same parties involving the same works); *Microsoft Corp v Lindows.com, Inc*, 319 F Supp 2d 1219 (WD Wash 2004) (trademark). Compare *Euromarket Designs, Inc v Crate & Barrel Ltd*, 96 F Supp 2d 824 (ND Ill 2000) (discussing claim for infringement of US trademark rights in mark 'Crate & Barrel') with *Euromarket Designs, Inc v Peters*, [2000] ETMR 1025 (Ch 2000) (England) (claim for infringement of UK trademark rights in same mark); compare *Improver Corp and Sicommerce v Remington Prods*, 24 IIC 838 (Dusseldorf Ct. App. 1991) (FRG) (discussing action in Germany for infringement of patent on Epilady shaver) with *Improver Corp and Others v Remington Consumer Prods Ltd*, 1990 FSR 181 (High Court 1989) (UK) (action in the UK for infringement of patent on same invention).

occur? The place of such acts would be the place of infringement.[32] The law of this place would thus be the applicable law, which meant that this would be where the plaintiff sued and where enforcement occurred. So, complex multinational intellectual property litigation appears in practice to have been quite rare.

National courts thus had little trouble with, and did not readily develop, rules of private international law for intellectual property disputes. And, they had very little engagement with the rules of public international intellectual property found in treaties, because these were not the source of the rules of decision in the cases before them. There was, therefore, very little dynamic between public and private international intellectual property laws.

Part II Changes to the Classical System

Over the last 15 to 20 years we have witnessed some changes to the foregoing description of the international intellectual property system. However, some things have not altered. The prevailing doctrinal premise is still one of territoriality;[33] rights remain largely national in nature;[34] and the principal

32 Trademark law is, to some extent, concerned more with effects (e.g. consumer confusion). Thus, although some courts and scholars have sought to elevate the nature of the defendant's use in assessing whether an act amounts to infringement, localization of trademark infringing activity will often turn on where consumers are alleged to have been confused. See World Intellectual Property Organization, 'Joint Recommendation Concerning the Protection of Marks, and Other Industrial Property Rights in Signs, on the internet' (October 2001), available at <http://www.wipo.int/documents/en/document/govbody/wo_gb_ab/pdf/a36_8.pdf> (last visited 11 May 2007) (defining the location of use online by reference to commercial effect).

33 See *Computer Associates*, note 31 above, 365 (copyright); *Rotec Indus, Inc v Mitsubishi Corp*, 215 F3d 1246, 1251 (Fed Cir 2000) (requiring that in order to violate the patent holder's exclusive right to offer its patented invention for sale, the allegedly infringing offer must occur within the United States); *Johns Hopkins Univ v Cellpro, Inc*, 152 F3d 1342 (Fed Cir 1998) (patent); *Sterling Drug, Inc v Bayer AG*, 14 F3d 733, 736, 744–48 (2d Cir 1994) (taking territorial nature of trademark rights into account when fashioning relief); *Subafilms, Ltd v MGM-Pathé Communications Co*, 24 F3d 1088, 1089 (9th Cir 1994) (copyright); *Person's Co Ltd v Christman*, 900 F2d 1565, 1569 n18 (Fed Cir 1990) (declining to revise territorial understanding to reflect the 'world economy'); *Playboy Enters v Chuckleberry Publ'g, Inc*, 939 F Supp 1032, 1036–37 (SDNY 1996) (taking territorial nature of trademark rights into account when fashioning relief).

34 Even those exceptional modifications of national rights that exist, such as unitary trademark rights over the entire region of several nations within a free trade agreement (most notably, the European Union: see Council Regulation 40/94 of 20 December 1993 on The Community Trademark, 1994 OJ (L 11), available at: <http://oami.europa.eu/en/mark/aspects/pdf/4094enCV.pdf> (last visited 11 May 2007)), could plausibly still be regarded as territorial in nature, albeit with a territory now defined by the regional 'superstate' rather than individual nation states.

intellectual property agreements remain structured around the dual principles of national treatment and substantive minima.[35]

But in that time, our social and economic environment has become more global in nature. Intellectual property products, like their creators and users, move through international commerce and international communities with speed and in quantities that we could not previously have imagined. This has prompted demands for intellectual property laws that are more global in reach, and the sometimes inconsistent demand for intellectual property laws that respond more quickly to new problems and new technologies.[36] In this climate, the principles of territoriality and national autonomy over intellectual property policy have come under pressure. In this Part, I will briefly highlight some of the most important changes to the public international intellectual property system, the network of obligations among nation states.

A. Lessons from Copyright

Intersecting Vectors of Balance

One of the dominant justifications tendered for the existence of copyright protection is that it encourages the generation and distribution of knowledge.[37] Copyright can be and is supported on other grounds (especially outside common law countries).[38] And the precise dynamic by which copyright effectuates its knowledge-positive purpose is unclear: different groups of producers and distributors no doubt respond to a different balance of incentives, and the inter-relationship between incentives to produce and incentives to distribute is complex. But the incentive theory is given substantial weight in most countries throughout the world.[39] If, as conventional theory suggests, a certain level of copyright protection enhances the supply of knowledge then, it might be argued,

---

[35] See TRIPs Agreement, note 11 above, Art 2(1) (requiring compliance with stated provisions of the Paris Convention), Art 3 (national treatment), and Art 9(1) (requiring compliance with stated provisions of the Berne Convention); see also United States–Section 211, note 17 above (discussing national treatment obligations of TRIPs), at <http://www.worldtradelaw.net/reports/wtoab/us-section211(ab).pdf> (last visited 7 June 2002).

[36] See Dinwoodie, 'A New Copyright Order', note 12 above, 477 (discussing these pressures in copyright law).

[37] See *Mazer v Stein*, 347 US 201, 219 (1954); William M Landes & Richard A Posner, 'An Economic Analysis of Copyright Law' (1989) 18 *J Leg Stud* 325.

[38] Stephen M. Stewart, *International Copyright and Neighboring Rights*, 2nd ed (Lexis Law Publishers 1989) (discussing justifications grounded in cultural diversity and natural rights); Paul Goldstein, *International Copyright: Principles, Law, and Practice* (Oxford University Press, 2001).

[39] World Intellectual Property Organization, 'Intellectual Property on the Internet: A Survey of the Issues,' (December 2002) WIPO Doc. No. WIPO/INT/02.

extending this beneficent force to other countries through the development of an international copyright system will, *inter alia*, enhance the global store of knowledge.[40] In this sense, international copyright law might be understood as a mere spatial extension of the conventional instrumentalist proposition.[41]

Of course, even within *single countries*, the incentive argument can be pressed too simplistically. Intricate balancing of competing considerations is necessary to ensure that copyright does not undermine the public objectives that it purports to advance. More incentive does not necessarily mean more production and distribution of knowledge. In some instances, gaps in protection lead not only to a reduced incentive but also to enhanced opportunities for creation and distribution. The argument for copyright protection relies on the increase in knowledge from enhanced incentive not being outweighed by a reduction in knowledge supply that would otherwise occur through gaps in protection.

Those institutions that develop international copyright rules must, no less than national law makers, pursue the same elusive goal of substantive balance. International copyright law must likewise be based on an assessment of what types and levels of protection best further the purposes of copyright law. Thus, in shaping treaties, policy makers consider the access/incentive dynamic in ways not unfamiliar in the domestic copyright context. Indeed, they may do so in a manner far too similar to that which occurs at the domestic level.[42] But constructing the international copyright regime is doubly difficult. The international system must wrestle not only with the copyright dilemmas confronted on the national level but also with broader questions of balance that pervade international relations generally.[43] In particular, what is the appropriate balance between universal rules and national autonomy? Every international instrument and institution implicitly addresses the competing claims of universality and national autonomy (or sovereignty). Emphasizing the autonomy

[40] In *Eldred v Ashcroft*, 537 US 186 (2003), the United States Supreme Court suggested that Congress could rationally view the development of the international copyright system, and the fullest US participation therein, as a factor that could result in greater incentive for the creation and dissemination of works in the United States. This argument rests on more systemic concerns, namely, that anything that facilitates a more secure environment for the distribution of authors' work (which, in a digital era where works cross borders with ease, includes protection abroad) will encourage the generation and distribution of works. See Shira Perlmutter, 'Participation in the International Copyright System as a Means to Promote the Progress of Science and Useful Arts' (2002) 36 *Loyola LA LR* 323, 323–325.

[41] Historically, adherents to natural rights theories of copyright could use the universalist character of natural rights to support international copyright laws.

[42] See Graeme B. Dinwoodie, 'The WIPO Copyright Treaty: A Transition to the Future of International Copyright Lawmaking' (forthcoming, 2007) *Case Wes Res Univ LR*.

[43] Moreover, the notion of balance can be seen as even more complex; identifying two vectors is itself a vast over-simplification. See ibid.

of nation states in international copyright law ensured that states could tailor national laws to their own social, cultural and economic demands. The incentives likely to maximize the generation and distribution of knowledge may vary widely from country to country. And, it allowed countries to serve as laboratories in which to determine whether certain norms were superior to others as determinants of knowledge supply.[44] Discussion of international copyright policy thus extends not only to substantive norms of copyright law, but also to whether certain norms should be allowed to evolve differently at the national level in lieu of articulating an international rule.[45]

Moreover, once a decision is made to develop an international norm, and thus limit the capacity of nation states to make fully autonomous determinations regarding the optimal level and form of intellectual property protection, what will that norm be? How fully will it constrain national choice? Can one construct an international rule that, by providing some room for cultural and economic difference, maximizes social utility in different countries?

Over the past century, the international intellectual property system sought to pursue the commonly-held objectives of copyright law while recognizing that the values of diversity and self-determination might caution against moving too quickly in the direction of universal norms.[46] The principle of national treatment, in tandem with the Berne Convention's substantive minima, ensured the availability of basic copyright protection for foreign works and foreign authors in a signatory country. Under conventional theory, it would also enhance the access to works in the new country by encouraging foreign authors to expand their distribution to that country.[47] Moreover, the availability of property rights consistent with minimum substantive norms would encourage local production of knowledge in the country newly acceding to the copyright regime.[48] Taken together, global production of, and access to, creative works, is enhanced by

[44] Graeme W. Austin, 'Valuing "Domestic Self-Determination" in International Intellectual Property Jurisprudence' (2002) 77 Chi–Kent LR 1155, 1194–1195; Dinwoodie, 'A New Copyright Order', note 12 above, 503.

[45] Those who see copyright as a natural right might be expected to argue for intrusive international norms with strong binding effect. Those who view copyright in more instrumental terms would likely prefer an approach that allowed each country, pursuing the same general objectives, to develop policies closely tied to a country's own social and economic conditions.

[46] See Austin, note 44 above, 1172.

[47] Moreover, the opening of new, secure markets in turn might enhance the incentive offered to authors in all countries, further enhancing the global incentive to creation. See Peter M Gerhart, 'Reflections: Beyond Compliance Theory—TRIPS as a Substantive Issue' (2000) 32 *Case W Res J Int'l L* 357.

[48] Arguments for international copyright protection are thus strengthened by measures designed to ensure an indigenous economy that takes advantage of the enhanced incentive. With respect to developing countries in particular, that calculation may be contingent on variables (e.g. disposable

the availability of protection internationally.[49] But these basic (and internationally shared) copyright objectives could be achieved without the imposition of universal copyright norms, optimizing overall access to creative works by allowing for nation-by-nation adjustment, and taking advantage of initial periods of national experimentation.

The Pressure to Internationalize Promptly

These, then, were the structural or institutional norms that guided the development of international copyright law. In recent years, however, these norms have been subjected to intense pressure to change. In particular, copyright owners have sought the adoption of more intrusive international rules, earlier in the stage of norm development and with respect to a larger array of copyright issues.[50] Thus, in 1996 the European Union and the United States advanced a proposal for an international treaty mandating a new form of protection for databases, notwithstanding that the EU Database Directive was of relatively recent vintage and the US Congress was baulking (and continues to baulk) at domestic adoption of such a system.[51] Debate about the appropriate level and form of protection for electronic databases was occurring in a number of countries but an immediate international consensus looked unlikely.

Although the Database Treaty was effectively shelved at the 1996 Geneva Diplomatic Conference, that conference did adopt two other treaties, namely, the WIPO Copyright Treaty and the WIPO Performances and Phonograms Treaty. These so-called 'Internet Treaties' sought to retrofit copyright and neighbouring rights for the digital era, a task upon which national policy makers were only just embarking. Indeed, while the classical international system typically worked with the raw data of enacted and interpreted national laws, in 1996 negotiators of the Internet Treaties drew inspiration from several pieces of proposed legislation that were contemporaneously being considered at the national level.[52]

income, skills and investment necessary to develop indigenous industry) that differ substantially from country to country and that are not in any event within the exclusive control of copyright law.

49 The conventional argument prevails on the theory that authorized versions of works are likely in the long term to be more numerous (or more reliably available) than the number of pirate copies that would be available in the second country in a copyright-free environment. The accuracy of this premise may vary between countries, differ as between different types of works, and be rendered quite unstable by the advent of digital communication technologies (especially as these technologies proliferate in lesser-developed countries).

50 Dinwoodie, 'A New Copyright Order', note 12 above, 477–483; Dinwoodie, 'The WIPO Copyright Treaty', note 42 above.

51 See Daniel J Gervais, 'The Protection of Databases' (forthcoming, 2007) 82 *Chi–Kent LR*.

52 WIPO Copyright Treaty, WIPO Doc CRNR/DC/94, 20 December 1996, 36 ILM 65; WIPO Performances and Phonograms Treaty, 20 December 1996, 36 ILM 76. See Dinwoodie, 'The WIPO Copyright Treaty', note 42 above.

More recently, the WIPO Standing Committee on Copyright and Related Rights (the SCCR) has been moving towards a broadcasting treaty that might create international rules on webcasting at a time when the market and technological significance of webcasting remains uncertain.

Of course, there may be good reasons to seek international solutions in a speedier fashion than in the late nineteenth century. In the digital world of instantaneous global exploitation and easy, faithful reproduction, universal rules are seen as more efficient and necessary to ensure the effectiveness of domestic policy choices. The level of effective enforcement of intellectual property rights might plausibly be figured into the balance of creator and user rights that default rules of copyright law strive to strike. If so, the ease with which offshore infringing activity can undermine the incentives established by national law is in fact a matter of distinct local concern.

As discussed below, the argument for early development of international norms has also been sustained by invocation of contemporary trade theories, which have assumed greater prominence because of the incorporation of intellectual property within the broader trade apparatus. In addition, rising resistance to certain copyright policies in the domestic political arena may have persuaded proponents of particular measures strategically to shift institutional focus to the international stage (where, to their dismay and surprise, the same competing forces are now arrayed).[53]

The Trade Prism

These arguments, in favour of more rapid and intrusive international copyright law making, have been assisted by viewing intellectual property through the prism of international trade. International intellectual property policy making has, in large part, been subsumed within the broader apparatus of trade relations. This first occurred unilaterally in the form of annual reviews by the United States Trade Representative under the Special 301 provisions of the Trade Act[54] and the (more recent) equivalent procedure in the European Union under the Trade Barriers Regulation.[55] A parallel shift was effected multilaterally, in 1994, by the

---

53 See Pamela Samuelson, 'The U.S. Digital Agenda at WIPO' (1997) 37 *Va J Intl'l L* 369; Dinwoodie, 'The WIPO Copyright Treaty', note 42 above.

54 See, e.g. Office of The United States Trade Representative, '2002 Special 301 Report' (April 2002), available at <http://www.ustr.gov/Document_Library/Reports_Publications/2002/2002_Special_301_Report/Section_Index.html>; see generally Kim Newby, 'The Effectiveness of Special 301 in Creating Long-Term Copyright Protection for US Companies Overseas' (1995) 21 *Syracuse J Int'l L & Com* 29.

55 See Council Regulation (EC) No 3286/94 of 22 December 1994 (laying down Community procedures in the field of the common commercial policy in order to ensure the exercise of the

inclusion of intellectual property provisions (i.e. TRIPs) within the Agreement Establishing the World Trade Organization.[56] The precise ways in which this overarching trade context may transform international intellectual property law remain unclear, but that context surely has altered the character of international intellectual property relations.[57]

Most obviously, many of the public international obligations undertaken by states in the classical era (and some added by TRIPS itself in 1994) are now backed by an effective dispute settlement system (that of the WTO) among states to ensure compliance with the internationally agreed-upon standards.[58] International intellectual property law now has real teeth. The latitude for member state autonomy has been reduced, in both the formation and interpretation of international norms, though it undoubtedly remains too early to make final judgments on the effect of the WTO system on international copyright law.

Nine WTO dispute settlement panel reports addressing TRIPs violations, including one that was copyright-specific, have been handed down thus far (three of which also gave rise to reports by the Appellate Body). Although all, bar one, find some transgression of the TRIPs Agreement, these proceedings probably involve the clearest cases of TRIPs non-compliance. Nor should we draw too much significance from the outcomes of these proceedings alone.[59] Indeed, the methodology of panels has been quite strict in tying decisions to the literal language of the TRIPs Agreement; *Webster's Dictionary* has become an essential research tool in

Community's rights under international trade rules, in particular those established under the auspices of the World Trade Organization, 1994 OJ (L 349) 71, as amended by Council Regulation (EC) No 356/95 of 20 February 1995, 1995 OJ (L 41) 3; see generally David Rose, 'The EU Trade Barrier Regulation: An Effective Instrument for Promoting Global Harmonisation of Intellectual Property Rights?' (1999) 21 EIPR 313.

56 Uruguay Round Agreements Act 1994, Pub L No 103–465, 108 Stat 4809 (1994). The conclusion of TRIPs did not prevent the United States from publishing annual Special 301 reviews of foreign intellectual property protection. Indeed, the Uruguay Round Agreements Act, which implemented the TRIPs Agreement in US law, expressly contemplated that those reviews would continue.

57 See Neil W Netanel, 'The Next Round: The Impact of the WIPO Copyright Treaty on TRIPS Dispute Settlement' (1997) 37 *Va J Int'l L* 441, 451–52; Dinwoodie, 'A New Copyright Order', note 12 above, 501–18; David Nimmer, 'The End of Copyright' (1995) 48 *Vand LR* 1385.

58 See Understanding on Rules and Procedures Governing the Settlement of Disputes, 15 April 1994, WTO Agreement, Annex 2, Legal Instruments–Results of the Uruguay Round, Vol 31, 33 ILM 112 (1994); United States–Section 211, note 17 above (reversing Panel Report that offered a narrow interpretation of the scope of TRIPs).

59 See Dinwoodie, 'Development of International Norms', note 18 above, 765–66 (stressing, in the context of the United States–Section 110(5) report, the importance of distinguishing between the outcome and the reasoning of the panel); Austin, note 44 above.

WTO TRIPs litigation.[60] Moreover, at least in some respects, the WTO panel in the sole copyright case to date did not try to alter radically the mix of national autonomy and universal standards embodied in the international intellectual property agreements.[61]

Yet, over time, the narrowness of the panels' reasoning in intellectual property disputes may unduly restrict national copyright law making, if not sufficiently infused with normative values drawn from the stated purposes and objectives of the TRIPS Agreement as well as the broader intellectual property literature.[62] Regardless of the long-term effect of cautious panel formalism, it is clear that the balance between national autonomy and universal norms will be a central (if sometimes unexpressed) consideration underlying WTO panel determinations, just as it was in the drafting and revision of the classical conventions.[63] Importantly, however, any recalibration of that balance may now be effected, not only by nation state negotiators but also (and perhaps more easily) by panellists in the WTO dispute settlement body.

An appreciation of the *rhetoric, philosophy and values* of the trade regime is also important in seeking to understand how the trade context has influenced the international intellectual property system. The enhancement of international intellectual property obligations has been bolstered, in particular, by invocation of contemporary free trade philosophies, most notably that of

60 See Dinwoodie, ibid, 775 (discussing United States–Section 110(5) panel report); Jerome H Reichman, 'Securing Compliance with the TRIPs Agreement After *US v India*' (1998) 1 *J Int'l Econ L* 585, 594–97 (discussing *India–Pharmaceutical Patents* Appellate Body report); see also United States–Section 211, note 17 above, ¶¶137, 172, 187, 215, 219 (citing dictionary definitions of 'as is', 'derogate', 'owner', 'available', and 'substantiate').

61 See Dinwoodie, ibid, 764–65 (discussing United States–Section 110(5) panel report); see also Reichman, ibid, 594–97 (discussing *India–Pharmaceutical Patents* Appellate Body report).

62 See Dinwoodie, ibid, 764–65 (discussing failure of United States–Section 110(5) panel to follow through on the normative component of its definition of 'normal'). I have written in greater detail about the emerging WTO TRIPS jurisprudence and its effects on national policy making choices and processes in a series of articles co-authored with Rochelle Dreyfuss. For more detailed explanations, see Graeme B Dinwoodie and Rochelle C Dreyfuss, 'Diversifying Without Discriminating: Complying with the Mandates of the TRIPS Agreement', vol 13, p 445 (2007) *Michigan Telecommunications and Technology LR*; Graeme B Dinwoodie and Rochelle C Dreyfuss, 'Patenting Science: Protecting the Domain of Accessible Knowledge', in Guibault and Hugenholtz (eds), *The Future of the Public Domain in Intellectual Property* (Kluwer, 2006); Graeme B Dinwoodie and Rochelle C Dreyfuss, 'TRIPS and the Dynamics of Intellectual Property Lawmaking' (2005) 36 *Case W Res J Int'l L* 95; Graeme B Dinwoodie and Rochelle C Dreyfuss, 'WTO Dispute Resolution and the Preservation of the Public Domain of Science Under International Law' in *International Public Goods and Transfer of Technology under Globalized Intellectual Property Regime*, Maskus and Reichman eds (Cambridge University Press, 2006); Graeme B Dinwoodie and Rochelle C Dreyfuss, 'International Intellectual Property Law and the Public Domain of Science' (2004) 7 *J Int'l Econ L* 431.

63 See Dinwoodie, 'Development of International Norms', note 18 above, 764–66.

comparative advantage. If one country has a comparative advantage in knowledge-based products then, the argument goes, global protection of intellectual property rights is essential to permit exploitation of that comparative advantage. This philosophy is one of the explanations for the inclusion of copyright (indeed, all intellectual property) within the heart of the trade regime in 1994. In political terms, the TRIPS Agreement (which contains a significant copyright component) can be seen as simply the product of a trade-off in which developing countries received access to the markets of the developed world in return for enhanced levels of intellectual property protection.[64] But the language of comparative advantage provides an arguably less power-centered explanation and justification for international copyright law.

Of course, this does not immunize contemporary trade theory from criticism. Thus, while the theory of comparative advantage touts the benefits of efficiency, one can question the moral force of an argument that is grounded in the premise that the developed world can take advantage of its strengths in financially lucrative technology while leaving the developing world its 'strength' of low-wage manufacturing jobs. Indeed, there is an inherent tension between the theory of comparative advantage, which in large part accepts present-day advantages as acceptable, and the obligations of technology transfer that are included in the TRIPS Agreement and which are an important part of development policy. The same is true with cultural products: comparative advantage philosophy celebrates cultural concentration; all countries have cultural goods, but because only some have a comparative advantage this is not a problem under contemporary trade theory. But copyright theory traditionally has valued a diverse cultural and informational ecology, particularly if copyright is understood as playing a significant role in constructing the marketplace of ideas.

Moreover, one might also fear that the incorporation of intellectual property agreements within trade mechanisms might (if economic concerns become paramount) deprive intellectual property policy making of the rich palette of human values that historically has influenced its formulation. International copyright debates would be less multidimensional if law makers sought only to enable states to exploit their comparative advantage in copyright. Of course, the outcome of these changes may depend not only upon whether the trade context affects the values underlying nation-to-nation negotiating— 'let in my bananas, we'll cut you some slack on CDs' becomes a more ready and explicit form of discussion—but also upon how the binding dispute settlement system of the

[64] See Gerhart, note 47 above, 370–373.

World Trade Organization (to which the TRIPS obligations are subjected) deals with the trade/intellectual property interface.[65]

Finally, one of the (arguably) unintended consequences of using the trade system to effect the geographical expansion of intellectual property has been an increase in critical public attention on a worldwide basis. That is, in part, because the effects of intellectual property rights are inevitably more stark when viewed in a context where they implicate core aspects of human subsistence more directly. In many countries that are new to the intellectual property regime, the claims of strong intellectual property rights are claims to be able to save the lives of vast proportions of the community afflicted at a young age with terminal illness, to raise large swathes of people from severe poverty through the stimulation of economic development, and to bring benefits such as literacy to more socially isolated groups and thus enable a broader range of valuable human experience. Critics of strong copyright protection argue that a maximalist vision of proprietary control impedes and imperils these very same important social objectives. Bringing the intellectual property debate into the global context has inevitably sharpened the tenor of debate because the stakes seem far more fundamental, and might ultimately move the trade debate itself into a debate that transcends economic efficiency. Certainly, the nominal title of the current round of trade negotiations—the Development Round—suggests that this is not out of the question. The rich set of social values implicated by intellectual property is likely to be affected by, and contribute to, such an expanded vision of trade negotiators.

B. Lessons from Trademark: Faster and Softer Norms

A study of recent international trademark law making confirms that international intellectual property law is now effectively generated by a wide range of different processes.[66] In response to some of the same pressures discussed above, existing international institutions have introduced new law making processes designed to enable quicker reactions to new social and technological developments. In this category, one might include the structural reorganization of

---

65 See generally Rochelle C Dreyfuss & Andreas F Lowenfeld, 'Two Achievements of the Uruguay Round: Putting TRIPs and Dispute Settlement Together' (1997) 37 *Va J Int'l L* 275; see also Dinwoodie, 'Development of International Norms', note 18 above, 766–69 (discussing the influence of the trade context on the first report issued by a WTO dispute settlement panel regarding a copyright law question).

66 See Graeme B Dinwoodie, 'The International Intellectual Property Law System: New Actors, New Institutions' (2004) New Sources of, 98 *Proc Am Soc'y Int'l L* 213, reprinted in (2006) 10 *Marq Intell Prop L Rev* 205.

the World Intellectual Property Organization (WIPO). WIPO has formed, and made use of, standing committees to present proposals to the WIPO Assemblies for adoption in the form of non-binding recommendations rather than pursuing these same substantive goals through the mechanism of formal treaties adopted after a longer negotiation process.[67] This device has been most prevalent in the trademark context, with the 1999 non-binding recommendation on the treatment of well-known marks, and later adoption of a recommendation on rules governing the concept of 'use' on the internet, being notable examples.[68]

The adoption of the Uniform Domain Name Dispute Resolution Policy (UDRP)[69] by the Internet Corporation for Assigned Names and Numbers (ICANN)[70] in late 1999 is another example of speedy (and novel) international intellectual property law making. ICANN requires every registrar, offering to register domain names in the most commercially significant generic top-level domains, to include in its registration agreement a contractual provision whereby domain name registrants submit to the application of the UDRP. As a result, certain disputes between domain name registrants and trademark holders (known as cyber-squatting disputes) are resolved by quasi-arbitral panels appointed by ICANN-authorized dispute settlement providers and according to substantive rules that were developed in an unconventional process of international intellectual property law making.[71]

---

67 See 'Report of the Director General of WIPO', WIPO Doc No WO/GA/23/1 ¶¶1–12 (4 September 1998) (discussing the proposal to establish standing committees), available at <http://www.wipo.int >;Joint Recommendation Concerning Provisions on the Protection of Well-Known Marks, WIPO Doc. No. A/34/13 at 3 (August 1999) (discussing the non-binding nature of the recommendation), at <http://www.wipo.int/about-ip/en/development_iplaw/pub833.htm> (last visited 7 June 2002) [hereinafter 'Well-Known Marks Joint Recommendation'].

68 See Well-Known Marks Joint Recommendation, ibid; 'Joint Recommendation Concerning the Protection of Marks, and Other Industrial Property Rights in Signs, on the Internet' (October 2001), available at <http://www.wipo.int/about-ip/en/development_iplaw/pub845.htm> (last visited 12 May 2007); see also 'Joint Recommendation Concerning Trademark Licenses' (October 2000), available at <http://www.wipo.int/about-ip/en/development_iplaw/pub835.htm> (last visited 12 May 2007).

69 See 'Uniform Domain Name Dispute Resolution Policy' (24 October 1999) [hereinafter UDRP], available at <http://www.icann.org/udrp/udrp-policy-24oct99.htm> (last visited 7 June 2002); see also 'Rules for Uniform Domain Name Dispute Resolution Policy' (24 October 1999), available at <http://www.icann.org/dndr/udrp/uniform-rules.htm> [hereinafter UDRP Rules] (last visited 7 June 2002).

70 ICANN is a not-for-profit corporation that was created by the US government to operate the domain name system, among other things, in accordance with parameters set by the Commerce Department. Management of Internet Names and Addresses, 63 Fed Reg 31, 741 (10 June 1998).

71 See generally Laurence R Helfer and Graeme B Dinwoodie, 'Designing Non-National Systems: The Case of the Uniform Domain Name Dispute Resolution Policy' (2001) 43 *Wm & Mary LR* 141 (analysing the development of the UDRP at length); Graeme B Dinwoodie, '(National) Trademark Laws and the (Non-National) Domain Name System' (2000) 21 *U Pa J Int'l & Econ L* 495

Without unduly minimizing the ambiguities of that process,[72] in essence WIPO acted at the request of a single member state (the United States) to produce a report that, by virtue of delegation of *de facto* control of the domain name registration process from that single government,[73] could be implemented by ICANN as substantive law without the usual airings found in the intergovernmental law making process of which WIPO is a part.[74] And, as the Australian government recognized in a submission to the TRIPs Council not long after the UDRP was adopted, the UDRP has indeed become the international standard for resolution of cybersquatting disputes.[75]

To be fair to WIPO, the Organization did try to solicit comments regarding the proposals through alternative channels. Yet the process was quite different from the classical intergovernmental model to which WIPO formerly adhered (and largely still adheres). Instead, the development of the UDRP occurred outside the traditional intergovernmental process, thus reducing the direct involvement of nation states and moving at a much brisker pace than found in the treaty revision process.[76]

To be sure, both of these developments are expressly intended to produce only soft law. The recommendations that emanate from the WIPO standing committees and are later adopted by the WIPO Assembly are non-binding; nations may decide without penalty whether to introduce reforms to national law in order to comply with the recommendations.[77] Likewise, the results in UDRP proceedings can be overcome by contrary determinations in national courts and those courts are not obliged to defer (or even refer) in any way to the conclusions of the UDRP panel.[78] Indeed, orders of UDRP panellists may

(explaining the clashes between trademark law and the domain name system that gave rise to the non-national solution).

72 For a much fuller account, see Helfer and Dinwoodie, ibid.

73 See Andrew Christie, 'The ICANN Domain-Name Dispute Resolution System as a Model for Resolving Other Intellectual Property Disputes on the Internet' (2002) 5 *J World Intell Prop* 105, 107–10.

74 See Helfer and Dinwoodie, note 71 above, 167–68.

75 See Council for Trade-Related Aspects of Intellectual Property Rights, WTO, Electronic Commerce Work Programme: Submission from Australia, IP/C/W/233, ¶44 (7 December 2000) (suggesting that the UDRP has 'arguably become a *de facto* international standard' for the resolution of cybersquatting disputes), available at <http://docsonline.wto.org>.

76 See Helfer and Dinwoodie, note 71 above, 168.

77 See Well-Known Marks Joint Recommendation, note 67 above, 3 ('this creates no legal obligation for any country, but following such a recommendation would produce practical benefits').

78 See UDRP, note 69 above, ¶4(k) (providing that parties to UDRP disputes are not precluded 'from submitting the dispute to a court of competent jurisdiction for independent resolution before such mandatory administrative proceeding is commenced or after such proceeding is concluded'); see also *Sallen v Corinthians Licenciamentos LTDA*, 273 F3d 14 (1st Cir 2001) (noting that UDRP panel decisions are not entitled to any deference in subsequent national court proceedings) (citing

be stayed by nothing more than the losing party filing a complaint in the appropriate national court.[79]

But in practice these new forms of law making may produce harder law. This solidification may happen in different ways. It can occur through traditional public law mechanisms. For example, a number of bilateral trade agreements entered into by the United States require signatory states to ensure that their trademark laws comply with the WIPO Joint Recommendation on Well-Known Marks.[80] WIPO also asked member states to consider whether the different non-binding trademark recommendations adopted from 1999–2001 should be incorporated in treaties harmonizing trademark law.[81] The Revised Trademark Law Treaty, concluded in Singapore in 2006, incorporated large parts of the earlier non-binding Recommendation on Trademark Licensing.

Alternatively, the practical structure of the soft law mechanism might cause it to possess more enduring force than would first appear. The soft law character of the UDRP, for example, is arguably belied by the minuscule number of cases in which the losing party has had recourse to national courts. This pre-eminence of the

cases); compare Holger P Hestermeyer, 'The Invalidity of ICANN's UDRP Under National Law' (2002) 3 *Minn Intell Prop Rev* 1 (suggesting that certain UDRP panel decisions may be vulnerable to attack under French and German law because of the failure of the contractual provision submitting disputes to the UDRP to conform with national consumer protection laws regulating such contractual provisions).

79 See Well-Known Marks Joint Recommendation, note 67 above, 3 (providing that a losing respondent's filing a complaint with a court of mutual jurisdiction within ten business days of the panel's decision will automatically stay the panel's order transferring or cancelling the contested domain name). Courts of mutual jurisdiction are determined when the trademark owner files a UDRP complaint. See, e.g. UDRP Rules, note 69 above, Rule 3(b)(xiii) (requiring that the complainant must agree to submit to jurisdiction of a court in at least one specified 'mutual jurisdiction' with respect to 'challenges to a decision... canceling or transferring the domain name'). The trademark owner must select the courts based either where the registrar that issued the domain name registration is located, or at the address of the domain-name holder as shown in the registrar's Whois data. See ibid at Rule 1.

80 See Free Trade Agreement, 6 May 2003, US–Singapore, Art 16.2(b)(1) (providing that each party shall give effect to the Joint Recommendation on Well-Known Marks), available at <http://www.ustr.gov/Trade_Agreements/Bilateral/Singapore_FTA/Section_Index.html> (last visited 7 October 2004); compare Free Trade Agreement, 6 June 2003, US–Chile, Art 17.2(9) (recognizing the importance of the Joint Recommendation and undertaking to be guided by its principles), available at <http://www.ustr.gov/Trade_Agreements/Bilateral/Chile_FTA/Section_Index.html> (last visited 7 October 2004).

81 See Proposals for Further Harmonization of Formalities and Procedures in the Field of Marks, WIPO Doc. No. SCT/8/2, ¶1 (26 April 2002) (noting that the WIPO programme for 2002–2003 includes consideration by the Standing Committee on Trademarks of the incorporation of the three non-binding recommendations adopted from 1999–2001 in the framework of harmonization of trademark law), available at <http://www.wipo.int/edocs/mdocs/sct/en/sct_8/sct_8_2.pdf> (last visited 12 May 2007); Suggestions for the Further Development of International Trademark Law, WIPO Doc. No. SCT/8/3, ¶1 (26 April 2002), available at <http://www.wipo.int/edocs/mdocs/sct/en/sct_8/sct_8_3.pdf> (last visited 12 May 2007).

UDRP may, in part, be attributable to the advantages of UDRP proceedings in comparison to national litigation.[82]

If soft law is so easily hardened, these new law-making processes deserve equal care and attention, notwithstanding the advantages that new and faster law-making processes offer.[83] As the Argentinian delegation stressed in the 1999 WIPO Assembly meeting, circumspection is appropriate where there is 'creation of *de facto* norms without the permanent transparency of the negotiation and decision-making processes'.[84]

C. The Climate for Law Making: Forum Shifting, Balance, Evidence, Process, and the Development Agenda

Substantive Impasse

To some extent, many of these changes could have been predicted in 1994 when the TRIPS Agreement was concluded and when the ambitious EU legislative (and member state expansion) agenda was apparent. As momentum toward internationalization of intellectual property law grew, it might not have been apparent, however, that this movement would still meet substantial resistance. The agenda built in to the TRIPS Agreement, particularly the negotiation of a multilateral register for the protection of geographical indications, review of provisions on the patentability of plants and animals other than micro-organisms, and the protection of plant varieties, has made little progress in the TRIPS Council.[85] On the copyright side, although the Internet Treaties

---

[82] Empirical evidence of challenges in national courts is hard to gather because developing precise data would require coordination among the different registrars to ascertain the number of panel orders that have not been implemented because of the receipt of notice of a court action. One (extremely useful, but now out of date) database of national court challenges to UDRP rulings lists only 51 cases (including a mere 3 non-US cases) out of the first 4,800 UDRP panel decisions. See The UDRP–Court Challenge Database, at <http://www. udrplaw.net/UDRPappeals.htm>. This small number is consistent with anecdotal evidence, although some decisions (of US courts in particular) have been handed down. See *Sallen v Corinthians*, note 78 above (reversing the dismissal of an action under US law by a US domain-name registrant against a Brazilian trademark owner seeking to override a UDRP panel decision in favor of the trademark owner); *Barcelona.com, Inc v Excelentisimo Ayuntamiento de Barcelona*, 330 F3d 611 (4th Cir 2003)(dispute between a Spanish trademark owner and the domain-name registrant from whom a UDRP panel had previously ordered transfer of the registration in question).

[83] See Helfer and Dinwoodie, note 71 above, 245–48 (discussing pace of law making through interpretation of the UDRP).

[84] 'General Report of the Assemblies of the Member States of WIPO,' 34th Annual Meeting, Doc A/34/16, ¶178 (September 1999), available at <http://wipo.int>.

[85] See Paul Vandoren, 'The Implementation of the TRIPS Agreement' (1999) 2 *J World Intell Prop L* 25.

were concluded in 1996, the Database Treaty that was also scheduled for discussion at the Geneva Diplomatic Conference has been shelved.[86] The 2000 Diplomatic Conference on an audiovisual performers' treaty collapsed without agreement.[87] And, important issues relevant to copyright in the digital era (for example, service provider liability) have been dealt with by intergovernmental organizations only in the context of informational workshops. Similarly, negotiations on a version of the draft Hague Agreement on Jurisdiction and Recognition of Judgments that broadly encompassed intellectual property reached an impasse in 2001, with intellectual property proving to be a principal sticking point. The prospects for new subject-specific treaties, let alone a broad-based TRIPS II, seem dim.

Yet, reaching this impasse has taken substantial work on all sides. As noted above, intellectual property owners have continued to push an ambitious agenda for international law making and have done so on a range of issues where widespread international experience (let alone international consensus) has been lacking. For example, although developing countries are only now establishing the patent regimes required by TRIPS (because of transitional provisions that postponed implementation dates), the WIPO Standing Committee on Patents (SCP) has been considering further harmonization of substantive patent standards.[88]

To some extent, the advocacy of greater internationalization of intellectual property can generally be explained by the reasons discussed above in the copyright context. But institutional competition may also partially explain the phenomenon. The decision to deploy trade mechanisms was in part a reflection of 15 years of little perceived progress at WIPO (at least as viewed by the developed world and by the United States in particular).[89] But the sudden emergence of the WTO as part of the international intellectual property law-making process seemed to energize WIPO, resulting in the conclusion of several new treaties in

86 WIPO Copyright Treaty, and WIPO Performances and Phonograms Treaty, both at note 52 above.

87 See, e.g. 'WIPO Members Fail to Agree on Performers' Rights for Audiovisual Treaty' (2001) 61 *Pat Trademark & Copyright J* (BNA) 231.

88 See Chapter 13 below (Rochelle C Dreyfuss and Jerome H Reichman).

89 See Susan K Sell, 'Intellectual Property Protection and Antitrust in the Developing World: Crisis, Coercion and Choice' (1995) 49 *Int Orgs* 315, 321; Peter Drahos, 'Global Property Rights in Information: The Story of TRIPs at the GATT' (1995) 13 *Prometheus* 6, 9.

copyright,[90] patent,[91] and trademark law[92] and the promulgation of non-binding recommendations.

Despite all this activity, however, with the exception of the Internet Treaties, the only formal treaties concluded at WIPO have been primarily procedural: the Patent Law Treaty, the Revised Trademark Law Treaty and a revised Hague Designs Convention. Thus, despite the efforts of intellectual property owners, and despite the incentive for WIPO to reassert its primacy in a trade-structured system of international intellectual property law, WIPO has not been much more successful than the WTO in turning the pressure for greater internationalization into new substantive treaties.

Multiplication of Fora

There are several causes for this impasse and each highlights an important aspect of the current law-making climate. Those opposed to further internationalization (or further international enhancement of intellectual property rights, at least) mimicked the strategy adopted by the developed world in 1986 and have engaged in what some have called forum shifting.[93] This has involved raising issues of intellectual property in a number of international fora other than the WTO or WIPO, many of which were more philosophically or structurally sympathetic to the cause of developing countries. These initiatives seek not only to enrich (and complicate) the debate in ways that decelerate the law-making process, but also in the long term to generate rival norms that will compete in the international arena with any norms emanating from international institutions more supportive of intellectual property interests.[94] Thus, at the multilateral level, we have seen numerous policy making initiatives in an

[90] See WIPO Copyright Treaty and WIPO Performances and Phonograms Treaty, both at note 52 above.

[91] See Patent Law Treaty, 2 June 2000, 39 ILM 1047.

[92] See Trademark Law Treaty (27 October 1994) WIPO Doc No WO027EN, available at <http://www.wipo.int/clea/docs_new/en/wo/wo027en.html> (accessed 12 May 2007).

[93] See Laurence R Helfer, 'Regime Shifting: The TRIPS Agreement and New Dynamics of International Intellectual Property Lawmaking' (2004) 29 *Yale J Int'l L* 1 (discussing 'regime shifting'); John Braithwaite and Peter Drahos, *Global Business Regulation* (Cambridge University Press, 2000), 564 (suggesting different forms of 'forum shifting'); Chapter 11 below (Peter Drahos).

[94] This proliferation of political institutions raises hard questions. Is there to be a normative reconstruction of the system away from 'intellectual property organizations', or will the more complex debate still operate entirely within the rubric of the existing system? More strategically for developing countries, while forum shifting has proven to be a very good strategy for the blocking of further international agreement, it may cause too much of a cacophony when pursuing a positive international agenda, such as mandatory users' rights. See below. Moreover, forum shifting worked for the developed world in 1994 because there was a package trade deal to be concluded. Is the developing world ready to trade away user rights in one field for enhanced intellectual property protection in others, and what will that do to the existing coalitions?

increased number of international fora (some of which had not previously addressed intellectual property law).[95]

Users' Rights and 'Balance'

As an inevitable part of generating counter-norms, the international intellectual property system is beginning to grapple with the idea of internationally mandated ceilings on protection to accompany the floors that have been established over the past century. These ceilings, which might be called 'users' rights' or 'substantive maxima', are, conceptually, not well fleshed out at present.[96] But user groups and developing countries have come to accept that the ultimate substantive outcome of international negotiations will be closer to that which they desire (typically, national autonomy to maintain lower levels of protection) if their agenda assumes a positive form.[97] The development of such users' rights is an important part of the political movement which, though it adopts many names, might best be labelled as the 'Access to Knowledge' or 'A2K' movement.

The Development Agenda advanced in a number of more formal institutional settings by a group of developing countries self-styled as Friends of Development is the institutional cousin of A2K. WIPO has acknowledged the importance of the Development Agenda by creating a Provisional Committee (the PCDA) to consider more concretely what shape a development component of WIPO's work would take. Although developing countries have been gratified by an institutional focus on development, they have been careful to ensure that the creation of the PCDA does not prevent the discussion of so-called

[95] The multiplication of fora has extended to the judicial, as well as treaty making, arena. See *Anheuser–Busch, Inc v Portugal*, Application No 73049/01, (Judgment of Grand Chamber, ECtHR, 11 January 2007) (holding that trademark applications were protected 'property' within the meaning of the European Convention on Human Rights).

[96] See Dinwoodie and Dreyfuss, 'Patenting Science', note 62 above.

[97] Of course, we should not expect these changes, the international adoption of substantive rights, to ensure ideal substantive balance. If one were to devise the ideal first phase of substantive maxima or users' rights, it might be appropriate that the binding scope of such instruments be limited. As with efforts to develop substantive minima in the late nineteenth century, lasting results might best be achieved by securing widespread agreement on the basic concept, and then building on that over time. Moreover, there is a tension between mandating extensive users' rights and respecting the value of national autonomy, one aspect of balance that distinguishes national from international policy making. Member states should, at some level, be permitted room for choice as to the exceptions they wish, and as to the form of implementation. There may need to be a users' rights parallel to Art 1(1) of TRIPS. See Dinwoodie and Dreyfuss, note 62 above. Of course, one can minimize this tension by viewing national autonomy in terms broader than simply being free from formal constraints on national law making. Instead, if national autonomy possessed a more affirmative resonance, we might understand the term to mean the capacity of a nation state effectively to achieve its potential unimpeded by international constraints.

development agenda issues in other contexts, highlighting that the Development Agenda has strategic as well as substantive objectives.

The debate about substantive maxima, or users' rights, is part of a broader debate regarding the concept of 'balance' that has routinely been invoked in domestic intellectual property law making and is now become a nominal touchstone (or rhetorical ploy) in international intellectual property policy discussions.[98] Thus, domestic policy makers have sought to accord sufficiently generous rights to achieve the social goals that underlie the grant of protection without conferring so much exclusivity that we in fact impede the pursuit of those very social objectives. Courts frequently claim to be guided by the same concern of balance in interpreting ambiguous or open-ended provision.

Even at the domestic level, the assessment of 'balance' operates almost as a Rorschach test. The balance (let alone the oft-cited 'delicate balance') that intellectual property strives to achieve is a rather protean concept. Yet, it is now increasingly common to hear international instruments decried or celebrated depending upon their concern for balance. Every side claims the mantle of balance. For critics of enhanced international protection of intellectual property, this is an attractive rhetorical tool because, unlike domestic political processes, the classical international intellectual property system did not purport to establish a particular substantive balance. Thus, most international treaties established floors below which protection could not fall, but imposed no ceilings on protection. For critics, this was incontrovertible proof that the classical international system produced unbalanced intellectual property policy, which the contemporary regime must correct.[99]

Of course, this assessment somewhat ignored the more complex balancing that the classical international system was pursuing, including the balance of national with international regulation.[100] Also, the classical system typically gave great weight to national autonomy, establishing only loose parameters within which national political processes could strike a substantive balance appropriate to the circumstances of each domestic order.[101] Yet, as the realities of national political economies and the pressures created by bilateral trade agreements began to produce national laws that increasingly favoured intellectual property interests, critics have sought to inject discussion of substantive balance into the international debate.

98 I discuss the complexities of 'balance' in greater length in Dinwoodie, 'The WIPO Copyright Treaty', note 42 above.
99 See ibid.
100 See ibid.
101 See ibid.

This enrichment of the debate is surely appropriate given the enhanced role of international norms in framing national laws, the feedback loop between national and international law making, the bilateral trade pressures that seek to exploit the path-dependent character of an international system that only imposes floors, and the different historical conditions to which the classical and contemporary system are each responding. However, it must also be recognized that the balancing performed in the international system has always been more complex than in the domestic environment and has become more so in recent years. TRIPS, for example, added new vectors of balance, such as that between ideal rules of intellectual property and other gains that developing countries might wish to pursue in trade negotiations, for example market access or technology transfer.[102] Moreover, just as the classical balance between national autonomy and universal standards may need revision in the light of digital technologies, so too the substantive balance of rights might need to be altered as the mix of legal rights and effective enforcement generates new practical levels of exclusivity.[103]

Evidence-Based Law Making

In addition to the development of rival substantive norms to ensure substantive balance, critics of further international intellectual property law making have deployed a number of arguments directed towards international process or the structure of international law making. The most common such refrain is that an international solution is premature, or that there is no evidence on the national level that would suggest an ideal international norm. Evidence-based intellectual property law making has become a drag on what many intellectual property owners would seek to achieve.

The call for evidence and experimentation clearly echo an essential feature of the classical system. Rochelle Dreyfuss, writing about ambitious patent law harmonization,[104] has helpfully characterized the alternative approach of extensive international standards as 'trickle down', in that new approaches to problems would have to be devised first at the international level and then implemented by states.[105] Such experimentation will inevitably lack the comparative and

102 See ibid.

103 In quite which direction adjustment would be made is an open question: digital technology may make works more vulnerable to appropriation, but it might also allow copyright owners to capture greater rents through the application of technological protection measures. See note 166 below (discussing Copyright Directive provision on levies and digital rights management).

104 See also Chapter 13 below.

105 See Rochelle C Dreyfuss, 'Creative Law Making: A Comment on Lionel Bently, Trade Development and Multiple Layers of Lawmaking: Copyright, Translations and Relations Between

context-specific character of the historical lessons of which the classical system made good use. Instead, Dreyfuss argues that Professor Reichman's call for a moratorium on further public international law making might make sense: 'a trickle up approach, one that internationalizes law only after disparate regimes have had time to operate, is a better way to develop a jurisprudence that meets emerging needs'.[106] While this observation holds true as a general matter, the classical model might still need at least two modifications to meet contemporary demands while holding true to the merits of national autonomy and experimentations: there may be a greater need to internationalize quickly today than was the case in the late nineteenth century; and if the concept of users' rights gains a foothold, international law making may be important to constrain expansions in rights under national laws.[107]

Like the rhetoric of balance, the call for evidence-based law making at the international level mirrors long-standing debates at the domestic level.[108] Indeed, there has been a resurgence in calls for empirical evidence as a prerequisite to new rights at the national level too.[109] And, the European Union has pioneered the development of empirical studies assessing the effect of new rights with the introduction into many directives of requirements that the Commission produce a report on the operation of a new law five years after implementation.[110] (Of course, in the European Union, these reports have typically, with some exceptions,[111] been commissioned after the introduction of new rights, and

---

Britain and India 1880–1914' (forthcoming, 2007) 82 *Chi–Kent LR*. This is a somewhat different and more limited form of experimentation. It replicates to some extent how the European Union has merged a desire for empirically sound laws with its impetus to harmonize. Thus, in its initial copyright directives, the EU adopted a harmonized solution and has required the Commission to produce a study after five years analysing the success of the harmonization instrument. Putting aside the much less varied experiments that this allows, the experience of the Database review casts some doubt about the value that the Commission will attach to negative reviews of the harmonization exercise. Institutional economics suggests that it will be hard to undo the harmonization.

106 Ibid.

107 See Dinwoodie, 'The WIPO Copyright Treaty', note 42 above (noting tension between users' rights and national autonomy).

108 See Robert W Kastenmeier and Michael J Remington, 'The Semiconductor Chip Protection Act of 1984: A Swamp or Firm Ground?' (1985) 70 *Minn LR* 417.

109 See 'Gowers Review of Intellectual Property' (5 December 2006), available at <http://www.hm-treasury.gov.uk/media/583/91/pbr06_gowers_report_755.pdf>; see also Chapter 1 above (Daniel J Gervais).

110 See, for example, Institute for Information Law, *Recasting of Copyright & Related Rights for the Knowledge Economy* (2007) (report on the Copyright Directive), available at <http://www.ivir.nl/publications/other/IViR_Recast_Final_Report_2006.pdf>.

111 The exceptions have tended to be where some policy makers proposed constricting rights, such as studies on whether to move from EU to international exhaustion. Advocates of users' rights should thus be aware of the capacity of calls for evidence-based law making to preserve the status quo.

the appetite for repeal of rights is often non-existent even after reports sceptical of the economic benefits of the new rights.)[112]

Again, the call for evidence mirrors a mindset that operated under the classical international system. It too is emblematic of a different approach to international law, and thus, its persuasiveness is affected, on a case-by-case basis, by some of the arguments above regarding the need for speedier and more extensive international solutions in an era of global trade and porous borders. It surely would have been a persuasive argument that, in the classical era, counselled caution that a proposed international agreement would require changes to 169 different laws of a signatory party, as critics of a recent US–Korea trade agreement charged of one draft of that agreement.[113]

By the same token, the rhetorical assertion by critics that the free trade agreement would 'violate 169 Korean laws' suggests a commitment to nationalism at odds even with the classical era's lax approach to enforcement of international law. Instead, what that rhetoric reflects is the imbalance in the extent of obligations being undertaken in international agreements. At the point in time when the Korean delegation had agreed to change 169 laws, the United States had not made any concessions requiring amendment of its laws. Thus, although critics of contemporary international law making may adopt some of the language of the classical system, they are also effectively seeking to broaden that debate by reference to the substance of the commitments undertaken and not merely the process-type questions of national autonomy, or evidence-based law making.[114]

Process Critiques

Process-based critiques of the international intellectual property political system have also become a dominant refrain in recent debates. For example, critics of the recent webcasting treaty proposal complained that there was law making taking place in Geneva by 'unelected officials' without a proper airing domestically first. To some extent, the process-based critiques of the international intellectual property system are critiques of the system of international law in general: a lack of accountability, democracy deficit, lack of transparency, and 'one size fits all'.

Thus, one could simply subsume debate about these issues within the broader ongoing discussion about the contemporary system of international law. But

112 See Commission of the European Communities, 'First Evaluation of Directive 96/9/EC on the legal Protection of Databases' (Brussels, December 2005), available at: <http://ec.europa.eu/internal_market/copyright/docs/databases/evaluation_report_en.pdf>.

113 See 'SK–US Free Trade Deal Would Violate 169 Korean Laws: Critics,' *The Hankyoreh*, 17 January 2007, at <http://www.bilaterals.org/article.php3?id_article=6933>.

114 See note 97 above (suggesting a recasting of 'national autonomy').

reforms at both the national and international level can help to preserve the flexibilities that enabled countries to adopt balanced intellectual property laws under the classical system. Rochelle Dreyfuss and I have suggested, for example, formalizing and institutionalizing values of transparency and inclusiveness by requiring APA-like notice and comment procedures prior to the adoption of bilateral trade agreements; these bilateral agreements are currently operating as the primary brake on the exercise of the flexibilities that remain in the multilateral system.[115]

The Role of NGOs

There has been exponential growth in the number of non-governmental organizations who are working on issues of international intellectual property. This can be explained, in part, by a number of developments, including the use of the internet to develop cross-border advocacy, which are by no means specific to intellectual property. But this is also, in part, a function of increased awareness (and funding) that has come from the global expansion of the discipline.

The increase in NGO activity on all sides raises a number of problems. While it has surely enhanced the range of views that contribute to the global debate, it has added to the problems of cacophony. And, NGOs suffer from many of the same process problems (lack of accountability, representativeness deficits, cultural imperialism, and 'one size fits all') that NGOs highlight when states act internationally contrary to the positions advocated by NGOs. Indeed, at least states acting internationally are typically accountable at some level of remove from the decision in question; that cannot even be said of NGOs.

To be sure, NGOs do not possess the power to bind countries and thus we might not wish to hold them to the same standards as nation states. However, it does, at least, make them somewhat unsteady bearers of the banner for process or institutional reform. Indeed, typically, NGOs are not animated by process concerns, but rather by substantive social goals. Few activist groups clamour under the banner of national autonomy, transparency or accountability. NGOs use all these arguments, of course, but only to serve their particular substantive goals.

115 See Chapter 4 below (Anselm Kamperman Sanders).

Part III Private Litigation and Private Ordering

The broader process of harmonization, which some of the developments discussed above exemplify, presents many challenges.[116] To the extent that these different law-making forces are causing a convergence around common rules of intellectual property, however, one might suggest that a more intrusive substantive international intellectual property law is growing through public law mechanisms.[117] Yet rules of similarly *de facto* global reach may be occurring in private litigation and through private ordering. The universalizing effects of each of these law-making forces—not considered part of the classical public international intellectual property system—offer similar benefits, but may implicate similar concerns, as the results achieved through the public international law-making process. Typically, however, they receive relatively little scrutiny.

A. Private Litigation

Ad Hoc Development of Private International Law

The panel decisions issued under the UDRP by ICANN-authorized dispute-settlement providers, previously discussed, have clearly established international norms on the practice of cybersquatting.[118] Likewise, any efforts by national courts to adjudicate domain-name disputes clearly have an effect beyond national borders; domain-name/trademark rules in the generic top-level domains are truly non-national.[119] Or, stated less tendentiously, such decisions by national courts may have substantial effects in a number of countries. The only means by which this proposition could be altered radically might be through relief mandating the deployment of measures that effect virtual territorialization.[120]

---

116 See Graeme B Dinwoodie, 'The Integration of International and Domestic Intellectual Property Lawmaking' (2000) 23 *Colom–VLA JL & Arts* 307, 310 (discussing EU harmonization of intellectual property laws).

117 See Ginsburg, note 16 above.

118 See text accompanying note 71 above.

119 See, e.g. *Sallen v Corinthians*, note 78 above (action by US domain-name registrant to recover registration from Brazilian trademark owner without equivalent US trademark registration); *Heathmount AE Corp v Technodome.com*, 2000 WL 33666935, 60 USPQ2d 2018 (ED Va 2000) (applying US law to dispute between Canadian parties because domain name registered with registrar located in the United States).

120 See 'Geography and the Net: Putting It in Its Place' (11 August 2001) *Economist*, 18–20.

There are many other (apparently more traditional) contexts in which national courts are beginning to tackle cases with broader international ramifications and thus contribute to the effective creation of international rules. This has occurred most perceptibly, and most readily, in the copyright context. Several courts in the United States, with the encouragement of the Second Circuit,[121] one of the leading appellate courts in copyright matters, have permitted plaintiffs to pursue actions alleging claims under several disparate foreign copyright laws;[122] courts are more consciously separating jurisdiction to adjudicate from questions of applicable law. There is also growing acceptance throughout the United States of a doctrinal device, first used by the Second Circuit, whereby relief will be granted in respect of both domestic and overseas acts of infringement where a predicate act of infringement occurred within the United States and enables further reproduction abroad.[123] In both these ways, US courts have provided multinational relief and, in the latter case, have effectively applied a single rule to international conduct.[124] (Even copyright courts that forswear

121 See *Boosey & Hawkes Music Publishers, Ltd v Walt Disney Co*, 145 F3d 481, 484 (2d Cir 1998) (reversing district court's dismissal of claims under foreign copyright laws on *forum non coveniens* grounds).

122 See, e.g. *Carell v Shubert Org, Inc*, 104 F Supp 2d 236, 257–59 (SDNY 2000) (permitting claims based on foreign copyright laws to proceed notwithstanding the plaintiff's failure to specify in her complaint the particular countries under whose laws the claims were made); *Armstrong v Virgin Records, Ltd*, 91 F Supp 2d 628, 637–38 (SDNY 2000) (entertaining claims based on unspecified foreign copyright laws on the basis of diversity jurisdiction and pendent jurisdiction); *Frink Am, Inc v Champion Road Mach, Ltd*, 961 F Supp 398, 404–05 (NDNY 1997) (declining to dismiss claim under Canadian copyright law). But see *ITSI*, note 29 above (refusing motion to amend complaint to assert claim under Mexican copyright law).

123 See *Los Angeles News Serv v Reuters TV Int'l, Ltd*, 149 F3d 987 (9th Cir 1998), later proceeding, 340 F3d 926 (9th Cir 2003); see also *Peter Rosenbaum Photography v Otto Doosan Mail Order*, 76 USPQ2d 1759 (ND Ill 2005). The device had long been accepted by the Second Circuit. See *Sheldon v Metro-Goldwyn Pictures*, note 22 above, 52. But the Ninth Circuit had previously expressed some doubt regarding the rule. See *Subafilms*, note 33 above, 1094.

124 Although courts applying this theory have applied a single law to the multinational event, it is not inevitable that courts seeking to provide relief for multinational infringement in a single proceeding must apply a single law. Courts could assume jurisdiction over all the related claims but apply different national laws to the different heads of conduct occurring in different jurisdictions, determining liability on a country-by-country basis. See Austin, note 44 above, 130–31. Indeed, the new willingness of courts to assume jurisdiction over claims of infringement of foreign copyright law makes this a more plausible alternative. See text accompanying notes 69–74 above. For reasons I have explained at length elsewhere (Dinwoodie, 'A New Copyright Order', note 12 above, 542–79) I favour the application of a single substantive rule (but not necessarily one found in the domestic law of a single nation state, let alone one determined using the vagaries of the predicate act or root copy theory) to copyright disputes that are inherently international. Moreover, in the context of online posting of allegedly infringing material, this possibility of applying different laws on the question of liability is very difficult in practical terms. And, although one could award damages in respect only of countries where posting would amount to infringement, injunctive relief is more difficult to fashion absent a willingness to issue orders regulating the nature of online use or imposing technologically-grounded obligations. See note 126 below (discussing Yahoo! litigation).

the extraterritorial application of the copyright statute may to some extent be regulating globally when they apply choice of law rules that easily localize any internet conduct in the United States.)[125]

These trends are less evident in patent and trademark cases, where the classical role of national courts has remained more constant. Yet even here, some US courts have been willing to become embroiled in multinational disputes and apply what in practice is a rule of much more than national scope.[126] Whereas copyright law has formally adhered to a rule proscribing extraterritorial application,[127] US courts have been less restrained in applying the Lanham Act to conduct with a much more tenuous US connection,[128] other than some of the parties involved.[129] And the enactment of the Anti-Cybersquatting Consumer Protection Act in 1999 has occasioned even more intrusive US judicial regulation of international domain-name space, particularly (though not exclusively) through the capacious *in rem* cause of action granted to trademark owners who cannot obtain jurisdiction *in personam* over a domain-name registrant.[130] In the patent context, the

125 See Dinwoodie, 'A New Copyright Order', note 12 above, 537 (discussing the ease with which internet copyright-infringing conduct can be localized in the United States).

126 Some courts, however, have sought to be careful in fashioning relief in ways that respect the foreign interests in the dispute before them. See, e.g. *Playboy v Chuckleberry*, note 33 above; *Sterling Drug v Bayer*, note 33 above. Although the use of injunctive relief tailored to accommodate competing interests occurs more frequently (and thus, perhaps, more easily) in trademark cases (see 'Joint Resolution Concerning the Protection of Marks, and Other Industrial Property Rights in Signs, on the Internet', note 68 above (suggesting the remedies to be afforded successful plaintiffs in online trademark disputes)) it is also possible in copyright cases. See Dinwoodie, 'A New Copyright Order', note 12 above, 558–69 (applying substantive law method to choice of law dilemma in international copyright disputes). This makes somewhat surprising the response of US courts and (most) US commentators (in a non–intellectual property context) to the efforts of the French judge in the well-publicized *Yahoo!* litigation to find a solution that took account of the values of different affected nation states. See *Yahoo! Inc v Le Ligue Contre Le Racism et L'Antisémitisme*, 145 F Supp 2d 1168 (ND Cal 2001), rev'd, 433 F3d 1199 (9th Cir 2006).

127 See *Subafilms*, note 33 above.

128 Lanham (Trademark) Act 1946—Title 15 of the US Code. See *Nintendo of Am, Inc v Aeropower Co*, 34 F3d 246, 249 n5 (4th Cir 1994).

129 See, e.g. *Ocean Garden, Inc v Marktrade Co*, 953 F2d 500 (9th Cir 1991).

130 Anti-Cybersquatting Consumer Protection Act, Pub L No 106–113, 113 Stat 1501A–545 (codified as 15 USC § 1125(d)(2)); see also *Heathmount v Technodome*, note 119 above (exercising *in rem* jurisdiction over a domain name registered with a registrar located in the United States in a dispute between Canadian parties); *Globalsantafe Corp v Globalsantafe.com*, 250 F Supp2d 610 (ED Va 2003); *America Online Inc v AOL.org*, 259 F Supp2d 449 (ED Va 2003). More all-encompassing US regulation of the domain-name space in the long term might occur through the operation of a complementary, but largely unheralded, provision also introduced by the Anti-Cybersquatting Consumer Protection Act, even if this provision has been surprisingly under-used to date. This provision, codified as §32(2)(D)(v) of the Lanham Act, permits domain-name owners aggrieved at the loss of a UDRP proceeding, and hence of their domain-name registration, to bring a claim in US federal court seeking (i) a declaration that their domain-name registration does not violate the Lanham Act, and (ii) an order returning the domain-name registration. The Court of Appeals for the First Circuit, in the first appellate consideration of this provision, read §32(2)(D)(v) to offer 'disappointed

Court of Appeals for the Federal Circuit has just issued an opinion narrowly interpreting the jurisdiction of US courts to adjudicate foreign patent claims along with their US counterpart patents in US courts, as Japanese and German courts have done. But that opinion did so over a vigorous dissent by Judge Newman.[131] Similarly, although the US Supreme Court recently narrowed the broad extraterritorial scope given by the Federal Circuit to the provisions of the US patent statute consciously aimed at effecting some external regulation, judicial interpretation of other terms of the patent statute in a transborder context has effectively resulted in the application of US patent law to activities legally occurring abroad.[132] As a practical matter, these new private law developments occurring in national courts increasingly may come to comprise and generate the content of international intellectual property law.

Moreover, courts have expressed some interest in the dynamic between public international intellectual property standards and the role of national courts. One court has found that a plaintiff could, through the vehicle of section 44(b) of the Lanham Act, advance a claim based upon violation of standards found in the

---

[UDRP] participants with a chance to have any unfavorable UDRP decision reviewed in a US court.' *Sallen v Corinthians*, note 78 above, 28 (emphasis in original). A textual analysis of §32(2)(D)(v) suggests that the US court's determination of non-infringement (and hence of the ownership of the domain-name registration) would turn on the application of US law. And, under a traditional view of US trademark principles, the ability of the successful UDRP trademark complainant to resist a §32(2)(D)(v) claim by the domain-name registrant would appear to rest upon the trademark owner possessing US rights. I am unaware of any similar provision in other countries that might redress this elevation of US courts and US rights. In any event, the number of 'appeals' of UDRP decisions filed in the US courts (see note 82 above) suggests that US law may come essentially to apply to most domain name disputes because of broader social and economic forces. See also Dinwoodie, 'A New Copyright Order', note 12 above, 577–79 (discussing copyright law).

131 See *Voda v Cordis Corp*, 476 F3d 887 (Fed Cir 2007) (Newman J, dissenting); see also *KK Coral Corp v Marine Bio KK*, Case No 1943(wa)/2002 (Tokyo District Court, 16 October 2003); see also Nahoko Ono, 'Cross-Border Patent Infringement: The *Coral Powder* Case, Where a Japanese Court Applies US Law' (July, 2005), Report Prepared for Annual Meeting of ATRIP (Montreal); *Hitachi v Seji Yonezawa*, Case No H16 (ju) 781, Supreme Court of Japan (17 October 2006), reported at WIPO Intellectual Property Report 10–11 (December 2006) (interpreting the statutory right of employee-inventors to receive reasonable compensation for the transfer of rights as permitting account to be taken of the profits that the employer derived from foreign patents). The capacity of German courts to continue this practice may have been adversely affected by a recent ruling of the European Court of Justice regarding the interpretation of the Brussels Regulation. See Case C–4/03, *Gesellschaft für Antriebstechnick mbH & Co KG (GAT) v Lamell und Kupplungsbau (LUK)*, 37 IIC 742 (2006)(ECJ 13 July 2006); *Roche Nederland BV*, 37 IIC 865 (2006)(ECJ 13 July 2006); see generally Annette Kur, 'A Farewell to Cross-border Injunctions? The ECJ decisions *GAT/LuK and Roche Nederland BV/Primus and Goldberg v Primus*' (2006) C–593/03, 37 I.I.C. 844.

132 See *NTP Inc v Research in Motion, Ltd*, 418 F3d 1282 (Fed Cir 2005), replacing 392 F3d 1336 (2004); *Microsoft Corp v AT & T Corp*, 127 S. Ct 1746 (2007), *reversing*, *AT & T Corp v Microsoft Corp*, 414 F3d 1366 (Fed Cir 2005); see generally Graeme B Dinwoodie, 'Developing a Private International Law of Intellectual Property' (forthcoming).

Paris Convention rather than being limited to the causes of action expressly delineated in the Lanham Act.[133] The development and content of public international intellectual property law has also informed judicial analysis of *forum non conveniens* issues in several international copyright and trademark cases.[134]

Scholars have also suggested that the choice of law methodologies that US courts have developed in copyright cases, acting free of the constraints of treaty provisions regarding choice of law, might include reference to substantive public international copyright law. I refer here, not only to my own proposal that well-established international principles contribute to the identification of a substantive governing rule in international copyright cases, but also to suggestions previously made by Jane Ginsburg that provisions in international copyright treaties might serve as a baseline standard to ensure that the foreign law a national court applies complies with international minimum standards. In this fashion, Professor Ginsburg would ensure that the country whose law was applied does not act as a haven for copyright infringers.[135]

In each of these contexts, one finds an echo of the tension underlying the public law debate in the 1880s: the contest remains one that pits notions of universality against those of national autonomy. This is seen in the public international context proper, as might be expected, but also in the development of

133 See *Gen Motors Corp v Lopez*, 948 F Supp 684 (ED Mich 1996). The majority of cases have read US law less expansively. See *Mattel, Inc v MCA Records, Inc*, 296 F3d 894, 907–08 (9th Cir 2002) (limiting benefits of §44 to the right of national treatment); *Int'l Cafe, SAL v Hard Rock Cafe Int'l (USA), Inc*, 252 F3d 1274, 1277–78 (11th Cir 2001) (same).

134 See *Murray v British Broadcasting Corp*, 81 F3d 287, 290–91 (2d Cir 1996) (analysing the national treatment obligation in international copyright law); *Creative Tech, Ltd v Aztech Sys, Ltd*, 61 F3d 696, 700–01 (9th Cir 1995) (giving weight to the principles of national treatment and territoriality); ibid, 706 (Ferguson J, dissenting) (same); see also *Heathmount*, note 119 above (considering the nature of ICANN proceedings); see also *Subafilms*, note 33 above, 109–98 (taking into account recent developments in international copyright law in determining the territorial scope of the copyright statute). The dynamic between public and private international law is complex. A British court recently invoked the public international process of intellectual property harmonization as support for revision of long-standing rules of private international law. See *Griggs Group v Evans*, 2005 Ch D 153 (HC 2004), later proceeding, 2005 FSR 31 (CA 2005) (UK). In contrast, the Canadian Supreme Court appears to see private international law as an interim solution pending public law harmonization. *Society of Composers, Authors & Music Publishers of Canada v Canadian Assn Of Internet Providers* ('Tariff 22'), 2004 SCC 45, 32 CPR (4th) 1 (SC 2004) (Canada). This disagreement reflects a philosophical debate that has been taking place for centuries within the field of private international law itself. See Arthur Taylor von Mehren, 'Special Substantive Rules for Multistate Problems: Their Role and Significance in Contemporary Choice of Law Methodology' (1974) 88 *Harv LR* 347 (discussing competing objectives of avoiding forum shopping and ensuring apt results).

135 See Ginsburg, 'Private International Law Aspects', note 23 above; Jane C Ginsburg, 'Private International Law Aspects of the Protection of Works and Objects of Related Rights Transmitted Through Digital Networks, 2000 Update' (2000) WIPO Doc No PIL/01/02, available at <http://wipo.int>.

rules that encourage national courts in private litigation to develop multinational solutions and to engage with public law standards. National courts, it may properly be said, now contribute to the development of international intellectual property law.

Systematic Approaches

Efforts to create a more systematic approach to transborder intellectual property disputes began in the 1990s with the draft Hague Convention, later built upon by the Dreyfuss–Ginsburg proposal. Strictly speaking, such treaties as were proposed might best be described as 'public private international law', to borrow Steve Burbank's nomenclature.[136] These treaties would not directly have determined the appropriate rules of substantive international intellectual property law, but rather would have framed the manner in which we determine the appropriate rules.

The treaty route appears unlikely to succeed in the foreseeable future. But other efforts to develop a more systematic approach to these disputes remain active, most notably the ALI Project on the development of a set of Principles, and the ongoing work of the Max Planck Group on Conflicts of Laws in Intellectual Property (CLIP). At their most basic, these proposals address the practical problems of litigating national rights in an increasingly non-national world. More systemically, they would establish the basic conditions under which national courts would contribute to and develop a form of international intellectual property law. Thus, these proposals would instal the elemental architecture of this (nationally constructed) part of the international intellectual property system, with the precise design to be decided on an ongoing basis by national courts (checked by legislatures) operating within that structure.[137]

But why should we expend any effort on developing these systems of private international intellectual property law? The development of substantive international rules, and the mediation of the competing values of national autonomy and universal rules, through national court jurisprudence may possess advantages over public law processes (whether classical or new). When compared with the traditional negotiation of treaties, national court development of 'international law' is more responsive to social conditions and hence more dynamic; and it is more

136 See Stephen B Burbank, 'Jurisdictional Equilibration, The Proposed Hague Convention, and Progress in National Law' (2001) 49 *Am J Comp L* 203, 204.

137 Obviously, if there is no single treaty establishing the system of transborder adjudication, no immediate 'elemental architecture' will arise. That would depend upon the extent of the adoption of the soft law principles by countries, and the extent of the reference to the ALI Principles by courts. See Dinwoodie, 'Developing a Private International Law', note 132 above.

readily subject to refinement by a range of national political institutions. Moreover, the articulation of cross-border relief under a single rule by a national court, or (to use the language of my own earlier proposal) the development of a substantive rule of national law applicable to international cases, would not result in the premature entrenchment of such a rule as a higher norm of international law in the way that WTO dispute-settlement body rulings in practice might do. At bottom, national court decisions are local law that remains subject to national legislative reversal or modification. And, while courts would be expected to refer to other national court decisions (both domestic and foreign), they would also be formally free to depart from those decisions, retaining the value of national experimentation that is crucial to the classical model of international intellectual property law.[138]

Moreover, this means of developing international intellectual property law is less subject to the political demands that historically have burdened the public international process and that continue to limit its efficacy. To the extent that agreement on substantive harmonized rules (especially forward-looking rules) is fast becoming impossible because of the number of interested parties with disparate agendas in the intellectual property law-making process, this alternative form of law making offers a greater prospect of progress. It is uncertain whether the systems of active national court involvement facilitated by the procedural mechanisms adopted by the ALI and under consideration elsewhere would produce rules more favourable to supporters or opponents of expansive intellectual property protection. But one value of these systems as law-making instruments may in fact lie in the common uncertainty as to the rules that they might produce. Negotiating for certainty, whether in substantive rules of intellectual property law or in the allocation of prescriptive authority between international and national law, has proven a difficult endeavour of late.

Critics of this purported procedural neutrality might argue that such systems embed quite partisan values, although broader systemic values than those underlying intellectual property policy alone. For example, almost every proposal would establish procedural rules that clearly contemplate the possibility of some degree of cross-border relief, of decisions that effect change beyond national borders, or of the universalization of certain values and rules. This critique is descriptively accurate, but unpersuasive as a rebuttal to the development of the systems proposed. Consider the alternative—and this is, I would suggest, a crucial perspective—of cross-border relief being developed on a purely ad hoc basis, in other words of a greater number of decisions by national courts that (without reasoned

138 See Austin, note 44 above.

contemplation) affect conduct beyond their borders. Let us not be naive about the choice: there is no idealized, 'national' world of hermetically sealed borders within which national courts decide disputes without spillover effects. The choice is between two scenarios, both of which involve a departure from a theorized territorial model: (1) courts providing relief that extends their law beyond their borders, but doing so without considering explicitly the external effects of their application of local law or why to offer cross-border relief; and (2) the development of a system in which courts offer conscious explanations of why cross-border relief is appropriate and why the internal effects of one state outweigh the external effects on another. It is, in effect, the difference between a systematic and transparent development of these rules of international intellectual property law, bounded by outside parameters established (whether through treaty or less formal adoption) by nation states, and a spate of competing decisions with universal effects but unaccompanied by any effort at justifying or explaining the same.

Moreover, I am less troubled than others by the notion that we are moving in some respects toward a different balance of universal and national values—though the precise balance is a point of genuine debate. Proper respect for national values, especially as long as national political structures remain the primary voice for the expression of political viewpoints, is important. But the balance between national and non-national sources of affinity is shifting; legal institutions that reflect the impulses of the citizenry are more likely to endure than those which resist or counter those impulses.[139]

B. Private Ordering

As the public international law-making process has reached impasse, other institutions have stepped forward. As noted above, national (especially US) courts have begun to offer interpretations of the scope of their national laws that can easily extend their local norms into international space, particularly in the

[139] See Dinwoodie, 'A New Copyright Order', note 12 above, 550–51. Having urged a realist perspective on those who find these proposals unsettlingly close to the imposition of global values, let me also suggest a reality check for those who seek to advance enlightened systems of so-called 'public private international law'. It may be some time before judges in national courts can function in ways that routinely defer to the application of foreign law. But there are signs of progress in judicial awareness of the experience and decisions of other national courts. The increased specialization of the intellectual property judiciary may assist in developing this common knowledge (see Dinwoodie, 'Developing a Private International Law', note 132 above), although specialized courts raise a number of other issues that might caution against too ready an embrace of that concept. See Rochelle C Dreyfuss, 'The Federal Circuit: A Case Study in Specialized Courts' (1989) 64 *NYU LR* 1.

online context.[140] But when courts do so, at least nominally (if, to my mind, inadequately), they consider the international implications of their decisions under the rubric of private international law concerns of jurisdiction, applicable law, recognition of judgments, and comity.

Other institutions have, however, begun to articulate and *sub silentio* develop international copyright norms in ways that do not involve the conscious consideration of either the balance of copyright law or the additional concerns of international copyright law. The remainder of this chapter discusses two such examples, but first situates them within the broader context of private ordering and copyright law.

Private Ordering and Copyright Law

Any rule of copyright law must encourage an optimal supply of knowledge in a vast array of different social and economic settings: copyright law covers a wide range of different works created and used in many different industries. Inevitably, default rules of copyright law are a blunt (and, some would say, inefficient) instrument for achieving an optimal level of protection. By tailoring protection to particular settings and enabling price discrimination, private ordering might make the creation and distribution of knowledge more efficient.

Private ordering of the treatment of copyrighted works has occurred through the use of both contract and technology. In the online context, contractual ordering has primarily taken the form of click-wrap contracts. Technological measures take private ordering further. Like click-wrap contracts, DRMs enable price discrimination and tailored access rights. But, they also hold out the prospect of self-enforcement and there is not even the nominal involvement of the user in the negotiation of the terms of access.

Proponents of these forms of private ordering also claim efficiency gains that implicate international copyright principles. Online delivery of works is almost inevitably international in nature. Yet, the discordance between territorial copyright laws and the ubiquity of the internet presents immense problems of jurisdiction and applicable law which international copyright law has not yet resolved. As discussed in Section A of this Part, developing a system of conflict

[140] See Austin, note 44 above, 1183; Michael Geist, 'Cyberlaw 2.0' (2003) 44 *BCL Rev* 323, 323–358. The phenomenon is even more pronounced in trademark law. See, e.g. *Heathmount*, note 119 above (BNA); *Sallen v. Corinthians*, note 78 above; *Harrods Ltd v 60 Internet Domain Names*, 302 F3d 214 (4th Cir 2002); see generally Graeme B Dinwoodie, 'The Extended Reach of the ACPA: The Domination of Trademark Rights or the Domination of US Law'(24 April 2003) Paper Presented to Eleventh Annual Fordham Conference on International Intellectual Property Law and Policy, New York.

rules for copyright law is on the agenda of several institutions, but a solution has proved hard to find. In contrast, parties to a contract can agree to norms that are limited to a particular nation state, or detached from any nation state (e.g. the *lex mercatoria* applied by arbitrators in international commercial arbitration). Technology, likewise, can be programmed to permit access that corresponds to certain national norms, international norms or to no existing norms at all. Both contract and technology are seen, therefore, as instruments for avoiding not only the inefficiencies flowing from the bluntness of rules of copyright law, but also the uncertainties that impede the generation and distribution of knowledge in an international environment.

However, private ordering of the supply of knowledge through contract and technology has tended to result in a balance of rights and obligations more favourable to the content provider than would be the case under default rules of national copyright law. Thus, persons disadvantaged by this shift might be expected to argue for the overriding application of copyright norms, notwithstanding the efficiency benefits that are claimed for private ordering. Such arguments can be grounded either in substantive concerns regarding the appropriate balance of rights or in the uninclusive nature of the private 'law-making process'.[141] Copyright law is devised through a democratic process. Notwithstanding public choice concerns that have made recent legislative activity unattractive to some scholars, that process confers a degree of legitimacy on the norms that are applied by courts. Private ordering lacks that form of legitimacy. Instead, proponents of private ordering rest their claim of legitimacy on its concordance with the parties' wishes and on the nominally limited reach of that ordering, namely, only as far as the parties to the transaction. Of course, in practice many parties to transactions are powerless to influence the terms of the deal. Moreover, such purportedly private activity (especially when replicated in the mass market) impinges directly and indirectly upon non-parties to the transaction (i.e. the public).

Private Ordering and the Creation of International Copyright Norms

Private ordering, therefore, clearly has costs and challenges to its displacement of copyright norms may yet succeed.[142] But in other online intellectual property

141 This may, but need not, be entirely grounded in efficiency. It is an open question whether the efficiency gains of binding, technologically (largely) self-enforcing bargains outweighs the arguable efficiency costs of an unbalanced allocation of rights and privileges. But, even if there are efficiency gains, a variety of non-efficiency-grounded values might support trumping private ordering (e.g. free speech, encouragement of heterodoxy, etc.).

142 Challenges to private ordering that ousts copyright norms have, however, been unsuccessful, at least in the United States. The majority of challenges to click-wrap licenses (like challenges to

contexts, private ordering has become the means of (at least, initially) overcoming the jurisdictional and enforcement issues presented by the ubiquity of the internet. Most notable in this regard is the UDRP, adopted by ICANN in late 1999, which has become the international standard for resolving cybersquatting disputes through a powerful cocktail of contract and technology. The UDRP shows that private actors may create 'international law' with virtually as much ease (and certainly as much effect) as nation states. The two examples discussed below suggest equivalent potential in copyright law.

Notice and Take-Down Procedures

The Digital Millennium Copyright Act 1998 (DMCA) introduced a set of provisions, now found in section 512 of the Copyright Act 1976, which created 'safe harbours' for internet service providers alleged to have contributed to copyright infringement by subscribers.[143] Among these safe harbours is one that enables an ISP to escape monetary relief for copyright infringement where it has hosted a subscriber's website containing infringing material, provided that once the ISP receives a notice from a copyright owner reporting an alleged infringement it expeditiously takes down the infringing material and otherwise complies with the provisions of the notice and take-down procedure in section 512.

Copyright owners are not obliged to use the notice and take-down procedures to pursue infringers. If they so desire, copyright owners may simply bring an infringement action against the user (and, contributorily, the ISP) under traditional principles of liability (which were not altered by the DMCA). But, because the copyright owner may not know the user, and because the primary relief sought (the removal of the infringing material) can be achieved more cheaply and more quickly through the offices of the cooperating ISP than the offices of the courts, copyright owners have readily turned to the notice and take-down procedure.

shrink-wrap licenses previously) have failed, and the contractual terms have been allowed to prevail. See Mark A. Lemley, 'Intellectual Property and Shrink-wrap Licenses' (1996) 68 *S Cal LR* 1239, 1239–1240. There are exceptions, see. e.g. *Step-Saver Data v Wyse Tec*, 939 F2d 91 (3d Cir 1991), and recent case law is mixed, but the trend is still toward enforcement. See *Bowers v Baystate Technologies*, 230 F3d 1317 (Fed Cir 2003); *Specht v Netscape Comms*, 306F3d 14 (1st Cir 2001). Most successful challenges have been grounded in contract doctrine, rather than insisting on the supremacy of copyright norms. But see *Vault Corp v Quaid Software*, 847 F2d 255 (5th Cir 1988). Similarly, arguments that the norms of copyright law should be elevated over technological measures imposing restrictions inconsistent therewith have been rebuffed by the courts. See *Universal City Studios v Corley*, 273 F3d 419 (2d Cir 2001).

[143] Digital Millennium Copyright Act, Pub L No 105–304, 112 Stat 2860 (1998); Copyright Act, 1976 (17 USC 512).

Likewise, ISPs are not obliged to comply with notices that they receive. ISPs may take the position that their subscriber's use is not infringing, or that they are not contributorily liable. But the immunity offered cooperating ISPs by section 512 greatly incentivizes compliance; indeed, it incentivizes over-compliance (and little independent analysis) by ISPs that are in receipt of notices from copyright owners.[144] Indeed, that is the value of the procedure, both to the copyright owner (who obtains complete cooperation) and the ISP (who is relieved of uncertainties over liability without any need to expend resources on making judgement calls or monitoring subscribers). As a result, take-down normally occurs within 24 hours.[145]

Under the DCMA, ISPs in the United States have through their responses to notices under section 512 effectively served as first-instance private adjudicators of infringement disputes between copyright owners and users who post copyrighted content to websites.[146] But they are adjudicators who largely do not adjudicate; instead they process and enforce claims without consideration of the merits of the defendant's arguments.

Of course, the take-down notice is not the sum of the section 512 procedure. In theory, these disputes are designed to precede litigation and the parties involved are always free to resort to judicial resolution. Thus, a subscriber who is informed that its ISP has received a notice of alleged copyright infringement may serve the ISP with a counter-notification contesting the claim of infringement. The statute then incentivizes the ISP's restoration of the allegedly infringing material by granting the ISP immunity for complying with the restoration request (after informing the copyright owner, who may then initiate litigation, which will stay restoration). Practice under the statute, however, reveals that the overwhelming

[144] See Rights Watch Report 5 (2003). The Rights Watch Report, which contemplated policies to be adopted in the EU, suggests that although ISPs might be incentivized to have scant regard for residential subscribers, that might not be true of a large corporation paying for dedicated hosting. This might in fact exacerbate concerns about this form of norm development, but there has been no evidence that ISPs operating under the DMCA have made this distinction. However, if they had, it would be hard to detect, highlighting the need (discussed below) for transparency to be a guiding principle of any public structuring.

[145] Department of Trade and Industry, *Combating Internet Copyright Crime* (The Publisher's Association, London, 2003) 20–25 available at <http://www.publishers.org.uk/paweb/paweb.nsf/pubframe!Open>.

[146] See 'Activist Network in New York City Evicted from Internet by Dow, *Verio*', (23 December 2002), available at <http://slash.autonomedia.org/article.pl?sid=02/12/23/153204>. Of course even in the offline context, different intermediaries (depending upon the type of work involved) often limit access to allegedly infringing work after receiving notice from the copyright owner. But in the online environment, ISPs become central actors in all copyright disputes, regardless of the type of work involved, and are thus able to determine the online availability of a broad spectrum of copyrighted works. The centrality of ISPs to the supply of knowledge online makes the *ex ante* structural incentives that will guide their conduct, and any *ex post* external checks, crucial.

majority of disputes are resolved with no counter-notification and no judicial intervention.[147]

The practices of ISPs are so central to the success of the notice and take-down procedure that they clearly have the capacity to develop norms both as regards the substantive scope of copyright protection, and with respect to the enforcement of copyrights. The discussion above suggests that these practices are likely, because of incentives built into the DMCA, to shift the balance of rights toward copyright owners. But the DMCA also contains provisions that are designed to balance the incentives that it creates to favour the copyright owner in the implementation of the notice and take-down procedure. In addition to ISP immunity for restoring material when requested to do so by a properly-served counter-notification, section 512 provides civil liability for knowing material misrepresentations that cause unjustified removal of material (or unjustified restoration). These causes of action, plus the various immunities created by the statute, and an important provision that entitles copyright owners to obtain from ISPs the identity of the ISP's subscribers who are alleged to have engaged in copyright infringement by subpoena and without court order, are different elements[148] of the 'public structuring' of private ordering.[149]

If the practices of ISPs were shown to be altering the scope of protection afforded to copyright owners, what should policy makers do? Assuming that copyright law embodies a balance more likely to produce an optimal knowledge supply, policy makers would need to revise the elements of public structuring currently found in the Copyright Act. The fact that some might describe ISP practices as 'private' transactions should be of no moment. Beyond the mythic qualities of the distinction that this presupposes, the description of section 512 above highlights that those practices are intensely structured and supported by public legislation, the Copyright Act.[150]

147 See Steven J Metalitz, 'Implementation of the DMCA: The Practical Experience' (20 April 2001) Working Paper, Ninth Annual Fordham Conference on International Intellectual Property Law and Policy, 7; *Combating Internet Copyright Crime*, note 145 above, 45. Of course, it might be argued that in most cases, the infringement is clear. See Shira Perlmutter, 'Comments from SOFTIC International Symposium' (20–21 November 2001) Tokyo.

148 In order to make the notice and take-down procedure work efficiently, copyright owners also need reliable Whois data. Again, the apparent private ordering of ISPs and copyright owners in fact requires substantial public underpinning.

149 See Michael Warnecke, 'DMCA's False Notification Provision Gains Traction in Complaints, Case Law', 73 Pat Trade Cop J 332 (26 January 2007) (discussing district court decision in *Online Policy Group v Diebold*, 337 F Supp 2d 1195 (ND Cal 2004), as well as more recent reported opinions and complaints filed).

150 See Radin and Wagner, note 6 above.

For this to be achieved, however, the ISP practices have to be known. While the DMCA contains many elements of public structuring that suggest an effort to maintain a fair balance of rights, the practices that it engenders are not easily accessible to the public. The Copyright Office maintains no relevant records and does not monitor the notices.[151] At present, the practices are being monitored by non-governmental organizations and these forms of monitoring may ultimately cause governmental action.[152] But transparency is lacking.[153] Efforts to replicate or revise the notice and take-down procedure should tackle this important question, which will lend legitimacy to the procedures adopted. [154]

ISP practices under the DMCA may also be giving rise to an international copyright norm. At present, no multilateral treaty provisions expressly govern ISP liability. The Diplomatic Conference of the WIPO Copyright Treaty in 1996 did not adopt any provision regulating service provider liability (though countries did adopt an Agreed Statement accompanying Article 8, which required states to offer copyright owners the exclusive right to make a work available to the public, acknowledging that 'the mere provision of physical facilities for enabling or making a communication does not in itself amount to communication within the meaning of this Treaty or the Berne Convention'). Yet this is a topic that cries out for international agreement, or cooperation.[155] WIPO has tried to encourage convergence of standards through workshops on ISP liability[156] and intellectual property owners in the United States have lobbied

151 See *Combating Internet Copyright Crime*, note 145 above, 20–25.

152 See ChillingEffects.org, <http://www.chillingeffects.org> (last visited 2003).

153 In this regard, although the UDRP system is lacking some of the structural design elements that inject balance into the notice and take-down procedure, such as a cause of action where complainants are found to have engaged in reverse domain-name hijacking, the decisions of panellists are all public. This has enabled intense scrutiny, and has validated concerns that certain structural elements skew the system (such as the choice of dispute-settlement provider being reserved exclusively to the trademark owner).

154 Directive 2000/31/EC of the European Parliament and of the Council of 8 June 2000 on certain legal aspects of information society services, in particular electronic commerce, in the Internal Market, OJ L 178, 1. Although the EU Directive was adopted seven years ago, many Member States of the European Union are still considering how best to implement a similar notice and take-down system. Art 14 of the E-Commerce Directive obliged member states to enact an immunity from liability similar to section 512, but contained significantly less detail. The recitals to the Directive instruct member states to encourage the development of a notice and take-down system by means of 'voluntary agreement between all parties concerned', Recitals 40–46. In constructing and revising these agreements, member states should be alert not only to the elements of public structuring in section 512, but also to the demand for transparency. Law making by private agreements always raises concerns of voice and legitimacy. This is particularly likely to be so where there is no mechanism to publicize or monitor the application of these rules. The EU 'voluntary agreements' must take these transparency concerns into account, because the directive itself makes no such provision.

155 See Perlmutter, 'Comments from SOFTIC International Symposium', note 147 above.

156 See WIPO Workshop on Service Provider Liability (1 December 1999) Geneva, available at <http://www.wipo.int/documents/en/meetings/1999/osp/pdf/osp_lia1.pdf>.

hard (directly, and by asking the United States government to make provision for DMCA replication in bilateral trade agreements) for other countries to adopt the DMCA model.[157]

And, in fact, ISP practices under the DMCA are coming to establish the international norm. US copyright owners are serving notices on ISPs worldwide under section 512[158] and receiving surprisingly high levels of compliance.[159] To be sure, discrete (though similar) practices continue to evolve in other countries, and this is not the first occasion when the law of a single country has purported to have broad territorial reach. As noted above, although national courts nominally apply their intellectual property laws territorially, US courts have applied their copyright and trademark law in a fashion that has arguably made US law the dominant law online. But, there, the extended reach of US law has occurred through its public application by courts, nominally restrained by rules of private international law, a context that is both apparent and subject to contest by courts of other countries. As those rules codify, through the public debate that the decisions themselves generate, one would expect a more diverse range of prescriptive influences.

ISP practices under the DMCA might, in addition, shift the balance between the application of national and international rules, a shift which is itself construction of a new international copyright norm. As noted above, an implicit element in every aspect of the international copyright regime is the allocation of prescriptive authority to national or international institutions. Where this balance is adjusted via ISP practices, however, the allocation between national and international sources will likely not occur through a conscious decision that for reasons of efficiency, already existing harmonization, or the maintenance of divergent and fundamental national values, certain values require to be set at one level or the other. Instead, this allocation might be the product of such serendipitous forces as the governance structure of multinational ISPs, or the market for ISP services (itself potentially the subject of regulation), or the geographic composition of an ISP's subscribers (which may be affected by any number of variables).

Alternatively, and still speculatively, the balance of national and international norms could be altered by a contractually grounded extension of the UDRP model into the copyright realm. If ISPs acquire customers from several different countries, ISPs might wish to establish a single policy for responding to alleged

---

[157] See *Combating Internet Copyright Crime*, note 145 above, 20–25.
[158] Metalitz, note 147 above, 8; *Combating Internet Copyright Crime*, note 145 above, 45.
[159] Geist, note 140 above, 377.

acts of copyright infringement. Indeed, because ISPs may (acting collectively) offer a choke point not unlike that made available in the domain name context by ICANN's control of the root server, one might envision a system that sought to expose a larger number of these copyright complaints to the light of day and provide some form of adjudication of their merits. An ISP could contractually require subscribers to submit to dispute settlement of infringement claims by third-party copyright owners with respect to postings of copyrighted materials on the ISP's servers. The dispute-settlement providers, like the panellists in the UDRP context, could be authorized to apply some designated body of rules, be they national or international copyright laws or some hybrid, to determine whether the ISP must remove such allegedly infringing materials.

In such an event, the rules applicable to notice and take-down disputes may well evolve away from purely national roots toward contract-enshrined norms and practices not tied to any particular prescriptive authority. Such rules might evolve quite independently of the norms of any particular nation state. If such a system were to develop,[160] it would even more directly raise the challenges of private ordering: rights of users coercively (though, nominally, contractually) subjected to adjudication before fora of private adjudication.[161]

Whether non-national or international norms develop by dint of practice or through a contractually constructed system, it is important to remember the role of public structuring. This is not to deny the benefits of dynamic, non-national specific standards that such a system might embody, or the efficiency gains that are generated by fast processing of routine complaints. Rather, for the benefits of these rules not to be outweighed by corresponding costs, any procedural mechanism that is established must address, not only the substance of the norms, but the structural incentives for their application in one direction or another, and the publicizing of the practices in ways that facilitate active national legislative or judicial involvement if that is appropriate. Moreover, there must be a public-oriented input towards the allocation of certain issues to the national, and other issues to the international, realm.

160 Copyright owners are content with the current system and would be unlikely to agree to any such experiment, which they would view as unnecessary and blind to the benefits of an automatic process that deals quickly and cheaply with routine cases of piracy. Moreover, they would argue, users already have the capacity to force content owners to court in order to vindicate their claim. These arguments are most easily rebutted, of course, if over-reaching by copyright owners is shown.

161 As in the case of the UDRP, one could not imagine national courts deferring to such decisions simply because they are the product of institutions established by private arrangement and 'affect only' those private parties.

Agreements contemplated by Article 6(4) of the EU Copyright Directive

The EU E-Commerce Directive contemplates agreements among ISPs, content-providers and users regarding notice and take-down procedures.[162] But, while that directive contains no mandatory administrative review of those agreements, the EU Copyright Directive goes further (procedurally, if not substantively) in acknowledging that private ordering should, to some extent, be subject to publicly-defined limits. The Directive (in Article 6) implements Articles 11 and 12 of the WIPO Copyright Treaty, which obliged signatory countries to protect effective technological measures (i.e. DRMs) against unauthorized circumvention. (The treaties still left national law much room for experimentation.)[163] Like the DMCA, the Copyright Directive validates DRMs as a form of private ordering. Like ISP practices in response to notices from copyright owners, technology need not be nationally configured. Technology is not inherently territorial, and thus to the extent that national laws validate DRMs that are not tied to national copyright rules, they may be validating international norms (if the DRMs are replicated by content owners generally). Indeed, it may add expense to make the terms of use or access country-specific (but enable greater price discrimination).

Alternatively, geographically-oriented technological measures have the capability to re-territorialize international knowledge markets in ways that bring product distribution back to the historical premises of international copyright law, rather than reconfigure copyright norms to the basis of contemporary product distribution. Region-coding of DVDs exemplifies this option.[164] Thus, decisions made in the construction of DRMs by content owners may determine whether norms of access to works are set nationally or internationally. And, as suggested above, they have the capacity to set norms without reference to the balance of rights established in copyright law (whether national or international). Private ordering thus, once more, can affect the structural norms of international copyright law: according to which set of values will the decision whether to universalize or territorialize be made?

---

162 E-Commerce Directive, note 154 above, 12–13. Directive 2001/29/EC of the European Parliament and of the Council of 22 May 2001 on the harmonisation of certain aspects of copyright and related rights in the information society, OJ 22 June 2001 at 10 (L167) (Copyright Directive).

163 Samuelson, note 53 above, 530–533.

164 In an early draft of the Finnish implementation of the Copyright Directive, region-coding of DVDs was expressly excluded from the definition of 'technological measure', thus enabling the sale of devices that circumvent region-coding. But see *Kabushiki Kaisha Sony Computer Entertainment Inc v Gaynor David Ball* [2004] EWHC 1738 (Ch) (UK). Region-coding clearly limits the ability of the technological protection measure to establish international norms.

This discussion, of course, assumes wholesale validation of private ordering. But the legislative inclination, thus far, does appear to be in favour of DRMs effecting norms regarding the distribution of knowledge, whether inconsistent with national copyright law (though some limited exemptions patrol that boundary), and whether inconsistent with international copyright norms (concerning which no legislative intent can be discerned).

The EU recognized the potential problem of unbalanced private ordering and the possibility that an unduly strict application of the new quasi-copyright prohibition might have the effect of denying users the right to engage in acts that would otherwise be permitted by copyright law. To redress any imbalance, Article 6(4) of the Copyright Directive relies in the first instance on 'voluntary measures taken by the right-holders, including agreements between right-holders and other parties concerned' to ensure that those benefiting from exceptions are able to exercise those exceptions.[165] Thus, it seeks to ensure that certain[166] copyright values will be preserved notwithstanding technological protection measures inconsistent therewith.[167]

Moreover, if such measures are not taken voluntarily, Article 6(4) of the Directive provides that 'Member States shall take appropriate measures to ensure that

165 See Art 6(4). The only type of 'voluntary measure' expressly referenced in Art 6(4) is 'agreements between right holders and other parties concerned'. But reaching such agreements will be a difficult task. As the range of stakeholders with interests implicated by copyright law expands, reaching consensus becomes difficult (even assuming you can identify the stakeholders). Indeed, because some of the exceptions at issue are linked to certain types of use and not defined categories of users (i.e. are purpose exceptions, not identity exceptions), the beneficiaries may be quite diverse. Thus to the extent that private contractual arrangements among interested parties will be the means by which the ability to take advantage of copyright exceptions is guaranteed, there will likely have to be a complex web of agreements. Of course, agreements are not the exclusive form of 'voluntary measure', so rights holders might also consider modification of technological measures in ways that enable beneficiaries to take advantage of the exceptions in question.

166 Art 6(4) only applies to certain stated exceptions, and only in so far as those exceptions are recognized in the national copyright law in question. See Jerome H Reichman, Graeme B Dinwoodie and Pamela Samuelson, 'A Reverse Notice and Takedown Regime to Enable Public Interest Uses of Technically Protected Copyrighted Works' (2007) 22 *Berk Tech LJ* (forthcoming).

167 The Copyright Directive also regulates the relationship between compensation rights of authors under 'private copying' schemes in national copyright laws, and the use of technological protection measures. Art 5 provides that the appropriate rate of return for authors under such compensation schemes should take into account the extent to which technological protection measures have been deployed. Indeed, a recital to the directive contemplates that the compensation under the copyright scheme might be reduced to zero where technological protection measures enable the author to obtain payment. But this provision regulates the technological protection measures only minimally: it does not make the copyright norm prevail but rather, simply ensures that the public system does not duplicate payments already extracted by private ordering. The payment extracted by private ordering may, however, exceed the payment that would have been available under the public system. Thus, as discussed below, Art 6(4) may be closer to a mechanism that ensures the predominance of the default norms of copyright law.

right-holders make available to the beneficiary [...] the means of benefiting from' certain exceptions and limitations to copyright.[168] Thus, unlike the agreements contemplated by the E-Commerce Directive, here there is a shadow in which the bargaining will take place. Substantively, it is a narrow shadow: only a very few exceptions and limitations are listed (and this is a major failing as a public structuring control element). But procedurally, it presents great latitude to member states.

What appropriate measures might member states adopt under Article 6(4)? Different member states are experimenting with different mechanisms. These differ in several respects, but most importantly, they vary in terms of institutional allocation of authority among courts, magistrates, and the administrative and legislative branches.[169] If these differences persist, then we may be presented with a series of experiments in how best to control and monitor private ordering in ways that preserve the benefit of DRMs without conceding control on the important public question of how to ensure a balance of rights between copyright owners and users.

If the inconsistency of DRMs with national copyright law is resolved by initial agreement between rights holders and the beneficiaries of exemptions, there is a possibility that the DRMs might seek to impose the same technological protection measures on products distributed internationally, raising the prospect that the DRMs (as modified by agreements between interested parties) will come to create international norms.[170] This is likely, at least within the European Union. Whether such norm creation by a mix of technology and contract should have a broader geographical remit should ideally be determined by the set of structural international copyright norms that guided the historical balance (contemporarily interpreted) between national autonomy and universality. More likely, it will be determined by whether, within industry groups, there is

168 The German implementation of the Copyright Directive contains an interesting provision that reflects comments above regarding transparency. Private ordering proponents frequently assert that any imbalance that occurs can be corrected by the competitive market; consumers will not buy goods protected by oppressive DRMs. But the market is constructed on massive information asymmetry. Germany proposes to partially correct that asymmetry by public regulation, namely, by requiring any work protected by DRM to be labelled in a fashion that discloses the restrictions on its use. See Foundation for Information Policy Research, 'Implementing the EU Copyright Directive' (September 2003) Cambridge. Recent attacks on over-protective DRM systems in a number of European countries (e.g. Germany, the Netherlands, France, Finland and Norway) have relied on consumer protection or unfair competition law. See David Ibson, 'Norway declares Apple's iTunes Illegal,' *Financial Times*, 24 January 2007.

169 See Foundation for Information Policy Research, ibid; Urs Gasser and Silke Ernst, *Best Practice Guide: Implementing the EU Copyright Directive in a Digital Age* (2006).

170 If ensuring compliance with exceptions available under national law falls to the safeguard mechanisms contemplated by Art 6(4), it is more likely that any solution will be tied to national norms.

the political will to extend any agreement reached within the European Union to the United States and elsewhere. Article 6(4) is a creditable (if overly limited and undefined) effort at imposing public checks on private ordering. But the values of the international copyright system, with their attendant affects on the generation and distribution of knowledge, are noticeably absent.

The Role for Public Structuring and International Norms

As both of these examples demonstrate, private ordering has (as its proponents have argued) substantial ability to overcome the persistent problem of territorial rights in a less than fully territorial world. Yet both are ultimately dependent upon an underpinning of public regulation, even if that regulation consists of a decision to forbear from acting. The mix of public structuring that will be essential to buttress effective private ordering will vary from one context to another. In some, it will be forbearance from intrusive regulation; in others it will be laws supplying the instruments (e.g. subpoena power to obtain information about alleged infringers) by which parties are able to engage in efficacious private ordering; and in yet others, it will consist in a set of related liabilities (or immunity therefrom) that incentivize private conduct.

It is clear that private ordering is dependent upon public structuring for its effectiveness. The central political question, however, that is essential to the legitimacy of publicly-structured private ordering, is whether the forms of structuring are sufficiently balanced to ensure that—when implemented through private ordering—the outcomes produce a balance of rights and access that furthers the optimal supply of knowledge. For those who are sceptical of the wholly 'private' nature of any social activity, it is not difficult to justify conscious political choices surrounding the nature of the public structuring. But even for those who attach the ('do not disturb') label of 'private' to what ISPs do in response to notices from copyright owners, or what content owners do in implementing DRMs, it is surely evident that their favoured system is heavily dependent upon public structuring, and thus not immune from the public oversight that is appropriate in return for public support.[171]

[171] In offline contexts, rarely was the availability of content of all types at the mercy of a single group of technological providers. Certainly, distribution channels for particular types of works contained dominant market players; the mass availability of hard copy books offline is increasingly (in the United States) a function of the proximity of Barnes & Noble and Borders. And, the availability of performance licenses for musical works was heavily dependent upon the practices of ASCAP and BMI. But these institutions acted subject to legal restraints (e.g. antitrust laws) rather than under the protection of legal immunities. This is public structuring in the offline world that was effective, and important. If copyright owners asserted egregious over-reaching, possible causes of action did exist (whether constructed creatively or expressly sanctioned, as is the case in the UK).

Even with conscious attention to the nature of that public structuring, because some of the ways that the private ordering will play out will likely flow from such unpredictable forces as the organizational structure of firms and inter-industry political bargains, it will be important for public structuring to be prospective and dynamic (no less than copyright law itself must be able to react to change). The provisions in Article 6(4) of the EU Copyright Directive, if expanded in scope, appear to possess that potential, even if in the Directive they assume only abstract and muzzled form. And, for such assessment to be made on an ongoing basis, whatever private ordering occurs must be subjected to the light of day. This can be done by non-governmental organizations, but more importantly such transparency must itself be built into the public structuring of the private system. If open government is a mantra of liberal democratic polities, then transparent private ordering must equally be the obligation of those who purport (beneficently) to arrive at the same results through private governance.

Finally, each of these forms of private ordering has the potential to create international norms, both substantively and structurally in the allocation of certain norms to the national or international level. Yet, no public structuring that currently exists holds private law makers to account for their decision to alter the balance of national autonomy and universal rules. International copyright law embodies important structural, or institutional, norms that impinge directly upon the generation and distribution of knowledge: national autonomy, diversity of values, and resistance to orthodoxy, are all valuables tools in optimizing the knowledge supply. Public structuring that fails to account for these international values has failed to account for an important part of a system that purports positively to affect the creation and availability of knowledge.

Conclusion

The international intellectual property system has always been driven, to some extent, by trade concerns. However, the recent incorporation of intellectual property within the apparatus of the World Trade Organization, along with other social and economic developments, has caused the rapid evolution of the international intellectual property system. The contours of that system are now quite different than when the system first took shape in the late nineteenth century. Yet, appreciating the important role of trade institutions in changing the

See Paul Heald, 'Payment Demands for Spurious Copyrights: Four Causes of Action' (1994) 1 *J Intell Prop L* 259.

intellectual property system should not distract commentators from other developments that are now effecting the creation of international intellectual property norms equally. In particular, private ordering activities have the capacity to regulate extensive international activity, and to do so without full public scrutiny. Thus, these activities also must be scrutinized, with a view to both how they affect the balance of rights between right holders and users, and how they affect the balance between national and international regulation.

3

ECONOMIC GROWTH AND INTELLECTUAL PROPERTY RIGHTS PROTECTION: A REASSESSMENT OF THE CONVENTIONAL WISDOM

Robert L Ostergard, Jr

Introduction

In 1994 more than 100 states signed the Marrakech Agreement establishing the World Trade Organization (WTO) and the implementation of the Uruguay Round of the General Agreement on Tariffs and Trade (GATT). As a result of a strong lobbying effort by the United States the agreement included a global trade regime for the protection of intellectual property rights (IPR).

The agreement bound all signatory states to implementing a 'Western-style' intellectual property (IP) regime within 16 years of ratification. The agreement itself was the final product of a long process that elevated the IPR issue from an obscure, esoteric legal field to a critical economic and political issue that brought states to the brink of trade wars.

Traditionally, IPR have been the concern of lawyers protecting their clients' ideas and discoveries. Economists took notice of the issue following the seminal work of Joseph Schumpeter, who argued that innovation and technology were the driving forces behind industrial growth and development.[1] Economists focused their attention on the importance of IPR to domestic economic growth through mediums such as foreign investment and technology transfers. In the conventional literature on the relationship between IPR and economic growth, the argument for strong IPR protection is predicated on the assumption that a positive relationship exists between strong IPR protection and economic growth (and development). This chapter is dedicated to the task of providing an empirical reassessment of the economic growth and IPR protection relationships. The research presented here indicates that there is reason to question at least part of the assumed relationship between IPR and economic growth. Moreover, with this relationship in question, additional evidence suggests that IPR protection is not always enacted as part of sound economic policy, but rather as a result of political pressure.

Part I The Measurement of Intellectual Property Rights Protection

With the increased global attention to IPR issues, scholars and policymakers have begun to focus more on IPR protection and its economic impact. One problem in conducting this research has been the measurement of IPR protection. Past attempts seem to be limited in their ability to capture IPR protection, focusing on the laws with limited attention paid to how countries enforce those laws. The importance of the enforcement component, however, becomes even more critical given the Agreement on Trade-Related Aspects of Intellectual Property Rights (TRIPS) administered by the WTO. The TRIPS Agreement requires that most developing countries should be in compliance with the minimum

[1] Joseph Schumpeter, *Capitalism, Socialism and Democracy* (Allen & Unwin, 1976).

standards for IPR protection by the year 2006.[2] However, in practical terms the distinguishing factor among countries in the protection of IPR will often be in how they enforce those laws, rather than in the existence of formal legislation.

The enforcement of IP laws has been a critical issue, particularly in trade relations between developed and developing countries. The measurement of such practices will be crucial in the assessment of national performance in protecting IP. This section presents an alternative method for measuring IPR protection that incorporates the strength of national IP laws and states' enforcement practices of those laws. The measure is a better gauge of IPR protection than just using the strength of laws, which may lead to greater estimation error in states' IPR protection. For scholars, the measures can offer insightful perspectives into micro-level questions about the nature of corporate inventive activity, investment trends, research and development and corporate strategic investments, property rights, and institutional effectiveness. At the macro level these data can also help address questions about the relationship between IPR and trade, foreign investment flows, and economic growth and activity. Practitioners in international business may find these data and the approach taken here valuable tools in assessing IP investment risk in countries, particularly in industries that are sensitive to the protection of IPR (e.g. pharmaceuticals and chemical industries, the entertainment and software industries, and marketing and licensing enterprises).

A. Empirical Research

Intellectual property has long been a concern for many industries, particularly for those with a heavy reliance on the protection afforded by national IPR laws. In many ways, as technology has advanced, industries have been victims of their own success, because with greater advances in technology have come easier methods for duplicating that same technology and associated products. For instance, the introduction of video recorders to consumer markets also brought with it the capacity to duplicate videotapes, bringing about potentially massive copyright piracy problems, a situation greatly exacerbated by the combination of the digital format of copyrighted material and the dissemination capacity and reach of the internet. As such, advances in technology have made some industries more reliant on IP protection than other industries. The pharmaceutical and chemical industries are highly dependent on patent protection as a consequence

2 This date includes the ten-year exception for implementation of the Agreement's provisions by developing countries established in Art 65 of the Agreement. The full text of the TRIPS Agreement can be found at the World Trade Organization website at <http://www.wto.org/english/docs_e/legal_e/27-trips_01_e.htm>.

of technology that has reduced the difficulties in duplicating chemical compounds.[3] Others such as the entertainment and computer software industries have reliance on copyrights and patents for the same reasons.[4] Much of this research, however, has been qualitative, with few quantitative studies. One obstacle to doing quantitative IPR research has been in constructing measures of IPR protection. A number of studies have attempted to measure IPR protection cross-nationally; among them are Rapp and Rozek, Seyoum, Sherwood, and Ginarte and Park.[5]

Rapp and Rozek's study was one of the first attempts to quantify IPR protection in some form. Scholars used this measure in their studies,[6] and the US government cited this study as providing additional evidence to support its position on global IPR.[7] Hence, Rapp and Rozek's measure warrants closer scrutiny. They used patent laws as a proxy for IPR protection and measured the strength of 159 countries' patent laws on a 0–5 scale, where 0 represents a country with no patent laws and 5 represents a country that has laws consistent with the minimum standards established by the US Chamber of Commerce Intellectual Property Task Force.[8] The Rapp and Rozek measure is presented in Table 3.1.

---

3 J Nogues, 'Patents and Pharmaceutical Drugs: Understanding the Pressures on Developing Countries', [1990] *J of World Trade* 24, 81–104; WD Noonan, 'Patenting Medical Technology', [1990] *J of Legal Medicine* 11, 263–319; Robert M Sherwood, *Intellectual Property and Economic Development* (Westview Press, 1990); William S Comanor, 'The political economy of the Pharmaceutical Industry', [1986] *J of Econ Literature*, Vol 24, No 3, 1178–1217; Stanley M Besen and Leo J Raskind, 'An Introduction to the Law and Economics of Intellectual Property', [1991] *J of Econ Perspectives*, Vol 5, 1, 3–27.

4 J Band and M Katoh, *Interfaces on Trial: Intellectual Property and Interoperability in the Global Software Industry* (Westview Press, 1995); KD Ebanks, 'Pirates of the Caribbean Revisited: An Examination of the Continuing Problem of Satellite Signal Piracy in the Caribbean and Latin America', [1989] *Law and Policy in Int'l Business* 21, 33–52; US Congress, Office of Technology Assessment, *Intellectual Property Rights in an Age of Electronic and Information*, OTA CIT–302 (Washington: US Government Printing Office, 1986); Besen and Raskind, ibid.

5 Richard Rapp and Richard P. Rozek, 'Benefits and Costs of Intellectual Property Protection in Developing Countries', [1990] *J of World Trade* 75I77, 75–102; Belay Seyoum, 'The Impact of Intellectual Property Rights on Foreign Direct Investment', [1996] *Columbia J of World Business* 31, 51–59; Robert M. Sherwood, 'Intellectual Property Systems and Investment Stimulation: The Rating of Systems in Eighteen Developing Countries', [1997] *IDEA* Vol 37 No 2, 261–370; JC Ginarte and WG Park, 'Determinants of Patent Rights: A Cross-national Study', [1997] *Research Policy* 26, 283–301.

6 David M Gould and William C Gruben, 'The Role of Intellectual Property Rights in Economic growth', [1996] *J of Development Econ* 48, 323–350.

7 Dana Wichterman, 'Intellectual Property Rights and Economic Development: An Issue Brief', (Washington: Agency for International Development, Center for Development Information and Evaluation, 1991).

8 Rapp and Rozek, note 5 above, 75–77; Richard Rapp and Richard P Rozek, 'Benefits and Costs of Intellectual Property Protection in Developing Countries', National Economic Research Associates, Inc Working Paper No 3 (1990); R Michael Gadbaw and Rosemary E Gwynn, 'Intellectual Property Rights in the New GATT Round', in R Michael Gadbaw and Timothy

Table 3.1 Rapp and Rozek's Patent Protection Scale

Score	Description
0	No intellectual property protection laws
1	Inadequate protection laws; no law prohibiting piracy
2	Seriously flawed laws
3	Flaws in laws, some enforcement laws
4	Generally good laws
5	Protection and enforcement laws consistent with minimum standards proposed by the US Chamber of Commerce

Source: Rapp and Rozek, 'Benefits and Costs of Intellectual Property Protection in Developing Countries', National Economic Research Associates, Inc Working Paper No 3 (1990), Appendix 4.

Seyoum also used the US Chamber of Commerces minimum standards for his criteria. However, his 0–3 scales for IPR protection components were constructed from surveys sent to IPR practitioners. After validating the responses against each other and against existing literature, Seyoum constructed four variables (patents, copyrights, trademarks and trade secrets) for use in his analysis.

Sherwood proposed a third measure of IPR protection that combined personal knowledge and experience with professional interviews. The protection scores theoretically range from 0–103 and were developed for 18 countries. Eight major components comprised Sherwood's measure summarized in Table 3.2.[9]

Table 3.2 Sherwoods Intellectual Property Rights Components

Description	Assigned Points
Enforceability	25
Administration	10
Substantive Law	
Copyright	12
Patents	17
Trademarks	9
Trade Secrets	15
Life Forms	6
Treaties	6
Total	100
Public Commitment	3
Total Possible Points Added	3

Source: Sherwood 'Intellectual Property Systems and Investment Stimulation: The Rating of Systems in Eighteen Developing Countries', [1997] *IDEA* Vol 37 No 2, 265.

J Richards (eds), *Intellectual Property Rights: Global Consensus, Global Conflict?* (Boulder, Col, Westview Press, 1988), 51–55.

9 Sherwood, 'IP Systems', note 5 above, 265.

The conditions for rating countries were derived from the US Chamber of Commerce Guidelines, but the relative weights were derived mostly from the author's experience.[10] Similarly, the points assigned to a country under any category were also based on the author's experience.[11] Interviews with local attorneys augmented the author's experience, particularly with the enforceability component.

Each major component contained sub-categories for which each country could lose points based on observed deficiencies in the total points allocated for that major component. For instance, the enforceability component (worth 25 points in the coding scheme) contains eight separate areas of interest to the author: judicial independence (up to 12 points), quality of judges (up to 10 points), lack of legal tools for enforcement (up to 10 points), judicial knowledge of IP concepts (up to 7 points), reliability of prosecutors, police, and customs officials (up to 6 points), civil and criminal sanctions (up to 6 points), delays in enforcement proceedings (up to 4 points), and the lack of transparency for final decisions (up to 2 points). Deficiencies in these components resulted in the subtraction of points ranging from a high of 12 for judicial independence to a low of up to 2 points for the final transparency issue. The amount to be subtracted was again based on interviews and the author's experience.

The sub-category point deductions were then subtracted from each component total score. All component scores were then added to obtain the aggregate IPR measure for each country. Finally, an impressionistic assessment of the public's commitment to IP accounted for up to three additional points, which were then added to the eight major components. This final step made the theoretical total points for each country 103. In practice the final scores ranged from a high of 83 for the Bahamas to a low of 13 for Guatemala.

Perhaps the most ambitious attempt to measure the strength of IPR protection has come from Ginarte and Park.[12] In their study of the economic characteristics that determine the strength of patent rights, they create an index of such rights for 110 countries over the period 1960–1990. In their index, five categories of patent law were coded: (1) extent of coverage, (2) membership in international organizations, (3) provisions for the loss of patent protection, (4) enforcement mechanisms, and (5) duration of protection. For each category, a set of conditions had to be met for a country to attain a perfect score. If the country did not attain a perfect score, it received a fractional score based upon the number of conditions within the category. For instance, if a country's patent laws satisfied

[10] Ibid, 265–267.
[11] Ibid, 267.
[12] Note 5 above.

only one of three conditions for international agreements, it received a score of 1/3 or 0.33 for the international agreements components. The resulting scores for all five categories were then summed to create an index of patent protection that ranges from 0–5.

B. Research Assessment

While each study makes important contributions in assessing the strength of IPR protection in countries, they raise several conceptual and methodological issues. The first conceptual issue is which IPR laws must be examined to gauge protection. Rapp and Rozek's measure assumes patent laws *ipso facto* represent all IPR laws. However, services increasingly are accounting for larger portions of economic growth. The value of a name or identification therefore has significant economic impact. Particularly in Western countries, the economic contributions of copyrighted software production, entertainment products, and publishing are significant. To discount trademark and copyright protection would be to underestimate their economic impact. Similarly, it has been argued elsewhere that states do not treat all IP rights equally.[13] In other words, some forms of IP are more important to countries' economies than others and using patents as a proxy for all IPR may overlook this issue. While Seyoum assesses the strength of these laws individually, Sherwood's measure blends five different forms of IPR law into a single score. The combining of various laws into one conceptual measure of IPR protection may present some theoretical and methodological difficulty.

A second conceptual issue relates to the enforcement of the laws. Neither Rapp and Rozek nor Seyoum include an enforcement component in their study, though Rapp and Rozek recognize the issue. [14] The logic behind this proposition is intuitively simple. States may have in place the institutional structures and financial resources to enforce these laws, but others that do not have these structures and resources may not be able to enforce the laws adequately. Sherwood too recognizes this issue by including an enforceability component in his measure, but it does not significantly address the behaviour of the governing regime in enforcing the IP laws. The enforcement component Sherwood uses reflects an assessment of the *potential* to enforce IPR laws and not an assessment of the regime's *actual* performance.

[13] Robert L. Ostergard, 'Intellectual Property Rights: A Universal Human Right?' [1999] *Human Rights Quarterly* 21(1), 156–178; Edwin C Hettinger, 'Justifying Intellectual Property', [1989] *Philosophy and Public Affairs* 18, 31–52.

[14] Ostergard, ibid, 170–178.

From a measurement perspective, all three researchers assign scores based on the laws in force at the time they coded their data. Changes and amendments to the laws that might have occurred during any specific time period are not taken into account. The temporal element becomes critical, particularly when using such measures to gauge the effect of IPR on foreign direct investment, technology levels, and industry and economic growth. The missing temporal element means that their measure will not capture the impact of changes to these laws.

Another measurement concern is the replicability of these measures. For instance, Rapp and Rozek do not adequately explain what constitutes the difference between a score of two and a score of three. What is the difference between 'inadequate' laws and 'seriously flawed' laws, or between 'generally good laws' and laws that are 'fully consistent' with the minimum standards? Without clearer criteria, an element of subjectivity is introduced, which casts doubt on the measurement's validity and reproducibility. In Seyoum's study, it is unclear how the raw data were reduced to a 0–3 scale. Similarly, because Sherwood's study is based preponderantly on the author's expertise, the ability to replicate the results without that vast experience is limited. Moreover, because the procedures use on-site interviews in the country measured, the practicality of duplicating these measures across time and across countries is limited as well.

A second concern with Sherwood's procedures is that, because they are largely based on his experience, they may be more subjective than is desirable. For instance, when judging how many points to subtract for judicial independence, no set rules exist for what constitutes such independence. What criteria are used to subtract five points rather than six points? We cannot be certain about distinctions, given that the assessment is grounded in personal perception. Moreover, there seems to be some incongruity between the total points assigned to the major components and the total points that can be subtracted in the sub-categories. For instance, the enforceability component itself is worth 25 points, but the sub-category points that can be subtracted total 57 points. Is it possible that countries could have a negative score for enforceability? In theory, it is a possible scenario.

The Ginarte and Park measure is perhaps the most extensive temporally and cross-sectionally. But, like the other studies, it too has conceptual and methodological drawbacks that should be taken into account. Methodologically, Ginarte and Park address the issue of weighing the categories within their index. Whereas each category represents 1/5 or 20 per cent of the potential five points that a country could attain, Ginarte and Park recognize that each category is weighted equally in the index construction. All categories, in this sense, are weighted equally.

However, the construction of each individual category creates an unintended weighting system within the categories.

An example of this can be illustrated with two of the categories—coverage and membership in the international agreements. The coverage variable contains seven components: patentability of pharmaceuticals, chemicals, food, plant and animal varieties, surgical products, micro-organisms, and utility models. The membership in international treaties includes membership in three treaties: the Paris Convention for the Protection of Industrial Property of 1883 and its revisions until 1967, the Patent Cooperation Treaty, and the International Convention for the Protection of New Varieties of Plants (known as 'UPOV' based on the acronym of the French version of the agreement). If we assume, hypothetically, a country only protects micro-organisms and is only a member of the Paris Convention, that means they have a score of 1 out of 7 (1/7) for coverage and 1 out of 3 (1/3) for international treaty membership. Conceptually, this means that membership in international treaty bodies, which only illustrates a willingness to extend patent coverage to foreign patent holders, is weighted more than the coverage of a particular patentable category. From a practical perspective, Ginarte and Park present no argument as to why one should be weighted more than the other. Moreover, it would seem that, in practice, the extent of coverage for particular types of patents would be more important than whether a country has signed up to an unenforceable treaty.

Additionally, they underestimate the importance of the practical enforcement of laws *versus* the statutory provisions for enforcement. To their credit, they recognize this, but then dismiss it with a bit of false logic: '[t]he concern should mostly be with the measured indexes of the OECD countries rather than those of the less-developed, since the main concern about the latter is the absence of laws. Hence, if there is any overestimation of patent rights and protection, it should be with the OECD's measures.'[15] The underlying logic here is that developing countries do not have either the capacity or the need to pass strong patent laws. In practice, this logic is quite contrary because it is easy to pass laws. Ginarte and Park's index can be used to illustrate this point. If we examine their scores for three developed countries and three developing countries, this point becomes quite clear in Table 3.3.

Based on Ginarte and Park's scores, South Africa has had better patent laws than Finland and Norway and lags behind Germany only marginally. Sri Lanka's patent laws have been on par with Norway's and better than Finland's in most years.

[15] Ginarte and Park, note 5 above, 289.

Table 3.3 Ginarte and Park's Patent Scores for Six Countries, 1960–1985

Country	1960	1965	1970	1975	1980	1985	1990
Finland	1.99	1.99	2.14	2.14	2.95	2.95	2.95
Norway	2.66	2.66	2.80	2.80	3.29	3.29	3.29
Germany	2.33	2.66	3.09	3.09	3.86	3.71	3.71
South Africa	3.04	3.37	3.37	3.37	3.57	3.57	3.57
Nigeria	2.71	3.05	3.05	3.05	3.05	3.05	3.05
Sri Lanka	2.60	2.60	2.60	2.60	2.769	3.12	3.12

Source: Ginarte and Park, 'Determinants of Patent Rights: A Cross-national Study', [1997] Research Policy 26, 285–6.

Likewise, Nigeria's patent laws have been comparable to Norway's and better than Finland's laws. Despite these similarities, it has been the developing countries that have experienced the bulk of problems in international trade relations over the issue of IPR protection.[16] As mentioned previously, the major variation between developed and developing countries' patent laws has not necessarily been between the existence of the laws (though in a number of cases this is a problem), but in the strength of the enforcement. While there are differences between the two groups of countries in terms of the strength of the laws, it can also be the case that somewhat weaker laws that are enforced (i.e. Finland and Norway) can be more effective than stronger laws that are weakly enforced (i.e. Nigeria and South Africa). Ginarte and Park dismiss this complex variation as simply a manifestation of developing countries.

Part II The Concept of Intellectual Property Rights Protection

The measurement of IPR must incorporate both a statute component and an enforcement component. Roughly categorized, countries can range from having no laws to having the strongest laws, and their practices can range from having no enforcement of the laws to having strong enforcement of the laws. As Sherwood also notes, a nation can have strong laws or weak laws, but unless those laws are enforced, they are virtually non-existent in terms of the protection afforded IP owners and investors.[17]

16 See for instance Robert L. Ostergard, 'The Political Economy of the South African–US Patent Conflict', [1999] *J of World IP*, Vol 2. No 6, 875–888, for an examination of the dispute.

17 See note 5 above.

A. Law Measurement

To measure the strength of IPR laws, two issues must be addressed: what IPR laws are to be measured and by what standards? I have settled for using just patents, copyrights and trademarks because the bulk of IP is protected under these laws and the information on cross-national patent, copyright, and trademark laws is more readily available than for other types of IP law.[18] Following the practice of the other studies, this study is based on the minimum criteria for IPR laws established by the US Chamber of Commerce. Using these criteria, separate code sheets were created for patent, copyright and trademark laws to conduct a content analysis of countries' IP laws.[19] A number of legal sources were used to complete code sheets for each country in this study. All sources used pertained to IP statutes only, without reference to past judicial review, trial histories or customs. The laws for 76 countries were coded twice with different coders utilizing the same code sheets.[20] A comparison of the two codings showed inter-coder agreement to be high: all inter-coder agreement scores were .90 or higher (i.e. 90 per cent or higher agreement between coders on all items coded) which indicates that these code sheets were constructed in such a way that coding replication could reasonably be achieved. The laws for each nation were coded for three time intervals, 1988, 1991 and 1994. Intervals of three years were used because the laws were not expected to change much on an annual basis. The time period was chosen because of the temporal limits of the enforcement component.

B. Enforcement Measurement

The enforcement score of the IPR protection measure was obtained through content analysis as well. Under the 1988 Omnibus Trade and Competitiveness Act, the US Department of State was mandated to track the status of the IP laws and enforcement practices of the United States' trading partners. These assessments appear in the US State Department's book, *Country Reports on Economic and Trade Practices*. These reports are produced semi-annually and

---

[18] Robert P Benko, *Protecting Intellectual Property: Issues and Controversies* (American Enterprise Institute for Public Policy Research, 1987).

[19] While not perfect, content analysis provides set criteria for coding elements, making the coding less subjective. Of course, it does not eliminate subjectivity in deciding what to code. For a classic statement on content analysis, see Klaus Krippendorff, *Content Analysis: An Introduction to Its Methodology* (Sage Publications, 1980).

[20] The countries were determined by the countries listed in the initial editions of the State Department's *Country Reports on Economic and Trade Practices*. The other coders were research assistants independent of the author.

began in 1989.[21] Hence, the data set is temporally limited to the post-1988 period. The early reports do not distinguish between the different types of IPR laws as the later reports do. The enforcement code sheet, which contains only one variable, was constructed to gauge a general assessment of the enforcement of IPR laws in the country. Coding of enforcement practices was done for 1988, 1991 and 1994 (although the reports began in early 1989, it was assumed information gathered was for 1988 and reported in 1989). Two separate coders coded the laws for each country, using the same code sheet. Again, all inter-coder reliability scores were over .90.

Scale scores of the IPR laws were obtained using Guttman scaling procedures.[22] Any polychotomous items were converted to dichotomous variables. A gamma matrix, measuring the strength of association among all variables, revealed that not all the variables clustered together (with a gamma score of .80 or higher) to form one scale of IPR laws. In fact, the clustering that did occur was within each individual type of law. This finding has *theoretical significance* in that it confirms the idea that states *do* treat these laws differently and that there is no unidimensional concept of IPR law. Each type of law *must* be treated distinctly from others. This procedure produced three scales: patents (0–5), copyrights (0–10) and trademarks (0–8). In these scales, 0 represents no laws while the other ends of the scales represent the strongest laws. Tests of reproducibility and scalability were conducted on the scales. Coefficients of reproducibility were above .90 and all coefficients of scalability were above .60, the minimum acceptable levels for Guttman scaling.

Reliability and stability coefficients for the IPR protection scores were calculated across the three panel waves.[23] The coefficients show that the measures are reliable across the three-wave panel design, with all reliability coefficients at .98 and higher. However, the stability of these measures varies. The stability of the copyright variable is high across all time periods (.879, .950, .830). Patents are stable over the first two waves (.993), but the stability decreases over the second and third waves (.769) and from the first to the third waves (.764). Trademarks reflect

[21] The US Congress terminated the production of these reports in 2002; however the coverage of the IPR issue has been maintained by the United States Trade Representative through its Section 301 reports, which highlight the countries seen as most problematic for the United States with respect to the protection of IPR.

[22] David Garson, *Handbook of Political Science Methods* (2nd Edn, Holbrooke Press, 1976); Duncan MacRae Jr, *Issues and Parties in Legislative Voting: Methods and Statistical Analysis* (Harper and Row, 1970); John P McKiver and Edward G Carmines, *Unidimensional Scaling* (Sage Publications, 1981).

[23] David R. Heise, 'Separating Reliability and Stability in Test–Retest Correlation', in HM Blalock, Jr (ed), *Causal Models in the Social Sciences* (Chicago, Aldine Atherton, 1971).

the greatest decline in stability over the three waves. While highly stable over the first and second waves (.984), the stability coefficients show a large decline over the second and third waves (.595) and from the first to the third waves (.588). This finding indicates that trademarks have undergone the most change over the six-year period.

To obtain complete IPR protection scores for each nation and each type of law, the scale score for each nation and law was multiplied by the enforcement score for each nation, which ranged from zero to four. Zero represents no enforcement of IPR laws while four represents the strongest enforcement. The multiplication of these two measures signifies that the law *and* the enforcement component are both *necessary conditions*. Because enforcement information could not be obtained for each type of law for each year, it is assumed that the enforcement practices apply to all the laws.

The multiplication of the enforcement and law components is not problem-free. First, it creates great variation in the data from country to country. For instance, the multiplication of a country's patent score of 3 by its enforcement score of 3 creates a score of 9. The same procedure for a country with a patent score of 3 and an enforcement score of 1 creates a score of 3. Is the relationship between the enforcement and the law component multiplicative or additive? And, by inference, what weights should be given to the enforcement component? Two ways of dealing with both questions exist; the first is grounded in the assumptions of the research question, the second is methodological.

In multiplying the two scores together, the underlying assumption is that the laws and their enforcement are *necessary* conditions for IP *protection*. Laws must be enforced in order to provide substantive protection. Researchers, however, may be inclined to believe that the enforcement is not a necessary and separate policy issue from the enactment of the laws, but rather that enforcement is simply another component of protection and is weighted no differently to the laws. The researcher may even find that the laws themselves have a deterrent effect and that the correct approach is to consider the scores to be additive. However, the issue is one of formulating the research assumptions. The benefit of these data is that both assumptions can be accommodated. Because the laws and the enforcement components are separate entities, the researcher is free to make the assumptions deemed appropriate. Should the researcher assume a multiplicative relationship, then some additional work is needed to address the question of how to weigh the enforcement component in the multiplicative relationship.

By taking the log of each of the variables, the data distances are reduced and the researcher can utilize the data in linear-log or log-log models. Moreover, the weights for each of the components are adjusted automatically by virtue of the log function.[24] Both model types are quite common in business, economics and political science studies where data are often characterized by wide variations cross-sectionally or temporally.

Part III The Debate: Intellectual Property Rights and Economic Growth

One study has empirically tested the relationship between IPR and economic growth. Gould and Gruben found that stronger IPR protection corresponds to higher economic growth rates across countries though the effects may be tempered in less competitive, closed markets.[25] Their findings lend support to the developed countries' claims of significant economic benefits to be derived from increasing patent protection.

Gould and Gruben begin with a benchmark model for comparative purposes. The purpose of this model is to gauge the effects of IPR on economic growth once major economic factors are considered. Their dependent variable is the log of the average annual per capita gross domestic product (GDP) between 1960 and 1988.[26] The independent variables include the log of GDP in 1960, the log of gross domestic investment as a share of GDP, and literacy rates in 1960, which measures the stock of human capital. In an addition to the model, the log of government consumption is added, plus dummy variables for assassinations, revolutions and coups, and for geographic location in Latin America and Africa. Assassinations, revolutions and coups are used as proxy variables for political stability; no theoretical justification is given for the geographic indicator variables. Gould and Gruben then add the IPR variable, which is Rapp and Rozek's patent protection measure, to the model.

---

24 The proof of this follows from logarithmic transformations. In using the IPR protection variables in a linear regression, the equation is $Y = \mu + b_1(\text{laws} \cdot \text{enforcement})$. By logarithmic transformation, the equation becomes $\text{Log}_e Y = \mu + b_1 \text{Log}_e(\text{Laws}) + b_2 \text{Log}_e(\text{Enforcement})$; when this equation is restated with respect to Y, the retransformed version of the log equation is $Y = e^{\mu} (\text{Laws}^{b1}\text{Enforcement}^{b2})$.

25 Note 6 above, 345

26 Gould and Gruben use a log function in their analysis for two reasons. First, the function has a base in standard economic production function literature. Second, the log function will minimize the mean squared error (ibid, 330).

Using OLS regression, they find *no significant relationship* between IPR and economic growth.[27] They then proceed to apply an instrumental variable approach to the analysis, which assumes that the IPR variable is a proxy for other variables. This procedure is tantamount to two-stage least squares analysis. Based on their assumption, instrumental variables were used to predict the IPR scores. The predicted scores were then used in the model. The results showed that IPR have a marginally significant ($p<.10$) effect on economic growth. This finding is supported in qualitative research prior to Gould and Gruben.

Qualitatively, the work of Joseph Schumpeter is cited in support of IPR protection. Schumpeter's work focused on the idea that innovation and technology are the driving forces in industrial development. Hence, the protection of IPR becomes even more crucial if one falls into the Schumpeterian school of thought. Those supporting IPR argue that strong protection provides several benefits:[28]

- increased domestic research and development;
- increased flow of new products;
- enhanced value of patent rights;
- increased inward investment and technology transfer; and
- improvements in the local knowledge base.

What makes these five points noteworthy is that they are most often characteristic of advanced, industrialized countries that do not face the specific issues that developing countries confront. Most developing countries do not have the capacity for domestic research and development, giving developed countries a decided advantage in the production of new products and processes.

The third point, the enhanced value of patent rights, is least important to developing countries and one of the most important to developed countries. In industrially developed countries, a patent (and other IPR forms such as copyrights and trademarks) is a source of monetary value for ideas and is a guarantee that others cannot legally copy the idea. It is also the basis for the incentives argument that proponents of strong IPR make. Incentives are needed to induce people to produce particular objects beneficial to society. Again, this point is well taken, but it has more application to developed countries than to developing countries that may be trying to acquire existing technologies and processes to help in their development processes.

---

[27] OLS (ordinary least squares) is an optimization technique which attempts to find a function that approximates the data when given a series of measured data.

[28] Alan S Gutterman, 'The North–South Debate Regarding the Protection of Intellectual Property Rights', [1993] *Wake Forest LR* 28, 89–139.

What are most important to developing countries are investment, technology transfer and local knowledge building. With these issues comes a complex myriad of social and economic problems associated with them. While investment and technology transfers are seen as goals to strive for, they can act as a double-edged sword in that they also increase expectations and change attitudes in developing countries. Of the potential problems, the influence of developed country social and economic standards on developing country salary scales, elite lifestyles, and wealth accumulation provide a basis for caution in seeking investment and technology transfer.[29] Moreover, when such investment and technology transfer does occur, there is no basis for believing that local knowledge may be increased. In fact, transnational corporations may be reluctant to allow certain types of technology to be adopted for fear of losing their competitive advantage in these markets. Hence, often the promise of increasing local knowledge bases is hollow. Given these associated issues, there is reason to exercise caution in accepting the prima facie arguments of improved economic benefits for developing countries if they adopt strong IPR.

Part IV The Economic Model

To gauge the effect that IPR protection has on economic growth, a benchmark or base model of economic growth must be established. Following Gould and Gruben I established a base model with four variables that provide measures of consumption, investment, and labour capacity. These variables include government consumption, investment as a percentage of GDP, population, and the physical quality of life index (PQLI). Population is used to control for the size of the country while the PQLI is used as a measure of human capital. In addition to these variables, GDP_{t-1} is used to account for the assumptions made by the partial adjustment model used in the estimation.

A. The Partial Adjustment Model

The partial adjustment model assumes that countries have a target or a preferred level of GDP in a given year (t). It also accounts for the idea that countries may be able to attain only a fraction ($1-\alpha$; where $0<\alpha<1$) of what they want toward their target on average each year. GDP is a function of the previous

[29] Michael P Todaro, *Economic Development* (5th Edn, Longman, 1994).

period's level of GDP plus an adjustment toward their target, which can be represented by the following equation:

$$\text{Log}\,(\text{GDP}_t) = (1-\alpha)\,\text{Log}\,(\text{GDP}_{t-1}) + \alpha(\text{Log}\,(\text{GDP}_t))$$

The coefficient $1-\alpha$ is an adjustment coefficient since it indicates the rate of adjustment of GDP_{t-1} to GDP_t. After one period, $1-\alpha$ of the gap between GDP_{t-1} and GDP_t is closed so that α of the gap remains. After N periods, the gap closed will be $1-a^N$ (Kmenta 1986: 530).[30] Thus, it can be written that $1-a^N=p$ and the number of periods to close the gap can be written as

$$N = \frac{\log(1\text{-}p)}{\log(p)}$$

By including GDP lagged in the equation, we can estimate both the short-term and the long-term effects of IPR protection on GDP across countries. With this, the base model can be written as

$\text{GDP}_t = f\,(\text{GDP}_{t-1}$, Government Consumption, Investment/GDP, Population, PQLI)

This model is used to analyse data for two periods, 1995 and 1991. Data for IPR protection could not be obtained prior to 1988. The first two models are for GDP 1995 regressed on variables at times t–1 and t–2 while the third model represents GDP 1992 regressed on variables at time t–1.

The variables used in the model represent standard economic factors used in the analysis of economic growth. Gould and Gruben chose government consumption as a proxy for government spending in the economy. As the government demands more goods and services in the economy through expenditures, the output of the economy can be expected to increase. Investment in GDP serves as a proxy for the amount of physical capital savings in the economy or how much capital is present in the economy. Gould and Gruben use literacy rates to approximate human capital; however I have substituted for this the PQLI, which includes literacy rates and other factors affecting human capacity or potential.[31] All these variables are expected to have a positive effect on GDP, both in the short term and the long term.

30 Jan Kmenta, *Elements of Econometrics* (Macmillan, 1986).

31 Morris Morris, *Measuring the Condition of the World's Poor: The Physical Quality of Life Index* (Pergamon Press, 1979).

B. Base Model Results

The results of the base model are presented in Tables 3.4 to 3.6. They show that population, PQLI and GDP in the preceding periods are generally significant, though PQLI drops out of significance in the third equation. Surprisingly, consumption and investment, standards in econometric models of GDP, are insignificant. This finding may be the result of the short time period used in these analyses. GDP is typically analysed using time-series data. However, these models are limited temporally due to the lack of available data. The interpretation of the coefficients in the partial adjustment model does not differ from that of ordinary least squares regression (OLS) except for the inclusion of the long-term parameter estimates. In the long term, each coefficient is divided by the adjustment coefficient (1–a) where a represents the coefficient of the lag GDP variable.

With the base model established, the variables of particular interest, the IPR protection variables, may be added to gauge their effect. These results are presented

Table 3.4 Model Results Dependent Variable GDP 1995

Variable	Short-Term Estimate		Long-Term Estimate
	Coefficient	t-stat	Coefficient
Intercept	–0.42	–1.22	–4.99
Ln(GDP 89)	0.91	***33.31	10.75
Ln (Cons 88)	0.12	1.45	1.39
Ln (Inv/GDP 88)	0.03	0.40	0.35
Ln (Pop 88)	0.16	***3.69	1.35
PQLI 1988	0.004	**2.83	0.058

Adj R^2 =0.99; n=72 * $p<0.05$; ** $p<0.01$; *** $p<0.001$

Table 3.5 Model Results, Dependent Variable GDP 1995

Variable	Short-Term Estimate		Long-Term Estimate
	Coefficient	t-stat	Coefficient
Intercept	–0.16	–0.95	–3.19
Ln(GDP 92)	0.95	***59.94	18.71
Ln (Cons 91)	0.037	0.70	0.73
Ln (Inv/GDP91)	0.034	0.67	0.67
Ln (Pop 91)	0.063	***3.74	1.24
PQLI 1988	0.003	***3.36	0.06

Adj R^2 =0.99; n=72 * $p<0.05$; ** $p<0.01$; *** $p<0.001$

Table 3.6 Model Results, Dependent Variable GDP 1992

Variable	Short-Term Estimate		Long-Term Estimate
	Coefficient	t-stat	Coefficient
Intercept	–0.28	–1.121	–6.59
Ln(GDP 89)	0.95	***47.22	21.99
Ln (Cons 88)	0.09	1.50	2.08
Ln(Inv/GDP 88)	0.009	0.17	0.21
Ln (Pop 88)	0.06	**2.62	1.39
PQLI 1988	0.002	1.60	0.04

Adj R^2 =0.99; n=72 * p<0.05; ** p<0.01; *** p<0.001

in Tables 3.7 to 3.9. The results including the IPR protection variables are inconsistent. While the base model variables remain consistent, with population, PQLI, and GDP being significant, the significance of the IPR variables is inconsistent. However, the slope values and directions are consistent over the three periods. Most surprising are the negative slopes on the patent and trademark variables. In substantive terms, for GDP 1995, a one-point increase in patent protection in 1988 would lead to a 0.013 per cent decrease in GDP in the short term and a 0.17 per cent decrease in the long run. A one-point increase in trademark protection would lead to a 0.011 per cent decrease in GDP in the short term and a 0.141 per cent decrease in the long term. Copyright protection has a positive slope and in the short term, for each point increase in copyright protection, a 0.009 per cent increase in GDP would result. In the long term, that point increase would yield a 0.12 per cent increase in GDP. These results are inconsistent for the second 1995 analysis, but consistent with the 1992 analysis. One possible reason for this discrepancy may be the severe economic recession in the Western economies, which may be reflected in the 1991–1992 data.

Table 3.7 IPR Model Results, Dependent Variable GDP 1995

Variable	Short-Term Estimate		Long-Term Estimate
	Coefficient	t-stat	Coefficient
Intercept	–0.67	*–1.90	–8.77
Ln(GDP 89)	0.92	***34.62	11.99
Ln(Cons 88)	0.16	*1.96	2.13
Ln(Inv/GDP 88)	0.02	0.31	0.30
Ln(Pop 88)	0.11	***3.75	1.45
PQLI 1988	0.006	**3.47	0.07
Patent 88	–0.01	–1.48	–0.17
Copyright 88	0.009	**2.67	0.12
Trademark 88	–0.01	**–2.44	–0.14

Adj R^2 =0.99; n=72 * p<0.05; ** p<0.01; *** p<0.001

Table 3.8 IPR Model Results, Dependent Variable GDP 1995

Variable	Short-Term Estimate		Long-Term Estimate
	Coefficient	t-stat	Coefficient
Intercept	–0.31	–1.54	–7.77
Ln(GDP 92)	0.96	***49.89	24.03
Ln(Cons 91)	0.07	1.32	1.86
Ln(Inv/GDP 91)	0.01	0.18	0.25
Ln(Pop 91)	0.05	***3.06	1.39
PQLI 1991	0.003	**3.36	0.08
Patent 91	–0.008	–1.61	–0.18
Copyright 91	0.003	1.16	0.07
Trademark 91	–0.008	–0.70	–0.06

Adj R^2 =0.99; n=72 * p<0.05; ** p<0.01; *** p<0.001

Table 3.9 IPR Model Results, Dependent Variable GDP 1992

Variable	Short-Term Estimate		Long-Term Estimate
	Coefficient	t-stat	Coefficient
Intercept	–0.38	–1.47	–10.17
Ln(GDP 89)	0.96	**49.30	25.54
Ln (Cons 88)	0.10	*1.69	2.75
Ln (Inv/GDP 88)	0.008	0.14	0.21
Ln (Pop 88)	0.05	***2.60	1.51
PQLI 88	0.003	*2.07	0.06
Patents 88	–0.004	–0.592	–0.10
Copyright 88	0.006	**2.522	0.17
Trademark 88	–0.01	***3.16	–0.27

Adj R^2 =0.99; n=72 * p<0.05; ** p<0.01; *** p<0.001

The results show significant features regarding IPR protection. First, when compared to other economic factors, the effects that IPR have cross-nationally are relatively small, with IPR protection contributing marginally to GDP. Second, should a nation adopt a policy of full, strong protection across the three types of IPR, the net impact is estimated to be negligible or negative, given the direction of the patent and trademark coefficients. While these results apply to all countries in the dataset, the question that still needs to be addressed is: do these results vary for developed and developing countries? As noted earlier, one primary assumption being made in this research is that developed and developing countries have different objectives, which mean they will emphasize policies differently. As discussed previously, the benefits of strong IPR protection may be different for developed countries than they are for developing countries. Thus, it would be beneficial to look at these groups of countries separately.

C. Developed and Developing Countries

To compare the impact that IPR protection has on economic growth, I follow the same procedure established in the previous sub-section of this chapter. The data set is split on the mean PQLI score in 1988. Countries above the mean are scored one and those below the mean are scored zero. The partial adjustment model equation was then run for each sub-group. The base model results are presented in Tables 3.10 to 3.12.

The results for the developed countries are consistent, though the population and PQLI variables drop in significance. This finding is not surprising given that there is much less variance in these variables as a result of sub-setting the data. The results from the second equation in Table 3.11 appear to be unusual. A clear indication of this is the lagged GDP variable. The coefficient is .998, which indicates the close correspondence between GDP 1995 and GDP 1992. Compare this

Table 3.10 Model Results, Dependent Variable GDP 1995, Developed Countries

Variable	Short-Term Estimate		Long-Term Estimate
	Coefficient	t-stat	Coefficient
Intercept	–0.74	0.95	–11.71
Ln(GDP 89)	0.93	***18.50	14.68
Ln (Cons 88)	0.26	1.57	4.139
Ln (Inv/GDP88)	–0.003	0.02	–0.05
Ln (Pop 88)	0.09	1.41	1.49
PQLI 1988	0.002	0.31	0.04

Adj R^2 =0.99; n=33 * $p<0.05$; ** $p<0.01$; *** $p<0.001$

Table 3.11 Base Model Results, Dependent Variable GDP 1995, Developed Countries

Variable	Short-Term Estimate		Long-Term Estimate
	Coefficient	t-stat	Coefficient
Intercept	0.19	0.45	170.34
Ln(GDP 92)	0.99	***37.57	893.45
Ln (Cons 91)	–0.03	–0.38	–27.67
Ln (Inv/GDP91)	0.07	1.05	71.54
Ln (Pop 91)	0.005	0.19	5.35
PQLI 1988	–0.003	–0.58	–3.00

Adj R^2 =0.99; n=33 * $p<0.05$; ** $p<0.01$; *** $p<0.001$

Table 3.12 Model Results, Dependent Variable GDP 1992, Developed Countries

Variable	Short-Term Estimate		Long-Term Estimate
	Coefficient	t-stat	Coefficient
Intercept	–1.06	–1.74	–17.27
Ln(GDP 89)	0.93	***23.81	15.24
Ln (Cons 88)	0.27	*2.08	4.40
Ln (Inv/GDP88)	–0.05	–0.48	–0.87
Ln (Pop 88)	0.08	*1.68	1.43
PQLI 1988	0.006	1.07	0.11

Adj R^2 =0.99; n=33 * p<0.05; ** p<0.01; *** p<0.001

with the GDP 1992 and GDP 1988 coefficient, which is .93. This coefficient shows less of a correspondence with GDP 1992 than GDP 1992 has with GDP 1995. Hence, the recession in developed economies during the early 1990s is illustrated clearly, with little growth in the 1992–1995 period. The interpretation of the coefficients is the same as in the previous section in both the short term and the long term. The one surprise in these results is the negative coefficient on the investment and consumption variables. These run counter to expectations, but may be a function of the cross-national design of the test. The next step is to add the IPR protection variables. The results for these are presented in Tables 3.13 to 3.15. The directions of the copyright and trademark coefficients are consistent across the three tests. However, only the trademark coefficient in the last equation is significant. Consistent with the results from the full dataset, the IPR variables appear to have a negligible effect on GDP.

Table 3.13 IPR Model Results, Dependent Variable GDP 1995, Developed Countries

Variable	Short-Term Estimate		Long-Term Estimate
	Coefficient	t-stat	Coefficient
Intercept	–1.01	–1.37	–16.73
Ln(GDP 89)	0.93	19.56	15.40
Ln (Cons 88)	0.30	*1.94	5.01
Ln (Inv/GDP88)	–0.02	–0.18	–0.39
Ln (Pop 88)	0.11	*1.83	1.88
PQLI 1988	0.002	0.33	0.04
Patents 88	0.003	–0.35	0.06
Copyright 88	0.004	1.08	0.08
Trademark 88	–0.01	**–2.56	–0.23

Adj R^2 =0.99; n=33 * p<0.05; ** p<0.01; *** p<0.001

Table 3.14 IPR Model Results, Dependent Variable GDP 1995, Developed Countries

Variable	Short-Term Estimate		Long-Term Estimate
	Coefficient	t-stat	Coefficient
Intercept	–0.02	–0.06	–27.37
Ln(GDP 92)	00.99	***29.12	989.09
Ln (Cons 91)	0.01	0.14	13.08
Ln (Inv/GDP91)	0.06	0.78	63.02
Ln (Pop 91)	0.01	0.29	10.54
PQLI 1991	–0.002	–0.39	–2.33
Patents 91	–0.005	–0.81	–5.05
Copyright 91	0.004	1.26	4.07
Trademark 91	–0.004	–0.97	–4.62

Adj R^2 =0.99; n=33 ** p<0.001

Table 3.15 IPR Model Results, Dependent Variable GDP 1992, Developed Countries

Variable	Short-Term Estimate		Long-Term Estimate
	Coefficient	t-stat	Coefficient
Intercept	–1.14	*–2.07	–21.07
Ln(GDP 89)	0.94	***26.73	17.49
Ln (Cons 88)	0.28	**2.42	5.18
Ln (Inv/GDP88)	–0.06	–0.65	–1.14
Ln (Pop 88)	0.09	*2.12	1.80
PQLI 1988	0.005	1.01	0.10
Patents 88	0.003	0.43	0.06
Copyright 88	0.002	0.62	0.03
Trademark 88	–0.01	***–3.24	–0.24

Adj R^2 =0.99; n=33 * p<0.05; ** p<0.01; *** p<0.001

The same procedures are followed for those below the mean 1988 PQLI. The results (Tables 3.16 to 3.18) show a closer resemblance to the full dataset's results than did the results for the developed countries. PQLI and the population variables remain significant in the first two models, though they drop out of significance in the third.

Again, we add the IPR variables to the model. These results are presented in Tables 3.19 to 3.21. The results again show no consistent pattern illustrating significant effects of IPR protection on economic growth. What little consistency there is comes from the patent protection variable. The negative direction of this

Table 3.16 Base Model Results, Dependent Variable GDP 1995, Developing Countries

Variable	Short-Term Estimate		Long-Term Estimate
	Coefficient	t-stat	Coefficient
Intercept	–0.58	–1.00	–9.080
Ln(GDP 89)	0.93	***20.52	14.61
Ln (Cons 88)	0.06	0.73	1.05
Ln (Inv/GDP88)	0.02	0.23	0.34
Ln (Pop 88)	0.09	*2.28	1.48
PQLI 1988	0.006	***3.20	0.10

Adj R^2 =0.99; n=38 * p<0.05; ** p<0.01; *** p<0.001

Table 3.17 Base Model Results, Dependent Variable GDP 1995, Developing Countries

Variable	Short-Term Estimate		Long-Term Estimate
	Coefficient	t-stat	Coefficient
Intercept	–0.26	–0.91	–4.10
Ln(GDP 92)	0.93	***29.29	14.30
Ln (Cons 91)	0.05	0.74	0.85
Ln (Inv/GDP91)	0.04	0.57	0.68
Ln (Pop 91)	0.07	**2.79	1.19
PQLI 1988	0.005	***4.04	0.08

Adj R^2 =0.99; n=38 * p<0.05; ** p<0.01; *** p<0.001

Table 3.18 Base Model Results, Dependent Variable GDP 1992, Developing Countries

Variable	Short-Term Estimate		Long-Term Estimate
	Coefficient	t-stat	Coefficient
Intercept	–0.13	–0.36	–3.89
Ln(GDP 89)	0.96	***29.57	27.58
Ln (Cons 88)	0.02	0.44	0.83
Ln (Inv/GDP88)	0.01	0.20	0.38
Ln (Pop 88)	0.04	1.60	1.35
PQLI 1988	0.002	1.61	0.07

Adj R^2 =0.99; n=38 * p<0.05; ** p<0.01; *** p<0.001

Table 3.19 IPR Model Results, Dependent Variable GDP 1995, Developing Countries

Variable	Short-Term Estimate		Long-Term Estimate
	Coefficient	t-stat	Coefficient
Intercept	–0.76	–1.36	–11.07
Ln(GDP 89)	0.93	***18.61	13.55
Ln (Cons 88)	0.09	0.82	1.35
Ln (Inv/GDP88)	0.07	0.73	1.12
Ln (Pop 88)	0.10	**2.21	1.45
PQLI 1988	0.007	***3.07	0.10
Patents 88	–0.007	–0.62	–0.10
Copyright 88	0.007	1.11	0.11
Trademark 88	–0.001	–0.16	–0.02

Adj R^2 =0.99; n=33 * $p<0.05$; ** $p<0.01$; *** $p<0.001$

Table 3.20 IPR Model Results, Dependent Variable GDP 1995, Developing Countries

Variable	Short-Term Estimate		Long-Term Estimate
	Coefficient	t-stat	Coefficient
Intercept	–0.60	*–1.73	–14.15
Ln(GDP 92)	0.95	***26.15	22.52
Ln (Cons 91)	0.12	1.57	2.93
Ln (Inv/GDP91)	–0.04	–0.53	–1.07
Ln (Pop 91)	0.07	**2.51	1.68
PQLI 1991	0.005	***3.72	0.12
Patents 91	–0.15	*–1.89	–3.71
Copyright 91	–0.007	–1.29	–0.17
Trademark 91	0.01	*1.82	0.34

Adj R^2 =0.99; n=33 * $p<0.05$; ** $p<0.01$; *** $p<0.001$

Table 3.21 IPR Model Results, Dependent Variable GDP 1992, Developing Countries

Variable	Short-Term Estimation		Long-Term Estimation
	Coefficient	t-stat	Coefficient
Intercept	–0.33	–0.85	–9.32
Ln(GDP 89)	0.96	**27.56	26.94
Ln (Cons 88)	0.04	0.58	1.27
Ln (Inv/GDP88)	0.06	0.91	1.88
Ln (Pop 88)	0.04	1.52	1.34
PQLI 1988	0.002	1.57	0.07
Patents 88	–0.007	–0.58	–0.21
Copyright 88	0.008	*1.81	0.24
Trademark 88	–0.006	–0.96	–0.17

Adj R^2 =0.99; n=33 * $p<0.05$; ** $p<0.01$; *** $p<0.001$

variable holds across all three models, but its significance does not. The patent variable is significant only in the second 1995 GDP model.

D. Discussion

Earlier studies have suggested that IPR have a positive effect in a number of ways in promoting economic growth, and that these benefits are universal in nature. The underlying assumption of this research is that all countries behave similarly and have similar goals that would motivate them to adopt a strong IPR regime. This assumption, however, is misleading. Past empirical work on this topic found only marginal benefits to be gained from strong IPR protection in developing countries.

Using a different measure of IPR protection, no consistent evidence emerged to show that IPR contributed significantly to economic growth cross-nationally. Furthermore, when the countries are split into developed and developing countries, results to suggest otherwise did not emerge. More important are the negative coefficients attached to many of the IPR variables. The negative coefficient implies that states may see negligible effects and quite possibly negative effects from adopting strong IPR protection, though the significance of these effects is low.

One possible reason for the weak findings in this chapter is that the temporal range of the study is limited. A time-series dataset might have produced stronger results. It may be possible that IPR protection takes a long time to work through the economic system of a country, limiting our ability to show any short-term impact. Also, time-series analyses of individual countries over a longer period would provide better comparisons amongst different types of countries in terms of how IPR protection affects developed and developing countries. Further research on the measurement of IPR protection needs to be conducted as well. With the TRIPS Agreement establishing near-universal standards for IPR protection, measures that use these standards should be pursued.

Despite the drawbacks with the analysis, the findings give researchers and policy makers some evidence to justify caution regarding the assumed relationship between IPR and economic growth. In fact, the analyses raise additional research questions to be explored, particularly regarding the role of IPR in promoting economic growth in developing countries. For instance, the coefficient for patent protection in developing countries is consistently negative and larger than the same coefficient for developed countries. This finding suggests that the impact of patent protection varies according to the level of a country's development. The two obvious questions that emerge, then, are: what motivates a developing country to adopt strong IPR protection, particularly if it might be harmful; and how does a country incorporate TRIPS-consistent IP protection without endangering its economic development (and ideally promoting such development)?

Part V The Determinants of Intellectual Property Rights Protection

Economists and legal scholars have argued that nations should adopt strong IPR policies as a matter of promoting economic growth. But the governments of some states at a lower level of economic development might perceive the benefits of a weak IPR regime as being greater than the benefits derived from a enacting a strong regime. A weak IPR regime allows states to acquire inexpensive technology by not paying royalties and licensing fees that IPR protection requires for the use of IP, and these may more than offset possible gains in increased FDI, for example. So why would a state adopt an IPR regime stronger than the one that would be the most beneficial (optimal) to its development? In answering this question, the beneficiaries of a strong domestic IPR regime must be explored—industries whose IP is most commonly stolen. If states perceive a weaker domestic and global IPR regime as beneficial to their interests, then the only reason to deter them from this strategy is the demands placed on them by special interests that can make it worthwhile for them to adopt stronger IPR protection.

With regard to interest groups, a few clarifying points are needed. All states are not equal in their level of political and economic development, which means interest groups domestically have different political effects across different states. The type of interest groups and how they operate will vary from one state to the next. Groups and their behaviour in the United States will be different from those in China or in South Africa. Moreover, not all states are at the same economic development level, which means that certain interest groups are not present in some countries. The influence in the US of the software and semiconductor industries is not equivalent to that of the same industries in India or Brazil. Because of the importance of these industries to the US economy, they exert substantial influence on the political process. These conceptions of interest groups in political and economic development portray them as domestic actors that exercise control and influence within the confines of the state. But this limitation must be relaxed to achieve an understanding of the IPR issue.

Interest groups can also be foreign actors, such as other states and transnational corporations (TNCs). State and non-state actors compete in the international system to achieve goals that may or may not coincide with those of other state and non-state actors. Thus, another issue is that developed states pursue different goals than do developing states and therefore behave differently in the international system. Developed countries have attained a level of economic and political development that provides a high standard of living for their people. Their goal, at minimum, is to maintain that level of development. Developing countries have not attained the same level of economic or political development. Their goals reflect the desire to improve the standard of living for their people. But different forces affect how developed and developing countries pursue these goals. Actors and circumstances that effect behavior at both the domestic and international levels confront both groups of states.

In fact, the state is active in the interplay of two distinct 'societies': domestic and international, each possessing forces that influence the state. The state does not operate exclusively in the realm of one *or* the other; instead, the state attempts to temper or to enhance the effect that each society has on the other. The state's role is to filter the extreme demands placed on the two societies by each other without compromising its own security and stability.

With respect to IPR, the debate between the developed and developing countries emerged in its most contentious form in the 1980s as nations began moving from protectionist policies to free trade and free market-oriented economies. The developed countries collectively sought to pry open large, untapped consumer markets in the developing world. But as trade with and investment in developing countries increased, developed countries expressed strong dissatisfaction with the fairness of the domestic markets in these countries, particularly with regard to the treatment of foreign products. Specifically, corporate leaders voiced concern over the lack of protection from pirating and imitation their products were afforded in foreign markets. They contended that foreign piracy of their IP had cost them billions of dollars and had eliminated millions of jobs in their home countries. Ideas had become the new economic battleground between developed and developing countries.

When IPR became a central trade issue, a number of states modified or completely overhauled their IPR systems to benefit (or continue to benefit) from preferential trade status with key industries and nations. However, given the findings previously presented, a state's decision to adjust IPR protection is not necessarily voluntary or purely IPR-related, but may be a product of internal and external conditions. States are faced with domestic pressure to strengthen or to enforce existing IPR laws, pressure from foreign governments demanding strong protection for the IP of their TNCs, or a combination of both. The goal here is to examine both the domestic and international factors that affect a state's IPR policy. Two questions are to be addressed: (1) which factors both domestically and internationally affect states' IPR protection policies and (2) do these factors differ for developed and developing countries? The evidence presented here suggests that both domestic and international factors have a role in determining a state's IPR policies and that these factors do differ for developed and developing countries.

A. Empirical Research

Empirical research on the determinants of IPR protection is scarce, though innovation and invention are recognized as major components of economic growth and development.[32] Rapp and Rozek addressed factors that affected how states protect IP. Using regression analysis, they found that the level of economic development correlates closely with the level of patent protection.[33] Rapp and Rozek interpret this finding as clear evidence of the need for strong IPR protection to promote economic development. In their study, patent protection is used as a proxy measure of IP protection. As noted previously, the measure they use has drawbacks given the nature of IPR, which cannot be viewed as a unidimensional concept to be measured by patent laws only. Moreover, Rapp and Rozek do not present the results of their regression analysis. No regression coefficients or standard errors are presented with their findings. Despite these issues, the importance of the Rapp and Rozek study cannot be overlooked. They present one of the first attempts to measure IPR protection and to explore the relationships associated with it. Though they do not present the empirical results, their study is one of the first to proclaim an empirical relationship between economic development and IPR protection.

A more recent attempt to understand the determinants of patent protection is Ginarte and Park (1997).[34] Using their index of patent rights discussed previously, they find that a country's level of development was not a significant factor in explaining the country's patent protection level; rather, it is the determinants of economic development, such as research and development, market freedom, and openness that determine how strongly a country will protect patents. Still in a later study, Shadlen, Schrank and Kurtz (2005) find that software piracy rates are negatively affected by international treaty obligations (specifically WTO

[32] Simon Kuznets, 'Innovations and Adjustments in Economic Growth', [1972] *Swedish J of Econ* 4, 431–451; Edward J Malecki, *Technology and Economic Development: The Dynamics of Local, Regional, and National Change* (Longman Scientific and Technical, 1991).

[33] Rapp and Rozek, note 5 above, 75–77.

[34] See note 5 above.

membership) and bilateral pressure from the United States.[35] In doing so, they use software piracy rates as an output or effect of copyright policies in 80 countries from 1994–2002. Their study is significant in that it takes full consideration of the distinction between the actual enforcement of laws and just the enactment of those laws. Needless to say, additional empirical research on this question is warranted.

B. The Pressure for Intellectual Property Rights

To understand the factors that contribute to a state's IPR protection policies, we must be concerned with the sources of pressure that come to bear on governments. These pressures emanate from both the domestic and international levels. At the domestic level, industries that have an interest in protecting their IP exert pressure on governments to enhance IPR protection. These industries tend to be high technology industries, or industries that are on the technological cutting edge and whose products are susceptible to IP piracy, or whose product life is short due to rapidly changing technology. In the US, for example, the chemical and pharmaceuticals industry, the computer industry, and the motion picture industry have been most vocal in pressing the government to increase protection at home and abroad.[36]

At the international level, states that are the recipient of large amounts of trade and investment come under pressure from foreign governments, particularly of developed countries, to increase IPR protection. The most watched example of this in recent years has unfolded in China. The opening of China's domestic market to foreign investment has proven to be an economic boom to investors and a major problem for IP owners. Corporations whose investments and trade are dependent on strong IPR protection protested vehemently to their home governments about the lack of adequate protection for IP in China. Under the threat of trade wars with the United States, the Chinese government increased the protection afforded IP under its laws and stepped up enforcement of existing laws. Cases where foreign pressure has been applied to increase IPR protection are not limited to China. Developed countries, led by the United States, pressured Taiwan, South Korea, Japan, Thailand, Philippines and numerous other countries to change their IPR protection practices.

35 Kenneth C Shadlen, Andrew Schrank, and Marcus J Kurtz, 'The Political Economy of Intellectual Property Protection: The Case of Software', (2005) 49 *Int'l Studies Qly* 1, 45, 27.

36 Robert L Ostergard, Jr, *The Development Dilemma: The Political Economy of Intellectual Property Rights in the International System* (LFB Scholarly Publishing, 2002); Susan K Sell, *Power and ideas: North–South politics of intellectual property and antitrust* (State University of New York Press, 1988); Michael P Ryan, *Knowledge diplomacy: Global competition and the politics of intellectual property* (Brookings Institution Press, 1988); Peter Drahos and John Braithwaite, *Information Feudalism* (The New Press, 2002).

C. The Empirical Model

The empirical model to be tested here is on the assumption that states do not voluntarily adopt strong IPR protection, particularly at early levels of development. The most relevant factors are sources of either domestic or foreign pressure on the existing regime. For this model, technology and democracy represent factors at the domestic level while global integration and foreign direct investment represent international level factors. From these, four specific hypotheses about IPR protection can be tested.

H_1: The more technologically advanced a state is, the stronger will be its IPR protection.

H_2: The more democratic a nation is, the stronger will be its IPR protection.

H_3: The more globally integrated a nation is, the stronger will be its IPR protection.

H_4: The more foreign investment a state receives, the stronger will be its IPR protection.

Theoretically, states that have higher levels of technology should want to protect the investments their citizens make in IP products. Those states with lower levels of technological development would be better off 'stealing' innovations. The costs of implementing patents and licensing agreements might prove too expensive to implement. Thus, even at low levels of technological development, some nations may be better off having weak IPR protection in order to stimulate the adoption of technologically sophisticated products.[37] States therefore adopt IPR policies strategically, based on their technological needs. Additionally, states with higher levels of technology should experience greater pressure to implement and enforce strong IPR regimes, particularly from those industries that are IPR-dependent, such as the chemical and entertainment industries.

Additionally, the political nature of the regime should have a positive impact on the IPR protection a state will accommodate. This relationship is based on two factors. First, democratic governments generally recognize and attempt to protect property rights of any kind. Government respect for property rights historically has been a critical issue in the relationship between governments and their citizens. Second, democratic governments, by their nature, are open to greater influences from pressure groups that are dependent upon IPR protection for their goods.

---

37 Sanjaya Lall, 'The Patent System and the Transfer of Technology to Less-Developed Countries', [1976] *J of World Trade L* 10, 1–16; see also Gutterman, note 28 above, 122.

At the international level, two relationships are postulated. The more states are integrated into the global economy, the more likely they are to protect IPR. Integration in this case is defined as how much a country trades. If states do not adequately protect IP, foreign governments may intervene on behalf of their TNCs to pressure target states to strengthen IPR protection. IPR protection has also been cast in terms of trade issues because corporations exporting IP to states with weak IPR protection lose export market share to those companies that freely pirate IP products in a target country. On the one hand, the more a state trades, the more likely it will be exposed to pressure to increase its IPR protection. On the other hand, it is also possible that the more a state trades, the less likely it will be to protect IPR. This argument has to do with the protection of domestic industry. If a country has strong IPR protection, this creates an artificial monopoly in that country for any product. If the protection is for a foreign product, then domestic producers will be legally blocked from entering markets to produce these products. States therefore may want to delay, either by legislation or in practice, strong IPR. By not having weak laws, or not enforcing laws, states create a non-tariff barrier to entry into domestic markets by foreign producers. Foreign producers cannot compete with the lower production costs of pirates who duplicate IP from foreign sources. Therefore, there is an incentive to keep IPR protection weak to enhance domestic industry production.

Similarly, calls to increase IPR protection come from those that invest in states. Investors who are willing to invest money in a country to produce goods will want strong IP protection so that their investments will be guaranteed. If they lose money due to IPR infringement, they may seek assistance from their home governments in pressuring the target country to increase IPR protection. Theoretically, the more a country receives in foreign investment, the greater the pressure will be from foreign sources to protect IPR.

D. Data and Measurement

The data set for this study is the IPR dataset developed previously. Variables for technology, democracy, foreign investment and integration have been added, based upon the procedures described below.

Technology Levels

The measurement of technology levels is a complicated and controversial process. Aggregate science and technology indicators have been addressed by a number of scholars across several disciplines. Each procedure has both positive and negative aspects. Three measures of note have been looked at for this study: bibliographic indicators, domestic patents issued by a country, and technology component measures. Frame discussed the use of bibliographic information (the number of scientific articles published in a country) as an indicator of a country's level of scientific achievement.[38] This measure is appropriate for addressing questions that deal with the structure of a country's research system, research trends, scientific dependency on outsiders, or scientific communication patterns in some countries.[39] However, its use as an aggregate indicator of scientific achievement is questionable because research may be hidden by several factors, including inability to write in English, time-sensitive research where there is no time to publish results, lack of clerical support, and disinterest in local country problems.[40] Hence, these numbers may seriously under-represent scientific activity in a country.

Another measure of science and technology used by Frame is the number of domestic patents issued by a country.[41] Frame argued that this measure is a good indicator of a country's technological capacity. However, the use of this measure in this study would present obvious methodological problems. These data are also misleading because they do not distinguish the type of technology patented. A child's toy is treated the same way as a pharmaceutical product. While these data may measure inventive capacity, it seems doubtful that they are able to measure technological capacity with any confidence.

What both these measures lack is a conceptual foundation for exactly what comprises technology, and how to measure those components. Reynolds and Krivo address this idea when they call attention to Frisbie and Clarke's work on comparative technology measures.[42] Frisbie and Clarke conceptualize technology as having six distinct components, which are shown in Table 3.22.[43]

Each component measures a particular type of technology. As Reynolds and Krivo discussed, each component is in no way a complete indicator of leading technology. Collectively, they tap into a society's basic capacity for subsistence, productive, supportive and informational technology cross-nationally and temporally.[44]

---

38 Davidson J Frame, 'Problems in the Use of Literature-based S&T Indicators in Developing Countries', in Hiroko Morita-Lou (ed), *Science and Technology Indicators for Development* (Westview Press, 1984).

39 Ibid, 121.

40 Ibid, 120.

41 Ibid.

42 John R Reynolds and Lauren J Krivo, 'Change in Societal Technology and Development, 1950–1990', [1996] *Soc Science Research* 25, 95–124.

43 WP Frisbie and CJ Clarke, 'Technology in evolutionary and ecological perspective: Theory and measurement at the societal level', [1979] *Social Forces* 63, 750–766.

44 Reynolds and Krivo, note 41 above, 102–103.

Table 3.22 Frisbie and Clarke's Technology Measurement Model

Component	Indicator
Energy Use	1. Consumption of coal, lignite, petroleum, natural gas, hydroelectric and nuclear energy
Agriculture	2. Tractors in use 3. Fertilizer consumed
Manufacturing	4. Cement produced 5. Steel consumed in industry 6. Tin consumed in industry
Transportation	7. Aviation (km flown) 8. Railway freight (ton–km) 9. International sea-borne shipping (metric tons) 10. Motor vehicles in use, passenger and commercial
Communication	11. Radios in use 12. Telephones in use 13. Televisions in use 14. Newsprint consumed 15. Domestic telegrams 16. Domestic mail 17. Total daily circulation of newspapers
Information	18. Scientists, technicians, and engineers 19. R&D expenditures per scientist and engineer 20. R&D expenditures as a percentage of GNP

Source: Reynolds and Krivo 'Change in Societal Technology and Development, 1950–1990' [1996] *Soc Science Research* 25.

In replicating Frisbie and Clarke's measure, Reynolds and Krivo transformed the data. Each indicator was divided by population and then the natural log was taken for these measures. The measures were then converted to z-scores relative to the mean and standard deviation of each indicator for the entire time period. According to Reynolds and Krivo, this was done to achieve a constant scale across the various indicators of technology.[45] A score for each component of technology was then calculated as the mean of the z-scores for a component indicator. They collapsed the component indicators to five by combining the transportation and communication components. Scores for all the components were then added to achieve a single index and then adjusted to a scale of 0–100, with 0 representing the lowest technology and 100 the highest. This procedure was used in a data set comprising 98 countries from 1950–1990 with data every 10 years for each country.

Conceptually, this index has appeal. It attempts to include major facets of what intuitively is a country's base technological capacity. The major drawback to this measure is the availability of data. While these data are available for the

45 Ibid, 105.

1950–1990 time periods (every ten years), they were not available for the time period of this study, 1988–1994 (the chosen time period of this study will be discussed in detail later). Developing countries in particular are not able to report these data frequently due to resource and data collection problems. Even in Reynolds and Krivo's study, the information technology component could only be included for dates prior to 1990. Therefore, in attempting to replicate this measure, a number of changes had to be made due to the availability of data.

Variables that indicated any measure of the consumption of a particular commodity were changed to production variables. This change allowed for easier gathering of some data. More importantly, the change reflects a stronger interest in being able to tap into a nation's productive capacity. Because of data availability problems, some variables could not be obtained. Of the 18 variables used, complete and uniform data could be obtained for 11 of them. These variables are listed below in Table 3.23.

Following Reynolds and Krivo, all variables were divided by population. Instead of transforming these data as Reynolds and Krivo did, I chose to factor analyse these data separately for each of the three years in this study. This procedure is not a major departure from Reynolds and Krivo, as they report that various transformations of their data all yield highly correlated indices of technology. Among the transformations they attempted was to obtain factor scores by factor analysis, which correlated at .95 or higher with the procedure they decided to use. I then derived factor scores for each country. Correlation analysis and reliability and stability coefficients among all three years showed a high level of reliability and stability among the new technology measures.[46]

Table 3.23 Technology Index Variables

Component	Indicator
Energy Use	1. Total Production of Energy (TPES), which includes all of Frisbie and Clarke's energy indicators
Agriculture	2. Tractors in use
Manufacturing	3. Cement produced
	4. Tin produced
Transportation	5. Railway freight (ton–km)
	6. International sea-borne shipping (metric tons)
	7. Motor vehicles in use, passenger and commercial
Communication	8. Radios in use
	9. Telephones in use
	10. Televisions in use
	11. Total daily circulation of newspapers

[46] Heise, note 23 above.

Global Integration

The term global integration, or globalization, connotes several different definitions incorporating both political and economic concepts. Globalization, as it has been termed by some, has been the subject of much literature that tries to define it in some precise manner. This task seems to be dependent upon the research question at hand. For the purposes of this study, I am particularly interested in a country's relationship to the global economy. I adopt van Bergeijk and Mensink's definition of globalization or global integration as the basis of a network of nations that links economies through various financial transactions, particularly trade, foreign direct investment, and labour migration.[47]

Most developed countries are major exporting countries whereas developing countries tend to be import dependent. Relative to the concept of integration into the global economy, this may create discrepancies in the importance of exports to one set of countries (developed countries) and the importance of imports to another set of countries (developing countries). One way of thinking about this is that, without those countries importing, exporting countries would have fewer markets. By using exports only, the importance of the importing country is marginalized. Also, by using exports as a proportion of GDP, the measure is capturing the significance of exports to the domestic economy, but it really says little about how much exposure the country has in the global economy. The argument that is being made here is that the more exposure a country has at the international level, the more likely it will be to have stronger IPR protection. By using total trade, the importance of both import- and export-dominant countries is taken into account. To weigh a country's relative importance in the global economy, the total trade figure is then taken as a proportion of world total trade. The exposure that a country has to the global economy is recognized without prejudice to the type of exposure, be it exports or imports.

Democracy

To measure the level of democracy in states, I have adopted Tedd Robert Gurr's democracy scale.[48] This variable, often used in international relations literature and empirical modelling, measures a state's level of democracy on a 0–11 additive scale, with 0 representing absolutely no democracy in the country and 11

[47] Peter AG van Bergeijk and Nico W Mensink, 'Measuring Globalization' [1997] *J of World Trade* 31, 159–168.

[48] Tedd R Gurr, *Polity III* [computer file]: regime type and political authority, 1800–1994. Ann Arbor: Inter-University Consortium for Political and Social Research [distributor], (1996).

representing a democratic government. Gurr and Jaggers[49] operationalize democracy based on three criteria: (1) the competitiveness and openness of executive recruitment, (2) the competitiveness of political participation and (3) the level of constraints placed on the chief executive. Other aspects of democracy, such as the rule of law, checks and balances, and civil rights are treated as means to or manifestations of the three institutional criteria. Their theoretical conceptualization of democracy is thus broken down into five separate dimensions and appropriate scores for each dimensional component (see Gurr 1996 and Gurr and Jaggers 1995 for these dimensions). The scores are then added to obtain the democracy scores for each country.

Foreign Direct Investment

Foreign direct investment is measured by a country's net capital inflow investment from overseas. These data are taken as a proportion of the nation's GDP in order to control for the size of the economy

E. Model Results

Two initial methodological problems had to be addressed. First, using the PQLI in the model to evaluate differences between developed and developing countries was problematic because of the PQLI variable's high correlation with the technology variable, which created problems of multicollinearity (the two variables correlated at .72). This presents a problem if we are to understand what factors contribute to a state's IPR protection level. Instead of utilizing the PQLI variable, I split the data using the mean of the technology variable. Second, because the dependent variable IPR protection contains ordinal level data, OLS regression analysis is inappropriate.[50] Instead, ordered logistic regression was used to test the models. The results of the analysis for developed countries are presented in Tables 3.24 to 3.26.

49 Tedd R Gurr and Keith Jaggers, 'Tracking Democracy's Third Wave with the Polity III Data', [1995] *J of Peace Research* 32, 469–482.

50 Tim Futing Liao, *Interpreting Probability Models: Logit, Probit, and Other Generalized Linear Models*, Sage University Paper series on Quantitative Applications in the Social Sciences, no. 07–101 (Sage Publications, 1994); Scott R Eliason, *Maximum Likelihood Estimation: Logic and Practice*, Sage University Paper series on Quantitative Applications in the Social Sciences, no. 07–096 (Sage Publications, 1993); Michael S Lewis-Beck, *Applied Regression: An Introduction*, Sage University Paper series on Quantitative Applications in the Social Sciences, no. 07–022 (Sage Publications, 1980); David G Kleinbaum, *Logistic Regression: A Self-Learning Text* (Springer Verlag, 1994); Gary King , *Unifying Political Methodology: The Likelihood Theory of Statistical Inference* (Cambridge University Press, 1989).

Table 3.24 Ordered Logit Model for IPR Protection, Patents 1988–1994, Developed Countries

Variable	Estimate	Standard Error
Integration	12.38	8.71
Democracy	0.02	0.08
Technology	2.26	***0.43
Foreign Investment	2.07	0.06

n=77
Log–Likelihood=298.85
c2(4)=46.86 Prob.>c2=0.000 Pseudo R2=0.46

***p<0.01

Table 3.25 Ordered Logit Model for IPR Protection, Trademarks 1988–1994, Developed Countries

Variable	Estimate	Standard Error
Integration	–3.19	8.73
Democracy	0.23	***0.09
Technology	2.45	***0.44
Foreign Investment	2.18	8.20

n=77
Log–Likelihood=288.85
$c^2(4)=53.53$ Prob.> $c^2=0.000$ Pseudo $R^2=0.50$

***p<0.01

Table 3.26 Ordered Logit Model for IPR Protection, Copyrights 1988–1994, Developed Countries

Variable	Estimate	Standard Error
Integration	12.06	8.90
Democracy	0.34	***0.10
Technology	2.08	***0.42
Foreign Investment	1.92	8.23

n=77
Log–Likelihood=322.36
$c^2(4)=53.35$ Prob.>$c^2=0.000$ Pseudo $R^2=0.51$

***p<0.01

The results for the three types of IPR protection measures are generally consistent. The two variables that represent domestic sources of pressure, democracy and technology, are all positive factors in determining the probability of a state's IPR protection level. Though democracy is not significant for patent protection, the technology variable remains a key factor in all three model results. For developed countries, the push for stronger IPR protection, according to the results, emanates from domestic forces. Does this condition hold for developing countries? Tables 3.27 to 3.29 present results for these countries.

The results for the developing countries have several interesting aspects when compared to those for the developed countries. First, the overall model for the developing countries tends to be a weaker predictor of IPR protection levels than the model for the developed countries. Both the log–likelihood estimate and the pseudo-R^2 are weaker for the developing countries than for the developed countries. Second, the factors that are consistent across the three model results are the sources of pressure for increased levels of IPR protection. For all the models, foreign sources (integration and foreign investment) are the significant variables in predicting IPR protection levels for developed countries. In all three models,

Table 3.27 Ordered Logit Model for IPR Protection, Patents 1988–1994, Developing Countries

Variable	Estimate	Standard Error
Integration	56.09	**24.67
Democracy	–0.04	0.04
Technology	–.12	0.58
Foreign Investment	–3.23	7.74

n=129
Log–Likelihood=522.07
$c^2(4)=8.31$ Prob.$>c^2=0.08$ Pseudo $R^2=0.06$

**p<0.05

Table 3.28 Ordered Logit Model for IPR Protection, Trademarks 1988–1994, Developing Countries

Variable	Estimate	Standard Error
Integration	47.76	**24.04
Democracy	–0.06	0.04
Technology	0.62	0.58
Foreign Investment	12.70	7.74

n=129
Log–Likelihood=572.90
$c^2(4)=9.821$ Prob.$> c^2=0.04$ Pseudo $R^2=0.07$

**p<0.05

Table 3.29 Ordered Logit Model for IPR Protection, Copyrights 1988–1994, Developing Countries

Variable	Estimate	Standard Error
Integration	55.62	**24.12
Democracy	–0.01	0.04
Technology	0.15	0.58
Foreign Investment	17.28	**7.77

n=129

Log–Likelihood=637.21

$c^2(4)=10.95$ Prob.$>c^2=0.02$ Pseudo $R^2=0.08$

**p<0.05

the integration variable is significant while the foreign investment variable is significant only for copyright protection. What these results clearly illustrate is that the more developing countries are exposed to international trade and investment, the greater will be the pressure on those states to increase the level of protection for IP. Domestic factors, democracy and technology, had no significant role in any of the models for the developing countries.

F. Discussion

The results predicting the level of IP protection for developing countries take on a distinct importance. We expect states to act rationally in deciding what type of protection to afford IPR. They must balance competing factors in devising policy in this area that is suited to their needs at that moment in time. What the analysis illustrated was that there were no clear domestic economic benefits for developing countries to maintain strong IPR protection. The economic growth benefit has been the primary argument that developed countries use in trying to persuade developing countries to adopt strong protection measures. Clearly, that argument is, at best, on shaky ground. If this is the case, why would developing countries adopt stronger IP regimes? The answer to this comes from the analysis just presented.

Most developing states have little incentive to adopt TRIPS-compatible (unmodulated) IPR protection measures on their own. It is rational for these states to obtain IP as inexpensively as possible and grow their IP protection level in parallel with economic development and according to their own industrial and commercial strengths. There is historical precedent for this rationale. Modern developed countries often undertook policies that would be considered 'piracy' by today's standards. In practice, the rationale is a proven method for advancing technological and economic development, tested frequently and successfully by many of today's developed countries during their history. Developing countries that have weak IP protection are doing nothing more than following historically proven methods for advancing development. This proposition, however, is too simple and does not convey the dynamics at work in the IPR problems between developed and developing countries.

While the methods for acquiring IP may not have changed much, with piracy being a centuries-old practice, the *environment* in which piracy occurs has changed. In the information age the nature of industry and time have manipulated the environment in which states and other actors operate. Entire industries are sometimes dependent upon strong IP protection to maintain a competitive edge in international markets. IP protection creates monopoly market conditions that industries utilize for greater profits. However, these conditions have been compromised with the advancement of technology that can rapidly disseminate information across the globe. The rapid spread of information compromises market exclusivity for industry producers. On the one hand, these conditions alone appear to promote developed countries' arguments for strong IP protection. On the other, the need for strong IP protection must be placed into an appropriate context.

Developed countries' calls for strong protection are advanced in the name of protecting overseas markets for their industries. These countries are acting to protect a major source of economic growth—foreign trade—for domestic industries. The irony is that developed countries have promoted policies that are intended to encourage developing countries to open their domestic markets to foreign competition. The logic behind free trade policies is that every state engaged in trade will benefit. When developing countries have opened their markets, developed countries have applied strong political and economic pressure for developing countries to protect foreign IPR. These pressures have produced the odd scenario of developing countries financing not just or even primarily their own growth, but promoting the economic growth of developed countries, possibly to the detriment of their own economic development. This represents *the development dilemma* faced by developing countries: if they open their domestic markets to trade, they face political and economic pressure to protect foreign IP; if they protect foreign IP, they create conditions that force them to abandon their goal to obtain IP as inexpensively as possible.

4

INTELLECTUAL PROPERTY TREATIES AND DEVELOPMENT

Anselm Kamperman Sanders

Introduction

Including issues of harmonization and enforcement of intellectual property rights (IPRs) in the setting of the Uruguay Round of negotiations is commonly understood to be a balancing act: safeguarding Western interest in return for access to Western markets. In the multilateral setting of the World Trade Organization and the TRIPS Agreement, this *quid pro quo* approach has since been hailed as a global breakthrough for IP rights holders. With the TRIPS Council to provide a platform for ensuring TRIPS compliance and early dispute resolution, and with the WTO Dispute Settlement Understanding in place to resolve differences without trade wars, the future development of intellectual property law seems set for multilateralism.

Bilateral treaties involving intellectual property chapters are flourishing, especially in the context of Bilateral Investment Treaties (BITs) and Free Trade Agreements (FTAs). The key to understanding the reasons behind continued bilateral activity in the face of intellectual property multilateralism is the perceived need to further economic development and the development of IPRs themselves. This chapter explores the flourishing of bilateralism against the backdrop of the remaining controversies, flexibilities, and loose ends of the TRIPS Agreement.

Part I Investment and Intellectual Property

The key to development, for a developing nation, is the ability to attract foreign direct investment (FDI). For example, intangibles such as patents, know-how and other intellectual capital absorb US$1 trillion of investment funds every year.[1] Not only is this on par with the corporate investment in physical assets, but the current trend of shifting investment into the knowledge-based economy also suggests that investment in intellectual capital may surpass investment in physical assets in developed economies.[2] Investment in a knowledge-based economy[3] is central to any effort seeking to bridge the gap in development[4] between markets in developing nations and markets in developed nations.[5] But what is the role of intellectual property in economic development? Because of its monopolistic nature, many economists approach IPRs with a great deal of caution.

Free and unrestricted competition lies at the heart of the generally accepted western economic theory—free play of market forces. Free competition between enterprises is thought to be the best means to satisfy supply and demand and to maximize wealth in society as a whole. Central to this proposition is the axiom that market participants can compete on a level playing field so that all competitors face the same market barriers, thus facilitating freedom of entry into the market. From this point of view, legal interference in the market should be kept to a minimum. This does not mean, however, that the policy towards markets should be one of *laissez faire*. There is a compelling argument for *laissez faire* policy insofar as interference in the market brings with it administrative costs that are incurred from the transfer of the costs of competition from one market participant to the other. Therefore, market intervention should result in a clear

---

1 B Lev, 'Sharpening the Intangibles Edge', (June 2004) *Harvard Business Review* 109, 110.

2 T Stewart, *Intellectual Capital—The Wealth of Organizations* (Currency, 1998); and T Stewart, *The Wealth of Knowledge: Intellectual Capital and the Twenty-First Century Organization* (Currency, 2003).

3 D Potter, 'Wealth Creation in the Knowledge Economy', available in the series of British Prime Minister's Millennium lectures at <http://www.number-10.gov.uk/output/Page3051.asp>.

4 On the risk of a widening digital divide due to TRIPS see Consumers International, 'Copyright and Access to Knowledge—Policy Recommendations on Flexibilities in Copyright Laws', available at <http://www.consumidoresint.org/a2k/documents/a2k-report.pdf>.

5 C Braga, K Fink and C Sepulveda, 'Intellectual Property Rights and Economic Development', World Bank Discussion Paper No 412 (World Bank, 2000); see also R Mansell and U When (eds.), *INK—Knowledge Societies: Information Technology for Sustainable Development* (Oxford University Press, 1998).

social benefit, such as the release of more low-priced high quality products for which there is consumer demand. In competitive markets, the process of spreading market information helps to shape the opinions of market participants with regard to profit-making activities,[6] and is seen as socially beneficial. Government intervention to enhance this aspect of competition is generally acceptable, even in classical economic theory. This adage gives rise to the premise in neo-classical theory that perfect knowledge will induce a situation where the spontaneous interaction between knowledge possessors will lead to a state of equilibrium and the optimum distribution of resources in society.[7] This means that disturbances in knowledge creation, leading to imperfect knowledge, need to be countered. Therefore, legal interference should aim to provide a level playing field of 'market information' in which perfect knowledge induces perfect competition. Laws on the protection of intellectual property and competition can be seen in this light. Entitlements are allocated to specific creators, to safeguard their information against expropriation, so that bargaining can facilitate an exchange thus creating a market. With most intellectual and industrial creations, the establishment of a market for ideas is possible only if the value of the idea can be assessed in advance. This generally means revealing that idea to a potential buyer, who will then already have acquired the idea at no cost.[8]

An example of government intervention through the creation of a property right facilitating the bargaining process and the creation of a market has been demonstrated in the case of copyright. After the creation of the entitlement, the role of the state is finished, leaving the transfer of the entitlement to the market, where a voluntary bargain can be made between buyer and seller. This implies that the value of the entitlement is also determined by the market and not by the state. This means that the value determination and maximization require the least state intervention.[9] According to the Coase Theorem, the allocations of initial entitlements by the state are unimportant, since they are transferred to their 'highest value use' through private bargaining leaving the total output of the economy unaffected. One system of property rights is no more efficient than another in this view.[10] This means, however, that the transaction costs of the

[6] F Hayek, 'Economics and Knowledge' in *Individualism and Economic Order* (University of Chicago Press, 1948) 106: '[c]ompetition is essentially a process of the formation of opinion: by spreading information [i]t creates the views people have about what is best and cheapest'.

[7] R Cooter and T Ulen, *Law and Economcs* (2nd edn, Addison Wesley, 1997) Chapter 2.

[8] K Arrow, 'Economic Welfare and the Allocation of Resources for Invention' in *The Rate and Direction of Economic Activity Economic and Social Factors* (Princeton University Press, 1962) 609 and 615.

[9] G Calabresi and A Melamed, 'Property Rules, Liability Rules, and Inalienability: One View of the Cathedral', (1972) 85 *Harvard LR* 1089 at 1092 and 1105.

[10] R Coase, 'The Problem of Social Cost' (1960) 3 *J of Law and Economics*, 1.

(re)allocation of property rights and the rules governing the exchange determine the efficiency of one system over the other.[11] In addition, the cost effectiveness of a protective regime depends on the social costs that are incurred when protection is afforded in error, and when the likelihood of overprotection by the system is real. The economic rationale for the patent system,[12] commonly described as a system of incentives and rewards and perhaps more aptly described as a monopoly that creates a barrier to entry,[13] forces a licensing practice to evolve. This serves two ends. First, the competitor faces a market barrier, equivalent to that encountered by the first market entrant, thus levelling the playing field. Just like the first market entrant the competitor has to pay for the innovative features of his product or means of production. As a free-rider he would not have faced the same barrier to market entry as the first market entrant and there would be no incentive for a free-rider to be creative. Second, more creators produce a wider variety of works that the public may be willing to pay for. This gives the consumer more choice and facilitates the creation of new markets. Without the protective regime of the patent system, which excludes free-riders, a situation of asymmetric market failure could emerge. Market failure is a situation where creators are not rewarded for their creative efforts. This makes it economically more attractive to copy than to create. Why would one spend creative energy and risk failure in the market when existing market success can be copied? The result is that creators produce fewer works than the public would be willing to pay for. The aspect of asymmetry is the situation where one party, the creator, faces a market barrier and the other, a copyist, does not.[14] If a combination of market failure and asymmetry occurs, a pattern emerges that holds true for all forms of intellectual property law.

Just like the patent system, which serves to stimulate disclosure of the invention and thus encourage further development, one of the purposes of the copyright system is to allow for the communication and use of information expressed in a copyright work, either by additions to the public domain or by rights acquisition

---

[11] R Merges, 'Of Property Rules, Coase, and Intellectual Property' (1994) 94 *Columbia LR* 2655 at 2664–7.

[12] E Kaufer, *The Economics of the Patent System* (Harwood Academic Publishers GmbH, 1989) and P Heald, 'Federal Intellectual Property Law and the Economics of Preemption' (1991) 76 *Iowa LR*, 962–65.

[13] H Demsetz, 'Barriers to Entry' (1982) 72 *American Economic R*, 47: '[t]he problem of defining ownership is precisely that of creating properly scaled legal barriers to entry'.

[14] For a definition of asymmetric market failure and the role of intellectual property law in providing a remedy against the resulting loss in wealth see W Gordon, 'Asymmetric Market Failure and Prisoners Dilemma in Intellectual Property' (1992) 17 *University of Dayton LR*, 853.

on a licensing basis.[15] Where a new work relies on previous work and ideas, the new work should not benefit the copyright holder through monopoly rents in excess of the value the new work has added to total welfare.[16] It would be wasteful competition[17] to gain benefits on the basis of the value of the underlying work, which often consists of contributions by others that may already be in the public domain, or never have been susceptible to copyright.[18] If there are many potential users of the work, it may become too costly to negotiate individual licences for every use that is made of it. This is especially true when works have become *de facto* industry standards, which may be the case in database or software or industries.[19] Disclosure of the source code and interface information and the fair use doctrine in copyright law can redress the economic imbalance that this increase in transaction costs entails.[20]

The trademark system displays different characteristics, in that it was not envisaged as a system of incentives and rewards, but as a regulation of marketing efforts.[21] As an identifier of products and their sources, a trademark performs the role of a communicator, a messenger that spreads information about what is best, the level and consistency of quality, and what is cheapest. Protection of

[15] For a representation of traditional patent and copyright protection and the varying level of creativity required, see E Mackay, 'Legal Hybrids: Beyond Property and Monopoly?' (1994) 94 *Columbia LR*, 2630.

[16] W Landes and R Posner, 'An Economic Analysis of Copyright Law' (1989) 18 *J of Economic Studies* 325, 347–353, offer the economic rationale for not protecting ideas.

[17] S Besen and L Raskind, 'An Introduction to the Law and Economics of Intellectual Property' (1991) *J of Economic Perspectives* 3, 5.

[18] F Warren-Boulton, K Baseman and G Woroch, 'The Economics of Intellectual Property Protection for Software: The Proper Role for Copyright' (1995) 3 *Standard View*, 68–78.

[19] See *US v Microsoft* 97 F Supp 2d 59 (JS App 253–279). The findings of fact of the District Court are reported at 84 F Supp 2d 9 (JS App 46–246). The conclusions of law of the District Court are reported at 87 F Supp 2d 30 (JS App 1–43). The final judgment of the District Court is reported at 97 F Supp 2d 59 (JS App 253–279). The order of the District Court certifying the case under the Expediting Act is found at JS App 284–285, 20 June 2000. The settlement information and final (modified) judgment of 7 September 2006, are available at <http://www.usdoj.gov/atr/cases/ms_index.htm>.

[20] See W Gordon, 'Fair Use as Market Failure: A Structural and Economic Analysis of the *Betamax* Case and Its Predecessors' (1982) 82 *Columbia LR* 1600, as to the extent of the fair use doctrine. See also Landes and Posner, note 16 above, 357–61. However, see also *Sony Corp of America v Universal City Studios*, 464 US 417 (1984), in which the US Supreme Court found that distributors of Grokster and Morpheus P2P file-sharing software, although capable of being used for non-infringing purposes, are liable for users' copyright violations; and similarly *MGM Studios, Inc v Grokster, Ltd*, 545 US 913 (2005).

[21] W Cornish and J Phillips, 'The Economic Function of Trademarks: An Analysis With Special Reference to Developing Countries' (1982) 13 *Int'l R of Industrial Property and Copyright Law*, 41; N Economides, 'The Economics of Trademarks' (1988) 78 *Trade Mark Reporter*, 523; W Landes and R Posner, 'Trademark Law: an Economic Perspective' (1987) 30 *J of Law and Economics*, 265.

trademarks ensures that the consumer can make correct purchasing decisions,[22] thus lowering the transaction costs.[23] The 'confusion rationale' is also expressed in the doctrine of passing off, where it also serves to prevent the consumer from incurring increased transaction costs by seeking to minimize a consumer's potential for confusion, guaranteeing to the marketer that his or her message is heard without interference.

Protection of trade secrets is underpinned again by the notion of incentives and rewards, but may be located in the realm of unfair competition law.[24] As an item of sensitive information, a trade secret may have commercial value and may attract the interest of competitors. Here lies one of the major differences from the fixed costs associated with obtaining a patent, in that the value of the trade secret and the costs that have to be incurred in order to protect it are directly related to the willingness of another to try to steal it. The parties do not bargain themselves, nor are they able to, since one of the parties intends to keep the asset secret. A regime that protects trade secrets, therefore, veers towards a 'liability-rule-based system' in which the transfer of an entitlement is protected and its value determined by the state. In the patent system, independent invention, reverse engineering and public disclosure do not detract from the proprietary right in the patent,[25] but in the case of trade secrets they do. Someone who sets out to uncover and apply another's trade secret may bring about social gain by increasing competition, but equally he may reduce the incentive to invent by inducing asymmetric market failure.[26] Trade secrecy protection serves to reduce the social costs that comprise expenditures for protection of trade secrets on one hand, and the cost of 'not investing resources designed to effect a transfer of wealth' on the other.[27] In balancing those costs associated with the upkeep of a protective regime and the costs associated with the absence of a market structure that facilitates bargaining and sale of information, trade secrecy protection is limited

22 According to S Diamond, 'The Public Interest and the Trademark System' (1980) 62 *J of the Patent Office Soc*, 529, the consumer is the 'unnamed third party in every action for trademark infringement, since the interest of the consumer lies in the ability of the trademark to facilitate choice on the basis that a trademark guarantees uniformity of quality at a consistent level'.

23 G Akerlof, 'The Market for "Lemons", Quality Uncertainty and the Market Mechanism' (1970) *Q J of Economics*, 488, demonstrated that this also applies to the quality function of the trademark. In his work he succinctly describes the market breakdown that occurs when the consumer can no longer trust the quality message a mark convers.

24 Besen and Raskind, note 17 above, 23–4.

25 Provided that the entitlement is enforced by the state.

26 D Friedman, W Landes and R Posner, 'Some Economics of Trade Secret Law' (1991) *J of Economic Perspectives*, 69–70.

27 W Landes and R Posner, *The Economic Structure of Tort Law* (Harvard University Press, 1987) Chapter 6.

to tortious interference with an entitlement that is not absolute in nature. An inventor relying on a trade secret cannot prevent the application of independent research and, if the resulting invention is patentable, he cannot even prevent a second market entrant from patenting the invention and forcing the original inventor out of the market. In the first instance, all market entrants face the same market barriers. This places reverse engineering, for example, in a peculiar position as it is not a method of independent research and may be considered theft. Friedman, Landes and Posner advance two reasons against liability for reverse engineering, namely the administrative cost associated with proof that independent research did not take place and the public disclosure argument.[28] The line between piracy and acceptable reverse engineering then lies in the presence of substantial investment and innovation. This means that reverse engineering does not create a monopolistic barrier to entry and the investment and innovation associated with it do not induce asymmetry in the market, since all market entrants face similar market barriers.

Seen from these economic perspectives of intellectual property, the grant of private rights serves to create a market for intangibles that would otherwise be common goods, and the enforcement of IPRs serves to safeguard not only the investment in innovation, but the prevention of market failure, by erecting the same barriers to market entry for all competitors. Furthermore, property in intangibles facilitates trade in them, with the transfer of the underlying technology as a result. Without an effective IP system, innovators will shy away from investment and technology transfer, especially when piracy rates are high and the enforcement of rights is weak. Therefore, it would seem that it would be wise for a developing country to invest in protection and enforcement of intellectual property. However, although the TRIPS Agreement provides the international framework for IP protection and enforcement, bilateral arrangements are increasingly relied on to secure enhanced IPRs and protection.

Part II Multilateralism, Bilateralism, and Economic Development

TRIPS implementation is a prerequisite for WTO members with pay-offs in respect of market access and FDI. In fact, TRIPS standards are now a permanent fixture in international trade and are integral to many bilateral trade and

[28] Note 26 above, 70.

investment agreements.[29] The US is the largest user of FTAs. After the 1985 US–Israel FTA, and the North American FTA of 1992, the US concluded FTAs with no less than 14 countries.[30] Since 2000, there have been more FTAs and some,[31] like the well-publicized US–Thai FTA, that are still being negotiated.[32] The number of BITs is close to 2,400 and these investment arrangements have been described by UNCTAD as 'the most important protection of international foreign investment'.[33]

In fact, although most countries that conclude BITs are developed, developing countries are catching up fast.[34] It is interesting to note that China has concluded 112 BITs, second only to Germany.[35] Intellectual property is usually part of an FTA or BIT and falls within the definition of 'investment'. This allows it to be covered not only by national and most favoured nation (MFN) treatment principles,[36] but also under investment protection provisions.[37]

At the 2005 WTO Hong Kong Ministerial Conference, the development issues related to TRIPS that dominated the agenda concerned finding flexibility in the implementation of TRIPS obligations, and balancing the monopoly of the IP rights holder with the interests of third parties and of society as a whole. Flexibility is, however, something that sits uneasily with the current trend in intellectual property policy. The trend has been one of strengthening IPRs, to stamp out serious issues of piracy, and of harmonization, to provide a 'one size fits all' level playing field of rights. Flexibility to curb the full exercise of the intellectual property monopoly, to accommodate the interests of users, competitors or developing countries, is not popular among industrialists. In fact, the focus

---

29 D Vivas-Eugui, 'Regional and Bilateral Agreements and a TRIPS-plus World: the Free Trade Area of the Americas (FTAA)' (2003) TRIPS Issues Papers No 1, QUNO/QIAP/ICTSD, Geneva.

30 FTAs have been concluded with Australia, Bahrain, Chile, Jordan, Oman, Morocco, Singapore, Peru and the six Central American parties to CAFTA (Costa Rica, Dominican Republic, El Salvador, Guatemala, Honduras and Nicaragua).

31 Korea, Panama, United Arab Emirates, Columbia and Ecuador, and the SACU countries (Botswana, Lesotho, Namibia, South Africa and Swaziland).

32 A Christie, S Waller, K Weatherall, 'Exporting the DMCA through Free Trade Agreements', in C Heath and A Kamperman Sanders (eds), *International Intellectual Property and Free Trade Agreements* (Hart Publishing, forthcoming).

33 UNCTAD, *International Investment Arrangements: Trends and Emerging Issues* (United Nations, 2006).

34 Ibid, 12.

35 Ibid, 13, listing the total for China up to 1 June 2005.

36 Agreement on Trade-Related Aspects of Intellectual Property Rights, April 15 1994, Marrakech Agreement Establishing the World Trade Organization, Annex 1C, Legal Instruments—Results of the Uruguay Round Vol. 31; 33 ILM 1197 (TRIPS Agreement), Arts 3 and 4.

37 See G Gagné and J-F Morin, 'The Evolving American Policy on Investment Protection: Evidence from Recent FTAs and the 2004 Model BIT', (May 2006) *Journal of International Economic Law* 9(2), 357–382.

of the US negotiation strategy is seen as favouring harmonization at all costs. This is especially true for patent law covering technological inventions, including those categorized as biotechnological or pharmaceutical inventions. This focus has led Maskus, a renowned development economist, to comment that:

> [w]hile enforcement initiatives have not been absent from trade policy, the United States has devoted far more effort to negotiating globally harmonized patent standards or, failing that, to markedly strengthening patent regulations in developing countries through trade agreements. Indeed, US trade policy places a strong priority on international patent harmonization at high levels of protection—a questionable ranking of priorities.[38]

Still, following a decision reached by member governments on 29 November 2005, least-developed WTO Member states have been given an extension until 1 July 2013 to provide protection for trademarks, copyright, patents and other intellectual property under the WTO's TRIPS Agreement. This extension can be explained as stemming from a continued challenge by a growing number of developing countries to the TRIPS 'one size fits all'[39] approach as the best way to ensure their and their nationals' needs. The United Nations Development Programme has gone as far as stating that the 'relevance of TRIPs is highly questionable for large parts of the developing world', and recommends that developing countries 'begin dialogues to replace TRIPs . . . with alternate intellectual property paradigms'.[40]

The mandate of the Development Agenda is to come up with a humane policy that takes into account the needs of developing nations.[41] The recognition that access to medicine is a human right was seen as the first step in formulating a humane policy. Yet the adoption by the UN Commission of Human Rights of a declaration on the right of access to medicine remains merely symbolic if the IPR system remains unclear on the appropriate balance of rights and interests. Rather than looking to other or higher legal principles like human rights to forge humane IPR policy, the IPR system must recognize the interests of individual rights holders, consumers, citizens and society at large, who all share a common interest in innovation and development of, and access to, industrial and intellectual creativity.[42]

---

38 K Maskus, 'Reforming US Patent Policy, Getting the Incentives Right' (2006) CSR No 19, Council on Foreign Relations, available at <http://www.cfr.org/publication/12087/>, 27.

39 Commission on Intellectual Property Rights, *Integrating Intellectual Property Rights and Development Policy* (CIPR, 2002).

40 UNDP, *Making Global Trade Work for People* (Earthscan Publications, 2003), 221–22.

41 A Koury Menescal, 'Changing WIPO's Ways? The 2004 Development Agenda in Historical Perspective' (2005) 8 *J Of World Intellectual Property*, 761.

42 C Geiger, 'Fundamental Rights, a Safeguard for the Coherence of Intellectual Property Law?' (2004) 35 *Intl R of IP & Comp L*, 268; RL Ostergard, 'Intellectual Property: A Universal Human Right?' (1999) 21 *Human Rights Q* 1, 156.

The recognition of the interests of both developed and developing nations is therefore part of a wider concern regarding the fundamental basis of the current IPR system. WIPO, as the UN's office for the development of IPR, should take a leading role in tailoring the IPR system to accommodate the needs of all stakeholders.

A Cooperation Agreement with the WTO in 1995 put WIPO in charge of providing technical assistance for TRIPS implementation to developing country members of the WTO. Providing assistance is, after all, one of the areas in which WIPO specializes. In fact according to Article 4 of the WTO–WIPO Cooperation Agreement:

> The International Bureau [WIPO] shall make available to developing country WTO Members which are not Member States of WIPO the same legal–technical assistance relating to the TRIPS Agreement as it makes available to Member States of WIPO which are developing countries. The WTO Secretariat shall make available to Member States of WIPO which are developing countries and are not WTO Members the same technical cooperation relating to the TRIPS Agreement as it makes available to developing country WTO Members.[43]

Under the agreement WIPO offers its expertise in the area of intellectual property law to WTO and non-WTO Member States so as to ensure a successful implementation of the TRIPS Agreement.

Part III Innovation and Intellectual Property

The level of innovation in a country is often measured against the number of patent applications and grants. According to WIPO:

> Patent statistics are increasingly recognized as useful indicators of inventive activity and of technology flows. Patents are a unique information resource because they contain very detailed, publicly available information about inventions which can be matched with other indicators to provide insight into the evolution of technology . . . [T]he use of the patent system remains highly concentrated with only five patent offices (United States of America, Japan, Republic of Korea, China and the European Patent Office) accounting for 75% of all patent applications and 74% of all patents granted.[44]

43 The WTO–WIPO agreement can be found at <http://www.wto.org/english/tratop_e/trips_e/wtowip_e.htm>.

44 WIPO Patent Report, 'Statistics on Worldwide Patent Activity' (2006), available at www.wipo.int/ipstats, 1.

Still, it is no longer self-evident that more patents equate to more innovation. In fact a recent report prepared for the Council on Foreign Relations, an influential and independent, non-partisan foreign policy membership organization and think tank on foreign policy and America's role in the world, called for a reform of the US patent system, noting a marked increase in the number of US patents, and stating:

> [t]his increase in patents, however, does not necessarily correspond to an increase in innovation. Available evidence does not support the view that enhanced patent protection necessarily stimulates more innovation. For example, surveys of technology officers reveal that, except in pharmaceuticals, biotechnology, and some forms of machinery, inventing firms do not view patents as significant reasons to invest in technology.[45]

A 2005 World Bank publication on intellectual property and development[46] shows that neither strong IPR, nor bilateral investment or free trade agreements (FTAs) automatically yield an increase in technology transfer and FDI.[47] Figures show that countries with weak protection of IPR, such as Brazil and China, have been more successful in attracting FDI than many developing countries that have made strong IPR central to their development strategy.[48] Brazil and China are high growth, large market economies with an increasingly adequate regulatory system involving taxes, investment regulations, production incentives, trade policies and a hint of competition rules.[49] Investors have also viewed favourably increased attention to policies for fighting corruption and lack of market transparency.[50] The strength of IPR protection is clearly not the only factor in investment decision making. Economic studies show that the relationship between IPR and FDI in developing countries is highly varied with respect to industry type, the stage of economic development factors (for example transparency, openness, stable financial institutions, sound economic governance, competition law, low corruption) and the natural and labour resources of the country in question. Although econometric evidence of positive effects of strong

---

45 Maskus, note 38 above, 15–16.

46 C Fink and K Maskus (eds), *Intellectual Property and Development—Lessons from Recent Economic Research* (World Bank/Oxford University Press, 2005).

47 C Correa, *Bilateral investment agreements: Agents of new global standards for the protection of intellectual property rights?* (GRAIN, 2004), 3, available at <http://www.grain.org/briefings/?id=187>.

48 K Maskus, 'The Role of Intellectual Property Rights in Encouraging Foreign Direct Investment and Technology Transfer', in Fink and Maskus, note 46 above, 54, where examples cited comprise Sub-Saharan Africa and Eastern Europe.

49 See M Williams, *Competition Policy and Law in China, Hong Kong and Taiwan* (Cambridge University Press, 2005).

50 See the statements of the 18th APEC Ministerial Meeting at <http://www.apec.org/apec/ministerial_statements/annual_ministerial/2006_18th_apec_ministerial.html>.

IPR on FDI and technology transfer is not conclusive,[51] strengthening IPR and providing effective enforcement is seen as a strong signal indicating that a country is willing to provide a more business-friendly environment that is capable of absorbing and safeguarding foreign investment and technology transfer interests.[52]

The ability to absorb knowledge and human capital drives the capacity to innovate. Past economic fiascos may even prove to be beneficial for developing countries in this respect. For example, when the dot-com bubble burst in 2001, investments, made during the 1990s, in high-speed networks spanning the globe were written off. Simultaneously thousands of IT workers that had been attracted from all over the world to work in the once-overheating Western economies were laid off. Moreover, a succinct example of capitalizing on opportunities of technology transfer can be found in India, where inexpensive access to the web and returning trained human capital helped to propel India into the position of outsourcing haven for Western industry, further spawning Bangalore Silicon Valley.[53] Sharing information and absorbing knowledge, rather than proprietizing intellectual effort, appears to have been key to economic development. The irony is that the dot-com's business model relies on bringing about network effects by giving products away to build market share. Profit would have to be realized later through brand awareness and additional services that are not free of charge. The dot-com survivors took the whole of the available market while others perished. Bangalore, on the other hand, was not really a survivor, but an heir to the dot-com legacy.[54] This example shows that the capacity to absorb technology and human capital, rather than the intellectual property system in and by itself, is the key to economic development. Therefore, in order for people to absorb science, technology and research, they need to be educated. Developing countries without a trained population will not be able to participate optimally in the global knowledge economy.

---

51 Maskus, 'The Role of IPRs', note 48 above, 63–66.

52 M Schiappacasse, 'Intellectual Property Rights in China: Technology Transfers and Economic Development' (2004) 2 *Buff Intell Prop LJ*, 164, who concludes that China's need to acquire growth-enhancing intellectual property through technology transfer should provide the incentive for strengthening IP protection.

53 See T Friedman, *The World is Flat* (2nd edn Farrar, Straus and Giroux, 2006), in which he describes how in a triple convergence the combination of the PC with the microprocessor, internet, and fiber optics enabled citizens to interact, collaborate, access information and innovate globally, giving rise to a global community. On the issue of India's transformation from socialism to global trade, see pp. 214–224 and 561: 'India only twenty years ago, before triple convergence, was known as a country of snake charmers, poor people, and Mother Teresa. Today its image has been recalibrated. Now it is also seen as a country of brainy people and computer wizards.'

54 See <http://www.bangaloreit.in/index.asp> for an overview of the Bangalore IT and biotechnology base and its impressive growth figures.

A report on access to knowledge by Consumers International's Asia Pacific Office points to the negative effects, brought about by heightened standards in copyright protection and enforcement in developing countries. Implementation of TRIPS Agreement obligations, in particular, appears to act as a barrier to accessing books, journals and teaching materials. In fact the price of books has increased upon implementation to the extent that many materials are no longer accessible. According to the report:

> [t]he Berne Convention (1886) . . . specified limitations and exceptions to the rights it conferred. These limitations and exceptions were further expanded in the Appendix (1971) due to representations made by developing countries . . . . The TRIPS Agreement (1995) altered the balance . . . and extended copyright protection in terms of scope and varied the limitations and exceptions to the rights provided to copyright owners. Developed countries have used their influence at the WIPO and through bilateral and regional trade agreements to further enhance copyright protection. The space available to developing countries to adopt policy options suited to their development needs [has] consequently in each instrument been reduced.[55]

This fact is even more perverse in view of the advice contained in a recent European Commission DG Internal Market study on copyright for the knowledge economy, wherein flexibility in limitations and exceptions is deemed essential for consumers and users of copyright works in dynamic information markets.[56] Now that developed economies have started to recognize that strengthening intellectual property, without providing for robust limitations and exceptions to these rights, may be too much of a good thing, it is of the utmost importance to make sure that developing trading partners are not encouraged or even forced to adopt a complex array of legal regimes that might widen the knowledge divide and decrease their ability to participate in a global knowledge economy which is rapidly absorbing more investment than physical assets do. Missing out on laying a base for a knowledge economy will inevitably mean losing the favour of the investor.

---

55 Consumers International, note 4 above, 39.

56 *The Recasting of Copyright & Related Rights for the Knowledge Economy* (IVIR, 2006), available at <http://ec.europa.eu/internal_market/copyright/docs/studies/etd2005imd195recast_report_2006.pdf>, p III: 'EC legislature should strive to establish a more flexible and forward looking regime of limitations on copyright and related rights. A non-exhaustive list of limitations would allow Member States to respond more quickly than the EC legislature to urgent situations that will arise in the dynamic information market.'

Conclusion

The flexibilities of the TRIPS Agreement can be used to allow WTO members to develop at their own pace. IPRs serve to create a market for intellectual and industrial creativity and serve as a conduit for technology transfer. Still, stronger and more substantive IPRs do not automatically lead to more investment or innovation. After all, it is the market that supports and rewards innovation. Market conditions in developing countries are often marred by corruption, lack of transparency, market access and human capital, and the inability to absorb technology and knowledge. Inclusion of developing countries in the world economy, however, does offer opportunities for development. This is supported by the economic progress in developing economies like India, China and Brazil. Effective enforcement and the establishment of minimum IPR standards form the conditions for including developing economies in the global marketplace. Multilateral and bilateral regimes harmonizing IPRs to the highest possible standard, however, appear to have an exclusionary effect, especially where capacity building necessary for the reception and embedding of technology in a developing economy is impaired. From an IPR development perspective, this means that capacity building for IPRs, with an emphasis on effective and transparent enforcement mechanisms, may be much more useful than efforts to harmonize and increase substantive rights according to a 'one size fits all' philosophy.

Part II

INTELLECTUAL PROPERTY, TRADE AND DEVELOPMENT: THE REGIONAL LINKAGES

5

INTELLECTUAL PROPERTY, ECONOMIC DEVELOPMENT, AND THE CHINA PUZZLE

Peter K Yu *

Introduction

Since the late 1980s, the Chinese economy has been growing at an enviable average annual rate of about ten per cent.[1] China's imports 'tripled from $225 billion in 2000 to $600 billion in 2005', and the country 'accounted for about 12 per cent of the growth of global trade', an impressive jump from only 4 per cent in 2000.[2]

1 CF Bergsten, B Gill, NR Lardy and D Mitchell (eds), *China: The Balance Sheet: What the World Needs to Know Now About the Emerging Superpower* (Public Affairs, 2006) 18. Some early research has placed China's annual growth rate at a more modest rate of seven to eight per cent: 'Symposium, China and the WTO: Progress, Perils, and Prospects' (2003) 17 *Colum J Asian L* 1, 3.

2 Bergsten, Gill, Lardy and Mitchell, note 1 above, 73.

Today, China has become one of the world's largest surplus countries, possessing one of the most sizeable foreign exchange reserves in the world.[3]

Accompanying this unprecedented economic development and growth was the maturation of the modern Chinese intellectual property system. Since the reopening of its market to foreign trade in the late 1970s, China introduced its first modern copyright, patent, and trademark laws.[4] A decade later, China revamped its intellectual property system in response to US pressure and did so again in preparation for its accession to the World Trade Organization (WTO).[5] At present, China is a proud member of many multilateral intellectual property agreements, including the Berne Convention, Geneva Convention, Paris Convention, the Patent Cooperation Treaty, and UPOV (International Union for the Protection of New Varieties of Plants).[6]

Notwithstanding these developments, the enforcement of intellectual property rights in China remains inadequate. Every year, US industries are estimated to have lost billions of dollars due to piracy and counterfeiting in the country. As the International Intellectual Property Alliance stated in its recent Special 301 Report, copyright piracy in China resulted in $2.2 billion of US trade losses in 2006 alone.[7] Of particular concern is the considerable quantity of the infringing products that have been exported to other foreign markets. To protect American industries, the United States has recently requested consultations with China over its failure to comply with the Agreement on Trade-Related Aspects of Intellectual Property Rights (TRIPS Agreement) concerning protection and enforcement of intellectual property rights.[8]

Although commentators often link intellectual property protection with economic development, China thus far has presented a puzzle to those who study this link. While some commentators consider China a paradigmatic case for showing that rapid economic development can take place despite limited

[3] Ibid, 4.

[4] PK Yu, 'From Pirates to Partners: Protecting Intellectual Property in China in the Twenty-First Century' (2000) 50 *Am U LR* 131, 136–141.

[5] Ibid, 141–151; PK Yu, 'From Pirates to Partners (Episode II): Protecting Intellectual Property in Post-WTO China' (2006) 55 *Am U LR* 901, 906–923.

[6] For a list of the international treaties to which China is a member, see C Sun, *China Intellectual Property for Foreign Business* (LexisNexis, 2004) 8.

[7] International Intellectual Property Alliance, *2007 Special 301: People's Republic of China—Amended* (2007) 96.

[8] For discussions of the United States's potential WTO complaint against China before the WTO Dispute Settlement Body concerning a lack of general enforcement of intellectual property rights, see Yu, 'From Pirates to Partners II', note 5 above, 923–946; PK Yu, 'Still Dissatisfied After All These Years: Intellectual Property, Post-WTO China, and the Avoidable Cycle of Futility' (2005) 34 *Ga J Int'l & Comp L* 143.

intellectual property protection, others have noted gradual improvements in the Chinese intellectual property system as the country became more economically developed.[9] In fact, history suggests that China is now simply following the economic development paths of Hong Kong, Japan, Singapore, South Korea, Taiwan—or even Germany and the United States.[10] It is only a matter of time before China is converted from a pirating nation to a country that respects intellectual property rights.

This chapter examines the relationship between intellectual property protection and economic development. It begins by exploring the conventional linkage between intellectual property protection and foreign direct investment (FDI).[11] Part I argues that, even though intellectual property protection can attract FDI in a country that has a strong imitative capacity and a sufficiently large market, foreign investors are likely to be attracted to China because of its low production costs and considerable market potential. Drawing on recent research that focuses on the 'push' explanation of FDI, this Part also shows that the country's inefficient economic system and preferential treatment of foreign investors have enticed local entrepreneurs to seek out FDI from firms in Greater China. Thus, instead of considering China the proverbial exception to the causal relationship between intellectual property protection and FDI, this Part contends that China illustrates rather well the ambiguity of that relationship and the complex interplay of the different location advantages that affect private investment decisions.

---

9 FM Abbott, 'Toward a New Era of Objective Assessment in the Field of TRIPS *and* Variable Geometry for the Preservation of Multilateralism' (2005) 8 *J Int'l Econ L* 77, 81; D Chow, 'The Role of Intellectual Property in Promoting International Trade and Foreign Direct Investment' in PK Yu (ed), *Intellectual Property and Information Wealth: Issues and Practices in the Digital Age* (Praeger, 2007) 4:187, 199.

10 As one commentator noted:

> From the start of the industrial revolution, every country that became economically great began by copying: the Germans copied the British; the Americans copied the British and the Germans, and the Japanese copied everybody. The thrust of the TRIPS Agreement is to ensure that this process of growth by copying and learning by doing will never happen again.

W Kingston, 'An Agenda for Radical Intellectual Property Reform' in KE Maskus and JH Reichman (eds), *International Public Goods and Transfer of Technology Under a Globalized Intellectual Property Regime* (Cambridge University Press, 2005) 653, 658. Similarly, Assafa Endeshaw noted that '[h]istorically, each of the advanced countries today was determined to industrialize first before . . . "opening up" to forces and interests that they might previously have dreaded and before calling for a stronger international IP system'. A Endeshaw, *Intellectual Property Policy for Non-industrial Countries* (Dartmouth, 1996) 120.

11 Keith Maskus, for example, defined FDI as 'the act of establishing or acquiring a foreign subsidiary over which the investing firm has substantial management control': KE Maskus, 'The Role of Intellectual Property Rights in Encouraging Foreign Direct Investment and Technology Transfer' (1998) 9 *Duke J Comp & Int'l L* 109, 119.

Part II examines why China expanded its intellectual property protection even though such expansion was unnecessary for attracting FDI. Tracing the growing protection to both external pressure and internal push, this Part underscores the intertwined relationship between intellectual property protection and economic development in China. While external pressure from the United States and the Chinese leaders' willingness to align intellectual property reforms with the national modernization goals provided the momentum needed for early intellectual property reforms, the development of local stakeholders who benefited from stronger protection, the determination to develop a knowledge-based economy, the economic and reputational gains of China's WTO accession, and the country's increasing shift towards an export-driven economy were primary drivers for later reforms. This Part argues that, even though stronger intellectual property protection was unnecessary for attracting FDI and, in fact, might have incurred significant social costs, such protection promoted economic development in certain parts of the country and resulted in the creation of local stakeholders who benefited from and lobbied for stronger protection.

Despite the growing benefits of stronger intellectual property protection to China, it remains intriguing to see *when* China will find it in its self-interest to offer stronger intellectual property protection. To provide a more accurate forecast of when China will reach this crossover point, and to better understand the socio-economic impact of the expansion of intellectual property protection in China, Part III highlights the country's regional and sectoral disparities, its inadequate development of an enabling environment for effective intellectual property protection, and its improvements in intellectual property protection at both the microscopic and qualitative levels. Taking account of these emerging developments is important, because a failure to do so not only would obscure the study of the relationship between intellectual property protection and economic development, but would also make it difficult for policy makers and rights holders to develop solutions to respond to the rampant piracy and counterfeiting problems in the country.

Part I Intellectual Property, FDI, and the China Exception

A. The Theory

Conventional wisdom holds that strong intellectual property protection is needed to attract foreign investment in less developed countries, because firms are reluctant to invest in a foreign country unless they are assured of protection of their intellectual assets and financial investment. However, recent empirical research questions this conventional wisdom. As Carsten Fink, Keith Maskus, Carlos Primo Braga, and other economists have shown, intellectual property protection is more likely to attract FDI only when two additional conditions are met.[12] First, the country needs to have a strong capacity to imitate foreign products and technologies. If local competitors are unable to copy these products and technologies, the business interests of foreign firms are unlikely to be threatened, and intellectual property protection will be unnecessary. Second, the country needs to have a sufficiently large market to enable foreign firms to capture economies of scale or scope.[13] In a country that lacks such a market, foreign firms are unlikely to find it advantageous to move their productions abroad.

Even if these two conditions are met, policy makers still have to question what form of protection needs to be strengthened in order to promote economic development. Paul Heald and Keith Maskus each suggested that firms that seek to establish manufacturing or research-and-development plants are unlikely to require more protection than what is needed to ensure the non-disclosure of technologies brought in by foreign firms.[14] While these firms need trade secrets and contractual protection, firms seeking to establish markets for finished products need copyright, patent, and trademark protection instead. Thus, it is important to separate investment decisions that seek to relocate manufacturing or research-and-development facilities from those that seek to market finished products.

While strong intellectual property protection is a main concern for marketing decisions, a decision to relocate manufacturing facilities is likely to be determined by such 'location advantages' as 'market size and growth, local demand patterns, transport costs and distance from markets, low wage costs in relation to labour productivity, abundant natural resources, and trade protection that could encourage "tariff-jumping" investments'.[15] Likewise, a decision to relocate research-and-development facilities is likely to be affected by 'the level of education and training of the local workforce, the condition of its financial sector, the health of its legal system, and the transparency of governmental procedures'.[16]

[12] See, for example, KE Maskus, *Intellectual Property Rights in the Global Economy* (Institute for International Economics, 2000); Maskus, 'The Role of IP Rights', note 11 above, 130–131; CA Primo Braga and C Fink, 'The Relationship Between Intellectual Property Rights and Foreign Direct Investment' (1998) 9 *Duke J Comp & Int'l L* 163, 164.

[13] PJ Heald, 'Mowing the Playing Field: Addressing Information Distortion and Asymmetry in the TRIPS Game' (2003) 88 *Minn LR* 249, 266.

[14] Ibid, 258–260; Maskus, 'The Role of IP Rights', note 11 above, 119–128.

[15] Maskus, 'The Role of IP Rights', note 11 above, 123.

[16] Heald, note 13 above, 259.

To make things more complicated, firms can resort to many different investment strategies, and FDI is only one of them. Using John Dunning's ownership–location–internalization framework,[17] economists have shown that, even in the presence of favourable location advantages, firms still need to decide whether they want to serve foreign markets through FDI, export finished products to the less developed market, conduct arm's-length technology licensing, set up joint ventures with local manufacturers or distributors, or ignore the foreign market entirely.[18] As Carlos Primo Braga and Carsten Fink explained:

> In order for firms to invest abroad, two further conditions must be met. First, the foreign country must offer location advantages that make it more profitable to locate business abroad. Location advantages are usually associated with factors such as high transportation costs and tariffs, low input prices, access to distribution networks, and local regulatory environments. Second, it must be more profitable for firms to internalize production rather than to sell or license their intellectual assets to independent local firms in the foreign country. Internalization advantages take the form of avoiding transaction costs with potential licensees, controlling inputs, and protecting quality.[19]

While the strength or weakness of intellectual property protection will 'influence a firm's decision to internalize or externalize its intellectual assets', it is only one of the many location advantages that influence such a decision.[20] As Keith Maskus put it in the FDI context, 'IPRs are an important component of the general regulatory system, including taxation, investment regulations, production incentives, trade policies, and competition rules. The joint implementation of an overall pro-competitive business environment matters most for FDI.'[21]

Paradoxically, the strengthening of intellectual property protection may encourage firms to conduct more arm's-length technology licensing, which in turn will result in a reduction of FDI. As Primo Braga and Fink explained, intellectual property protection can affect foreign investment in two negative ways: 'First, stronger IPR protection provides title holders with increased market power and could, at least theoretically, cause firms to actually divest and reduce their service to foreign countries. Second, higher levels of protection may cause [transnational corporations] to switch their preferred mode of delivery from foreign production to licensing.'[22] Whether a firm will choose to license will depend on transaction costs—in particular, the robustness of the local regulatory regimes, the existence

[17] JH Dunning, *International Production and the Multinational Enterprise* (George Allen & Unwin, 1981) 110–112.

[18] Maskus, 'The Role of IP Rights', note 11 above, 130.

[19] Primo Braga and Fink, note 12 above, 170.

[20] Ibid, 171.

[21] Maskus, 'The Role of IP Rights', note 11 above, 129.

[22] Primo Braga and Fink, note 12 above, 172.

of a contracting culture and experience, and the availability of information needed to evaluate the transactions. In places where there is limited intellectual property protection, the firm's need to internalize foreign production to maintain direct control over their proprietary assets may also affect licensing decisions.[23] If the firm chooses to externalize its production through, say, licensing, stronger intellectual property protection arguably would have the 'cancel out' effect of reducing FDI.

Finally, most firms do not need to make the difficult decision between relocating their entire facilities and not relocating at all. They can simply decide which type of operations they want to relocate abroad and whether they want to combine FDI with other investment strategies, such as export, licensing, or establishment of joint ventures. Even if they choose to relocate abroad, they can still decide 'where to invest and in what kind of facilities, whether to purchase existing operations or construct new plants (so-called "greenfield investments"), which production techniques to pursue, and how large an equity position to take with potential local partners'.[24]

Economists generally distinguish between 'horizontal FDI' and 'vertical FDI'. While the former refers to the investment made when 'firms establish plants abroad to produce the same or similar goods for local or regional markets', the latter 'occurs if plants in different countries produce outputs that serve as inputs in other plants'.[25] Although intellectual property protection affects both horizontal and vertical FDI, the amount and composition of FDI vary according to the impact of such protection on the particular production process.

For example, Edwin Mansfield observed in his influential study for the World Bank that, '[w]hile US firms may be quite willing to invest considerable amounts in sales and distribution outlets and in rudimentary production and assembly facilities in countries with weak protection, their investments in R and D facilities or in facilities to manufacture components or complete products may be more likely to go to countries with stronger protection systems'.[26] Because '[v]ertical FDI is more prevalent among [multinational enterprises] that invest in developing (low-wage) economies, while horizontal FDI tends to characterize

[23] Ibid, citing MJ Ferrantino, 'The Effect of Intellectual Property Rights on International Trade and Investment' (1993) 129 *Rev World Econ* 300, 303.

[24] Maskus, 'The Role of IP Rights', note 11 above, 113.

[25] Primo Braga and Fink, note 12 above, 172–173. Some commentators have added a third type of FDI, distribution FDI, referring to 'investment in local sales offices, distribution networks, and services facilities': KC Kennedy, 'A WTO Agreement on Investment: A Solution in Search of a Problem?' (2003) 24 *U Pa J Int'l Econ L* 77, 79 n 5.

[26] E Mansfield, *Intellectual Property Protection, Foreign Direct Investment and Technology Transfer* (World Bank, 1994) 17.

the investment decisions of [multinational enterprises] operating across borders within the industrialized, developed nations', the amount and proportion of each type of investment may fluctuate with the country's economic development.[27] As the country becomes more developed economically, the amount of horizontal FDI may increase while that of vertical FDI may decrease.

In sum, countries that lack a strong imitative capacity and a sufficiently large market are unlikely to benefit from stronger intellectual property protection. However, even if countries meet these two prerequisites, stronger intellectual property protection may be unnecessary for attracting FDI. It depends on the complex interactions between the different location advantages, especially when some of these advantages are significant enough to compensate for the lack or ineffectiveness of strong intellectual property protection. Thus, the relationship between the strength of intellectual property protection and FDI remains theoretically ambiguous.

B. The Practice

Commentators often consider China as an exception to the causal relationship between intellectual property protection and economic development. However, China is not the exception they suggested. Rather, it illustrates the ambiguous relationship between intellectual property protection and economic development and the complex interplay of the different location advantages that can affect private investment decisions.

To begin with, China has met the two prerequisites needed for a country to benefit from stronger intellectual property protection. Since the reopening of its market to foreign trade in the late 1970s, China has developed a strong imitative capacity. In fact, such capacity explains China's ability to produce a large amount of pirated and counterfeit products. Moreover, China has seen tremendous economic growth in the past two decades. Today, China boasts a healthy market of hundreds of millions of customers, even though it has yet to offer one billion customers as some would hope.

Nevertheless, intellectual property protection in the country remains inadequate and ineffective, and it is unlikely that foreign firms were attracted to China because of its intellectual property system. Instead, firms often relocate to China to take advantage of the lower production costs and the emerging market. To many of these firms, the lower costs and the promise of an enormous

[27] Maskus, 'The Role of IP Rights', note 11 above, 120.

market would easily make up for the losses incurred by ineffective intellectual property protection.[28] While these firms certainly welcome greater intellectual property reforms, they do not find stronger protection a prerequisite for obtaining profits in the first place. In fact, many major Western firms—like Coca-Cola, Kodak, Motorola, Procter & Gamble, and Siemens—have already been enjoying substantial profits for years despite serious piracy and counterfeiting problems.[29] Thus, instead of seeing strong intellectual property protection as the necessary precursor to profitability, they see it more as a means to 'increas[e their] already acceptable profit ratios'.[30]

Other firms, especially those that are new to China or are unfamiliar with the local conditions, have been less successful. Nevertheless, they consider the emerging Chinese market too large to ignore. While some consider the losses unavoidable as they build up their market share and improve their position in this emerging market, others write off their piracy-related losses as promotional expenses. The latter approach easily reminds one of the remark Microsoft's founder Bill Gates made a few years ago. When questioned about the widespread piracy of Microsoft software in China, Gates observed: 'Although about three million computers get sold every year in China, people don't pay for the software. Someday they will, though. And as long as they're going to steal it, we want them to steal ours. They'll get sort of addicted, and then we'll somehow figure out how to collect sometime in the next decade.'[31]

Recent research, however, has revealed a more complicated picture concerning FDI in China. The amount of FDI in a country does not depend only on 'pull' factors, but also on 'push' factors, such as those that have made the country unappealing for local production. As Huang Yasheng pointed out in his provocative book, *Selling China*, the inefficiencies of the Chinese economic system and the country's preferential treatment of foreign investors have led to a large amount of FDI in the country.[32] Because commentators tend to focus on the attractions of the Chinese market, they often ignore how '[t]he poor profitability of the state sector, the credit constraints on the part of Chinese private firms,

[28] P Tackaberry, 'Intellectual Property Risks in China: Their Effect on Foreign Investment and Technology Transfer' *J Asian Bus* (Fall 1998) 1, 26 quoted in Y Li, 'The Wolf Has Come: Are China's Intellectual Property Industries Prepared for the WTO?' (2002) 20 *UCLA Pac Basin LJ* 77, 79 n 9.

[29] Sun, note 6 above, 4–5.

[30] Ibid, 5.

[31] B Schlender, W Buffett and B Gates, 'The Bill & Warren Show' *Fortune* (20 July 1998) 48.

[32] Y Huang, *Selling China: Foreign Direct Investment During the Reform Era* (Cambridge University Press, 2005).

the insecurity of private property rights, and the weaknesses of domestic firms have all driven up China's demand for FDI'.[33]

To Professor Huang, the considerable amount of FDI in China may reflect the weakness, rather than the strength, of the Chinese market. As he explained: 'China's low labour—and land—costs do not automatically motivate a Hong Kong firm to *invest* in China; instead, they motivate a Hong Kong firm (or any other firm) *to do more business* with China, as opposed to doing more business with, say, Mexico. China's low labour costs tell us something about the location of a labour-intensive production facility, but not about who owns it.'[34] Professor Huang therefore credited the superior regulatory and legal treatments of foreign-invested enterprises as an important motivation for private entrepreneurs in China to seek out FDI from its neighbours.[35] His thesis also illuminates why a substantial amount of investment was derived from businesses in Hong Kong and Taiwan as well as those owned by the Chinese diaspora.[36] After all, if local firms have to reach out for FDI, they are more likely to turn to firms in the so-called Greater China.

In sum, the drastically lower production costs, the country's enormous market, its inefficient economic system, and the preferential treatment of foreign investors have all helped to attract FDI in China. Because these factors more than compensate for the country's weak intellectual property protection, FDI in China increased substantially despite limited intellectual property protection in the country. China therefore is not an exception to the causal relationship between intellectual property protection and FDI, but an ideal case study to illustrate the ambiguity of this relationship and the complex interactions between the many location advantages that affect private investment decisions. After all, as Keith Maskus pointed out, if stronger intellectual property protection always led to more FDI, 'recent FDI flows to developing economies would have gone largely to sub-Saharan Africa and Eastern Europe . . . [rather than] China, Brazil, and other high-growth, large-market developing economies with weak IPRs'.[37]

33 Ibid, 81.
34 Ibid, 57.
35 Ibid, 90.
36 See, for example, MJ Enright, EE Scott and K Chang, *Regional Powerhouse: The Greater Pearl River Delta and the Rise of China* (John Wiley & Sons, 2005); WV Kemenade, *China, Hong Kong, Taiwan, Inc.: The Dynamics of a New Empire* (Vintage, 1998).
37 Maskus, 'The Role of IP Rights', note 11 above, 129.

Part II Intellectual Property and Economic Development

'Since 1983, FDI [in China] has grown from less than $1 billion a year to more than $60 billion, and it is projected to soon reach $100 billion annually.'[38] Today, China is one of the world's largest recipients of FDI with capital inflows of about $50 billion, behind the United States and the United Kingdom.[39] Such an influx of FDI not only provides China with the foreign capital needed for economic modernization, but also results in technology transfer, job creation, development of human capital, and generation of tax revenues.[40] Although economists have pleaded for caution in considering the benefits of FDI to recipient countries, there is no denial that the influx of foreign capital has contributed to China's recent rise to its status as an emerging economic superpower.[41]

As Part I of this chapter points out, strong intellectual property protection is not always needed for attracting FDI. In fact, stronger protection may reduce investment by encouraging investors to conduct arm's-length transactions by licensing their products. Such protection would also reduce the net gains in economic welfare from increased FDI by incurring significant costs, such as administrative and enforcement costs, adjustment costs due to labour displacement, social costs associated with monopoly pricing, higher imitation and innovation costs, and potential costs resulting from the abuse of intellectual property rights.[42] Stronger intellectual property protection therefore would drain the country's scarce governmental resources, render cutting-edge foreign technologies inaccessible, and stifle the development of local industries.[43] Given the significant costs of strengthening intellectual property protection, Chinese policy makers and commentators understandably were worried that

---

38 P Navarro, *The Coming China Wars: Where They Will Be Fought and How They Can Be Won* (Financial Times Press, 2007) 13.

39 Chow, note 9 above, 198.

40 RM Sherwood, *Intellectual Property and Economic Development* (Westview Press, 1990) 191–199.

41 As Keith Maskus noted, '[t]he idea that foreign direct investment and the acquisition of new technologies through FDI and licensing are beneficial for the recipient country seems to be increasingly taken for granted. While a strong presumption in this direction exists, it is not a necessary outcome in all situations': Maskus, 'The Role of IP Rights', note 11 above, 146.

42 KE Maskus, SM Dougherty and A Mertha, 'Intellectual Property Rights and Economic Development in China' in C Fink and KE Maskus (eds), *Intellectual Property and Development: Lessons from Recent Economic Research* (World Bank and Oxford University Press, 2005) 295, 302–306.

43 TK Giunta and LH Shang, 'Ownership of Information in a Global Economy' (1993) 27 *Geo Wash J Int'l L & Econ* 327, 331; Yu, 'From Pirates to Partners I', note 4 above, 189–190.

stronger protection would slow down the country's economic progress and therefore would make it difficult for the country to catch up with its Western developed neighbours.

Indeed, as Rod Falvey, Neil Foster, and David Greenaway have shown recently, although intellectual property protection promotes innovation in high-income countries and technology flows in low-income ones, middle-income countries may suffer from offsetting losses due to the reduced scope of imitation.[44] Likewise, as the UK-based Commission on Intellectual Property Rights cautioned, 'rapid [economic] growth is more often associated with weaker IP protection. In technologically advanced developing countries, there is some evidence that IP protection becomes important at a stage of development, but that stage is not until a country is well into the category of upper middle income developing countries.'[45]

If the costs of strong intellectual property protection are not enough, the costs of introducing an inappropriate intellectual property system can be quite high for less developed countries. Although overprotection of intellectual property rights harms both developed and less developed countries, it usually harms less developed countries more than it would harm their developed counterparts. Many less developed countries lack the economic strengths and established correction mechanisms to overcome problems created by an unbalanced system.[46] As the Commission noted, 'if anything, the costs of getting the IP system "wrong" in a developing country are likely to be far higher than in developed countries. Most developed countries have sophisticated systems of competition regulation to ensure that abuses of any monopoly rights cannot unduly affect the public interest.'[47] Even if stronger intellectual property protection is beneficial to less developed countries in the long run, they may lack the needed wealth, infrastructure, and technological base to take advantage of the opportunities created by the system in the short run.

In sum, all of these potential negative impacts of stronger intellectual property protection lead one to wonder why China introduced reforms to offer stronger intellectual property protection at all. After all, both theories and actual practice

---

44 R Falvey, N Foster, and D Greenaway, 'Intellectual Property Rights and Economic Growth' (2006) 10 *Rev Dev Econ* 700.

45 Commission on Intellectual Property Rights, *Integrating Intellectual Property Rights and Development Policy: Report of the Commission on Intellectual Property Rights* (2003) 22, available at <http://www.iprcommission.org/papers/pdfs/final_report/CIPRfullfinal.pdf>.

46 PK Yu, 'The International Enclosure Movement' (2007) 82 *Ind LJ* 827, 890; PK Yu, 'TRIPS and Its Discontents' (2006) 10 *Marq Intell Prop LR* 369, 382–383.

47 Commission on Intellectual Property Rights, note 45 above, 4.

have suggested that China would have limited net economic benefits from stronger intellectual property protection during the first decade of the reopening of the Chinese market to foreign trade. Acknowledging the Chinese leaders' lack of focus on these net benefits in the early development of the modern Chinese intellectual property system, this Part traces the intellectual property reforms to both external pressure and internal push. While external pressure from the United States and the Chinese leaders' alignment of intellectual property reforms with the national modernization goals provided the momentum needed for early intellectual property reforms, the development of local stakeholders who benefited from stronger protection, the determination to develop a knowledge-based economy, the economic and reputational gains of China's WTO accession, and the country's increasing shift toward an export-driven economy were primary drivers for later reforms.

A. External Pressure

Shortly after China reopened its market to foreign trade in the late 1970s, China and the United States signed the Agreement on Trade Relations Between the United States of America and the People's Republic of China, which, among other things, called for reciprocal protection of copyrights, patents, and trademarks owned by the nationals of the other party.[48] Pursuant to this agreement, China became a member of the World Intellectual Property Organization (WIPO). It also promulgated a new trademark law in 1982 and a new patent law in 1984 and joined the Paris Convention in 1985. Notwithstanding these new developments, China afforded authors and inventors very limited protection, due to the leaders' concern about establishing new private property interests in a socialist economic system, their belief that strong intellectual property protection is inappropriate for a less developed country like China, and their inexperience with Western forms of intellectual property protection.[49] While the new laws granted individuals rights in their marks and inventions, these statutes included many limits that rendered the original grants largely insignificant.

Concerned about the lack of intellectual property protection in China, copyright in particular, US businesses lobbied their government heavily for

48 Agreement on Trade Relations Between the United States of America and the People's Republic of China (PRC–US, 7 July 1979; 31 UST 4652).

49 WP Alford, *To Steal a Book Is an Elegant Offense: Intellectual Property Law in Chinese Civilization* (Stanford University Press, 1995) 66, 70; AC Mertha, *The Politics of Piracy: Intellectual Property in Contemporary China* (Cornell University Press, 2005) 84–86.

stronger pressure on China. In the late 1980s and early 1990s, the US government repeatedly threatened China with a series of economic sanctions, trade wars, non-renewal of most-favoured-nation status, and opposition to China's entry into the WTO.[50] Such threats eventually led to the issuance or signing of two memoranda of understanding in 1989 and 1992,[51] an 'agreement' regarding intellectual property rights in 1995 which appeared in the form of an 'exchange of letters' with an attached action plan,[52] and an 'accord' reiterating China's commitment to strengthening intellectual property protection in 1996.[53]

Although the seldom-mentioned 1989 memorandum of understanding reassured the United States that China would strengthen its protection for computer software, the 1992 memorandum was the 'first full bilateral IPR agreement' between China and the United States.[54] In retrospect, the 1992 memorandum was effective in revamping China's intellectual property system. Pursuant to that document, China acceded to the Berne Convention and ratified the Geneva Convention. China also amended its 1990 Copyright Law, issued new implementing regulations, and adopted a new unfair competition law that provided trade secret protection.

Likewise, the 1995 Agreement was effective in helping China create an institutional infrastructure conducive to protecting and enforcing rights created under this new intellectual property regime. The Agreement introduced the State Council Working Conference on Intellectual Property Rights, which was later replaced by the State Intellectual Property Office, as well as the Enforcement Task Forces.[55] To protect CDs, laser discs, and CD–ROMs, the agreement established a unique copyright verification system, proposing to punish by administrative and judicial means any manufacturer of audiovisual products who failed to comply with the identifier requirement. The agreement also called for title registration with the National Copyright Administration and local copyright authorities

50 Yu, 'From Pirates to Partners I', note 4 above, 140–151.

51 Memorandum of Understanding Between the People's Republic of China and the United States (PRC–US, 19 May 1989) in 'PRC Agrees to Push for Copyright Law That Will Protect Computer Software' *World Intell Prop Rep* (July 1989) 3(7):151; Memorandum of Understanding Between the People's Republic of China and the United States on the Protection of Intellectual Property (PRC–US, 17 January 1992; 34 ILM 677 (1995)).

52 Agreement Regarding Intellectual Property Rights (PRC–US, 26 February 1995; 34 ILM 881 (1995)).

53 China Implementation of the 1995 Intellectual Property Rights Agreement (PRC–US, 17 June 1996), available at <http://tcc.export.gov/Trade_Agreements/All_Trade_Agreements/exp_005361.asp>.

54 JA Massey, 'The Emperor Is Far Away: China's Enforcement of Intellectual Property Rights Protection, 1986–2006' (2006) 7 *Chi J Int'l L* 231, 235.

55 Yu, 'From Pirates to Partners I', note 4 above, 152.

of foreign audiovisual products and computer software in CD–ROM format. In addition, the agreement required customs offices to intensify border protection for all imports and exports of CDs, laser discs, CD–ROMs, and trademarked goods. The agreement further stipulated that relevant authorities would conduct training and education on intellectual property protection throughout China. Finally, the agreement provided that the Working Conference would develop a transparent legal system while compiling and publishing guidelines regarding application and protection in various areas of intellectual property law.

Notwithstanding these two agreements, piracy remained rampant in China in the mid-1990s, and the United States was estimated to have lost $2 billion of revenues annually due to copyright piracy.[56] To make things worse, the ineffectiveness of the coercive tactics used by the United States Trade Representative (USTR) has become apparent to not just Chinese negotiators and seasoned commentators, but also the US industries and the American public. Although the two countries reached another 'accord' in 1996, that document clearly revealed the limitation of the coercive approach. The document included neither significant new terms nor terms that improved market access of American products; instead, it merely reaffirmed China's commitment to protect intellectual property rights made under the intellectual property agreement signed the year before.[57]

As industry support decreased, the Clinton administration abandoned its strong-arm tactics shortly after the 1996 negotiations.[58] Although the United States continued to exert pressure on China during the negotiation of China's accession to the WTO, and undertook frequent consultations with Chinese officials, the United States has yet to revive its coercive approach—partly because of the approach's limitations and partly because of its impracticality after China's WTO membership. Under the WTO, countries are prohibited from taking retaliatory measures before they have exhausted all of the actions permissible under the rules.[59] Except in areas that are outside the scope of the TRIPS Agreement, China's WTO membership has greatly constrained the United States's ability to exert external pressure on China in the intellectual property area. To make up for the lack of external pressure, US businesses now exert pressure from within the

56 S Faison, 'China Turns Blind Eye to Pirated Disks' *NY Times* (28 March 1998) D1.

57 PK Yu, 'Piracy, Prejudice, and Perspectives: An Attempt to Use Shakespeare to Reconfigure the US–China Intellectual Property Debate' (2001) 19 *BU Int'l LJ* 1, 14.

58 PK Yu, 'The Copyright Divide' (2003) 25 *Cardozo LR* 331, 365.

59 Panel Report, United States—Sections 301–310 of the Trade Act of 1974 (WT/DS152/R, 22 December 1999).

country—through persuasion, business pressure, and alliances with local stakeholders and authorities.

In February 2005, US policy makers and trade groups again urged the administration to file a formal complaint against China with the WTO Dispute Settlement Body concerning inadequate intellectual property protection.[60] A few months later, the United States, in conjunction with Japan and Switzerland, invoked article 63(3) of the TRIPS Agreement to formally request 'clarifications regarding specific cases of IPR enforcement that China has identified for the years 2001 through 2004, and other relevant cases'.[61] In April 2007, the United States finally requested consultations with China concerning its failure to protect and enforce intellectual property rights in pursuance to the TRIPS Agreement. As of this writing, the United States, however, has yet to request the establishment of a WTO dispute settlement panel. If the United States did so, and if China were found to have violated the TRIPS Agreement, external pressure again might play an important role in unleashing and accelerating intellectual property reforms in China.

B. Internal Push

Alignment with the National Modernization Goals

While researchers have explored extensively the relationship between intellectual property protection and economic development, they rarely examine the rhetorical effects of the claim that stronger intellectual property protection will promote economic development. The lack of such an examination is understandable considering the difficulty in quantifying and assessing rhetorical effects. Nevertheless, rhetoric is needed to persuade the populace to accept a new government policy, and may also provide the direction and psychological incentives needed for promoting economic development.

To some extent, the rhetorical significance of the claim that stronger intellectual property protection will promote economic development is similar to the significance of the claim that intellectual property is property. Despite the uneasy analogy of intellectual property to real property, intellectual property rights holders have widely used the rhetoric of private property to push for

[60] Yu, 'From Pirates to Partners II', note 5 above, 923.

[61] Letter from Peter F. Allgeier, United States Trade Representative, to HE Mr Sun Zhenyu, Ambassador, Permanent Mission of the People's Republic of China to the World Trade Organization (25 October 2005), available at <http://www.ustr.gov/assets/Document_Library/Reports_Publications/2005/asset_upload_file115_8232.pdf>.

stronger protection.[62] Meanwhile, foreign rights holders and governments have also used the economic development rationale to entice foreign leaders and policy makers to ratchet up intellectual property protection and, more specifically, to establish the TRIPS Agreement within the WTO. As Daniel Gervais recounted, developed countries and the lobbies that pushed for stronger intellectual property protection believed that 'TRIPS was a difficult but essential measure to jump-start global economic development', while less developed countries 'were told to overlook the distasteful aspects of introducing or increasing intellectual property protection and enforcement in exchange for longer-term economic health'.[63] Similarly, Edmund Kitch argued that less developed countries agreed to stronger intellectual property protection during the TRIPS negotiations because they found such protection in their self-interests, although the negotiation records and the reactions of less developed countries offered very limited support for Professor Kitch's account.[64]

While the rhetorical linkage of intellectual property to economic development is important to induce less developed countries to offer stronger protection, it is particularly important to a country like China, which has placed heavy emphasis on symbols and political movements and was emerging from autarky and diplomatic isolation. Since the reopening of the Chinese market to foreign trade in the late 1970s, Deng Xiaoping and other reformist leaders advocated a pragmatic 'economics in command' approach to replace Mao Zedong's 'politics in command'. Seeing economic wealth as the foundation of China's power, the reformist leadership believed 'whether China could have a rightful place in the world of nations depended on China's domestic economic development'.[65] These leaders therefore vigorously pushed for the Four Modernizations to develop China's world-class strengths in agriculture, industry, science and

62 For discussions or critiques of the use of the private property rhetoric to expand intellectual property protection, see TW Bell, 'Authors' Welfare: Copyright as a Statutory Mechanism for Redistributing Rights' (2003) 69 *Brook LR* 229, 273–277; NW Netanel, 'Impose a Noncommercial Use Levy to Allow Free Peer-to-Peer File Sharing' (2003) 17 *Harv JL & Tech* 1, 22; RM Stallman, 'Did You Say "Intellectual Property"? It's a Seductive Mirage' (12 February 2005), <http://www.fsf.org/licensing/essays/not-ipr.xhtml>; SE Sterk, 'Intellectualizing Property: The Tenuous Connections Between Land and Copyright' (2005) 83 *Wash U LQ* 417, 420.

63 DJ Gervais, 'The TRIPS Agreement and the Doha Round: History and Impact on Economic Development' in Yu, *Intellectual Property and Information Wealth*, note 9 above, 4:23, 43.

64 EW Kitch, 'The Patent Policy of Developing Countries' (1994) 13 *UCLA Pac Basin LJ* 166; Maskus, 'The Role of IP Rights', note 11 above, 138. For my earlier discussion of the self-interest narrative, see Yu, 'TRIPS and its Discontents', note 46 above, 376–379.

65 Y Zheng, *Discovering Chinese Nationalism in China: Modernization, Identity, and International Relations* (Cambridge University Press, 1999) 17.

technology, and national defence.[66] They also established Special Economic Zones to transform socio-economic conditions in coastal areas and renewed diplomatic and commercial ties with the United States, Japan, and other Western developed countries.[67] The 1979 US–China trade agreement was a product of this urgent push for greater internationalization.

While economic development was easily justified by the severe need for reforms following the Cultural Revolution, the death of Mao Zedong, and the subsequent arrest of the infamous Gang of Four, the justification for intellectual property reforms remained elusive. Indeed, when China reopened its market to foreign trade in the late 1970s, both the Chinese leaders and the populace considered intellectual property an alien concept transplanted from Western soil. As William Alford pointed out in his seminal work, *To Steal a Book Is an Elegant Offense*, the notion of intellectual property protection did not take root in China despite earlier attempts to transplant the concept onto the country through bilateral commercial treaties at the turn of the twentieth century and intellectual property reforms during the Republican era.[68] Even if those reforms introduced the concept to the Chinese populace, the numerous class struggles, mass movements, and the Cultural Revolution that rejected ownership of private property virtually eliminated from public consciousness the concept of intellectual property.[69]

Thus, when this concept was reintroduced in the 1980s, the justification for such a concept was badly needed. In his well-cited chapter concerning justifications for intellectual property protection, William Fisher identified four possible justifications—utility, labour, personality, and social planning.[70] For a society that was making a transition from a command economy, rather than today's socialist market economy, the first and second justifications were easily deemed unsuitable. Indeed, early Chinese intellectual property laws were filled with compromises that resulted in what commentators called 'socialist legality with Chinese characteristics'.[71] While the Chinese leadership was anxious to create a stimulus for inventions and to rehabilitate scientists, inventors, and

---

66 For a comprehensive overview of the Four Modernizations, see ICY Hsü, *The Rise of Modern China* (6th edn, Oxford University Press, 2000) 803–814.

67 For a discussion of the Open Door Policy adopted by the Chinese Communist Party in December 1978, see ibid, 858–869.

68 Alford, note 49 above, 36–55.

69 Yu, 'Piracy, Prejudice, and Perspectives', note 57 above, 21–22.

70 W Fisher, 'Theories of Intellectual Property' in SR Munzer (ed), *New Essays in the Legal and Political Theory of Property* (Cambridge University Press, 2001) 168, 169–173.

71 Alford, note 49 above, 70.

academics, to make up for the time lost to the Cultural Revolution,[72] the leaders remained gravely concerned about the impact of new intellectual property rights on the country's socialist economic system.

The third justification, which was based on personality theories, was attractive to the Chinese, because it sat well with Communist ideology and the Soviet notion of non-property-based protection of authorship. Recent research by Mira Sundara Rajan, for example, has shown that the Russian Copyright Act of 1928 granted limited recognition to the authors' property interests by 'plac[ing] them within the broader context of a non-property theory of authorship'.[73] As a 1938 commentary on the Russian Law noted, the Soviet author's right 'has the objective of protecting to the maximum the personal *and property* interests of the author, coupled with the assurance of the widest distribution of the product of literature, science and the arts among the broad masses of the toilers'.[74] Nevertheless, the personality justification—in particular, its emphasis on moral rights—was inconsistent with foreign demands for stronger intellectual property protection, which reflected the interests of and the more utilitarian approach embraced by Western rights holders.

The most suitable justification was therefore what Professor Fisher described as 'social planning', which ranges from the development of the economy to the nurturing of an attractive intellectual culture.[75] As he explained, '[t]his approach is similar to utilitarianism in its teleological orientation, but dissimilar in its willingness to deploy visions of a desirable society richer than the conceptions of "social welfare" deployed by utilitarians'.[76] This justification therefore fitted well with China in the early 1980s, and economic modernization provided the needed 'social planning' justification for a new intellectual property system. Since then, intellectual property reforms have been linked to the country's rapid economic development and have benefited from the push for continuous economic reforms.

Politically, backing the newly-established intellectual property system with rhetoric that was consistent with the national modernization goals was

72 Ibid, 65.

73 MT Sundara Rajan, 'Copyright and Free Speech in Transition: The Russian Experience' in J Griffiths and U Suthersanen (eds), *Copyright and Free Speech: Comparative and International Analyses* (Oxford University Press, 2005) 315, 333.

74 Ibid, 334, quoting 'A Text Writer's Opinion' in Grazhdanskoe Pravo (Civil Law) 1:254–255 (1939) translated in JN Hazard, *Materials on Soviet Law* (Columbia University, 1947) 35 (emphasis added by Professor Rajan).

75 Fisher, note 70 above, 192–193; NW Netanel, 'Copyright and a Democratic Civil Society' (1996) 106 *Yale LJ* 283, 288.

76 Fisher, ibid, 172.

very important. As David Zweig suggested, directions from the leadership and rhetoric that conveys these directions are critical to a country that is undergoing 'a fundamental change in [its] international orientation'.[77] Because the Chinese leaders were inexperienced with intellectual property protection, and had to constantly struggle with unfamiliar concepts and models introduced during the transitional period, the alignment of intellectual property reforms with the national modernization goals also allowed leaders to defend intellectual property reforms on more familiar terms.

In addition, because reformist leaders were constantly challenged by their more conservative counterparts, who were uncomfortable with the country's rapid socio-economic changes and the social ills brought about by these changes, the rhetoric allowed the reformist leaders to deflate criticisms of their kow-towing to foreign interests, especially in times of considerable external pressure from the United States. Instead, the leaders could highlight the economic benefits of stronger intellectual property protection and justify intellectual property reforms as an important leapfrogging tool to enable China to catch up with its more advanced trading partners. The reformist leadership could also tie the reforms to the growing nationalist sentiments that longed for China's regaining its rightful place following centuries of humiliation and semi-colonial rule.[78]

Moreover, the fact that stronger intellectual property protection is unnecessary for attracting FDI does not mean that an increase in protection would not result in more economic development. In fact, it would, at least in certain parts of the country or in selected industrial sectors. The more profits a firm can obtain, the more likely it is to expand its business, and the greater is its investment in or trade with the country. This is particularly true with respect to a country that has a strong imitative capacity and an enormous growing market. Indeed, stronger intellectual property protection may also provide to foreign investors important signals of a favourable investment climate.[79] As Claudio Frischtak noted, a country's overall investment climate is often more influential on FDI

[77] D Zweig, *Internationalizing China: Domestic Interests and Global Linkages* (Cornell University Press, 2002) 27, quoting CF Hermann, 'Changing Course: When Governments Choose to Redirect Foreign Policy' (1990) 34 *Int'l Stud Q* 3.

[78] Hsü, note 66 above, 660–661. As Professor Hsü noted, Mao Zedong and other Chinese leaders 'were fired with a burning desire to restore China's rightful position under the sun, to achieve the big-power status denied it since the Opium War, and to revive the national confidence and self-respect that had lost during a century of foreign humiliation': ibid.

[79] Alford, note 49 above, 68; Maskus, 'The Role of IP Rights', note 11 above, 137–138.

decisions than the strength of intellectual property protection it offers.[80] Likewise, Carsten Fink and Keith Maskus stated that '[a] poor country hoping to attract inward FDI would be better advised to improve its overall investment climate and business infrastructure than to strengthen its patent regime sharply, an action that would have little effect on its own'.[81] Thus, stronger intellectual property protection might result in more foreign investment from existing investors as well as those who otherwise would not invest in the country. While serious questions remain concerning whether stronger protection would result in net gains in economic welfare within the country, and whether such protection, on balance, would benefit the country, those questions do not negate the fact that stronger intellectual property protection would induce *some* economic development in the country.

In sum, even though stronger intellectual property protection is unnecessary for promoting economic development, the claim that stronger intellectual property protection would promote economic development provided the needed internal push for intellectual property reforms in the first decade and a half following the reopening of the Chinese market to foreign trade. In retrospect, that claim, to some extent, was similar to what psychologists have termed a 'self-fulfilling prophecy'. Although people might not be able to prove conclusively whether stronger intellectual property protection would lead to greater economic development, they would accept a higher level of protection if they believed such a link existed. This higher level of protection, in turn, would result in greater economic development in certain parts of the country and in selected industrial sectors. As more local stakeholders stood to benefit from stronger protection, they would lobby for even stronger protection. Eventually, the belief in the benefits of stronger intellectual property protection would result in more economic development, regardless of whether the link existed in the first place. And the cycle would repeat itself.

Development of Local Stakeholders

China experienced major economic setbacks after Tiananmen in 1989 and the subsequent turbulent bilateral relationship with the United States and other Western countries. Fortunately, its economy quickly recovered following Deng Xiaoping's famous 'tour' of southern China in 1992. In March 1993, the National

[80] CR Frischtak, 'Harmonization *Versus* Differentiation in Intellectual Property Rights Regime' in MB Wallerstein, ME Mogee and RA Schoen (eds), *Global Dimensions of Intellectual Property Rights in Science and Technology* (National Academy Press, 1993) 89, 99–100.

[81] C Fink and KE Maskus, 'Why We Study Intellectual Property Rights and What We Have Learned' in Fink and Maskus, note 42 above, 1, 7.

People's Congress incorporated into the Chinese Constitution the concept of the socialist market economy, which contrasted powerfully with a command or centrally-planned economy.[82] Four years later, the private sector was designated an important component of the changing economy, and 'red capitalists' were invited to join the Chinese Communist Party at the Sixteenth Party Congress in 2001.[83] Today, the Constitution stipulates that '[c]itizens' lawful private property is inviolable',[84] and booming real estate markets appear in many major Chinese cities. Most recently, the National People's Congress enacted a much-anticipated, yet controversial law to offer explicit protection to private property.[85]

Accompanying this rapid economic development and growth was the emergence of local stakeholders who stood to benefit from stronger intellectual property protection. Consider, for example, the software industry, which has experienced tremendous growth since the mid-1990s. By 1997, the value of the software market had doubled from RMB 6.8 billion in 1995 to RMB 12.6 billion.[86] The Chinese government also has been active in developing the local software industry, establishing bases in Liaoning, Hunan, Shandong, and Sichuan Provinces and in Beijing, Shanghai, and Zhuhai districts.[87]

Today, the number of private software companies has greatly increased. Although state-owned enterprises once dominated the Chinese economy, a large number of employees of these enterprises are now entering the private sector—or, in the Chinese parlance, 'plunging into the sea' (*xiàhǎi*). As the late Zheng Chengsi and Xue Hong, two leading commentators on Chinese intellectual property law, observed:

> In recent years . . . many software engineers resigned from state enterprises or research institutes, taking software products (finished or unfinished) created during the course of employment with them, and joined private software companies or established their own companies. These private companies immediately produced and marketed the software products, and became competitors of state software enterprises.[88]

82 The amended Art 15 now reads: 'The State has put into practice a *socialist market economy*. The State strengthens formulating economic laws, improves macro adjustment and control and forbids according to law any units or individuals from interfering with the social economic order.' Xianfa 1982, Art 15 (amended 2004) (PRC) (emphasis added).

83 C Prestowitz, *Three Billion New Capitalists: The Great Shift of Wealth and Power to the East* (Basic Books, 2005) 27.

84 Xianfa (1982), Art 13 (amended 2004) (PRC).

85 J Kahn, 'China Approves Property Law, Strengthening Its Middle Class' *NY Times* (16 March 2007) A1.

86 H Xue and C Zheng, *Software Protection in China: A Complete Guide* (Sweet & Maxwell Asia, 1999) 8.

87 Ibid, 9.

88 H Xue and C Zheng, *Chinese Intellectual Property Law in the 21st Century* (Sweet & Maxwell Asia, 2002) 104–105.

In the late 1990s, intellectual property reforms were given a further push by the emerging consciousness of the need to develop a knowledge-based economy. As Lester Thurow noted, '[k]nowledge is the new basis for wealth . . . . In the past, when capitalists talked about their wealth, they were talking about their ownership of plant and equipment or natural resources. In the future when capitalists talk about their wealth, they will be talking about their control of knowledge.'[89] Perhaps under the influence of the internet boom in other parts of the world, the phrase 'knowledge economy' suddenly began to appear in major Chinese newspapers, such as *The People's Daily* and *Guangming Daily*. Government officials used the phrase frequently in their presentations,[90] while Chinese businesses quickly adopted words like 'e-commerce' and 'e-business' to enhance public image and stock market value.[91]

Although the internet bust a few years later slowed online developments throughout the world, the drive for the development of a knowledge-based economy in China continued, and the Chinese internet population grew exponentially. In October 1997, there were only 299,000 computers connected to the internet and 620,000 internet users.[92] Based on the most recent survey by the China Internet Network Information Center (CNNIC), there are now 58.4 million computers connected to the internet and 137 million internet users, second only to the United States.[93]

As the use of the internet and new communications technologies continues to increase, Chinese policy makers have paid greater attention to issues concerning intellectual property rights in the digital environment. For example, the 2001 copyright law amendments addressed for the first time online copyright issues.[94] In May 2006, the State Council promulgated the Regulations on the Protection of the Right of Communication Through Information Network.[95] Most recently, China acceded to the WIPO Copyright Treaty and the WIPO Performances and Phonograms Treaty. These developments make a lot of sense. Greater certainty over the scope of rights protected on the internet is important

89 LC Thurow, *Building Wealth: The New Rules for the Individuals, Companies, and Nations in a Knowledge-Based Economy* (HarperBusiness, 1999) xiii.

90 Xue and Zheng, *Software Protection in China*, note 86 above, 7.

91 Xue and Zheng, *Chinese IP Law*, note 88 above, xl.

92 Yu, 'The Copyright Divide', note 58 above, 371.

93 China Internet Network Information Center, *19th Statistical Survey Report on the Internet Development in China* (2007) 5.

94 Copyright Law of the People's Republic of China, Arts 10(12), 37(6), 41, 47, available at <http://www.sipo.gov.cn/sipo_English/flfg/xgflfg/200204/t20020416_34754.htm>.

95 Regulations on the Protection of the Right of Communication Through Information Network (PRC), available at <http://www.ncac.gov.cn/GalaxyPortal/inner/bqj/include/detail.jsp?articleid=9400&boardpid=175&boardid=11501010111602> (in Chinese).

to both local and foreign content providers and will greatly facilitate electronic commerce and broadband deployment.

The biggest push for intellectual property reforms in the 1990s was China's accession to the WTO. As China prepared to join the international trading body, it undertook a complete overhaul of its intellectual property system, amending its copyright, patent, and trademark laws.[96] In addition, it introduced a large number of implementing regulations and administrative measures, such as those concerning the registration of computer software and those on the protection of topographies of integrated circuits.[97] To help courts interpret these new laws and regulations, the Supreme People's Court also issued a number of judicial interpretations.[98]

In November 2001, the WTO members finally approved the proposal to admit China to the international trading body during the Fourth Ministerial Conference in Doha, Qatar. After 15 years of exhaustive negotiations, China formally became the 143rd member of the WTO on 11 December 2001. Although the accession process was complicated and involved many inextricable factors, it would not be far-fetched to argue that China might still remain outside the WTO had it not strengthened its protection of intellectual property rights.[99] Indeed, some commentators considered the WTO membership a major impetus for China's recent improvements in intellectual property protection. As Professors Zheng and Xue explained:

> In general, China's entry to the WTO significantly influenced the speed and scope of the development of the Chinese IP law system. It is interesting to note that IP rights reforms kept pace with Chinese WTO negotiations. When the negotiations encountered obstacles, the IP rights reform slowed down; when the negotiations reached agreements to promote the accession process, the IP rights reform accelerated noticeably. Since China has become a member of the WTO, Chinese IP law reform has also peaked.[100]

To some extent, the economic benefits and reputational gains that were associated with China's accession to the WTO far exceeded the socio-economic costs

---

96 Chinese Copyright Law, note 94 above; Patent Law of the People's Republic of China (PRC), available at <http://www.sipo.gov.cn/sipo_English/flfg/zlflfg/200203/t20020327_33872.htm>; Trademark Law of the People's Republic of China (PRC), available at <http://www.sipo.gov.cn/sipo_English/flfg/xgflfg/200204/t20020416_34755.htm>.

97 Measures on the Registration of Computer Software, translated in <http://www.chinagate.com.cn/english/433.htm> (last accessed 15 May 2007); Regulations on the Protection of Layout-Designs of Integrated Circuits (PRC), available at <http://www.sipo.gov.cn/sipo_English/flfg/zlflfg/200204/t20020402_33873.htm> (last accessed 15 May 2007).

98 Sun, note 6 above, 66–67.

99 Yu, 'The Copyright Divide', note 58 above, 372.

100 Xue and Zheng, *Chinese IP Law*, note 88 above, xxxix.

incurred by increased intellectual property protection. By linking the two issues together, the Chinese began to understand that the stakes for the lack of intellectual property protection extended beyond the intellectual property arena, covering almost every other area that implicates international trade, including agriculture, banking, electronics, insurance, professional services, securities, telecommunications, and textiles.[101] While they might not be excited about introducing stronger intellectual property protection, they certainly were reluctant to give up WTO-related trade benefits that were linked to such protection.

Moreover, the moderate costs of stronger protection required by the TRIPS Agreement were incomparable to the high costs of other reforms required by the WTO accession. If the leaders and the Chinese public were willing to accept the costs of these other reforms, it was natural for them to accept the costs of TRIPS-related reforms. In fact, one could make a strong claim that China could easily recoup its losses in the intellectual property area by obtaining gains in such other trade areas as agriculture or textiles. Even critics of the overall economic benefits of China's accession had a tough time responding to the strong nationalistic sentiments that considered the WTO accession an important means for China to regain its past glory, not to mention the general excitement, rejuvenation, and other psychological benefits brought about by the accession.

Nevertheless, one needs to be cautious about how much one attributes the recent intellectual property reforms to China's WTO accession. Although commentators and policy makers have widely credited the recent changes in the Chinese intellectual property system to the WTO accession,[102] it is important not to overlook the many internal developments within the country, including the Chinese leaders' changing attitude toward the rule of law, the emergence of private property rights and local stakeholders, the increasing concerns about ambiguities over relationships in state-owned enterprises, and the government leaders' active push for modernization.[103] While the WTO accession may be important, China's *guóqíng*, or national conditions, continues to play a very important role in shaping intellectual property reforms in China.

---

101 Yu, 'The Copyright Divide', note 58 above, 371.

102 See, for example, Office of the US Trade Representative, *2005 National Trade Estimate Report on Foreign Trade Barriers* (2005) 95, available at <http://www.ustr.gov/Document_Library/Reports_Publications/2005/2005_NTE_Report/Section_Index.html?ht=>; M Shi, 'China's Participation in the Doha Negotiations and Implementation of Its Accession Commitments' in H Gao and D Lewis (eds), *China's Participation in the WTO* (Cameron May, 2005) 23, 32.

103 Yu, 'From Pirates to Partners II', note 5 above, 908.

Increasing Shift toward an Export-Driven Economy

Today, China is 'the world's fourth largest economy and the third largest trading nation'.[104] Its factories 'make 70 per cent of the world's toys, 60 per cent of its bicycles, half its shoes, and one-third of its luggage'.[105] China also 'builds half of the world's microwave ovens, one-third of its television sets and air conditioners, a quarter of its washers, and one-fifth of its refrigerators'.[106] As the Chinese economy becomes increasingly driven by exports to other countries, intellectual property protection will become even more important than it was a decade ago. As Daniel Chow explained:

> [g]lobal competitiveness in the modern age is directly linked to the level of technology in goods and services. Studies indicate that the higher the level of technology involved in goods and services, the higher the growth rate of exports . . . . In the 1990s, China began to build a trade surplus with many nations based upon its low manufacturing costs. While China has been able to dominate in low-technology/labor-intensive industries, China realizes that to continue its growth in exports, it must move up the ladder into more technology-intensive goods and services. To do so, China must acquire access to advanced technology.[107]

Indeed, 'China, like most nations, encourages exports because export sales contribute to a favorable trade balance and can earn United States dollars or other forms of hard currency.'[108] While Chinese companies were content to serve as original equipment manufacturers (OEM) for foreign firms a decade ago, they have now moved into high-end technology markets, such as those for cars and regional jets, while seeking to maintain their competitive edge over low-cost products.[109] Thus, some commentators and pundits suggested that China's export-driven economic growth is likely to lead to greater future confrontations with the United States. As Peter Navarro observed, '[a]ny complete understanding of the Coming China Wars must begin with this observation: China's hyper-rate of economic growth is export driven; and the ability of the Chinese to conquer one export market after another, often in blitzkrieg fashion, derives from their ability to set the so-called China Price.'[110]

---

104 Bergsten, Gill, Lardy and Mitchell, note 1 above, 3.

105 O Shenkar, *The Chinese Century: The Rising Chinese Economy and Its Impact on the Global Economy, the Balance of Power, and Your Job* (Wharton School Publishing, 2005), 2.

106 Ibid, 3.

107 DCK Chow, 'Why China Does Not Take Commercial Piracy Seriously' (2006) 32 *Ohio NU LR* 203, 206.

108 Ibid, 214.

109 Ibid, 207–208; Shenkar, note 105 above, 161–162.

110 Navarro, note 38 above, 2.

Consider, for example, trademark protection, which is particularly important to an export-driven economy. The usual criticism of strong trademark protection in an emerging economy is that such protection would force local consumers to pay a premium for well-known foreign brands in exchange for no or very limited benefits. This is particularly true when local consumers are brand-conscious or when their purchase decisions are distorted by their obsession with social status, which they seek to gain by buying or owning more expensive foreign products. Because most of the branded products are made in China, local consumers are often asked to pay a higher price even though the quality of the products is no different from that of products made by local brand owners.

Moreover, by intentionally not offering trademark protection, countries may be able to take a free ride on the investment of foreign trademark holders, by earning profits as if they were selling genuine goods that bear the infringing marks. As foreign brand owners continue to advertise and promote their products, the local copycats would also benefit from the goodwill of the original products without incurring any advertising expenses. Such a competitive strategy, however, is ill-advised, especially for a country that has now become one of the world's largest exporters. As Professor Kitch explained, that strategy 'will result in a parasitical business that will always be dependent on the willingness of the targeted countries to tolerate the infringing imports . . . [and that] will never have an established market position that can lay a foundation for the development of an internationally competitive business'.[111]

To be certain, local firms can ensure the marketability of their products in foreign countries by using non-infringing trademarks in foreign markets. Indeed, global firms have used that strategy to avoid infringement in selected markets. Nevertheless, such a strategy is costly, because it will not allow for the economies of scale commonly found in global production. That strategy also makes it difficult for local firms to learn how to establish market position by experimenting in the local market with brand development and trademark portfolio management. To some extent, one can see the local market as a 'playground' for Chinese export businesses to acquire the needed skills to set up internationally competitive businesses.

A case in point is the leading Chinese personal computer manufacturer, Lenovo (*Liánxiǎng*). When the company sought to expand business overseas a few years ago, it found out that its English name 'Legend' had already been registered and used as a trademark or trade name in many foreign countries. To avoid potential infringement, and to ensure that it could become an official

111 Kitch, note 64 above, 168.

sponsor of the 2008 Beijing Olympics, it had no choice but to develop the new 'Lenovo' mark, which combined the first two letters of the Legend mark with the word 'novo'.[112] Interestingly, the Lenovo mark has now become famous as a result of the worldwide media coverage of its purchase of IBM's personal computers division.

Lenovo, however, is not the only one. Compared to a decade ago, a number of Chinese companies have now achieved prominence in the international market, with their trademarks being recognized as well-known outside China.[113] Examples of these famous local brands include Galanz (for microwave ovens), Haier (for household appliances), Huawei Technologies (for telecommunications equipment), Konka (for televisions), and TCL (for televisions). As China increases its exports of goods branded with globally recognized local trademarks, the importance of intellectual property protection to the country's future economic development cannot be ignored.

From the standpoint of internal economic development in China, trademark protection is even more beneficial than the protection afforded by other forms of intellectual property. The development of globally recognized trademarks requires neither considerable technological expertise nor initial heavy capital investment. Although the global market has been dominated by brands developed by major corporations in developed countries, less developed countries and smaller enterprises have their fair share of famous trademarks that are recognized throughout the world, especially in the fields of beer and liquor production—Bacardi (for Bermuda rum), Corona (for Mexican beer) and Tsingtao (for Chinese beer) easily come to mind.[114] In fact, according to Interbrand, 'Bacardi is the world's 75th most valuable global brand, and with a valuation in excess of $3 billion, is worth comfortably more than the GDP of the country which produces it'.[115]

---

112 Z Ling (M Avery (trans)), *The Lenovo Affair: The Growth of China's Computer Giant and Its Takeover of IBM–PC* (John Wiley & Sons, 2006) 334–335.

113 For interesting profiles of successful Chinese local brands in the areas of information technology, telecommunications equipment and services, food and beverage, and electronic appliances, see DN Sull with Y Wang, *Made in China: What Western Managers Can Learn from Trailblazing Chinese Entrepreneurs* (Harvard Business School Press, 2005).

114 JH MacLaughlin, TJ Richards and LA Kenny, 'The Economic Significance of Piracy' in RM Gadbaw and TJ Richards (eds), *Intellectual Property Rights: Global Consensus, Global Conflict?* (Westview Press, 1988) 89, 104. For a detailed discussion of emerging brands in less developed countries, see S Anholt, *Brand New Justice: How Branding Places and Products Can Help the Developing World* (2nd edn, Butterworth-Heinemann, 2005) 43–77.

115 Anholt, ibid, 60.

From the standpoint of consumer welfare and economic self-sufficiency, it is also helpful to encourage local companies to catch up and compete with famous Western brands by developing more attractive products and better brand positioning.[116] Instead, this brand building strategy 'fits [well] with the government's strategy of consolidating strategic industries . . . to create national champions that can hold their own in global markets and . . . to restore its imperial glory'.[117] Compared to foreign firms, local firms thus far have been very successful in the Chinese market. In this dynamic, yet immature market, 'consumers are still experimenting, and brands come and go with great speed'.[118] As a result, local firms have the opportunity to attain market position and develop the next promising brands.

The ability of local firms to improve consumer loyalty and establish market position has been further enhanced by the failure of foreign firms to understand or adjust to the local market conditions. Studies, for example, have 'estimated that less than 10 percent of Chinese consumers have the level of disposable income that can afford to buy Western products'.[119] Yet many foreign businesses ignore this financial reality and insist on focusing on the high-end market, perhaps due to benefits from economies of scope and scale in global production, or to the firms' reluctance to lower the quality, and often the international reputation, of their products.

A case in point is the microwave market, which Galanz has overtaken recently. '[I]n 1993 only 1 per cent of Chinese consumers had microwaves. Consumption grew—but not in the pattern expected. By early 2000, nearly 90 per cent of the market was in cheaper models, with the Chinese company Galanz dominating.'[120] Similarly, although Whirlpool and Kelon were competitors for the manufacture of washing machines, the local manufacturer quickly won the race.[121] Today, '[a]fter losing more than $100 million and shutting down most of its factories, Whirlpool . . . manufactures washing-machines for Guangdong Kelon'—a scenario that Whirlpool certainly did not foresee when it began its investment in China.[122]

116 Yu, 'From Pirates to Partners II', note 5 above, 996.

117 Shenkar, note 105 above, 158.

118 H Chee with C West, *Myths about Doing Business in China* (Palgrave Macmillan, 2004) 30; R Yan, 'Short-Term Results: The Litmus Test for Success in China' in *Harvard Business Review: Doing Business in China* (2004) 79, 95.

119 Chee, ibid, 31.

120 Ibid.

121 Huang, note 32 above, 193–194.

122 Anholt, note 114 above, 64.

As China continues to increase exports and develop products under globally recognized trademarks, especially after the much-anticipated push around the 2008 Beijing Olympics (and again during the 2010 World Expo in Shanghai), the existence of effective intellectual property protection is likely to be of paramount importance. Significant improvement in trademark protection is therefore likely to be more important to China than similar improvement in the protection of other forms of intellectual property. In fact, the improved ability of Chinese businesses to develop globally famous brands may ultimately hold the key to converting those Chinese who are sceptical of intellectual property protection to global missionaries for greater intellectual property reforms.

Part III In Search of a Crossover Point

Although piracy and counterfeiting problems remain widespread in China, history suggests that intellectual property protection will vastly improve when the overall benefits of such protection begin to outweigh its overall costs. After all, similar changes occurred in Japan in the 1970s, and in Hong Kong, Singapore, South Korea, and Taiwan in the 1980s. At some point in the near future, the development of the Chinese economy will reach a crossover point at which the country will gradually abandon its infamous pirate past to become a champion of intellectual property protection.[123] Similar transformation, indeed, happened in virtually every developed country, including the United States—a former haven for pirated works of Charles Dickens, Anthony Trollope, Gilbert and Sullivan, and many other British and French authors.[124]

Notwithstanding the importance of this crossover point and the considerable historical evidence suggesting the potential for such a dramatic change, there is little, if any, empirical research concerning when this point will be reached. To provide a more accurate forecast of when China will reach this proverbial crossover point, and to better understand the socio-economic impact of the expansion of intellectual property protection in China, this Part highlights the country's regional and sectoral disparities, its lack of an adequate enabling environment for effective intellectual property protection, and its improvements in intellectual property protection at both the microscopic and qualitative levels.

123 Abbott, note 9 above, 81–82.
124 Yu, 'The Copyright Divide', note 58 above, 342.

A. Regional Disparities

The fact that China is not a homogeneous country has been stated repeatedly since Westerners first encountered China many centuries ago. China is large, complex, diverse, and 'sometimes internally contradictory'.[125] The Chinese speak different languages, enjoy different cuisines, grow up with different cultures, and subscribe to different historical and philosophical traditions. Conditions in Beijing are often very different from those in Guangzhou, and the intellectual property strategies that are effective in Shanghai are likely to fail in a village in western China. The trade patterns found in the coastal areas are also very different from those found in the inland areas.

To make things more complicated, during the rapid economic development in China in the past two decades, 'some regions have been positively encouraged to become wealthy before others'.[126] As Deng Xiaoping noted in the early 1980s in response to the country's growing inequality, 'some people have to get rich first'.[127] As a result, across the country there were enormous disparities in the levels of wealth and income, the purchasing power of local consumers, and the stages of economic and technological development.

The goods that are in high demand in the inland and rural areas are often very different from those in the major cities and the coastal areas. Because of these differing market conditions, local people in the less developed parts of China understandably are less aware of the importance of intellectual property protection. Nor do they have much need for it. Those places are also likely to present greater structural problems for intellectual property enforcement, such as inefficient administration, low penalties, shortage of funds, local protectionism, and severe conflicts of interests.[128] Meanwhile, the limited economic and technological developments in these areas have heavily constrained the local resources devoted to research and development efforts.

Sadly, despite all of these divergent regional conditions, intellectual property developments in China are often analysed as if the country were homogeneous. While it is logical for policy analysts to swap analytical accuracy for practical convenience, the end result unsurprisingly presents only half of the picture—at

125 JJ Hamre and CF Bergsten, 'Preface' to Bergsten, Gill, Lardy and Mitchell, note 1 above, ix.
126 DSG Goodman, 'The Politics of Regionalism: Economic Development, Conflict and Negotiation' in DSG Goodman and G Segal (eds), *China Deconstructs: Politics, Trade and Regionalism* (Routledge, 1995) 1–20.
127 Bergsten, Gill, Lardy and Mitchell, note 1 above, 31.
128 Maskus, Dougherty and Mertha, note 42 above, 309.

times a very misleading, if not inaccurate, half. As the Chinese market has expanded further away from the major cities and the coastal areas, a more complete and deeper analysis of the country's regional economic developments is in order.

In June 2006, the Office of the United States Trade Representative altered its decades-old emphasis on country-based assessments in China. Instead of calling for only information about the entire country, for the first time the Office requested information concerning provincial developments. As the announcement in the *Federal Register* stated, '[t]he goal of this [special provincial] review is to spotlight strengths, weaknesses, and inconsistencies in and among specific jurisdictions'.[129]

This new approach not only will promote the interests of US rights holders, but also will help facilitate a better understanding of the divergent protection offered in different parts of the country. To some extent, China is what I have described as 'a country of countries'.[130] The economic conditions in different parts of this country are drastically different, and intellectual property protection and enforcement in each of these different parts are unlikely to be the same. Any overall nationwide assessment of intellectual property enforcement is likely to be misleading, if not meaningless.

Since the reopening of the Chinese market to foreign trade in the late 1970s, the country has become heavily decentralized, and problems of local protectionism are now widespread. Today, there are considerable differences between protection at the national, provincial, and local levels.[131] As far as these differences are concerned, the Chinese proverb 'the mountains are high, and the Emperor is far away' (*shān gāo huángdì yuǎn*) could not provide a more accurate description. Joseph Massey, the former Assistant United States Trade Representative for Japan and China, recounted the story of a senior USTR official's visit to the southern part of China following the signing of the 1992 memorandum of understanding. In Guangdong province, the official 'was told by a senior provincial government leader that "Beijing's agreement" with the US was "*mei you guanxi*" (irrelevant) in that southern province'.[132]

Like the level of intellectual property protection, the level of innovation varies considerably among the different parts of China, adding another factor to this

---

[129] Office of the US Trade Representative, Special Provincial Review of Intellectual Property Rights Protection in China: Request for Public Comment, 71 Fed Reg 34,969 (16 June 2006).
[130] Yu, 'From Pirates to Partners II', note 5 above, 963.
[131] Mertha, note 49 above, 93–100.
[132] Massey, note 54 above, 235.

already complicated picture. For example, in 2000, '[r]esidents of Guangdong applied for more than 21,000 patents, while people in Hebei applied for only 3,848'.[133] A regional breakdown of 1995 technology data supplied by the State Science and Technology Commission of China showed that while Beijing and Shanghai spent 2.6 and 1.4 per cent of the local GDP, Sichuan and Liaoning, the provinces that came next, spent only 0.6 per cent.[134] Given the inter-relationship between intellectual property protection and economic development, the considerable regional disparities within the country will provide important clues to the future development of intellectual property protection in China.

When China joined the WTO, commentators were divided as to their views of the impact of its accession to intellectual property protection. The so-called China optimists suggested that intellectual property protection in China would improve, because the WTO accession would lead to better economic and living conditions, which in turn would result in greater demand for higher-priced genuine products and luxury goods. When people are poor, they have limited disposable income and are more willing to settle for fake Prada handbags, Gucci shoes, or low-quality video compact discs (VCDs). When they become richer, however, they may start looking for better and fancier legitimate products, especially when they can distinguish between genuine and fake products.[135] Indeed, Ernst & Young recently forecasted that the Chinese luxury market 'is expected to grow 20 per cent annually until 2008 and then 10% annually until 2015, when sales are expected to exceed US$11.5 billion'.[136] Thus, some optimists predicted that 'pirates and counterfeiters will . . . gradually move into legitimate businesses[,] and the focus of counterfeiting and piracy will shift away from China to lesser developing countries, such as Vietnam'.[137]

By contrast, the so-called China pessimists suggested that intellectual property protection would be likely to deteriorate in China, due to an influx of foreign products, the growing economic disparity within the country, and the increased desire for products that many people could not afford. As these pessimists claimed, the growing access of foreign products to the Chinese market and the increase in foreign investment and trade would enhance the economic conditions that gave

133 Maskus, Dougherty and Mertha, note 42 above, 317.

134 Ibid, 320.

135 Chow, 'Commercial Piracy', note 107 above, 215.

136 Ernst & Young, *China: The New Lap of Luxury* (2005) 1, available at <http://www.ey.com/global/download.nsf/China_E/050914_Report_E/$file/China-The%20New%20Lap%20of%20Luxury_Eng%20(Final).pdf>.

137 DCK Chow, *A Primer on Foreign Investment Enterprises and Protection of Intellectual Property in China* (Kluwer Law International, 2002) 254.

rise to piracy and counterfeiting in the first place.[138] Even worse, the reduced restrictions on export privileges and the elimination of state monopoly over trading rights—both results of China's WTO commitments—would further allow pirates and counterfeiters to trade more aggressively with markets that have 'a strong appetite for low-priced counterfeit goods', such as Southeast Asia and Eastern Europe.[139] The WTO accession might also create a disincentive for the country to carry out further immediate reforms, while providing China with 'leverage against any future pressure to improve its piracy problem'.[140] In the end, according to the pessimists, the market for counterfeit exports would grow substantially.[141] As Professor Chow summarized:

> Recent estimates by the PRC State Council in 2001 indicate that the Chinese economy was flooded with counterfeits valued at $19–24 billion and that counterfeiting accounted for eight percent of China's GDP. Multi-national companies in China indicate that fifteen to twenty percent of their brands in China are counterfeit, causing annual losses in the hundreds of millions of dollars. Counterfeits made in China are now exported to markets in all parts of the world; there are indications that exports from China will increase sharply for the foreseeable future. According to some accounts, China now accounts for eighty percent of all counterfeits in the world. Counterfeiting and commercial piracy are vital to the economy of many local municipalities and there are now millions of people in China involved in the counterfeiting industry.[142]

By now, it is quite clear that regional disparities in China have undermined the forecasts of both the optimists and pessimists. While stronger intellectual property protection and the emergence of intellectual property-based industries in Beijing, Shanghai, Guangzhou, and other major cities and coastal regions have led to greater improvement of protection in the affected places, piracy and counterfeiting have not migrated out of the country. Instead, they have spread to other parts of the country, whose conditions are no different from those of the big cities a decade ago when intellectual property protection began to strengthen. In light of this migration, intellectual property problems are likely to remain in the country in the near future, even if some of these problems have migrated to countries in Southeast Asia. Thus, it is misleading to look for nationwide solutions to China's counterfeiting and piracy problems, and the USTR's new provincial review offers a refreshing change for collecting information about intellectual property developments in the country.

---

138 Ibid.
139 Ibid; Chow, 'Commercial Piracy', note 107 above, 216.
140 Chow, *Primer on Foreign Investment Enterprises*, note 137 above, 253–254.
141 Chow, 'Commercial Piracy', note 107 above, 205.
142 Ibid, 204–205.

That approach is also attractive because it will help reduce the frustration of many Chinese, especially those in regions that have undertaken successful intellectual property reforms or made considerable sacrifices in the transition to a regime that is more respectful of intellectual property rights. While intellectual property protection continues to be a problem for foreign rights holders throughout China, one cannot deny the many important developments in the major cities and coastal areas in the last two decades. Following the introduction in the early 1990s of specialized courts filled with judges who possess intellectual property expertise, courts in the major cities have also been greatly improved. These courts now attract foreign rights holders to use the judicial process in lieu of the alternative approach of administrative enforcement. In 2002, for example, a total of 2,080 patent cases (an increase of 30.24 per cent over 2001) and 707 trademark cases (an increase of 46.68 per cent) were adjudicated.[143]

Moreover, a continued insistence on the overall improvement in the country is unrealistic, ineffective, and counterproductive. By ignoring the important successes governments and businesses have made in major cities and coastal areas, such an insistence would create resentment among a large portion of the Chinese, which regard the repeated threats and demands 'as American excesses'.[144] Such insistence would also foster a misimpression among local Chinese leaders that, no matter what they do, the US government and foreign businesses will never be satisfied. This misimpression will only erect further barriers to future cooperation, not to mention the lost opportunities for cultivating local allies.

Finally, regional disparities may affect decisions by foreign investors on which provinces to invest in, how much to invest, what forms the investment should take, and what type of technologies will be used in the facilities in a particular region. As regional and local governments fight hard to attract FDI, the picture we will see in China is likely to be more complicated in the near future than it is today. Because gains in one region may also result in losses in another, many local authorities have been particularly concerned about the unemployment and labour displacement problems created by the closure of pirate and counterfeit factories.[145] While the costs of adjustment to job losses and labour displacement are often limited, due to the fact that 'copying is typically done in footloose firms with limited capital requirements . . . [and] that former unauthorized factories are [often] licensed to produce by copyright holders because of their expertise',[146] some regions will certainly suffer more job losses and unemployment than

143 Sun, note 6 above, 12.
144 NM Lam and JL Graham, *China Now* (McGraw–Hill, 2007) 321.
145 Yu, 'From Pirates to Partners II', note 5 above, 954.
146 Maskus, Dougherty and Mertha, note 42 above, 305.

others, due to a lack of skilled labour, education, technological infrastructure, and training facilities.[147] The closures induced by intellectual property reforms therefore may sometimes shift production out of a region or a locality. If problems are likely to linger for a significant period of time, rights holders are likely to encounter severe local resistance and lax enforcement. The divergent protection may even lead to 'interregional disputes over intellectual property infringement and enforcement'.[148]

B. Sectoral Disparities

While regional disparities have greatly affected the analysis of intellectual property protection in China, the country's divergent sectoral developments present challenges that are common for analyses of emerging, transition, and other less developed economies. Because industries develop at different paces, and because not all industrial sectors can simultaneously benefit from strong intellectual property protection, these countries are unlikely to have a coherent national intellectual property policy. Instead, the positions taken by national governments often vary depending on the impact of the proposed protection on their fast-growing industries.

For example, based on its existing developments, China is likely to prefer stronger protection of intellectual property rights in entertainment, software, semiconductors, and selected areas of biotechnology, to increased protection in areas concerning pharmaceuticals, chemicals, fertilizers, seeds, and foodstuffs. This rather 'schizophrenic' position is understandable because China has fast-growing movie, software, semiconductor, and biotechnology industries. These industries are likely to obtain greater benefits if intellectual property protection is strengthened. Even when policy makers fail to recognize the need for stronger protection, they will provide the information needed to lobby for intellectual property reforms.

By contrast, in fields concerning pharmaceuticals, chemicals, fertilizers, seeds, and foodstuffs, China is unlikely to benefit from greater protection, due to its huge population, continued economic dependence on agriculture, the worries about public health issues, and concerns about the people's overall well-being. Indeed, because stronger intellectual property protection in these areas is likely to drain the country's limited economic resources, local leaders would hesitate to use their hard-earned political capital to introduce reforms that would provide

[147] Maskus, 'The Role of IP Rights', note 11 above, 112.
[148] Maskus, Dougherty and Mertha, note 42 above, 298.

benefits primarily for foreign rights holders and their export countries. The likelihood of success for the intellectual property reforms is also greatly reduced by the increased frustration among the local people who would bear the costs of increased protection, and by the development of organized efforts against increased protection.

Politics aside, it makes good economic sense for policy makers to develop intellectual property protection that is in line with the country's economic development. For example, economists have shown that the 'length of protection for a given product should be inversely related to the elasticity of demand and the social rate of discount, and positively related to R&D returns'.[149] Edwin Mansfield also found that '[t]here is often little correlation between one industry's evaluation of the strength or weakness of intellectual property rights protection in a particular country and another industry's evaluation of the same country'.[150] As he pointed out in his study for the World Bank, intellectual property protection played a major role in the chemical, pharmaceutical, machinery, and electrical equipment industries, but has only marginal significance for the transportation equipment, metals, and food industries.[151] Likewise, Keith Maskus found that '[i]nvestment in lower-technology goods and services, such as textiles and apparel, electronic assembly, distribution, and hotels, depends less on the strength of IPRs and relatively more on input costs and market opportunities. Investors with a product or technology that is costly to imitate may also pay little attention to local IPRs in their decision making.'[152]

In recent works, Dan Burk and Mark Lemley have shown how policy levers in patent law have allowed courts to take account of the different types of innovation in different industries.[153] As they noted, 'there is no reason to assume that a unitary patent system will optimally encourage innovation in the wide range of diverse industries that it is expected to cover'.[154] Likewise, Michael Carroll and Glynn Lunney each highlighted the problem of uniformity cost in intellectual property law.[155] As these commentators have recognized, the divergence of protection in different industrial sectors will allow a country to better tailor

149 Frischtak, note 80 above, 97 citing W Nordhaus, *Invention, Growth and Welfare* (MIT Press, 1969).

150 Mansfield, note 26 above, 19.

151 Ibid, 2.

152 Maskus, 'The Role of IP Rights', note 11 above, 131–132.

153 DL Burk and MA Lemley, 'Policy Levers in Patent Law' (2003) 89 *Va LR* 1575.

154 Ibid, 1577.

155 MW Carroll, 'One for All: The Problem of Uniformity Cost in Intellectual Property Law' (2006) 55 *Am U LR* 845; GS Lunney Jr, 'Patent Law, the Federal Circuit, and the Supreme Court: A Quiet Revolution' (2004) 11 *Sup Ct Econ Rev* 1.

its intellectual property system to the needs of local industries. Such tailoring, in turn, would allow the country to take better advantage of its comparative and competitive advantages. After all, a country that has a strong pharmaceutical industry is more likely to benefit from an intellectual property system tailored to that industry's needs than one that is designed to support a strong software industry.

In addition, the problems an industry faces vary according to the nature of its products. In China, for example, 'copying rates vary considerably across types of goods, with business applications software experiencing the highest rates and entertainment software next . . . [and] music recordings and motion pictures hav[ing] lower copying rates'.[156] Thus, at least for China, there may be more urgent needs to strengthen the protection for business software applications than that for music recordings and motion pictures.

Under the TRIPS Agreement, countries are prohibited from offering discriminatory protection in the patent area. Article 27 states specifically that 'patents shall be available and patent rights enjoyable without discrimination as to the place of invention, the field of technology and whether products are imported or locally produced'.[157] The TRIPS Agreement therefore prohibits countries from deciding whether they want to offer protection to the pharmaceutical industry without offering protection to the biotechnology industry. Put differently, countries cannot pick and choose; they have to offer protection to all industries as long as they remain members of the WTO.

Nevertheless, Article 27 allows all members, including those with great sectoral disparities, to carefully tailor the country's protection to local needs. Because the TRIPS Agreement covers only minimum standards of protection offered by each WTO member, it does not dictate the scope of protection beyond what the agreement requires.[158] The TRIPS Agreement also does not require countries to offer protection of equal scope and strength to all industries. As long as countries do not discriminate between national and foreign rights holders and between the different types of industries, countries are free to introduce legislation that provides additional protection to benefit local industries.

In fact, the preamble of the TRIPS Agreement recognizes 'the special needs of the least-developed country members in respect of maximum flexibility in

156 Maskus, Dougherty and Mertha, note 42 above, 303–304.

157 Agreement on Trade-Related Aspects of Intellectual Property Rights (TRIPS Agreement), Art 27(1), Marrakech Agreement Establishing the World Trade Organization, Annex 1C, Legal Instruments—Results of the Uruguay Round (Marrakesh, 15 April 1994, 33 ILM 1197 (1994)).

158 Ibid, Art 1(1).

the domestic implementation of laws and regulations in order to enable them to create a sound and viable technological base'.[159] Article 8 of the agreement states that 'Members may, in formulating or amending their laws and regulations, adopt measures necessary to protect public health and nutrition, and to promote the public interest in sectors of vital importance to their socio-economic and technological development, provided that such measures are consistent with the provisions of this Agreement'.[160] Moreover, as Professor Heald pointed out:

> Nothing in the TRIPS Agreement prevents other countries from similarly favoring local creators of sub-patentable innovation by protecting their work. Although a developing country is unlikely to have numerous strong sectors in its economy, it may have some modest innovators worthy of special protection from competition. For example, if a country has a strong textile industry that occasionally improves its dyeing and weaving techniques, protection of new (but obvious) methods should tend to favor local firms, even if protection is not discriminatory on its face.[161]

For example, commentators have described the benefits of offering *sui generis* or utility model protection, which offers protection of limited duration to minor or incremental innovations that involve low levels of novelty.[162] '[S]tudies in Brazil and the Philippines suggested that effective systems of utility models can promote innovation. Another study demonstrated econometrically that Japan's system of utility models and widespread licensing of new technologies contributed positively and significantly to its postwar rise in productivity.'[163]

In sum, if we are to fully understand the relationship between intellectual property protection and economic development, we need to pay attention to the different forms of intellectual property and the varying scope of each form of protection. It would be misleading to explore the impact of intellectual property protection as if all of these various forms of protection are based on identical models, offer protection of similar scope and characteristics, and incur similar social costs. With increasing *sui generis* protection for new subject matters and technologies, a clear understanding of the impact on each industrial sector becomes even more important.

---

159 Ibid, Preamble.

160 Ibid, Art 8(1).

161 Heald, note 13 above, 270.

162 Commission on Intellectual Property Rights, note 45 above, 21; Maskus, *IP Rights in the Global Economy*, note 12 above, 148; Maskus, Dougherty and Mertha, note 42 above, 299; JH Reichman, 'From Free Riders to Fair Followers: Global Competition Under the TRIPS Agreement' (1997) 29 *NYU J Int'l L & Pol* 11, 62–74. For a recent study of utility models, see U Suthersanen, *Utility Models and Innovation in Developing Countries* (2006), available at <http://www.unctad.org/en/docs/iteipc20066_en.pdf>.

163 KE Maskus, 'The Economics of Global Intellectual Property and Economic Development: A Survey' in Yu, *Intellectual Property and Information Wealth*, note 9 above, 4:159, 164.

Moreover, in China, the protection for different forms of intellectual property varies according to the *xìtǒng*, or functional bureaucratic system, that governs each form of protection. As a result, the philosophies behind such protection and the support it receives from related industrial sectors may affect the level of protection in a particular area. As Andrew Mertha pointed out in his book, *The Politics of Piracy*, a better understanding of the different *xìtǒng* will enable one to understand better the effectiveness of the protection involved, and the potential resistance confronting the push for greater protection in the area.[164] In fact, because of the different degree of effectiveness of each form of protection, rights holders and their attorneys often have to plan which form of protection they want to use to protect intellectual assets. As Keith Maskus, Sean Dougherty, and Andrew Mertha recounted:

> One person involved in enforcement claimed that although 90 percent of his investigations involve trademark allegations and 10 percent involve patents, up to 60 percent of these cases could be patent violations. However, enforcement is easier if the case is pursued as a trademark violation. One reason for this bias seems to be that, to date, Chinese authorities have been reluctant to entertain patent cases, evidently in the belief that patent infringement embodies technology transfer and helps meet national technology development goals.[165]

The differences inherent in each *xìtǒng* may further affect the pace of reforms for each form of intellectual property. Out of the three dominant forms of intellectual property, trademarks present the least problems for legal reforms.[166] By contrast, copyrights encounter the greatest challenge because of their association with propaganda, thought work, and information control.[167] Patents are somewhat in between, due to their considerable impact on technology transfer and the potential for slowing down the country's modernization efforts by draining foreign exchange reserves in the form of royalty and license fee payments.[168] As Professor Mertha explained, '[t]he copyright bureaucracy . . . is embedded within a *xitong* that concerns itself with cultural, ideological, and value-laden media and is therefore involved in a more politically sensitive environment, even if technical copyright issues themselves are no more or less "political" than those pertaining to patents or trademarks'.[169]

164 Mertha, note 49 above, 15.

165 Maskus, Dougherty and Mertha, note 42 above, 310.

166 Yu, 'From Pirates to Partners II', note 5 above, 995.

167 Mertha, note 49 above, 140. For discussion of the Chinese censorship and the information control policy, see Yu, 'Piracy, Prejudice, and Perspectives', note 57 above, 28–32.

168 Yu, 'From Pirates to Partners II', note 5 above, 995.

169 Mertha, note 49 above, 133–134.

Thus, it is no surprise that trademarks have been protected even during the Cultural Revolution. When China reopened its market for foreign trade in the late 1970s, the trademark law was also the first to be (re)introduced. Meanwhile, the patent law was filled with compromises, while the copyright law was the last to be enacted. Had there not been continuous pressure from the US government and the intention to rebuild international ties after Tiananmen, the introduction of the copyright law might not even have taken place in 1990.

In sum, like regional disparities, sectoral disparities greatly affect the analysis of the relationship between intellectual property protection and economic development. At times, sectoral disparities are the partial result of regional disparities. Taken together, regional and sectoral disparities not only affect the types of industry that are fast-growing in the region, but also the types of pirated and counterfeit products that will become available there. As one commentator suggested:

> According to the China United Intellectual Property Protection Centre (CUIPPC), a private business that has been representing Western companies like Coca-Cola, Microsoft and Kodak in China since 1994, there are even regional centres of counterfeiting expertise: imagine Silicon Valley for fakes. So if you are manufacturing in Chaosan, in Guangdong Province, your specialty is likely to be electronics, cigarettes, pharmaceuticals or CDs. For car parts, it's more likely you'll be in Wenzhou City or the Pearl River Delta. In Yuxiao County, the expertise is in manufacturing fake cigarettes; in Jintan City, it's pesticides.[170]

C. Inadequate Enabling Environment

With the expansion of intellectual property protection and the growing interdependence between different bodies of law, a focus on intellectual property laws and enforcement alone often does not fully account for the full extent of such protection. Instead, one may need to understand better the political, economic, and judicial environments that enable effective intellectual property enforcement—something I describe here as the enabling environment for effective intellectual property protection.

So far, commentators have underscored the importance of these complementary factors. Edwin Mansfield noted that 'one should recognize that a country's system of intellectual property protection is inextricably bound up with its entire legal and social system and its attitudes toward private property; it involves much

170 T Phillips, *Knockoff: The Deadly Trade in Counterfeit Goods* (Kogan Page, 2005) 59.

more than the passage of a patent or copyright law'.[171] Robert Sherwood reminded us that 'some things cannot be legislated'.[172] As he put it bluntly, 'until judicial systems in developing and transition countries are upgraded, it will matter little what intellectual property laws and treaties provide'.[173] Paul Heald stated that 'a rational strategy for developing countries must not only consider compliance options, but must also account for institutional competency—legislative, judicial, executive, and diplomatic—in order to make the most of available options'.[174] As Maskus, Dougherty, and Mertha summarized in the Chinese context:

> Upgrading protection for IPRs alone is a necessary but not sufficient condition for th[e] purpose [of maximizing the competitive gains from additional innovation and technology acquisition over time, with particular emphasis on raising innovative activity by domestic entrepreneurs and enterprises]. Rather, the system needs to be strengthened within a comprehensive and coherent set of policy initiatives that optimize the effectiveness of IPRs. Among such initiatives are further structural reform of enterprises, trade and investment liberalization, promotion of financial and innovation systems to commercialize new technologies, expansion of educational opportunities to build human capital for absorbing and developing technology, and specification of rules for maintaining effective competition in Chinese markets.[175]

As they noted, the effectiveness of intellectual property protection in expanding economic growth and promoting technology development not only depend heavily on economic circumstances and the existence of a sufficiently developed technological base and infrastructure, but also on such complementary factors as 'further structural reform to increase entrepreneurship and flexibility of enterprises; expanded liberalization of restrictions on trade, investment, and technology agreements; and additional steps to ensure competition in domestic markets among firms and across regions'.[176]

In China, the oft-cited barriers to intellectual property reforms include 'the difficulties in monitoring a large territory, in collecting evidence of infringement, and in collecting judgments, widespread corruption, abuse by government officials, different values placed on intellectual property infringement, the indistinguishability between public and private entities, local protectionism, and the decentralization of government'.[177] Ironically yet crucially, none of these

171 Mansfield, note 26 above, 20.
172 RM Sherwood, 'Some Things Cannot Be Legislated' (2002) 10 *Cardozo J Int'l & Comp L* 37.
173 Ibid, 42.
174 Heald, note 13 above, 252.
175 Maskus, Dougherty and Mertha, note 42 above, 297.
176 Ibid, 307.
177 Yu, 'From Pirates to Partners I', note 4 above, 230–231.

barriers is directly covered by the TRIPS Agreement or by the many international intellectual property treaties China has ratified.

As I pointed out elsewhere, one of the major defects of the United States's potential WTO complaint against China over its lack of general enforcement of intellectual property rights is the inability by the United States to show that China's enforcement in the intellectual property area is worse than its enforcement in other areas.[178] Article 41(5) of the TRIPS Agreement stated specifically that a WTO member state is not required to devote more resources to intellectual property enforcement than to other areas of law enforcement.[179] If China were able to show that their enforcement problems with piracy and counterfeiting were no more excessive than their problems with, say, tax collection (which are very serious), China would be likely to prevail.[180] After all, it is hard to imagine any country putting intellectual property protection ahead of tax collection. Nor does the WTO require it to do so.

Finally, it is important not to ignore the additional protection that is offered outside the intellectual property regime. To protect their intellectual assets, rights holders have increasingly relied on mass-market contracts, such as shrink-wrap or click–wrap licenses.[181] They have also used alternative technological protection measures, such as encryption technology for protecting copyrighted works in digital media[182] and genetic use restriction technologies (GURTs) for protecting seeds.[183] Whether this additional protection will help protect the important intellectual assets will ultimately depend on the additional legal protection in the contract area, or in related areas that govern the circumvention of technological protection mechanisms.

In sum, one has to look beyond the intellectual property system to examine the various complementary factors that are needed to build an enabling environment for effective intellectual property protection. Although the addition of

178 Yu, 'From Pirates to Partners II', note 5 above, 935.

179 TRIPS Agreement, note 157 above, Art 41(5).

180 For discussion of China's problems with the collection of tax revenues, see JL Chan, *China Streetsmart: What You MUST Know to Be Effective and Profitable in China* (Prentice Hall, 2003) 103; JH Jackson, 'The Impact of China's Accession on the WTO' in DZ Cass, BG Williams and G Barker (eds), *China and the World Trading System: Entering the New Millennium* (Cambridge University Press, 2003) 19, 27; DL Yang, 'Reform and the Restructuring of Central–Local Relations' in Goodman and Segal, note 126 above, 59–98.

181 PK Yu, 'Five Disharmonizing Trends in the International Intellectual Property Regime' in Yu, *Intellectual Property and Information Wealth*, note 9 above, 73, 91–94.

182 PK Yu, 'Anticircumvention and Anti-anticircumvention' (2006) 84 *Denv U LR* 13.

183 T Swanson and T Goeschl, 'Diffusion and Distribution: The Impacts on Poor Countries of Technological Enforcement Within the Biotechnology Sector' in Maskus and Reichman, note 10 above, 669–694.

these factors will complicate the analysis and make it more difficult to clearly identify the determinants for economic development, such addition will also provide a more complete analysis that will assess intellectual property enforcement more accurately and realistically.

D. Micro-level, Quantitative Improvements

Bilateral intellectual property discussions are inevitably state-centred. As a result, documents emanating from these discussions tend to overemphasize developments at the macroscopic level, rather than the microscopic level. In February 2006, for example, the USTR completed a 'top-to-bottom review' of US–China trade relations.[184] Although the importance of undertaking this comprehensive study cannot be ignored, the top-down approach used in conducting the study is somewhat misguided.

First, studies that are conducted using the top-down approach often contain quantitative analyses that rely on the use of basic indicators as proxies for the effectiveness of the country's intellectual property protection. For example, Section 301 submissions or similar reports are filled with information about which laws have been enacted, which new taskforces have been established, how many patents or trademarks have been applied or granted, how many intellectual property cases have been brought or tried, how cases have been disposed of, and how many criminal prosecutions the local authorities have pursued or completed. Likewise, reports supplied by the Chinese authorities are filled with similar, and often impressive, statistics as well as 'war stories' about the efforts these authorities have launched or completed to crack down on piracy and counterfeiting.

To be certain, proxy measures are sometimes needed, and basic indicators can be selected in a way that will tell not only 'on the books' stories, but also how written laws have been translated into practice.[185] In fact, these statistics may provide important and useful information about recent intellectual property reforms in China. Nevertheless, just like indices used for ranking intellectual property protection in empirical surveys, the basic indicators are unlikely to 'fully capture the complexities and multiple dimensions of modern IPR systems'.[186] An overemphasis on quantitative analysis therefore will lead researchers to

---

184 Office of the US Trade Representative, *US–China Trade Relations: Entering a New Phase of Greater Accountability and Enforcement: Top-to-Bottom Review* (2006), available at <http://www.ustr.gov/assets/Document_Library/Reports_Publications/2006/asset_upload_file921_8938.pdf>.

185 Commission on Intellectual Property Rights, note 45 above, 21.

186 Primo Braga and Fink, note 12 above, 180.

overlook the important developments that can be revealed only through qualitative or case-by-case analyses.

Indeed, as seasoned China observers have pointed out, many of the most interesting developments in China were not taking place at the macroscopic level, but rather at the microscopic level. For example, commentators have suggested how village and township elections have provided hope for China's democratic reforms,[187] while the proliferation of bulletin boards, chatrooms, and web logs has resulted in an expansion of free expression and political discourse in the country.[188] One might even remember David Sheff's insightful observation in his book about the transformation of mass communication in China, in which the ringing mobile phone in the backroom of a Chinese restaurant belonged to a waiter, rather than the businesspeople inside.[189] Had researchers focused solely on top-down developments or the statistics supplied by governments or industry groups, they would have missed these important developments.

Like other reforms in China, the most interesting developments in the intellectual property area are now taking place at the microscopic and qualitative levels. For example, many of today's copyright- or patent-based piracy cases are no longer disputes about verbatim copies of protected goods, although such disputes still exist and piracy of music, movies, and computer software remains rampant in the country. Many of these cases also do not involve underground or fly-by-night operations, but rather legitimate businesses that either are ignorant of intellectual property laws or are testing the limits of the law.[190] This line of disputes include those concerning the unauthorized translation or adaptation of copyrighted works, or the infringing use of patented processes in the manufacture of competing finished products.

Moreover, although many of today's intellectual property disputes may sound like traditional piracy stories, they have more complex storylines. Elsewhere, I have discussed how the recent invalidation of Pfizer's patent on Viagra by the State Intellectual Property Office, which was subsequently overturned by a Chinese court, has shown a promising development in which local pharmaceutical manufacturers took the legal route to challenge the patent owned by

---

187 JP Horsley, 'A Legal Perspective on the Development of Electoral Democracy in China: The Case of Village Elections' in CS Hsu (ed), *Understanding China's Legal System: Essays in Honor of Jerome A. Cohen* (New York University Press, 2003) 295–352.

188 BL Liebman and T Wu, 'Chinese Network Justice' (2007) 8 *Chi J Int'l L* (forthcoming).

189 D Sheff, *China Dawn: The Story of a Technology and Business Revolution* (HarperBusiness, 2002) 91.

190 Yu, 'From Pirates to Partners II', note 5 above, 977.

a major foreign company. In the past, local manufacturers were likely to ignore the law and rely on counterfeits to compete.[191]

Similarly, the celebrated dispute between General Motors and Chery Automobile Company, in which General Motors claimed that the Shanghai-based carmaker copied its Chevy Spark in designing the Chery QQ, was far from a typical intellectual property dispute. That dispute included complicated legal issues raised by the territorial nature of intellectual property rights, General Motors's lack of patents in China, and the complexity created by General Motors's acquisition of Korea-based Daewoo Motor.[192] Had the dispute been a simple infringement case, one has to wonder why it eventually took three years and required the 'assistance' of the Chinese government to reach an out-of-court settlement to end the dispute.[193]

In addition to the nature of the disputes, one can explore whether and to what extent the consciousness of intellectual property rights has grown among the Chinese populace. One of the more promising copyright-related developments is the growth of private collective copyright administration bodies. The first of these bodies, the Music Copyright Society of China, was established on 17 December 1992. Today, it represents more than 2,500 'local stakeholders', including Chinese singers, composers, music adaptors, heirs, music publishers and recording companies of Chinese nationality.[194] Meanwhile, a few other collective bodies have been established since 2000.[195] With the recognition of these private administration bodies in the recently revised copyright law, their number is likely to grow substantially.[196] In fact, one commentator has recently suggested the possibility of the institution of a private levy system in light of the country's changing conditions.[197]

---

191 Ibid, 986.

192 Ibid, 950.

193 As reported, 'GM and Chery extended their appreciation to Chinese government for helping to resolve the dispute.' 'Intellectual Property Battle Between GM and Chery Reaches Settlement', *China IP Express* (1 December 2005), available at <http://www.iprights.com/cms/templates/china-ipx.aspx?articleid=2319&zoneid=4>. Although Chery agreed not to use the 'Chery' trademark in the United States, which is likely to be confusingly similar to General Motors' 'Chevy' trademark, Malcolm Bricklin, Chery's American partner, claimed that 'Chery [was] not required to pay any compensation to GM under the settlement agreement . . . [and that] the agreement clears the way for a smoother introduction of the newly designed, Chinese-made, vehicles into the United States, starting in 2007'.

194 Sun, note 6 above, 63.

195 Ibid.

196 Art 8 of the revised copyright law provides that copyright holders 'may authorize an organization for collective administration of copyright to exercise the copyright or any copyright-related right'. Chinese Copyright Law, note 94 above, Art 8.

197 E Priest, 'The Future of Music and Film Piracy in China' (2006) 21 *Berkeley Tech LJ* 795.

Finally, it is important to analyse the impact of changes in the intellectual property system on consumers, in both tangible and intangible forms. Are consumers getting products of better quality and higher reliability? Are they getting products that are more suitable or desirable? Do they have more confidence in shopping in the open market? Do they have more product choices? Do they respect others' legal rights more than they used to? To some extent, finding the answers to some of these questions is just as difficult as examining whether Mark Twain was right that stronger copyright protection in nineteenth-century United States would have prevented young Americans from being polluted by foreign novels that 'fill[ed] the imagination with an unhealthy fascination with foreign life, with its dukes and earls and kings, its fuss and feathers, its graceful immoralities, its sugar-coated injustices and oppressions'.[198] Nevertheless, a better account of the many intangible improvements in intellectual property protection is likely to enhance the quality of the overall economic analysis.

In the near future, the type of intellectual property infringement in China is likely to be as important as the amount and frequency of the infringement. Thus, the use of the top-down approach and the reliance on basic indicators are likely to be of limited use. Instead of questioning how often infringement takes place, one also has to examine what type of infringement has occurred. Because policy compromises are needed to respond to regional and sectoral variations within the country, region-based, sector-specific, micro-level, qualitative analyses are likely to be more illuminating than those focusing on nationwide, cross-sector, macro-level, quantitative developments. In fact, if researchers continue to use a top-down, nation-based approach, they will not be able to fully account for the progress China has made in recent intellectual property reforms.

---

198 As Mark Twain wrote in *Century Magazine* in 1886:

> The statistics of any public library will show that of every hundred books read by our people, about seventy are novels—and nine-tenths of them foreign ones. They fill the imagination with an unhealthy fascination with foreign life, with its dukes and earls and kings, its fuss and feathers, its graceful immoralities, its sugar-coated injustices and oppressions; and this fascination breeds a more or less pronounced dissatisfaction with our country and form of government, and contempt for our republican commonplaces and simplicities; it also breeds a longing for something 'better' which presently crops out in the diseased shams and imitations of the ideal foreign spectacle: Hence the 'dude.'

S Vaidhyanathan, *Copyrights and Copywrongs: The Rise of Intellectual Property and How It Threatens Creativity* (New York University Press, 2001) 61.

Conclusion

Many commentators have considered China the proverbial exception to the causal relationship between the strength of intellectual property protection and economic development. This chapter rejects that position and contends that China illustrates rather well the ambiguity of the relationship and the complex interplay of the different location advantages that affect private investment decisions. Whether one can develop a complete and accurate picture of this relationship will depend on whether one understands and properly analyses the many different factors that affect those decisions. Compared to other countries, the study of this relationship in China has been made particularly difficult by the uneven development and continuous economic transition.

Nevertheless, a better understanding of this relationship will help provide a more accurate forecast of when China will reach a crossover point at which it will find stronger intellectual property protection in its self-interests. Interestingly, despite the urgency of finding when China will reach this crossover point and the importance of fully understanding the socio-economic impact of stronger intellectual property protection, the relationship between intellectual property and economic development has been largely under-explored by commentators—Chinese commentators in particular. As Maskus, Dougherty, and Mertha observed:

> University scholarship in China (and in other countries) in IPRs is overwhelmingly addressed to legal issues. Many scholars are actively involved in assessing shortcomings in the law and in drafting revisions, and they also participate in training new intellectual property lawyers. Few economists study the processes of technical change in China and how they are affected by market structure, competition, and exposure to foreign technologies and investment. Fewer still examine the relationship between IPRs, technical development, and growth. Accordingly, economists in China either remain unaware of IPR issues or are skeptical about the potential for IPRs to increase technological advance and business development.[199]

Hopefully, this chapter, and the larger volume, will convince policy makers that intellectual property protection should be measured not only in legal terms, but also in socio-economic ones. Although intellectual property protection may not be a prerequisite for economic development and growth, it is an integral and essential part of a complex innovation system that serves as a catalyst for economic development. The sooner Chinese policy makers understand the dynamics of this complex innovation system, the quicker they can harness the system to promote the country's economic development.

---

199 Maskus, Dougherty and Mertha, note 42 above, 311.

6

TRIPS AND TRIPS-PLUS PROTECTION AND IMPACTS IN LATIN AMERICA

Carlos M Correa

Introduction

The linkages between intellectual property and economic and social development are difficult to establish. In particular, it is extremely difficult to determine the causal relationship between certain levels of intellectual property protection and indicators of trade, investment, innovation, and technology transfer.[1] Although several econometric studies have explored the relationship between

[1] See, e.g. C Fink and K Maskus, *Intellectual Property and Development. Lessons From Recent Economic Research* (World Bank and Oxford University Press, 2005).

intellectual property and some of these variables, their results are far from being conclusive.[2]

Despite the paucity of evidence on the impact of intellectual property rights, enormous changes have taken place in this area in the last 15 years. Such changes have not been based on a rational assessment of available evidence on the effects of such rights. In developed countries, they have essentially been driven by persuasive actions and lobbying of particular industries, while in developing countries they have largely been the result of the implementation of the TRIPS Agreement, of developed countries' demands and, more recently, of free trade agreements (FTAs) that provide for TRIPS-Plus standards.[3]

Given their status as 'developing countries', Latin American countries were allowed, under the transitional periods provided for in Article 65 of the TRIPS Agreement, to implement its obligations as of 1 January 2000. They could also delay the granting of product patent protection to areas of technology not so protectable in its territory on that date for an additional period of five years. As discussed below, however, no Latin American country made full use of this possibility. The use by Latin American countries of the flexibilities built into the TRIPS Agreement has been uneven.[4] Some countries which did use them have stepped back in the context of FTAs signed with the USA, as examined below.

This chapter briefly reviews, first, the literature on economic and social impact of intellectual property in the region. Second, it highlights the main changes in legislation that took place in Latin America since the 1990s and, in particular, the extent to which domestic laws and standards were calibrated to respond to local conditions and needs.[5] Third, it considers measures regarding the protection of traditional knowledge (TK) adopted in some Latin American countries. Although there are other measures that share some of the objectives

---

[2] See, e.g. *Assessing the impact of new IPR provisions on public health*. Summary of key points raised during the two day ICTSD–WBI–WHO workshop in Geneva, 31 July to 1 August 2006. Note prepared by the organizers, available at <http://www.iprsonline.org/unctadictsd/dialogue/2006–07–31/Workshop%20summary_Impact%20Assessment.pdf>, and the studies available at <http://www.iprsonline.org/unctadictsd/dialogue/2006-07-31/2006-07-31_docs.htm>.

[3] Agreement on Trade-Related Aspects of Intellectual Property Rights, 15 April 1994, Marrakech Agreement Establishing the World Trade Organization, Annex 1C, Legal Instruments—Results of the Uruguay Round Vol. 31; 33 ILM 1197 (TRIPS Agreement). See, e.g. Susan K Sell, *Private Power, Public Law: The Globalization of Intellectual Property Rights* (Cambridge University Press, 2003). Many Latin American countries were threatened or (Brazil in 1987 and Argentina ten years later) actually subject to retaliations under the special s 301 of the US Trade Act.

[4] See, e.g. Carlos Correa, 'Implementing the TRIPs Agreement in the Patents Field—Options for Developing Countries',(1998) 1 *J of World Intell Prop* 1.

[5] The analysis made is not exhaustive; it only aims at providing an overview of the main aspects of the reform of intellectual property regimes in Latin America after the beginning of the Uruguay Round.

of intellectual property rights—the promotion of creativity and innovation—the range of such measures is too broad and cannot be systematically considered here.[6]

Part I Assessing the Impact of Intellectual Property Rights

The possible effects of intellectual property rights, particularly of the adoption of higher standards of protection, has raised considerable debate and stimulated a few studies on the matter in Latin America. Of special concern has been the likely impact of patents and protection of medical test data.[7]

A number of prospective studies about the impact of the outcomes of the Uruguay Round in the area of intellectual property rights were conducted during the 1990s, particularly with regard to pharmaceuticals. For instance, Nogués estimated the welfare losses that the introduction of pharmaceutical patents would generate in Argentina, Brazil, Mexico and other countries, as well as the potential benefits in terms of technology transfer, foreign direct investment, domestic innovation and avoiding trade retaliation by developed countries. He estimated that substantial price increases would result from the introduction of pharmaceutical patents.[8]

More recently, several studies were conducted to assess the possible impact on public health of TRIPS-Plus provisions contained in FTAs negotiated between the USA and Andean countries.[9] Most of these studies anticipated that provisions

6 For instance, research and development subsidies, tax breaks and prizes. A variety of instruments of this type can be found in Latin American countries. See e.g. D de Ferranti, G Perry, I Gill, J Guasch, C Sanchez-Paramo, N Schady, *Closing the Gap in Education and Technology* (World Bank, 2003). See also, with regard to incentives for innovation in Brazil, Denis Borges Barbosa (org),Ana Beatriz Nunes Barbosa, Ana Paula Machado, Marcelo Siqueira e Mariana Loja Tápias, *Direito da Inovação* (Comentários à Lei 10.973/2004, Lei Federal da Inovação) (Lumen Juris, 2006).

7 See, e.g. J Bermudez and MA Oliveira, *Intellectual Property in the Context of the WTO TRIPS Agreement* (WHO/PAHO, Fiocruz, ENSP, 2004).

8 L Nogués, 'Patents and Pharmaceutical Drugs: Understanding the Pressures on Developing Countries', (1990) 24 *J of World Trade* 6, 81–104. See also P Challú, *Patentamiento de productos farmacéuticos. Consecuencias* (Mercado, 1991); A Chambouleyron, 'La nueva ley de patentes y su efecto sobre los precios de los medicamentos. Análisis y propuestas' (1995) XVIII *Estudios*, 75.

9 Organización Panamericana de la Salud –Colombia – Fundación IFARMA, 'Modelo prospectivo del impacto de la protección a la propiedad intelectual sobre el acceso a medicamentos en Colombia' 2004, available at <www.col.ops-oms.org>; National Institute for the Defense of Competition and the Protection of Intellectual Property (INDECOPI), 'Serie estudios de investigación. Balance del conocimiento y propiedad intelectual en el comercio' May 2005; INDECOPI, 'Serie estudios de investigación. Incidencia de los derechos de propiedad intelectual en el gasto de las familias en el marco del TLC' May 2005, both available at <www.indecopi.gob.pe>; República del Perú. Ministerio de Salud. Gerardo Valladares *et al*, 'Evaluación de los potenciales efectos sobre el

requiring the extension of patent term, or granting exclusive rights with regard to test data, would lead to price increases and a negative impact on access to medicines—in the case of delays in the examination of patents, or approving the marketing of a pharmaceutical product. For instance, a study for Peru relating to 43 products that could have been subject to data exclusivity estimated that the average price of such products would have been between 94.3 and 114.4 per cent higher than what they have actually been in the absence of such protection.[10]

The sectoral impact of patents has been examined in the case of Argentina. The study found that patenting in medium- and high-technology industries is dominated by foreign applicants, and that there is little relationship between domestic innovation and the patent system,[11] A similar conclusion was reached by Aboites in Mexico, who found that the strengthening of the patent regime introduced in 1991 did not encourage local innovation, but instead a significant increase in foreign patenting.[12]

Some studies have also been conducted on the economic importance of copyright in MERCOSUR member countries[13] and Chile. They indicated a considerable weight of copyright-related industries in Argentina and Brazil (around 6 per cent of GNP) but noted that most value added is contributed by the distribution of imported copyright works rather than by the local production thereof, and found significant trade deficits in this area.[14]

Jeroen van Wijk examined the impact of the protection of plant varieties in Latin America. He concluded that it may reduce germplasm flows and competition, and that such protection may help the domestic seed industry 'to restrict the trade in seed saved from their varieties and to increase their income. There is little

acceso a medicamentos del tratado de libre comercio que se negocia con los Estados Unidos de América', available at <www.minsa.gob.pe>; Corporación Andina de Fomento (CAF)/Fedesarrollo/ Fundación Santa Fé de Bogotá: Emilio j Archila *et al*, 'Estudio sobre la propiedad intelectual en el sector farmacéutico Colombiano' June 2005; CAF/Apoyo Consultoría, 'Impacto de las negociaciones del TLC con Estados Unidos en materia de propiedad intelectual en los mercados de medicamentos y plaguicidas' April 2005; Juan Pichihua Serna, 'Possible Impact of US–Peru FTA on Access to Medicines Due to Data Exclusivity Protection for Drugs', available at <http://www.iprsonline.org/unctadictsd/dialogue/2006-07-31/9Peru%20Study-PichihuarevisedAug10.pdf>.

10 CAF/Apoyo Consultoría, 'Impacto de las negociaciones', note 9 above.

11 Centro de Estudios para la Producción, 'Lógica sectorial del uso del sistema de patentes en Argentina, Síntesis de la Economía Real N° 51—Segunda Epoca 2006'.

12 J Aboites, 'Innovación, patentes y globalización', in J Aboites and G Dutrénit (eds) *Innovación, aprendizaje y creación de capacidades tecnológicas* (UAM, 2003) 163–206.

13 Argentina, Brazil, Paraguay, and Uruguay.

14 OMPI–Universidade Estadual de Campinas, 'Estudio sobre la importancia económica de las industrias y actividades protegidas por el derecho de autor y los derechos conexos en los países de de MERCOSUR y Chile', 62–63.

evidence, however, that this additional income leads to the availability of more and better varieties for farmers.'[15]

These studies show that different countries and sectors are affected differently by intellectual property rights, depending on the strength of the scientific and technological capacity, the availability of capital for funding innovative activities, and the nature of the products involved, among other factors. As noted by Professor Boyle, the assumptions that 'to promote intellectual property is automatically to promote innovation and, in that process, the more rights the better' are incorrect.[16] Obviously, like any other incentive, the impact of intellectual property rights will depend on the context in which they apply. Such rights cannot encourage innovation in Latin America as they may in countries with more sophisticated innovation systems. Likewise, there is no evidence suggesting that the increased levels of protection resulting from the implementation of the TRIPS Agreement have been instrumental in attracting more foreign direct investment or technology transfer.[17]

Part II Changes in Intellectual Property Legislation[18]

A. Patent Law

The implementation of the TRIPS Agreement entailed significant changes in patent legislation in Latin America, as most countries in the region excluded the protection of pharmaceutical products, and did not provide for the reversal of

---

[15] Jeroen van Wijk, 'How does stronger protection of intellectual property rights affect seed supply? Early evidence of impact', (1996) *Natural Resources Perspectives*, No. 13; Overseas Development Institute, site at <http://www.oneworld.org>; Jeroen van Wijk and W Jaffé, *Intellectual Property Rights and Agriculture in Developing Countries*, (University of Amsterdam, 1996); and Jeroen van Wijk and W Jaffé, 'The Impact of Plant Breeders' Rights in Developing Countries: Debate and experience in Argentina, Chile, Colombia, Mexico, and Uruguay', (1995) *Biotechnology and Development Monitor* No 23, 15–19, available at <http://www.biotech-monitor.nl/2306.htm>.

[16] James Boyle, 'A Manifesto on WIPO and the future of intellectual property', (2004) *Duke L & Tech R* No. 9, available at <http://www.law.duke.edu/j Law 9.279 (Industrial Property Code), May 14, 1996.ournals/dltr/articles/PDF/2004DLTR0009.pdf>.

[17] Contrary to pledges about a positive impact of stronger intellectual property protection on foreign direct investment, there is some evidence of disinvestment in the pharmaceutical sector after pharmaceutical product patents were introduced in Latin America. For instance, in Colombia there remained only seven out of 32 manufacturing plants owned by foreign companies; in Peru, 15 such plants closed down in the last ten years and only two remained; while in Venezuela 21 closed down and only four remained. In Chile all such manufacturing plants were closed down. See G Holguin, *La Bolsa y la vida. Impacto de los TLC en acceso a medicamentos* (Misión salud, 2004), 78.

[18] This section is partially based on previous works of the author, particularly Carlos Correa 'Reforming the intellectual property rights system in Latin America', (2000) 23 *The World Economy* 6.

burden of proof nor for the extension of the protection to products directly made with a protected process, among other standards required by the Agreement. In some cases, very old laws were applied at the time the TRIPS Agreement was adopted,[19] which did not incorporate these concepts.[20]

Despite the right to delay the introduction of product patents for pharmaceuticals, most countries in Latin America started to grant such patents before the expiry of the transitional period on 1 January 2005.[21] This was mainly due to pressure exerted by the US government and pharmaceutical industry. Argentina, for instance, changed its patent law in 1995 after a turbulent legislative process, and granted pharmaceutical product patents as of October 2000. Uruguay started to grant patents for pharmaceutical (and agrochemical) products as of 1 November 2001. Brazil went even further in adopting the 'pipeline' solution actively promoted by US industry and government. The new law permitted the retroactive recognition of pharmaceutical product and process patents[22] based on applications made before its entry into force, provided that the covered inventions had not previously been commercialized in any market, nor serious preparation for the exploitation of the invention been made in Brazil.[23]

Eligible Subject Matter

Latin American patent laws generally exclude plants and animals from patentability, in accordance with the exception allowed under Article 27.3(b) of the TRIPS Agreement.[24] Those countries that have entered into FTAs with the

19 Such as in the case of Argentina, which applied Law No 111 of 1864.

20 Only Brazil and Cuba have signed the Patent Law Treaty (which has not yet entered into force in those countries). Latin American countries have generally opposed or only reluctantly considered the further harmonization of patent law as proposed in the context of the draft Substantive Patent Law Treaty (SPLT) in WIPO. See generally, e.g. Carlos Correa and S Musungu, 'The WIPO Patent Agenda: the risks for developing countries', Working Paper No 12, South Centre, Geneva, 2002, available at <http://www.southcentre.org/publications/workingpapers/wp12.pdf>.

21 Mexico and the members of the Andean Community substantially modified their intellectual property regimes even before the formal adoption of the TRIPS Agreement in 1994. In 2000, the Common Andean Regime on Industrial Property was reviewed again (through Decision 486) in order to ensure consistency with all aspects of the TRIPS Agreement.

22 In Brazil neither product nor process patents for pharmaceuticals were allowed under the previous law.

23 Article 230, Law No 9.279 (Industrial Property Code), 14 May 1996. Though Decision 344 of the Andean Community did not accept the 'pipeline' principle, in the framework of a bilateral agreement with the United States, Ecuador (one of the members of the Andean Community) accepted that solution and retroactively granted some patents with respect to pharmaceutical products which were not 'new'. The Junta del Acuerdo de Cartagena initiated an action against Ecuador for non-compliance with the Andean regime. The Andean Court of Justice decided (on 30 October 1996) that the novelty requirement was absolute and that the Andean Group had explicitly rejected the 'pipeline' principle. The High Court declared that patents granted in Ecuador in accordance with said principle were void.

24 In the case of Argentina, the exclusion is not contained in the law but in the implementing regulation, Decree 260/96.

United States, however, may be bound to recognize patents for plants. Chile, for instance, committed in its FTA to undertake 'reasonable efforts', through a transparent and participatory process, to develop and propose legislation within four years from the entry into force of the agreement for that purpose. In the DR–CAFTA a pledge is made to undertake all reasonable efforts to make patent protection for plants available by the date the agreement enters into force. These obligations[25] would make available patent protection, *inter alia*, for transgenic plants.[26]

In addition, several countries have clarified that substances existing in nature are not 'inventions', thereby using the leeway left by the TRIPS Agreement to define what an invention is.[27] Decision 344 of the Andean Community considered non-patentable substances that exist in nature, or which 'replicated' them. Decision 486—which replaced Decision 344—considers non-patentable substances that exist in nature.[28] Similarly, the Mexican and Argentine laws exclude the patentability of substances existing in nature, although it is unclear to what extent isolated materials may be deemed patentable in the case of Mexico. The 1996 Brazilian Industrial Property Code is more precise in this respect. It excludes the patentability of living beings or 'biological materials found in nature', even if isolated, including the 'genome or germplasm' of any living being (Article 10.IX). The Biodiversity Law of Costa Rica (1998) establishes the non-patentability, *inter alia*, of sequences of DNA *per se*.[29]

---

25 Similar commitments are contained in the FTAs with Peru and Colombia.

26 No equivalent obligation is established with regard to animals. This has raised the criticism of the USTR advisory body, IFAC–3, which noted its disappointment because there is no explicit requirement in CAFTA to implement patent protection for transgenic animals: 'IFAC–3 notes that the United States provides for the patenting of animals that are new, involve an inventive step and are capable of industrial application and that the Singapore FTA requires the patenting of both transgenic plants and animals' (IFAC–3 Report to USTR on CAFTA, available at <http://www.ustr.gov/assets/Trade_Agreements/Bilateral/CAFTA/CAFTA_Reports/asset_upload_file571_5945.pdf>.

27 See, e.g. J Straus, 'Implications of the TRIPs Agreement in the field of patent law', in F-K Beier and G Schricker (eds), *From GATT to TRIPs—The Agreement on Trade-Related Aspects of Intellectual Property Rights* (Max Planck Institute for Foreign and International Patent, Copyright and Competition Law, 1996), 187.

28 Art 15 of Decision 486: 'The following shall not be considered inventions: . . . Any living thing, either complete or partial, as found in nature, natural biological processes, and biological material, as existing in nature, or able to be separated, including the genome or germplasm of any living thing'.

29 The Biodiversity Law established that the following matters are not protectable: sequences of DNA *per se;* plants and animals; non-genetically modified micro-organisms; essentially biological processes for the production of plants and animals; natural processes or cycles as such; inventions essentially derived from knowledge which is associated with traditional or cultural biological practices in the public domain; inventions which, to be commercially exploited through a monopoly, can affect farming or fishing processes or products which are considered basic for the food and health of the inhabitants of the country.

All these laws have explicitly excluded from patentability (as permitted by Article 27.3(a) of the TRIPS Agreement) methods of surgical, therapeutic or diagnostic treatment. The exclusion of therapeutic methods may entail the non-patentability of the 'second use' of a known product, since patents on the new use of a known medicine are essentially equivalent to patents on therapeutic methods. Decisions 344 and 486 of the Andean Community explicitly excluded the patentability of second uses.[30] On this basis, the Andean Community Secretariat challenged the granting of a patent over the second use of sildenafil (Viagra) by the patent office of Ecuador,[31] while the Andean Court of Justice subsequently declared the patent invalid.[32]

In other Latin American countries, the granting of second use patents depends on the criteria applied by the patent office. In Argentina, the patent examination guidelines of the patent office exclude second use patentability.[33] In Brazil there has been a divergence between the patent office and ANVISA, the national health regulatory authority, which has been given the power to reject the granting of pharmaceutical patents.[34] According to the 'Diretrizes para o exame de pedidos de patentes nas áreas de biotecnologia e farmacêutica depositados após 31.12.1994' issued by the Instituto Nacional de Propriedade Industrial, patents covering the second use of a pharmaceutical product can be granted under so-called 'Swiss claims'.[35] This is not acceptable, however, to ANVISA.[36]

Patent Term

The TRIPS Agreement requires a minimum protection term of 20 years (Article 33). Although, as mentioned above, the Agreement only became binding for Latin American countries on 1 January 2000, in some cases rights holders attempted to force an early application of it. In Argentina, for instance, some foreign companies initiated judicial actions before that date, (unsuccessfully) attempting to extend the patent term—of 15 years from grant—to 20 years

30 Decision 486, Art 21: '[p]roducts or processes already patented and included in the state of the art within the meaning of Article 16 of this Decision may not be the subject of new patents on the sole ground of having been put to a use different from that originally contemplated by the initial patent'.

31 See Resolution 476 of the La Secretaria General De La Comunidad Andina (2001), available at <http://www.comunidadandina.org/normativa/res/r476sg.htm>.

32 See Proceso N° 34–Ai–2001 Sumario por Incumplimiento de Sentencia (2003), available under 'Documentos' within the main Community site, <http://www. comunidadandina.org>.

33 See Resolución P–243—Directrices sobre Patentamiento, <http://www.inpi.gov.ar/templates/novedades/p243.pdf>.

34 Law No 10.196/2001.

35 See <http://www.agif.com.br/download/INPI-diretrizes%20para%20exame.doc>.

36 See e.g. M. Basso, 'Intervention of Health Authorities in Patent Examination. The Brazilian Practice of the Prior Consent', 1 *Int'l J of Intell Prop Mgmt* 1, forthcoming 2006.

from the filing date, in accordance with Article 33 of the Agreement. Similar cases were reported in Brazil.[37]

The FTAs negotiated by the USA with Chile, Colombia, Peru, as well as the DR–CAFTA oblige the parties to extend the patent term to compensate for unreasonable delays beyond a certain period (a) in the obtaining of marketing approval of a medicine and (b) in the examination of patent applications.

US FTAs require each party, at the request of the patent owner, to adjust the term of a patent 'to compensate for unreasonable delays that occur in granting the patent' (e.g. Chile FTA, Article 17.9.6; DR–CAFTA, Article 15.9.5). This adjustment was introduced by the US Patent Term Guarantee Act (1999), when the 17 years of protection from the date of granting was replaced by 20 years from the filing date.[38]

The provisions in the FTAs contain a definition of what unreasonable or unjustified delay means: more than five years from the date of filing the application in the Party, or three years after a request for examination of the application has been made, whichever is later in the case of the Chile FTA and CAFTA.

The extension to compensate delays in the examination of patent applications is not recognized in most countries (such as in Europe), and is not required by the TRIPS Agreement.[39] It overlooks that patent laws often confer rights to applicants after the application has been published (normally within 18 months after the date of filing). Such extension is based on the unproven presumption that 20 years less the period required for the examination would not be sufficient to reward the inventor for whatever contribution he has made.

Another common feature in US FTAs (e.g. Chile FTA, Article 17.10.2(a); CAFTA, Article 15.9.6(b)) is a provision requiring compensation of the patent owner for an 'unreasonable' delay in the marketing approval of pharmaceuticals. Most US FTAs do not mention whether the extension shall apply only to delays in the country where approval is sought (although it would be legitimate to

37 See, e.g. *EI Dupont de Nemours and Co v INPI* (Superior Court of Justice—STJ), Third Jurisdiction no: 2004/0048736–1, Appellate Review no 652172/RJ, original case no. 98.0001955–3 (Origin: 14th Federal District) Patent no 8401507–1.

38 The term must be extended when the USPTO does not issue a patent within three years after the filing date (35 USC 154).

39 According to Art 62(2) of the Agreement, 'where the acquisition of an intellectual property right is subject to the right being granted or registered, Members shall ensure that the procedures for grant or registration, subject to compliance with the substantive conditions for acquisition of the right, permit the granting or registration of the right within a reasonable period of time so as to avoid unwarranted curtailment of the period of protection'.

interpret that this is the case), or whether the delay in the country where the first approval was obtained should also be taken into account.[40]

No maximum period is provided for the extension. This constitutes a remarkable difference between the FTAs and the current law in the United States, where some time limits are provided for. The extension in the United States to compensate for delays in the marketing approval process shall not exceed five years and, in no case, shall exclusivity exceed 14 years from the date of approval by the Food and Drug Administration (35 USC §156). In addition, the extension applies to only one patent per product.

Since the grounds for the extension of patent terms under the FTAs are *independent, cumulative* and with *no maximum period*, nothing—unless this is precluded by national legislation—seems to prevent a patent from being extended for *x* years due to a delay in its granting, and for *y* more years due to a delay in the marketing approval process. In other words, patents on pharmaceutical products may last for several months or years after the 20-year term required by the TRIPS Agreement.

The possibility of an extension creates uncertainty for generic producers and, when effective, has obvious consequences for public health: it delays the introduction of competing products with the ensuing loss of consumer welfare and increased barriers in the way of access to medicines by the population. The positive impact on research and development of the additional income obtained by patent owners is minimal, as Latin American markets contribute a tiny portion of the global income of the pharmaceutical industry.[41]

Exceptions to Exclusive Rights

Article 30 of the TRIPS Agreement makes clear that the patent holder does not enjoy absolute exclusive rights, as they may be subject to 'limited exceptions'.[42] One of the possible exceptions is for third parties' use of the protected subject matter for experimentation or research. While experimentation or research *as such* are not enumerated exclusive rights of the patent owner, in order to conduct those activities it is normally necessary to make or use the patented product, or to use the patented process. This is the reason why an exception may be necessary regarding experimentation or research on a patented invention. The extent to

[40] This is clarified, however, in the case of the US FTA with Bahrain (Art 15.6.(b)(ii)), which obliges account to be taken of delays in a foreign country.

[41] In accordance with PhRMA's *Pharmaceutical Industry Profile 2005—From Laboratory to Patient: Pathways to Biopharmaceutical Innovation* only between five and seven per cent of profits are generated in low- and middle-income countries. See also F Scherer, 'Global Welfare in Pharmaceutical Patenting' (2004) *World Economy*, July.

[42] See generally on this issue, C Garrison, 'Exceptions to patent rights in developing countries' (UNCTAD–ICTSD, 2006).

which third parties can undertake experimentation, including for commercial purposes is, in particular, an important element to promote innovation based on or around a patented invention.

An exception of this type has been incorporated into the laws of European and many other countries,[43] while research without the authorization of the patent owner has only been narrowly admitted in the USA. The Federal Circuit Court of Appeals held in *Madey v Duke* that, regardless of whether a particular institution or entity is engaged in an endeavour for commercial gain, so long as the act is in furtherance of the alleged infringer's legitimate business and is not solely for amusement, to satisfy idle curiosity, or for strictly philosophical inquiry, it does not qualify for the very narrow and strictly limited experimental use defence. Moreover, the profit or non-profit status of the user is not determinative.[44]

Acts for experimental purposes are specifically considered as an exception to the exclusive rights in some Latin American countries (see Table 6.1) only if such acts are done for non-profit. This limitation may prevent follow-on innovation by competitors and slow down the pace of technological development.

Table 6.1 The experimental exception in patent laws of selected Latin American countries[45]

Where?	Law	Provisions
Argentina	Law No 24.481 on Patents and Utility Models(as amended by Law No 24.572).	*Article 36(a)*—[excepts] a third party who privately or in an academic environment and without gainful intent, conducts scientific or technological research activities for purely experimental, testing or teaching purposes, and to that end manufactures or uses a product or applies a process identical to the one patented.
Bolivia, Ecuador, Colombia, Peru, Venezuela[46]	Decision No. 486, Common Provisions on Intellectual Property—of the Commission of the	*Article 53* The owner of the patent may not exercise the right referred to in the foregoing Article in relation to the following acts: (a) acts performed in a private circle for non-profit-making purposes;

[43] See, e.g. W Cornish 'Experimental Use of Patented Inventions in European Community States', (1998) 29 *Int'l R Indus Prop & Copyright L* (IIC) 7, 736. See also Carlos Correa, 'International Dimension of the Research Exception', SIPPI Project, AAAS, available at <http://sippi.aaas.org/intlexemptionpaper.shtml>.

[44] 64 USPQ 2d 1737 (Fed Cir 2002).

[45] Compiled with the assistance of D Shabalala. The table does not include legislation of the Dominican Republic and Central American countries, which are in the process of amendment for the implementation of DR–CAFTA.

[46] It is to be noted that Venezuela has withdrawn from the Andean Community and a new patent regime is under consideration by its Parliament.

Table 6.1 (*cont.*)

Where?	Law	Provisions
	Andean Community, December 2000.	(b) acts performed for exclusively experimental purposes on the subject matter of the patented invention; (c) acts performed solely for the purposes of teaching or scientific or academic research; (d) acts referred to in Article 5ter of the Paris Convention for the Protection of Industrial Property; (e) where the patent protects biological material, that can be reproduced, other than plants, using that material as the basis with which to obtain viable new material, except where to do so requires repeated use of the patented subject matter.
Brazil	Law No 9.279, May 1996, entered into force May 1997, as amended by Provisional measure 2014–1, December 1999; and Law 10.196, of 14 February 2001.	*Article 43(II)* The provisions of the previous Article do not apply: to acts carried out by unauthorized third parties for experimental purposes, in connection with scientific or technological studies or researches; *Article 43(VII)*—to acts performed by non-authorized third parties, regarding patented inventions, which aim exclusively [at] the production of information, data and test results directed to procure commerce registration, in Brazil or any other country, to allow the exploitation and commercialisation of the patented product, after the termination of the terms provided in Article 10.
Chile	Industrial Property Law No 19.039, January 1991.	*Article 52* The following persons shall be liable to a fine of 100 to 500 monthly accounting units payable to the State: (c) any person who fraudulently makes use of a patented procedure. This provision shall not apply where the use of the patented procedure is exclusively for experimental or teaching purposes.
Mexico	Ley de la Propiedad Industrial publicada por decreto de Agosto de 1994, reformada de Diciembre de 1997 y de Mayo de 1999. (Tr: Industrial Property Law,	*Article 22(I)*—[excepts] a third party who, in the private or academic sphere, and for non-commercial purposes, engages in scientific or technological research activities for purely experimental, testing or teaching purposes, and to that end manufactures or uses a product or process, identical to the one patented.

Table 6.1 (*cont.*)

Where?	Law	Provisions
	published by decree in August 1994, amended in December 1997 and in May 1999).	
Panama	Ley de Propiedad Industrial No 35. (Tr: Law on Industrial Property No 35), May 1996.	*Article 19* The right conferred by a patent shall have no effect whatever against: (1) a third party who, in the private sphere and on a non-commercial scale, or for a non-commercial purpose, engages in acts involving the patented invention; (2) an industry or enterprise in the general sense, or an educational or scientific body, that engages in acts of manufacture or use of the invention for experimental purposes relating to the subject matter there or for the purposes of scientific or educational research.
Paraguay	Law on Patents for Invention No 1630, November 2000.	*Article 34* The patent shall not provide the right to prevent: (a) acts made exclusively for the purpose of experimentation without commercial intent of the subject matter of the patented invention; (b) acts made exclusively for the purpose of teaching or scientific or academic research.
Uruguay	Law No 17.164 regulating Rights and Obligations relating to Patents, Utility Models and Industrial Designs, September 1999.	*Article 39* The rights conferred by patents shall not cover the following acts: (a) acts carried out in private for non-industrial or non-commercial purposes, provided that they do not cause economic prejudice to the owner of the patent; (c) acts carried out solely for experimental purposes, including acts anticipating future commercial exploitation, carried out during the year prior to expiry of the patent; (d) acts carried out for teaching, scientific or academic research purposes.
Andean Community	Decisión No. 486, Régimen Común sobre Propiedad Industrial—Comisión de la Comunidad	*Article 53* The owner of the patent may not exercise the right referred to in the foregoing Article in relation to the following acts: (a) acts performed in a private circle for non-profit-making purposes;

Table 6.1 (*cont.*)

Where?	Law	Provisions
	Andina, diciembre 2000. (Tr: Decision No 486, Andean Community Common Provisions on Industrial Property, December 2000).	(b) acts performed for exclusively experimental purposes on the subject matter of the patented invention; (c) acts performed solely for the purposes of teaching or scientific or academic research; (d) acts referred to in Article 5*ter* of the Paris Convention for the Protection of Industrial Property; (e) where the patent protects biological material, that can be reproduced, other than plants, using that material as the basis with which to obtain viable new material, except where to do so requires repeated use of the patented subject matter.

Like under European law, in other Latin American countries the exceptions explicitly or implicitly seem to allow for experimentation, including for commercial purposes. Thus, in Argentina, although the patent law established a narrow exception for research activities 'without gainful intent', later on an experimental exception for commercial purposes was introduced by Law No 24.766 of December 1996 (Article 8). Article 42 of the Brazilian Industrial Property Code states that a patent confers the right to prevent a third party from producing, using, offering for sale, selling or importing with those purposes. Among the admissible exceptions, the law lists those 'acts practiced by non-authorized third parties, with an experimental purpose, related to scientific or technological studies or research'. Article 53 (b) and (c) of Decision 486 of the Andean Community establishes that there is no infringement where the invention is used for experimental or academic purposes, without specifying whether for commercial purposes or not.

An important exception for public health relates to the 'early working'—also known as the '*Bolar* exception'—of a patent on a pharmaceutical product, that is, the use of the invention before the date of patent expiry in order to apply for registration of a generic product to be marketed after that date. An exception of this kind is recognized in the USA, Canada, Australia and many other countries, and has also been incorporated into recent FTAs signed by the USA with a number of developing and developed countries.[47]

[47] These agreements, however, provide that '... if the Party permits exportation, the product shall only be exported outside the territory of that Party for purposes of meeting marketing approval requirements of that Party', thereby limiting the possibility of seeking regulatory approval in a foreign country.

Despite the importance of the *Bolar* exception in allowing generic competition as soon as a patent expires, it has only been provided for in a relatively small number of countries in the region: Argentina (Law No 24.766, 1996), Dominican Republic (Law No 20–00 on Industrial Property, April 2000) and Brazil (Law No 10.196/2001). The absence of this exception in most laws in the region suggests that national parliaments have failed to take public health considerations fully into account in designing the patent regimes. Since this exception has been recognized as legitimate by a WTO panel[48] and is currently accepted in the USA and Europe,[49] complaints under WTO rules relating to this exception are unlikely.

Based on the principle of exhaustion of rights (Article 6 of the TRIPS Agreement) WTO members may also admit parallel imports of products legitimately put on a foreign market, and thereby promote competition and lower prices for consumers. A number of Latin American countries, such as Argentina, Andean Community, Dominican Republic, Honduras and Panama,[50] have provided for the principle of international exhaustion, thereby admitting parallel imports, although in some cases subject to some limitations.[51] In Mexico, however, there is no such provision under the patent regime[52] and in Brazil parallel imports are not permitted, except in certain cases where a compulsory license has been granted (Industrial Property Code, Article 68(4)). This limitation is in contrast to the position that Brazil has held in international fora on the matter, particularly on occasion of the debates leading to the adoption of the Doha Declaration on the TRIPS Agreement and Public Health.[53]

Compulsory Licences

WTO Member countries may provide for different forms of compulsory licenses, which are explicitly authorized by the TRIPS Agreement (Article 31). Such licenses mitigate the monopolistic rights conferred by a patent and may, therefore, promote competition by third parties without denying the patent holder's right to receive a remuneration for the use of his invention.

---

48 See *European Communities – Patent Protection for Pharmaceutical and Agricultural Products*, complaint by Canada (WT/DS153/1).

49 The *Bolar* exception was introduced into European Community law by a Directive adopted by the European Council of Ministers on 10 March 2004.

50 See Maria Auxiliadora Oliveira, Jorge Antonio Zepeda Bermudez, Gabriela Costa Chaves and Germán Velásquez 'Has the implementation of the TRIPS Agreement in Latin America and the Caribbean produced industrial property legislation that favors public health policy?' (2004) *WHO Bulletin*, November, 82 (11).

51 In the case of Argentina, for instance, Decree 260/96 that implements the Patent Law of 1995 (No. 24.766) restrains the scope of parallel imports as permitted by the patent law No 24.481.

52 Parallel imports might instead be allowable, under certain conditions, for trademarks.

53 See WT/MIN(01)/DEC/W/2, 14 November 2001.

Most countries in the world provide for compulsory licenses. They have been extensively used in the USA in order to remedy anticompetitive practices and as part of government's eminent right to exploit any patented invention.[54] The use of compulsory licenses in developing countries has generally encountered opposition from the USA. For instance, in 1997, the US threatened to enforce sanctions on Thai exports if Thailand did not drop its plan to use compulsory licensing provisions. In 1998, 40 pharmaceutical manufacturers brought suit against South Africa's law on parallel imports and compulsory licensing.[55] Only recently some developing countries have started to make effective use of this safeguard.[56] Brazil is the only Latin American country so far that has granted a compulsory license (in May 2007) after an agreement with the patent holder to reduce the price of an antiretroviral failed. It had also threatened the use of such licenses in 2001, but without actually granting them, since the prices of the targeted patented medicines were substantially reduced as a result of the government's threat.[57]

The possibility of granting compulsory licenses or allowing for the government use of patented inventions is provided for in Latin American laws, on a number of grounds (see Table 6.2).

Table 6.2 Compulsory licenses in Latin American legislation[58]

Grounds for issuing a compulsory license	Countries
Failure to exploit patent	Andean Community, Argentina, Brazil, Dominican Republic, Honduras, Mexico
Public interest	Andean Community, Brazil, Dominican Republic, Honduras, Mexico
National emergency	Andean Community, Argentina, Brazil, Dominican Republic, Honduras, Mexico
Remedy anti-competitive practices, unfair competition	Andean Community, Argentina, Brazil, Dominican Republic

54 See, e.g. Jerome Reichman, 'Nonvoluntary Licensing of Patented Inventions: The Law and Practice of the United States' (UNCTAD–ICTSD, forthcoming 2006).

55 See JF Morin, 'Tripping Up: TRIPS Debates, IP and Health in Bilateral Agreements', 1 *Int'l J of Intell Prop Mgmt,* 1, forthcoming 2006; Justice Nowobike, 'Pharmaceutical corporations and access to drugs in developing countries: The way forward', (2006) 4 *Sur—Int'l J on Human Rights* 3, available at <http://www.surjournal.org/eng/conteudos/artigos4/ing/artigo_nwobike.htm>.

56 See e.g. C Oh, 'Compulsory licences: Recent experiences in Developing Countries', 1 *Int'l J of Intell Prop Mgmt* 1, forthcoming 2006.

57 See Commission on Intellectual Property Rights, Innovation and Public Health, *Public Health, Innovation and Intellectual Property Rights* (World Health Organization, 2006), available from <http://www.who.int>, 135.

58 Elaborated on the basis of Oliveira *et al,* note 50 above, 819.

Table 6.2 (*cont.*)

Grounds for issuing a compulsory license	Countries
Failure to obtain license under reasonable terms	Andean Community, Argentina, Dominican Republic, Honduras
Failure to produce locally	Brazil
Dependent patents	Andean Community, Argentina, Brazil, Dominican Republic, Honduras
Refusal to deal	Argentina, Dominican Republic
No apparent CL provision	Panama

In several countries the lack of exploitation of a patent may constitute a valid ground for the granting of a compulsory license, but the import of the covered product is deemed to be exploitation. Only Brazil has provided for the possibility of granting compulsory licenses in cases of lack of local industrial use of the patent (Article 68 of the Industrial Property Code).[59] Argentina and the Dominican Republic explicitly allow for the granting of compulsory licenses in cases of 'refusal to deal', that is, when the patent holder rejects to grant a voluntary license which has been requested on reasonable commercial terms.[60]

Some FTAs restrain the WTO members' freedom, confirmed by the Doha Declaration on the TRIPS Agreement and Public Health, to determine the grounds for compulsory licenses.[61] Thus, in the case of the US FTAs with Jordan, Australia and Singapore, such grounds are limited to cases of anticompetitive practices, public non-commercial use, national emergency or other circumstances of extreme urgency. This limitation does not appear in other FTAs entered into with developing countries after the adoption of the Declaration. However, some provisions in the FTAs, namely data exclusivity and the

59 The USA requested a panel against Brazil under the WTO Dispute Settlement Understanding in relation to this provision, arguing that it was inconsistent with Article 27.1 of the TRIPS Agreement. The complaint was, however, withdrawn by the US government before the panel was set up, upon agreement by the Brazilian government to inform the US government prior to the granting of a compulsory license on such grounds. See *Brazil – Measures Affecting Patent Protection*, Request for the Establishment of a Panel by the United States, 9 January 2001, WT/DS199/3.

60 See e.g. Carlos Correa, 'Refusal to deal and access to an essential facility: balancing private and public interests in intellectual property law', in Yvon Blais (ed) *Mélanges Victor Nabhan*, (Série Les cahiers de Proprieté Intellectuelle, 2004).

61 Ministerial Declaration on the TRIPS Agreement and Public Health, 14 November 2001, 41 ILM. 755, available at <http://www.wto.org/english/thewto_e/minist_e/min01_e/mindecl_trips_e.pdf>.

patent–registration linkage,[62] may limit, in practice, the use of patented inventions under compulsory licensing and for governmental non-commercial purposes.[63]

No Latin American country has introduced amendments to its legislation in order to implement the WTO Decision of 30 August 2003 establishing waivers allowing supply of pharmaceutical products to countries with no or inadequate pharmaceutical manufacturing capacity. El Salvador is one of the few countries to have ratified said Decision so far.[64]

Disclosure

Some Latin American countries, notably Brazil and Peru as well as Ecuador and Venezuela, have led an initiative to amend the TRIPS Agreement in order to introduce an obligation to disclose the origin of biological resources in patent applications.[65] Developing countries have elaborated the arguments justifying the disclosure of origin obligation within the patent system as follows:

> . . . a legally binding obligation to disclose the source and country of origin of biological resources and/or traditional knowledge used in inventions will guide the patent examiners in ensuring that all relevant prior art information is available to the patent examiners. Disclosure will also be relevant in helping patent examiners determine whether the claimed invention constitutes an invention that is excluded from patentability under Article 27 paragraphs 2 and 3 of the TRIPS Agreement. Further, disclosure would serve as part of a process to systematise available information of biological resources and traditional knowledge that will continuously build the prior art information available to patent examiners and the general public.[66]

---

62 The US FTAs require a linkage between drug registration and patent protection which is absent in the TRIPS Agreement. As a result of this linkage, the national health authority may be obliged to refuse marketing approval to a generic version of a product if a patent thereon is in force, unless with the consent or acquiescence of the patent owner. In addition, such authority must inform the patent owner about applications for the approval of generic products. See, e.g. J Rius Sanjuan, 'Patent–Registration Linkage', CPTech Discussion Paper No. 2, 3 April 2006, available at <http://www.cptech.org/publications/CPTechDPNo2Linkage.pdf>.

63 See, e.g. Carlos Correa 'Bilateralism in intellectual property: defeating the WHO system for access to medicines' (2004) 36 *Case W Res J of Int'l Law*. 1, Winter.

64 As of 31 October 2006, the amendment to the TRIPS Agreement (Article 31*bis*) that incorporated the Decision of 30 August 2003.

65 See WTO document IP/C/W/474, available at <http://www.wto.org/spanish/tratop_s/trips_s/art27_3b_s.htm>.

66 See, e.g., 'Elements of the obligation to disclose the source and country of origin of biological resources and/or traditional knowledge used in an invention', submission from Brazil, India, Pakistan, Peru, Thailand, and Venezuela, IP/C/W/429 of 21 September 2004, para. 4–5. See also J Sarnoff and Carlos Correa, 'Analysis of Options for Implementing Disclosure of Origin Requirements in Intellectual Property Applications' (2006) UNCTAD/DITC/TED/2005/14), Geneva, 2006, available at <http://www.unctad.org/en/docs/ditcted200514_en.pdf>.

An obligation for disclosure of the type proposed is contained in the Biodiversity Law No 7.788 of Costa Rica (Article 80), in Decision 486 (Article 26(h)) and in the Brazilian Provisional Measure 2.186–16 (Article 31).

Provisional Measures

In many Latin American countries, the TRIPS Agreement has been deemed self-executing, including in the case of provisions included in Part III on enforcement.[67] This was particularly the case for Argentina, where courts generously granted preliminary injunctions based on infringement allegations, including in cases of weak patents covering salts, polymorphs and other minor modifications of products in the public domain. In order to prevent disruptions to legitimate competition, Argentina introduced an amendment to the patent law under terms negotiated with the USA on the occasion of the WTO dispute procedures mentioned above. Law No 25.859 (2004) subjected the grant of provisional injunctions to a number of requirements[68] similar to those established under US law.[69]

---

[67] This was the case, for instance, of Article 50 of the TRIPS Agreement in Argentina. See, e.g. Carlos Correa, 'Medidas cautelares en material de patentes de invención', *Lexis Nexis Jurisprudencia Argentina*, (2002) JA–2002–IV, No 8, 21–28; J Kors (coordinador), *Patentes de invención. Diez años de jurisprudencia–Comentarios y fallos* (La Ley–Colección CEIDIE, 2005).

[68] The amended Art 83 reads as follows:

> The judicial authorities shall have the authority to order provisional measures in relation to a patent granted in conformity with Articles 30, 31 and 32 of the Law, in order to:
>
> (1) prevent an infringement of the patent and, in particular, to prevent the entry into channels of commerce of goods, including imported goods, immediately after customs clearance;
> (2) preserve relevant evidence in regard to the alleged infringement, whenever the following conditions are met:
>   (a) there is a reasonable likelihood that the patent, if challenged by the defendant as being invalid, shall be declared valid;
>   (b) it is summarily proven that any delay in granting such measures will cause an irreparable harm to the patent holder;
>   (c) the harm that may be caused to the title holder exceeds the harm that the alleged infringer will suffer in case the measure was wrongly granted;
>   (d) there is a reasonable likelihood that the patent is infringed.
>
> Provided that the above conditions are met, in exceptional cases such as when there is a demonstrable risk of evidence being destroyed, the judicial authorities can grant such measures *inaudita altera parte*. In all cases, before granting a provisional measure, the judicial authority shall request that an expert appointed *ex officio* examine items (a) and (d) above within a maximum period of 15 days. In the case of granting of any of the measures provided for under this article, the judicial authorities shall order the applicant to provide a security or equivalent assurance sufficient to protect the defendant and to prevent abuses.

[69] See, e.g. Jerome Reichman and M Zinnani (2002), 'Las medidas precautorias en el derecho estadounidense: el justo balance entre las partes', *Lexis Nexis Jurisprudencia Argentina*, 2002–IV, No 8, 15–21.

B. Copyright and Neighbouring Rights

Significant changes were introduced in some Latin American countries in order to implement the TRIPS standards on copyright and related rights, such as with regard to the duration of protection for works of juridical persons, rental rights and the protection of computer programs.

Decision 351 (1993) of the Andean Community introduced, even before the adoption of the TRIPS Agreement, protection for computer programs and databases, in line with Article 10 of the Agreement. Decision 351 also defined the extent of protection (with respect to the 'form' of expression) in terms similar to Article 9.2 of the Agreement, and explicitly incorporated 'rental rights'. In Mexico, a new copyright law was approved in December 1996. Computer programs are protected as literary works and the title holder can exercise 'rental rights' (which are also conferred to phonogram producers). Interestingly, Mexico is the only Latin American country where not only are original databases protected as 'compilations'—as required by the TRIPS Agreement—but non-original databases also receive protection for a five-year period (Article 108). The Mexican law is, thus, the only one in Latin America to follow the model of protection adopted by Directive 96/9/EC of the European Parliament and of the Council of 11 March 1996 on the legal protection of databases. In Argentina, Law No 25.036 explicitly extended copyright protection to computer programs, including criminal sanctions for cases of unauthorized reproduction and commercialization thereof. Brazil enacted a special law for the protection of software (Law No 9.609 of February 1998) whereby computer programs were assimilated to literary works, as mandated by the TRIPS Agreement. Other countries, such as Honduras (1993) and Costa Rica (1994), introduced copyright protection for computer programs as well.

In 2002, a significant number of Latin American countries joined the WIPO Performances and Phonograms Treaty (WPPT) of 1996. They include Argentina, Chile, Colombia, Costa Rica, Ecuador, El Salvador, Guatemala and Honduras.[70] Also, Argentina, Bolivia, Colombia, Costa Rica, Ecuador, El Salvador, Guatemala, Panama, Parguay, Uruguay and Venezuela joined the 1996 WIPO Copyright Treaty (WCT).[71]

70 See <http://www.wipo.int/treaties/en/documents/pdf/wppt.pdf>.

71 See <http://www.wipo.int/treaties/en/ShowResults.jsp?country_id=ALL&start_year=ANY&end_year=ANY&search_what=C&treaty_id=16>.

The TRIPS Agreement allows Members to establish exceptions to exclusive rights, subject to a three-step test, in line with Article 9.2 of the Berne Convention. Such exceptions may be crucial to ensure access to copyrighted work for education and personal use. Latin American copyright laws generally enumerate a number of exceptions, more or less narrowly defined. Some allow for the reproduction for educational purposes of copyright works[72] as well as certain uses by libraries.[73]

Several Latin American countries have, however, voiced the need to establish minimum international standards on limitations and exceptions to copyright and related rights. At the 12th Session of the WIPO Standing Committee on Copyright and Related Rights, Chile made a proposal to define internationally exceptions and limitations to copyright and related rights.[74] It argued that the lack of regulation and harmonization of exceptions and limitations at the international level has made difficult in developing countries implementation of initiatives of social priority, such as access to copyright works by public libraries, handicapped people, and for distance education purposes.[75]

The FTAs signed with the USA by a number of Latin American countries have triggered a new set of reforms in copyright legislation, but in the direction of expanding the protection. Of particular importance has been the strengthening in the context of such agreements of the rights of recording producers and performers, which under the FTAs receive a protection comparable in many aspects to that conferred to copyright holders.[76] In addition, Chilean and Peruvian FTAs,

[72] For instance, Art 22 (b) of Decision 351 of the Andean Community allows the reproduction 'by reprographic means for teaching or for the holding of examinations in educational establishments, to the extent justified by the purpose, articles lawfully published in newspapers or magazines, or brief extracts from lawfully published works, on condition that such use is made in accordance with fair practice, that it does not entail sale or any other transaction for payment and that no profit-making purposes are directly or indirectly pursued thereby'.

[73] For instance, Art 22 (c) of Decision 351 of the Andean Community allows the reproduction of 'a work in single copies on behalf of a library or for archives whose activities are not conducted for any direct or indirect profit-making purposes, provided that the original forms part of the permanent stocks of the said library or archives and the reproduction is made for the following purposes: (i) to preserve the original and replace it in the event of loss, destruction or irreparable damage; (ii) to replace, in the permanent stocks of another library or archives, of an original that has been lost, destroyed or irreparably damaged'.

[74] See WIPO document SCCR/12/3, 2 November 2004. The proposal was supported, *inter alia*, by Argentina, Paraguay, Uruguay, Brazil, Costa Rica and the Dominican Republic.

[75] See, e.g. S Shashikant, 'Development: Debate at WIPO on limitations and exceptions to copyright', available at <http://www.cpsr-peru.org/lpi/internacional/sscr/excepciones/debate>.

[76] Despite that, in the case of the FTA with Peru, a differentiation between authors' rights and related rights is maintained. See, e.g. Report of the Industry Trade Advisory Committee on Intellectual Property Rights (ITAC–15), available at <http://www.ustr.gov/assets/Trade_Agreements/Bilateral/Peru_TPA/Reports/asset_upload_file473_8978.pdf>, 11.

and DR–CAFTA, extended the term of protection to the life of the author plus 70 years for most works. The term of protection for sound recordings and audiovisual works is also extended to 70 years from publication. Other standards introduced by the FTAs include: [77]

- the reproduction right covers transient copies (such as those made in the RAM of a computer);
- the right to control any technological manner of transmitting works, including interactive transmissions over electronic networks like the internet, with minor exceptions for analog performances and broadcasts of sound recordings and performances;
- technological protection measures (TPMs) with narrowly crafted exceptions; and
- prohibiting the removal or alteration of electronic rights management information.

The introduction of TPMs may be problematic in countries that need to dramatically increase access to information and education, like the Latin American countries. Although the original objective of TPMs has been to prevent infringing copyright activities in the digital environment, if the anti-circumvention legislation that legally backs them up does not require a connection between the anti-circumvention prohibition and copyright infringement, such measures can prevent access to and use of any content, whether copyrighted or not. Also, prohibiting the trade in circumvention devices even when they might be necessary to access to or use copyrighted works in ways that are allowed, may deter the exercise of permitted uses, such as fair use.[78] Hence, the new standards introduced by FTAs should be carefully implemented, in a manner that preserves the possibility of accessing information vital for the public and for research and education.

C. Trademarks

Like in other areas, the implementation of the TRIPS Agreement brought about some important changes in the area of trademarks in many Latin American countries,[79] particularly with regard to well-known trademarks, one of the key

---

77 Ibid, 11–12.

78 See, e.g. Carlos Correa 'Fair use in the digital era', (2002) IIC, Vol 33 No 5.

79 Costa Rica, Cuba, the Dominican Republic, Mexico and Uruguay are the only Latin American countries that signed the Trademark Law Treaty. See <http://www.wipo.int/treaties/en Show Results. jsp?country_id=ALL&start_year=ANY&end_year=ANY&search_what=C&treaty_id=4&treaty_id=5&treaty_id=16>.

aspects dealt with by the TRIPS Agreement.[80] For instance, Decision 344 of the Andean Community generally reinforced the protection of such trademarks.[81] They became protected if 'confusingly similar without regard to the type of product or service for which registration is sought' (Article 83e), as well as when the mark is a 'total or partial reproduction, imitation, translation or transcription of a distinctive sign that is commonly known to the sectors concerned in the country in which registration is sought or in sub-regional or international business' (Article 83d). As required by the TRIPS Agreement, the 'scale and scope of promotion' was one of the elements to be taken into account (Article 84b).[82]

Mexico also improved the protection of well-known trademarks, in line with the TRIPS standards (including of trademarks known on the basis of their promotion or publicity) through the industrial property law as amended in 1991 and 1994. The new law approved in Brazil in 1996 also introduced a 'special protection' for well-known trademarks, an area in which weaknesses had been often noted in the past.

Another important development was the revision, in 1994, of the Central American Convention for the Protection of Industrial Property. The revision addressed a number of issues in which the original Convention was inconsistent with the TRIPS Agreement, notably the protection of well-known trademarks, including service marks. The revised treaty also stipulated that the bona fide use of a trademark before registration in any party contracting to the Convention conferred a preferential right to obtain the title.

The FTAs signed by some Latin American countries with the USA increase the level of protection conferred to trademarks and may require new changes in the legislation of parties to such agreements. Eligible signs are not limited to visible signs, as 'sound marks' need also to be protected.[83] In addition, FTAs modify the standard contained in Article 20 of the TRIPS Agreement.[84] For example Article 15.2.2 of DR–CAFTA provides that

> [i]n view of the obligations of Article 20 of the TRIPS Agreement, each Party shall ensure that measures mandating the use of the term customary in common language as the common name for a good or service ('common name') including, *inter alia*, requirements concerning the relative size, placement, or style of use of the trademark

[80] See, e.g. Daniel Gervais, *The TRIPS Agreement: Drafting history and analysis* (2nd edition, Sweet and Maxwell, 2003) 171–175.

[81] See, e.g. P Bueno Martínez, 'La marca notoria y la interpretación prejudicial del Tribnal de Justicia de la Comunidad Andina', (2001) *Revista del Derecho Industrial y de la Competencia* 5, 61–106.

[82] Decision 486, which replaced Decision 344 in 2000, introduced changes to these provisions.

[83] See, e.g. Art 15.2.1 of DR–CAFTA.

[84] See, e.g. Gervais, note 80 above, 179–182.

in relation to the common name, do not impair the use or effectiveness of trademarks used in relation to such goods.

This article might be interpreted as a limitation on the use of generic names in the labelling of medicines, an important measure that many countries adopt in order to promote generic competition and more affordable prices to patients.[85]

D. Geographical Indications

Geographical indications have traditionally received scant attention in Latin American legislation. Some countries, however, now show increasing interest in protecting their own indications.[86] The process of adaptation to the TRIPS Agreement standards has not been completed yet, as some countries (e.g. Brazil) have not concluded the process of legislative reform in this area.[87]

While the TRIPS Agreement does not require a specific form of protection for geographical indications and, in particular, it does not impose the *sui generis* model adopted in European countries, many Latin American countries have followed this approach. Thus, in 1993, Decision 344 of the Andean Community introduced the protection of the right to the exclusive use of officially recognized 'appellations of origin'. The revised Central American Convention for the Protection of Industrial Property (1994) also requires the protection of geographical indications where a given quality, reputation or other characteristics of a product is essentially attributable to its geographical origin, as required by Article 22 of the TRIPS Agreement. In Brazil, in accordance with the 1996 law, both 'designations of origin' and 'geographical indications' are protectable

[85] See, e.g. the report of IFAC–3 (Industry Functional Advisory Committee on IPR for Trade Policy Matters) of 12 March 2004, to the President, the Congress and USTR (available at <http://www.ustr.gov/assets/Trade_Agreements/Bilateral/Australia_FTA/Reports/asset_upload_file813_3398.pdf>) with regard to a similar provision contained in the FTA with Australia ('. . .Article 17.3 reaffirms TRIPS Article 20 that the use of one's trademark should not be encumbered. Thus the article clarifies and enhances existing TRIPS obligations prohibiting interference with the use of trademarks, rights and products such as pharmaceuticals that are also subject to requirements regarding the use of the generic or common name of the product').

[86] See, e.g. INDECOPI, Perú. 'Los intereses nacionales en la propiedad intelectual y los Tratados de Libre Comercio' (2005), 7; D Vivas Eugui, 'Negotiations on geographical indications in the TRIPS Council and their effect on the WTO agricultural negotiations: implications for developing countries and the case of Venezuela', (2001) 4 *J of World Intell Prop*.

[87] There are considerable differences between Latin American countries regarding the level of protection for geographical indications, which has become apparent in the negotiations at the TRIPS Council on an international registration regime for wines and spirits, and on the possible enhancement of protection for all geographical indications. See, e.g. S Bowers, 'Location, location, location: the case against extending geographical indications under the TRIPS Agreement', (2003) 31 *AIPLA Quarterly J*,2, 129–164.

(Articles 176–178), except if they have become the customary name of a product or service (Article 180).

Clearly, the European Union—and not the USA, like in the case of other areas of intellectual property rights—has been the main *demandeur* of protection in this area. It has actively sought bilateral agreements to ensure protection for European geographical indications that might be exempted under the provisions of the TRIPS Agreement.

Despite the progress made in Latin America, in some countries further action seems necessary in order to align domestic legislation with the standards of the TRIPS Agreement, particularly for indications relating to wines and spirits. The FTAs signed with the USA require the protection of geographical indications as marks consisting of any sign, or any combination of signs, capable of identifying a good or service as originating in the territory of a party, or a region or locality in that territory, where a given quality, reputation, or other characteristic of the good or service is essentially attributable to its geographical origin.[88]

E. Industrial Designs and Utility Models

Many Latin American countries provide *sui generis* forms of protection for industrial designs of an aesthetic nature, while protection under copyright is also available. In addition, they protect functional designs under utility models. The protection of the latter is not required under the TRIPS Agreement nor under the FTAs established with the USA. This is an area where Latin American countries consider intellectual property rights may play a positive role, and where legislation is not just a way of complying with international obligations, or essentially satisfying foreign interests.[89]

Although the evidence on the impact of utility models is scant, the World Bank reported that in Brazil utility models helped domestic producers gain a significant share of the farm-machinery market by encouraging adaptation of foreign technologies to local conditions.[90] In Brazil, 3,258 utility models were applied for in 2002, while 358 were granted. 98.5 per cent of applications were made by nationals and 94.6 per cent of the titles were granted to national applicants, in sharp contrast to the situation in the area of patents, where foreign applications

88 See, e.g. Article 15.2.1 of DR–CAFTA.

89 Utility models are protected, for instance, in Argentina, Brazil, Colombia, Costa Rica, Ecuador, Guatemala, Honduras, Mexico, Peru, Uruguay and Venezuela.

90 World Bank, *Global Economic Prospects and the Developing Countries 2002* (2001), 123.

and grants largely prevail.[91] A similar pattern is found in other Latin American countries for which statistics are available (see Table 6.3).

Table 6.3 Applications for and grants of utility models in some Latin American countries

	Applications for registration filed by			Registrations effected in the name of		
Country	Residents	Non-residents	Total	Residents	Non-residents	Total
Brazil	3,211	47	3,258	338	20	358
Colombia	169	9	178	169	9	178
Ecuador	11	5	16	4	1	5
Mexico	394	60	454	72	15	87
Uruguay	46	12	58	11	11	22

Source: WIPO, IP/STAT/2002/A

With the exception perhaps of Brazil, the number of applications and grants of utility models does not seem to meet the expectations about their role as an incentive to incremental innovations. The number of applications and grants in most Latin American countries is low, as compared, for instance, to China (93,139 applications, 57,848 grants), Germany (23,428 applications, 17,188 grants)[92] and South Korea (39,193 applications, 39,957 grants).[93]

F. Integrated Circuits

The protection of integrated circuits has not given rise to much litigation on a world scale nor to any complaint under the Dispute Settlement Understanding of the World Trade Organization.[94] Latin America has almost no role in semiconductor production, with the noticeable exception of Costa Rica, where Intel started manufacturing them in 1998.

As for geographical indications and industrial designs, the TRIPS Agreement does not mandate a specific form of protection for the layout designs (topographies)

91 See WIPO, 'Utility Models Statistics', IP/STAT/2002/A, available at <http://www.wipo.int/ipstats/en/statistics/models/pdf/umodels_02.pdf>.

92 Ibid. It should be noted that the scope of protection was broadened in Germany in 1987 in order to include inventions concerning chemicals and polymers, in addition to mechanical devices.

93 Ibid.

94 See, e.g. A Millard, 'Integrated Circuit Topography Protection: Why Bother?' (2004) 21 *Canadian IPR* 1.

of integrated circuits. Some Latin American countries protect them in the context of industrial property laws. Mexico, for instance, incorporated provisions on the matter into the Industrial Property Law (Law published on 26 December 1997). Protection is granted for ten years from the date of application for registration. The same approach was followed by the Andean Community (Decision 486). Some Latin American countries (e.g. Argentina, Brazil) have not adopted specific legislation on the matter.[95]

G. Undisclosed Information

The TRIPS Agreement obliges members to protect undisclosed information of commercial value (Article 39.2), as well as undisclosed data submitted for the registration of new chemical entities (Article 39.3). Protection is conferred under the heading of unfair competition, as regulated in Article 10*bis* of the Paris Convention and, hence, no exclusive rights on such information are mandated.

Special legislation on undisclosed information was first introduced in the region by Mexican law in 1991. This law in turn largely inspired the Andean Community Decision 344, which literally incorporated some articles of the draft TRIPS Agreement on the matter (Articles 39.2 and 39.3), but introduced some elements which are not in the Agreement. Like the Mexican law, the Decision required that, in order to be protected, the information should not be 'obvious to a person skilled in the art' (Article 76). In addition, the information should be fixed.[96] These non-TRIPS requirements disappeared, however, in Decision 486 which, as mentioned, replaced Decision 344.

With regard to information submitted to national authorities for the registration of pharmaceutical and agrochemical products involving new chemicals, Decision 344 recognized a period of exclusive use of the data (Article 78) and, hence, went beyond the standards of the TRIPS Agreement in a way comparable to Article 1711 of NAFTA. Decision 486, however, also suppressed the requirement of an exclusivity period.

Colombia adopted an exclusivity period for test data under Decree 2085 of 2002. The provision of this protection, however, was challenged before the Andean Court of Justice as violating Decision 486. The Court determined the existence

95 The topographies of integrated circuits, however, may be deemed eligible for protection under copyright, patent or other titles, provided that the relevant requirements of protection are met.

96 This requirement is also contemplated by NAFTA, but not by the TRIPS Agreement.

of such violation in December 2005,[97] at the time Colombia negotiated with the USA an FTA including an obligation to provide data exclusivity for five years for pharmaceuticals and ten years for agrochemicals.[98] In April 2006, the Commission of the Andean Community adopted (without the support of Colombia, Ecuador and Peru) Decision 632, which authorized member countries to provide for an exclusivity period for test data.

In December 1996, Argentina passed legislation on 'confidential information'. It literally reproduces Article 39.2 of the Agreement. Protection is given in the framework of unfair competition. Data submitted for the approval of agrochemical and pharmaceutical products is protected against disclosure, again following the Agreement's standards (Article 39.3). The Argentine law allows for the registration of pharmaceutical products by 'similarity', i.e. without requiring the applicant to duplicate clinical tests. This means that no period of exclusive use of data is provided for.

The United States retaliated against Argentina in January 1997 (that is, before the end of the transitional period established by Article 65.2 of the TRIPS Agreement), arguing that Argentine confidentiality law contradicted 'international standards'. Argentina was subject to a commercial sanction by the US government consisting of the withdrawal of 50 per cent of the General System of Preferences. In 2000, the US government requested consultations under the WTO Dispute Settlement Understanding in relation to the protection of data for agrochemical products. After nearly two years of discussions, the dispute was settled at the consultation stage.[99] Argentina did not accept the US claim that exclusive rights should be granted for test data and maintained its law unchanged. No further action in the framework of the WTO has been taken by USA against Argentina, nor against any other country that does not recognize data exclusivity.[100] A number of foreign companies have recently sued local companies, arguing that the use of test data they had developed was illegal, since such data constituted a constitutionally protected 'property' and that Article 39.3 obliged WTO members to grant an exclusivity period.[101]

---

97 Proceso 114–AI–2004, available under 'Documentos' within the main Community site, <http://www. comunidadandina.org>.

98 The same TRIPS-Plus obligation is contained in the FTA signed with Peru and in the DR–CAFTA.

99 See Notification of Mutually Agreed Solution According to the Conditions Set Forth in the Agreement (IP/D/18/Add.1, IP/D/22/Add.1), available at <http://www.wto.org>.

100 However, the USTR has regularly listed, under the special Section 301 of the US Trade Act, countries that, according to USTR, do not confer adequate (that is, exclusive) protection for test data.

101 Decisions are pending on 13 cases where these allegations were made. Courts refused plaintiffs' requests of preliminary injunctions.

Guatemala adopted 15 years of data exclusivity for drugs in 2000, that is three times the period established in the USA. A turbulent legislative process that set public health-concerned non-governmental organizations, on the one hand, against the US government and industry, on the other, subsequently led to the derogation of data exclusivity, its reinstatement for five years, and its derogation again in November 2004.[102]

In Brazil, Article 195 of the Code on Industrial Property (1996) punishes the unauthorized disclosure or use of confidential information, excluding information publicly known or 'evident' for a technical person on the matter. It also, in line with Article 39.3 of the TRIPS Agreement, forbids the disclosure of undisclosed results of tests and other data submitted to government authorities to obtain the approval for the marketing of a product, provided that the production of such data 'involved a considerable effort'. Law No 10.603/2002 introduced data exclusivity in Brazil but limited to agrochemicals and veterinary products. Marketing approval for generic pharmaceutical products is not subject to any exclusivity period.[103]

The FTAs signed with the USA require the establishment of five years of data exclusivity for pharmaceutical products that contain new chemical entities, and ten years for agrochemicals. In the case of DR–CAFTA, a waiting period of five years is also provided for, within which the originator of data can submit an application for registration with the other party.[104] As mentioned above, several studies have been conducted with the aim of estimating the costs of the introduction of this TRIPS-Plus modality of protection in some Latin American countries.

H. Breeders' Rights

During the 1990s, several Latin American countries introduced legislation for the protection of plant varieties. Despite the wide room for manoeuvre left by Article 27.3(b) of the TRIPS Agreement, they opted to join the UPOV

102 See, e.g. Médicos Sin Fronteras (MSF), 'Efectos del CAFTA sobre la salud pública en Guatemala' (2005) available at <http://www.perufrentealtlc.com/files/Analisis%20Carlos%20Correa%20CAFTA%2025%2002%2005.pdf>.

103 See, e.g. A da Silveira e Silva and J Viera Borges Vallini, 'A proteçao a informaçao no divulgda na área da saúde: una abordagem internacional' in *Propriedade intelectual. Estudos en homenagem a profesora maristela Basso* (Juruá Editora, 2005), 307–314.

104 For a proposal for the implementation of DR–CAFTA provisions regarding data protection, see Carlos Correa, *Implementación de la Proteccion de Datos de Prueba de Productos Farmacéuticos y Agroquímicos en DR–CAFTA–ley Modelo* (2006), available at <http://www.iprsonline.org/unctadictsd/docs/ICTSD%20CAFTA%20proteccion%20de%20datos_Carlos_C.America.pdf >.

Convention as revised in 1978. Eleven Latin American countries are currently members of this Convention. However, some have incorporated elements of UPOV 1991, such as the Brazilian law of 1997, which introduced the concept of 'essentially derived variety' contained in the Convention. Most notable is the case of the Andean Community countries, which under Decision 345 have largely adopted the rules of UPOV 1991.

Part III Protection of Traditional Knowledge[105]

A number of Latin American countries have adopted legislation to protect TK, particularly that associated with genetic resources. This Part reviews some of the adopted or proposed regimes. There are so far no studies on the impact of the TK protection regimes mentioned here. Most of them are, in fact, too recent to allow for an observation and assessment of their implementation and effects.

In 1996 the Andean Community of Nations adopted a Common Regime on Access to Genetic Resources (Decision 391). This regime was one of the first access regimes established to implement the Convention on Biological Diversity. Genetic resources covered by Decision 391 are deemed subject to the sovereign rights of the Andean States, and as 'goods or patrimony of the Nation or of the State' (Article 5). The rights over such resources are, in addition, considered 'inalienable and imprescriptible', without prejudice, however, to property regimes of the biological resources that contain them, the land on which they were found, or the associated 'intangible component' (Article 6). In order to enter into an access contract with the national competent authority, an accessory contract must be signed between the applicant and the provider of the 'intangible component', whether an indigenous community or not.[106]

The Second Complementary Provision of Decision 391 provides that Member States will not recognize rights, including intellectual property rights, over genetic resources, derived or synthesized products, and intangible associated components, obtained or developed on the basis of access activities which do not comply with

[105] This Part is substantially based on Carlos Correa, 'Protecting traditional knowledge: lessons from national experiences', (UNCTAD, 2004) available at <http://r0.unctad.org/trade_env/test1/meetings/tk2/correa.draft.doc>. See also M Ruiz Mueller, *La protección jurídica de los conocimientos tradicionales: algunos avances políticos y normativos en América Latina* (UICN, SPDA, BMZ, 2006).

[106] See, e.g. Carlos Correa 'The access regime and the implementation of the FAO International Treaty on Plant Genetic Resources for Food and Agriculture in the Andean Group countries', (2003) 6 *J of World Intell Prop* 6, November.

the Decision. Member States may also request the cancellation of rights conferred in non-member countries in violation of these rules. Further, the Third Complementary Provision establishes that, where national intellectual property offices have reasonable or concrete evidence that the product or process for which protection is being requested has been obtained or developed from genetic resources or their derived products for which any Member State is a country of origin, such offices may require the applicants to submit the registration number of the access contract and a copy of it, as a prerequisite for the granting of the respective rights. Article 26(h) of Decision 486 requires patent applicants to include, if applicable, a copy of the access contract, when products or processes for which protection is requested have been obtained or developed on the basis of genetic resources or the derived products for which any of the Member States is a country of origin.

Article 3 of Decision 486 also provides that

> 'Member countries shall ensure that the protection conferred on the various forms of industrial property shall be granted in such a way as to safeguard and respect their biological and genetic heritage and also the traditional knowledge of their indigenous Afro-American or local communities. By virtue of the foregoing, the grant of patents relating to inventions developed on the basis of material derived from that heritage or knowledge shall be subject to that material having been acquired in accordance with international, community and national legal provisions. Member countries shall recognize the right and competence of indigenous Afro-American or local communities to decide on matters pertaining to their collective knowledge.'

In Brazil, the Provisional Measure No. 2.186–16, of 23 August 2001, established a regime for access to genetic resources,[107] including a specific chapter on the 'Protection of Associated Traditional Knowledge'. The main aim of the Measure is to prevent bio-piracy.[108] It applies to 'traditional knowledge of indigenous and local communities relating to the genetic heritage', which encompasses 'the cultural heritage of Brazil'. Such knowledge is protected 'against illegal use and exploitation and other actions that are harmful or have not been authorized' by the Management Council established by the same Measure or by an accredited institution (Article 8).

---

[107] Under Brazilian constitutional law, a 'provisional measure' requires periodic renewal in order to be kept in force.

[108] On 22 May 2006, the Brazilian government released a list with the scientific names of about 3,000 species of Brazilian flora. The list, with names such as *cupuacu*, *kiwi*, *carambola* (starfruit), *pequí* (souari nut), *babosa* (aloe), and *catuaba*, aims at preventing foreign companies from registering the names used in Brazil to refer to these plants. See 'Brazil Fights To Make Case For International Biodiversity Protection', in *Intellectual Property Watch*, 31/5/2006, available at <http://www.ip-watch.org/weblog/index.php?p=322&res=1024&print=0>.

Under this legislation, the state recognizes the right of indigenous and local communities to decide on the use of the traditional knowledge associated with their genetic heritage. Indigenous or local communities that create, develop, hold or preserve traditional knowledge associated with the genetic heritage are guaranteed the right to:

(1) have the origin of the access to traditional knowledge mentioned in all publications, uses, exploitation and disclosures;
(2) prevent unauthorized third parties from:
    (a) using or carrying out tests, research or investigations relating to associated traditional knowledge;
    (b) disclosing, broadcasting or rebroadcasting data or information that incorporate or constitute associated traditional knowledge; and
(3) derive profit from economic exploitation by third parties of associated traditional knowledge the rights in which are owned by the community.

The protection instituted by the Provisional Measure shall not affect, prejudice or limit rights pertaining to intellectual property.

Costa Rica[109] adopted, in 1998, an access regime for genetic, biochemical resources and the traditional associated knowledge, as a component of the Biodiversity Law (No 7.788).[110] According to this Law, the state recognizes and protects, as *sui generis* community intellectual rights, the knowledge, innovations and practices of indigenous peoples and local communities, related to the use of biodiversity elements and related knowledge. This right exists and is legally recognized merely on the basis that the cultural practice or knowledge related to the genetic and biochemical resources exists. It does not require any prior declaration, express recognition or official registration.

In order to determine the scope and nature of *sui generis* community intellectual rights, the Law established that within the 18 months following its entry into force, a participatory procedure should be established with the indigenous and peasant communities for this purpose. The Law further provides for an inventory to be drawn up of specific *sui generis* community intellectual rights that the communities wish to protect. The registration of these rights will be voluntary and free of charge. The law also requires the prior informed consent of local

---

109 See G Aguilar, 'Access to Genetic Resources and Protection of Traditional Knowledge in Indigenous Territories', in Christophe Bellmann, Graham Dutfield and Ricardo Meléndez-Ortiz (eds) *Trading in Knowledge* (EARTHSCAN, 2003), 179–182.

110 The law is in force since its publication (April 1998). However, a legal action filed by the General Attorney's Office—alleging the unconstitutionality of powers granted to the (National Commission for the Management of Biodiversity (CONAGEBIO)—has in practice impeded the full application of the Law.

communities as a condition to granting access to genetic resources. Indigenous peoples are recognized the right to oppose access to their resources and related knowledge, for cultural, spiritual, social, economic, or other reasons. The basic requirements for access also include, *inter alia*, technology transfer and equitable sharing of benefits. The Law further requires that any application for access to biodiversity elements be accompanied by proof of prior informed consent issued by the authority of the indigenous community when the activity is located within their territories, and by the director of the conservation area.

Law No 20 of 26 June 2002, of Panama established a Special Regime of Intellectual Property on the Collective Rights of Indigenous Peoples, for the Protection and Defence of their Cultural Identity and their Traditional Knowledge.[111] Its objective is to protect the collective intellectual property rights and traditional knowledge of indigenous communities through the registration, promotion, commercialization and marketing of their rights in such a way as to give prominence to indigenous socio-cultural values and cultural identities and for social justice. Another key objective is the protection of the authenticity of crafts and other traditional artistic expressions.

The subject matter of protection encompasses customs, traditions, beliefs, spirituality, cosmovision, folkloric expressions, artistic manifestations, traditional knowledge and any other type of traditional expression of indigenous communities which are part of their cultural assets (cultural heritage). 'Collective intellectual property rights' and 'traditional knowledge' are protected, as embodied in creations such as inventions, models, designs and drawings, innovations contained in images, figures, graphic symbols, petroglyphs and other material, cultural elements of history, music, arts, and traditional artistic expressions.

'Collective indigenous rights' means the indigenous cultural and intellectual property rights relating to art, music, literature, biological, medical and ecological knowledge, and other subject matter and manifestations that have no known author or owner, and no date of origin, and constitute the heritage of an entire indigenous people. 'Traditional knowledge' means the collective knowledge of indigenous people based on the traditions of centuries, which are tangible and

---

[111] The following description is essentially based on B Espino, 'Experiencia de Panamá en la protección de los conocimientos tradicionales con énfasis en las artesanías', a paper presented to the UNCTAD Expert Meeting on Systems and National Experiences for Protecting Traditional Knowledge, Innovations and Practices Geneva, 30 October–1 November 2000, available at <http://r0.unctad.org/trade_env/docs/panama.pdf>; and A López Martinez, 'Sistemas *sui generis* para la protección del conocimiento tradicional', a paper presented to the UNCTAD Expert Meeting on Systems and National Experiences for Protecting Traditional Knowledge, Innovations and Practices Geneva, 30 October–1 November 2000, available at <http://www.unctad.org/trade_env/docs/lopez.pdf>.

intangible expressions encompassing their science, technology, and cultural manifestations, including their genetic resources, medicines and seeds, their knowledge of the properties of fauna and flora, oral traditions, designs, and visual and representative arts. Several examples of protected subject matter are given by the Law and the implementing Decree, such as traditional dresses of certain indigenous communities, musical instruments, music, dances, performances, oral and written expressions, working instruments, and traditional art and techniques for making them, such as basket and bead work.[112]

In order to be protectable, the subject matter must be capable of commercial use, be based upon tradition (although it need not be 'old'), and fit within the classification system established by the Decree. It must also be 'collective', i.e. the subject matter must have no known author or owner and no date of origin and constitute the heritage of an entire indigenous people, or must be regarded as belonging to one or more of the indigenous communities of Panama. More than one community can be registered collectively as holders of the rights.

Collective rights permit right-holders to authorize or prevent:

(1) use and commercialization;
(2) industrial reproduction;[113]
(3) acquisition of exclusive IPRs over the subject matter; and
(4) the certification of cultural expressions as works of indigenous traditional art or handicraft and handmade by natives.

Protection is dependent on the registration of the relevant TK.[114] An application for this purpose must indicate that the object applied for belongs to an indigenous community, the technique used, the history, a brief description of the object, and a specimen thereof. Applications are examined by an examiner on indigenous collective rights (for whom a special position is established in the industrial property office). Registrations are published and appeals may be lodged against them.

The government of Peru elaborated a first proposal of a Regime for the Protection of the Collective Knowledge of Indigenous Peoples related to Biological Resources in May 1998. Broad consultations were held with the private sector, NGOs

---

112 Executive Decree No 1 (20 March 2001).

113 Exemptions are allowed in certain cases for folkloric dance groups and small non-indigenous artisans. They are able to manufacture and market reproductions, but they will not be able to claim the collective rights recognized by the Law.

114 Regulations for the use of 'Mola Kuna Panama' were submitted on behalf of the indigenous Kuna people and registered accordingly under Resolution No 1 of 21 November 2002.

and sectors representing indigenous communities.[115] Despite the efforts made by the government to elaborate and adopt the proposed regime, traditional and indigenous communities showed little enthusiasm and support for the initiative.[116]

The regime was finally adopted and published in August 2002. It recognizes that the traditional knowledge of the indigenous peoples contributes to conserve and make sustainable use of the components of biodiversity. Its objectives are to:

(1) promote respect, protection, preservation, wider application and development of the collective knowledge of indigenous peoples;
(2) promote the fair and equitable distribution of the benefits derived from the use of that collective knowledge;
(3) ensure that the use of knowledge takes place with the prior informed consent of indigenous peoples;
(4) promote the strengthening and development of the capabilities of indigenous peoples, and of the mechanisms traditionally used by them, to share and distribute collectively generated benefits; and
(5) avoid the patenting of inventions obtained or developed using the collective knowledge of the indigenous peoples of Peru.

The Peruvian regime establishes a *sui generis* system that recognizes the indigenous people's ownership and associated rights over their traditional knowledge, as well as their right to decide on how it should be used. For access to knowledge that is not within the public domain, prior informed consent by the relevant community is required independently of the purposes for which access is sought.

The law stipulates the need to negotiate and sign a written licensing agreement for the use of collective knowledge, on terms that ensure an adequate payment and an equitable distribution of the benefits derived from its use. The agreement must provide for an initial payment and a royalty of no less than 5 per cent of the value, before taxes, of the gross sales resulting from the marketing of the products developed directly or indirectly from the said collective knowledge, as the case may be. Sufficient information on the purposes, risks, and implications of the access activity must also be supplied. The licensing agreements must be registered with the INDECOPI.

---

[115] See B Venero Aguirre, 'The Peruvian Law on Protection of the Collective Knowledge of Indigenous Peoples Related to Biological Resources', in Bellmann, Dutfield and Meléndez-Ortiz, note 109 above.

[116] See Report of the Multistakeholder Dialogue on Trade, Intellectual Property and Biological and Genetic Resources in Latin America, Cusco, Peru, 22–24 February 2001 (available at <http://www.ictsd.org/dialogueweb/texts/report2.htm>).

The law provides that if the collective knowledge has passed into the public domain in the last 20 years, a percentage of the pre-tax value of the gross sales resulting from the marketing of products developed from this knowledge shall be set aside for the Fund for the Development of Indigenous Peoples. The Fund will also receive a minimum 10 per cent of the gross sales, before taxes, resulting from the marketing of products developed from collective knowledge.

Voluntary registers of protected indigenous knowledge are set up by the law. There are three kinds of register: the National Public Register, the National Confidential Register and the Local Registers of Collective Knowledge of Indigenous Peoples. Registration is not a condition for protection: indigenous peoples have rights over the collective knowledge they possess whether it is registered or not. Indigenous peoples may apply for the registration of their collective knowledge through their representative organizations. They may also create their own local registers. No registration of TK under this law has taken place so far.

Protection is granted against disclosure, acquisition or use of collective indigenous knowledge, when any of those acts has taken place in an unfair manner. The law does not grant, hence, exclusive rights. Neither does it contain a definition of what 'unfair' would mean in this context. Though the concept evokes the notion applied under unfair competition law, it is clearly different from the latter, since under unfair competition law unfairness is judged in relation to commercial practices, as they may affect competitors and, in some cases, consumers.[117]

This review suggests that a great diversity of approaches, scope, types of rights, and modes of implementation exist for the protection of TK in Latin America. In the case of Panama and Peru, autonomous regimes have been established, while in other countries the protection of TK is provided for in the context of regimes more broadly dealing with biodiversity laws or access to genetic resources. The protection of TK is conceived in some cases as a defence against misappropriation, while other regimes rather assert positive rights, such as the right to exclude unauthorized parties from using the protected knowledge.

In most cases, protection is limited to biodiversity-related knowledge or to knowledge held by indigenous peoples (like in Peru). Panama's law provides, however, an example of an all-encompassing regime applicable to cultural

[117] See, e.g, Stephen Ladas, *Patents, Trademarks, and Related Rights. National and International Protection* (Cambridge University Press, 1975), Vol III, 1688.

expressions as well as knowledge of technical nature, and to both intangible and material elements.

Registration of TK is voluntary under some regimes (Peru) while in others (Panama) it is a condition for the granting of rights. Some regimes provide for exclusive rights, while others are based on the more flexible concept of unfair or disloyal conduct.

Conclusion

Intellectual property legislation has undergone dramatic changes in Latin America in the last 15 years. The need to amend existing regimes and to introduce new modalities of protection consistently with the TRIPS Agreement was central to that process. External pressures, namely from the US government and industry, also influenced legislative processes in the region, in some cases decisively. The adoption of reforms (like the patent law in Argentina and data protection in Guatemala) showed in some cases strong tensions that led to turbulent legislative processes.

By 2000 most Latin American countries had completed the revision of their intellectual property regimes in line with the TRIPS Agreement. Although some outstanding issues remained (such as in the area of integrated circuit topographies) and there are still controversies about the implementation of certain provisions of the TRIPS Agreement (such as Article 39.3), only two Latin American countries (Argentina and Brazil) were subject to complaints before the WTO, in 2000, based on the alleged violation of TRIPS standards. In both cases an agreement was reached and no panel was established to rule on the matters under dispute. No further complaints have been filed before the WTO against a Latin American country since then.

Latin American countries have used to a varying degree, but not to the fullest possible extent, the room for manoeuvre left by the TRIPS Agreement to design a pro-competitive intellectual property regime. Many countries have used such room broadly to develop compulsory licensing systems. Few countries, however, have explicitly established exceptions for early working of a patented invention, and many do not allow for parallel imports. In several cases, foreign companies have attempted to reduce such room for manoeuvre through strategic litigation, including preventing the application of the transitional periods provided for by the TRIPS Agreement, and trying to obtain exclusivity for the use of test data.

While, as mentioned, after massive reforms of their legislation Latin American countries had generally complied with the TRIPS Agreement by 2000, a new wave of changes has been triggered in some countries by the signature of FTAs with the USA. Chile, Colombia, Peru, the Dominican Republic and the Central American countries have already undertaken that process, which implies, *inter alia*, the extension under certain circumstances of the patent term, exclusivity for test data, and patent–registration linkage for pharmaceutical products.

Not all elements in the intellectual property regimes of Latin American countries have been determined, however, by the TRIPS Agreement and FTAs. In addition to joining the WCT and WPPT, many Latin American countries have introduced the protection of utility models, as a means to promote minor or incremental innovations that characterize the innovation path in countries without a sophisticated scientific and technological infrastructure. Some countries have also been active in developing *sui generis* regimes, in some cases based on intellectual property concepts, for the protection of TK. Rather than as an incentive for the development of such knowledge (which is still evolving), those regimes mainly aim at preventing bio-piracy and ensuring benefit sharing in cases of commercial exploitation of TK.

In Latin America the relationship between intellectual property and development remains as nebulous as elsewhere. There is very little evidence so far about the impact of intellectual property rights on variables such as investment and technology transfer, but several studies point to considerable costs derived from the implementation of higher standards of protection, notably increased prices and more limited access to medicines. Such a relationship is a matter of concern for many Latin American countries, which have voiced the need to examine the way in which intellectual property rights may affect development. In particular, Argentina and Brazil, supported by other Latin American and developing countries, have led a process to establish, a 'development agenda' within WIPO.[118] Their proposal aims at profoundly refashioning the WIPO agenda towards development objectives, and working on new approaches to support innovation and creativity.[119] If successful, this agenda may permit the avoidance of commonplace simplifications about the relationship between intellectual property and development, and eventually explore new mechanisms to strengthen the innovation systems in Latin America and other developing countries.

[118] See 'Proposal By Argentina And Brazil For The Establishment Of A Development Agenda For WIPO', WIPO document WO/GA/31/11, available at <http://www.wipo.int/documents/en/document/govbody/wo_gb_ga/pdf/wo_ga_31_11.pdf>.

[119] See, e.g. South Centre, 'Establishing a 'Development Agenda' for the World Intellectual Property Organization (WIPO): commentary on proposal by Argentina and Brazil'.

7

TRIPS AND TRIPS-PLUS IMPACTS IN AFRICA

Ikechi Mgbeoji

Introduction

The emergence of the World Trade Organization (WTO)[1] as the juridical framework for global trade is one of the most fundamental changes in the second half of the last century.[2] No less epochal is the linkage of intellectual property rights (hereafter, IPR) issues to global trade governance. Prior to the WTO era, matters of IPR at the global level were usually dealt with at various fora of the United

1 Agreement Establishing the World Trade Organization, 15 April 1994, 33 ILM 81, available at <http://www.wto.org/english/docs_e/legal_e/04-wto.pdf> (last accessed 5 March 2007) [hereafter, WTO Agreement].

2 The substance and negotiating history of the TRIPS Agreement has been exhaustively dealt with elsewhere and need not detain us here. See D Gervais, *The TRIPS Agreement: Drafting History and Analysis* (Sweet & Maxwell, 2003). See also M Blakeney, *Trade-Related Aspects of Intellectual Property Rights: A Concise Guide to the TRIPS Agreement* (Sweet & Maxwell, 1996).

Nations, especially the United Nations Conference on Trade and Development (UNCTAD) and the World Intellectual Property Organization (WIPO).[3]

The implication in this transformation has not been lost on commentators. Vincent Chiappetta describes TRIPS as a 'dramatic shift away from the traditional view that intellectual property law primarily serves the interest of national cultures, values, and politics'.[4] On his part, Endeshaw opines that 'the characterization of intellectual property lawmaking and enforcement as a trade issue was a shrewd device which transposed the internal policies and legal formula concocted by the US in 1974[5] to the international fora from 1984 onwards'.[6] No matter the perspectives on the changes wrought by TRIPS, there is a consensus that the annexing of intellectual property rights issues by the WTO under the Agreement on Trade-Related Aspects of Intellectual Property Rights, [7] hereafter TRIPS, is a radical restructuring of world trade.

How has this transformation of the ground rules in IPR protection affected African countries? For many people, Africa is the place of exotic wild animals, of diseases, political anomie, and the continent where often, 'terrible things happen'.[8] Africa is a huge continent, indeed, the second largest continent. Despite its enormous size—the African continent is four times the size of the United States; it is as large as the United States, Europe, Japan and China put together—little has been said about the impact of TRIPS in Africa.[9] Indeed, absent ubiquitous public commentaries and scholarly ruminations on the alleged relationship between TRIPS, the Doha Declaration,[10] and access to HIV/AIDS antiretroviral

---

3 L Helfer, 'Regime Shifting: The TRIPS Agreement and New Dynamics of International Intellectual Property Lawmaking' (2004) 29 *Yale J Int'l L* 1; R Gutowski, 'The Marriage of Intellectual Property and International Trade in the TRIPS Agreement: Strange Bedfellows or a Match Made in Heaven?' (1999) 47 *Buffalo LR* 713.

4 V Chiappetta, 'The Desirability of Agreeing to Disagree: The WTO, TRIPS, International IPR Exhaustion and a Few Other Things' (2000) 21 *Mich J Int'l L* 333.

5 Section 301 of the Trade and Tariff Act of 1974.

6 A Endeshaw, 'The Paradox of Intellectual Property Law-Making in the new Millennium: Universal Templates as Terms of Surrender for non-industrial Nations; Piracy as an Offshoot' (2002) 10 *Cardozo J of Int'l and Comp L* 47–77. Some commentators have commented on the decisive influence of US pharmaceutical corporations on the tenor of TRIPS.

7 Agreement Establishing the World Trade Organization, Annex 1C, Agreement on Trade-Related Aspects of Intellectual Property Rights, 15 April 1994, 33 ILM 1197, available at <http://www.wto.org/english/docs_e/legal_e/27-trips.pdf> (last accessed 5 March 2007) [hereafter, TRIPS Agreement or TRIPS].

8 Apologies to Richard Falk, see 'Collective Insecurity: The Liberian Crisis, Unilateralism, & Global Order' [Book Review], (2005) 43 *Osgoode Hall LJ* 203.

9 R Mallet, 'Sub-Saharan Africa in the Global Economy' (1999) 30 *Law and Policy in Int'l Business* 569. Africa holds 54 per cent of the world's gold, 40 per cent of its diamonds, 75 per cent of its platinum and 12 per cent of world population.

10 *Ministerial Declaration on the TRIPS Agreement and Public Health*, 14 November 2001, 41 I.L.M. 755, available at <http://www.wto.org/english/thewto_e/minist_e/min01_e/mindecl_trips_e.pdf> (last accessed 5 March 2007) [hereafter, Doha Declaration].

drugs, the larger issue of the impact of TRIPS in Africa has somewhat escaped rigorous scholarly attention. The welter of publications on access to HIV/AIDS antiretroviral drugs could lead one to the erroneous conclusion that in the 53 African countries, the TRIPS Agreement is all about HIV/AIDS and nothing more!

In the light of the fact that issues of pharmaceutical patents and HIV/AIDS have been amply documented elsewhere by countless numbers of authors, this chapter would focus, as much as possible, on the overall impact of TRIPS in various African countries. The central objective of this chapter is to gain an understanding of the various linkages that exist between intellectual property rights, trade rules, and socio-economic development of African member states of the WTO by a careful deliberation and analyses of trends and developments in African countries.[11]

It must be noted at the outset that IPRs affect various societies or types of country in different ways. As a generally convenient method of analysis (but not necessarily accurate in all material respects), one may divide the various countries of the world into three large groups, namely, the industrialized economies (ICs), the non-industrialized economies (non-ICs) and the emerging industrialized economies (emerging ICs).[12] The desirable level of IPR protection to be accorded to innovations and products in these different groups is a subject that historically has elicited significant scholarly inquiries and controversies.[13] Despite the near-canonical status of the alleged roles of IPRs in influencing economic and technological development, much of the recent discussion on the subject merely rehashes earlier arguments in the guise of studying the impact or implementation of TRIPS.[14]

The pertinent question is whether and to what extent the accession of African countries to the TRIPS Agreement has impacted on Africa. This is a difficult task and indeed, in several respects, an impossible mission to accomplish within

---

[11] For a discussion of the policy options before developing countries see Carlos Correa, *Intellectual Property Rights, the WTO and Developing Countries: The TRIPS Agreement and Policy Options* (Zed Books, 2000).

[12] Endeshaw, note 6 above.

[13] E Penrose, *The Economics of the International Patent System* (Johns Hopkins Press, 1951); H Grundmann, 'Foreign Patent Monopolies in Developing Countries: An Empirical Analysis' (1976) 12 *J Dev Stud* 186.

[14] For example, as Endeshaw observes, regarding Robert Sherwood's often-quoted work, 'The TRIPS Agreement: Implications for Developing Countries', 'while purporting to study the impact of TRIPS on non-industrialized economies [Sherwood] was merely rehashing the alleged role of IP in industrialized economies as being synonymous with its significance for non-industrialized economies and ended up by merely explaining the TRIPS agreement'. See Endeshaw (note 6 above).

the constraints of space and available empirical tools. Indeed, it must be emphasized that Africa is a vast continent of diverse and complex states, not a monolith. In particular, access to measurable data and statistics are often non-existent. Added to this complexity is the fact that various segments of industries in different African countries have varying needs or competences in some forms of actual or emerging forms of IPR. For example, South Africa is much industrialized and also a leading producer of wine. On the other hand, Nigeria is not as industrialized as South Africa but she is home to Africa's largest and most vibrant home-video industry. Again, Ghana's globally acclaimed Kente cloth is in serious need of an effective IPR protection mechanism. It therefore stands to reason that certain forms of IPR that have resonance in one country may be of marginal significance in another. Indeed, in some cases, new forms of IPR may be necessary.

Notwithstanding the aforesaid constraints, this chapter is divided into five parts including this introduction. Part II offers a brief introduction to the historical and theoretical development of IPRs in Africa prior to the emergence of WTO/TRIPS. It also situates the analysis within a comparative and holistic framework. The importance of historical context in the study of IPRs cannot be overemphasized. Scholars can no longer persist in the fallacy that economic, technological, and cultural conditions do not influence the structure and content of IP laws.[15] For too long, many scholars and institutions have pretended that IPRs are universal verities lacking in local flavour and cultural affinities. As Endeshaw laments, this trend is evident in 'standard IP textbooks and even WIPO publications.[16] Pick up any of these writings and you will see a discussion beyond the concrete; an outpouring of rules and policies that do not tie in with specific conditions of countries. Perhaps this had to do with the misfortune of IP being in the suffocating care of lawyers and not economists.'[17] Part II affords a historical background to the subsequent analyses of the impact of TRIPS in African countries.

Part III explores the significance and normative impact of TRIPS on Africa. Sections A to E of this Part are more detailed in their treatment of the scope and impact of the implementation of TRIPS in African countries. Given the complexity and manifold impacts of TRIPS in Africa, and the palpable differences among various African states and regions, Part III adopts a regional and in some cases, country-by-country approach. The macro-regions identified

[15] See for example F K Beier, 'The Significance of the Patent System for Technical, Economic, and Social Progress' (1980) 11 *Int'l R Indus Prop & Copyright L* (IIC) 569.

[16] WIPO, *Introduction to Intellectual Property: Theory and Practice* (1997).

[17] Endeshaw, note 6 above, 55.

by the United Nations Department of Statistics are adopted in this analysis.[18] There are five African regions in the UN schemata: Northern Africa, East Africa, West African, Southern Africa, and Middle/Central Africa. Part III is thus sub-divided into five mini-parts.

Northern Africa is the northernmost region of the African continent and comprises Algeria, Egypt, Libya, Morocco, Sudan, Tunisia, and Western Sahara. The West African sub-region comprises 16 countries, namely Benin, Burkina Faso, Cape Verde, Côte d'Ivoire, The Gambia, Ghana, Guinea, Guinea-Bissau, Liberia, Mali, Mauritania, Niger, Nigeria, Senegal, Sierra Leone, and Togo. Central or Middle Africa comprises Angola, Cameroon, Central African Republic, Chad, Democratic Republic of Congo, Equatorial Guinea, Gabon, São Tomé and Principe. The East African sub-region comprises Kenya, Tanzania, Uganda, Djibouti, Eritrea, Ethiopia, Somalia, Mozambique, Madagascar, Malawi. Southern Africa comprises Botswana, Lesotho, South Africa, and Zimbabwe. Part IV is the concluding part of this chapter.

Part I The Colonial Origins and Historical Development of IPRs in Africa

Although IPRs are often promoted as universal verities,[19] there is no doubt that the specific forms of IPRs recognized by TRIPS have their origins in the cultural, legal, and economic traditions of continental Europe and of Western jurisprudence and economic tradition.[20] The prevalent notion that TRIPS-compatible IPRs are universal truths distanced from the cultural and genetic fingerprints of its European origins and unmediated by economic impulses is simply false. A careful study of the cultural and ideological impulses of the dominant forms of IPR is crucial in understanding the full range of arguments in support of IPRs, and explicating the inherent challenges faced by policy makers in transplanting IPRs to Africa.

Arguments for the existence or maintenance of IPRs are virtually anchored on the hypothesis that IPRs encourage innovation and commercialization of new

18 Available at <www.un.org/depts/dhl/maplib/worldregions.htm>. Last accessed on 5 March 2007.

19 For a critique of this view see P Drahos, 'The Universality of Intellectual Property Rights: Origins and Development' (1998) *Intell Prop and Human Rights* 13. Available at <http://www.wipo.int/tk/en/hr/paneldiscussion/papers/pdf/drahos.pdf>.

20 I Mgbeoji, 'The Juridical Origins of the International Patent System: Towards a Historiography of the Role of Patents in Industrialization' (2003) 5 *J of the History of Int'l L* 403.

technologies, products, artistic and literary works.[21] Notwithstanding the axiomatic status of this notion, the most rigorous studies by some of the most reputable economists in the field are undecided as to the veracity of the assumption that TRIPS-compatible protection of IPRs necessarily leads to innovation and economic progress in every society, or that such progress demonstrably outweighs the social cost of TRIPS compliance, especially within the short transitional periods provided under TRIPS.[22] Curiously, the history of industrialized states shows clearly that they did not adopt strong IP regimes when they were at early stages of industrialization.[23]

As this author has argued elsewhere,[24] there is a powerful body of evidence and literature showing that the industrialized economies of today tweaked and adapted their domestic IP policies to suit their perceived industrial and economic needs.[25] For example, between 1790 and 1836, as a net importer of technology, the USA restricted the issue of patents to its own citizens and residents. Further, in 1836, patent fees for foreigners were fixed at ten times the rate for US citizens and two-thirds as much for British inventors. Indeed, numerous restrictions placed by the USA on foreign copyright delayed US entry to the Berne Convention[26] until 1989.[27] Indeed, a 1986 study for the US Congress admitted that the USA was a 'pirate': 'when the United States was a relatively young and developing country it refused to respect international intellectual property rights on the grounds that it was freely entitled to foreign works to further its social and economic development'.[28]

Although empirical evidence on the alleged relationship between IP regimes and economic development in poorer countries is generally inconclusive, it is becoming increasingly fashionable for policy makers to assert that strong

21 J Homere, 'Intellectual Property Rights Can Help Stimulate the Economic Development of Least Developed Countries' (2004) 27 *Columbia J of L and Arts* 277.

22 See for example F Machlup, *An Economic Review of the Patent System* (Study No 15 of the Sub-committee on Patents, Trademarks, and Copyrights of the Committee of the Judiciary, United States Senate, 85th Congress, Second Session).

23 E Schiff, *Industrialization Without National Patents—The Netherlands, 1869–1912, Switzerland, 1850–1907* (Princeton University Press, 1971); D Brenner-Beck, 'Do as I say, Not as I Did' (1999) 11 *UCLA PAB Asian LJ* 84.

24 I Mgbeoji, *Global Biopiracy: Patents, Plants, and Indigenous Knowledge* (UBC Press, 2006).

25 D Brenner-Beck, note 23 above.

26 Berne Convention for the Protection of Literary and Artistic Works, 9 September 1886, revised by 14 July 1967, 828 UNTS 221.

27 O Arewa, 'TRIPS and Traditional Knowledge: Local Communities, Local Knowledge, and Global Intellectual Property Frameworks' (2006) 10 *Marq Intell Prop LR* 155.

28 US Congress, Office of Technology Assessment, *Intellectual Property Rights in an Age of Electronics and Information* (1987) at 230. Switzerland did not grant product patents until 1977; Italy engaged in 'knock-off' productions until 1978.

IP regimes potentially generate benefits for poor countries.[29] Some of the alleged benefits include greater trade, inflows of foreign direct investment,[30] and technology transfers.[31] Of course, there are costs[32] which include restricted access to protected technologies, increased price of goods and services, and other social welfare costs.[33] Regardless of the merits (or lack thereof) of the purported benefits of IPRs,[34] there is hardly any question that IPRs moved from the peripheries to the core of global regulation of trade.[35]

Despite the globalization of IPRs,[36] the successful transplanting of IPRs to African countries has been beset with several challenges, including the brutal legacies of colonialism, domestic economic difficulties, and cultural dissonance. Historically, the structure and process of international intellectual property regulation has marginalized the Third World,[37] especially Africa.[38] This phenomenon is epitomized by the colonial imposition of IP laws and institutions in Africa, and the contemporary limited relevance of African countries in global IP law-making processes.[39]

---

29 K Maskus, 'Lessons From Studying the International Economics of Intellectual Property Rights' (2000) 53 *Vanderbilt LR* 2219; K Maskus, 'Intellectual Property Rights and Economic Development' (2000) *Case W Res J of Int'l L* 471.

30 FDI may be described as the act of establishing or acquiring a foreign subsidiary over which the investing firm has substantial management control. Scholarly opinion is divided on whether strong IPRs are necessary for FDI.

31 K Idris, *Intellectual Property: A Power Tool for Economic Growth*, WIPO, Geneva (2002); R Sherwood, *Intellectual Property and Economic Development* (Westview Press, 1990); B Frischmann, 'Innovation and Institutions: Rethinking the Economics of US Science and Technology Policy' (2000) 24 *Vermont LR* 347.

32 H K Manion, 'A Global Perspective on Intellectual Property Rights: A Social Work' (48) 1 *Int'l Social Work* 77–87.

33 E Su, 'The Winners and the Losers: The Agreement on Trade-Related Aspects of Intellectual Property Rights and its Effects on Developing Countries' (2000) 23 *Houston J of Int'l L* 169.

34 K Maskus, 'Intellectual Property Challenges for Developing Countries: An Economic Perspective (2000) *U of Illinois LR* 457.

35 In 2000, intellectual property assets represented 40 per cent of the net value of corporations in the United States. Similarly, IPRs account for more than 33 per cent of corporate assets in Europe. See Idris, note 31 above, 61–62.

36 F Abbott et al (eds), *The Making of the International Intellectual Property System* (Kluwer Publications, 1999).

37 For a definition of the Third World see, B Rajagopal, 'Locating the Third World in Cultural Geography' (1998–1999) *Third World L Studies* 1, (contending that the concept of global south or third world should not be inflexibly moored to a fixed geographical location). For a consideration of the complexity of the Third World see K Mickelson, 'Rhetoric and Rage: "Third World" Voices in International Legal Discourse' (1998) 16 *Wisconsin Int'l LJ* 353 at 360, (describing the Third World as a 'chorus of voices that blend, though not always harmoniously, in attempting to make heard a common set of concerns').

38 D Gervais, 'The Internationalization of Intellectual Property: New Challenges From the Very Old and the Very New' (2002) 12 *Fordham Intell Prop Media & Ent LJ* 929.

39 Endeshaw, note 6 above.

With respect to colonialism, the colonial legacy of Africa has also left indelible prints and influences in both the law and structural framework of IPR in the continent.[40] The vestiges of the European scramble for Africa is reflected in the discordant and often competing IPR laws and institutions in decolonized African countries. For example, English common law applies in Anglophone countries while Francophone countries operate the French Civil Law system. Lusophone countries in Africa operate the Romano–Germanic civil system. The result is a gaggle of IP laws and institutions in Africa which, in several instances, are a verbatim reproduction of IP laws in the colonial states.

In short, European laws were simply re-enacted in African colonies without regard to local sensibilities and practical realities. Until 1962, patent law in French Africa was governed by French laws. Administratively, the French National Patent Rights Institute (INPI) was the National Authority for members of the African French Union.[41] Similarly, barely two decades ago, a person wishing to obtain patent protection in most British colonies in Africa could do so by re-registering a British patent in the local office in the particular African country. In effect, the content and process of IP governance in Africa was an appendage to colonial dictates and preferences.

At the normative level, the ideological values and world view encoded in the IPRs of the colonizing European powers were often alien to indigenous African ethos and economic traditions.[42] The internationalization of IPRs which started in Europe in the nineteenth century and culminated with the conclusion of the Paris and Berne Conventions was an extension of colonial diktat in Africa.[43] African countries did not participate meaningfully in the law-making process at the international level. This, again, was a re-enactment of domestic alienation from IP law-making processes.[44] A major consequence of this phenomenon was the non-protection of indigenous categories of IPR such as folklore,[45] and the

---

40 A Adewopo, 'The Global Intellectual Property System and Sub-Saharan Africa: A Prognostic Reflection' (2002) 33 *U Tol LR* 749.

41 Otherwise known as the Union Française, the group is composed of 16 French-speaking African colonies outside French North Africa. These are Benin, Burkina Faso, Cameroon, Central African Republic, Congo, Côte d'Ivoire, Equatorial Guinea, Gabon, Guinea, Guinea-Bissau, Mali, Mauritania, Niger, Senegal, Chad, and Togo.

42 C Farley, 'Protecting Folklore of Indigenous Peoples: Is Intellectual Property the Answer?' (1997) 30 *Conn LR* 1.

43 A Adewopo and C Oguamanam, 'The Nigerian Trademark Regime and the Challenges of Economic Development' (1999) 30 IIC 632.

44 Large-scale African participation in IP matters started in the late 1970s.

45 P Kuruk, 'Protecting Folklore Under Modern Intellectual Property Regimes: A Reappraisal of the Tensions Between Individual and Communal Rights in Africa and the United States' (1999) 46 *Am U LR* 769.

congealed perception in African countries that IP laws were part of the repertoire of colonial oppression and subjugation of Africa.

The process of political independence did not bring about radical changes. Indeed, shortly after formal decolonization, with the singular exception of South Africa, none of the newly-decolonized African states operated functional patent offices. Save for trademarks, which were used to protect merchandise from the imperial states, there was little domestic effort on the protection of IPRs. Consequently, any fruitful discussion of the impact of TRIPS in contemporary Africa must, of necessity, be situated within the contexts of the colonial legacies and absence of infrastructure in several African countries. Such discussion must take into account the fact that a vast majority of Africans live in abject poverty, without adequate food, clean water, sanitation, healthcare, or education.[46] Again, it should be borne in mind that a large number of Africans have been either directly embroiled in civil wars for upwards of five years, or hugely impacted by the effects of civil wars in neighbouring countries.

At the continental and macro-levels, the colonial rupture of Africa left in its wake competing continental institutions and frameworks for the regulation and governance of IPRs. The two continental organizations which deal in IPRs are the African Intellectual Property Organization (OAPI)[47] and the African Regional Industrial Property Organization (ARIPO). The former comprises 14 French colonies in Africa (North Africa excluded). The French colonies decided in 1962 to create The African and Malagasy Patent Rights Authority by the agreement known as the Libreville Agreement. The Libreville agreement was signed to form the African Malagasy Patent Rights Authority (OAMPI).[48] Following the withdrawal of Madagascar and the need to expand coverage to other categories of intellectual property, the Libreville Agreement was revised and a new convention signed in Bangui on 2 March 1977 gave birth to OAPI.[49]

46 A Zikonda, *Institutional Issues for Developing Countries in IP Policy-Making, Administration and Enforcement* (Sub-Saharan Africa), Country Case Study for Study 9, Commission on Intellectual Property Rights. Available at <http://www.iprcommission.org/papers/pdfs/study_papers/sp9_SSAfrica_case_study.pdf > (last accessed 17 May 2007).

47 The acronym OAPI is derived from the French name of the organization, which is Organisation Africaine de la Propriété Intellectuelle. OAPI is constituted by French-speaking countries.

48 The Libreville Agreement was based on three fundamental principles. These are: (1) the adoption of a uniform legislation by the putting in place and application of common administrative procedures resulting from a uniform system of patent rights protection; (2) the creation of a common authority for each of the member states; and (3) the centralization of procedures.

49 Bangui Agreement of 2 March 1977, as revised on 24 February 1999; available at <http://www.oapi.int/doc/en/bangui_agreement.pdf>. Art 19 of the Paris Convention permits members to belong to regional IP groupings provided there is no contradiction between the Paris norms and the obligations created by such regional groupings.

The Bangui Agreement deals with the following categories of intellectual property: Patents; Utility Models, Trademarks and Service Marks; Industrial Designs; Trade Names; Appellations of Origin; and Copyright. With respect to trademarks, the Agreement provides that only visible marks are registrable.[50]

Although every member of the Bangui Agreement has domestic patent-granting agencies, the OAPI office is invested with powers to grant patents that have efficacy across the board of member states. The patent law of all OAPI members is that set out in the Bangui Agreement. The OAPI office also serves as the registration office for OAPI members of the Trademark Registration Treaty.[51] In addition, members of OAPI submit notifications of their domestic legislation to WIPO.[52] The Bangui Agreement was amended in 1999 to make it TRIPS-compliant. The revised version of the Bangui Agreement entered into force for all OAPI members in early 2002 following ratification by 16 OAPI member states.

For most of Anglophone Africa, there was the Lusaka Agreement of 1976 which came into effect in 1978. In December 1985, the Lusaka Agreement was amended in order to admit all African states interested. This change gave birth to ARIPO.[53] The Harare Protocol adopted by ARIPO members in 1982 empowers the ARIPO office to receive and process patent and industrial design applications on behalf of states party to the Protocol. A patent granted under the Harare Protocol has the same effect in the designated contracting state as a national patent. The Banjul Protocol on marks was adopted by the administrative council of ARIPO in 1993. It establishes a trademark filing system similar to the Harare Protocol. The Protocol came into effect on 6 March 1997.

With respect to the issue of limited African relevance in the law-making processes on international IPRs, the key problem is the absence of congruence between

50 T Kongolo, 'Trademarks and Geographic Indications Within the Frameworks of the African Intellectual Property Organisation Agreement and the TRIPS Agreement' (1999) 2 *J of World Intell Prop* 832.

51 Art 2 (3) (4) of the Trademark Registration Treaty, 550 UNTS 45.

52 Côte d'Ivoire, Congo, Gabon, Senegal, Togo, Niger, Benin, Guinea, Guinea-Bissau, Malawi, and Mauritania have all notified WIPO on their domestic legislation. Chad simply affirmed that it will abide by the terms of the TRIPS Agreement.

53 Agreement on the Creation of theAfrican Regional Intellectual Property Organization (ARIPO)(as adopted by the Diplomatic Conference at Lusaka (Zambia) on 9 December 1976, and amended by the Administrative Council of ARIPO on 10 December 1982, 12 December 1986 and 27 November 1996, and as amended by the Council of Ministers on 13 August 2004) (Lusaka Agreement); Protocol on Patents and Industrial Designs within the Framework of the African Regional Intellectual Property Organization (ARIPO), 10 December 1982, amended 13 August 2004 (Harare Protocol); Banjul Protocol On Marks, adopted by the Administrative Council at Banjul, The Gambia on 19 November 1993 and amended on 28 November 1997, 26 May 1998 and 26 November 1999 and as amended by the Council of Ministers on August 13, 2004 (Banjul Protocol). There are currently 15 members of ARIPO. See <http://www.aripo.wipo.net>.

the formulae adopted in TRIPS, on the one hand, and the domestic and cultural requirements of non-industrialized countries (non-ICs) on the other hand. As Endeshaw observes,

> the extant literature on the nature, forms, and impact of IP does not distinguish between the roles of non ICs and ICs in IP lawmaking. It tends to jumble them together as if the state of economic and technological development of nations matters little to the forms and scope of the IP law they adopt. All nations are hence perceived as having to subscribe to universal standards irrespective of any diversity they may have.[54]

Yet for decades commentators have made the point that the economic and cultural imperatives of many nations are different. As Hanns Ulrich observed in the late 1980s, '. . . is there any hope that laws which have been pressed upon these countries (non-ICs) really will be applied by domestic authorities with any degree of effectiveness? The danger is that [TRIPS] will either remain a dead letter or else become a source of permanent dispute.'[55]

Part II The Significance and Normative Impact of TRIPS in Africa

As already indicated, an inquiry into the impact of TRIPS in Africa inevitably implicates a host of factors such as the colonial experience and legacies in the continent, the marginal roles by African countries in IPR law making, and of course, the persistent lack of infrastructure and chronic political instability in the continent. Amidst these peculiar endemic factors, the debate among African countries on the implementation of TRIPS and the expected impact of TRIPS has often revolved on what level of protection IPRs should be accorded in the continent.

Policy makers from African countries are virtually unanimous in their belief that the standards set out in TRIPS are the ceiling and not the floor of the protection they are willing to accord IPRs. On the other hand, powerful and influential entities from industrialized economies clamour for a TRIPS-Plus regime of protection of intellectual property rights in Africa.[56] A TRIPS-Plus regime would

---

54 Endeshaw, note 6 above.

55 H Ulrich, 'GATT: Industrial Property Protection, Fair Trade and Development', in F K Beier and G Schricker (eds), *GATT or WIPO? New Ways in the International Protection of Industrial Property* 148 (VCH Publishers, 1989). See also F Abbott, 'TRIPS in Seattle: The Not-So-Surprising Failure and the Future of the TRIPS Agenda' (2000) 14 *Berkeley J Int'l L* 165.

56 K Maskus and J Reichman, 'The Globalization of Private Knowledge Goods and the Privatization of Global Public Goods' (2004) 7 *J of Int'l Econ L* 279.

generally reflect the type of more stringent protections often embedded in most US bilateral trade agreements.[57] The growing spread of TRIPS-Plus rules via bilateral trade agreements or free trade agreements (FTAs) is a subject of increasing concern to some scholars.[58] The scepticism towards TRIPS-Plus levels of IPR protection derives from the economic and political realities on the ground, and the general perception that the benefits from such strong IPR enforcement are unidirectional and a drain of scarce resources from the continent.[59] While several African countries grapple with political instability, poverty, and other crises, there is little doubt that the greatest beneficiaries of strong IP regimes in the continent are the powerful Western states.[60]

Despite the divergent narratives[61] on the alleged benefits of strong IP regimes, why have African countries suddenly embraced such regimes?[62] The answer may well be located in the immense political and economic pressure mounted on African states by powerful Western states. Why pressurize African states to adopt strong IPR laws and institutions? Again, the answer to this is probably to be found in the increasing industrialization of many states and the narrowing technological divide between industrialized states (ICs) and the newly industrializing states (new ICs).[63] Curiously, at the time when the industrial know-how and manufacturing abilities of the industrialized parts of the world were beyond the reach of other parts, IPRs were not accorded serious and rigorous protection. However, as the technological gap narrowed, it became apparent that the value of innovative products lies not in the paper, metal, or plastic used in making such products. Rather, the value of new products is in the cost of innovation, research, design, testing and marketing involved.[64]

---

[57] Conference Report of the House of Representatives on the Trade and Development Act of 2000, Joint Explanatory Statement of the Committee of Conference on Subtitle B—Trade Benefits for Caribbean Basin Countries.

[58] A Endeshaw, 'Free Trade Agreements as Surrogates for TRIPS-plus' (2006) *EIPR* 374–380.

[59] K Aoki, 'Sovereignty and the Globalization of Intellectual Property: Neocolonialism, AntiCommons Property, and Biopiracy in the (Not-so-Brave) New World Order of International Intellectual Property Protection' (1998) 6 *Ind J of Global L Studies* 11.

[60] P McCalman, 'Reaping What You Sow: An Empirical Analysis of International Patent Harmonization' (2001) 55 *J of Int'l Economics* 161–186.

[61] R Okediji, 'The International Relations of Intellectual Property: Narratives of Developing Country Participation in the Global Intellectual Property System' (2003) 7 *Sing J Int'l & Comp L* 315.

[62] E Smith, 'Worldwide Copyright Protection Under the TRIPS Agreement' (1996) 29 *Vand J Transnat'l L* 559.

[63] F Abbott, 'The WTO TRIPS Agreement and Global Economic Development' (1996) 72 *Chi–Kent LR* 385.

[64] P Drahos, 'Developing Countries and International Intellectual Property Standard-Setting' Study Paper 8, Commission on Intellectual Property Rights. Available at <http://www.iprcommission.org/papers/pdfs/study_papers/sp8_drahos_study.pdf> (last accessed 17 May 2007).

In short, the emergence of inexpensive and accessible reproduction technologies in new ICs made it possible for newly-industrializing countries to free-ride on the technological breakthroughs of the industrialized states.[65] Coupled with increased access to Western education and significant development of a domestic technological base, cheaper labour, and inexpensive copycat technologies in the newly industrialized countries, the manufacturing advantage hitherto possessed by industrialized states began to dwindle.[66] TRIPS was thus created to plug a hole in the declining industrializing capacity of the US and to deal with the increasing trade deficits in the 1980s and 1990s.[67] It was therefore considered important by the industrialized states that greater attention be paid to the knowledge embedded in innovative products rather than to the actual embodiment of the products. This new era, the birth of the so-called 'information economy',[68] makes the protection of IPRs an economic and ideological imperative.[69]

The template shift has global ramifications. A fundamental question is why new ICs should be made to protect assets produced elsewhere[70] in circumstances that largely speak to rent-seeking, especially when non-Western forms of knowledge lack international legal protection.[71] Although opinions are strongly divided on the benefits or lack thereof of the WTO/TRIPS arrangement,[72] the benefits of WTO membership may be twofold: namely, a transparent and systematic review of the acceding country's trade law and policy, and secondly, the right to use the WTO's dispute settlement process.[73]

---

65 'Cosmopolitan Legalism Meets "Thin Community"; Problems in the Global Governance of Intellectual Property' (2004) 39 *Government and Opposition* 393.

66 Report of the President's Commission on Industrial Competitiveness, Vol 11 (1985).

67 WP Alford, 'How Theory Does—And Does Not—Matter: American Approaches to Intellectual Property Law in East Asia' (1994) 13 *UCLA Pac Basin LJ* 8.

68 P Drahos and J Braithwaite, *Information Feudalism: Who Owns the Knowledge Economy*? (The New Press, 2002).

69 K Maskus, *Intellectual Property Rights in the Global Economy* (Institute for Int'l Economics, 2000); G Evans, 'A Preliminary Excursion into TRIPS and Non-Violation Complaints' (2000) 3 *J of World Intell Prop* 1; S Cho, 'GATT Non-Violation Issues in the WTO Framework: Are they the Achilles Heel of the Dispute Settlement Process'? (1998) 39 *Harvard Int'l LJ* 311.

70 T Lewis, 'Patent Protection for the Pharmaceutical Industry: A Survey of the Patent Laws of Various Countries' (1996) 30 *Int'l Law* 835.

71 D Downes, 'How Intellectual Property Could be a Tool to Protect Traditional Knowledge' (2000) 25 *Columbia J Envtl L* 253; P Kuruk, 'Protecting Folklore Under Intellectual Property Regimes: A Reappraisal of the Tensions Between Individual and Communal Rights in Africa and the United States' (1999) 46 *Am U.LR* 769.

72 C Primo Braga, 'The Economic Justification for the Grant of Intellectual Property Rights: Patterns of Convergence and Conflict' (1996) 72 *Chi–Kent LR* 439.

73 J Bacchus, 'Groping Towards Grotius: The WTO and the International Rule of Law' Address at Harvard Law School, 1 October 2002; R Gilpin, *Global Political Economy: Understanding the International Economic Order* (Princeton University Press, 2001); R Hudec, *Enforcing International Trade Law: The Evolution of the Modern GATT Legal System* (Butterworth, 1993).

However, there are costs too. For example, upon accession, a WTO member has to undertake and bear the costs of adopting, institutionalizing, and implementing an array of heavy legal commitments to honour concessions and agreements negotiated with other trading partners.[74] The administration of IPRs involves receiving of applications, formal examination, granting or registration of the IPRs, etc. All these would have to be backed up with appropriate laws, personnel, and institutions. Indeed, it costs several million dollars to enact necessary laws, create the relevant institutions and enforcement structures for IPRs in poor countries.[75]

Failure to honour these commitments will ultimately result in direct legal and economic consequences. Whatever benefits are believed to accrue from institutionalized IPRs, protection and enforcement of intellectual property rights directly impacts on vital matters of national policy, especially for weak and impoverished states.[76] Primarily, the capacity and ability of poor states to set policy and standards on matters of grave national importance have been significantly removed.[77] Beyond the issue of diminished local capacity to legislate on IPR issues, the key question is whether TRIPS has made any significant impact in Africa. On this question, the spectre of the HIV/AIDS crisis looms large in sub-Saharan Africa.

Part III TRIPS in Africa—An Overview

For many commentators, the impact of TRIPS in Africa is all about HIV/AIDS and patented antiretroviral drugs.[78] Since the 'Africanization',[79] indeed global

[74] For example, following its ratification of the WTO Agreement, the Philippines had to change at least 40 per cent of its laws and regulations and enact new ones. See W Bello, *Multilateral Punishment: The Philippines in the WTO, 1995–2003* (Focus on the Global South, Manila, 20 June 2003).

[75] For a summary of the UNCTAD study on the cost implications of acceding to WTO/TRIPS see UNCTAD, *The TRIPS Agreement and Developing Countries* (UNCTAD/ITE/1, 1996).

[76] R Okediji, 'Public Welfare and the Role of the WTO: Reconsidering the TRIPS Agreement' (2003) 17 *Emory Int'l LR* 819.

[77] S Sell 'TRIPS and Access to Medicines Campaign' (2002) 20 [3] *Wisconsin Int'l LJ* 481.

[78] The question whether patents for antiretroviral drugs actually constrain access to HIV/AIDS treatment in Africa is a controversial one, with the contenders in combative and deeply entrenched positions. In a study financed by the major manufacturers of patented HIV/AIDS antiretroviral drugs, two researchers concluded that patents and patent laws are not major barriers to treatment in and of themselves: A Attaran and L Gillespie-White, 'Do Patents for Antiretroviral Drugs Constrain Access to AIDS Treatment in Africa?' [2001] 286 *J of the AMA 15*, 1886–1892. For a somewhat contrary view see J Lanjouw, 'The Introduction of Pharmaceutical Patents in India: "Heartless Exploitation of the Poor and Suffering"?' NBER Working Paper 6366, available at <http://www.nber.org/papers/w6366> (last accessed 5 March 2007).

[79] In the late 1980s and early 1990s there was unprecedented media campaigning and hysteria on the HIV/AIDS 'epidemic', generally believed to have the gay community in the United States

construction of the HIV/AIDS crisis as a peculiar problem of poor but sexually promiscuous peoples of the Third World, especially sub-Saharan Africa and Thailand, the perceived impact of TRIPS in Africa has been limited to issues of patented HIV/AIDS retroviral drugs.[80] The problematic definition of HIV/AIDS[81] in Third World countries, and the insinuations of reckless sexual habits among sub-Saharan Africans[82] are touchy subjects, especially having regard to the many vested interests in the global HIV/AIDS crisis industry.

Be that as it may, it is beyond doubt that the linkage of the HIV/AIDS crisis in Africa with TRIPS provisions on patents helped precipitate an impact on the TRIPS Agreement as encapsulated in the Doha Declaration of 2001.[83] More impetus for a reinterpretation of TRIPS comes from the attempt by multinational pharmaceutical companies and the US government to prevent the implementation of measures by the South African government to address the HIV/AIDS epidemic,[84] and the complaint brought by the US government against Brazil in relation to compulsory licenses.[85] These incidents were perceived as manifestations of a conflict between the recognition of IPRs and essential public health objectives, especially in the developing world.

as its epicentre. The end of humanity was predicted unless there was a radical change in human sexual behaviour. Since the repeated redefinition of the AIDS illness (for a definition of HIV/AIDS, see WHO, Workshop on AIDS in Central Africa, Bangui 22–25 1985, Document WHO/CDS/AIDS/85.1, Geneva, 1985) the current epicentre is sub-Saharan Africa, and latterly, India. On the redefinition of HIV/AIDS, see CDC, 'Revision of the Case Definition of AIDS for National Reporting—United States' (1985) Vol 34 MMWR 373–5; CDC, 'Revision of the CDC Surveillance Case Definition for AIDS' (1987) Vol 36 MMWR 1–15; CDC, '1993 Revised Classification System for HIV Infection and Expanded Surveillance Case Definition for AIDS Among Adolescents and Adults' (1992) Vol 14 MMWR 17. Stehr-Green *et al*, 'Potential Effect of Revising the CDC Surveillance Case Definition for AIDS' (1988) 5 March, *Lancet* 520–1.

80 E Seiguer, 'AIDS in the Developing World' [1998] 1 *Princeton J of Foreign Affairs* 10–15.

81 In many African countries, HIV/AIDS is largely 'diagnosed' on the basis of unspecific symptoms. Needless to say, in a continent where infectious diseases, poverty, and unhygienic living conditions have kept the average life expectancy at 50 years, it is not a coincidence that people who are suffering from well-known infectious diseases are often officially described as suffering from AIDS. See for example, T Irova & J Ninane, 'AIDS-Resembling Disease in a non-HIV-Infected African Born to an HIV-Positive Mother' (1995) 12 *Pediatric Hematology and Oncology* (September–October) 495–8.

82 D Gisellquist & J Potterat, 'Heterosexual Transmission of HIV in Africa: An Empiric Estimate' (2003) 14 *Int'l J of STD & AIDS* 162–173.

83 Ministerial Declaration on the TRIPS Agreement and Public Health, 14 November 2001, 41 ILM 755 (Doha Declaration). See generally E 't Hoen, 'TRIPS, Pharmaceutical Patents, and Access to Essential Medicines: A Long Way from Seattle to Doha' (2002) 3 *Chicago J of Int'l L* 27 at 27–38.

84 W Nagan, 'International Intellectual Property, Access to Health Care, and Human Rights: South Africa v United States' (2002) 14 *Florida J of Int'l L* 155.

85 P Champ and A Attaran, 'Patent Rights and Local Working Under the WTO TRIPS Agreement: An Analysis of the US–Brazil Patent Dispute' (2002) 27 *Yale J of Int'l L* 365.

This chapter does not concern itself with the juridical status and effect of the Doha Declaration.[86] It would suffice to observe that the Doha Declaration affirms that the TRIPS Agreement should be interpreted and implemented so as to protect public health and promote access to essential pharmaceuticals, and represents a significant development in international law.[87] At the normative level, the Doha Declaration represents a significant political adoption by WTO members that provides members with the capacity to enact measures necessary to ensure access to healthcare under the framework of the TRIPS Agreement.

Since the adoption of the Doha Declaration, the WTO council responsible for IPR, on 27 June 2002, approved a decision extending until 2016 the transition period during which least-developed countries (LDCs) are exempted from providing patent protection for pharmaceuticals. This decision formalized part of paragraph 7 of the Declaration on the TRIPS Agreement and public health. In addition, Article 31 of the TRIPS Agreement has been amended to make it easier for poorer countries to import cheaper generics made under compulsory licensing, if they are unable to manufacture the medicines themselves. The decision covers patented products or products made using patented processes or methods in the pharmaceutical sector. This is a temporary waiver that would last until the WTO's intellectual property agreement is amended.[88] However, as subsequent pages would demonstrate, there is often a huge gap between juridical prescriptions and actual ability and capacity of African countries to make use of those prescriptions. Thus, notwithstanding the amendment to Article 31 of the TRIPS Agreement, it is doubtful whether African countries have fared much better in terms of developing local industrial manufacturing capacity and

---

86 Under Art 31 §1 of the Vienna Convention a treaty is to be interpreted in good faith using the ordinary meaning of its terms in context and in light of the treaty's object and purpose. See Agreement Establishing the World Trade Organization, Annex 2, Understanding on Rules and Procedures Governing the Settlement of Disputes, 15 April 1994, 33 ILM 112, Art. 3.2, available at <http://www.wto.org/english/docs_e/legal_e/28-dsu.pdf> (last accessed 20 April 2003). The legal status of the Declaration under international law, specifically the Vienna Convention, has been suggested to include three separate possibilities:

(1) as a subsequent agreement under Art 31 §3(a) of the Vienna Convention regarding the interpretation and application of the TRIPS Agreement;
(2) as a subsequent practice under Art 31 §3(b) of the Vienna Convention in the application of the TRIPS Agreement, establishing an agreement of WTO members regarding the interpretation of the TRIPS Agreement; or
(3) as a declaration of commitment and intent that does not constitute an enforceable legal obligation.

See J Gathii, 'The Legal Status of the Doha Declaration on TRIPS and Public Health under the Vienna Convention on the Law of Treaties' (2002) 15 *Harvard J of L and Technology* 291, 299.

87 FM Abbott, 'The Doha Declaration on the TRIPS Agreement and Public Health: Lighting a Dark Corner at the WTO' (2002) 5:2 *J of Int'l Econ L* 469, 496.

88 Doha Work Programme, Ministerial Declaration, WT/MIN (05) /DEC, 22 December 2005, adopted on 18 December 2005.

thus significantly addressing the dire health challenges in Africa that compelled the amendment of Article 31 of the TRIPS Agreement.

A. TRIPS in Northern Africa

Northern Africa comprises Algeria, Egypt, Libyan Arab Jamahiriya, Morocco, Sudan, Tunisia, and Western Sahara. Northern African countries are a reflection of historical patterns of conquests, colonialism, Arabization, and Islamization of the Maghreb, Nile Valleys, and the Saharan parts of the African continent. The Arab conquests of the seventh century AD, and European (mainly French) colonialism of the eighteenth century have largely defined the legal framework of Northern African countries. However, the economies of some Northern African countries such as Algeria, Libya, and Sudan have been affected by the discovery of oil and natural gas in their deserts. Like many other countries with low levels of industrialization, the economies of many northern African countries are often dominated by agriculture and extractive activities such as mining. Egypt, however, has the most diversified industrial base of North African countries. The general picture, thus, is that IPRs have played marginal roles in the economies and juridical life of northern African countries.

With specific reference to Algeria, there are various legislations dealing respectively with patents,[89] trademarks,[90] industrial designs,[91] copyrights,[92] appellations of origin,[93] and topographies of integrated circuits.[94] Algeria, however, is not a member of the WTO[95] and therefore need not detain us here. [96]

Egypt is a member of the WTO and arguably has the most diversified industrial base in northern Africa. Like many African countries, prior to the emergence of TRIPS, pharmaceutical products were not eligible for patent protection under Egyptian law. Since its accession to TRIPS, however, Egypt has enacted a TRIPS-compliant patent law.[97] It is arguable that the accession to TRIPS has

89 Law No 03–19, November 2003.
90 Law No 03–18, November 2003.
91 Decree No 66–87, April 1966.
92 Executive Decree No 98–366, November 1998.
93 Decree No 76–121, July 1976.
94 Law No 03–20, November 2003.
95 J Goodman, '"Stealing our Heritage?": Women's Folksongs, Copyright Law, and the Public Domain in Algeria' (2002) March 22 *Africa Today* 85–97.
96 For a summary of the national IPR system in Algeria, however, see the Algerian National Institute of Industrial Property (INAPI) website at <http://www.inapi.org>.
97 Intellectual Property Law No 82 of 2002 (Egypt).

had legal and economic impacts in Egypt.[98] On the legal plane, as already indicated the Egyptian patent law has been modified to permit the patenting of pharmaceutical products and processes. Additional changes have been made with respect to mailbox applications with respect to patents; protection of undisclosed information; and the regulation of compulsory licensing in compliance with Articles 30 and 31 of TRIPS. These new legal changes came into effect in January 2005.

Despite the changes to Egyptian patent law, a significant problem in the Egyptian pharmaceutical industry is the unauthorized use of data by generic drug manufacturers desirous of obtaining quick approvals for their drugs.[99] However, with the passage of the new Egyptian patent law, the Ministry of Health is obliged to ensure that there is no access to the test data except for the purposes of examining the application of the originator of the information.[100] In some respects, the Egyptian patent law exceeds the minimum requirements of TRIPS.

Changes to Egyptian patent law have come with some severe costs. For example, the cost of establishing a patent office in Egypt was conservatively put at about US$2 million.[101] Economically and socially, given the economic and healthcare infrastructures' limited ability to absorb or redistribute the higher costs of patented products through effective health insurance, there is an increase in the costs of those items; a burden that now falls on the poor. Roughly 20 per cent of Egypt's 70 million people live below the poverty line and thus millions of people are hit by increases in the prices of pharmaceuticals. Studies have shown that since the introduction of TRIPS in Egypt, prices of drugs have increased.[102] Whether this is a coincidence or a direct cause and effect relationship is unclear.

In addition to its patent law, Egypt has enacted TRIPS-compliant legislation on trademarks and industrial designs. With respect to copyright protection, collective management societies have been created. Some Egyptian policies such as the imposition of higher taxes on foreign-produced films, and a screen quota that gives priority to Egyptian films,[103] may be problematic in the context of TRIPS.

---

98 N Al-Ali, 'The Egyptian Pharmaceutical Industry After TRIPS—A Practitioner's View' (2003) 26 *Fordham Int'l LJ* 274.

99 Niveen Washish, 'At Loggerheads Over Patent Rights', *Al-Ahram Weekly Online* (May 24–30, 2001), available at <http://www.ahram.org>.

100 Arts 55 and 56 of Law 82.

101 UNCTAD, TRIPS and Developing Countries, note 75 above, 23–24.

102 A S Saleh, 'Impact of Globalization on Drug Industry: Possible Risks and Means to Overcome Them', 7th International Conference on 'The Impact of Globalization on Development and Healthcare Service in Islamic Countries' (March 23–27, 2002). See also J Quick, 'Ensuring Access to Essential Medicines in the Developing Countries and Least Developed Countries—Framework for Action', IOMS Conference.

103 Office of the United States Trade Representative, 1991 National Trade Estimate Report on Trade Barriers 79 (1995).

On enforcement, infringement of IPRs may be litigated in Egyptian courts. Statistics show that Egypt has one of the busiest IPR offices in Africa. In 2002, more than 1,400 patents were granted by the Egyptian patent office. Nearly 2,000 industrial designs were granted, and nearly 200,000 trademarks were approved within the same period. There is little doubt that Egypt's significant industrial base accounts for the large number of activities in the IP sectors.

Morocco is located at the north-western tip of Africa. Until 1953 Morocco was a French colony. Consequently, Morocco has been largely influenced by French civil law traditions. Morocco promulgated a new industrial property law to comply with its obligations under TRIPS.[104] Under the new law, the following categories are considered industrial properties: patents, integrated circuit topographies, industrial designs, trade- and service marks, trade names, geographical indications, and appellations of origin.[105] The new law came into effect on 9 March 2000. The law on patents in Morocco permits the patenting of most subject matters except discoveries, theories, computer programs, and aesthetic creations.[106] Plant varieties are not yet protected under Moroccan law. Sudan is different because it is not a member of the WTO.[107] Tunisia has enacted TRIPS-compliant laws on patents,[108] trademarks,[109] industrial design, copyright, and integrated circuit topographies. Although Tunisia has one of the best IPR offices in Africa, Egypt grants more patents and trademarks than either Tunisia or Morocco.

B. TRIPS in Western Africa

Western Africa comprises Benin, Burkina Faso, Cape Verde, Côte d'Ivoire, The Gambia, Ghana, Guinea, Guinea-Bissau, Liberia, Mali, Mauritania, Nigeria, Senegal, Sierra Leone, and Togo. The colonial imprint on West African countries is palpable in the present day. Throughout the colonial era, Britain controlled a wide swath of West Africa including The Gambia, Sierra Leone, Ghana and

104 Morocco Industrial Property Act, Act No 17–97 (9 February 2000).

105 Ibid.

106 T Kongolo, 'Morocco's Patent System and its International Connection' (2002) 42 *IDEA* 181.

107 V Mosoti, 'The Legal Implications of Sudan's Accession to the World Trade Organization' (2004) 103 *African Affairs* 269–282.

108 For example Law No 2000–84 of August 2000; Decree No 2001–328 of January 2001, setting out the terms for keeping a national register of patents; Decree No 2001–836 of April 2001, establishing fees relating to patents.

109 Law No 2001–36 of April 2001, on the protection of trademarks; Decree No 2001–1603 of July 2001, setting out the terms for the registration and the raising of objections against the registration of trademarks; Decree No 2001–1985 of August 2001, establishing fees relating to trade- and service marks.

Nigeria. On the other hand, France controlled Senegal, Guinea, Mali, Burkina Faso, Côte d'Ivoire and Niger. The remainder territories were controlled by Portugal (in Guinea-Bissau) and Germany (Togo until the end of the First World War). Liberia is the only country in West Africa to escape direct imperial control, although it saw itself as an American outpost in Africa.

Since the attainment of formal political independence in the 1960s, West Africa has been plagued by political convulsions including chronic coups and counter-coups, civil wars of continental dimensions, and political corruption. Indeed, West Africa is the most politically unstable region in Africa, with more military coups in the region than all other regions combined. The economies of most West African countries are agrarian and extractive, especially of petroleum. With respect to industrialization, there have been spasms of industrial activity in the sub-region, especially in Ghana and Nigeria. Despite the absence of a strong manufacturing and industrial base, West African countries have historically filled their statute books with IP law and, in recent times, TRIPS-compliant legislation. On a case-by-case analysis, West Africa presents a mixed picture.

The Republic of Benin, a founding member of OAPI, has enacted TRIPS-compliant laws on patents, trademarks, and industrial designs. As a member of OAPI, Beninoise laws on patents and trademarks are anchored on the 1999 amendment to the Bangui Agreement. Like most African countries, the supervision of IP matters is generally handled by government ministries such as the Ministry of Industry and the Ministry of Culture. Virtually the same as in Benin may be said for the republic of Burkina Faso. With a special Industrial Property Tribunal and a Copyright Tribunal, Burkina Faso in theory has complied with its obligations under TRIPS. As a member of OAPI, Côte d'Ivoire's regulations on patents, trademarks, and industrial designs are premised on the annexes to the Bangui Agreement as amended in 1999. A new copyright bill has recently been enacted. There is also a collective management society for copyright royalties. Enforcement of IP matters are handled by the courts, the police and the Customs. Records from the relevant IPR offices in Côte d'Ivoire show that trademarks and industrial designs often dominate in the grants issued by the relevant offices.

Further west, like most British colonies in Africa, the acquisition of patent rights under Gambian law was largely dependent on re-registration of patents already issued by the British Patent Office. However, since 1989, The Gambia has enacted a local patent law. Similar laws have been made with respect to trademarks, utility models, unfair competition, and industrial designs. This legislation is generally compatible with TRIPS. However, the position with respect to copyright is different. The Gambia is a member of ARIPO. In the year 2001, nearly 100 patents were granted in The Gambia through the auspices of ARIPO.

Ghana has recently enacted TRIPS-compliant laws on patents, trademarks, copyrights, and industrial designs. A law on plant variety protection is pending before the Parliament. The situation in Ghana compels a careful reappraisal of the peculiar needs of some African countries for certain IP laws. Ghana is a member of ARIPO and thus uses the examination processes established under the ARIPO framework. It is significant that Ghana's world-famous Kente cloth designs are often the victim of illegal copying and dumping from Asian countries, especially China. Perhaps, if IPRs are to have local relevance and resonance in African countries, products such as Kente cloth ought to anchor the move towards making IPRs relevant to the local populace.

Guinea is a former colony of France and a member of OAPI. Hence, her laws on patents, trademarks, and industrial designs are premised on the terms of the Bangui Agreement. The Guinean copyright law[110] needs to be amended to comply with the minimum requirements of TRIPS. The situation in Guinea-Bissau is slightly different. A former colony of Portugal, Guinea-Bissau's laws on patents,[111] trademarks, and industrial designs are TRIPS-compliant. A law on copyright and neighbouring rights is currently under consideration. Liberia is not a member of the WTO and thus need not detain us here.

Like fellow signatories to and members of OAPI, Malian laws on patents, trademarks, and industrial designs are all governed by the annexes to the Bangui Agreement as last amended in February 1999. These international provisions are generally compatible with TRIPS. With respect to copyrights, Malian Law No 84/AN–RM of October 1994 on copyright and neighbouring rights is compatible with the minimum requirements of TRIPS. Mauritania is also a member of OAPI and the position in Mali is comparable to what obtains in Mauritania, save for the absence of TRIPS-compliant legislation on copyright and neighbouring rights. Like other OAPI members, Niger is a signatory to the TRIPS-compliant annexes to the Bangui Agreement on patents, trademarks and industrial designs. Its 1993 law on copyrights, neighbouring rights and expressions of folklore exceeds the standards set by TRIPS by its protection of folklore. There are Tribunals respectively created for the purposes of dealing with industrial property and copyright cases.

Despite the existence of TRIPS-compliant laws on patents, trademarks, and industrial designs, it is virtually impossible to highlight benefits that have accrued to Guinea, Guinea-Bissau, Ghana, Mali, Mauritania, or Niger solely on the basis of their accession to TRIPS. In any event, Guinea, Guinea-Bissau and

110 Law No 043/APN/CP/80, of August 1980.
111 Decreto lei No 6/96, Capitulo 1, February 1997.

The Gambia are desperately poor countries. It is therefore doubtful whether any reasonable or compassionate person would expect such countries to spend their meagre resources on creating IP laws and institutions at the expense of health, education, and shelter. Yet, the usual refrain from advocates of the WTO is that such countries have 'an urgent need . . . to enact a new Industrial Property Legislation which will take into account new developments in the field'.[112]

Nigeria is a member of WIPO and a signatory to several international IPR treaties and conventions including the Universal Copyright Convention, the Berne Convention, and the Paris Convention (Lisbon text).[113] Nigeria is generally regarded as the largest and most important market in the African region. Its patents and trademarks offices are relatively busy. However, a huge proportion of patents granted by the Patent Office belong to foreigners. For example, in 1999–2002 1,458 patents were issued to foreigners while local applicants obtained 986 grants. Records from the trademarks office shows that for the same period, 4,613 approvals went to foreigners while local applicants obtained a total of 8,694 approvals. In Nigeria, the regulation of technology transfer associated with patented technology is handled by the National Office of Technology Acquisition and Promotion (NOTAP). The registration of licenses and agreements on technology transfer is voluntary.[114] Failure to register a license or contract does not nullify the contract under NOTAP.

Nigeria's current IPR laws are TRIPS-compliant. This may be related to the fact that, unlike many African countries that have flirted with several economic ideologies such as communism, socialism, etc, Nigeria has consistently been a capitalist economy and has participated in international IP conventions. Thus, Nigeria has a comprehensive body of IP law and boasts a growing segment of the population with vested interests in the protection of diverse forms of intellectual property, especially, copyrights and trademarks. Notwithstanding the availability of modern IP laws, the USTR alleges that Nigeria has done little to eradicate the widespread production and sale of pirated tapes, videos, computer software, and books.[115] Analysts have pointed out, however, that the problem is with the lack of institutional capacity, low morale among enforcement personnel, poor training, and limited resources. More worrisome, the court process in Nigeria is notoriously slow and cumbersome.

---

[112] Zikonda, note 46 above, Annex Two, 1.

[113] Paris Convention for the Protection of Industrial Property, 20 March 1883, revised 14 July 1967, 21 UST 1629.

[114] *Beecham Group Ltd. v Essdee Food Prods Nig Ltd* (1985) 3 NWLR Pt 11, 112.

[115] B Sodipo, *Piracy and Counterfeiting: GATT, TRIPS and Developing Countries* (Kluwer 1997).

However, Nigerian authorities, especially the Nigerian Copyright Commission and the National Agency for Food, Drug Administration and Control (NAFDAC) have been quite active in combating the menace of piracy and counterfeit drugs, respectively, in the country. In many cases, people operating video rental clubs have been arrested and prosecuted by the Nigerian Copyright Commission.[116] In such arrests thousands of pirated videocassettes and equipment worth millions of dollars have been seized and confiscated. A number of high-profile charges have been laid against IP violators. There are collective management societies in Nigeria and also a Copyright Council. With respect to counterfeit drugs, NAFDAC has gained global fame and recognition in its fights with importers and retailers of counterfeit drugs.

With respect to Senegal, as a member of OAPI, its patents, trademarks and industrial design regimes are governed by the annexes to the Bangui Agreement as amended in 1999. Its copyright law, however, does not meet the standard set out in the TRIPS Agreement. There are cases of piracy and illegal copying of copyrighted products. The situation in Sierra Leone is typical of unstable and strife-ridden Africa. Sierra Leone was embroiled in a bloody war for nearly ten years. As a former British colony, however, its IP laws were largely premised on British laws and institutions. Given that Sierra Leone has been the theatre of one of the most brutal and savage conflicts in modern history, it is not surprising that modernization of IP laws and institution is not a priority. Togo is very much in the same situation as all Francophone West African countries but the noticeable difference is that Togolese copyright law protects folklore expressions and thus is superior to the minimum standards set out in TRIPS.

C. TRIPS and Post-TRIPS in Eastern Africa

Eastern Africa comprises Burundi, Comoros, Djibouti, Eritrea, Ethiopia, Kenya, Madagascar, Malawi, Mauritius, Mozambique, Rwanda, the Seychelles, Somalia, Uganda, United Republic of Tanzania, Zambia, and Zimbabwe. Like most of the smaller and poorer African member states of the WTO, little IP business is done by the Burundian IP offices. Indeed, in 2002, only ten patents were issued by the Patent Office in Burundi. Similarly, only 152 trademarks were issued in 2002. The situation in Djibouti is bleaker. Currently, laws dealing with patents, trademarks, industrial designs, appellations of origin, and copyright respectively are under consideration. Djibouti is one of the Least Developed Countries in Africa.

116 'Copyright Commission Arrests 30 Over Piracy' *Thisday* 7 August 2006.

With respect to Kenya, the situation is very much different. Kenya has witnessed significant positive developments in its Trademark Act of 1994 which has expanded the scope of trademark protection to cover service marks, and shapes and packaging of goods. Similarly, the Kenyan Copyright Act of 2001, Industrial Property Act of 2001, and the Seed and Plant Variety Act of 1977 are all compatible with the minimum requirements of TRIPS. Kenyan patent law is equally TRIPS-compliant.[117] In 2004, nearly 150 patents were issued by the Kenyan patent office, 89 of which were granted to foreign inventors. In the same year, 1,303 trademarks were issued to foreigners while 539 trademarks were issued to domestic applicants. Similarly, 46 industrial designs were approved for foreign applicants while local applicants obtained 193 approvals. 326 plant breeders' grants went to foreign applicants while the number for local applicants was 252. On the aspect of IPR enforcement, the customs authorities in Kenya have reportedly made 50 seizures of counterfeit goods. In addition, more than 50 IP-related criminal cases were dealt with by Kenyan authorities in 2004. Kenya has a functional collective management society. The courts in Kenya regularly deal with cases involving IP matters.

Madagascar has a relatively effective system of laws and institutions for the protection of IPRs. Its patent and trademarks offices issue patents and trademarks to both domestic and foreign applicants. Malawi has not modified its IPR laws to conform to the standards set by TRIPS. Similarly, Mauritius and Mozambique have not yet modified their IPR laws to conform with TRIPS standards. Rwanda has emerged from one of the worst genocides in world history. Not surprisingly, it has not yet modified its IPR laws to conform to TRIPS standards.

Tanzania and Uganda present a somewhat similar case. In both cases, domestic laws on patents, trademarks, industrial designs, and copyright hitherto were anchored on colonial British laws that have now been reformed to meet the minimum standards set out in the TRIPS Agreement. Tanzania has also created a collective management society. The High Courts of Tanzania are empowered to adjudicate on suits pertaining to IP matters. Uganda is a LDC and a staunch supporter of the WTO.[118] The Ugandan patent law of 1991 is compatible with TRIPS. Its copyright and other laws on IPRs are currently being revised. There is a pending law on the protection of plant varieties. For the year 2001, 14 trademarks were approved in respect of foreign applicants while local applicants obtained three approvals. In the same year, 406 patents were granted to foreigners while local applicants obtained two grants.

[117] Section 80(1)(a) of Kenya Industrial Property Act 2001.
[118] Trade Policy Review Uganda, 21 November 2001, WT/TPR/93.

Uganda's international trade is small and lopsided with agriculture as the backbone of the Ugandan economy.[119] Uganda exports agricultural produce and imports merchandise goods. As a member of the Common Market for Eastern and Southern Africa (COMESA), Uganda is part of an ambitious economic liberalization agenda. However, it is generally accepted in Uganda that few benefits have flowed from its membership of the WTO. Indeed, Uganda's GDP has deteriorated significantly in the past six years. The deterioration in GDP has been blamed inter alia on 'deterioration in terms of trade'.[120]

The Zambian experience with TRIPS is somewhat similar to the situation in Kenya, albeit on a smaller scale. Prior to formal political independence, IP matters in Zambia were administered from Harare in Zimbabwe. It was only in 1968 that an IP office was created in Zambia. Currently, the Patents, Companies Registration Office (PCRO) administers the industrial property aspects of IPRs, while the Ministry of Information and Broadcasting deals with copyright and neighbouring rights issues. The PCRO was transformed into an executive agency in 1998. In terms of administration, lack of adequate funding of the PCRO has stunted the development of the office.[121] From the juridical perspective, the administration of IPRs in Zambia is governed by five statutes.[122] IPRs, however, are enforced by the High Court of Zambia. There is a collective management society for the collection and sharing of royalties from certain copyrighted rights in Zambia. However, commentators have pointed that Zambia's huge foreign debt and domestic poverty make it unlikely that IPR enforcement would receive priority attention from government funds.

Zimbabwe is a signatory to the WIPO Convention of 1981, the Paris Convention, the Berne Convention, the Patent Cooperation Treaty, and also a member of ARIPO. Domestic laws were enacted after 2000 specifically to meet Zimbabwe's obligations under the TRIPS Agreement with particular respect to copyrights,[123] trademarks, geographical indications, industrial designs, plant varieties,[124] and

119 WT/MIN (01)/ST/111, Doha, 9–13 November 2001.

120 Ibid. This is often explained in terms of increased price of crude oil and the relative decline in the price of coffee.

121 Zikonda, note 46 above, 3.

122 The respective statutes are: The Patents Act, Chapter 400 of the Laws of Zambia; The Trade Marks Act, Chapter 40 of the Laws of Zambia; The Registered Designs Act, Chapter 402 of the Laws of Zambia; The Copyrights and Performance Act, Chapter 406 of the Laws of Zambia, and The Competition and Fair Trading Act, Chapter 417 of the Laws of Zambia.

123 Copyright Act (Chapter 26:1) 1966 (1981), available at <http://www.wipo.int/clea/en/index.jsp> (last accessed 5 March 2007).

124 Plant Breeders' Rights Act, Chapter 18'16, October 1974; Plant Breeders' Rights Regulations 1998 SJ 113/98; Plant Breeders' Right Amendment Act No 11, July 2001.

integrated circuit topographies.[125] Given that the Zimbabwean Patent Act of 1972 passes the minimum threshold set out in TRIPS, Zimbabwe did not have to amend its patent law. The Zimbabwean copyright law provides protection for literary, dramatic, musical or artistic work, cinematograph films, sound recordings, broadcasts and computer programs as provided for in the TRIPS Agreement. The ambit of works covered in the Zimbabwean copyright law is not different from what is provided for under the Berne Convention.[126] There is, however, no express mention or definition of 'databases' in Zimbabwean legislation. An argument has been made that Zimbabwe should amend her laws to provide for the protection of databases, preferably in accordance with the EC Database Directive.[127] Be that as it may, by the combined operations of sections 5(1) and 42 of the Zimbabwe Copyright Act, copyright protection is extended to Zimbabwean nationals, persons domiciled in Zimbabwe, and nationals of states who are signatories to the Berne Convention.

Although Zimbabwean law guarantees protection for the holders of copyright, copyright infringement is common. This is particularly serious and rampant with respect to the piracy of videocassettes and computer software. There is evidence that, while Zimbabwean law protects the rights of copyright holders, enforcement in this area is lax. However, legal actions against resellers of pirated computer software are usually successful. It is noteworthy that Zimbabwean jurisprudence in this area is heavily influenced by European law as implemented or interpreted by English courts.[128]

Zimbabwe protects trademarks under the Trade Marks Act.[129] The general incidents of rights associated with ownership of trademarks in member states of the WTO apply with equal force to rights holders in Zimbabwe. Geographical indications are protected under the Geographic Indications Act.[130] Theoretically,

125 F Maonera, 'Implementing the World Trade Organization (WTO) Agreement on Trade-Related Aspects of Intellectual Property Rights (TRIPS) in Zimbabwe' March 2005, Trades & Development Studies Centre, Harare, available at <www.tradescentre.org.zw> (last accessed 5 March 2007).

126 Copyright Act, note 123 above; Berne Convention, note 26 above.

127 Directive on the Legal Protection of Databases, 96/9/EC, Official J L077/ 27/03/1996.

128 C Ncube, 'Copyright Protection of Computer Programs, Computer-Generated Works and Databases in Zimbabwe' (2002) 2 *J of Info L & Technology* 6–11, available at <http://www2.warwick.ac.uk/fac/soc/law/elj/jilt/2002_2/ncube/> (last accessed 5 March 2007).

129 Trade Marks Act (Chapter 26:04) 1974 (1994).

130 Geographic Indications Act 2002, Chapter 26:06. Under the Zimbabwe Geographic Indications Act, no person shall apply a misleading geographical indication to any product, and no person shall sell any product; import any product for sale in Zimbabwe; export any product for sale outside Zimbabwe, or manufacture any product for sale, if a misleading geographical indication is applied to the product.

protecting geographical indications serves to stimulate and ensure fair competition and to protect consumers from misleading geographical indications.

Patents in Zimbabwe are protected under the Patent Act.[131] Needless to add, the impact of the Doha Declaration on matters pertaining to access to HIV/AIDS antiretroviral drugs in Zimbabwe has not yet been empirically settled.[132] Interestingly, on 30 August 2003, the TRIPS Council granted extra flexibility to poor countries so that countries that are unable to produce pharmaceutical products domestically can import patented drugs made under compulsory licensing. This waiver would last until 2016. Pursuant to sections 34 and 35 of the Zimbabwean Patent Act, the Minister of Justice, Legal and Parliamentary Affairs issued a notice declaring a period of emergency on HIV/AIDS for the purpose of enabling the state or a person authorized in writing by the Minister to make or use any patented drug, including any antiretroviral drug, in the treatment of persons suffering from HIV/AIDS. The declaration, initially made for a period of six months, was extended in January 2003 to December 2008.[133] Zimbabwe is one of the few countries in the industrializing world that has issued a compulsory license.

With respect to enforcement, the Zimbabwean Parliament enacted the Intellectual Property Tribunal Act[134] which puts in place a specialist court for the enforcement of IPRs in the country. Presently, all intellectual property rights are enforced by the High Court of Zimbabwe sitting as a copyright tribunal pending the actual operation of the Intellectual Property Tribunal. Pursuant to the law setting up the Intellectual Property Tribunal, a series of subsidiary court procedures and regulations governing the procedural aspect of IPRs in the country have been put in place.

D. TRIPS in Central Africa

Central Africa comprises Angola, Cameroon, Central African Republic, Chad, Congo, the Democratic Republic of the Congo, Equatorial Guinea, Gabon, and the twin islands of São Tomé and Principe. Central Africa has been the stage of one of the most chronic and brutal wars in Africa, the Congo war, otherwise known as Africa's World War. Similarly, the Congo war is the widest interstate war in modern African history. The war has involved nine African countries. Between 1998 and 2004, more than 3.8 million people have died, either directly

131 Patents Act, Chapter 26:03, (as amended by Act 20/1994 (s.7)).
132 Abbott, 'Lighting a Dark Corner', note 87 above, 469–505.
133 Statutory Instrument 32 of 2003, Minister of Justice, Zimbabwe. The declaration also permits the import of generic antiretroviral drugs.
134 (Chapter 26:08) 2001.

in the conflict or from circumstances precipitated by it. The contextual circumstances and experiential exigencies in Central Africa are imperative factors in any useful analysis of the impact or lack thereof of the TRIPS Agreement in that region of Africa.

Angola fought a long war of independence and also witnessed a bloody post-independence conflict. However, as a member of the WTO, Angola has enacted TRIPS-compliant laws on patents,[135] trademarks, industrial designs and copyright.[136] There are also laws on utility models, appellations of origin/geographic indications, and unfair competition. The administration of patents and utility models is undertaken by a special office attached to the Angolan Ministry of Industry. Copyright matters are overseen by the Ministry of Education and Culture. There are presently no collective management societies for copyright royalties in Angola. With respect to enforcement, there is an Industrial Property Tribunal for infringement of patents and a Copyright Tribunal for copyright-related cases. Despite these remarkable efforts, and perhaps as a result of the long years of civil conflict, in the past 29 years only 30 trademarks were registered on Angolan industrial products.[137]

The situation in Cameroon is somewhat different, maybe because Cameroon has been one of the most politically stable countries in Africa. As a signatory to the WTO treaty, Cameroon has amended its IPR laws to conform to the requirements of TRIPS. Being a member of OAPI, Cameroonian laws on patents, trademarks and industrial designs are anchored on the provisions of Annexes 1–IV of the Bangui Agreement as last amended in February 1999. For copyrights and neighbouring rights, Cameroon has enacted Law No. 2000/011 on Copyright and Related Rights. This legislation meets the minimum standards set out in the TRIPS Agreement. With respect to enforcement, Cameroonian courts regularly hear cases on infringement of IPRs. However, there is a high level of piracy in Cameroon despite its modern patent law, and industrial and technological activities in Cameroon are at insignificant levels. Like Cameroon, in the Central African Republic (CAR) the regulation of patents, trademarks, and industrial designs respectively are anchored on the provisions set out in the annexes to the Bangui Agreement as last amended in February 1999. The independent legislation on copyright is in conformity with the requirements of TRIPS.[138] Virtually the same pattern of compliance with TRIPS is repeated in Chad.

---

135 Industrial Property Law No 3/92, February 1992.

136 Copyright Law No 4/90, March 1990.

137 Press Release, Angola Press Agency, 'Angola Struggling to Make Inroads Into Intellectual Property' (17 September 2004), available at <http://www.tralac.org/scripts/content.php?id=2919>.

138 Ordinance No 85–002 on Copyright.

The epicentre of the Congo war, the Democratic Republic of the Congo (formerly Zaire) adhered to the WTO in January 1997. Congo enacted a law in 1986 for the protection of copyright. The 1986 law abrogated the colonial decree of 1948. Congolese copyright law provides for the protection of both the economic and moral rights of the author. As a signatory to the Berne Convention, Congolese copyright law covers most of the recognized categories and types of copyright.[139] Congolese copyright law is generally TRIPS-compliant notwithstanding its omission of folklore from copyrightable categories.[140] However, despite the apparent compliance with TRIPS, it has been observed that 'works of authors are not adequately protected, particularly in respect of neighbouring rights. The collective society in charge of safeguarding author's rights is incompetent to cope with these complex issues and it lacks the means to bar the export or import of infringing works and fight against pirated works'.[141] It has been suggested by one scholar that a special police be created to deal with this problem. One wonders how a country beset for decades with civil war, and where daily life is fraught with grave personal risk, should be asked to create a special police for the enforcement of copyright.

The situation in Gabon is akin to what obtains in Cameroon, CAR, Chad, and Congo. Gabon's laws on patents, trademarks, and industrial designs are premised on the Bangui Agreement as last amended in February 1999. With respect to copyright, the Copyright Law No. 1/87 of July 1987 makes provisions for the regulation and enforcement of copyright-related rights in Gabon.

In sum, in spite of grave political and social challenges Central African countries have generally complied with their obligations under TRIPS. However, it is difficult to point out the benefits that they have derived from changing their IPR laws and creating the institutions for the enforcement of IPRs. The paradox here is that Central Africa is home to some influential and world-respected genres of music such as 'Makosa', 'Lingala', etc. These are expressions and products which ordinarily should have benefited from certain forms of IPR such as copyrights.

E. TRIPS in Southern Africa

Southern Africa is composed of Botswana, Lesotho, Namibia, South Africa, and Swaziland. Save for South Africa, with its very diverse industrial base, much

139 Article 4 of the Copyright and Neighbouring Rights Act.

140 T Kongolo, 'Does the Congo's Copyright and Neighboring Rights Law Conflict with the TRIPS Agreement?' (1999) 2 *J of World Intell Prop* 311.

141 Ibid.

of southern Africa is dependent on mining, agriculture, and tourism. As a member of WTO/TRIPS since 1995, Botswana has largely complied with its obligations under the WTO regime. Patents-related issues in Botswana are governed by the Industrial Property Act No. 14 of 1996 as amended in 1997.[142] Appellations of origin and geographic indications are also covered under the 1997 legislation. A bill on Layout Designs of Integrated Circuits is under consideration. Botswana also enacted the Copyright and Neighbouring Rights Law in 2000. In terms of implementation and enforcement of IPRs, the patents office in Botswana is supervised by the Ministry of Trade and Commerce. The High Courts of Botswana have jurisdiction to hear cases of infringement of IPRs.

Lesotho is the only country in the continent that is completely surrounded by another country—South Africa. Lesotho is also the only LDC in the Southern Africa Customs Union (SACU). Despite this status, Lesotho benefits from the good rail, road, and air transport links with South Africa. Lesotho has various laws dealing with a variety of IPRs such as patents, trademarks, industrial designs, copyrights, utility models, unfair competition, and employee's inventions. The patents and trademarks offices in Lesotho issue patents and trademarks. Litigation on matters pertaining to IPRs are resolved by the High Court of Lesotho. The garment and apparel industry in Lesotho is its largest employer and this sector has grown largely as a result of trade preferences, such as the now-defunct Multi-Fibre Agreement (MFA).[143] Indeed, more than 250,000 jobs were lost in Africa when the MFA was ended. Namibia also enacted a Copyright and Neighbouring Rights law, in 2002. This bill contains measures intended to implement the WIPO treaties.[144] Namibia's trademarks law is also TRIPS-compatible. However, Namibia has not yet made the necessary changes to its patent law. As with Lesotho, the demise of the MFA agreement was a big blow to Namibia.[145]

South Africa signed the TRIPS Agreement in 1994 and has since then taken various steps to comply with its treaty obligations. Prior to the TRIPS agreement, South Africa's Patent Act No 57/1978 reflected the perceived national economic interests of South Africa in that it permitted compulsory licensing. That Act was amended by the Intellectual Property Laws Amendment No 38/1997 in an

142 Chapter 68:02, The Laws of Botswana, Revised Edition 1997.

143 G Mutume, 'Loss of Textile Market Costs African Jobs' (2006) 20 *Africa Renewal* 1, 18.

144 G Mossinghoff and R Oman, 'The World Intellectual Property Organisation: A United Nations Success Story' (1997) [Fall] *World Affairs* 104–108.

145 A !Naruseb, 'The End of the WTO Fibre Agreement and its Impact on the Local Textile Industry: Implication on the Namibian Economy and Employment' Address to the Namibia Economic Society, 5 August 2005.

obvious attempt to comply fully with the TRIPS Agreement.[146] It must be noted, however, that in the wake of the HIV/AIDS crisis, South Africa amended its Medicines and Related Substances Control Act to allow the Health Minister to abrogate patent rights for pharmaceuticals, to issue compulsory licenses and to allow parallel imports of pharmaceuticals.[147]

In addition, the government of South Africa in 2002 enacted the Electronic Communications and Transactions Act which contains strong provisions on service provider liability.[148] The bill also contains anti-hacking provisions against the unauthorized access to data, or the unlawful manufacture of devices that circumvent technological protection measures on a specified computer system to protect data. Further, South Africa has enacted a TRIPS-compliant copyright law. However it may be argued that, despite this legislative initiative, there is an impression that widespread copyright piracy exists in South Africa. Indeed, the Business Software Alliance reported that US copyright holders lost an estimated $196 million in South Africa during 2004.[149]

The impression of rampant piracy is largely fostered by the low number of convictions by the courts. Some of the problems implicated in the low level of convictions in South Africa include the lack of evidentiary presumptions of subsistence and ownership in copyright infringement cases.[150] Beyond the issues of procedural law, some critics have argued that South African courts accord low priority to copyright infringement cases.[151] This argument fails to take into consideration the political and economic challenges that South Africa has had to deal with, especially gun violence and gross economic disparities, since the demise of apartheid. Further, it has to be noted that the advancement of technologies that facilitate copying makes it exceedingly difficult to apprehend pirates.

146 D Sheppard, 'Patent Law in South Africa With Particular Reference to the TRIPS Agreement' (1999) 2 *J of World Intell Prop* 607.

147 R Ostergard, 'The Political Economy of the South Africa–United States Patent Dispute' (1999) 2 *J of World Intell Prop* 875.

148 No 25/2002.

149 It is arguable that these figures, representing the full market price of each pirated copy, are somewhat inconsistent with common market practices. Publishers rarely sell copyright items at full market prices, especially to poorer countries. In addition, it is well known that prices of copyright items are usually reduced for a variety of factors. Accordingly, the figures estimated by the BSA represent the highest end of the market, a position inconsistent with common experience.

150 According to the International Intellectual Property Alliance, 'whereas in certain former Commonwealth countries, ownership by the plaintiff is presumed unless proof to the contrary is introduced, in South Africa a mere denial by the defendant shifts the burden to prove ownership to the plaintiff'. See IIPA Comments to the TPSC on IPR Provisions in AGOA, 13 October 2005. On file with the author.

151 There is evidence, however, that South African prosecutors are indeed very active and that more cases on infringement have gone to court.

Cultural factors may also influence attitudes to copying.[152] At the economic level, legitimate products are not available to consumers, thus leaving pirates with an open lucrative market. These are real challenges that may be dealt with in constructive ways rather than the name-calling that has largely characterized Western attitudes to illegal copying and piracy in southern African countries.[153] Like South Africa, Swaziland has enacted a copyright law which contains WIPO treaty language on implementation. However, Swaziland has not yet amended its law on patents to comply with TRIPS.

Part IV TRIPS in Africa: The Paths Not Taken

From the foregoing, it seems clear that African states have stocked their statute books with various laws on IPR issues. At the continental level, African states are also making efforts to join the IPR bandwagon. For example, in addition to complying with TRIPS, African countries have developed a continental treaty on access to plant genetic resources.[154] The Ministerial Council of the OAU has recommended that African States enact domestic legislation based on the draft law and that they develop a common African negotiating position on the revision of Article 27(3) of the TRIPS Agreement. Indeed, African members have shown significant willingness to grant broad exceptions to enable farmers to save and exchange seeds.[155] The model legislation includes an array of provisions impacting on intellectual property rights. A key provision in the draft legislation prohibits the collector of the biological resource from applying for any form of IPR over the resource, or over any community innovation, practice, knowledge, or technology, without the prior informed consent of the original provider. A potentially controversial aspect of the draft legislation is the provision removing recognition of patents over life forms and biological resources. How the draft legislation seeks to enforce this is unclear.

Another area where there has been some interesting international activity with potential relevance for African countries is geographic indications and

152 W Alford, *To Steal a Book is an Elegant Offence: Intellectual Property Law in Chinese Civilization* (Stanford University Press, 1995).

153 P Yu, 'From Pirates to Partners: Protecting Intellectual Property in China in the Twenty-First Century' (2001) 50 *Am U LR* 131.

154 OAU Model Law on Access to Plant Genetic Resources 2000, available online at < http://www.grain.org/brl_files/oau-model-law-en.pdf >.

155 D Collier, 'Access to and Control Over Plant Genetic Resources for Food and Agriculture in South and Southern Africa: How Many Wrongs Before a Right?' (2006) 7 *Minn JL Sci & Tech* 529.

appellations of origin. Under WIPO's initiative, a pilot project for the promotion of geographic indications has been launched. The first areas covered are Côte d'Ivoire, Burkina Faso, Cameroon and Guinea. In addition, WIPO has begun a process of identifying two or three products within the textile sector, capable of potential protection and development in four countries of Africa, namely Ethiopia, Ghana, Kenya and Nigeria, with a 'view to illustrating how intellectual property can contribute to wealth creation in small and medium-sized enterprises (SME)'.[156]

But beyond the outbreak of IP laws, the second and perhaps more profound issue is whether the chasm between the promise of law and the redemption of that promise has been bridged. In this regard, it bears repeating that there is significant evidence that most African members of the WTO have enacted or are in the processes of enacting IP laws that are compatible with their minimum obligations under the TRIPS Agreement. Indeed all but three of the 30 LCDs in Africa are 'apparently already providing patent for such products despite not having to do until 2016 at the earliest'.[157] However, it seems that there is a huge gap between what exists in the statute books and the practical realities on the ground. This may be a function either of a theoretically flawed thesis that laws by themselves give rise to 'development'; or, the anomalous situation in Africa may be a function of the adoption of the wrong laws. Whatever the cause, the result so far is the same: IP laws have not delivered on their promises.

For example, while it may be said that some African members of the WTO are cognizant of the legislative possibilities provided under TRIPS, there is little evidence that many have taken advantage of the flexibilities embedded in TRIPS. In particular, the provision for international patent exhaustion and the use of patented product without the consent of the patent holder for regulatory approval purposes, otherwise known as the Bolar exception, has not been generally utilized by African states.[158] Interestingly, a majority of the patents issued in Africa go

---

156 Eleventh Session of the Consultative Committee of the Quadripartite Agreement Between ARCT, ARIPO, OAPI and WIPO, Geneva, 11 and 12 June 2002, 6.

157 P Thorpe, 'Study on the Implementation of the TRIPS Agreement by Developing Countries', Study Paper 7, Commission on Intellectual Property Rights, Commission Secretariat, 2. Available at < http://www.iprcommission.org/papers/pdfs/study_papers/sp7_thorpe_study.pdf> (last accessed 17 May 2007).

158 Named after the case of *Roche Products Inc v Bolar Pharmaceutical Co* (733 F 2d 858, Fed Cir, *certiorari* denied 469 US 856, 1984) in which the US Court of Appeal found infringement where, before patent expiry, the patented product was made and used in research to obtain data necessary for an application for approval of the generic drug. It is now settled law that Art 30 of TRIPS allows for exceptions to exclusive patent rights in the case of early working. In response to *Bolar*, the first early-working provision was introduced in the Drug Price Competition and Patent Term Restoration Act (1984) of the US, under which a generic producer is allowed to import, manufacture and test a

to medicines. Ironically, industrialized states are the most frequent users of compulsory licenses.[159] It may therefore be argued that a majority of African countries have focused more on letter compliance than on a pragmatic use or deployment of TRIPS in the service of perceived national economic interests. It seems to be the trend that patent laws play marginal roles in the domestic policy making of African states. Perhaps African countries would need to learn some lessons from India and Brazil, two countries that achieved significant domestic competence in industrialization through a deft manipulation of the patent system.[160]

The chasm between the promises of IP laws and industrial development in Africa may also be a result of institutional problems and challenges, rather than a demerit in the laws themselves. For example, in many cases, 'patent offices' in African countries tend to be located in the office of the Minister for Justice and are usually headed by a registrar who performs other functions unrelated to the business of running a fully-fledged patent office. Neither are the Patent Offices staffed with scientists, or other qualified officials. More worrisome, there is often an absence of organic relationship between the Patent Office and other relevant government departments or agencies.

At the macro-level, patent law and other IPR subjects are not often taught in the universities. Further, it is plausible that the gulf between IP laws and industrialization in Africa is a function of the low level of educational and scientific training in the continent. There is little question that technical progress can help stimulate the economies of poor countries.[161] If technical progress is to be made in Africa, there would have to be strong focus on areas such as science education, and the training of technologists. In comparative terms, African countries have a pathetic number of researchers, scientists, mathematicians, etc working in them. The truth of the matter is that African states have not devoted significant resources to education, research and development. Creating world-class patents or copyrights offices in African state capitals cannot transform the continent into a net producer of innovations. Indeed, evidence shows that while industrialized states

---

patented product before the expiry of its patent, for the purpose of meeting regulatory requirements. Naturally, the ability to do this prior to the expiry of the patent enables the generic producer to have its product ready for marketing as soon as the patent protection for the original branded product ends.

159 T Haag, 'TRIPS Since Doha: How Far Will the WTO go Toward Modifying the Terms for Compulsory Licensing?' (2002) 84 J of Patent, Trademark Office Soc 950.

160 B Naomi, 'Implications of the TRIPS Agreement for Developing Countries: Pharmaceutical Patent Laws in Brazil and South Africa in the 21st Century' (2002) 34 George Washington Int'l LR 191–222.

161 E Malecki, *Technology and Economic Development: The Dynamics of Local, Regional and National Competitiveness* (2nd ed., Longman, 1997) at 192.

spend an average of 2.0 per cent of their GNP on R&D, Africa spends only 0.28 per cent of her GNP on R&D.[162] An UNCTAD Report also shows that there are only 83 scientists and engineers per 1 million of the population in sub-Saharan Africa, while developing countries have an average number of 514 scientists and engineers per million of their population.[163]

The low number of formally trained scientists in African countries would help account for the low number of patents issued to Africans in Africa. Statistics from the UN Development Program and US Patent Office reflect that in 2001: 2.5 technology patents per 1 million people in South Africa compared with 25 in Australia and 779 in South Korea.[164] The analysis above clearly shows that IP laws are not enough in and of themselves to transform a politically unstable and economically dysfunctional continent into an innovative and technologically advanced society. Africa desperately needs to accelerate the pace at which human capital is built. It would be silly to expect modern IP laws and ultra-modern IP offices to be a catalyst for technological growth, when children are dying of preventable diseases, and adults cannot feed themselves, or live in a secure and peaceable environment.

Another area of disconnect between statutory provisions and practical realities is the enforcement of IP laws. The institutional framework for the administration of IPRs are woefully inadequate, and in some cases non-existent. Of course, it would cost a fortune to implement IPRs in poor African countries.[165] Although WTO Agreements have provisions for technical assistance that member countries, upon accession, could theoretically utilize to create or improve domestic technical capacity to implement the agreements entered into, the reality is that such provisions are neither legally binding nor enforceable.[166] Indeed, non-industrialized states have not received technical assistance and support from richer and more experienced member states.[167] Given that TRIPS may be construed as

162 C Jebuni, 'Trade-Related Intellectual Property Rights and African Economic Development' (Centre for Policy Analysis, Accra, Ghana, August 2003).

163 World Investment Report, 1999 (Foreign Direct Investment and the Challenge of Development), UNCTAD.

164 A Katsnelson, 'South Africa Fights Low Patent Rate' (2004) 14 October *Nature*, available at <http://www.nature.com/news/archive/041011.html>.

165 WIPO, 'WIPO's Legal and Technical Assistance to Developing Countries for the Implementation of the TRIPS Agreement From January 1, 1996 to December 31, 2000', WIPO, Geneva.

166 R Sherwood, 'Study on the Financial and Other Implications of the Implementation of the TRIPS Agreement for Developing Countries', WIPO, Geneva (2000).

167 On the unenforceability of WTO provisions on technical assistance see E Kessie, *Legal Enforceability of the Legal Provisions Relating to Special and Differential Treatment in the WTO Agreements*, WTO paper available at <http://www.wto.org/english/tratop_e/devel_e/sem01_e/kessie_e.doc>.

a rent-seeking mechanism in poor countries, it would be immoral to ask impoverished countries of Africa to spend their scarce resources in enacting and implementing laws that would only exacerbate the divide between rich and poor countries. Indeed, as the World Bank has pointed out,

> Given other pressing needs in education, health and policy reform it is questionable whether the LDCs would be willing to absorb these costs, or indeed whether they would achieve much social payoff from investing in them. Moreover, note that poor countries are extremely scarce in trained administrators and judges, suggesting that one of the largest costs would be to divert scarce professional and technical resources out of potentially more productive activities. Indeed, in many poor countries, devoting more resources to the protection of tangible property rights, such as land, could benefit poor people more directly than the protection of intellectual property.[168]

In the circumstances, the relevance of TRIPS for poor African countries is questionable.[169] As noted by a Judge of the Court of Appeal of South Africa, 'many of those living in the South reside in insulated communities cut off by a lack of infrastructure and education. They cannot benefit from IP. How can they understand the merits of its protection? . . . If one does not have bread, why should one protect gourmet recipes?'[170]

In a just world, intellectual property rights would be made to accommodate the diverse range of stakeholders to ensure that the limited monopoly costs of the protection afforded do not outweigh the welfare gains. A credible way of achieving this is to ensure that only innovative products truly deserving of protection enjoy the benefits conferred by IPRs. At present, there is a palpable feeling across the African continent that IPR rights holders are over-compensated. It can hardly be doubted that while many industrialized countries of Africa have the necessary intellectual property laws in their books, such laws are underutilized and barely serve any useful purpose save to satisfy powerful states that the poor states have 'complied' with their international obligations.

Since the emergence of economic liberalism in the 1980s, industrializing countries have been fed with the message that attraction of foreign direct investment (FDI), with the attached conditions of strong IPRs will automatically yield economic development.[171] Yet, since the accession of African countries to the

168 World Bank, 'Intellectual Property: Balancing Incentives With Competitive Access' in *Global Economic Prospects and the Developing Countries 2002*, (World Bank, 2002).

169 UN Dev Programme, *Making Global Trade Work for People* (2003), available at <www.undp.org/dpa/publications/globaltrade.pdf>.

170 L T C Harms, 'Offering Cake for the South' (2000) 22 *Euro Intell Prop R* 451.

171 M Correa, 'Some Assumptions on Patent Law and Pharmaceutical R&D' Occasional Paper 6, Quaker United Nations Office, June 2001.

WTO, there is virtually no empirical work on the relations between IPRs and FDI in Africa.[172] It is arguable that if TRIPS has any influence in Africa, such influence might be limited to the perceptions of foreign investors about the African environment generally rather than any direct relation between strength or lack thereof of IPRs with FDI.

Another touted benefit of membership in the WTO is the dispute settlement mechanism. While much scholarly ink has flowed on the WTO dispute settlement system, it should be noted that it is an extremely complex and expensive mechanism with little tangible benefit to poor African countries.[173] African countries are only minimally involved in the WTO dispute settlement system.[174] Indeed no African country has ever been a complainant in any dispute and 'in only six cases has an African country been a respondent. Of the six disputes, Egypt was a respondent in four, while South Africa was a respondent in two.'[175] Many African countries cannot afford the princely fees commanded by international experts in trade/IP laws.

In sum, it seems that the impact of TRIPS on a country would depend on the economy and current technological state of that country.[176] For example, Egypt and South Africa have felt a noticeable impact on their drug policies, especially on the price of drugs and medicines, since the emergence of TRIPS. On the other hand, agrarian African countries such as Uganda and Tanzania can hardly point to any noticeable impact arising from the TRIPS Agreement. Second, despite adopting strong IP regimes, sub-Saharan African countries have attracted little FDI.[177] Third, despite their dubious merits, desperately poor African countries are required to internalize the enormous costs associated with IPRs, especially patents[178]

---

172 For a contrary view see R Sherwood, 'Intellectual Property Systems and Investment Stimulation: The Rating of Systems in Eighteen Developing Countries' (1997) 37 [2] *IDEA* 1.

173 See *Negotiations on the Dispute Settlement Understanding: Proposal by the Least Developed Countries' Group*, WTO Doc TN/DS/W/17 (9 October 2002) and *Negotiations on the Dispute Settlement Understanding: Proposal by the African Group*, WTO Doc TN/DS/W/15 (10 October 2003). The entire list of documents is available on the WTO website at <http://www.wto.org/English/tratop_e/dispu_e.htm>.

174 V Mosoti, 'Africa in the First Decade of WTO Dispute Settlement' (2006) 9 [2] *J of Int'l Econ L*, 427–453.

175 Ibid.

176 R Sherwood, 'The TRIPS Agreement: Implications for Developing Countries' (1997) 37 *IDEA* 491.

177 K Maskus and M Penubarti, 'How Trade-Related are Intellectual Property Rights?' (1995) 39 *J of Int'l Econ* 227; S Oddi, 'The International Patent System and Third World Development: Reality or Myth?' (1987) *Duke LJ* 831.

178 For a detailed analysis of the costs attributable to a patent system see D Turner, 'The Patent System and Competitive Policy' (1969) 44 *NYU LR*, 450.

while foreigners are the main beneficiaries of IPRs in those countries.[179] Fourth, the small size of the African economy relative to other regional economies of the world has not been mitigated by strong IPRs. Only 1 per cent of US trade is tied to sub-Saharan Africa.[180] The economy of the city of Los Angeles is larger than the entire economy of South Africa. Yet South Africa has the largest economy in Africa. Indeed, all sub-Saharan African countries, with the exception of Nigeria and South Africa, are classified as small economies.

Fifth, there is some evidence that since the advent of the WTO, there has been a stagnation of GDP in Africa. Recent statistics from the World Bank show that gross national income per capita in sub-Saharan Africa actually declined by 0.2 per cent from 1990 to 2001. Life expectancy has decreased over the past two decades. Poverty levels have increased. Africa's share of world trade and FDI has decreased.[181] Despite the scramble to enact IPR laws across the continent, there is little or no funding for research on diseases that afflict Africans. In fact, most of the medicines in Africa for the treatment of tropical diseases have no relationship with the institutionalization of modern patent laws. According to MSF [Médecins Sans Frontières],

> [n]eglected diseases which threaten the lives of tens of millions of people, mainly in Africa, accounted in 2002 for less than 0.001% of the $60–70bn spent a year on medical research throughout the world. Most of the treatments now available in Africa were devised during the colonial period and destined for use by the white population, or else developed by the US Army with the aim of protecting its soldiers.[182]

Conclusion

What, then, is the way forward? Perhaps it is time for African countries to focus on those industrial and economic activities in Africa that would best respond to certain types of IPR. For example, many African state economies are largely agrarian.[183] In this regard, it would be sensible to adopt and implement IP regimes that are proven to be responsive to agriculture and agri-based industries. For example, a considerable number of African countries such as Kenya, Ethiopia,

179 D Greer, 'The Case Against Patent Systems in Less-Developed Countries' (1973) 8 *J of Int'l Law and Econ* 223.

180 H Clark, 'African 'Renaissance and US Trade Policy' (1999) 27 *Ga J Int'l & Comp L* 265.

181 *The Washington Post*, 10 June 2003.

182 *The Guardian Weekly*, 5 June 2003.

183 J H Reichman, 'Universal Minimum Standards of Intellectual Property Protection Under the TRIPS Component of the WTO Agreement' (1995) 29 *Int'l L* 345.

etc are known to produce high-quality coffee. Others such as Mali and Sudan produce world-class cotton. Nigeria, Côte d'Ivoire, Ghana, etc produce some of the finest cocoa in the world. These countries have been known to have significant problems marketing their produce. An IP regime such as certification marks could have resonance and relevance to such producers of high quality, niche-market agricultural produce. Similarly, some African countries produce distinctively designed cloths such Ghana's Kente, Nigeria's Adire, etc. It would be useful for such countries to devise and implement IPRs that are particularly responsive to those niche markets.

As a net importer of technology, there is no question that modern IPR laws *per se* have not worked for African countries.[184] We may therefore need to reject a 'one size fits all' mentality when it comes to IPRs. African countries would do well to reflect critically on what they need in terms of technology, how such technological needs are to be addressed via the instrumentality of IPRs, and how best to create a local critical mass in those identified niche areas of need and competence. For example, countries such as South Africa, with an emerging global reputation in wine-making would benefit from a functional regime on appellations of origin and geographic indications. On the other hand, countries such as Nigeria, with an emerging home movie industry would benefit a lot from an efficient and responsive copyright regime. Africa can no longer remain a dumping ground for both ill-considered ideas and irrelevant technologies.

Ultimately, it has to be noted that development economists have long discarded the notion that more laws are more synonymous with more development.[185] Economic and cultural life cannot be reordered merely on the diktat from a Tsarist ukase. The creeping notion that the existence of rigorous IP laws on the statute books of nations and the construction of ultra-modern IP offices is a reliable indicator of their level of technological and economic development is simply silly. The rash of IP laws in Africa may be of intellectual or academic interest to lawyers and policy makers but the facts show that those laws have not transformed the lives of ordinary Africans. The current state of IP laws in Africa, that is, theoretical compliance but practical public indifference to actual implementation, may be characterized as one form of 'passive resistance'.[186]

184 K Martin, 'Rethinking IPRs and the TRIPS Agreement' (2001) *Third World Network*.

185 R B Seidman, *The State, Law and Development* (St Martin's Press, 1978); D M Trubek and M Galanter, 'Scholars in Self-Estrangement: Some Reflections on the Crisis in Law and Development Studies in the United States' (1974) *Wis LR* 1062.

186 F M Abbott, 'The New Global Technology Regime: The WTO TRIPS Agreement and Global Economic Development' (1996) 72 *Chi–Kent LR* 385.

IP laws in Africa have largely remained fig leaves for the inadequate concealment of serious economic and socio-political challenges in the continent. The tragedy here is that if the multilateral arrangements fail, there is a real prospect of a return to bilateral relationships with its grave implications of a divide-and-rule pattern;[187] a method of governance that Africans are painfully familiar with.[188]

[187] R Okediji, 'Back to Bilateralism? Pendulum Swings in International Intellectual Property Protection' (2004) 1 *U Ottawa L & Technology J* 127.

[188] S Oddi, 'TRIPS—Natural Rights and a "Polite" Form of Economic Imperialism' (1996) 29 *Vand J Transnational L* 415.

8

TRADEMARK POLICY: THE CASE OF ARAB COUNTRIES

Amir H Khoury

Introduction

The global economy has created a 'New World Order' with respect to intellectual property. The most potent characteristic of this order is its attempt to produce an ever-increasing unified system of protection for intellectual property rights in the form of the Agreement on Trade-Related Aspects of Intellectual Property Rights (TRIPS) and other subsequent agreements.[1]

While these attempts have been largely successful, mainly because of decisive backing by influential states and business interests, the value that such attempts have for developing countries is questionable. Indeed, doubts about the

[1] WIPO Copyright Treaty, 20 December 1996, 36 ILM 65, available at <http://www.wipo.int/documents/en/diplconf/distrib/94dc.htm> (last accessed 5 March 2007). WIPO Performances and Phonograms Treaty, 20 December 1996,36 ILM 76, available at <http://www.wipo.int/clea/docs_new/pdf/en/wo/wo034en.pdf> (last accessed 17 May 2007).

justification for intellectual property protection generally, and trademarks specifically, have always existed.[2]

In a nutshell, the debate surrounding trademark policy revolves around the perceived benefits of trademark law. The proponents of trademark protection contend that a trademark regime benefits the economies of those countries that endorse it. According to those in favour of trademark protection the modern standards of trademark protection (e.g. the TRIPS Agreement) assist domestic producers to reap income that would otherwise be lost to counterfeiters. They also argue that protecting foreign brands encourages brand owners to invest in developing countries and establish an industrial or commercial presence therein. This in turn facilitates the opening of those countries' respective markets while creating new jobs. Thus, trademark protection is said to carry a promise of economic benefit for developing and developed countries alike.

However, those rejecting this proposition assert that the abovementioned benefits are not feasible because developing countries generally consume, rather than own, intellectual property. These sceptics further argue that foreign investments do not contribute to the economies of developing countries because those investments are primarily 'turnkey' projects that do not entail a substantial transfer of technology or expertise.

This chapter will examine the policy debate described above and explain how Arab countries ultimately have opted to settle it in their respective national laws and their reasons for doing so. I will begin with a brief overview of the theoretical backdrop of this debate, which is also dealt with in other chapters, and end with the presentation of the results from an empirical study pertaining to the protection of trademarks in a number of Arab countries.

Part I Theoretical Backdrop of the Policy Debate

The debate between those who advocate immediate compliance with TRIPS and other recent international agreements and those who favour a more progressive

[2] One unlikely venue for such a debate took place during the legislation process of the United States trademark law—Lanham (Trademark) Act 1946 (15 USC 22)—Title 15 of the US Code—contains the federal statutes governing trademark law in the United States of America.

Initially, the US Department of Justice considered the Act to be 'too strongly favouring big business and allowing for illegal monopolies'. C Oakley, 'The United States Trademark Century in Review: Prosperity in the U.S. Leaps and Lulls 1930 to 1959' (2001) International Trademark Association. According to Oakley the Lanham Act was eventually accepted and viewed 'as a means to protect consumers from deception and essential for businesses to secure protection in the United States and abroad'.

or even differential implementation of international intellectual property norms is rooted in opposing theories; namely, the 'Development Theory' and the 'Dependency Theory'. These theories are widely used in the context of Development Studies as well as literature dealing with the political economy of development. The two theories reflect fairly polarized positions that exist within the academic discourse on the development of 'Third World' countries. It is worth mentioning that these theories are not limited to the argument surrounding intellectual property but rather extend to all spheres including economic structure and social values. For example, Development theorists might argue that adopting democracy, freedom of speech, free market and other values, are crucial preconditions for attaining development.[3]

During the 1950s and 1960s, various scholars associated with 'Comparative Politics' formulated the 'Modernization Theory', also referred to as the 'Development Theory', as a tool for explaining the development (or lack thereof) of so-called 'Third World' countries.[4] Despite some variations among these Development theorists, they urged developing countries to adopt methods, undertaken by developed countries, aimed at securing economic and political modernization. In practical terms, developing countries were advised to 'acquire modern cultural values and create modern economic and political institutions'[5] that would prompt them to act 'more like us' (i.e. the West).[6]

Evidently, the Development theory is based on the premise that the only way for non-industrialized countries to develop is by following in the footsteps of developed countries by adopting the latter's standards and values. In essence, this theory advocates a fairly mechanical adoption of norms by developing countries as they strive to achieve economic development and long-term prosperity. This theory is said to form the 'backbone of general economic studies as well as the

---

[3] ME Latham, 'Modernization, International History, and the Global Cold War World', 1, in DC Engerman, N Gilman, MH Haefele, and ME Latham (eds), *Staging Growth: Modernization, Development, and the Global Cold War*, (University of Massachusetts Press, 2003), DC Engerman, 'West Meets East: The Center for International Studies and Indian Economic Development' in Engerman *et al*, ibid; V Koschmann, 'Modernization and Democratic Values: The "Japanese Model" in the 1960s', 225 in ibid; C Leys, *The Rise & Fall of Development Theory* (Indiana University Press, 1996); PW Preston, *Development Theory: An Introduction* (Blackwell, Cambridge, 1996); CV Scott, *Gender and Development: Rethinking Modernization and Dependency Theory* (Rienner Publishers, 1995); EM Rogers, *Diffusion of Innovations* (Free Press, 1983); T Spybey, *Social Change, Development, and Dependency: Modernity, Colonialism and the Development of the West* (Polity Press, 1992).

[4] SP Huntington, *Political Order in Changing Societies* (Yale University Press 1968); G Almond and J Coleman (eds), *The Politics of Developing Areas* (Princeton University Press, 1960); L Pye and S Verba, *Political Culture and Political Development* (Princeton University Press, 1965); CE Black, ed, *Comparative Modernization: A Reader* (Free Press, 1976).

[5] H Handelman, *The Challenge of Third World Development* (Prentice Hall, 1996), 12.

[6] M Levy, Jr, 'Social Patterns (Structures) and Problems of Modernization', in W Moore and R Cooke (eds), *Readings on Social Change* (Prentice Hall, 1967), 207.

justification for aid programs and policies aiming to solve problems of development in non-industrialized countries'.[7]

In its attempt to tackle economic and technological underdevelopment, the development theory also calls for a mechanical adoption or transplanting of norms that exist in industrialized countries, together with the legal and judicial systems designed to implement and enforce such norms. In this context, Development theorists appear to argue that, 'ICs (industrialized countries) have developed because of the existence of specific forms of laws and institutions, while non-ICs failed to do so because they had no such laws and institutions or were "traditional"'.[8]

The Development theory has not gone unchallenged. In fact, several researchers have criticized both its merits and its underlying concepts. Those critics typically argue against a unitary approach to development. They submit that, throughout history, people, nations and countries have charted different paths of development.[9] Accordingly, they contend that it is a misconception, and a mistake, to single out one developmental path and essentially rule out other factors and methods. It is further argued that re-enacting the developmental actions of today's industrialized countries is not a viable option. That is because it is not possible to repeat history and reconstruct the circumstances under which those countries had developed.[10] The opposition to the Modernization (Development) theory peaked during the 1960s and 1970s, when a number of social scientists in Latin America and the United States formulated the 'Dependency' theory.[11]

---

[7] A Endeshaw, *Intellectual Property Policy for Non-Industrial Countries*, Law Social Change and Development Series (Dartmouth, 1996), 2, 11–52; ZY Hershlag, *The Philosophy of Development Revisited* (Leiden, 1984); G Francis, 'Law and Development in Light of the Dependency Theory', (1980) 14 *L and Society R* 723; LJ Theberge, *Law and Economic Development*, 9 *Denver J of Int'l L and Policy* 231. B Hettne, *Development Theory and the Three Worlds* (Longman, 1990); D Seers (ed), *Dependency Theory: A Reassessment*, (Frances Pinter, 1981); D Seers, 'The Birth, Life and Death of Development Economics', 10 *Development and Changes*, 707–719; P Gabriel, 'Dependency and Development: A Critical Overview' in Seers, *Dependency Theory*, 20–78; C Furtado, *Development of Latin America: Historical Background and Contemporary Problems* (Cambridge University Press, 1970) 209; P Almeida, 'The Political Economy of Intellectual Property Protection: Technological Protectionism and Transfer of Revenue Among Nations' (1995) 10 *Int'l J of Technology Mgmt*, Special Issue on the Management of Intellectual Property, 214–229.

[8] Endeshaw, note 7 above, 5.

[9] NB Shamilov, *Economic Growth in the Third World* (trans M Habib and S Yosef), (Dar Al-Takadom Al-Arabi, Alzahra Al-Haditha Publishers, 1997). Shamilov makes a clear distinction between the circumstances of development of countries nowadays as compared with the circumstances in which countries had developed in the past.

[10] Shamilov, ibid; Endeshaw, note 7 above, 2.

[11] T Dos Santos, 'The Structure of Dependence' (1970) *American Econ R*, 1; W Baer, 'The Economics of Prebisch and ECLA', in *Latin America: Problems in Economic Development* (Free Press, 1969); A Gunder, 'Capitalism and Underdevelopment Latin America' (1967) Monthly Review Press.

The 'Dependency' theory is said to emanate from earlier economic theories by Karl Marx and Friedrich List.[12] List opposed Adam Smith's theories and suggested, instead, a theory of national economics based on building strong nations rather than focusing on 'exchanging value' between nations.[13] One could say that List favoured managed trade, rather than 'free' trade. He held the view that this was what most countries were in fact doing, in spite of their free trade rhetoric.[14]

In essence, Dependency theorists contend that the 'world capitalist economy has resulted from a relationship of domination by a few metropolitan countries ("*The Center*") and the "subjugation" and subordination of most of Africa, Asia and Latin America ("*The Periphery*")'.[15] Dependency theorists argue that the 'Center' has dominated the 'Periphery' by employing various tactics and strategies including the formulation of an international division of labour (starting from the 16th century) in which the 'Periphery' was 'condemned to agriculture'. According to this line of reasoning, the 'Periphery' was prevented from attaining industrialization and remained in the capacity of supplier of primary products. These theorists conclude that colonization of the 'Periphery' by the 'Center' cemented the relationship between the two into 'passivity' and 'dynamism', respectively.[16]

Supporters of the Dependency theory further claim that this unbalanced exchange (between 'Center' and 'Periphery') is evident in the permanent transfer of value-added products from the 'Center' to the 'Periphery'. That, in turn, is said to have caused a lack of foreign currency reserves and lack of capital accumulation in countries of the 'Periphery'.[17] Thus, a 'vicious circle' was created whereby countries of the 'Periphery' were largely relegated to the production and export of food and raw materials and forced to trade for industrial imports on unfavourable terms.[18]

---

12 F List, (trans SS Lloyd), *The National System of Political Economy* (Longman's, 1885); K Marx, *Capital* (Foreign Languages Publishing House, 1961), Vol 1.

13 W Henderson, Friedrich List: Economist and Visionary (Frank Cass, 1983).

14 List, note 12 above, at xxxvi. For a detailed survey of the synthesis between intellectual property and the 'Development' argument see M Chon, 'Intellectual Property and the Development Divide', (2006) 27 *Cardozo LR*, 2821, 2839–2872.

15 Endeshaw, note 7 above, 3.

16 Endeshaw, ibid, explains that this relationship has reflected negatively on countries of the 'Periphery' in various ways, including the exchange process, the freedom of independent economic decision-making, and the proliferation of technology.

17 Handelman, note 5 above, 15, 21.

18 Ibid.

While Development theorists urge developing countries to adopt the norms of industrial countries, as a means for development, Dependency theorists suggest that such adoption merely serves to widen the economic rift between the rich 'North' and the poor 'South' and accordingly, conclude that developing countries cannot progress by merely copying 'Western' values and standards because they will always be dependent on 'Western' capital and technology. Dependency theorists are pessimistic about the possibility of bridging the gap between the 'Center' and the 'Periphery'. They reject the concept that is professed by Development theorists. Consequently, Dependency theorists call for severing the ties of dependency.[19]

Part II Applying the Debate to Trademarks

In the narrower context of trademarks, Dependency theorists would likely contend that the Development theory does not justify stringent trademark protection in developing countries because the mere adoption of modern standards of trademark protection cannot guarantee significant economic benefits.[20] The approach advocated by Dependency theorists would suggest that 'excessive' protection of trademarks (as well as other forms of intellectual property) only serves the industries of developed countries and will hamper the efforts of developing nations to compete in the global marketplace. Consequently, those who oppose stringent intellectual property protection have advanced alternative industrialization strategies (such as 'Import Substitution') whereby countries are encouraged to aim for self-sufficiency instead of just protecting (foreign) brands.[21] Such self-sufficiency is ultimately expected to enable developing countries to compete for international markets.[22]

In light of the above, one can see that not everyone supports the adoption of modern standards of intellectual property protection in developing countries.

---

19 M Dobb, *Some Aspects of Economic Development* (Delhi School of Economics, 1955). Dobb notes that the problem of industrialization is not of finance, but of economic organization. He predicts that as long as developing countries do not do away with economic dependency they will remain prone to colonial theft.

20 Handelman, note 5 above, 29–30.

21 MP Ryan, 'Knowledge-Economy Elites, the International Law of Intellectual Property and Trade, and Economic Development (2002) 10 *Cardozo J of Int'l and Comp L*, 271, 292–297.

22 These 'industrialization strategies' include 'Import-Substituting Industrialization', which has been implemented by some countries of Latin America, and 'Export-Oriented Industrialization', an approach that has been adopted by countries in East Asia ('Asian Tiger Economies'). See Handelman, note 5 above, 226.

While some argue that such protection is a precondition for international trade and for the success of developing countries,[23] others regard trademarks, and other forms of intellectual property, as non-universal norms not 'applicable to non-industrialized societies'.[24] Some go even further by contending that intellectual property protection is merely an economic tool of Western monopoly.[25] Conversely, substantial literature emanating from developed countries and international organizations such as the World Trade Organization (WTO), WIPO and the International Trademark Association (INTA) suggests that standards of intellectual property protection, as formulated in TRIPS, strike a fair balance between the interests of all countries notwithstanding their levels of development. According to this literature, trademark protection is equally beneficial to both developed and developing countries.[26]

Other commentators are in doubt as to the effects of trademark protection on developing countries. They hold that modern standards of intellectual property protection are prone to create a monopoly by developed countries and widen the existing economic rift between developed and developing countries due to the unequal distribution of intellectual property (and brands) across countries. Hence, the need for a different intellectual property regime that is more attuned to the needs of developing countries.[27]

---

23 RM Sherwood, 'Human Creativity for Economic Development: Patents Propel Technology', (2000) 33 *Akron LR* 351; RJ Gutowski, 'The Marriage of Intellectual Property and International Trade in the TRIPS Agreement: Strange Bedfellows or a Match Made in Heaven?', 47 *Buffalo LR* 713, 715.

24 RL Gana, 'The Myth of Development, The Progress of Rights: Human Rights to Intellectual Property and Development', 18 *Law & Policy* 315, 326.

25 M Khor, 'How the South is Getting a Raw Deal at the WTO', in S Anderson (ed), *Views from the South: The Effects of Globalization and the WTO on Third World Countries* (Food First Books and the International Forum on Globalization, 2000) 19, 22–23, 26–27, W Bello, 'Building an Iron Cage: The Bretton Woods Institutions, The WTO and the South', in Anderson, ibid, 74–77.

26 P Gallagher, *Guide to the WTO and Developing Countries* (WTO and Kluwer, 2000), 16; KE Maskus, *Intellectual Property Rights in the Global Economy* (Institute for International Economics, 2000) x, contending that the 'balance of evidence strongly suggests' that intellectual property rights provide an important foundation for promoting technology transfer, local innovation and economic growth in the long run. Maskus notes that in Lebanon (and China) trademark and trade secret infringement was at least as costly to domestic as to foreign firms, and that the latter had greater resources to deal with it and more options to withdraw from the market. Maskus, 156 further submits that 'effective trademark enforcement raises the average quality of products over time and provides a wider range of qualities from which consumers may choose'. Also see Hon. JR Homere, 'Intellectual Property Rights Can Help Stimulate the Economic Development of Least Developed Countries' (2004) 27 *Columbia J of L and the Arts* 227.

27 See Chapter 11 below (Professor Drahos), and P Drahos, 'Developing Countries and International Intellectual Property Standard-Setting', The IPR Commission, in Report of the Commission on Intellectual Property Rights, *Integrating Intellectual Property Rights and Development Policy* (September 2002), available at <http://www.iprcommission.org/papers/word/study_papers/sp8_drahos_study.doc> (last accessed 5 March 2007); C May, *A Global Political Economy of*

Part III Trademark Policy in the Arab World

A. Globalization in the Arab World

Globalization sceptics in the Arab world are generally critical of modern international economic institutions such as the WTO, which, in their view, does not allow Arab countries to attain a heightened economic and trade standing in the international arena.[28] Other sceptics assert that 'globalization' serves Western financial and mercantile interests and capitalist industrial production. According to this position, developing countries are unable to maintain their economic independence and are coerced into adopting concepts of 'free trade' and 'competition', and abandoning concepts of 'self-sufficiency' and 'independence'. Consequently, these countries become 'victims' of globalization because they have effectively delegated their powers of economic decision making to transnational (Western) corporations.[29] They argue against 'market dictatorship' and 'modern imperialism', and focus instead on opportunities for growth and stability that can be achieved through equality, raising domestic production and self-sufficiency.[30] A striking example of this self-sufficiency involves the well-known 'Meccacola' brand

---

Intellectual Property Rights, The New Enclosure?, (Routledge, 2000), 155; GS Lunney, 'Trademark Monopolies', (1999) 48 *Emory LJ* 367. For an expansive discussion as to why TRIPS alone is not sufficient to ensure development, see DJ Gervais, 'Intellectual Property, Trade and Development: The State of Play', (2005) 74 *Fordham LR* 500; KE Maskus, 'Intellectual Property Rights and Economic Development' (2000) 32 *Case W Res J of Int'l L* 471. In order to complete the picture, it is worth noting that another body of research focuses on intellectual property protection *vis-à-vis* Western and Islamic values. While one position professes a divide between Islam and the West on issues pertaining to intellectual property protection, another position uncovers a substantial common denominator between both civilizations. See J Carroll, 'Intellectual Property Rights in the Middle East: A Cultural Perspective' (2000–2001) 11 *Fordham IP, Media and Ent LJ* 555; AH Khoury, 'Ancient and Islamic Sources of Intellectual Property Protection in the Middle East: A Focus on Trademarks' (2003) 43(2) *IDEA* 151.

28 AA Baidoos, 'The Arab Common Market: Arab Economic Integration between the Hurdles and the Prospects' (1997) *Lebanese Studies*, Ministry of Information, Beirut, 8, 37. This research contends that Arab countries have, thus far, failed to utilize their huge resources. This research calls for comprehensive and full regional economic cooperation in order to overcome these challenges and to allow Arab countries to realize their economic weight in the international arena. It encourages Arab countries to address international economic challenges in a collective manner and to refrain from approaching such challenges independently.

29 AO Al-Tom and AA Adam, *Globalization: An Analytical and Critical Study* (Dar Alwarrak, 1999), 16, 182–198, 204. Other research warns against the current technology transfers in the form of 'turnkey' projects, because those projects create a trap of 'technological and colonial' dependency that entails intellectual dependency; M Waridi, *The Role of Technology in the Backwardness of Countries*, Ministry of Education and Arts of the Iraqi Republic, A Series of Research, (Al-Talia'h, 1978), 9.

30 J Asfour, 'Globalization and Issues of Cultural Identity' (1998) 50 *Al-Nahj Magazine* 6. Asfour predicts that Arab countries will ultimately clash with certain aspects of globalization due to its inherent contradictions namely: 'development and poverty', 'tolerance and fanaticism', 'freedom of

that has successfully been introduced as a substitute for other (Western) cola brands.[31]

Critics of globalization also argue that, in the context of the trademark debate, the nature of the capitalist system is such that it is dependent on production that, in turn, is dependent on consumption. The critics contend that 'globalization' is preoccupied with creating needs and wants, within the consumer market, that are especially harmful to a country's economy when the majority of products are imported rather than locally produced. In this regard, those critics perceive the United States as the pioneer of the 'civilization of consumption' that has opened the door of developing markets to an 'imperialistic cultural invasion'.[32] This, in turn, has prompted some to refer to this 'civilization of consumption' as 'Americanization', 'McDonaldization', or 'Cocalization' of the world.[33] Some of the research is wary of the power of globalization, contending that it knows no compassion or leniency, and tolerates no competition.[34]

Conversely, proponents of globalization reject the notion that globalization is an extension of imperialism, because in their view, while imperialism achieved control by force, globalization does not employ methods of 'cultural imperialism'. Moreover, it may be argued that the 'cultural dimension' emanating from consumer brands is in fact a perception embraced by consumers in non-Western cultures and is not forced upon them by the 'Western' brand owners. The proponents further explain that producers (in the West) are not preoccupied with 'creating' new cultures but rather with increasing sales.[35] As such, globalization today should not be identified with Western imperialism, since some aspects of globalization (such as inventions and the environment) are in the interest of all countries and peoples.[36]

---

trade and new forms of domination'; see also Handelman, note 5 above, 2, 14, 15, 29–32, 213–227. Handelman considers a possible solution in the form of 'Industrialization Strategies'.

31 The Meccacola brand was launched in France in 2002 by entrepreneur Tawfik Mathlouthi. It tapped into demand for alternative carbonated beverage products in Europe. This cola drink is now extensively sold in the Middle East. The company is based in Dubai, UAE. For more on the Meccacola brand see <http://www.mecca-cola.com/en/company.php> (last accessed 5 March 2007).

32 Al-Tom, note 29 above, 98.

33 Al-Tom, note 29 above, 98–99 contends that this consumption represents a 'Trojan Horse' that is likely to deface and destroy local culture; see also J Tomlinson, 'Cultural Globalization: Placing and Displacing the West' (1996) 8 *European J of Development*, 22–36.

34 N Raghed, *The Seven Masks of Globalization* (Dar Gharib, 2001). This book analyses what it perceives are 'seven masks of globalization' namely politics, economics, culture, media, security, technology and civilization. According to this research, the consequent unraveling of those masks will reveal the real face of globalization.

35 GD Tella, 'The Manipulation of Demand: The Problem of Trade Marks' (1971) *World Development*, 35–42.

36 Carroll, note 27 above.

Additional research reflects a more balanced approach which acknowledges the market control that is exercised by owners of intellectual property while, on the other hand, recognizing the benefits of intellectual property for the local economy.[37] Similarly, one expert submits that, despite the fact that developed countries use intellectual property to serve their national interests, this should not eclipse the important role of intellectual property.[38] In this regard, Cornish and Phillips note that '[trademarks] play a variety of roles, which differ from industry to industry and which may produce different balances of advantages and disadvantages'.[39] This body of research recognizes that trademarks constitute a basic tool of trade in a free market economy, but does not fully take into account the different effects that trademark protection has on different countries.[40] Thus, it has been recommended that a thorough review of the TRIPS provisions be conducted to ensure that a balance is achieved between intellectual property rights and the national interests of developing countries.[41]

B. Trademark Impacts in the Arab World

Only a small portion of the literature in this field has studied the specific effects of trademark protection on developing countries. Typically, studies presuppose that trademark protection is beneficial to the economies of all countries, notwithstanding their level of development or economic infrastructure, because it helps fight 'piracy'.[42] This notion is generally based on theoretical assertions, and in some cases has anecdotal support, but rarely provides any empirical support.

---

[37] Maskus, *IPRs in the Global Economy*, note 26 above, Preface (by CF Bergsten): 'while there are reasons to be concerned about potential exercise of market power by firms endowed with greater intellectual property protection, the balance of evidence strongly suggests that intellectual property rights provide an important foundation for promoting technology transfer, local innovation, and economic growth in the long run'.

[38] Al-Zakout, 'Trademarks: Their Importance, Use and Protection', (1994) *IP Protection Magazine* 28.

[39] WR Cornish and J Phillips, 'The Economic Functions of Trade Marks: An Analysis with Special Reference to Developing Countries', (1982) *01 Int'l R of Ind Prop & Copyright L (IIC)*, 41–41.

[40] UNCTAD Secretariat, *The Impact of Trade Marks on the Development Process in Developing Countries*, TD/B/C, 6A/C 3.3, (1977) (republished in 1979 under the title *The Role of Trademarks in Developing Countries*); M Gabay, '*The Role of Trademarks and Development in Developing Countries*' (1981) 20 *Ind Prop* 102.

[41] F Hamed, 'Working Paper on IP and the expected changes in Light of GATT' (The Egyptian Academy of Scientific and Technological Research), 3–5. This commentary does not accept the TRIPS face value but rather recommends following a balanced approach; by identifying the virtues as well as the pitfalls of that Agreement.

[42] Abu-Ghazaleh, *Intellectual Property Laws of Arab Countries* (Kluwer, 2000), Introduction.

In this regard, a 1980 commentary observed that relevant existing literature, at the time:

> did not have in mind the detailed interests of developing countries, nor their intention to analyze the particular problems of these countries, nor to reflect on their specific problems in trademark law [thus in effect the] relationship between the socioeconomic structure of developing countries and between the role and function of trademarks, does not appear to have been discussed adequately.[43]

A substantial mass of literature addresses trademark protection from a strictly pragmatic angle by focusing on how to best protect trademarks.[44] For example, WIPO and its predecessor, the United International Bureaus for the Protection of Intellectual Property (BIRPI), introduced draft model trademark laws for developing countries.[45] This type of literature is predominantly preoccupied with the more technical, legal aspects of trademarks without due regard for the effect of such protection on developing countries.[46] Another study, that proposes to examine the effects of the TRIPS Agreement on Arab countries, does not consider empirical data, but rather focuses on the legislative amendments that are required from Arab countries in order to meet their obligations under the TRIPS Agreement.[47] Thus, most of the literature is preoccupied with debating the implementation of trademark laws rather than analyzing their effects on developing countries.[48]

---

43 A Vida, *Trade Marks in Developing Countries* (Akade'miai Kiiad'o, Licensing Executive Society International, 1981); see also RM Sherwood, 'Intellectual Property Systems and Investment Stimulation: The Rating of Systems in Eighteen Developing Countries', (1997) 37 *IDEA* 261; L Clarisa (ed), *Intellectual Property Rights in Emerging Markets* (The American Enterprise Institute (AEI) Press, 2000).

44 M Al-Moaasher, 'Procedures that Arab Countries Should Undertake in Order to Implement TRIPS in the Context of Pharmaceutical Products' (1995) *Jordan*,2, 8–9. This commentary focuses on the benefits that are gained by Arab economies as a result of protecting well-known marks in the pharmaceutical industry.

45 BIRPI, *Model Law for the Developing Countries on Marks, Trade Names and Acts of Unfair Competition* (Geneva, 1967).

46 Vida, note 43 above, 21; S Sarkis, 'The Protection of Trademark Rights Through Legislation and Adjudication in Syria' (1996) 49 *IP Protection Magazine* 10; Y Abu-Ala'az, 'Intellectual Property Infringements in the United Arab Emirates' (1996) 50 *IP Protection Magazine* 12; Article, 'An Analytical Look at the Trademark Law of the United Arab Emirates' (1992) *IP Protection Magazine* 46, 47 asserts that 'trademark law serves the needs of consumers, producers and exporters'; AA Bader, 'Legal Protection of Trademarks' (1996) 48 *IP Protection Magazine* 28.

47 IA Ibrahim, 'The Effects of the GATT Agreement on Intellectual Property Rights in Arab Countries' (1995) 44 IP Protection Magazine 23–25. Ibrahim looks at the underlying principles of National Treatment and Most Favoured Nation respectively set out in Arts 3 and 4 of TRIPS. However, his research does not point out that the MFN principle prevents any discrimination in intellectual property through secondary or regional agreements. The research refers to Arts 8 and 64 of TRIPS, which allow taking measures to protect intellectual property. However, the actual effect of those articles on Arab countries is not examined or discussed.

48 JR Olsen and SM Maniatis, *Trade Marks, Trade Names and Unfair Competition: World Law and Practice* (Sweet & Maxwell, 1998). E Horwitz, *World Trademark Law and Practice* (2nd Edn, Lexis Publishing, 2000).

The paucity of literature that adequately reflects upon the effects of trademark protection in developing countries is compounded by the lack of examination of empirical data regarding trademark protection in those countries. Studies tend to justify trademark protection based on moral justifications as well as possible losses due to trademark infringement. In this regard, the posited arguments are that infringement of intellectual property rights inflicts financial losses on the right owner in terms of lost revenues and legal costs, adversely affects consumers both in terms of the quality of the products and consumer safety (e.g. in foods and pharmaceuticals), and creates a disincentive for foreign investors.[49]

Typically, authors of this type of literature (in support of trademark protection), argue that trademarks are intended to regulate the market and to propel development by: preserving the incentive to produce; protecting the consumer from harmful counterfeits; maintaining the quality of products/services; assisting consumers to identify quality products; protecting producers; preventing unfair competition in trade; ensuring the expansion of international trade; and by allowing local products to more easily penetrate foreign markets.[50]

A related body of research contends that 'economic development is a dynamic process and that intellectual property may help convert "free riders" into "fair followers"'.[51] In this regard, WIPO has predicted that a robust intellectual property system would help developing countries secure a competitive edge in knowledge-based economies of the 21st century.[52] According to this approach, trademarks are perceived to be an indispensable tool of trade and their protection is said to carry a promise of economic benefits for developing countries.[53] Moreover, proponents of strong protection for intellectual property rights reason that 'today's

---

49 Al-Ksiwani, *Intellectual Property* (Al-Warrak Publishing, 1998), 57–59.

50 K Al-Ahmar, *The Role of IP and Industrial Property & E-commerce in Growth* (Dar Arrida Publications, 2000), 20; KE Maskus and M Lahouel, 'Competition Policy and Intellectual Property Rights in Developing Countries: Interests in Unilateral Initiatives and a WTO Agreement' (1999) U of Colorado 13 (this report was prepared for the World Bank Global Conference on Developing Countries, Geneva).

51 JH Reichman, 'From Free Riders to Fair Followers: Global Competition Under the TRIPS Agreement' (1993) 29 *J of Int'l L and Policy* 11.

52 AGIP, January 2002 News Bulletin; reporting that, in a meeting held in November 2001 at WIPO headquarters in Geneva, WIPO's Director General stressed Egypt's need for a robust intellectual property system. The Director General submitted (to the Egyptian Delegation) various methods in which Egypt could capitalize on its rich cultural heritage by exploring digital technologies, for example: by making museum collections visually available over the internet.

53 Al-Ksiwani, note 49 above, 8, 30, 58. According to this commentary trademarks constitute an important pillar in trade and economics, both internationally and domestically. Trademarks assist consumers to identify the products that they seek. Furthermore, trademarks allow manufacturers to distinguish their products from those belonging to others, thus boosting sales and creating an incentive to maintain quality; Al-Ahmar, note 50 above, 20, asserts that developing countries cannot achieve growth without protecting trademarks.

industrialized countries were once themselves developing countries and that their progress was strongly affected by intellectual property protection'.[54] Such assertions might conflict with the view that countries cannot replicate previously charted paths of development because it is impossible to recreate the circumstances that existed at the time.

The proponents of strong trademark protection hold that such protection affords many benefits. In this regard, Abu-Ghazaleh asserts that intellectual property protection is a crucial element for the region's development:

> Intellectual property protection in the Arab world has long been one of a number of weak links in the region's economic development framework. Despite desires to meet the social and economic demands of the region's growing population, development has long been held back by lack of sufficient IP protection both in terms of adequate legislation and enforcement of existing legislation. However, the last decade has witnessed significant changes in Arab countries' IP regimes and some of the most important changes in the region's history are on the immediate horizon.[55]

According to Al-Ksiwani the protection of intellectual property in Arab countries would foster 'noble competition', encourage personal initiative, and prompt development. Al-Ksiwani holds that the level of intellectual property protection is indicative of a society's development or lack thereof, and that 'a country that respects the intellectual property of others inspires confidence' and renders investors 'more inclined to invest in countries which protect their investments'.[56] He goes even further by attributing development in all fields including politics, economics, law, society, technology, science, industry, trade, and literature to intellectual property.[57] As such, he regards the infringement of intellectual property as not only an intrusion on private ownership but also as an act against civilization generally.[58] Therefore, he advocates the need to strengthen protection

54 Opening Remarks at the First Arab Intellectual Property Conference, 28 September 1995, Amman, Jordan, (speaker unspecified), 2.

55 Abu-Ghazaleh, note 42 above, x.

56 Al-Ksiwani, note 49 above, 11–12; T Zuwayyed, 'The Status of IP in Arab Countries, Aspects of Deficiency in the Arab Legislation, The Objectives of the Arab Countries to Develop the Field of Intellectual Property' (1997) 53 IP Protection Magazine 12: Zuwayyed asserts that 'the lack of intellectual property legislation in Arab countries did not last for long. They [Arab countries] have discovered the importance of providing economic security to create an environment of fair and legal commercial competition'.

57 Al-Ksiwani, ibid.

58 Ibid, 12. See also RD Anderson and H Wager, 'Human Rights, Development and the WTO: The Case of Intellectual Property and Competition Policy' (2006) 9 *J of Int'l Econ L* 707, 721–730.

of intellectual property rights and to acknowledge its contribution to the national economy.[59]

In this regard Leaffer, another supporter of trademark protection, believes that 'this new world of trademarks wears a happy face' that will bring about a 'progressive harmonization of trademark law among nations—one that will lead to ever greater simplification and expediency in the acquisition and protection of trademark rights worldwide' for the benefit of trademark owners and consumers alike.[60] Hausser, who also favours stringent trademark protection, asserts that trademarks constitute an indispensable tool of modern trade that is the backbone of a healthy economy and affects all countries in a similar manner, without regard to their economic development or the orientation of their economies:

> Intellectual property rights have proved to be of outstanding importance for the economic growth of a country and for its participation in international cooperation and competition . . . IPRs are necessary instruments for fair competition and an essential precondition for the economic development of a country, for its participation in international competition, and at the same time for the transfer of modern technology and for foreign investments.[61]

In sum, the mainstream in current literature falls back on generalized justifications of intellectual property protection while evading an empirical examination of the effects of trademark protection, and without distinguishing between various types of country and economy in the world.[62] Thus, one should welcome attempts made to determine the actual effect of introducing a TRIPS-compatible trademark regime. Along these lines, Vida suggests that, before turning to study trademark laws, one should inspect 'the role played by trademarks in developing countries in trade and in connection with the process of industrialization'.[63]

---

59 R Al-Kalubi, 'The Legal Aspects of Trademark Infringements in Saudi Law' (1996) 50 IP Protection Magazine 7 recommends that Arab countries should undertake to amend intellectual property laws; introduce more protection mechanisms; join/ratify international intellectual property agreements; and modernize the judicial system and make it more efficient.

60 MA Leaffer, 'The New World of International Trademark Law' (1998) 2 *Marq IP LR* 1.

61 E Hausser, 'The Importance of Intellectual Property Rights for the Economic Growth of a Country and for International Cooperation' (1997) 53 *IP Magazine* 6; IM Dalal, 'Trademarks and their Protection' (Dalal Law Office, 1995), 1.

62 M Dofash, 'Laws of Intellectual Property Protection Serve the National Interest' (1997) 53 *IP Magazine* 3. Dofash contends that intellectual property protection serves Arab national interests because such protection encourages Arab investors and scientists to register their patents in their home countries, thus slowing the brain drain from those countries. Notably, this commentary, like others, does not consider other types of intellectual property, e.g. trademarks, copyrights, etc.

63 Vida, note 43 above, 22; DF Greer, 'The Economic Benefits and Costs of Trademarks: Lessons for Developing Countries' (1997) 7 *World Development* 638; P O'Brien, 'Trademarks in Developing Countries' (1976) *J of Modern African Studies* 297; SJ Patel, (ed) 'Introduction to the Special Issue, Trademarks in Developing Countries' (1979) 7 *World Development* 649; SJ Patel, 'Trademarks and the Third World', 7 *World Development* 653 (1979), both available from <http://econpapers.repec.

Research has been undertaken to examine the use of intellectual property rights by examining data pertaining to the registration of patents and trademarks, and by considering the relationship between intellectual property rights and economic development worldwide.[64] The United Nations Conference on Trade and Development (UNCTAD) has employed similar research methods. In one study, UNCTAD examined the relationship between the number of trademark registrations originating in a given country and that country's export market.[65] Another study published by UNCTAD focused on statistical, economic and legal aspects of trademarks in developing countries,[66] while a third study examined the impact of trademarks on the development process of developing countries.[67] Additional UNCTAD studies in the early 1980s, dealing with industrial property protection, conveyed some criticism of the role of trademarks and patents in developing countries.[68]

Therefore, one can clearly see that literature which supports trademark protection refers to the basic attributes (and functions) of trademarks but refrains from crossing that threshold into the domain in which the rationales of trademarks are not taken for granted, but rather, are scrutinized vis-à-vis empirical data.[69] In this regard, a study by Maskus has observed that 'though there are extensive treaties on the subject by legal scholars and international relations specialists, they tend to take the basic economic impacts for granted rather than analyze their subtleties

org/article/eeewdevel/default7.htm>; R Rapp and RP Rozek, 'Benefits and Costs of Intellectual Property in Developing Countries' (1990) 5 *J of World Trade* 75.

64 Maskus, *IPRs in the Global Economy*, note 26 above, 10–11, 87–197 considers the following factors, including the number of patent and trademark applications: the level of demand for copyright products in selected countries; trade in intellectual property rights (IPR)-sensitive goods; trade in IPR-sensitive services, royalties and license fees; membership trends in key intellectual property conventions; estimated rates of software piracy and lost revenues; and simulated increases in total imports by sector into developing countries resulting from strengthened patent laws.

65 UNCTAD, *The Role of Trademarks in the Promotion of Exports from Developing Countries* (Geneva, 1977). That study focused on Argentina, Brazil, Mexico and India.

66 UNCTAD, *Systems Including Industrial Property Systems for Improving the National Scientific and Technological Infrastructure of Developing Countries* (Geneva, 1975).

67 UNCTAD, *Impact of Trademarks/Development Process*, note 40 above.

68 UNCTAD, *Study on Industrial Property* (1982) *IIC*, March, 412. The countries examined therein included Colombia, Peru, Ecuador, Mexico and the Philippines; UNCTAD, *Trademarks and Generic Names of Pharmaceuticals and Consumer Protection* (1987) concludes that trademarks and trade-related advertising by the pharmaceutical industry have been primarily responsible for product differentiation that, in turn, creates market power, inhibits price competition, and raises price levels. In order to find a remedy, that study entertained the possibility of substituting generic names for trademarks.

69 AH Khoury, 'The Effects of Trademarks on Arab Countries in the Middle East' (Doctoral Dissertation, Haifa University, Israel, 2004).

and test them with empirical evidence'.[70] Thus, it remains evident that the policy debate surrounding the optimal trademark regime remains unresolved.

C. How Arab Countries have Settled the Debate

In light of the aforementioned unsettled policy debate concerning the value and effects of trademark protection, various questions still loom: how have Arab countries elected to formulate their respective trademark regimes? Have these trademark regimes been shaped in the same 'mould' or is there a plurality among Arab countries? Are these regimes shaped regionally or are they merely a translation of conventional international standards of trademark protection? How do practitioners in Arab countries perceive their national trademark regimes?

Arab countries are not a homogeneous group of countries because they 'present a wide and diversified spectrum, both geographically and economically, apart from political, institutional and special aspects'.[71] Therefore, it would be logical to

---

[70] Maskus, *IPRs in the Global Economy*, note 26 above, 7. Maskus further notes, 2, that 'although patents have been studied in various ways for their role in developed country economies, literature relevant to developing countries is scant'. R Sherwood, *Intellectual Property and Economic Development* (Westview Press, 1990), 1 notes that 'the literature is replete with studies of the relation of innovation to economic growth, but the relation between intellectual property protection and innovation in developing countries rests largely on conjecture'.

[71] ZY Hershlag, 'Industrialization in Arab Countries: Patterns, Options and Strategies', 13 in R Alibani (ed), *Arab Industrialization and Economic Integration* (Croom Helm, Instituto Affari Internazionali, 1979). Typically, Arab countries are divided into three groups depending on their geographic location: the Arab Peninsula, Levant Countries and North Africa. Except for Yemen, countries located in the Arab Peninsula are also widely referred to as the 'Gulf States'. These countries include Saudi Arabia, The United Arab Emirates (UAE), Kuwait, Oman, Qatar, and Bahrain. These countries form the Gulf Cooperation Council (GCC). The largest, wealthiest and most powerful member of this group is the Kingdom of Saudi Arabia. The second group referred to as the 'Levant Countries' includes Lebanon, Jordan, Iraq, Syria, and the Palestinian Territories. The third group is composed of countries located in North Africa, which include Egypt, Sudan, Tunisia, Algeria, Libya, and Morocco. Egypt is the most prominent member in this group and has the largest population. Some regions of the Arab world are endowed with rich deposits of petroleum. Other Arab countries do not have such resources. Indeed, this distinction is regarded as the most important one because it separates the 'haves' from the 'have-nots'. Saudi Arabia, for example, represents the 'haves' and Syria, to a large extent, represents the 'have-nots'. Egypt is not only the Arab country with the biggest population but is also among the most influential of Arab countries and the most dominant on the political scene. What is more, during the past three decades, Egypt has been striving to attain better ties with the West through economic openness. Furthermore, Egypt was the first Arab state to sign a formal peace treaty with Israel. Syria, on the other hand, has a relatively closed and underdeveloped economy. Jordan has a relatively small population and an aspiring economy. It has strong ties with the United States and other Western countries and has signed a peace treaty with Israel. Saudi Arabia is the richest Arab country in the oil-rich Arabian Gulf. Much like Egypt, Saudi Arabia traditionally maintained firm connections with the West, which were strained in the wake of 'September 11'.

expect each of those countries to formulate laws in accordance with its respective national interests.

All Arab countries, like most countries around the world, have enacted national trademark laws. This is not surprising given the important value of trademarks. Originally, the role of trademarks was limited to indicating origin and guaranteeing the quality of products that are sold under the mark.[72] However, over the years, the role of trademarks has evolved into a tool for advertising one's brand. Eventually, leading and famous marks acquired a value that is independent from the respective goods/services that they covered.[73] This evolution of the function of trademarks entailed a substantial rise in their economic value, which in turn has led to increased legal protection for them.

In view of their ever-increasing economic value, trademarks, much like other types of intellectual property rights, received protection within a wide array of international as well as regional agreements and national laws. A number of conventions and treaties shape the basic elements of trademark protection. These international agreements can be divided into four functions, namely setting standards of protection, facilitating trademark registration, classifying marks, and harmonizing documentation.[74]

The two primary agreements that deal with setting standards of protection, of particular importance to this discussion, are the Paris Convention for the Protection of Industrial Property (1883) and the TRIPS Agreement (1994).[75]

---

[72] A Firth, *Trade Marks: the New Law* (Jordans, 1995), 9–11; P Drahos, *A Philosophy of Intellectual Property* (Dartmouth, 1996), 157, 168, 204, 205; IM Azmi *et al*, 'Distinctive Signs and Early Markets: Europe, Africa and Islam' (1997) 1 *Perspectives on IP* 123 (Sweet & Maxwell); PK Fletcher, 'Joint Registration of Trademarks and the Economic Value of a Trademark System' (1998) 36 *U of Miami LR* 297; M Ryan, 'What every Manager Should Know About Intellectual Property Law, Policy and Business Strategy', International Intellectual Property Institute (IIPI); D Shilling, *Essentials of Trademarks and Unfair Competition* (Wiley, 2000), 2.

[73] L Cratchley, 'The Brand Owner's View' (2000) 7 *Perspectives on IP* 1 (Sweet & Maxwell); H Norman, 'Schechter's *The Rational Basis of Trademark Protection Revisited*' (2000) 7 *Perspectives on IP* 191 (Sweet & Maxwell).

[74] For updated membership list pertaining to the Paris Convention; Madrid Agreement; Madrid Protocol; Lisbon Agreement; Trademark Law Treaty; Nairobi Treaty for the Protection of the Olympic Symbol; Nice Agreement; Vienna Agreement; and WIPO, see World Intellectual Property Organization (WIPO), <http://www.wipo.int> (last accessed 5 March 2007). Convention Establishing the World Intellectual Property Organization (WIPO) (1967), 21 UST 1749 (1970). Egypt, Algeria and Tunisia are members of most of these conventions and treaties. For more information pertaining to trademark laws in Arab countries, see <http://www.agip.com> (Abu-Ghazaleh Intellectual Property), WIPO, <http://www.sabaip.com> (Saba & Co Group, Intellectual Property), <http://www.infoprod.co.il> (Info Prod Research Middle East Ltd), <http://www.wto.org> (World Trade Organization).

[75] Marrakech Agreement Establishing the World Trade Organization: Annex 1C: Agreement on Trade-Related Aspects of Intellectual Property Rights 33 ILM 1197 (1994); The Paris Convention for the Protection of Industrial Property, as revised (1967), 21 UST 1583 (1970).

The Paris Convention was the first multilateral international agreement intended to protect trademarks. Since then, other agreements and treaties have been introduced culminating in the TRIPS Agreement.[76] Sixteen Arab countries are now party to the Paris Convention (Paris Union) and 11 Arab countries are party to the TRIPS Agreement, which constitutes an annex to the Agreement Establishing the World Trade Organization (WTO).[77] Table 8.1 includes a list of Arab countries that are party to the Paris Convention:

Table 8.1 Arab Membership in the Paris Convention for the Protection of Industrial Property (1883) as amended in Stockholm (1967)[78]

State	Entry into Force
Algeria	1 March 1966
Bahrain	29 October 1997
Egypt	1 July 1951
Iraq	24 January 1976
Jordan	17 July 1972
Lebanon	1 September 1924
Libya	28 September 1976
Mauritania	11 April 1965
Morocco	30 July 1917
Oman	14 July 1999
Qatar	5 July 2000
Saudi Arabia	11 March 2004
Sudan	16 April 1984
Syria	1 September 1924
Tunisia	7 July 1884
United Arab Emirates	19 September 1996
Yemen	15 February 2007

The TRIPS Agreement sets higher standards of protection, revamps enforcement of intellectual property rights, increases the efficiency of enforcement and raises fines. It came into effect on 1 January 1995. It deals with various trade-related norms pertaining to intellectual property rights including patents, trademarks, copyright and related rights, geographical indications, industrial designs, integrated circuit topographies, and undisclosed information (trade secrets). TRIPS regulates various issues pertaining to intellectual property rights including scope, protection, and enforcement of intellectual property rights. TRIPS requires

[76] Leaffer, note 60 above. For a concise summary of TRIPS, see South Centre, 'Main Provisions of the TRIPS Agreement', available at <http://www.southcentre.org/publications/trips/tripsmaintexttrans-02.htm>, 1–4 (last accessed 25 May 2007).

[77] See Part IV of this chapter for a list of Arab countries that are members of the WTO.

[78] Based on information provided by the WIPO website; see <http://www.wipo.int/treaties/en/ShowResults.jsp?lang=en&treaty_id=2> (current through 15 February 2007).

member states to establish a minimum level of intellectual property protection in their national law. With respect to trademarks, TRIPS sets various standards, including the recognition of service marks, setting a minimum (renewable) term of protection, defining use requirements, enhancing the role of Customs in enforcement, and recognizing well-known marks. In addition, TRIPS allows for cancelling the registration of a mark due to non-use (subject to exceptions), confirming the right to use a mark without conditions, and regulating issues of licensing and assignment.[79]

D. Recent Legislative Changes

During recent years many Arab countries have enacted new trademark laws. This process of legal reform began as early as 1999. In that year, a new intellectual property law was enacted in Jordan, which replaced Trademark Law No 33 of 1952. In addition, the Commercial Law of Kuwait (that also regulates trademark protection) was amended. A year later, in June 2000, Oman revised its trademark law (Royal Decree No 38/2000).[80] In that year (2000) Yemen revised its Unified Intellectual Property Rights Law of 1994. In 2001, Tunisia followed suit by amending its own trademark law (Law No 2001–36). In the same year, Lebanon amended its national trademark law, and began drafting a new Trademark and Geographical Indications Law.

The year 2002 saw a flurry of activity in terms of enacting or revising existing trademark legislation in Arab countries. In that year, Qatar revised its existing trademark law[81] and Saudi Arabia enacted new trademark regulations (law), which substituted its previous trademark regulations (in effect since 1984). In May 2002, a new and comprehensive intellectual property law was enacted in Egypt (Law No 82). The law not only covers trademarks but also patents, copyrights, plant varieties, industrial designs, and semiconductor chip topography. At around the same time (July 2002), the UAE enacted a new Federal Trademark Law (Law No 8). That law replaced the previous UAE law (Law No 37, for 1992).

In 2003, a similar legislative exercise (to that carried out in Egypt) was undertaken by Algeria. In March 2003, Algeria enacted its own intellectual property law covering patents, copyrights as well as trademarks. The year 2004 was no different: both Morocco and Iraq enacted new trademark provisions. In Morocco,

[79] D Gervais, *The TRIPS Agreement, Drafting History and Analysis* (Sweet & Maxwell, 1998).
[80] Effective as of 3 June 2000.
[81] Implementing regulations of the Qatari law are pending.

this has been achieved through the Unified Law Number 17–97 for the year 2004. In Iraq, trademark registration and protection is now governed by a 2004 amendment of the previous (1957) Iraqi Trademark Law (Law No 21). The amended Iraqi law has been renamed 'The Trademark and Geographical Indications Law'.[82]

These new laws, or amendments, are intended to mirror the standards of protection that were set out in the TRIPS Agreement. Generally, these laws possess similar distinctive features that include:[83]

(1) granting rights over a distinctive mark;
(2) awarding rights over a mark through use and/or registration in the relevant jurisdiction;
(3) allowing owners of registered or well-known marks to prevent others from using an identical or confusingly similar mark;
(4) facilitating opposition proceedings against the registration of confusingly similar marks;
(5) granting the right to obtain judicial 'cease and desist' and 'search and seizure' (*Anton Piller*) orders against an infringing party;
(6) providing that a trademark registration is valid for a period of between seven and ten years, and is renewable for consecutive periods of similar duration;[84]
(7) allowing the trademark-right owner to dispose of his mark through licensing or sale (assignment);
(8) granting trademark protection to service marks;
(9) expanding the scope of signs that could be recognized as trademarks; and
(10) setting specific procedures aimed at strengthening trademark protection, including specific powers delegated to the Customs authority allowing it to search (and to seize) infringing or counterfeit products at the ports of entry.

Evidently, trademark laws in Arab countries contain most of the standards of trademark protection that are prescribed by TRIPS and other trademark-related conventions, such as the Madrid Agreement and the Nice Agreement.[85]

---

82 The amended law was enacted in accordance with Order Number 80, issued by the Coalition Provisional Authority.

83 For more on the rights accorded by law to the owner of a mark, see R Jacob and D Alexander, *A Guide to Intellectual Property* (4th edn, Sweet & Maxwell, 1993), 65–92; WIPO, *Introduction to Intellectual Property* (Kluwer, 1997); also, see International Trademark Association (INTA), 'Frequently asked Questions' at <http://www.inta.org/index.php?option=com_simplefaq&task=display&Itemid=60&catid=284&getcontent=1> (last accessed 18 May 2007).

84 Those rights may continue indefinitely, as long as the trademark owner does not abandon his mark or the mark does not become generic.

85 Madrid Agreement Concerning the International Registration of Marks, available at <http://www.wipo.int/madrid/en/legal_texts/trtdocs_wo015.html>; Nice Agreement Concerning the

Moreover, despite the economic, political and social differences among Arab countries, their trademark regimes are in many respects one and the same.[86] This should come as no surprise, given that current trademark laws in Arab countries have been modelled on the provisions of the TRIPS Agreement.

In addition to this, the enforcement of intellectual property rights has been increasing in many Arab countries. Courts have been more active in granting *Anton Piller*-type injunctions in civil cases involving trademark infringement. In fact, raids against suspected counterfeiters have become commonplace.[87] Police and Customs are frequently authorized by the courts to conduct search and seizure raids relating to counterfeit products or products bearing infringing marks.[88]

International Classification of Goods and Services for the Purposes of the Registration of Marks, available at <http://www.wipo.int/treaties/en/classification/nice/trtdocs_wo019.html> (last accessed 5 March 2007).

86 This is evident not only in the case of countries that have attained WTO membership but also in the case of Syria which, although it has not attained membership yet, contains in its law provisions that closely resemble the standards that are prescribed by TRIPS; AH Khoury, 'The Development of Modern Trademark Legislation and Protection in Arab Countries of the Middle East' (2003) 16 *The Transnational Lawyer* 2; M Dallal, 'Trademarks and Copyrights in Jordan', in Price-Waterhouse-Coopers, *Building and Enforcing Intellectual Property Value: An International Guide for the Boardroom* (2003), 235. Notably, in September 2001, the Syrian Government issued a decree aimed at formally implementing the Syrian Copyright Law No 12 of 2001. This new law affords protection of copyrightable subject matter including written works, musical compositions, and computer software, where such materials have been duly registered in Syria in accordance with this new law. Syria is party to the Berne Convention (from 11 June 2004), another step towards enhancing copyright protection therein.

87 Saba, note 74 above, reports that the annual number of IP-related cases in Jordan have risen to 600. The beginning of 2001 brought a surge of activity on the anti-piracy front in Jordan. A raid carried out by Jordanian police in March of that year resulted in the seizure of unlicensed Microsoft software as well as 'pirated' CDs. The raid targeted a computer retailer located in Amman, who had loaded computers with unlicensed Microsoft software and sold counterfeit software. In July 2000, a raid was conducted in Jordan against traders selling chisels and screwdrivers bearing the well-known Stanley brand. These raids yielded a substantial cache of counterfeit products that were confiscated and later destroyed. See March 2001 News Bulletin, AGIP, at < http://www.agip.com/bulletin_sub.aspx?year=2001&month=3&lang=en> (last accessed 18 May 2007); and NJQ & Associates, 'STANLEY—Police Raid on Counterfeit Products in Jordan', <http://qumsieh.com/Newsletters/Newsletter_%20August_2000/Newsletter_August_2000.html> (last accessed 18 May 2007). In April 2001, a substantial search and seizure operation was simultaneously conducted at three Emirates in the UAE (Dubai, Sharjah and Abu Dhabi). The operation yielded a very large quantity of counterfeit items of clothing bearing the famous mark CK Calvin Klein. For a report on this operation (including pictures of some of the seized products) see NJQ & Associates, at <http://qumsieh.com/Newsletters/Newsletter_April_2001/Newsletter_April_2001.htm> (last accessed 18 May 2007). Towards the end of 2001 a raid on a tailor shop in Jeddah jointly conducted by Saudi police led to the arrest of those involved in the manufacture of articles of clothing bearing well-known marks (e.g. Levi Strauss): AGIP, January 2002 News Bulletin, at <http://www.agip.com/bulletin_sub.aspx?year=2002&month=1&lang=en> (last accessed 7 March 2007).

88 The TRIPS Agreement (Art 51) strongly emphasizes the enforcement role of the Customs authorities. For more on anti-counterfeiting activity in the Middle East see S Adams, 'Tackling Counterfeiters in the Middle East' (2000) 29 *Trademark World* 11.

As a result, the Customs authorities have become much more proficient in identifying suspected counterfeit products and preventing their entry into Arab countries.[89]

Egypt, Kuwait, Jordan and the UAE are generally considered to be the most active Arab countries in terms of complying with WTO standards pertaining to intellectual property.[90] Another report reiterates that Jordan and the UAE are among the 'best performing countries in the Middle East for pushing ahead with legislation to enforce intellectual property rights and clamp down on software piracy'.[91]

In addition to the enforcement by judicial and administrative entities within Arab countries, various domestic and foreign organizations are engaged in the promotion of intellectual property protection in Arab countries.[92] Substantial 'grass roots' promotion regarding intellectual property, through conferences and workshops, is taking place in these countries.[93] This is being achieved through academic, business, and international channels. WIPO has been active in raising the awareness of intellectual property protection in Arab countries and amending national legislation.

---

89 In April 2001, Jordanian Customs began to require trademark owners to provide it with copies of their respective trademarks in order to assist it to identify counterfeit products at the ports of entry. Under Amendment No 20 of the Jordanian Customs Law of 1998, the owner of an intellectual property right may petition the court to order Customs to seize certain shipments suspected of containing infringing goods. In such cases, the petitioner is required to substantiate his right. The courts are required, by law, to lend an expedited decision within three days of filing the petition; NJQ & Associates, Jordan: 'The Role of Customs Department in Intellectual Property Protection', Newsletter Circular December 2001, at <http://www.qumsieh.com/Newsletters/Newsletter_%20December_2001/Newsletter_December_2001.html> (last accessed 25 May 2007).

90 Ali and Partners, 'The Middle East and the World Trade Organization', available at <http://www.mideastlaw.com/article_middle_east_and_the_wto.html>, 1 (last accessed 5 March 2007).

91 Agence France Press (Report) 'King Abdullah Given Award for Efforts to Combat Software Piracy', (6 February 2001). The prize was awarded by the Business Software Alliance (BSA).

92 For example, the Arab Society for the Protection of Intellectual Property (ASPIP): <http://www.aspip.org>; the Jordanian Intellectual Property Association (JIPA); the Arab Internet Names Consortium (AINC): <http://www.icannwatch.org/article.pl?sid=01/03/27/071115>; the Jordanian Committee for Intellectual Property in E-Business and the Licensing Executive Society—Arab Countries (LESARAB).

93 For example, Jordan IP Week (Summer 2004): <http://www.jordanipweek.com> (last accessed 5 March 2007). Many organizations have been active in this regard including: the United States Patent and Trademark Office (USPTO), WIPO, US Agency for International Development (USAID), the International Anti-Counterfeiting Coalition (IACC) and the International Intellectual Property Institute (IIPI). The last IP week as of this writing was held on 11–12 December 2006 in Amman. Its focus was the economic costs of counterfeiting.

E. The Arab Opinion Survey

In order to gain a better understanding of how Arab countries have formulated their trademark laws against the backdrop of the policy debate, in late 2003 I conducted an opinion survey. The survey consisted of a questionnaire comprising ten multiple-choice questions that I sent by, e-mail, to a group of trademark practitioners in different Arab countries. The questionnaire pertains to various trademark-related issues including registration, protection and enforcement. The questions are listed below:

1. **Has there been a substantial increase in the number of trademark applications filed through your firm in the last four years, as compared with filings before the year 1999?**
   a. A substantial increase
   b. Moderate increase
   c. No real change
   d. Decrease

2. **What is the (approximate) ratio of trademark applications filed (in your country) through your firm by foreigners, to those filed by local persons or entities?**
   a. 4:1 (i.e. foreigners 4 times more than locals)
   b. 3:1
   c. 2:1
   d. 1:1
   e. Less than 1:1

3. **Do you detect, since 1999, any increased awareness by local persons/entities of the importance of registering their trademarks?**
   a. Yes, there is a notable rise in such awareness among the local business community.
   b. There is only some awareness of this issue.
   c. No real change is noted in this regard in the last four years (since 1999).
   d. The opposite; fewer local entities are registering their marks.

4. **Has there been a rise (since 1999), as compared with the period before 1999, in the number of trademark applications being filed by local business entities abroad (in trademark offices outside your country)?**
   a. Yes; a notable rise.
   b. Local businesses are making some inquiries. However, not many trademarks are actually being filed abroad.
   c. No change has been detected as compared with the period before 1999.
   d. Before 1999, more local entities were filing trademarks abroad.

5. **Is the period of examination (of a trademark application by the local trademark office) reducing, as compared with periods of examination before 1999?**
   a. Yes; there has been a drastic shortening in the time taken to examine new trademark applications.
   b. The local trademark office has made some attempts. However, for now, the period of examination remains almost the same.
   c. No change.
   d. The local trademark office is becoming even slower in its examination of new trademark applications; (this may be due to workload).

6. **Have the police, in the last four years (since 1999), become more active in investigating cases of trademark infringement?**
   a. Yes; the police are very active and efficient in this regard.
   b. Only to some extent. The activity of the police in this regard is still not satisfactory.
   c. The police are unable to deal with trademark infringements, due to other priorities.
   d. The police appear unwilling to deal with such cases.

7. **In the last four years (since 1999) have the local courts become more willing to grant interlocutory orders and issue search and seizure orders against suspected trademark counterfeiters?**
   a. Yes; the local courts have become very active in these functions.
   b. Courts are only granting these (orders) decisions in some cases involving trademark infringements.
   c. The court proceedings are still too slow; and as such are not efficient.
   d. Courts are becoming increasingly reluctant to give such orders.

8. **Would it be correct to state that: In most cases involving trademark infringements in your country, the plaintiffs are foreigners and the defendants/respondents are local persons/entities?**
   a. Yes. That is the situation.
   b. Generally so.
   c. It is not possible to generalize. There is a mixed pattern.
   d. In most cases, both parties are local.
   e. The opposite is true; in most infringement cases local persons/entities are (typically) the plaintiffs and the defendants are foreign entities.

9. **Do you think that, in your country, local brands are able to compete with foreign brands?**
   a. Yes.
   b. Only to a limited extent.

c. Not really.
d. Local brands have no chance in such competition.

10. Do you think that foreign trademarks (brands) benefit your country's economy/culture?
a. Very much so; by encouraging openness and boosting foreign investment.
b. Only to a limited extent.
c. No, because products/services sold under these marks are foreign owned/made and the revenue flows abroad.
d. Foreign brands harm the local economy/culture by dominating the market and by undermining social values.

In all, 28 substantive responses were e-mailed to me from law firms based in Jordan, Syria, Egypt, Kuwait, Oman, United Arab Emirates, Sudan, Yemen and Morocco. The results of the questionnaire are summarized in Table 8.2. The row numbers 1–10 refer to the corresponding questions in the questionnaire. The letters a–d (or a–e in the case of question 8) refer to the corresponding answers that are attached to each question. Table 8.2 also shows the number of responses received from each country and the general total of various options that were selected.

Table 8.2 Summary of Responses to Questionnaire

Question Number	Answer	Countries from which responses were received									
		Jordan	UAE	Kuwait	Egypt	Sudan	Syria	Yemen	Oman	Morocco	TOTAL
		Number of responses received from each country									
		9	4	4	5	2	1	1	1	1	**28**
1	a	4	2	2	3	1	1	–	1	1	**15**
	b	4	2	1	1	–	–	1	–	–	**9**
	c	1	–	1	1	1	–	–	–	–	**4**
	d	–	–	–	–	–	–	–	–	–	–
2	a	1	3	3	4	1	–	1	1	1	**15**
	b	4	1	1	1	–	1	–	–	–	**8**
	c	–	–	–	–	–	–	–	–	–	–
	d	2	–	–	–	1	–	–	–	–	**3**
3	a	7	4	2	3	1	1	1	–	1	**20**
	b	2	–	2	2	1	–	–	1	–	**8**
	c	–	–	–	–	–	–	–	–	–	–
	d	–	–	–	–	–	–	–	–	–	–
4	a	6	3	1	4	–	–	1	–	–	**15**
	b	3	1	2	1	1	1	–	–	1	**10**
	c	–	–	1	–	1	–	–	1	–	**3**
	d	–	–	–	–	–	–	–	–	–	–

Table 8.2 (*cont.*)

Question Number	Answer	Jordan	UAE	Kuwait	Egypt	Sudan	Syria	Yemen	Oman	Morocco	TOTAL
		Countries from which responses were received									
		Number of responses received from each country									
		9	4	4	5	2	1	1	1	1	**28**
5	a	6	3	2	1	–	–	–	1	–	**13**
	b	2	1	2	2	1	–	1	–	–	**9**
	c	–	–	–	1	1	–	–	–	–	**2**
	d	1	–	–	1	–	1	–	–	–	**3**
6	**a**	2	2	1	1	–	–	–	–	–	**6**
	b	6	2	1	2	2	–	–	1	1	**15**
	c	1	–	1	–	–	1	1	–	–	**4**
	d	–	–	1	1	–	–	–	–	–	**2**
7	a	5	–	–	1	–	–	–	–	1	**7**
	b	4	3	1	3	1	–	–	–	–	**12**
	c	–	1	2	1	1	1	1	1	–	**8**
	d	–	–	–	–	–	–	–	–	–	**–**
8	**a**	2	–	2	2	1	–	1	–	–	**8**
	b	5	4	2	2	–	1	–	–	1	**15**
	c	2	–	–	1	1	–	–	–	–	**4**
	d	–	–	–	–	–	–	–	–	–	**–**
	e	–	–	–	–	–	–	–	1	–	**1**
9	a	1	–	–	1	–	–	–	–	–	**2**
	b	3	4	1	4	–	1	–	–	1	**14**
	c	4	–	2	–	1	–	1	1	–	**9**
	d	1	–	1	–	–	–	–	–	–	**2**
10	**a**	3	3	1	3	–	–	–	–	1	**11**
	b	5	–	1	1	–	–	1	1	–	**9**
	c	1	1	2	1*	–	1	–	–	–	**6**
	d	–	–	–	1*	1	–	–	–	–	**2**

* One respondent chose both answers c and d for question 10. As such, both answers were counted.

The results prompt the following observations:

1. There has been a moderate to substantial increase in the number of trademark applications filed after 1999, as compared with filings before the year 1999.
2. In Arab countries the ratio of trademark applications filed by foreigners to those filed by local trademark owners is between 3:1 and 4:1.
3. Since 1999, there has mostly been a notable rise in awareness by local persons/entities of the importance of registering their trademarks.
4. Since 1999, there has been a moderate to notable rise in the number of trademark applications being filed by local business entities abroad (outside their home country).

5. Since 1999, the time taken by the trademark office to examine trademark applications is reducing in a moderate to drastic manner.
6. Police investigation of cases involving trademark infringement is still not regarded as satisfactory.
7. Since 1999, in most countries courts have been granting interlocutory and search and seizure orders in some, but not all, cases involving trademark infringement.
8. Generally, in trademark infringement cases, the plaintiffs are foreigners and the defendants are local persons/entities.
9. Local brands are able to compete with foreign brands to a very limited extent.
10. Generally, foreign brands do benefit Arab countries' economy/culture.

Broadly speaking, the trends identified by this survey match the general trends in literature supporting trademark protection. It is possible to conclude that in the past decade trademark laws in Arab countries have come a long way in conforming to international standards of protection.

Part IV Assessing Arab Countries' Policy Regarding their Trademark Regimes

After outlining the current trademark regimes in Arab countries, it is important to gain some understanding of why these legal systems have evolved in the way that they have. In the midst of, and despite, this long-running policy debate, it is quite apparent that Arab countries have knowingly adopted, into their national legislation, modern standards of trademark (and other intellectual property) protection as prescribed by various international agreements and mainly TRIPS. In so doing, Arab countries appear to have adopted the approach advocated by Development theorists; namely, that trademark protection will yield positive effects for Arab countries, despite the lack of econometric studies regarding the effects of trademark regimes on these countries.

Moreover, while legal literature is saturated with formalistic commentary as to the importance of trademark protection and theoretical arguments regarding the attributes of such regimes, it lacks analysis of data that might reveal how the law actually affects developing countries. As such, one must question the reasons that have prompted Arab countries to act in this manner.

It appears quite clear that there is a direct correlation between enacting new intellectual property legislation (or amending existing law) and attaining membership in the WTO.[94] Arab countries have initiated a process of revising all of their intellectual property-related legislation in order to bring it into conformity with the TRIPS standard of protection. Thus, the resulting trademark legislation is not a direct product of pure national choice, but rather a by-product of the bigger picture involving other interests of Arab countries, namely being a member of the WTO. This trend, towards the full adoption of (TRIPS-compliant) intellectual property norms of protection, appears to be part of a larger move by Arab countries towards opening their economies to the world through the WTO.[95]

Indeed, this should not come as a surprise, because the WTO is the most substantial mechanism for regulating international trade. Joining the WTO requires a rigorous process of accession involving the WTO Secretariat, as a whole, as well as its individual member states.[96]

---

94 Gallagher, note 26 above. The WTO came into effect on 1 January 1995 and is regarded as the most sophisticated trade organization. It is perceived as a mechanism for facilitating and unifying international trade. It comprises various multilateral and plurilateral agreements. The five main 'multilateral agreements' binding on all WTO members address various international trade issues including intellectual property: General Agreement on Tariffs and Trade (GATT); General Agreement on Trade in Services (GATS); Agreement on Trade-Related Aspects of Intellectual Property Rights (TRIPS); Understanding on the Dispute Settlement System (DSU); and Trade Policy Review Mechanism (TPRM). The WTO performs various functions including: administering and implementing the multilateral trade agreements that make up the WTO, including those dealing with IP issues; providing a forum for multilateral trade negotiations; assistance to the resolution of international trade disputes; supervision of international trade policies; and cooperation with other international institutions involved in global economic policy making. The WTO also has optional agreements that cover specific trade areas including Civil Aircraft and Government Procurement. In addition to these multilateral agreements, there are a number of supplementary ministerial decisions and declarations.

95 HL Stovall, 'Arab Commercial Laws—Into the Future', (1999–2000) 34 *Int'l Law*, 839, 847. Stovall observes that many Arab governments 'are no longer trying to protect their economies from the rest of the world, but rather selecting the advantages of participation in the global economy. As a result, Arab legal systems are facing new challenges, and at an ever increasing pace.'

96 For a concise summary of the WTO accession process see Jordanian Ministry of Industry and Trade, 'Policy Reform: World Trade Organization Membership Process and Requirements', (published with the assistance of AMIR Program/USAID). The accession process involves the following stages:

1. Applicant country initiates its accession process by submitting a letter to the WTO indicating its desire to join the WTO.
2. Applicant state is required to submit a memorandum detailing all aspects of its trade and economy which have a bearing on WTO agreements.
3. Following receipt of these documents, the WTO sets up a working party intended to review the memorandum.
4. Simultaneously, the applicant state is required to engage WTO members in negotiations aimed at establishing its concessions and commitments with respect to goods and services.
5. During these negotiations, applicant country must submit a special report dealing with its outstanding accession issues.

In the 11 years since the WTO's inception, 11 Arab countries have attained membership therein.[97] These countries are Bahrain, Kuwait, and Morocco (on 1 January 1995), Tunisia (29 March 1995), Mauritania (31 May 1995), Egypt (30 June 1995), [98] Qatar (13 January 1996), the UAE (10 April 1996), Jordan (11 April 2000), Oman (9 November 2000), and Saudi Arabia (December 11, 2005). Syria's application to rejoin the WTO is also pending and is now subject to the regular process of accession.[99] In addition, six other Arab countries have a status of 'Observer Governments' with the WTO, these being Algeria, Iraq, Lebanon, Libya, Sudan and Yemen.

Members of the World Trade Organization (WTO) are required, through TRIPS, to comply with the substantive provisions of international agreements and conventions dealing with intellectual property protection (most notably the Paris Convention), and to conform to the Paris-Plus elements contained in TRIPS itself.[100]

6. When the accession negotiations are concluded successfully, the applicant's policies are determined to be compatible with WTO requirements. At this stage, the issue is referred to the working party that conducts a revision of the applicant's tariff protections. The applicant, in turn, is required to undertake certain obligations that are to be performed within a designated timeframe.
7. Once the parties have done all of the above, the working party submits an accession report to the Ministerial Council. This report typically contains basic terms of the accession, draft protocol of the accession and agreed schedules.
8. The Ministerial Council is the WTO body authorized to adopt and approve accession reports. Following such approval, the applicant country signs and (where applicable) ratifies the protocol, thus attaining membership in the WTO.

[97] For more on WTO membership and compliance (with WTO standards) in the Middle East, see RI Ali and LW Haddad, 'WTO Membership and Compliance in the Middle East Countries', (1999) *Middle East Econ R* 11.

[98] Until mid-1999 Egypt had committed itself to only 4 of the 12 sectors covered by GATS, namely, construction, finance, tourism and transport. Not surprisingly, Egypt was subjected to pressure aimed at opening up more service sectors in accordance with its GATS–WTO obligations. Specifically, Egypt was required to 'open and liberalize' its telecommunications, insurance and banking sectors: HL Stovall and H Pullman, 'Middle East Commercial Law Developments' (1999) 33 *Int'l Law*, 753–755. For a comprehensive analysis of Egypt's obligations and commitments under the GATT/WTO agreement; Nathan Associates Inc, 'Development Economic Policy Reform Analysis (DEPRA) Project, Egypt: Obligations and Commitments Under the GATT/WTO Agreements' (1999)(Final Report), Submitted to the United States Agency for International Development (USAID–Egypt).

[99] Ali and Partners, note 90 above; in 1949, Syria withdrew its membership in the GATT following Israel's entry into it, and has not rejoined.

[100] The two main conventions in this regard are the Paris Convention for the Protection of Industrial Property 1883 and the Berne Convention on the Protection of Literary and Artistic Works 1886. The deadline for the implementation of the TRIPS obligations depends on that member's classification: 'developed countries' had until 1995, 'developing countries' had until January 2000. 'Least-developed countries' were granted 11 years with a possibility for extension in which to implement TRIPS, namely until 2006: this has since been extended until 1 July 2013.

The TRIPS Agreement constitutes a milestone in the protection of intellectual property rights. TRIPS prescribes minimum standards of protection which have become compulsory by way of incorporating TRIPS into the WTO framework.[101] TRIPS subjects non-complying countries to economic and trade sanctions imposed through the WTO dispute resolution mechanism.[102] Thus, TRIPS revolutionized the rules of intellectual property protection because of its substantive rules, its ability to harmonize national trademark legal regimes, and its ability to ensure the adoption and continued enforcement of these norms. Consequently, it is not surprising that TRIPS is regarded as the most central agreement in the context of intellectual property protection. In this regard, TRIPS differs greatly from previous intellectual property agreements in that it provides mechanisms that help ensure its effective implementation.[103]

The legal norms pertaining to intellectual property rights have ceased to be shaped in accordance with national norms and interests, and have become intertwined in the wider context of international trade regulation.[104] In fact, by including intellectual property protection within the WTO framework, the infringement of intellectual property has been placed in the same category as other impediments to trade, such as dumping and subsidies, that are also regulated by the GATT/WTO.[105] In this context, one commentator concluded that 'to assert

[101] May, note 26 above, 76. See, for example, DW Plant, *Resolving International Intellectual Property Disputes* (International Chamber Of Commerce (ICC) Publishing, 1999). Notwithstanding these unified standards, TRIPS allows its members to exercise some independence (e.g. rules pertaining to the regulation of parallel imports).

[102] TRIPS allows for settling disputes between member states over intellectual property issues by applying the WTO 'Dispute Settlement Understanding'. This mechanism also covers disputes pertaining to 'National Treatment' as well as issues of 'Most Favoured Nation' status. Grey Markets (parallel imports) have been excluded from TRIPS and this dispute settlement mechanism; Gallagher, note 26 above, 182. For a discussion on dispute settlement under the WTO: J Waincymer, 'Settlement of Disputes Within the World Trade Organization: A Guide to the Jurisprudence', (2001) 24 *The World Economy*, 1247. Ali and Partners, note 90 above; R Meyer-Reumann, 'The Endeavors of Gulf Countries to Meet WTO Requirements', (2001) *Arab L Qly* 49 (Kluwer).

[103] WIPO, *Introduction to Intellectual Property*, note 83 above, 475; INTA, 'TRIPS 2000 Subcommittee Treaty Analysis Committee, Developing Countries Compliance with the TRIPS Agreement' (Updated Version), available at <www.inta.org/downloads/tap_trips2000.pdf> (last accessed 24 May 2007).

[104] J Jackson *et al*, *Legal Problems of International Economic Relations* (3rd. edn, West Publishing, 1995) 291, 885–892.

[105] The Ministerial Declaration on the Uruguay Round, (September 1986, WT/MIN (96)/16) stated that 'in order to reduce the distortions and impediments to international trade, and taking into account the need to promote effective and adequate protection of intellectual property rights and to ensure that measures and procedures to enforce intellectual property rights do not themselves become barriers to legitimate trade, the negotiations shall aim to clarify GATT provisions and elaborate as appropriate new rules and disciplines'. Sherwood, note 70 above, 3, 67–92. Endeshaw, note 7 above, 121.

the trade relatedness of intellectual property is to make a claim for it to be legitimately included within the legal structure covering world trade'.[106]

The multilateral agreements within the WTO (including TRIPS) require members to provide 'National Treatment' (treating both imported and domestic products equally) and 'Most Favoured Nation' (treating all member states equally) status to goods, services, and intellectual property of every other member state. In addition, member states are required to coordinate their trade policies and national laws in line with their respective obligations.[107]

As clearly evidenced by the WTO accession process, countries wishing to join the WTO (including Arab countries) have had to amend their respective intellectual property laws or to enact new laws in accordance with the standards set by TRIPS. In other words, adopting modern standards of intellectual property protection is not simply a matter of choice but rather a matter of necessity in order to improve the chances of accession to the WTO or to retain membership therein.[108]

Conclusion

The bulk of literature dealing with protection of intellectual property in developing countries has approached the topic from a legalistic and formalistic angle, namely by highlighting basic moral concepts of fair competition and fair dealing in trade, and by identifying the amendments and measures that are necessary in order to comply with conventional standards of protection. This is especially puzzling in light of a substantial mass of literature that demonstrates

---

106 May, note 26 above, 78. The WTO is a result of the Uruguay Round of trade negotiations, which was concluded in December 1993; Jackson *et al*, note 104 above, 289–326. For more on WTO membership, see WTO, 'Members and Observers', at <http://www.wto.org/english/thewto_e/whatis_e/tif_e/org6_e.htm> (last accessed 9 April 2006). Notably, the majority of these countries (about 68 per cent), including Arab Countries, are classified as 'Developing Countries'. 30 other member states are categorized as 'Least-Developed Countries'. It is worth noting that the WTO does not provide any definition of what constitutes a 'Developed' or 'Developing' country. Developing countries in the WTO are classified as such based on 'self election.'

107 Member states have to negotiate and comply with other specific obligations under the Agreement, including reciprocity, equal treatment, and transparency in trade and legal regimes as well as reducing trade barriers. Member states are obliged to implement various measures, which include creating a transparent economic policy, setting clear tariffs on goods, opening national service industries to investors and service providers of other member countries, limiting antidumping and countervailing duties, and reducing levies on transit goods. All this in order to secure free trade that operates in accordance with the theory of comparative advantage.

108 For a different outlook on the formulation of TRIPS see BA Lehman, 'Intellectual Property Rights as a Trade, Health and Economic Development Issue' (2003) 17 *St. John's J*, Legal Comment, 417. Lehman asserts that 'the TRIPS Agreement was an agreement that was negotiated on the basis of *quid pro quos* among states. Each state gave something and got something.'

widespread scepticism about the benefits that trademark protection (and intellectual property protection in general) actually affords the economies of developing countries.

The debate between the proponents and the sceptics over the attributes of intellectual property protection is embedded in opposing theories; namely, the 'Development Theory' and the 'Dependency Theory'. These theories are not limited to the argument surrounding intellectual property but rather extend to all spheres of development, including economic structure and social values. In fact, those theories reflect the polarized positions that exist within policy discourse pertaining to the development of Third World countries.

While the 'Development Theory' urges developing countries to adopt modern norms of industrial countries, as a means for development, those citing the 'Dependency Theory' contend that such adoption merely serves to widen the economic rift between the rich 'North' and the poor 'South'(or what is also referred to as 'West' and 'East' respectively). According to the Dependency theorists, the mere adoption of legal and economic standards does not ensure development, and may even hamper the efforts of developing nations to compete in the global marketplace, while becoming dependent on the capital and technology of developed countries. Therefore, Dependency theorists advocate a proactive approach whereby developing countries should exercise self-sufficiency by producing and manufacturing what they consume ('Import Substitution').

Arab trademark laws, especially those enacted recently in most Arab countries, are in conformity with the standards of trademark protection as prescribed by TRIPS. Thus, despite this ongoing policy debate, it appears that Arab countries have opted for mechanical compliance without conducting a thorough examination of the implications of their actions.

The conduct of Arab countries appears to be driven by two primary concerns, namely the possibility of losing foreign investments, and the worry about economic sanctions that might be imposed due to the lack of protection for intellectual property rights.

It is possible to conclude that most Arab countries have been seeking to raise the level of intellectual property protection in their respective jurisdictions in order to facilitate or maintain membership in the WTO, without sufficient regard for the ongoing debate surrounding trademark policy.[109]

---

109 For a similar observation regarding intellectual property and developing countries see RE Evenson, 'Comment: *Intellectual Property Rights and Economic Development*, by Keith Maskus' (2001) 33 *Case W Res J of Int'l L* 187, 190: '[p]olicymakers in developing countries are being

While I remain steadfast in my support for trademark protection, based on its moral and even economic rationales, it is my contention that the law should also be formulated in accordance with the needs of developing countries, namely by ensuring that they are able to secure a competitive edge in the world economy.

pressured both domestically and internationally to build stronger IPRs.... Economists have traditionally been divided on the economic consequences of IPRs, even though developed countries' governments and courts have decidedly favored strong IPRs'.

9

INTELLECTUAL PROPERTY, TRADE AND DEVELOPMENT: A VIEW FROM THE UNITED STATES

Hon. Jean R Homere[1]

Introduction

Intellectual property has become an integral part of the economies of industrialized countries such as the United States. As their economies are becoming more information-based, industrialized countries have devoted greater resources to

[1] To my mother Anne-Mercie, my wife Marie-France, and my sons Christopher and David.

promoting innovation, to securing exclusive rights in information and to gaining competitive advantage in world markets.[2] Empirical evidence shows that industrialized countries with functioning intellectual property systems are more likely to experience economic growth, lower unemployment rates, stronger education systems, better quality of life, and greater research and development.[3] Intellectual property has been recognized as one of the most valuable assets in many commercial transactions, and it is increasingly gaining ground as a measure of corporate viability and future performance.[4] For instance, the global IP licensing market totalled more than $100 billion in 1999.[5] In the year 2000, intellectual property assets represented 40 per cent of the net value of corporations in the United States.[6] Similarly, in Europe, intellectual property accounts for more than 33 per cent of corporate assets.[7]

By contrast, the economies of several, perhaps most developing countries depend primarily on the export of agricultural goods and raw materials.[8] Developing countries, however, tend to limit the amount of agricultural goods that they produce as a way of balancing supply and demand of agricultural products. Consequently, they cannot achieve economic development solely through agricultural production.[9] According to Robert Solow, a leading developmental economist, the three factors that affect production are labour, capital and technical progress.[10] He recognizes that, because capital and labour are limited in developing countries, only technical progress can help stimulate their economies to increase growth and attain the economic levels found in industrialized countries.[11] Along the same line, another economist asserts that the key to continual economic success lies in the technological development within a country.[12] The 'Two Gap' theory, on the other hand, postulates that developing countries are unable to create and maintain the technological growth to promote economic

2 K Idris, *Intellectual Property, A Power Tool for Economic Growth* WIPO, Geneva (2002), 34.

3 KE Maskus, 'Intellectual Property Challenges for Developing Countries: An Economic Perspective' (2001) *U of Illinois LR* 457, 458–59.

4 Idris, note 2 above, 54–55.

5 Ibid, 61–62.

6 Ibid.

7 Ibid.

8 TD Larson, *International Political Economy: The Struggle for Power and Wealth* (Harcourt School, 1993), 181.

9 Ibid, 198.

10 R Solow, 'A Contribution to the Theory of Economic Growth' (1956) 70 *Quarterly J of Econ* 65, 66.

11 Ibid, [65].

12 EJ Malecki, *Technology and Economic Development: The Dynamics of Local, Regional and National Competitiveness* (2nd edn, Longman, 1997), 192.

development because they lack the necessary capital.[13] Their industrial imports often exceed their agricultural exports, which causes them to be eternally indebted to developed nations.[14]

By the turn of the twenty-first century, numerous developing countries began to foster a greater awareness and a deeper appreciation of intellectual property rights.[15] Many of them started to recognize that a functioning intellectual property right system can offer numerous economic benefits to them. In particular, a functioning intellectual property system can stimulate domestic innovation, and it can attract foreign direct investment, which in turn can be a conduit for technology acquisition and economic development.[16] Further, with the advent of TRIPS[17] requiring less industrialized countries to implement certain basic intellectual property laws in order to enjoy membership in the World Trade Organization (WTO), numerous developing countries have decided to implement an intellectual property system.[18] In most cases, however, developing countries tend to resist implementing strengthened IPR models similar to those of industrialized countries. Rather, developing countries have opted to implement IPR systems that integrate laws and enforcement procedures of intellectual property rights in an attempt to stimulate domestic innovation, foreign investment, and economic development while conforming to the TRIPS requirements.[19] For example, in 1987, Asian countries like Singapore, Malaysia, and Indonesia decided to implement more stringent intellectual property protection systems to prevent trade sanctions, and to encourage foreign investment.[20] They enacted stricter laws, and stepped up enforcement of these laws, as well, by imposing fines and criminal sanctions for infringement and piracy.[21] In contrast, countries like Vietnam and Thailand opted to resist such pressure from the West. As a result, piracy flourished in these nations, while it

[13] P Krugman, 'International Finance and Economic Development', in A Giovannini (ed), *Finance and Development Issues and Experience* (Cambridge University Press, 1993) 15.

[14] Ibid.

[15] RE Evenson, 'Review of *Intellectual Property Rights and Economic Development* by KE Maskus' (2001) 33 *Case W Res J of Int'l L* 187, 188.

[16] Ibid.

[17] MP Ryan, *Knowledge Diplomacy: Global Competition and the Politics of Intellectual Property* (Brookings Institution Press, 1988), 104–119.

[18] MW Smith, 'Bringing Developing Countries' Intellectual Property Laws to TRIPS Standards: Hurdles and Pitfalls Facing Vietnam's Efforts to Normalize an Intellectual Property Regime' (1999) 31 *Case W Res J of Int'l L* 213, 218.

[19] Ibid, 214.

[20] E Uphoff, *Intellectual Property and US Relations With Indonesia, Malaysia, Singapore and Thailand* (Cornell University, 1991) 12.

[21] Ibid.

was virtually eliminated in Singapore, Malaysia and Indonesia.[22] Additionally, Singapore, Malaysia, and Indonesia experienced a rising influx of foreign direct investment in the 1990s, while Vietnam and Thailand did not attract similar economic opportunities.[23]

Part I Intellectual Property and Trade Between Industrialized Countries and Developing Countries

A. Industrialized Countries Demand TRIPS Compliance in Developing Countries

During the mid-1980s, a number of industrialized countries were becoming increasingly concerned about infringing activities, which prevented them from fully reaping the economic benefits that intellectual property has to offer.[24] Their heavy investments in research and technology development were not realizing their full economic potentials in certain markets and infringing activities were among the leading causes of lost sales domestically and abroad.[25] For example, the International Intellectual Property Alliance (IIPA) reported that, in 1994 alone, the United States lost over $1.265 billion to infringing activities in Japan, $1.2 billion to such activities in Germany, $866 million to China, $805 million to Russia, $103 million to Malaysia and $5.2 million to Vietnam.[26] In 1994, domestic infringing activities, counted as the value that counterfeit goods would have if they were legitimate products, amounted to $2.9 billion in the United States.[27] Consequently, industrialized countries sought to implement more stringent protection domestically and abroad to prevent such 'economic rent' erosion.[28] These nations have attempted to harmonize intellectual property rights worldwide by encouraging the enactment of a number of multinational agreements.[29] Thus, developing countries and least-developed countries alike were admonished to strengthen their IPR systems by joining multinational

---

22 Smith, note 18 above, 234.

23 Ibid.

24 Ibid, 219.

25 Ibid, 220.

26 EH Smith, 'Worldwide Copyright Protection Under the TRIPS Agreement' (1996) 29 *Vand J of Transactional L* 559, 568.

27 Ibid, 562–63.

28 MW Smith, note 18 above, 213.

29 E Su, 'The Winners and Losers: The Agreement on Trade-Related Aspects of Intellectual Property Rights and Its Effects on Developing Countries' (2000) 23 *Houston J of Int'l L* 169, 178.

treaties, and particularly by complying with the TRIPS requirements.[30] Otherwise, industrialized countries vowed to impose trade sanctions upon such poorer countries for failing to crack down on these infringing activities that decrease their revenues in the international market for intellectual property.[31]

B. Developing Countries Resist TRIPS Compliance

Initially, many developing countries resisted joining the TRIPS Agreement.[32] They argued that TRIPS primarily favours the interests of industrialized countries, which are the main producers of intellectual property products.[33] Further, many developing countries argued that they do not have the necessary resources to monitor and enforce intellectual property rights to the extent required by TRIPS.[34] They also complained that stronger intellectual property protection would result in a technology transfer blockade and would act as an impediment to economic development in such poorer countries.[35] Most developing countries, however, have now decided to sign on with TRIPS to avoid trade sanctions, and to possibly attract foreign direct investment.[36]

A comprehensive economic study suggests that, while TRIPS is likely initially to impact the economies of most developing countries in a negative way, the intellectual protection that it provides is sufficiently strong to stimulate foreign direct investment.[37] According to the study, the impact of TRIPS on a country will depend on the economy and current technological state of that country.[38] For instance, least-developed countries (LDCs) have little to lose (though perhaps also little to gain) by implementing the stringent intellectual property requirements of TRIPS. This is due to the fact that they do not have the necessary technology and the required know-how to pirate the intellectual property of

30 Ryan, note 17 above, 104–119.

31 Ibid.

32 FM Abbott, 'The WTO TRIPS Agreement and Global Economic Development' (1996) 72 *Chi–Kent LR* 382, 387.

33 TB Lewis, 'Patent Protection for the Pharmaceutical Industry: A Survey of the Patent Laws of Various Countries' (1996) 30 *Int'l Lawyer* 835, 838.

34 Ibid.

35 FR Romano, 'Global Trademark and Copyright 1998: Protecting Intellectual Property Rights in the International Marketplace, in International Conventions and Treaties' (1998) Practicing Law Institute 561–63.

36 Abbott, note 32 above, 388–89. CA Primo Braga *et al*, 'The Economic Justification for the Grant of Intellectual Property Rights: Patterns of Convergence and Conflict' (1996) 72 *Chi–Kent LR* 439, 446.

37 RM Sherwood, 'The TRIPS Agreement: Implications for Developing Countries'(1997) 37 *IDEA* 491, 510.

38 Ibid, 494–95.

others to the extent of deriving any significant economic benefit from such domestic infringing activities.[39] However, in certain developing countries where such infringing activities are prevalent, an initial reduction in economic activity ensues upon implementing TRIPS.[40]

C. TRIPS Compliance, Foreign Investments and Technology Transfer in Developing Countries

The adoption of TRIPS is claimed in certain cases to have produced an increase in foreign investments in developing countries.[41] To put it bluntly, developing countries with stronger intellectual property regimes are in a better position to attract knowledge-related FDI flows.[42] In other words, the adoption of TRIPS in developing countries is likely to produce an inflow of FDI to such countries.[43] Multinational enterprises may undertake horizontal FDI by investing in high-skilled products or services in industrialized countries, or in vertical FDI by investing in low-skilled products or services in developing countries.[44] As a country moves through the FDI spectrum from vertical to horizontal, intellectual property rights (IPRs) take on an increasing role.[45] Studies have shown a positive correlation between stronger IPR protection, FDI, and the transfer of technology from industrialized countries to developing countries.[46] A study based on game theory reveals that the quality of transferred technologies rises with stronger IPRs.[47] Another related study shows that product innovation and technology diffusion increase as IPRs are strengthened.[48] According to these studies, provided that developing countries possess the necessary legal

39 Ibid.

40 Ibid.

41 MW Smith, note 17 above.

42 Foreign direct investment (FDI) is the act of establishing or acquiring a foreign subsidiary over which the investing firm has substantial management control. KE Maskus 'The Role of Intellectual Property Rights in Encouraging Foreign Direct Investments and Technology Transfer' (1998) 9 *Duke J of Comp and Int'l L* 109, 119. RA Caves, *Multinational Enterprise and Economic Analysis* (2nd edn, Cambridge University Press, 1996) 25.

43 Maskus, ibid, 119.

44 Ibid, 120.

45 *Ibid*, 125.

46 RM Sherwood, 'Intellectual Property Systems and Investment Stimulation: The Rating of Systems in Eighteen Developing Countries' (1997) 37 *IDEA* 261, 350–52); E Mansfield, 'Intellectual Property Protection, Direct Investment, and Technology Transfer' (1995) (International Finance Corporation Discussion Paper No. 27) 2.

47 ELC Lai, 'International Intellectual Property Rights Protection and the Rate of Product Innovation' (1998) 55 *J of Development Econ* 133.

48 S Vishwasrao, 'Intellectual Property Rights and the Mode of Technology Transfer' (1994) 44 *J of Development Econ* 381, 399.

infrastructure to protect intellectual property rights, they are likely to attract foreign investors from industrialized countries. This is due to the fact that foreign investors are more willing to invest in countries that provide adequate legal protection for intellectual property.[49] For instance, the implementation of a stronger IPR system in Singapore permitted joint ventures with computer companies who refused to do business there before stricter laws were enforced.[50] Similarly, in the early 1990s, Poland experienced a 40-fold increase in inward FDI following its rapid liberalization and deregulation programme.[51] After showing a willingness to strengthen its IPRs, China experienced a ten-fold increase in FDI between 1990 and 1995, receiving nearly $36 billion in 1995.[52] Additionally, Mexico experienced a sharp increase in FDI following the passage of NAFTA, as did Chile.[53]

According to an empirical economic study conducted by Edwin Mansfield, who surveyed executives of major US corporations and patent attorneys, increased foreign direct investments are positively correlated with higher levels of intellectual property protection.[54] Foreign investments in the electrical, chemical, and pharmaceutical sectors increased particularly with higher levels of protection.[55] Another economic study ranking the IPRs of 18 developing countries reveals that research and development of new technology bears higher financial risks than any other commercial activity, and that stronger protection can help reduce that risk and stimulate higher levels of investment in developing countries.[56]

According to Professor Maskus, however, developing countries with weak IPRs are likely to be isolated from modern technologies and end up developing technological knowledge from their own limited resources.[57] Further, the lack of IPR protection in these countries generally results in limited incentives for domestic innovation and relatively few inward technology transfers.[58] A survey reveals that 80 per cent of surveyed chemical firms indicated that they

---

49 B Frischmann, 'Innovation and Institutions: Rethinking the Economics of US Science and Technology Policy' (2000) 24 *Vermont LR* 347, 368.

50 MW Smith, note 18 above, 238.

51 Maskus, 'Role of IPRs', note 42 above, 115.

52 Ibid.

53 Ibid.

54 Sherwood, 'IP Systems and Investment Stimulation', note 46 above, 352.

55 CA Primo Braga *et al*, 'The Relationship Between Intellectual Property Rights and Foreign Direct Investment' (1998) 9 *Duke J of Comp and Int'l L* 163, 175–76.

56 Sherwood, 'The TRIPS Agreement', note 37 above.

57 KE Maskus, 'Intellectual Property Rights and Economic Development' (2000) 32 *Case W Res J of Int'l L* 471, 487.

58 Ibid.

would not invest in India because of the lack of IPR protection.[59] Similarly, nearly all surveyed managers of foreign enterprises were reluctant to invest in certain industrial sectors in China because of the rampant counterfeiting and misappropriation practices in that corner of the world.[60]

Certain studies, on the other hand, suggest that the strength of IPRs alone cannot generate strong incentives for FDI.[61] For instance, developing countries in Sub-Saharan Africa and Eastern Europe which have adopted strong IPR systems, have attracted little FDI, while China, Brazil, Argentina, and Thailand have attracted high levels of FDI despite their weak IPRs.[62]

Overall, empirical evidence seems to favour the position that countries with stronger IPRs attract a greater influx of FDI. Stronger IPRs are viewed as a signalling device that alerts potential investors that a particular country is serious about protecting IPRs within its borders.[63] Developing countries should thus strive to adopt stronger IPR protection as such measures are likely to result in the transfer to them of modern technologies from industrialized countries.[64] The implementation of strong IPRs, as shown in the following section, is also likely to result in a spur of domestic innovation in developing countries.

D. TRIPS Compliance and Domestic Innovation in Developing Countries

Innovation in developing countries primarily consists of minor adaptations of existing technologies, which in the aggregate stimulate economic activity.[65] Modern economists, however, have advocated the position that IPRs strengthened through the implementation of the TRIPS requirements are capable of stimulating domestic innovation and inducing greater research and development in developing countries.[66] Some economists argue that the loss of domestic investors and local scientists to other countries that offer better economic

59 Maskus, 'Role of IPRs', note 42 above, 132.

60 Maskus, 'IPRs and Economic Development', note 57 above, 487.

61 KE Maskus *et al*, 'How Trade-Related are Intellectual Property Rights?' (1995) 39 *J of Int'l Econ* 227, 229–30; S Oddi, 'The International Patent System and Third World Development: Reality or Myth?' 1987 *Duke LJ* 831, 848–50.

62 Maskus *et al*, ibid, 244. Abbott, note 32 above, 390–91.

63 RM Sherwood, *Intellectual Property and Economic Development* (Westview Press, 1990), 191–93.

64 R Everson, 'Intellectual Property Rights of Appropriate Invention', in JA Roumasset and S Barr (eds), *The Economics of Cooperation: East Asian Development and the Case for Pro-Market Intervention* (Westview Press, 1992) 51, 66–73.

65 Maskus, 'Intellectual Property Challenges', note 3 above, 460.

66 Ibid, 459–60.

incentives for intellectual property is among the principal problems that retard the development of many developing countries.[67] Often, developing countries lack the necessary legal infrastructure to protect innovations and expressions of ideas, causing them to be stolen and resold to third parties at lower price, and leaving intellectual property right owners with little reward for their hard work.[68] This lack of protection, in turn, results in the loss of the incentives to invent, invest and innovate. Such lack of incentives, consequently, discourages domestic research and economic development in developing countries, and causes local researchers and scientists to look for better protection abroad.[69]

Strengthened IPRs in developing countries can also help reduce the level of risk to foreign investors and scientists, and allow them to be more comfortable in sharing their technologies and resources with poorer countries.[70] Economists have also suggested reliance on utility models as a way to help improve domestic productivity in many developing countries.[71] For instance, in Brazil, domestic producers have adapted foreign utility models to local conditions, and they have gained a large share of production in the farm machinery market.[72] Similarly, in the Philippines, the adaptation of foreign utility models to local conditions has resulted in an increased production of rice threshers.[73]

Part II Cost–Benefit Analysis of Intellectual Property Rights Systems

According to Donald Turner, seven cost elements are generally attributable to a patent system in an industrialized country.[74] The first is the administrative cost of having a patent system, including the costs of patent prosecution, examination, infringement, litigation, and enforcement. The second is the cost of giving exclusive rights to inventors for inventions that would have been produced whether or not a patent system existed.[75] The third is the cost associated

---

[67] Abbott, note 32 above, 390; Primo Braga *et al, 'Patterns of Convergence'*, note 36 above, 443.
[68] Su, note 29 above, 204.
[69] Abbott, note 32 above, 392.
[70] Maskus, 'Intellectual Property Challenges', note 3 above, 462–66.
[71] Ibid, 460.
[72] Ibid.
[73] Ibid.
[74] DF Turner, 'The Patent System and Competitive Policy' (1969) 44 *New York LR* 450, 454–55.
[75] Ibid.

with the patent misuse and antitrust violations that result from the grant of monopoly to patentees. The fourth is the opportunity cost incurred in duplicative research efforts by competitors to solve a particular problem, and to design around a patented invention. The fifth is the cost incurred by a company to secure a patent in a given product for the sole purpose of precluding other competitors from marketing the invention. The sixth is the cost resulting in inhibiting inventive activities by providing little incentive to invest in an area heavily covered by competitors. The seventh is the cost incurred by over-allocating resources in the pusuit of researches capable of securing a patent, while dedicating very few resources in other basic areas.[76]

The seven costs mentioned above are exacerbated when extended to developing countries and LDCs, since rights holders (mostly foreigners from industrialized countries) are the primary beneficiaries of IPRs in those countries.[77] For instance, most patents granted by developing countries and LDCs are granted to foreigners.[78] Often foreigners secure patents in a developing country or an LDC, not for the purpose of developing that particular technology in that country, but rather to prevent other competitors from making or selling the patented invention in that country.[79] Thus, the grant of exclusive rights to foreigners often increases the administrative costs and the costs of getting the patented product to consumers in that poorer country, and seldom results in foreign investment and technology transfer.[80] Consequently, the net social cost of a developing country or an LDC granting the majority of its patents to foreigners tends to exceed the net social benefit of that patent system in that country.[81] Further, FDI changes the demand for labour in each country, and imposes the cost of technology transfer on developing countries by requiring them to train unskilled workers to meet the greater competition.[82] Since a strong IPR system is generally a prerequisite for FDI in poorer countries, stronger IP laws displace individuals that once made a living in the market for pirated and

76 Ibid, 454–455.

77 DF Greer, 'The Case Against Patents Systems in Less-Industrialized countries' (1973) 8 *J of Int'l Law and Econ* 223, 239; United Nations Conference on Trade and Development, *The TRIPS Agreement and Developing Countries*, 63–64 UN Doc UNCTAD/ITE/UN Sales No 96.II.D.10 1996. (explaining that UNCTAD estimated the administrative costs of complying with TRIPS to be around $718,000 in fixed costs for Chile with $837,000 in annual recurrent costs; $800,000 in fixed costs for Egypt with $1 million in annual training costs; $250,000 in fixed costs for Bangladesh with over $1.1 million for judicial work, equipment and enforcement efforts).

78 Greer, ibid, 228, 230 (table).

79 Ibid, 240–42.

80 Ibid, 226–27.

81 Oddi, note 61 above, 848.

82 Maskus, 'Role of IPRs', note 42 above, 112.

counterfeit goods.[83] For instance, in Lebanon, shortly after adopting a stronger IPR system, piracy and counterfeiting activities decreased while unemployment increased.[84]

Despite the upfront costs that developing countries may face, their decision to strengthen IPRs is likely to pay off in the long run.[85] These costs are counterbalanced by the greater incentives of FDI and domestic innovation, which have been shown to be capable of stimulating the economies of developing countries.[86] Besides, as noted by Professor Maskus, some of these costs can be defrayed in part by registration and examination fees, as well as by direct financial assistance from industrialized countries, the WTO and WIPO.[87] In sum, the benefits of IPRS to developing countries are likely to exceed the costs of implementing and enforcing them.

Part III Intellectual Property, Trade, and Least-Developed Countries

A. Intellectual Property Rights in LDCs

The economies of LDCs, similarly to those of developing countries, are primarily dependent upon agricultural production.[88] Unlike developing countries, however, LDCs do not have the luxury of producing adequate agricultural products to meet their internal demands. LDCs have relatively lower gross national products (GNP) and gross domestic products (GDP) than developing countries.[89] Additionally, they have poorly developed managerial and technical capacities in the private sector, weaknesses in the public administration, and deficiencies in physical infrastructure.[90]

---

83 Maskus, 'IPRs and Economic Development', note 57 above, 489.

84 Ibid (citing KE Maskus, 'Strengthening Intellectual Property Rights in Lebanon', in B Hoekman *et al* (eds), *Catching up with the Competition* (University of Michigan Press, 2000)).

85 Ibid, 495.

86 Vishwasrao, note 48 above, 396–99.

87 Maskus, 'IPRs and Economic Development', note 57 above, 494.

88 Su, note 29 above, 197.

89 'Socio-Economic Data on Least-Developed Countries for 2004', available at <http://www.wipo.int/ldcs/en/statistics/socio_economic_data.html>. The number of LDCs in 2004 was 50, 34 of which are in Africa, nine in Asia, six in the Pacific Islands, and one in Latin America and the Caribbean.

90 See 'Criteria for the Least-Developed Countries', available at <http://www.wipo.int/ldcs/en/criteria_ldcs.html>.

Due to extremely low productivity, education, and skills, LDCs attract very little FDI.[91] Underdeveloped infrastructures, political instability, and relatively closed markets are among other factors that repel foreign investments in LDCs.[92] To the extent that strong investments are made in the infrastructure and education in LDCs, however, vertical FDI is capable of thriving in such countries since the cost of labour is so low.[93]

Further, the costs of implementing TRIPS or strengthening IPRs in LDCs are even higher than those of developing countries. LDCs require greater investment in their infrastructures in order to establish working IPRs that can assimilate the provisions of the TRIPS Agreement. WIPO and other industrialized countries have helped LDCs defray the costs of meeting the 1 January 2006 deadline to comply with the TRIPS requirements.[94] Despite such assistance, LDCs are not able to justify their share of the costs to comply with TRIPS unless they seek to obtain a greater economic return from such compliance. For instance, LDCs can derive greater economic benefits from having complied with TRIPS by seeking to integrate traditional knowledge into their national IPRs and in multinational intellectual property jurisprudence.[95]

B. Traditional Knowledge as a Valuable Tool for Economic Development

Traditional knowledge generally refers to practices, and knowledge of indigenous and local communities inherited, developed, and preserved through local traditions, culture, and folklore.[96] Traditional knowledge is thus an integral

---

[91] Maskus, 'Role of IPRs', note 42 above, 124 (citing KH Zhang, 'Theory and Evidence Regarding Multinational Enterprises and International Trade' (1996) (unpublished PhD Dissertation, University of Colorado (Boulder)) 62–64, 166 (on file with Author).

[92] Ibid, 143.

[93] Ibid, 124.

[94] Su, note 29 above, 191–92. Maskus, 'Intellectual Property Challenges', note 3 above, 466–67. *Summary of WIPO Technical Assistance for the Least Developed Countries*, available at <http://www.wipo.int/ldcs/en/ip/tech_assistance.html>.

[95] A Adewopo, 'The Global Intellectual Property System and Sub-Africa: A Prognostic Reflection' (2002) 33 *U of Toledo LR* 749, 769.

[96] DR Downes, 'How Intellectual Property Could Be a Tool to Protect Traditional Knowledge' (2000) 25 *Columbia J of Environmental L* 253, 255; G Dutfield, 'TRIPS-Related Aspects of Traditional Knowledge' (2001) 33 *Case W Res J of Int'l L*; M Johnson, 'Research on Traditional Environmental Knowledge: Its Development and its Role', in M Johnson (ed), *LORE: Capturing Traditional Environmental Knowledge*, (Diane Pub Co, reprinted 1992), 3, 4, 7–8 (defining traditional ecological knowledge as 'a body of knowledge built by a group of people through generations living in close contact with nature. It includes classification, a set of empirical observations about the local environment, and a system of self-management that governs resource use.' . . . It 'derives its explanations of environmental phenomena from cumulative, collective and often spiritual

part of the cultural heritage of local communities that have developed and preserved it.[97] Traditional knowledge has been used as a significant source for commercial research, as well as a starting point for product development in the areas of medicine and pharmaceuticals (e.g. herbal treatment, medicinal plants, botanical medicine), agriculture and horticulture (e.g. recipes, farming and fishing techniques), and toiletries and cosmetics.[98] It is estimated that 74 per cent of the 119 plant-based compounds used in pharmaceutical medicine worldwide have used traditional knowledge as a starting point to develop such compounds.[99] In 1990, an estimated $61 billion of plant-based medicine was sold in OECD (Organization for Economic Cooperation and Development) countries.[100] Similarly, in India the use of traditional crops for rice breeding amounted to annual benefits of nearly $6.1 million, about 5.6 per cent of India's rice yields.[101]

Fostering traditional knowledge can stimulate the market for eco-tourism, which will in turn attract foreign investments in the tourism sector in developing countries and LDCs.[102] A survey of international visitors to Australia conducted during the months of February and March 1993 showed that one-third to one-half of visitors were desirous to experience the indigenous culture, including local performance, tribal shows and displays of artifacts.[103] Similarly, in Kaikoura, New Zealand, between the years of 1987 and 1995, eco-tourists increased from 3,400 to 188,000.[104] A study estimates the annual gross revenue

---

experiences. Such explanations are checked, validated, and revised daily and seasonally through the annual cycle of activities.')

97 Downes, ibid.

98 KT Kate *et al*, *The Commercial Use of Biodiversity: Access to Genetic Resources and Benefit Sharing* (Earthscan Publications, 2003), 20–28; WV Reid *et al*, 'A New Lease on Life' in WV Reid *et al* (eds), *Biodiversity Prospecting: Using Genetic Resources for Sustainable Development*, (World Resources Inst, 1993), 1–52; MJ Plotkin, 'The Outlook for New Agricultural and Industrial Products from the Tropics', in EO Wilson (ed), *Biodiversity* (National Academy Press, 1988), 106–16.

99 Dutfield, note 96 above, 244; NR Farnsworth, 'Screening Plants for New Medicines', in Wilson, ibid 83, 83, 91.

100 Dutfield, ibid [243–44]; P Principe, 'Economics and Medicinal Plants', in TR Tomlinson and O Akerele (eds), *Medicinal Plants: Their Role in Health and Biodiversity* (University of Pennsylvania Press, 1998) 42, 44–45.

101 RE Evenson, 'Economic Valuation of Biodiversity for Agriculture', in Pan American Health Organization (ed), *Biodiversity, Biotechnology, and Sustainable Development in Health and Agriculture: Emerging Connections* (PAHO, Pan American Sanitary Bureau, Regional Office of the WHO, 1996) 153, 162.

102 DE Long, 'The Impact of Foreign Investment on Indigenous Culture: An Intellectual Property Perspective' (1998) 23 *North Carolina J of Int'l L and Commercial Reg* 229, 230. Tourist activities in developing countries and LDCs are known to attract foreign investors in the construction of hotels, beaches and other attractions.

103 Ibid, 231.

104 R McKelvie, 'Shooting Very Very Big Fish (with a Nikon)', *The Independent* (2 November 1997) 4, available in 1997 WL 15214307.

from the sales of indigenous arts and souvenirs to international visitors to be around $46 million.[105] Another study reveals that artisans of various Native American tribes in the Southwest of the United States earned as much as $800 million in annual sales of arts and crafts.[106] Additionally, traditional knowledge has intrinsic spiritual and cultural value to which a dollar value cannot be assigned.[107]

Contrary to popular belief, indigenous folk generally establish their own procedures for sharing and acquiring traditional knowledge, as well as local schemes for regulating and maintaining it.[108] For instance, local shamans view shamanic knowledge as a commodity that can be lent, sold, exchanged, and stolen.[109] Similarly, locals from Melanesia trade their secret knowledge for food and/or money.[110] Consequently, it should be apparent that traditional knowledge is a valuable resource in the vein of technological knowledge, and similarly to intellectual property rights, it can provide economic advantage to its owners if it is protected.

C. Need for International Protection of Traditional Knowledge

The Conference on Biological Diversity (CBD) has sought to protect the value of traditional knowledge in the 170 countries affiliated with the Conference.[111] Particularly, Article 8(j) of the CBD requires that member countries respect, preserve and maintain such traditional knowledge within their borders.[112] Article 8(j) of the CBD also gives the member countries broad discretion to promote a wider application of traditional knowledge with the permission of its holders, and to encourage the equitable sharing of the benefits from its use.[113] The CBD has further sought to create IPRs in traditional knowledge, so that developing countries and LDCs can benefit from traditional knowledge in the same way

---

105 Ibid.

106 Downes, note 96 above, 270.

107 DPA Posey, 'Preface' to DA Posey (ed), *Cultural and Spiritual Values of Biodiversity* (*Practical Action*, 1999), xvii, xviii.

108 RL Barsh, 'Indigenous Knowledge and Biodiversity, in Indigenous Peoples, Their Environments and Territories', in Posey, ibid, 73.

109 JW Hendricks, 'Power and Knowledge: Discourse and Ideological Transformation among the Shuar' (1987)15 *American Ethnologist* 216, 222.

110 L Lindstrom, *Knowledge and Power in a South Pacific Society* (Smithsonian, 1990) 119.

111 'UN Conference on Environment and Development: Convention on Biological Diversity' (5 June 1992) 31 ILM 818 (defining Biological Diversity as 'the variability among living organisms from all sources, including, *inter alia*, terrestrial, marine, and other aquatic ecosystems and the ecological complexes of which they are part; this includes diversity within species and of ecosystems.')

112 Ibid, 827.

113 Ibid.

industrialized countries benefit from technical knowledge.[114] Despite the measures adopted by the CBD, numerous multinational corporations and individuals have increasingly been misappropriating traditional knowledge from indigenous localities to secure exclusive intellectual property rights on such knowledge in industrialized countries.[115] This misappropriation of traditional knowledge for private financial gain, sometimes referred to as biopiracy, has resulted in a significant loss of the value of traditional knowledge to indigenous communities.[116] Such practices translate to an exploitation of the bioresources of poorer countries by industrialized countries.[117] Misappropriated traditional customs, folklore, and rituals of indigenous peoples are often de-culturized through streamlined processes for mass production and consumption.[118] Such bastardized commercialization of native and indigenous cultures results in a loss of the cultural and religious significance of traditional culture in the public memory.[119] According to David Howes, this de-culturization causes two harms.[120] First, it dilutes traditions, causing the fundamental beliefs of certain cultures to be undermined and misconceived.[121] Second, it disseminates traditions, resulting in a loss of control over dissemination of culturally sensitive information.[122]

114 V Date, 'Global Development and its Environmental Ramifications—the Interlinking of Ecologically Sustainable Development and Intellectual Property Rights' (1997) 27 *Golden Gate U LR* 631, 662.

115 Turmeric, a spice derived from the root of *Cucuma long*, which has a long history in India for traditional use as flavouring, food colourant, and ingredient in medicine and cosmetics, was patented in the US in 1995 for its use to make powdered tumeric, which speeds the healing of wounds (US Patent No 5,401,504). Ayahuasca, a ceremonial drink produced by shamans of indigenous tribes throughout the Amazon Basin from the bark of *Banisteriopsis* and other rainforest plants, to diagnose and heal illnesses during religious and healing ceremonies, was patented in the US for its healing properties in 1986. (Plant Patent No 5,751). The Neem tree, traditionally known in India for its uses in toothpaste and pesticide, was patented in the US in 1990 as a technique for improving the storage stability of neem seed extracts containing azadirachtin (US Patent No 4,946,681), and for a storage stable insecticidal composition that includes a neem seed with increased stability (US Patent No 5,124,349). Downes, note 95 above, 278–281.

116 S Holowick, 'Developing Nations and the Agreement on Trade-Related Aspects of Intellectual Property Rights' (2000) 1999 *Colorado J of Int'l Env L and Policy* 183, 198.

117 Ibid.

118 Long, note 102 above, 243.

119 Ibid, (giving the following examples of traditions that have lost their traditional significance in public memory due to mass production and extensive commercialization: New Zealand tourists watch performers clad in bastardized versions of traditional Maori dress perform a welcoming ceremony, although the performers have no concept of, nor appreciation for, the cultural significance of such rituals; in Peru, local workers manufacture and sell replicas of golden artefacts symbolizing Incan culture with no remembrance or connection to the heritage that created such artefacts; in the US, the names of native American tribes and historical personages have been used to name and adorn every type of good imaginable, including sports teams, T-shirts and alcoholic drinks.)

120 D Howes, 'Cultural Appropriation and Resistance in the American Southwest: Decommodifying "Indian-ness"' (1996) *Cross Cultural Consumption: Global Market, Local Realities*, 142–43.

121 Ibid.

122 Ibid.

Many commentators deplore the fact that existing IPRs in most industrialized countries provide little protection for traditional knowledge.[123] Additionally, these key players in the IP arena are even unwilling to extend international protection to traditional knowledge.[124] They often view this traditional knowledge and practices as being archaic, and as being unsuitable for IPRs since they pertain to collective rights, which have no clearly identifiable inventors.[125] Such sentiment is reflected in the TRIPS Agreement, which does not provide specifically or differentially for the protection of traditional knowledge.[126] A commentator criticizes such view as overemphasizing the role of individuals in knowledge creation, by providing them with IP protection while failing to reward knowledgeable communities that supplied the intellectual raw materials which formed the true basis for the protected work.[127] Consequently, LDCs and developing country members of TRIPS should actively lobby WIPO and WTO for international IP protection to be extended to traditional knowledge in the same way technical knowledge is protected.[128]

D. Protecting Traditional Knowledge under the TRIPS Agreement

Numerous commentators have suggested that developing countries and LDCs can craft their IPRs in such a way to comply with the provisions of the TRIPS Agreement while protecting traditional knowledge within their borders.[129]

123 'Mataatua Declaration on Cultural and Intellectual Property Rights of Indigenous Peoples', (1993) (Geneva: Commission on Human Rights, Sub-Commission on Prevention of Discrimination and Protection of Minorities, Working Group on Indigenous Populations, Doc No E/CN.4/sub.2/AC.4/1993/CRP.5).

124 JH Reichman, 'The TRIPS Agreement Comes of Age: Conflict or Cooperation with the Developing Countries?' (2000) 32 *Case W Res J of Int'l L* 441, 452.

125 J Axt *et al*, *Biotechnology, Indigenous People and Intellectual Property Rights* (Congressional Research Service, 1993), 58.

126 ML Doane, 'TRIPS and International Intellectual Property Protection in an Age of Advancing Technology' (1994) 9 *American U J of Int'l L and Policy*, 477–78. TRIPS allows the exclusion from patentability of plants, animals, and biological processes to make plants and animals, diagnostic, therapeutic, and surgical methods. 'Final Agreement, Trade-Related Aspects of Intellectual Property Rights' (1994) reprinted in 33 ILM 1125, 1197, at Art 27, s2, 3(a), (b) (hereinafter TRIPS Agreement).

127 J Boyle, *Shamans, Software and Spleens: Laws and the Construction of the Information Society* (Harvard University Press, 1996), 192.

128 P Kuruk, 'Protecting Folklore Under Intellectual Property regimes: A Reappraisal of the Tensions Between Individual and Communal Rights in Africa and the United States' (1999) 48 *American U LR* 769, 815.

129 Long, note 102 above, 263; L Petherbridge, 'Comment: Intelligent TRIPS Implementation: A Strategy for Countries on the Cusp of Development' (2001), 22 *U of Pennsylvania J of Int'l Econ L* 1029, 1033.

Particularly, a strong IP system tailored to the specific needs of developing countries and LDCs will allow them possibly to attract foreign direct investments, to stimulate domestic innovation while generating additional revenues through the protection of their traditional knowledge. Along the same line, a commentator suggests that developing countries and LDCs can maximize their economic benefits from intelligently implementing the TRIPS Agreement.[130] Particularly, the commentator proposes that, while faithfully implementing the TRIPS Agreement, LDCs and developing countries might use their internal administrative and judicial policies cooperatively, to set standards for patentability in the life science industries to exceed those of industrialized countries.[131] Such intelligent implementations of the TRIPS Agreement are likely to culminate in a surge of R&D investments due to lower costs for research and fewer acts of piracy in these countries.[132] The rationale for this approach is that, although TRIPS sets minimum IPR standards for its member countries, its requirements for compliance are cast in broad language.[133] Since TRIPS permits member countries to adopt measures to protect their own socio-economic interests, developing countries and LDCs can afford to craft their domestic intellectual property laws to curb biopiracy and de-culturization of traditional knowledge.[134]

According to these commentators, LDCs and developing countries can integrate traditional knowledge in their IPR systems by crafting each of the intellectual property branches as follows.

Patents

Under the TRIPS Agreement, a patentable invention should meet three basic requirements: industrial application (patent eligibility), novelty, and the inventive step (non-obviousness).[135] TRIPS, however, does not provide a definition for these three requirements and has left it up to the member countries to provide their own definitions regarding which inventions are new, non-obvious and patent-eligible.[136] LDCs and developing countries might profit from such broad language provided in the TRIPS Agreement, to modulate their IP system to satisfy the TRIPS requirements while allowing traditional artefacts, recipes, the practice of folk medicines, and healing techniques to be patent-eligible.

130 Petherbridge, ibid, 1033.
131 Ibid.
132 Ibid, 1038–1043.
133 Long, note 102 above, 268.
134 Ibid.
135 TRIPS Agreement, note 126 above, 1208.
136 Petherbridge, note 129 above, 1049.

For instance, they can choose to exclude traditional knowledge from any 'on sale' or 'known or used' bars that they might have adopted.

Trademarks

Developing countries and LDCs can use geographical indications to preserve the traditional goodwill and reputation of members of an established group in lieu of focusing on rewarding innovation *per se*.[137] Consequently, geographical indications and trademarks, or *sui generis* analogies to them, could serve as tools capable of curbing biopiracy while protecting traditional knowledge for the economic benefit of local and indigenous communities in developing countries and LDCs.[138] The resulting economic benefits from the use of geographical indications would then include an increase in revenues from domestic and export markets for distinctive goods originating from developing countries and LDCs.[139] Additionally, LDCs and developing countries can integrate moral right into their IP system to preserve the cultural and spiritual integrity of their costumes, rituals, and artwork.[140] TRIPS does not require moral rights, but leaves it up to individual countries to integrate them in the IP system if they choose to do so.[141]

Copyright

TRIPS requires that artistic and literary works be fixed on a material form to be protected under copyright.[142] It does not require, however, that these works be fixed on a tangible medium of expression.[143] Thus, folkloric expressions such as traditional rhythms, dances, designs, costumes, handicrafts, fables, stories,

---

137 Geographical indications are useful where consumers are willing to pay a premium on the market for products manufactured in the relevant region according to that region's traditional knowledge, innovations and practices. Downes, note 96 above, 259.

138 'Indicators of geographic origin are especially suitable for use by indigenous and local communities since they are based upon collective traditions and a collective decision-making process; they protect and reward traditions while allowing evolution; they emphasize the relationships between human cultures and their local land environment; they are not freely transferable from one owner to another; and they can be maintained as long as the collective tradition is maintained.' Ibid, 268. Ibid, 256 (suggesting the creation of new categories of IPR specifically tailored to traditional knowledge, aka *sui generis* rights).

139 Ibid, 270–71.

140 Long, note 102 above, 274–75 (Art 9 of TRIPS exempts moral rights from the Berne Convention, Art 6*bis*). Moral right prohibits the alteration of protected work without the author's permission, and protects the author's reputation, rights, and the creative value of the work. JA Cline, 'Moral Rights: The Long and Winding Road Toward Recognition' (1990) 14 *Nova LR* 435.

141 Long, ibid.

142 TRIPS Agreement, note 126 above, 1201 (Art 9 incorporating the Berne Convention, which prescribes that works be fixed in some material form to be protected under copyright).

143 Ibid.

myths, rituals, and musical and dramatic performances that are elements of traditional people's cultural identity can find a niche for national IP protection in LDCs and developing countries under the copyright provisions of TRIPS.[144] Further, the TRIPS provisions on copyright have no originality requirement and are broad enough to cover oral work.[145] Consequently, the fact that traditional folklore does not identify a particular individual as the author will not preclude it from being protected under TRIPS. In addition, various indigenous groups have used copyright law to protect their traditional knowledge.[146] For instance, Russian copyright law protects oral work, including folklore.[147] Similarly, Chinese copyright law protects *quyi*, an unfixed ritual dance and pantomime.[148] Other developing countries like Tunisia, Kenya, Cuba, and Bolivia have also incorporated folkloric expressions into their copyright laws.[149] LDCs and developing countries could study these copyright models of developing countries to craft their own copyright laws that are compliant with TRIPS while protecting traditional knowledge within their borders.

Confidential Information (Trade Secrets)

Developing countries and LDCs can develop trade secret laws that comply with TRIPS while protecting traditional knowledge.[150] Under TRIPS' adoption of Article 10 *bis* of the Paris Convention, which requires that undisclosed information be protected, folk medicines and curing techniques that have been long held secret within indigenous communities could be preserved and protected.[151]

Conclusion

Intellectual property has been widely used as a tool in industrialized countries to promote economic growth, and to acquire technological advantage on the world market. It has also been used as a viable tool for economic development

[144] Long, note 102 above, 271–72.
[145] Ibid, 273 (citing Russian Federal Law on Copyright and Neighbouring Rights, Art 6 (1993)).
[146] CH Farley, 'Protecting Folklore of Indigenous Peoples: Is Intellectual Property the Answer?' (1997) 30 *Connecticut LR* 1, 4–7 (Aboriginal artists successfully suing for copyright infringement); T Greaves, 'Tribal Rights', in SB Brush and D Stabinsky (eds), *Valuing Local Knowledge: Indigenous Peoples amd Intellectual Property Rights* (Island Press, 1996) (indigenous groups in Canada suing foreigners for copyright infringement) 25, 31.
[147] Long, note 102 above, 273 (citing Russian Federal Law on Copyright and Neighboring Rights, Art 6 (1993)).
[148] Ibid, (citing Copyright Act of the People's Republic of China, Art 3 (1990)).
[149] World Intellectual Property Organization, *Intellectual Property Reading Material* (2nd ed, 1998) 53. Long, note 102 above, 273 (citing Cuban Law of Copyright, Arts 2, 6 (1997)).
[150] Long, ibid, 279.
[151] Ibid.

in developing countries and least-developed countries. In developing countries, the implementation of TRIPS-based intellectual property systems has for the most part helped enhance domestic innovation while attracting foreign direct investments. In least-developed countries, however, such traditional implementations of intellectual property are not very cost-effective or pragmatic. For such countries, it appears that a more suitable approach should involve the protection of traditional knowledge as part of their intellectual property systems. This approach would stimulate the interests of such countries by allowing them to participate in the intellectual property process in more active manner, as well as to fully derive the economic benefits that intellectual property has to offer.

Part III

OPTIMIZING DEVELOPMENT WITHIN AND OUTSIDE INTELLECTUAL PROPERTY NORMS

10

THE LIMITS OF DEVELOPMENT STRATEGIES AT THE INTERSECTION OF INTELLECTUAL PROPERTY AND HUMAN RIGHTS*

Ruth L Okediji

* This chapter is adapted from and develops ideas based on an ongoing project on the political economy of intellectual property rights. See Ruth L Okediji, 'The International Relations of Intellectual Property: Narratives of Developing Country Participation in the Global Intellectual Property System' (2003) 7 *Singapore J Int'l & Comp L* 315.

Introduction

The objectives of intellectual property rights are traditionally justified by the public policy interests of nation states. Accordingly, for much of its history, intellectual property regulation has been a territorial matter both as to subject matter and the scope of rights recognized. Scholars and courts relied with great confidence on the axiomatic international law principle of sovereignty and its concomitant attributes, most notably the right to make laws and exercise authority over nationals, as a starting point to assess conditions under which domestic laws could be extended extraterritorially.[1] Even such assessments, however, were generally directed at accomplishing domestic interests reflected in the national law at issue: after all, no state ever purported to enact intellectual property laws in the interest of a society other than its own. The central motivation, even in the earliest efforts to extend transborder protection for intellectual property rights, was the public interest of the nation (both economic and cultural). Exchanges of reciprocal obligations were premised on benefits flowing back to the domestic polity, with any gains to foreigners viewed merely as necessary incidents of a mutually beneficial alliance.

No less is true today of the current global system, yet long-established assumptions about the domestic welfare import of sovereignty and territoriality have been formally disrupted by the advent of the Agreement on Trade-Related Aspects of Intellectual Property Rights (TRIPS Agreement).[2] The Agreement advances a historical agenda for a truly transnational law of intellectual property by requiring incorporation of globally negotiated standards into each member country's domestic system. Unlike previous multilateral treaties, which established a framework for cooperation within which shared national interests could be pursued in a coordinated fashion, the TRIPS Agreement articulates the bare elements of an international public policy deeply enmeshed in an instrumentalist vision of intellectual property rights. Prescriptively, that policy is expressed in the preamble of the TRIPS Agreement, which identifies the rationale and objectives

1 See, e.g. *Steele v Bulova Watch Co* [1952] 344 US 280, 285 ('. . . legislation of Congress will not extend beyond the boundaries of the United States unless a contrary legislative intent appears'); *United Dictionary Co v G & C Merriam Co* [1908] 208 US 260, 263 (' . . . it [is] unlikely that [Congress] would require a warning to the public against the infraction of a law beyond the jurisdiction where that law was in force'); *Dowagiac Manufacturing Co v Minnesota Moline Plow Co* [1915] 235 US 641, 225 ('[t]he right conferred by a patent under our law is confined to the United States and its territories . . . .').

2 Agreement on Trade-Related Aspects of Intellectual Property Rights (TRIPS Agreement) (15 April 1994; Marrakech Agreement Establishing the World Trade Organization, Annex 1C: 1869 UNTS 299, 33 ILM 81 (1994)).

as a desire 'to reduce distortions and impediments to international trade, . . . taking into account the need to promote effective and adequate protection of intellectual property rights, and to ensure that measures and procedures to enforce intellectual property rights do not themselves become barriers to legitimate trade . . . .'[3] The Agreement is designed to accomplish primarily the goals of free trade by, *inter alia*, 'the provision of adequate standards and principles concerning the availability, scope and use of trade-related intellectual property rights', while acknowledging 'the underlying public policy objectives of national systems for the protection of intellectual property, including developmental and technological objectives'.[4] What is left glaringly undefined is precisely how the new global obligations will contribute to national development objectives, and more critically, the sphere within which states can meaningfully exercise sovereign prerogatives directed at those objectives.

As the social and economic costs of the TRIPS Agreement continue to spiral,[5] scholars, non-governmental organizations and inter-governmental organizations have become occupied with efforts to infuse these oblique prescriptions about 'developmental objectives' with substantive force. In one sense, these efforts are largely designed to identify and more fully define doctrinal space within the TRIPS Agreement itself, in which national interests of developing and least-developed countries can be effectively pursued—a sort of legitimate inconsistency with the spirit, if not text, of the robust rights negotiated. These can be described as 'intra-TRIPS approaches' to development, which focus primarily on the flexibilities inherent in intellectual property law to counterbalance the dangers of overly strong proprietary rights. Additionally, however, immense energy has been expended in leveraging institutions and other international obligations against the edifice of the TRIPS Agreement in an effort to transform the presumptive ascendancy of the free-trade system in evaluating the obligations

3 TRIPS Agreement, ibid, Preamble.

4 Ibid.

5 Various estimates have been proffered as reflective of the economic costs of the TRIPS Agreement to developing countries. For a recent review of estimates, see e.g. Tina Rosenberg, 'Reverse Foreign Aid', *NY Times*, 25 March 2007. When I consider the costs of the TRIPS Agreement, however, I include the spate of regional trade agreements which have further weakened the ability of developing countries to work around the consequences of heightened global intellectual property standards. See, e.g. David Vivas-Eugui, 'Regional and Bilateral Agreements in a TRIPS-Plus World: The Free Trade Area of the Americas (FTAA)' (Quaker United Nations Office Publication, 2003); Maria Julia Oliva, 'Intellectual Property in the FTAA: Little Opportunity and Much Risk' (2003) 19 *Am U Int'l LR* 45, 53; Alan Story, 'Burn Berne: Why the Leading International Copyright Convention Must Be Repealed' (2003) 40 *Hous LR* 763, 772 n.41; Hernan L Bentolila, 'Lessons from the United States Trade Policies to Convert a "Pirate": The Case of Pharmaceutical Patents in Argentina' (2002–2003) 5 *Yale J L & Tech* 1.

of states to secure the welfare interests of their citizens,[6] whether they are in developed or developing countries. I will refer to these as 'inter-TRIPS approaches' to development.

Both methods of approaching the international intellectual property system have as an end the advancement of welfare, and both draw increasingly from embedded norms in the fabric of the international system to delineate legitimate grounds on which states can justify less than complete adherence to the global mandatory standards. Of the various branches of the international system that have sourced various moves and countermoves in the pursuit of global welfare, it is international human rights law which has attracted the most attention and controversy. Broadly, human rights law holds a state accountable for its relationship to its citizens by imposing obligations on governments to create and/or promote an environment (political and economic) in which human aspirations can best be pursued. Through its direct application to states, human rights law constitutes a formidable doctrinal assault on the doctrine of sovereignty and justifies direct intervention in the internal affairs of nations for the benefit of their citizens.

Historically, international economic law did not enjoy or attempt to exercise a similar prerogative. States negotiating multilateral economic agreements did so in full exercise of political sovereignty, with little accountability to a broader principle of global welfare in the implementation of internal domestic policy choices. The TRIPS Agreement, with its mandatory provisions and the requirement of oversight by an international dispute settlement system, has brought the international economic system much closer to the conceptual foundations and assumptions of the human rights framework. Member states of the World Trade Organization (WTO) now have the right to observe the intellectual property laws and regulations of other Members, and to intervene by bringing a complaint before a dispute body with enforcement powers. The pulsating rationale for such strong oversight over national intellectual property laws is that protection of these rights is beneficial to national development aspirations, even if the direct beneficiaries of enforcement are other states in the international community who enjoy the large wealth transfers that accrue to rights holders. Given the strong justification for the free trade ideal as the improvement of national welfare through open access by non-citizens into local markets, notwithstanding adverse effects on local industries, mandatory intellectual property regulation embedded in the multilateral trade system and human rights appear to have much more in common, at least structurally in the global context, than ever before.

---

[6] Laurence H Helfer, 'Regime Shifting: The TRIPS Agreement and New Dynamics of International Intellectual Property Lawmaking' (2004) 29 *Yale J Int'l L* 1 (discussing the strategy of regime shifting used by developed and developing countries).

It is not yet clear what scholars mean by a 'human rights approach' to international intellectual property rights or how human rights can effectively compel and assure development outcomes beyond the moral force of making some connection between the two regimes.[7] Although there has been a recent turn of attention to the relationship between the two bodies of law, much of the work has been devoted to identifying how human rights and intellectual property conflict, cooperate, or collide. In this chapter, I examine tensions in the efforts to use human rights law as a source of norms capable of transforming the international intellectual property regime into an instrument of development. This is a large area and I do not attempt exhaustively to address all the development-related challenges that lie at the intersection of intellectual property and human rights. Instead, I seek to explore the contours of the human rights arguments designed to aid economic development, and to link these to intra-TRIPS narratives about the welfare prospects of intellectual property law. I conclude that human rights can be used instrumentally to deflect the moral appeal of certain affirmative rights of intellectual property holders, e.g. by justifying compulsory licenses for public health, or requiring national exceptions to copyright laws in the interests of freedom of expression. Further, I begin a tentative consideration of how intellectual property law might influence human rights rather than the converse. More specifically, how might intellectual property jurisprudence take on attributes uniquely tied to the cultural conditions of developing societies (something that the dominant political strains of human rights jurisprudence currently resist), and thus effect transformations of conceptions of human rights in aid of a more meaningful and sustainable development process?

Part I The Human Rights Narrative and its Efficacy in the International Intellectual Property System

A. Sovereignty, Universality and Responsibility for Development

Scholarly analysis of the human rights/intellectual property interface tends to focus on individual human rights evaluated against requirements of intellectual property protection and vice versa. Rarely is the right to development raised as part of the discourse; instead, tracking the organization of the discipline, human

---

7 See, e.g. Laurence H Helfer, 'Human Rights and Intellectual Property: Conflict or Coexistence?' (2003) 5 *Minn IP R* 47.

rights analyses are predicated on the articulation of rights best described as procedural and affecting the zone of individual autonomy. This particular analytical approach tracks very nicely with intellectual property rights, which fundamentally reflect a view of individuality and autonomy not that inconsistent with human rights. Indeed, the TRIPS Agreement recognizes intellectual property rights as private rights, an articulation that is immediately value-laden, reflecting theoretical premises that resonate most strongly in the Continental European intellectual property tradition. On the other hand, in addition to individual rights, human rights recognize certain collective rights, of which the right to development is most critical to the intersection of development goals and multilateral intellectual property regulation.

First articulated in 1972 and adopted as a United Nations Declaration in 1986, the right to development requires an inherent balancing act between individuals, groups, peoples, and states. As conceived and designed, the right to development was intended to serve as a mechanism with which to reconcile individual and collective rights, and civil and political rights with economic and social rights. It is a human right which countries in the South have closely aligned with the importance of maintaining sovereign discretion over intellectual property law to foster economic growth. Accordingly, it is important to understand the historical context in which the development discourse and the right to development emerged.

Self-Determination as Development

The independence of many countries in Africa and Asia occasioned significant disruption in the established method and structure of relations between existing sovereign states.[8] Very quickly, polarizing cultural differences were introduced into the international environment despite assertions of 'universal principles

[8] International law became very much preoccupied with the techniques and methods of dealing with newly independent states having distinct cultural, economic, and religious identities. The rise of international institutions is largely attributed to decolonization and the process of integrating former colonies into the international system. Of course, bridging differences between political units has been a part of international law since the Peace of Westphalia. Nonetheless, the sheer number of countries that had become independent added a new dimension to the post-War commitment to institutions in which sovereign power would devolve. The structure of these institutions,permitted developing countries to advance interests, challenge actions, and otherwise add to the cost of administering international 'law.' As some scholars have argued, however, international law, through a diversity of methods, has actively engaged in marginalizing these countries by its formal insistence on a universal set of values that are at least reminiscent of, if not entirely consistent with, European political traditions and experience. The question of international law's universality remains a central part of the discipline. For explorations of these issues, and how cultural difference has been treated by international law, see, e.g. David Kennedy, 'New Approaches to Comparative Law: Comparativism and International Governance' (1997) 2 *Utah LR* 545, 569. For an account of how international law enabled colonialism

of human society' that sought at once to transcend culture and to immunize international law from the experience of non-European societies.[9] The impetus for decolonization itself was the end of World War Two, and the euphoric principles associated with liberal democracy advanced by Western states.[10] Of course, one strain of liberalism had already made its presence known in international law most brutally, even if quietly, in the justifications for colonialism offered by international law,[11] and then in the creation of the mandate system to administer the former colonies of defeated European states after World War One.[12] Under the mandate system, former colonies were put under a trust system administered by the League of Nations. As scholars have pointed out, this 'halfway house' for former colonies was not fundamentally different from the colonial experience.[13] However, in part the system reflected two things: a conscious disquiet with the condition of the liberal premise, namely the insistence on

and an ongoing manifestation of colonial attributes, see Antony Anghie, 'Finding the Peripheries: Sovereignty and Colonialism in Nineteenth Century International Law' (1999) 40 *Harv Int'l LJ* 1.

[9] See Kennedy, ibid, 563–580 (describing the relationship between international law and culture). In broad terms, liberalism supplied the principal analytical tool used for assimilating former colonies into the international community of states. However, as Antony Anghie has argued, it was positivism that defined the conditions of participation in the international system. Thus engaged with liberalism, positivism controlled the terms of assimilation of non-European states into the system. Anghie, ibid, 1; Antony Anghie, 'Colonialism and the Birth of International Institutions: Sovereignty, Economy, and the Mandate System of the League of Nations' (2002) 34 *NYU J Int'l L & Pol* 513 (noting that universality in the interwar period was liberal in character).

[10] Abram Chayes, Thomas Ehrlich and Andreas F Lowenfeld, *International Legal Process: Materials for an Introductory Course* (Little, Brown, 1968); David Kennedy, 'When Renewal Repeats: Thinking Against the Box' (2000) 32 *NYU J Int'l L & Pol* 335; Mary Ellen O'Connell, 'New International Legal Process' (1999) 93 *Am J Int'l L* 334; Anne-Marie Slaughter Burley, 'International Law and International Relations Theory: A Dual Agenda' (1993) 87 *Am J Int'l L* 205.

[11] Anghie, note 8 above.

[12] The legal basis for the mandate system was Art 22 of the Covenant of the League of Nations, which provided in relevant part:

> To those colonies and territories which as a consequence of the late war have ceased to be under the sovereignty of the States which formerly governed them and which are inhabited by peoples not yet able to stand by themselves under the strenuous conditions of the modern world, there should be applied the principle that the well-being and development of such peoples form a sacred trust of civilisation and that securities for the performance of this trust should be embodied in this Covenant.
>
> The best method of giving practical effect to this principle is that the tutelage of such peoples should be entrusted to advanced nations who by reason of their resources, their experience or their geographical position can best undertake this responsibility, and who are willing to accept it, and that this tutelage should be exercised by them as Mandatories on behalf of the League.

On the mandate system, see Quincy Wright, *Mandates Under the League of Nations* (University of Chicago Press, 1930).

[13] See, e.g. H Duncan Hall, *Mandates, Dependencies and Trusteeships* (Carnegie Endowment for International Peace, 1948). See also Anghie, note 9 above, 580–608 (describing the various goals of the mandate system and how it extended and justified the colonial exercise).

sovereignty as the criterion for participation in the international community[14] of states, and the derivative formal acknowledgement of the equality of all peoples.[15]

The end of World War Two brought about a confrontation of these two factors. Self-determination blossomed both as a principle of political organization and identity against the world, and as an internal mechanism to deal with competing claims of people groups in non-European societies,[16] whose social organization could, did, and does at times threaten the stability and authority of the new invention of the post-colonial state.[17] As Thomas Franck described:

> [s]elf-determination was soon recognized not only as a writ for obtaining colonization but . . . it achieved the status of a fundamental right of all 'peoples' and became a prerequisite for the development of 'friendly relations among nations'. In other words the concept was, at least potentially, both universalized and internationalized, in that it could be said to portend a duty owed by all governments to their peoples and by each government to all members of the international community.

Thus, self-determination was both a right and an obligation,[18] ultimately codified in several constitutional instruments of international law—the UN Charter and joint Articles 1 of the 1966 Human Rights Covenants.[19]

It is difficult to understate the theoretical and normative significance of the human right to self-determination where development discourse is concerned. Self-determination in the 1966 Covenants broadly reflected a convergence of the liberal commitment to the supremacy of the nation state as the object of international law, the legacy of positivism in deciding how statehood is acquired,

---

14 Nigel Purvis, 'Critical Legal Studies in Public International Law' (1991) 32 *Harv Int'l LJ* 81, 93–94 (defining liberalism in international law as partly a philosophy that views sovereignty as 'the foundation of international life'). See also Martii Koskenniemi, *From Apology to Utopia: The Structure of International Legal Argument* (Helsinki: Finnish Lawyers' Pub Co, 1989) 1–51 (noting the difficulty of objectifying international law).

15 Gerry J Simpson, 'Imagined Consent: Democratic Liberalism in International Legal Theory' (1994) 15 *Austl YB Int'l L* 103 ('where domestic liberal theory appeals to a conception of the individual as a bearer of rights and a democratic actor, classical liberalism substitutes the State for the individual and posits the nation-State as the free and equal object and subject of international law'). See also Purvis, ibid, 88 (offering a critique of liberal international law as, among other things, internally incoherent).

16 Thomas M Franck, *Fairness in International Law and Institutions* (Clarendon Press, 1995) 94–95.

17 Kennedy, 'New Approaches', note 8 above, 571.

18 Franck, note 16 above, 94.

19 GA Res 2200A, International Covenant on Economic, Social and Cultural Rights, UN GAOR, 21st Sess, Supp No 16 at 49, UN Doc A/6316 (1966) (entered into force 3 January 1976); International Covenant on Civil and Political Rights, UN GAOR, 21st Sess, Supp No 16, at 53, UN Doc A/6349 (1966).

the immutability of naturalism in its willingness to pierce the sovereign veil,[20] and a complicity in the acceptance of Western legal and political traditions as an objective universal truth equally applicable and, more importantly, *relevant*, to all societies. This complicity has been addressed by scholars,[21] but not with direct application to intellectual property rights.[22] Although human rights attach to people and 'peoples', it is nonetheless usually a 'state' (or the international community) that owes an obligation to ensure the satisfaction of the demands imposed by these universal values. Thus, for human rights and for intellectual property, the state is the responsible agency for implementation of these 'universalist' norms and undertakes an obligation to foster their realization in the domestic environment. Within the specific context of intellectual property rights, self-determination requires that, at a minimum, states are obligated to address innovation models consistent with sociopolitical and economic realities present in the local market and legitimate within the cultural milieu. In this regard, the human right to self-determination offers enormous implications for the kind of intellectual property framework that would be consistent with development processes;

20 Naturalism had been the dominant analytical tool of international law prior to the nineteenth century. Naturalism did not distinguish between European and non-European peoples, but asserted that a universal international law derived from human reason was applicable to all people.

21 See, e.g. Makau Mutua, 'Savages, Victims, and Saviors: The Metaphor of Human Rights' (2001) 42 *Harv Int'l LJ* 201, 243 ('[t]he human rights movement must abandon the [savage–savior–victim] metaphor if there is going to be real hope in a genuine international discourse on rights. The relentless efforts to universalize an essentially European corpus of human rights through Western crusades cannot succeed. Nor will demonizing those who resist these efforts achieve a truly international approach'). Peter van Ness, 'Introduction' to *Debating Human Rights: Critical Essays from the United States and Asia*, Peter Van Ness (ed) (Routledge, 1999), 13 ('[m]ost in the non-Western world are determined not to let the United States impose its particular definitions of democracy and human rights upon them, especially if that imposition tends to violate central moral principles of their own cultural communities'); Abdullahi Ahmed An-Na'im, 'Problems of Universal Cultural Legitimacy for Human Rights' in *Human Rights in Africa: Cross-Cultural Perspectives*, Abdullahi Ahmed An-Na'im and Francis M Deng (eds) (The Brookings Institution, 1990), 15, 15–25 (questioning legitimacy of applying individualistic Western philosophies to African culture); Makau Mutua, 'Terrorism and Human Rights: Power, Culture, and Subordination' (2002) 8 *Buff Hum Rts LR* 1, 12.

22 For an early treatment of the relationship between human rights and intellectual property, see Ruth L Gana, 'The Myth of Development, The Progress of Rights: Human Rights to Intellectual Property and Development' (1996) 18 *Law and Policy* 315. For recent scholarship dealing with this relationship, see, e.g. Helfer, 'Human Rights and IP', note 7 above, 47; David Weissbrodt and Kell Schoff, 'Human Rights Approach to Intellectual Property Protection: The Genesis and Application of Sub-Commission Resolution 2000/7' (2003) 5 *Minn IP R* 1; Sol Picciotto and David Campbell, 'Whose Molecule Is It Anyway? Private and Social Perspectives on Intellectual Property' in *New Perspectives on Property Law, Obligations and Restitution*, Alistair Hudson (ed) (Cavendish, 2003) 279; Kelley A Friedgen, Comment, 'Rethinking the Struggle Between Health & Intellectual Property: A Proposed Framework for Dynamic, Rather than Absolute, Patent Protection of Essential Medicines' (2002) 16 *Emory Int'l LR* 689; Symposium, 'The Global AIDS Crisis: Human Rights, International Pharmaceutical Markets and Intellectual Property', (2002) 17 *Conn J Int'l L* 149; Symposium, 'Intellectual Property, Development, and Human Rights' (2002) 14 *Fla J Int'l L* 147.

as a human rights matter, the state would have an affirmative obligation to attend to innovation policy. As an intellectual property matter, the state's policy choice would have to foster creative endeavour and thus improve the prospects for development through technological growth and improved capacity to absorb any foreign direct investment flows. Self-determination thus offers a context in which the sovereign obligation to steward development would justify—perhaps demand—that a state devise a means to encourage innovation, which is a proven factor in economic growth. However, self-determination would also police the boundaries of that stewardship by legitimizing inter- and intra-TRIPS efforts to ensure the appropriate level of protection to secure incentives to create, use and adapt technology locally. Pursued to a meaningful end, the right of self-determination would probably be at odds with the harmonization of core principles of intellectual property, to the extent that these are inconsistent with domestic innovative capacity, creative culture, and competitive environment.

B. Human Rights Instruments and Intellectual Property: Functional Considerations and the Human Rights Narrative

Article 27(2) of the Universal Declaration of Human Rights provides that 'everyone has the right to the protection of the moral and material interests resulting from any scientific, literary or artistic production of which he is the author'. This fundamental position is repeated in other human rights instruments, most notably the International Covenant on Economic, Social and Cultural Rights (ICESCR).[23] Article 15 of the ICESCR acknowledges the right to 'benefit from the protection of the moral and material interests resulting from any scientific, literary or artistic production of which he is the author'.[24] These human rights, worded as broadly as other major constitutional sources of intellectual property law,[25] were obscure and largely unutilized by scholars or international institutions until recently, in light of the public health crises epitomized by the HIV/AIDS epidemic in sub-Saharan Africa. This public health crisis drew significant attention to the effects of strong patent rights for pharmaceuticals—a feat accomplished by the TRIPS Agreement—and the corresponding limited

23 Note 19 above, Art 15.

24 Ibid, Art 15(1).

25 In the United States, the Constitutional authority for patents and copyright grants Congress the power '[t]o promote the progress of science and the useful arts, by securing for limited times to authors and inventors the exclusive right to their respective writings and discoveries.' US Constitution, Art 1, Sec 8, cl 8.

opportunities for developing countries to secure access to medicines.[26] But what precisely does a human right to own works of innovation or authorship mean? Correspondingly, how might a 'human rights approach' transform the current international intellectual property system in a manner meaningful to developing countries' long-term interests?

There are two ways of thinking about the function of human rights claims in the international intellectual property system. The first is to consider the human rights discipline as a *situs* for 'public rights' to the fruits of innovative endeavour on equal footing with the right of the innovator. Each claim—the public and the individual—exerts its own force within the system, thus forcing a balancing act that provides room for the exercise of limitations and exceptions to promote public access. This approach would recognize the legitimacy of intellectual property rights, while requiring the development and enforcement of norms that can effectively contain those rights in a strategic balance. In essence then, users' interests are just as 'rights-based' as the interests of owners. A second approach is to view human rights claims as a means of introducing 'strategic incoherence' into the international intellectual property system in efforts to weaken the power of developed countries during multilateral negotiations. This approach is reflected partly in the strategies of 'regime shifting' and in efforts of international institutions to incorporate intellectual property concerns more substantively in their activities.[27]

The dominant treatment of the relationship between human rights and intellectual property has been dialectic. Most of the literature frames the relationship in terms of how human rights might be used as a countervailing force against intellectual property rights.[28] This containment or 'push back' strategy is the classic

26 Nabila Ansari, 'International Patent Rights in a Post-Doha World' (2002) 11 *Currents: Int'l Trade LJ* 57, 61 (2002) ('[t]he tremendous public pressure generated by global activists led to the slashing of AIDS drugs prices by pharmaceutical companies, and an executive order from President Clinton that supported the use of compulsory licensing for sub-Saharan Africa'); Susan K Sell, 'Industry Strategies for Intellectual Property and Trade: the Quest for TRIPS, and Post-TRIPS Strategies' (2002) 10 *Cardozo J Int'l & Comp L* 79, 106 (describing global mobilization 'to highlight the public health consequences of overly broad patent rights').

27 See, e.g. 'Implementation of the International Covenant on Economic, Social and Cultural Rights, Approaching Intellectual Property as a Human Right: Obligations Related to Article 15 (1)(c)', Committee on Economic, Social and Cultural Rights, E/C.12/2000/12, 2 October 2000. See also Helfer, note 6 above.

28 For examples of this approach, see, e.g. Alicia Ely Yamin, 'Not Just a Tragedy: Access to Medications as a Right under International Law' (2003) 21 *BU Int'l LJ* 325, 327–28 (arguing that a human rights framework 'imposes an obligation to interpret [treaties and statutes relating to trade, competition, and intellectual property] in the manner that most fully advances the public's health interests'); Leonard S Rubenstein, 'Human Rights and Fair Access to Medication' (2003) 17 *Emory Int'l LR* 525, 532 ('[b]oth sources of law [human rights and IP principles] are internationally recognized based on binding treaties, but one could also argue that human rights law should actually take precedence over intellectual property law'); Haochen Sun, 'A Wider Access to Patented Drugs under

balancing posture of the human rights discipline. Human rights push back on sovereignty in face of gross abuses of individual rights. The panoply of rights seeks not coherence but balance between groups and individuals, between political and economic concerns, and between the universal and the particular. The institutional revitalization of the relationship between human rights and intellectual property has largely been the work of the United Nations Sub-Commission on the Promotion and Protection of Human Rights.

In August 2000, the Sub-Commission adopted a resolution which, *inter alia*, noted an absence of human rights concerns and principles in intellectual property agreements, and called for a human rights approach to the implementation of intellectual property rights and the development of international intellectual property systems.[29] A human rights approach to intellectual property, as framed by Resolution 2000/7 and subsequent activities in this area,[30] does not at all entail an examination of intellectual property rights *stricto sensu*. Instead, a human rights approach so far appears to mean the development of structural responses to an imbalance between owners of knowledge products and users of such products, rather than dealing with state obligations to create substantive legal regimes to address innovation needs relevant to the specific national context. Resolution 2000/7 describes merely the incompatibility between human rights and the 'implementation' of the TRIPS Agreement.[31] Therefore, the primary focus of the 'human rights approach' to TRIPS appears to be on addressing the effects of the rights, and not the subject of the rights.[32] Such an emphasis seems consistent, given the recognition of a human right in ownership of innovative endeavour.

the TRIPS Agreement' (2003) 21 *BU Int'l LJ* 101, 136 ('[i]ntellectual property protection should keep a balance between the need to provide incentives to reward and spur innovation and the need to ensure that society benefits from having maximum access to new creations. Just as too little protection of intellectual property rights can impede innovation and trade, so can too much protection undermine fundamental human rights'). See also sources listed in Helfer, 'Human Rights and IP', note 7 above, 49 n.4.

29 See Weissbrodt and Schoff, note 22 above, 25–30 (describing the adoption of Resolution 2000/7).

30 See ibid, 34–41 (describing some of these activities).

31 For example, the Resolution speaks of actual or potential conflicts that exist 'between the *implementation of the TRIPS Agreement* and the realization of economic, social and cultural rights . . .' and that 'implementation of the TRIPS Agreement does not adequately reflect the fundamental nature and indivisibility of all human rights . . .' See Preface and ¶¶2 and 9. See Helfer, 'Human Rights and IP', note 7 above, 56 (describing additional initiatives).

32 See Weissbrodt and Schoff, note 22 above, 15 (stating that 'the imbalance in the way international obligations are realized under TRIPS and the human rights treaties was a significant motivating factor in the Sub-Commission's decision to adopt Resolution 2000/7').

C. Assessing the Impact of Human Rights on Intellectual Property Norms

The acknowledgement of a human right to intellectual property suggests that, despite the tension between the two subjects, the normative roots are essentially the same, namely the recognition of the value of the human person through the protection of the fruits of creative endeavour.[33] This is typically the position advanced even by the most ardent advocates of developing country interests.[34] The very idea of protecting rights to intangible goods is, of course, a feature of ideals regarding the dignity of labour, and how fundamental labour is to life and living. At its core, the human rights discipline does not encounter intellectual property as much as it complements it; it does not resist it as much as it attempts to contain its effects. The descriptive narrative at the intersection of the right to development and intellectual property rights thus frames human rights as a redemptive discipline important to the mission of recognizing and

---

33 This reflects, in part, the Continental tradition of valuing the creator primarily in intellectual property systems. Even in the utilitarian tradition of common law countries, however, strains of natural rights are evident in intellectual property jurisprudence. See Alfred C Yen, 'Restoring the Natural Law: Copyright as Labor and Possession' (1990) 51 *Ohio St LJ* 517, 527 (describing natural law elements of early copyright law); Jane C Ginsburg, 'A Tale of Two Copyrights: Literary Property in Revolutionary France and America' (1990) 64 *Tul LR* 991, 995 ('[s]imilarly, while the law of US letters predominantly reflects and implements utilitarian policies, US law was not impervious to authors' claims of personal right. Indeed, some of the earliest US state copyright laws set forth author-oriented rationales of which any modern Frenchman would be proud—and from which some revolutionary legislators might have drawn considerable inspiration').

34 See, e.g. Peter Drahos, 'The Universality to Intellectual Property Rights: Origins and Developments' in *Intellectual Property and Human Rights* (WIPO, 1999) 33, 34 ('[l]inking intellectual property to human rights discourse is a crucial step in the project of articulating theories and policies that will guide us in the adjustment of existing intellectual property rights and the creation of new ones . . . . Viewing intellectual property through the prism of human rights discourse will encourage us to think about ways in which the property mechanism might be reshaped to include interests and needs that it currently does not'); Rosemary J Coombe, 'Fear, Hope, and Longing for the Future of Authorship and a Revitalized Public Domain in Global Regimes of Intellectual Property' (2003) 52 *DePaul LR* 1171 (articulating 'two visions—one of fear and one of hope, and, to suggest a point of reconciliation of these visions located in a broader frame of reference, the place of creativity in the international human rights framework and its integral relation to issues of cultural life and identity'); ibid, 'Intellectual Property, Human Rights and Sovereignty: New Dilemmas in International Law Posed by the Recognition of Indigenous Knowledge and the Conservation of Biodiversity' (1998) 6 *Ind J of Global L Stud* 59–115 (urging protection of indigenous knowledge as a form of intellectual property 'through the prism of the major international human rights covenants'). 'Thus, all 130 States that are party to the CESCR have international human rights obligations to ensure that the IPRs recognized in their jurisdictions are established, granted, exercised, enforced, licensed, and otherwise used in a fashion that does not infringe upon the human rights recognized in the two international Covenants. Moreover, States may have human rights obligations not simply with respect to acts of violation in their own territory of jurisdiction, but also in countries other than their own under international law principles.' Ibid, 70.

protecting the ability of people to participate in the public interest goals animating the intellectual property system. The point of the human rights narrative is not to transform intellectual property rights, nor to decry their validity. Indeed, the human rights narrative sees the intellectual property system as a constitutive part of the universal values it seeks to affirm in and among states: hence the codification of a human right to own intellectual property in both the UDHR and the ICESCR.

Further, the human rights narrative considers intellectual property rights as a *necessary* complement to the discipline's mandate.[35] According to a report by the office of the High Commission on Human Rights, '[h]uman rights and the equitable treatment of authors and inventors . . . remain the underpinnings of IP systems'.[36] The report goes on to identify how provisions of the TRIPS Agreement correspond with rights granted by the ICESCR and adds:

> [t]he TRIPS Agreement also promotes other values deemed essential for the realization of human rights. For example, the TRIPS Agreement prohibits discrimination on the basis of nationality in the area of IPRs; this is supported by the non-discrimination principles contained in the human rights instruments. The Agreement promotes the rule of law at the national level; it requires *inter alia*, the observance of due process by requiring that judicial procedures are fair and equitable, decisions are in writing and reasoned, and that parties have an opportunity to appeal. The Agreement provides for international cooperation to fight copyright piracy and trademark counterfeiting, which often have links to organized crime. The TRIPS Agreement also promotes the rule of law at the multilateral level by commonly agreed rules and peaceful settlement of disputes through a multilateral system.[37]

Consequently, a principal feature of the human rights narrative is resistance to the effects of an 'unbalanced' IP system, and not the system itself.[38] As articulated at present by most scholars, non-governmental organizations and international institutions, this narrative accepts the implicit premise of the European justification for intellectual property rights, namely the rationalization of private

---

[35] But see Helfer, 'Toward a HR Framework', note 27 above (identifying a strand of the narrative that views human rights and intellectual property as contradictory). But see Helfer, note 7 above (short version).

[36] 'Intellectual Property Rights and Human Rights: Report of the Secretary-General, ESCOR', Commission on Human Rights, Sub-Commission on the Promotion and Protection of Human Rights, 52nd Sess, Provisional Agenda item 4, §II.B.2, UN Doc E/CN.4/Sub.2/2001/12, at 7 (2001), requested by Sub-Commission and prepared by the office of the High Commission of Human Rights.

[37] Ibid, 8.

[38] The report goes on to state that '[t]he challenge of the national and international rule-maker is to find the optimal balance between various competing interests with a view to maximizing the public good, while also meeting the human rights of authors and inventors.' Ibid.

property as an aspect of liberty.[39] Further, the narrative assumes the efficacy of the intellectual property system in cultures where liberty norms might find expressions in places other than the stronghold of private property, or individualism, thus reinforcing the constraint exerted on the right to self-determination.

In essence, then, the human rights narrative in its popular rendition is a source of authority for the international intellectual property system. Within the narrative, intellectual property internalizes the universality of human rights and relegates cultural differences to the realm of the domestic as a responsibility that lies outside the purview of intellectual property as it is currently constructed. This coy interplay *within* the human rights narrative, between human rights and intellectual property, perversely allows the narrative to remain consistent with the discipline's balance between the right to self-determination and the right to own intellectual property, while undermining the essence of the right to self-determination and development.[40] In other words, having internalized intellectual property as a norm, the narrative could mandate (as it has) that it is the responsibility of *states* merely to balance intellectual property rights against other interests.[41] Consequently, intellectual property rights and the treaties that promote them arguably can and should be honoured both as a matter of positivist international law, and as a moral obligation of human rights.

This result is troubling for several significant reasons. The protection of intellectual property in the Paris and Berne Conventions is not necessarily the only way to protect creative works.[42] In other words, as I have argued elsewhere, a human right to own or enjoy the fruits of creative endeavour does not lead us inexorably to the form or scope of protection required by TRIPS.[43] If anything, a human rights conception of intellectual property would suggest that the principle of self-determination, which guarantees to a people the freedom to

---

[39] Wendy Gordon, 'A Property Right in Self-Expression: Equality and Individualism in the Natural Law of Intellectual Property' (1993) 102 *Yale LJ* 1533.

[40] Gana, note 22 above, 336–341.

[41] This is precisely the position taken in the Sub-Commission Report:

> An optimal balance within IP systems at the national and multilateral level can be reached by properly determining the definition of protectable subject matter, the scope of rights, permissible limitations and the term of protection. This balance is constantly developing, both at the national and international level, in response to economic and technological as well as political developments. The TRIPS Agreement is a minimum rights agreement that leaves a fair amount of leeway to member countries to implement its provisions within their own legal system and practice and fine-tune the balance in light of domestic public policy considerations.

Report of the S-G, ESCOR, note 36 above, ¶7.

[42] Steven Shavell and Tanguy van Ypersele, 'Rewards Versus Intellectual Property Rights' (2001) 44 *JL & Econ* 525 (arguing that an optional reward system is superior to an intellectual property rights system).

[43] Gana, note 22 above, 323–326, 339–341.

determine their social, legal and political institutions—in essence, the right to self-governance—is the platform on which the content of Article 27(2) of the Universal Declaration of Human Rights is guaranteed, as the sole prerogative of the people or a state.

The effect of legitimizing the particular form of intellectual property embodied in the international agreements reflects an entrenched acceptance of the political ideals about property, liberty, and personhood that have long been foundational to Western liberal democracies. The universality of human rights through the agency of intellectual property rights may also be understood as continued affirmation of values inconsistent with non-European cultures, whether the intellectual property rights are 'balanced' or not. In other words, it can often be politically expedient for countries to assert that human rights and intellectual property rights are fundamentally incompatible with traditional societal culture. Finally, it is crucial to note the perverse effect and irony of using human rights discourse to limit a human right. Human rights then must serve as an arbiter between the equally valid claims of owners who have a human right to their intellectual creations, and users who have a right to demand from the state the conditions by which they can pursue their own welfare.[44] The state may address the demand of users in ways that do not involve violations of intellectual property rights, such as state purchase of the works in question. Using intellectual property rights to subsidize social welfare is, in the views of some, arguably just as serious a violation of human rights as is protecting intellectual property rights in a way that imperils public health and safety, or that limits investments in enforcing private rights to the full.[45]

These concerns about the limitations of the human rights narrative are amplified when we move from the context of essential medicines and access to drugs to the

---

[44] Owen Lippert, 'One Trip to the Dentist Is Enough: Reasons to Strengthen Intellectual Property Rights Through the Free Trade Area of the Americas' (1998) 9 *Fordham IP Media & Ent LJ* 241, 267 (arguing for strong IP protection on the grounds that IP rights are human rights): '[t]he court of world opinion would rightly condemn a country if it argued that upholding human rights imposed an unfair competitive disadvantage. Property rights are human rights, and intellectual property rights are property rights. All deserve respect.' Robert J Gutowski, Comment, 'The Marriage of Intellectual Property and International Trade in the Trips Agreement: Strange Bedfellows or a Match Made in Heaven?' (1999) 47 *Buff LR* 713, 745, 746:

> A common criticism levied against the TRIPS Agreement maintains that it violates the sovereign right of nations to development; however, Western industrialized countries contend that intellectual property rights are natural, human rights and are so recognized in the Universal Declaration of Human Rights (UDHR). TRIPS accentuates the tension between these discordant 'regimes of rights'. While those opposed to TRIPS see international protection of IP and the sovereign right to development in direct conflict, TRIPS adherents view these rights as complementary—that in order to develop, nations must recognize and employ IP protection.

[45] Lippert, ibid.

relatively banal and non-life-threatening domain of literary and artistic works. Limited access to copyright works may hinder long-term development prospects, but this is unlikely to evoke the emotive responses that are so intensely associated with the discourse over the effects of intellectual property rights. When the effects of TRIPS implementation cannot be measured in loss of human life, the human rights narrative loses much of its intuitive moral appeal and political force. This is not unlike the traditional tension between political human rights which enjoy strong approval and emphasis by developed countries, and economic human rights which have received significantly less attention, if not outright rejection as 'human rights'.

The implications of an uncritical application of human rights norms to affirm TRIPS and post-TRIPS agreements are echoed in an important discussion between two leading scholars regarding the relationship between international human rights and international trade. Professor Ernst-Ulrich Petersmann has argued in a robust collection of writings for the constitutionalization of economic rights, thus equating the right to trade (and by extension intellectual property) with other fundamental human rights which he argues are essential features of a democratic state.[46] In contesting the normative premises relied on by Professor Petersmann, Professor Philip Alston warns of the danger of 'epistemological misappropriation' evident in the argument that the international economic order of the WTO complements the guarantees of human rights.[47] As Alston argues, this kind of a 'human rights approach to trade' will 'fundamentally redefine' the contours of the human rights discipline with serious negative consequences.[48] The economic rights that emerged triumphant at the conclusion of the Uruguay Round are not '*per se* recognized as economic rights within the framework of international human rights law'.[49] Alston stresses that such rights arising from WTO agreements, including the TRIPS Agreement, which is arguably consistent with Article 15 of the ICESCR,

46 Ernst-Ulrich Petersmann, 'Time for a United Nations "Global Compact" for Integrating Human Rights into the Law of Worldwide Organizations: Lessons from European Integration' (2002) 13 *Euro J Int'l L* 621; ibid, 'Human Rights and International Economic Law in the 21st Century: The Need to Clarify Their Interrelationships' (2001) 4 *J Int'l Econ L* 3; ibid, 'Constitutionalism and International Organizations' (1996) 17 *Northwestern J In'tl L Bus* 398; ibid, 'How to Constitutionalize International Law and Foreign Policy for the Benefit of Civil Society?' (1999) 20 *Mich J Int'l Law* 1; ibid, 'Legal, Economic and Political Objectives of National and International Competition Policies: Constitutional Functions of WTO "Linking Principles" for Trade and Competition' (1999) 34 *New Eng LR* 145.

47 Philip Alston, 'Resisting the Merger and Acquisition of Human Rights by Trade Law: A Reply to Petersmann' (2002) 13 *Eur J Int'l L* 815.

48 Ibid, 816.

49 Ibid, 822.

> should not be considered to be analogous to human rights. Their purpose is fundamentally different. Human rights are recognized for all on the basis of the inherent human dignity of all persons. Trade-related rights are granted to individuals for instrumentalist reasons. Individuals are . . . empowered as economic agents for particular purposes and in order to promote a specific approach to economic policy . . . . Instrumentalism should not be confused with a human rights approach.[50]

Uncritically deployed outside of the context of self-determination, the human rights narrative affirms the premise that developing countries lag behind economically *because of* their failure to develop institutions of private property and the rule of law, and emphasizes the importance of protecting these 'indispensable ingredients' as human rights guarantees, effected through liberal trade and competition laws without any need to consider historical, cultural or global conditions that undeniably have significant effects on how economic development is best enhanced in poor countries.[51]

In focusing on the effects of the TRIPS Agreement, the human rights narrative falls far short of steering state responsibility to address core development concerns related to intellectual property regulation, including the adequate supply of public goods such as education and basic R&D, infrastructure to support cultural industries, and the design of laws that can accommodate unique aspects of the creative enterprise in collective societies. Undoubtedly, the current narrative is an important response to the serious and immediate threat to human life with respect to public health. Nonetheless, the narrative must outlast the current crisis—to do so, it must develop tools that will facilitate meaningful inquiry to assess how innovation is best stimulated in developing countries and whether or how intellectual property rights can aid that process in the current global scheme. Put differently, the human rights narrative must seriously re-engage the content of specific human rights guarantees and determine whether intellectual property rights *as they exist and in light of the conditions that produced them* can ever truly be reconciled with the core principles of international human rights law, which requires state and global attention to local conditions affecting the realization of

---

50 Ibid, 826.

51 To quote Petersmann,

> [w]herever freedom and property rights are protected, individuals start investing, producing and exchanging goods, services and income. Personal self-development and enjoyment of human rights require the use of dispersed information and economic resources that can be supplied most efficiently, and most democratically, through the division of labour among free citizens and through liberal trade promoting economic welfare, the freedom of choice and the free flow of scarce goods, services and information across frontiers in response to supply and demand by citizens . . . The moral 'categorical imperative' of maximizing personal autonomy and equal liberties across frontiers corresponds with the economic objective of maximizing consumer welfare through open markets and non-discriminatory competition.

Petersmann, 'Time for a UN Global Compact', note 46 above, 621.

improved social conditions. A framework for such consideration is partly evident in the Statement of the Committee on Economic and Cultural Rights.[52] The next major inquiry will be to develop a model consistent with the fundamental mission of the corpus of human rights norms. In this regard, it may be possible to conceive of human rights as a tool for redistributing *political* responsibility for development by requiring developed countries to address intellectual property rights as part of their human rights monitoring systems, not just to ensure conformity to global standards but also to evaluate how those standards have improved the welfare aspirations of the polity.

Part II Culture as Development and International Intellectual Property

A. The Relationship Between Culture and Human Rights: Are Cultural Claims Tenable?

Despite philosophical traditions that yield distinctive doctrines in intellectual property, the two major approaches to the justification of rights are uniformly European: the common law and civil law traditions. Globalization and ongoing efforts at harmonization continue to exert pressures for the essentialization of the normative underpinnings of each tradition. As several authors have pointed out, however, the traditions reflect cultural histories that are more alike than different.[53]

Cultural narratives of intellectual property are closely related to the human rights narrative and are premised generally on the principle of self-determination.[54] They typically begin with what I have described elsewhere as 'the rhetoric of difference'. The cultural narratives seek to maintain and sustain the legitimacy of differences between the interests, priorities, and preferences of developing countries, rather than overcome or manage those differences. The argument starts generally with the proposition that developing countries have different value systems, engage in creative endeavour for different reasons, and are organized communally through kinship ties rather than as individuals. These differences in

52 'Substantive Issues Arising in the Implementation of the International Covenant on Economic, Social and Cultural Rights, Human Rights and Intellectual Property', Statement by the Committee on Economic, Social and Cultural Rights, 14 December 2001, E/C.12/2001 15 (setting forth principles for assessing the human rights-compatibility of intellectual property rights).

53 Ginsburg, note 33 above; Yen, note 33 above.

54 Coombe, 'IP, HR & Sovereignty', note 34 above, 81 ('[t]hrough the concept of intellectual property rights we deploy widely accepted Western assumptions').

values, organization, and heritage in developing countries, the narrative argues, require different considerations for intellectual property rights to be meaningful. Most recently, the focus of the cultural narrative has been on the subject of protection for indigenous knowledge.

Indigenous knowledge 'refers to the knowledge held, evolved and passed on by indigenous peoples about their environment, plants and animals, and the interaction of the two'.[55] While indigenous knowledge does not often meet the criteria for current forms of intellectual property, the appropriation of such knowledge to produce commercially viable products has proved highly controversial.[56] In particular, the contributions of local citizens typically are never acknowledged, neither is any remuneration paid to them. This distinct problem has generated proposals for 'benefit-sharing' agreements[57] and other means by which traditional knowledge might be protected from appropriation.[58] Almost uniformly, participants in the cultural narratives reject the viability of intellectual property rights

---

55 Erica-Irena A. Daes, 'Some Observations and Current Developments on the Protection of the Intellectual Property of Indigenous Peoples' (23 July 1998) (available at <http://www.wipo.int/documents/en/meetings/1998/indip/pdf/daes.pdf>).

56 Larry Rohter, 'Brazil Moves to Protect Jungle Plants From Foreign Biopiracy' *NY Times*, 23 December 2001, A4; Andrew Pollack, 'Patenting Life: A Special Report; Biological Products Raise Genetic Ownership Issues' *NY Times*, 26 November 1999, A1.

57 The concept of 'benefit sharing' gained visibility in the Convention on Biological Diversity. Convention on Biological Diversity, 5 June 1992, 31 ILM 818, 837 (1992). It includes equitable arrangements between indigenous people and patent holders, and is designed to ensure that 'genetic resources or traditional knowledge are obtained on mutually agreed terms and with the approval of the traditional holders of that knowledge.' Vandana Date, '"Global "Development" and its Environmental Ramifications—The Interlinking of Ecologically Sustainable Development and Intellectual Property Rights' (1997) 27 *Golden Gate U LR* 631, 666–67; Gerard Bodeker, 'Traditional Medical Knowledge, Intellectual Property Rights & Benefit Sharing' (2003) 11 *Cardozo J Int'l & Comp L* 785, 799 ('[t]he concept of benefit sharing in the development of herbal medicines has only recently begun to find its place in the intellectual property sphere'). One of the most detailed articles about benefit sharing in the indigenous knowledge context is Ikechi Mgbeoji, 'Patents and Traditional Knowledge of the Uses of Plants: Is a Communal Patent Regime Part of the Solution to the Scourge of Bio Piracy?' (2001) 9 *Ind J Global L Stud* 163.

58 Shuba Ghosh, 'The Traditional Terms of the Traditional Knowledge Debate' (2001) 11 *Cardozo J Int'l & Comp L* 497 (noting modes of legal protection of traditional knowledge along four lines: (1) a 'public domain' model, where certain basic biological, genetic or other information is treated as unowned but appropriable; (2) a 'trust' model, where certain basic biological, genetic or other knowledge is treated as a sort of communal 'resource' by 'trustees' for the benefit of designated 'beneficiaries;' (3) a 'commercial use' model, where ownership rights in certain basic biological, genetic or other information are assigned to the first party to reduce such knowledge to a commercially marketable product; and (4) a 'private property' model, where rights in certain biological, genetic or other information are assigned by the geographically superordinate sovereign within which such resources are located and treated as the assignee's 'private property'); ibid, 'Traditional Knowledge, Patents, and the New Mercantilism (Part II)' (2003) 85 *J Pat & Trademark Off Soc'y* 885, 887 (suggesting an approach to establishing state regimes to protect indigenous knowledge from exploitation).

for indigenous knowledge.[59] The arguments tend to focus on the purposes for which creativity and creative works are used in developing countries, and the limited nature of intellectual property rights to protect the spiritual, religious, or moral interests associated with traditional knowledge.[60]

The cultural narratives seek to address or argue for the recognition and protection of innovation in developing countries under alternative systems. A vital component of these narratives also argues for the incorporation of non-European values into the international system. In both these efforts, however, the narratives overemphasize the cultural differences between intellectual property and indigenous knowledge, and underemphasize the cultural relevance of intellectual property rights to all societies. Specifically, the cultural narratives essentialize creativity in *developed* countries. As in developing countries, creativity in developed countries is motivated by different interests and reflects a diversity of values. Particularly with respect to copyright, these values are inevitably a reflection of cultural dynamics. The cultural narratives also implicitly accept the artificial standards of what constitutes patentable or copyrightable subject matter in order to make the argument for why intellectual property rights will not or cannot appropriately address the interests of peoples in developing countries.

B. Inventing a Cultural Intellectual Property Law

Creativity in developing countries may not be 'fixed' as required by copyright, or 'novel' as required by patent laws. Authorship and ownership may be difficult to determine in a communal setting, and 'non-obviousness' or utility may be an unwieldy standard for much of the innovation that occurs in developing countries. But these reasons do not ineluctably require a unique system of protection to accommodate these distinctions. To insist that this is the only or ideal response to the international intellectual property system is to accept Eurocentrism as the metric for the 'global' consensus. In essence, arguing *for* difference *because*

59 See, e.g. Paul Kuruk, 'Protecting Folklore Under Modern Intellectual Property Regimes: A Reappraisal of the Tensions Between Individual Rights and Communal Rights in Africa' (1999) 48 *American LR* 769 (asserting that IP laws are inadequate to protect indigenous knowledge); Christine Haight Farley, 'Protecting Folklore of Indigenous Peoples: Is Intellectual Property the Answer?' (1997) 30 *Conn LR* 1, 4 ('[a]pplication of intellectual property laws, whose underlying logic is to facilitate dissemination, is fundamentally inappropriate to prevent sacred indigenous images from circulation and re-use'). But see Helfer, 'HR and IP', note 5 above; Helfer, 'Toward a HR Framework', note 27 above.

60 Kuruk, ibid; Haight Farley, ibid. See also Ruth L Gana, 'Has Creativity Died in the Third World? Some Implications of the Internationalization of Intellectual Property' (1996) 24 *Denv J Int'l L & Pol'y* 109.

of difference exalts cultural dominance instead of challenging it; the status quo remains intact.

It is true that the value system and forms of creativity differ in developing countries. However, these differences in themselves do not justify the need for an entirely separate system of protection.[61] In the first place, such a strategy continues the disparate treatment between what is considered 'European' and what is considered 'different'. As mentioned earlier, the fact is that the criteria for granting patent or copyright are themselves culturally contingent.[62] Arguing that cultural differences make traditional knowledge unsuitable for protection under the intellectual property system ascribes a scientific validity to European-based intellectual property criteria that simply is not sustainable. For example, new technologies have stretched and, in some cases, transformed long-standing assumptions of intellectual property.[63] Cultural narratives tend to ignore the fact that the criteria for intellectual property change with time and with technology. There is an inherent elasticity in intellectual property categories that has sustained the institution of intellectual property throughout the centuries. Thus, as I have argued elsewhere, if there was a desire to admit them, certain types of creative work in indigenous societies and developing countries could fit comfortably within the modern intellectual property system.[64] To opt for an alternative is to avoid rather than confront the presumption of propriety associated with the current system.

Finally, the alternative to intellectual property proposed by the cultural narratives is to protect traditional knowledge under the 'customary law' of developing countries.[65] The narrative has ignored critical anthropological literature that demonstrates that customary law is not a product of dynamic indigenous life, but instead reflects indigenous interaction with colonial power, as institutionalized through the apparatus of colonial institutions. The path-breaking work of scholars such as Sally Falk Moore and Martin Chanock shows in historical detail how customary law 'was constituted out of the residue left after the colonial

[61] See generally Ruth L Okediji, 'Making Room at the Table: The Protection of Indigenous Knowledge at the Interstices of Human Rights, International Law, and Intellectual Property Law' (mimeo, 2004).

[62] Margo Bagley, 'Patently Unconstitutional: Geographical Limitations on Prior Art in a Small World' (2003) 87 *Minn LR* 679; ibid, 'Still Patently Unconstitutional: A Reply to Professor Nard' (2003) 88 *Minn LR* 239.

[63] Consider, for example, business method patents, the extension of copyright to cover software, para-copyright protection for content protection devices, and other recent developments.

[64] Okediji, note 61 above.

[65] Ibid.

modification of the [indigenous] . . . polity.'[66] What was an indigenous law metamorphosed into a new and discrete body of rules constructed, modified, or contrived between colonial and local rulers. Indigenous law was 'transposed' into a political and legal system set up by the colonial power, and applied in a socio-economic context altered both by the slave trade and colonial rules; hence, the essence of a true indigenous law was lost.[67] As Martin Chanock sums it up:

> The law was the cutting edge of colonialism, an instrument of the power of an alien state and part of the process of coercion. And it also came to be a new way of conceptualizing relationships and powers and a weapon within African communities which were undergoing basic economic changes, many of which were interpreted and fought over by those involved in moral terms. The customary law, far from being a survival, was created by these changes and conflicts. It cannot be understood outside of the impact of the new economy on African communities. Nor can it be understood outside of the peculiar institutional setting in which its creation takes place. African legal conceptions, strategies and tactics are formed both by the impact of capitalism and by the interaction of the communities thus affected with the concepts, strategies and power of British colonial legal institutions.[68]

The many diverse permutations of colonial rule as administered by various European powers lie beyond the scope of this chapter. But some highlights are worth noting. Commercial trade was the principal focus of initial interaction between European and non-European peoples. Eventually, this gave way to formal colonial rule either 'directly', by extending European laws to the territories as is generally associated with the French system, or 'indirectly' as in the style of rule perfected by the British, which utilized local institutions, law, and custom to enforce British laws, and thus blended local institutions with the colonial administration. Under both systems, regular invocations of pre-colonial customs or rules (approved by the colonial power, of course) were used to govern civil disputes between the indigenous populations. Criminal matters, or matters relating to interests that might bear directly on the objectives and interests of the European powers and their ability to control the territories, remained subject to European laws.[69]

66 Sally Falk Moore, *Social Facts and Fabrications: Customary Law on Kilimanjaro, 1880–1980* (Cambridge University Press, 1986), 317.

67 See generally ibid.

68 Martin Chanock, *Law, Custom and Social Order: The Colonial Experience in Malawi and Zambia* (Cambridge University Press, 1985) 4.

69 RF Betts and M Asiwaju, 'Methods & Institutions of European Domination' in A Adu Boahen (ed), *Africa Under Colonial Domination 1880–1935* (University of California Press, 1985) 324 (describing this practice as a 'dyarchical judicial arrangement'); Richard Roberts and Kristin Mann, 'Law in Colonial Africa' in Roberts and Kristin Mann (eds) *Law in Colonial Africa* (Heinemann, 1991) 3; Patrick Manning, *Francophone Sub-Saharan Africa, 1880–1995* (Cambridge University Press, 1998) 58, and generally at 57–78.

Regardless of its form, eventually the administration of European power had the same purpose of recreating non-European societies in Europe's image pursuant to the 'civilizing' mission of colonial powers. Literacy occupied a chief place in measuring what constituted a civilized people.[70] Ultimately, social changes in European society, combined with technology changes propelled by industrialization, made it possible for the balance of power between European powers and non-European peoples, in Africa particularly, to shift in favour of Europeans, who subsequently demanded and then imposed or superimposed European legal concepts to govern interactions with the local citizens.[71] The profound transformation occasioned by literacy, and later by the Industrial Revolution, shaped the European perception of their civilizational superiority, justifying their attempts to 'civilize' non-Europeans.[72] As expressed by Lord Lugard,

> [w]e develop new territory as Trustees for Civilisation, for the Commerce of the World . . . . As Roman imperialism laid the foundations of modern civilisation, and led the wild barbarians of these islands along the path of progress, so in Africa to-day we are repaying the debt, and bringing to the dark places of the earth, the abode of barbarism and cruelty, the torch of culture and progress, while ministering to the material needs of our own civilisation.[73]

Intellectual property law, which has played only an incidental role (if any) in the literature on the relationship between international law, colonialism, and developing countries, is paradigmatic of the motives, strategies, and justifications of the colonial experience in Africa and Asia, particularly as they reflected race consciousness.[74] European law was the central tool of control, power, influence,

---

70 David Armitage, 'Literature and Empire' in 1 *The Oxford History of the British Empire: The Origins of Empire* 100 (Oxford University Press, 1998) (listing printing as one of the skills distinguishing Europeans from non-Europeans).

71 Bruce Waller, 'Europe and the Wider World' in *Themes in Modern European History, 1830–90* (Unwin Hyman, 1990) 285–86 (listing armed steamboats (i.e. gunboats) and improvements in weapons technology such as the invention of the rifle as examples of innovations that enabled European powers to conquer non-European peoples).

72 See Gana, 'Has Creativity Died?', note 60 above, 112–116 (describing the link between European ideals of civilization, literacy and, more subtly, race).

73 FD Lugard, *The Dual Mandate in British Tropical Africa* (William Blackwood and Sons, 1922), title page.

74 A vital and growing body of international law scholarship has explored the link between race and international law, specifically in the justification of the colonial exercise. See, e.g. Anghie, 'Finding the Peripheries', note 8 above; Antony Anghie, 'Francisco de Vitoria and the Colonial Origins of International Law' (1996) 5 *Soc & L Stud* 231; BS Chimni, *International Law and World Order* (Sage Publications, 1993); Symposium, 'International Law and the Developing World: A Millenial Analysis' (2000) 41 *Harv Int'l LJ* 595; Symposium, 'Critical Race Theory and International Law: Convergence and Divergence' (2000) 45 *Vill LR* 827; Colloquium, 'International Law, Human Rights, and LatCrit Theory' (1997) 28 *U Miami Inter-Am LR* 177; James Thuo Gathii, 'Alternative and Critical: The Contribution of Research and Scholarship on Developing Countries to International Legal Theory' (2000) 41 *Harv Int'l LJ* 263; Ruth Gordon, 'Critical Race Theory and International

and change in the European colonies. So called 'customary laws' were in reality a synthesis of European values and local practices acceptable to the ruling authorities, with the application of local laws shaped by European institutional implementation.[75] To replace intellectual property categories with cultural customary law simply replicates, it does not escape, colonial history. Perversely, invocations of customary law neglect that customary law, as currently conceived in most African societies, is subject to static precedent, particularly in former British colonies such as Nigeria and Ghana. While a dynamic customary system for the protection of innovation in developing countries could be contrived, the challenge will remain how to 'translate' domestic customary protection into the global system of protection. It is in this relationship between the 'customary' and the 'modern' that innovation in developing countries is vulnerable to reincarnation as yet another form of intellectual property.

Part III Finding Development Goals in Intellectual Property Doctrine

A. Doctrinal Coherence and Normative Claims

Given incessant demands for ever-increasing levels of protection by intellectual property owners, commentators and members of the general public in developed countries have begun to consider the impact of strong intellectual property rights on public welfare in the United States.[76] The unexpected and unprecedented success of the TRIPS Agreement actually masked an uninterrupted agenda of strengthening protection for rights, as well as strengthening of rights *per se*, at home and abroad. In response, important doctrinal limitations to rights have been revived and advanced vigorously by academics, some policy makers, and public interest groups concerned about the destabilization of intellectual property policy and its effect on domestic welfare. Indeed, global welfare and domestic welfare became intertwined for the first time, thus providing

Law: Convergence and Divergence' (2000) 45 *Vill LR* 827; Elizabeth M Iglesias, 'International Law, Human Rights, and LatCrit Theory' (1997) 28 *U Miami Inter-Am LR* 177.

75 See generally Chanock, note 68 above; Falk Moore, note 66 above; Roberts and Mann, note 69 above.

76 See generally Lawrence Lessig, *The Future of Ideas: The Fate of the Commons in a Connected World* (Random House, 2001) (criticizing the growing scope of copyright and patent protection); Rosemary J Coombe, *The Cultural Life of Intellectual Properties* (Duke University Press, 1998) (arguing that copyright and trademark law can be used to suppress dissent); Jessica Litman, *Digital Copyright* (Prometheus Books 2001) (attacking recent extensions of copyright law).

developing countries with authoritative doctrinal arguments with which to delimit the incursion of intellectual property rights on their domestic legal frameworks. In essence, the vulnerability of knowledge goods to appropriation attendant to the effects of globalization intensified interest-group tactics of coordinating forces in an effort to entrench strong intellectual property rights on a global basis.[77] This compelled the convergence of public interest concerns worldwide, yielding a compelling body of literature that identifies how the expansionist trend undercuts the very goals of intellectual property in the Western tradition.

But the narratives comprise more than the concerns of developing countries and I focus here on the general arguments for limitations on international intellectual property rights, rather than specific prescriptions for developing countries. To start, I should observe that limitations to intellectual property rights serve to constrain sovereignty in much the same way as human rights. Rather than relying on the political weakness of developing countries to institute domestic welfare norms in the intellectual property framework, crafting limitations into the very fabric of the global system may serve to hold governments explicitly accountable for limitations as part of their trade and human rights obligations under international law.

Further, the doctrinal narratives look within intellectual property doctrine to make arguments about welfare-enhancing tools beneficial to developing countries. The narratives begin with an empathetic acknowledgment of the difficulty faced by developed countries by the challenge of the Information Revolution and the transition to a knowledge economy.[78] Doctrinal narratives mostly do not challenge the propriety of intellectual property protection *per se*, nor question its efficacy for stimulating innovation in developing countries. Indeed, a fundamental attribute of doctrinal narratives is the acceptance of the basic rationale of intellectual property rights in developed countries: that market failures justify the interdiction of property rights over public goods.

77 Saul Levmore, 'Property's Uneasy Path and Expanding Future' (2003) 70 *U Chi LR* 181, 186 (describing intellectual property rights as the product of interest-group pressures); Justine Pila, 'Bound Futures: Patent Law and Modern Biotechnology' (2003) 9 *BU J Sci & Tech L* 326, 365 (noting key role of 'effective lobbying' by the biotech industry in obtaining support for global patent protection); Susan K Sell, 'Trade Issues and HIV/AIDS' (2003) 17 *Emory Int'l LR* 933, 942 (tracing history of industry lobbying for global IP protection); Nermien Al-Ali, 'The Egyptian Pharmaceutical Industry after Trips—A Practitioner's View' (2003) 26 *Fordham Int'l LJ* 274 (describing industry lobbying at 1994 TRIPS negotiations).

78 Jerome H Reichman, 'From Free Riders to Fair Followers: Global Competition Under the TRIPS Agreement' (1996/97) 29 *NYU J Int'l L & Pol* 11; Frederick M Abbott, 'Protecting First World Assets in the Third World: Intellectual Property Negotiations in the GATT Multilateral Framework' (1989) 22 *Vand J Transnat'l L* 689.

Finally, doctrinal narratives do not necessarily oppose the extension of intellectual property to developing countries. Indeed, some variants within the narrative affirm the long-held position that intellectual property protection as defined and practiced in the United States is a positive economic value universally applicable for the good of all peoples, including those that live in different economic and cultural conditions.[79]

B. Doctrinal Coherence in International Intellectual Property Law

The major focus of the doctrinal narratives is the extent to which the US constitutional imperative of the 'progress of Science and the useful Arts', intended to benefit the public, has been sabotaged by private capital with organized access to the legislative process. Thus, the doctrinal narratives have, as their essence, a public choice problem and an economic welfare problem. As to the public choice problem, the question is how to ensure that legislation is affected and influenced by interests other than those of the owners of intellectual property. The implicit assumption, of course, is that what constitutes the 'public interest' is not itself embedded in the second contested problem, namely what measure of welfare most reflects the public interest.

The debates on this particular issue are not unfamiliar and the answers are not self-evident. For present purposes, the point is that the doctrinal narratives, like the human rights narratives, assume the essential rightness and universality of the current intellectual property system. In these narratives, developing countries are not the central objects at all. Instead, developing countries are part of an intellectual toolkit useful in the fight against the domestic aggrandizement of intellectual property owners. Essentially, developing countries at the international level serve as the 'public' face in defending or protesting demands for higher rights in multilateral fora. As a strategic matter, developing countries ameliorate the public choice problem that is cardinal to international law, namely the

[79] Robert M Sherwood, 'The TRIPS Agreement: Implications for Developing Countries' (1997) 37 *IDEA* 491, 544 ('it can be expected that developing countries will experience the solid economic benefits which flow from robust protection of intellectual property' once an adequate public administration is put in place); Anthony D Sabatelli and JC Rasserthe, 'Impediments to Global Patent Law Harmonization' (1995) 22 *N Ky LR* 579, 619:

> developing countries will not be able to participate adequately in world trade and encourage investment and technology transfers unless the need for strong and effective international patent protection is recognized. Initially, it may be difficult for the developing nations to upgrade their systems to conform to those of the developed nations. However, such conformity ultimately would be in their economic best interest because of the economic investments that would be encouraged.

inability of non-state actors to participate meaningfully in the development of international legal norms.[80] The important benefits of the doctrinal limitations in Western intellectual property law have become powerful tools for developing countries in circumscribing the expansive reach of the TRIPS and TRIPS-Plus regimes.[81]

The doctrinal narratives start from the baseline of American intellectual property discourse, utilitarianism. The narratives hold firmly to the ideals of welfare inherent in the policy objectives behind the recognition of proprietary interests in knowledge goods, and advance powerful legal, economic, and policy arguments directed at sustaining the robustness of the welfare component of intellectual property. The insistence on limits to the proprietary interests of intellectual property owners forced a powerful marriage between public interest advocates in developed countries and developing countries, concerned over the exercise of rights in their markets and the implications for their citizens for accessing protected material, be it drugs, literary works, or the benefits of the internet.

From a developed country perspective, the convergence of interests between public interest groups in the developed world and developing countries was of immense strategic importance in allowing these groups to overcome the public choice problem domestically by transferring the *locus* of the battle to international fora. In such international fora, developing countries with the requisite characteristics for participation in treaty negotiation (i.e. statehood and membership in the international institution) were able to advance arguments for limitations to treaty rights, at times supplementing these with normative constraints imposed by other agreements, such as the International Undertaking for Plant Genetic Resources,[82] or the Convention on Biological Diversity,[83] or more recently, the Convention on the Protection and Promotion of the Diversity of Cultural Expressions.[84]

---

80 In a positivist framework, this is still the case, although a notable feature of modern international relations is the strong presence of non-governmental organizations and other non-state actors, including most recently private interest groups.

81 For an influential account of an example of this phenomenon, see Pamela Samuelson, 'The US Digital Agenda at WIPO' (1997) 37 *Va J Int'l L* 369; Julie E Cohen, 'WIPO Copyright Treaty Implementation in the United States: Will Fair Use Survive?' (1999) 21 *Eur IP R* 236.

82 Available at <ftp://ftp.fao.org/ag/cgrfa/iu/iutextE.pdf>.

83 (1992) 31 ILM 818 (entered into force 29 December 1993).

84 Available at <http://portal.unesco.org/culture/en/ev.php-URL_ID=33232&URL_DO=DO_TOPIC&URL_SECTION=201.html>.

C. Advancing a Global Intellectual Property Jurisprudence: Whither Development?

While the instrumentalist face of intellectual property has helped to advance the interests of developing countries in obtaining access to protected goods, access is neither the end of what developing countries seek, nor is it the only interest at stake in a global intellectual property system. As both the human rights and cultural narratives suggest, the deeper question for developing countries is whether and how intellectual property rights make sense, given the present realities of life in these regions. Doctrinal narratives are vitally important in resisting the wholesale propertization of knowledge goods. However, they cannot replace the fundamental need of developing countries to determine how to stimulate innovation domestically, or whether intellectual property rights as constructed can viably contribute towards long-term economic development. The doctrinal narratives will likely remain a vital part of developing country engagement in the international intellectual property system. Practically speaking, doctrinal limitations in developed countries constitute an easy target for containing intellectual property expansion, since the presence of these limits (in domestic settings of countries arguing for stronger global intellectual property rights) makes the limitations arguably *de facto* legitimate under current international standards. The doctrinal narratives, as all the other narratives, offer a means for developing countries to translate their concerns within the existing context of the international economic system. However, they cannot substitute for a real discourse about the adequacy and relevance of the norms that underlie intellectual property rights with respect to developing countries.

International intellectual property treaties reinforce the fundamental assumption of international law, that developing countries are somehow endued, by their christening as 'sovereigns', with the freedom to interact with intellectual property in a way that is culturally meaningful, economically sustainable, and politically feasible. Yet the TRIPS Agreement fundamentally undermines that sovereignty by restraining the exercise of sovereign discretion to shape domestic intellectual property policy. Efforts to maintain a balanced intellectual property system, by creating resistance through the deployment of human rights doctrine and principles, or through contested cultural claims about indigenous knowledge, or by imposing limitations on recognized rights, all fall short of addressing how development can occur within the current global context, and whose responsibility it is to ensure that the prescriptive policy that identifies intellectual property as a development tool is endued with political and legal force. The narratives, in essence, are a discourse of interaction, not a reflection of the realities of the encounter between peoples of developing countries and the international intellectual property system.

Conclusion

Intellectual property rights have been extended to developing countries in an unbroken historical chain lasting over 500 years. Over the course of this period, international law has yielded doctrines that have been instrumental to the political independence of these countries and, to a lesser extent, through human rights law, political, social, and economic guarantees for the people groups and individuals of these countries. The manifestation of economic guarantees remains an issue in international law that is contested in terms of which particular mix of market and other institutions, particularly legal, will produce optimal results for development. In the highly technological age of the twenty-first century, the regulation of intellectual property occupies a crucial role in this debate. The narratives of developing country participation in the global system all seek to redeem the system from its own problematic history by restructuring terms of engagement between developed and developing countries to facilitate development objectives. To do so effectively will require as a minimum that the right of self-determination be considered as a means to re-engage sovereign responsibility for creating and enforcing domestic innovation systems conducive to the interests, cultural claims, and economic goals of the domestic polity. Such systems might look exactly like modern intellectual property regimes, or not. The crucial issue is to hold states and the global community accountable for their claims, via the TRIPS Agreement, that development goals can be pursued effectively within a harmonized system of mandatory rights. In the absence of evidence to support the success of the TRIPS Agreement as a development tool, a human right to own the fruits of creative enterprise cannot justify the social and economic costs of underdevelopment associated with insufficient access to existing technology and the failure of policy mechanisms to encourage domestic innovation.

11

A NETWORKED RESPONSIVE REGULATORY APPROACH TO PROTECTING TRADITIONAL KNOWLEDGE

Peter Drahos

Introduction

The origin of the link between traditional knowledge (TK) and biodiversity can probably be said to lie in a US proposal at the Governing Council of the United Nations Economic Programme in 1987 for a comprehensive treaty on the conservation of biodiversity.[1] That proposal initiated a sequence of events

[1] K ten Kate and S A Laird, The Commercial Use of Biodiversity (Earthscan, 1999) 4.

that ultimately led to the Convention on Biological Diversity (CBD) being opened for signature in 1992.

The CBD established a clear link between TK and biodiversity, most notably in Article 8(j), which creates obligations to preserve and maintain TK that relates to preservation and sustainable use of biodiversity. Since the CBD came into operation, an ever-increasing range of actors and policy networks have become involved in the issue of the protection of TK.[2] There has been an explosion of meetings, dialogues, workshops and policies on TK. Even more impressive has been the rapid production of regulatory norms at national and international levels. These norms range from hard law (for example, national statutory access regimes for biological resources and the protection of TK) to soft law (for example, model laws) to non-law forms (for example, codes of ethics and protocols).[3] In a decade or so, TK has come from policy obscurity to being an object of plural regulation.[4] Within the World Intellectual Property Organization (WIPO) an Intergovernmental Committee on Intellectual Property and Genetic Resources, Traditional Knowledge and Folklore (IGC) was established in 2000. The calls by member states for the IGC to draft and present to the WIPO General Assembly a legally-binding international instrument to protect genetic resources, traditional knowledge, and folklore have led to a set of draft 'Revised Provisions for the Protection of Traditional Knowledge' (Revised TK Provisions).[5]

The Revised TK Provisions could clearly form the basis of a treaty. But treaties may also arrive on the international scene as dead letters, their promised benefits never being seen. There is also the danger of symbolic regulation. A concerned public is assured, by the passage of fine-sounding legislation, that the problem in question has been dealt with; as a result public attention moves on to the next drama; in reality, the legislation (for one reason or another) does nothing to solve the problem. Intellectual property treaty law has its historical examples of symbolic regulation. In the 1960s the demands of developing countries for a better deal on copyright and textbooks eventually led, in 1971, to an Appendix to the Berne Convention for the Protection of Literary and Artistic

---

2 Overviews can be found in G Dutfield, *Intellectual Property Rights, Trade and Biodiversity* (Earthscan, 2000); C Correa, 'Traditional Knowledge and Intellectual Property', Discussion Paper, Quaker United Nations Office, Geneva, 2001; 'Intellectual Property Needs and Expectations of Traditional Knowledge Holders', WIPO (2001); The Crucible II Group, *Seeding Solutions*, Vol 1 (IPGRI, DHF, IDRC, 2000); C Bellman, G Dutfield and R Meléndez-Ortiz (eds) *Trading in Knowledge* (Earthscan, 2003) Chaps. 16–21.

3 There are dozens of these. See the list that is kept in relation to Art 8(j) at the CBD website: <http://www.biodiv.org/programmes/socio-eco/traditional/instruments.aspx?grp=GLN>.

4 Gervais observes that one reason why traditional knowledge has become an important international issue has to do with the increasing political influence of aboriginal communities. See D Gervais, *The TRIPS Agreement: Drafting History and Analysis* (2nd edn, Sweet & Maxwell, 2003) 57.

5 The draft provisions can be found in WIPO/GRTKF/IC/9/5.

Works which contained special provisions regarding developing countries.[6] These provisions did little to help developing countries solve the problem of gaining access to textbooks at affordable prices.[7] Similarly, the signs are that the recent decision of the WTO on the implementation of paragraph 6 of the Doha Declaration, concerning access to medicines by countries that lack pharmaceutical manufacturing capacity, will do very little in practical terms to solve those capacity problems.[8]

The purpose of this chapter is to suggest that, if a treaty on TK is to avoid the fate of becoming a failed promise, it has to be part of a larger regulatory strategy, a strategy that the treaty can itself help to coordinate. TK poses enormous challenges for policy and regulation because it is an intimate form of knowledge that is tied to people and localities and often relies on non-written forms of transmission and reproduction. Once information is captured through some process of codification (for example, a births and deaths register, patents register, a manual, etc) it becomes much easier to regulate for its preservation and uses. Much of TK is not recorded and registered. It is a matter of debate as to whether it should be.[9] Its continued existence is dependent on the survival of local cultural practices in a world where markets operate to commodify and standardize assets so that they can be sold to those who value them the most in economic terms. The tendency of markets to commodify and standardize as part of the process of achieving economies of scale means that markets are generally better at eliminating local customs than preserving them.

Drawing on the theory of responsive regulation and the regulatory pyramid, this chapter outlines the elements of a responsive regulatory response to TK and suggests a role that a treaty might play. In particular, the chapter argues that a treaty should concentrate more on the coordination of the enforcement of existing norms than on the setting of new standards. Over the last decade or so the proliferation of regulatory norms for TK has been remarkable, but the monitoring and enforcement of these norms has not received much attention. Yet it was enforcement that was the *raison d'être* of the Agreement on the Trade-Related Aspects of

---

6 See P Drahos with J Braithwaite, *Information Feudalism: Who Owns the Knowledge Economy?* (The New Press, 2002) 77.

7 See, for example, 'The Copy/South Dossier: Issues in the economics, politics, and ideology of copyright in the global South', The Copy/South Research Group, April 2006, available at <http://www.copysouth.org>.

8 See 'Implementation of paragraph 6 of the Doha Declaration on the TRIPS Agreement and Public Health', Decision of the General Council of 30 August 2003, WT/L/540, 1 September 2003. For the reasons why the decision is unlikely to work, see P Drahos, 'Four Lessons for Developing Countries from the Trade Negotiations Over Access to Medicines', (2007) 28 *Liverpool LR*, 11.

9 See J Gibson, *Community Resources: Intellectual Property, International Trade and Protection of Traditional Knowledge* (Ashgate, 2005) 141–145.

Intellectual Property Rights (TRIPS). It was the desire of US companies to be able to enforce international obligations with respect to intellectual property that led the US, in the 1980s, to link intellectual property to the trade regime.[10] Following this enforcement theme, the chapter argues that the key to enforcement in TK lies in the creation of an international enforcement pyramid. The coordinated use of this pyramid requires an international agency. The chapter suggests one possible model for such an agency in the form of the Global Bio-Collecting Society.

Part I Regulation, Responsive Regulation and Networks

Regulation used to be thought of as an activity carried out by governments using the tools of law. This traditional command–control model of regulation has been replaced by a multidimensional model which recognizes that non-state actors and non-legal norms also regulate.[11] At the core of the multidimensional model of regulation is the view that regulation is 'the intentional activity of attempting to control, order or influence the behaviour of others'.[12] So, for example, when a multinational threatens a government with the closure of a plant employing many people unless it receives some important economic concessions, and the government complies with its demand, the government is being regulated by that multinational. Confining the definition of regulation to the agency of states using law does not change the empirical reality that control and influence in the world has many agents and methods. Studying the intentional use of normative mechanisms by different actors lies at the heart of modern regulatory scholarship.

One distinctive approach to regulation is responsive regulation.[13] Responsive regulation is based on the idea that regulatory responses must take into account the motivations and conduct of those being regulated, and these must guide the

---

[10] See, for example, M Ryan, *Knowledge Diplomacy: Global Competition and the Politics of Intellectual Property* (Brookings Institution Press, 1998); Drahos with Braithwaite, note 6 above; D Matthews, *Globalising Intellectual Property Rights* (Routledge, 2002); S Sell, *Private Power, Public Law: the Globalization of Intellectual Property Rights* (Cambridge University Press, 2003).

[11] For an excellent overview of the decentred understanding of regulation see J Black, 'Critical Reflections on Regulation' (2002) 27 *Aust J of L Philosophy* 1.

[12] Ibid.

[13] The approach is developed in I Ayres and J Braithwaite, *Responsive Regulation: Transcending the Deregulation Debate* (Oxford University Press, 1992).

degree of intervention by the regulator. Its most distinctive idea is that the tools of regulation can be ordered in a way that enhances self regulation, thereby reducing the actual need for governmental coercion, while at the same time retaining it as an answer for some kinds of regulatory problem. Known as the enforcement pyramid, this approach always begins with persuasion and dialogue. If this does not work, the regulator moves up the pyramid, using responses that are increasingly severe. Creating an international enforcement pyramid for TK is key to a strategy of regulation for TK, because the actors that are most interested in the enforcement of ownership norms concerning TK are also likely to have the weakest capacity to take an enforcement action of some kind. For example, Indonesia, a country of some 200 million people and rich in TK, has approximately 40 registered patent attorneys, with only about ten of those having a full practice.[14] An indigenous group that was seeking advice on a matter related to TK and patents would find it difficult to take the first basic step of finding someone in Indonesia that could provide advice and expertise. Filling this kind of radical capacity deficit represents the next phase of protecting TK.

The example of the Indonesian capacity problem could be solved if the indigenous group gained access to networks that had the expertise and technical competence to solve patent-related problems. Access to networks, as a means of increasing capacities and power, has become a key theme of social science theory.[15] Increases in power occur when individuals enrol others with capacity and resources to help them achieve a goal. Power is less a matter of sovereign command over others, and more a matter of building a network of agents willing to share resources and information to achieve a common purpose. The potentially serious problems of coordinating a large network over time and space have been greatly reduced by information technology.[16] Recently, some have argued that even greater gains in power and capacity can be obtained by tying existing networks together—the networking of networks.[17] So, for example, a network of computer software companies, of the kind led by the Business Software Alliance, can do a lot to further an agenda of stronger enforcement of intellectual property rights. But even more can be accomplished if they join

14 Interview by the author in the Indonesian Patent Office, 24 January 2006.

15 Much of this work draws on Latour's theory of power: B Latour, *Science in Action* (Harvard University Press, 1987).

16 M Castells, 'Materials for an exploratory theory of the Network Society' (2000) 51 *British J of Sociology*, 5.

17 P Drahos, 'Intellectual Property Rights And Pharmaceutical Markets: A Nodal Governance Approach' (2004)77 *Temple LR*, 401; J Braithwaite, 'Methods of Power for Development: Weapons of the Weak, Weapons of the Strong'(2004) 26 *Michigan J of Int'l L*, 297.

with other networks of film studios and recording companies to persuade the US government to make the enforcement of intellectual property rights a global priority. When already powerful networks join forces regulatory achievements on a global scale can be achieved.

The strategies of building networks, enrolling others into those networks and then networking networks are also available to weak actors. In fact, in the modern world of networked governance these strategies are the only means by which weak actors have a chance of achieving their goals. By definition they lack capital or other sources of power that enable them to act alone. Drawing on the insights of networked governance, this chapter shows how capacity deficits in the enforcement of TK can be overcome using a networked regulatory pyramid.

There is another reason why this chapter argues for an approach based on networked responsive regulation for TK. Responsive regulation is an approach that places great emphasis on understanding the context of a regulatory problem, and the forms of self regulation and market structure that have evolved in a given business sector. Understanding the customary base of a given sector of business regulation is fundamental, because regulation that fails to engage with business is likely to fail altogether.[18] This emphasis on context and custom is crucial for the successful regulation of TK. It is simply a fact that there is enormous cultural and customary diversity amongst the owners of TK.[19] This means that any given problem over the use of TK is likely to be a stand-alone problem because the customary base of the TK in question will be unique. As a WIPO fact-finding mission observed 'traditional societies often have highly-developed, complex and effective customary systems for TK protection'.[20] The sheer diversity of customary systems for TK means that each problem relating to the use of TK will need an individually crafted solution that is responsive to the context of that particular problem. Under a responsive regulatory approach the specific customary institutional base of TK would be the natural starting point for solving individual problems.

18 J Braithwaite and P Drahos, *Global Business Regulation* (Cambridge University Press, 2001) 31.

19 For some sense of the huge variety of customary law in general see A Dundes Renteln and A Dundes (eds), *Folk Law: Essays in the Theory and Practice of* Lex Non Scripta, Vols 1 and 2 (University of Wisconsin Press, 1994).

20 *Intellectual Property Needs and Expectations of Traditional Knowledge Holders*, WIPO (2001), 221.

Part II Do We Need a Treaty on TK?

Treaties are costly to negotiate. They may also end up as dead letters. In the case of a treaty on TK it is worth drawing attention to Paul Heald's observation that there is an emerging consensus amongst scholars around the world that there is too much intellectual property protection.[21] General scepticism about the value of more and more intellectual property protection does not necessarily lead to a case against a treaty on TK, but it does at least raise the issue of whether a treaty is needed, and the closely related issue of what form the treaty might take. Paul Heald's point is part of a larger argument about the nature of intellectual property policy in the international arena. New forms of intellectual property are much more the product of the politics of rent-seeking than they are the product of careful social welfare analysis.

Applying the economics of intellectual property protection to TK is anything but straightforward. To begin with, TK is the paradigmatic example of group innovation that takes place over time. Well and truly before anybody thought of the term 'sequential innovation', indigenous communities were engaged in a collective process of incremental improvement of their various techniques and products.[22] Group innovation does not fit with the assumptions of conventional models of intellectual property protection. Conventional intellectual property systems operate on the assumption that it is possible to identify an individual or individuals who can claim clear title to an innovation that itself can be clearly demarcated. Once innovation is located in groups and complex networks, and the innovation itself takes the form of a living body of knowledge, rather large entitlement and demarcation problems start to surface. It becomes difficult, for example, to decide which individuals can claim ownership, what exactly is the subject of ownership, and how, if at all, ownership is extinguished. These problems exist for all forms of group innovation, but they are especially pressing for TK innovation because groups are so dominant in the innovation process.

There is another line of economic thinking that points away from an intellectual property-based model of TK protection. One of the important observations that came out of WIPO's fact-finding missions was that there was a great

21 P Heald, 'The Rhetoric of Biopiracy' (2003) 11 *Cardozo J Int'l & Comp L*, 519.

22 Sequential innovation involves successive inventions, each being an advance on its predecessor. See J Bessen and E Maskin, 'Sequential Innovation, Patents, And Imitation', Working Paper, Department of Economics, MIT, revised 2002, available at <http://www.researchoninnovation.org>.

deal of uncertainty about how to value TK.[23] This uncertainty is especially salient in the case of TK, because TK, if it is used by a company, will most likely be used as a further input into research by that company. At the time the knowledge is disclosed or the genetic resource handed over to a company, the value of that information cannot be fully known by either party. As Kenneth Arrow noted in his seminal discussion of market failure in innovation markets 'the value of information for use in developing further information is *much more conjectural* than the value of its use in production and therefore *much more likely to be underestimated*' (emphasis added).[24]

The possible implications of uncertainty over the economic value of TK are considerable. If developing countries commit themselves to a treaty that significantly raises the costs of TK to companies, the value of which is already uncertain, then the effect will most likely be to dampen demand.[25] This is particularly so if there are less costly substitutes available (for example, combinatorial chemistry, searching in non-member countries, exploring microbiological diversity in unregulated areas, etc).[26] The effect of a treaty, therefore, might be to discourage the commercialization of TK. WIPO's fact-finding mission suggests that at least some indigenous groups would be happy with this outcome, but clearly this would not meet the desires of the countries that are members of the Megadiverse Group. These countries see important commercialization possibilities in the field of TK.[27]

Economic analysis can provide some insight into the costs and benefits of a treaty-based approach to TK, but cannot itself answer the question of whether we ought to protect TK. This, in the final analysis, is a matter of moral argument. However, to some extent states may already be locked in to more concrete action

[23] Note 20 above, 230.

[24] K Arrow, 'Economic Welfare and the Allocation of Resources for Invention', reprinted in P Drahos (ed), *Intellectual Property* (Ashgate, 1999) 14.

[25] In this context it is worth noting that the effect of the CBD may be to have dampened demand for access to genetic materials. ten Kate and Laird report that one change in business practice as a result of the CBD is 'a decrease in corporate collecting': note 1 above, 323. Also, Brazilian scientists have called upon the Brazilian government to reform its laws to make it easier for scientists to collect genetic materials for non-commercial purposes, and the government has done this. See 'Brazil's biopiracy laws are stifling research' available at < http://www.scidev.net/content/news/eng/brazils-biopiracy-laws-are-stifling-research.cfm>, and 'Brazil eases restrictions on biodiversity researchers' available at <http://www.scidev.net/content/news/eng/brazil-eases-restrictions-on-biodiversity-researchers.cfm>.

[26] On this point see J Watal, *Intellectual Property Rights in the WTO and Developing Countries* (Aspen, 2001) 171. On the shift by pharmaceutical companies from searching at the macroscopic level to the microscopic, see 'Prospecting in New England Waters' (1995) 5(4) *LabNotes*, available at <http://www.mbl.edu/publications/pub_archive/labnotes/5.3/bioprospecting.html>.

[27] See para l of the Cancun Declaration of Like-Minded Megadiverse Countries.

on TK as a result of the web of international human rights standards that have emerged in treaty law, or through state practice or activity on this topic in international organizations.[28]

There is increasing evidence that TK is linked to a very obvious human rights issue—the survival of the holders of TK. A Composite Report in the CBD points out that in very many areas of the world indigenous groups are the victims of national governments rather than their partners:

> The report on Australia, Asia and the Middle East draws attention to the problem of persecution and lack of recognition of indigenous peoples, and other traditional knowledge holders, as one of the main causes of traditional knowledge loss. [29]

There are similar kinds of observation about other regions of the world. The Composite Report then goes on to make a fundamental observation about traditional knowledge:

> [A]ccess to the land upon which traditional knowledge is based, together with the opportunity to practice it, is paramount for retention of traditional biodiversity-related knowledge.[30]

Beneath the complexity of protection for TK there are two basic issues that have to be confronted and usually are not. First, protection for TK cannot be separated from human rights protection for indigenous peoples. Second, the protection of TK is inextricably linked to protection of land rights of indigenous people. These two issues are fundamental, and yet most of time they are ignored by a technocratic discourse aimed at developing models of protection for TK that treat TK independently of its holders and its links to land and territory. The drive by government policy makers to encourage the documentation and codification of TK, thereby opening up the possibility of it becoming an asset that can be protected independently of those who produce it, takes on sinister connotations. Little wonder that many indigenous groups are suspicious and distrustful of the documentation drive.

The answer to our question of whether a treaty on TK is needed is Yes, because such a treaty can help to strengthen the protection of the human rights of TK holders. The protection of TK has to be responsive to the values and practices of TK holders. The advantage of using a treaty to constitute such a regulatory

---

[28] L R Helfer, 'Human Rights and Intellectual Property: Conflict or Co-existence?' (2004) 22 *N'lands Quarterly of Human Rights*, 167; H M Haugen, 'Traditional Knowledge and Human Rights' (2005) 8 *J of World Intell Prop*, 663.

[29] See 'Composite Report on the Status and Trends Regarding the Knowledge, Innovations and Practices of Indigenous and Local Communities Relevant to the Conservation and Sustainable Use of Biodiversity', UNEP/CBD/WG8J/3/4, 6.

[30] Ibid, 6.

strategy is that treaties bind signatory governments. More importantly though, a framework treaty that articulates general principles may evolve over time into a powerful international regime with a high rate of compliance. Using framework treaties to build a regulatory strategy is an option that weak actors need to take seriously. There are many examples of treaties that begin as 'vague and platitudinous' and end up as highly specific and with an enforcement regime.[31] Many treaties in fact disappoint the aspirations of their original architects, but then over time, as opportunities and state groupings change, such treaties may evolve into something of genuine significance.[32]

Obviously, a framework treaty is the first critical step in this process because it creates the 'contracting space' for the evolution of more specific and enforceable obligations. Importantly, the WIPO Revised TK Provisions contain a set of comprehensive principles that could easily be incorporated into a framework treaty on TK. The globalization of a regulatory regime usually begins as a contest of principles in which different actors push in various ways for abstract principles that underpin the evolution of rules. Principles, as it were, lure parties into a process of adjustment and compromise. The principles in the Revised TK Provisions have been refined through WIPO's consultation and consensus approach and so form a natural starting point for inclusion in a framework treaty.

TK is an area that is characterized by radically different perceptions by actors as to what is or is not a problem, fragile alliances, and a diversity of actors with different values and goals. An obvious example of radically different perceptions is the long-running debate between developed and developing countries over the relationship between TRIPS and the CBD which started in the WTO with the review of Article 27.3(b) of TRIPS. Some groups see a need to harmonize the two agreements in order to avoid conflict, while others see no conflict in the first place.[33] Fragile alliances beset the TK issue. Developing country governments that advocate strong TK protection are also sometimes the same governments that are named by NGOs like Human Rights Watch for violations of the human rights of indigenous groups, especially in the context of land rights.[34] Following a cartelist logic, in 2002 a group of 12 countries representing roughly 70 per cent of the world's biological diversity met at Cancun in Mexico

---

31 Braithwaite and Drahos, *Global Business Regulation*, note 18 above, 620.

32 Ibid, 619–20.

33 See generally, 'The Protection of Traditional Knowledge and Folklore: Summary of Issues Raised and Points Made', Note by the Secretariat, IP/C/W/370, 8 August 2002.

34 The Crucible Group, noting the complexities of relations between indigenous groups and governments, recommended that governments adopt Art 29 of the Draft Declaration on the Rights of Indigenous Peoples. See The Crucible II Group, note 2 above, 78.

and formed the Group of Like-Minded Megadiverse Countries.[35] The Cancun Declaration that launched the Megadiverse Group contains a sweeping agenda that includes the pursuit of a new international regime for the fair and equitable sharing of benefits which arise from the use of biodiversity. Yet individual members of the Megadiverse Group have signed free-trade agreements with the US that undermine the position of the group on issues fundamental to it, such as a mandatory obligation to disclose the country of origin for biological materials and any related TK, when intellectual property rights are being sought over those materials.[36]

TK in international fora is a world characterized by multilayered debates, nested agendas, and opaque political games. In this world actors find it hard to read each other's motives and true positions. Trust and cooperation skate on the thinnest ice. In this negotiating jungle the prospects of obtaining a detailed rule-intensive treaty with a raft of enforceable obligations on TK appear slim. This is especially so when neither the US nor the EU can be said to have an overriding interest in seeing a treaty on TK emerge. In the absence of a hegemonic actor in favour of globalizing standards of protection for TK, the only way forward for weak actors, who would like to see a treaty, is to adopt the framework approach.[37]

The upshot of this Part is that the best strategy for TK holders is to use a framework treaty to establish guiding principles for the protection of TK, and then work towards an enforceable global regulatory regime that will support their rights. The justification for such a treaty lies in moral and legal obligations that states have under international standards of human rights protection. In the Part that follows, some of the elements that might make up this framework approach are discussed.

---

35 Brazil, China, Colombia, Costa Rica, Ecuador, India, Indonesia, Kenya, Mexico, Peru, South Africa and Venezuela. Since then Bolivia, Malaysia and the Philippines have joined the group. See Cancun Declaration of Like-Minded Megadiverse Countries, note 27 above.

36 A mandatory disclosure requirement remains a goal of the group. See the New Delhi Ministerial Declaration of Like Minded Megadiverse Countries on Access and Benefit Sharing, New Delhi, 21 January 2005. The US proposal is that issues related to use of genetic materials and traditional knowledge should be dealt with at the *point of access* to those materials rather than at the *point of commercialization*. See WTO Secretariat, 'The Protection of TK', note 33 above, 10. The US–Peru FTA contains an 'Understanding Regarding Biodiversity and Traditional Knowledge' (dated 12 April 2006) which states that the Parties recognize that access and benefit sharing issues 'can be adequately addressed through contracts'. This would appear to support the US position in the WTO much better than it supports the goal of the Megadiverse Group.

37 Sometimes a hegemonic actor, acting unilaterally, can globalize a form of regulatory protection. However, even in the case of the powerful actor certain conditions have to hold. The US was successful with its strategy of globalizing semiconductor chip protection using the principle of reciprocity, because foreign manufacturers in Japan and Europe wanted access to the lucrative US market, industry interests were concentrated, and there was only a small number of countries with which it was important for the US to come to a reciprocal arrangement (Japan was the other main producer in the 1980s). See Braithwaite and Drahos, *Global Business Regulation*, note 18 above, 76.

Part III Elements of a Framework Treaty on TK

A. Defining TK

A lot has been written about the legal terms appropriate to use to describe the knowledge assets of indigenous groups, local people, or traditional groups.[38] It is fairly clear that no one definition commands universal support. A report prepared by the WIPO Secretariat neatly summarizes the situation:

> There is . . . a diffuse range of potentially overlapping terms in current use in international, regional and national discussions related to TK, corresponding with a wide range of policy frameworks. Terms are not neutral, and the choice of term is neither arbitrary nor irrelevant.[39]

As a general observation one might say that perfect connotative definitions of subject matter are not usually the stuff of legal definition in any case. Rather, much of the law, whether civil or common law, operates on the basis of open-ended, inclusive definitions of its subject matter. The definition of intellectual property in the Convention establishing WIPO is a good example of this approach. Article 3 of the Revised TK Provisions takes an open-ended, inclusive approach to the subject matter of TK by including 'know-how, skills, innovations, practices and learning that form part of traditional knowledge systems', and not confining the subject matter of TK to any one technical field. As the High Court of Australia remarked (in one of its seminal judgements in patent law) when considering the definition of invention: 'it is an inquiry not into the meaning of the word so much as into the breadth of the concept which the law has developed . . .'.[40] Article 3 triggers precisely this kind of conceptual inquiry, and in a situation where definitions are contested this is all that can be hoped for.

B. The Land Issue—A Treaty Review Mechanism

A treaty that did not in some way recognize the territorial issues that are bound up in TK would ultimately undermine its credibility and effectiveness. The link between TK and land remains too powerful for a treaty to ignore. The Composite Report points out that, despite the land claims that have been

---

[38] For a survey see 'Traditional Knowledge—Operational Terms and Definitions', WIPO/GRTKF/IC/3/9.

[39] Ibid, 8.

[40] *National Research Development Corp v Commissioner of Patents* (1959) 102 CLR, 252.

pressed by indigenous activists around the world, many governments have made inadequate progress.[41] This sets a real problem for the successful evolution of any proposed treaty on TK. Yet at the same time, an attempt to deal with the issue of indigenous sovereignty over land in a treaty on TK would mean that the treaty would probably never see the light of day. National land policy, even in the era of globalization, remains the last bastion of state sovereignty.

One way in which a treaty on TK could recognize the link with land is by means of a modest review mechanism that could be used to track the progress that states make on land access issues as they relate to TK. The Composite Report pointed out that there were few initiatives in the world that were directed towards both the protection of TK and the conservation and sustainable use of biodiversity.[42] Currently in the CBD, where states submit national reports, the reporting mechanism is not working well on the issue of indigenous knowledge. The Composite Report itself recommends that thematic reports on Article 8(j) should be compiled.[43]

One of the problems with any reporting mechanism in the context of the CBD is that its efficacy might be diluted by the volume and complexity of the COP agenda under the CBD. A treaty on TK offers the opportunity to construct a specialist reporting mechanism on whether land policy is being used to support the goals of protecting TK and biodiversity. The exact model for a reporting and/or review mechanism is a matter for negotiation, but international organizations offer many examples of such a mechanism, including the WTO's Trade Policy Review Mechanism and the International Labour Organization's sophisticated dialogic machinery for securing compliance with its standards.[44]

The purpose of such a mechanism would be to commit states to a process of continuous improvement on the protection of TK. There are different approaches one might take to a treaty review mechanism, but one possibility is that states could agree on a set of performance indicators in this field. These could include reporting on the following:

- progress on land rights issues related to TK;
- assistance rendered to other states on TK enforcement issues; and

41 See note 29 above, 7.
42 Ibid, 4.
43 See Recommendation 1 in ibid, 10.
44 For a discussion of the ILO's work see Braithwaite and Drahos, *Global Business Regulation*, note 18 above, 238–239.

- assistance given to indigenous groups to develop representative commercial structures.

States could then agree, as is done in the WTO's Trade Policy Review Mechanism, that all Members would be subject to regular review. A review mechanism would magnify the transparency of domestic decision making by states on TK. The performance indicators would help to evaluate progress and might also provide a way of coordinating technical assistance to states that reported difficulties in making progress.

C. Operating Principles of a Treaty

One important issue that parties to a treaty in this field will have to decide is how the treaty will regulate the relationship between a given party's domestic standards for the protection of TK and another's standards. In particular, the parties will have to decide to what extent they will want to use the treaty as a means to converge on a given set of standards. Related to this is the question of whether the treaty itself will set positive minimum standards that each party must meet or, for that matter, maximum standards beyond which the parties cannot go. The issue of the convergence effects of a treaty on TK is a very sensitive one. States that have invested time and resources in developing national models and protection for TK will not want those models undermined by a treaty.

The core principles that regulate the interaction of national standards amongst members of a treaty are the principles of reciprocity, national treatment, most-favoured-nation (MFN), and mutual recognition. These principles can operate together in various ways in a treaty and they can be the subject of qualifications, exceptions and conditions. States might start with a robust statement of MFN or national treatment, for example, but then allow for certain exceptions based on subject matter or membership.[45] National treatment might be the subject of a 'list' approach, in which certain matters are listed for national treatment, or certain matters are excluded from national treatment.

Clearly states can use these principles to shape their rights and liabilities on any given subject matter in a wide variety of ways, including in the field of TK. The national treatment and MFN principle are essentially principles that

[45] For a discussion of the various ways in which these basic principles can be qualified see *Most-Favoured-Nation Treatment*, UNCTAD Series on issues in international investment agreements, (1999); *National Treatment*, UNCTAD Series on issues in international investment agreements (1999).

commit states to an equality of treatment. National treatment, whether it is applied to a class of goods or a group of individuals, aims to place those goods or individuals in the same position in terms of treatment or rights. However, the equalizing effect of MFN and national treatment does not necessarily produce a harmonizing effect. MFN and national treatment only require a state to extend its standards to goods or citizens from another state, not to match the standards of that other state.

D. National Treatment and Mutual Recognition

Article 14 of the Revised TK Provisions and its accompanying commentary suggest that the principle of national treatment is a suitable starting point for the international protection of TK. However, as the commentary also makes clear, a strict application of national treatment quickly runs into problems. The value of respect for difference, which is central to this whole area, is not strongly served by a principle that would require a state to treat an outside indigenous group, or the use of indigenous knowledge, in the same way that it treated its own indigenous groups. National treatment of itself does not oblige a state to recognize another state's standards. It follows that national treatment is not an especially suitable principle where states wish their own domestic standards to be recognized in a foreign state. Strong states such as the US have been able to take advantage of the principle of national treatment in intellectual property, but this is principally because in bilateral and regional treaty negotiations the US has been able to secure standards that match its own domestic standards. In the hands of a state that has the necessary leverage and bargaining power, the principles of national treatment and MFN can be used to promote convergence towards higher standards.

TK is more about recognizing the legal transportability of standards that, by virtue of custom, are personal to a group of TK holders, than about convergence on a set of common standards. In essence, TK raises a choice-of-law issue. The principle that many TK holders would like to see applied by states exercising jurisdiction over the matter is that courts recognize and apply those customary rules that regulate the origins and use of the TK. On this principle the customary rights and duties of TK holders would track TK knowledge wherever it was used. Clearly, this principle is radically extraterritorial in its operation.

On the face of it, the principle of mutual recognition would appear to have the greatest relevance, because it allows for the recognition of another party's standards. Mutual recognition is a principle that is important in cross-border provision of services such as banking and insurance. It can also be applied to the sale of goods that come from one jurisdiction to another (as it is for example under the Mutual Recognition Agreement and the Trans-Tasman Mutual Recognition Arrangement between Australia and New Zealand). Typically, the parties to a mutual recognition agreement will have agreed to at least some common standards that applicants for a licence to operate will have to have met.[46] It is also important to note that in this kind of situation the principle of mutual recognition will not have conferred extra rights on a commercial actor. The foreign beneficiary gains the benefit of entry, but not extra rights.

The effect of mutual recognition is different if it is applied to the holders of rights. In its simplest form, the principle would require a state to recognize the standards of rights protection of other states. However, states may be reluctant to commit themselves to such a principle because of potentially non-reciprocal effects. For example, State A might declare some aspects of folklore to be in the public domain while State B might subject all elements of folklore to property rights protection. An agreement between them based on mutual recognition would mean that the citizens of State B could draw on those elements of State A's folklore that were in the public domain. However, the citizens of State A could not draw on the folklore of State B. They would be restricted to what was in the public domain under their own law.[47] Mutual recognition essentially presupposes some mutually held standards. Yet in a survey carried out by WIPO in 2002, nine out of 21 states reported that their current standards of intellectual property did not afford protection for TK.[48] It would be surprising if states were prepared to recognize property rights for foreigners that they did not recognize for nationals. States that enacted weaker property rights regimes for TK might take the view that they were disadvantaged by mutual recognition because it required them to recognize the strong domestic standards of foreign states. Generally speaking, mutual recognition works well where trade in goods or services is already occurring and there is already some degree of convergence between the standards that are to be the subject of mutual recognition. The mutual recognition between Australia and New Zealand, for example, seems to have been successful in part because the 'close commonality of history, culture and objectives across Australia and New Zealand reduces

[46] See *Most-Favoured-Nation Treatment*, ibid, 23.

[47] A real example is reported in 'Introductory Observations' in the 'Model Provisions for National Laws on the Protection of Expressions of Folklore Against Illicit Exploitation and Other Prejudicial Actions', UNESCO/WIPO 1985, para 7. The law of Morocco restricted folklore to unpublished works, while the laws of Algeria and Tunisia did not.

[48] See 'Report on the Review of Existing Intellectual Property Protection of Traditional Knowledge', WIPO/GRTKF/IC/4/7, 5 November 2002.

significantly the risk that mutual recognition would compromise any jurisdiction's basic interests'.[49]

E. Misappropriation

Article 1 of the Revised TK Provisions creates an obligation to protect TK against misappropriation. Misappropriation is in many ways a natural starting point for the protection of TK because its vagueness can be used to accommodate a diversity of national approaches to protection. The fertile vagueness of misappropriation flows from the fact that its operation depends on an act being characterized as unfair. There is an irreducible component of subjectivity in deciding between fair and unfair acts, meaning that there would be an inevitable variety at the national level in the scope of protection against misappropriation offered to TK holders. It has been pointed out that, as a logical possibility, a general norm of misappropriation could replace all existing categories of intellectual property.[50] But it is also clear that some jurisdictions want to confine the operation of misappropriation. In the US, section 38 of the Restatement (Third) of Unfair Competition (1993) puts an end to the tort of misappropriation in the form of an independent action.[51] Posner has argued that one of the problems with misappropriation is that, in a market economy, it can potentially drive out efficient free-riding upon which competition depends.[52] Given the policy debates that a misappropriation norm is likely to trigger, it is better to think of misappropriation in the context of TK as a general term denoting different possible statutory and non-statutory actions. This seems to be the approach of WIPO's Revised TK Provisions.

Irrespective of whether or not a treaty on TK contains a misappropriation norm, it is clear that a wide variety of norms for the protection of TK are in fact evolving. The key issue in many ways is a practical one—how can TK holders find the means and capacity to make use of national forms of protection, especially if they are located outside the country in which they are seeking a remedy?

49 Productivity Commission, 'Evaluation of the Mutual Recognition Schemes', Commonwealth of Australia, Canberra (2003), 2.

50 See S Ricketson, 'New Wine into Old Bottles: Technological Change and Intellectual Property Rights' (1992) 10 *Prometheus* 53, 75.

51 See G Myers, 'The Restatement's Rejection of the Misappropriation Tort: A Victory for the Public Domain' (1996) 47 *South Carolina LR*, 673.

52 RA Posner, 'Misappropriation: A Dirge' (2003), 40 *Houston LR*, 621.

Part IV The Fair Trade Movement and TK

One of the significant contributions that a treaty might make is to help develop an approach to a system of certification that could be used by indigenous groups around the world for the marketing of their products. One of the recommendations of the Second Session of the Permanent Forum on Indigenous Issues was that states should promote 'the knowledge, application and dissemination of appropriate technologies and indigenous peoples' local products with certificates of origin to activate product activities, as well as the use, management and conservation of natural resources'.[53]

WIPO, in its report on its fact-finding missions, made reference to the Indigenous Label of Authenticity that was developed by the National Indigenous Arts Advocacy Association in Australia in 1999.[54] It was thought that the mark would help to ensure a fair and equitable return to Aboriginal and Torres Strait Islander communities, and that it would maximize consumers' certainty that they were getting the genuine product.

The results of the authentication mark, however, have been disappointing and the mark has been abandoned. The reasons have to do with debates about what constituted authenticity, the fact that one mark was not seen as being able to accommodate the needs of all indigenous groups, and the lack of proper funding for the administration of the mark.[55] This failure can be compared to a success story, namely the Fairtrade label. The contrast between this and the authenticity label could not be greater. Products selling under the Fairtrade label can be found in European, US, Canadian and Japanese markets. The Fairtrade Labelling Organizations International (FLO) represent some 352 certified producers and 449 licensees that are authorized to use the label in 17 consumer countries. Some 800,000 farmers and workers benefit as producers from the FLO systems of certification. Significantly, according to its website, FLO is moving down the path of a single International Fairtrade Certification Mark, because this helps consumer recognition and aids producers in international trade.

---

[53] See Report of the Second Session (12–23 May 2003) E/c.19/2003/22, 9.

[54] Two labels were developed and registered—the Label of Authenticity and the Collaboration Mark.

[55] See J Anderson, 'The Production of Indigenous Knowledge in Intellectual Property Law', unpublished PhD thesis, University of New South Wales, September 2003, 240–241. See also L Wiseman, 'The Protection of Indigenous Art and Culture in Australia: The Labels of Authenticity' (2001) 23 *Euro IP R*, 14.

It would be wise to study in detail the reasons for the failure of the authenticity label in Australia and compare this with the success of the Fairtrade label. One preliminary conclusion that could be drawn is that it pays to think big. In a world of increasing trade, trademarks can work large-scale effects in wealthy consumer markets. In the case of FLO, these large-scale effects have been won through an extended period of coordination amongst the National Initiatives, the individual country organizations that make up FLO. Labelling initiatives that are poorly financed, that do not look to global markets, and are isolated are likely to fail, as in the case of the authenticity mark in Australia. Crucial also is the idea that producers should unite around a few or, as FLO plans, one highly visible certification mark.

Labelling will be fundamental to the success of TK products in the vast consumer markets of developed countries. Drawing on the experience of the Fairtrade label, the potential members of a treaty on TK should use the treaty as a means of developing a coordinated approach amongst themselves to labelling and certification. WIPO's fact-finding missions revealed a clear demand by indigenous groups for the improved use of certification systems.[56] Indigenous groups need more than just assistance with matters relating to the registration of marks. The Fairtrade label example shows that labels linked to trade and development issues can become global brands if they are part of an overall commercial strategy in markets. Governments should explore the role that they can play in creating an infrastructure that allows for the creation of some small group of highly visible certification marks for the benefit of indigenous groups.[57] Significantly, through the agency of the European Parliament the European Union is moving towards creating a policy framework for fair trade.[58]

Care must be taken not to confuse the Fairtrade labelling issue with the issue of geographical indications. Geographical indications are one highly specialized form of intellectual property that potentially can divide developing countries in terms of trade gains and losses. Protection for geographical indications has

[56] WIPO, *Intellectual Property Needs*, note 23 above, 123. See also 'Consolidated analysis of the legal protection of traditional cultural expressions', WIPO/GRTKF/IC/5/3, 2 May 2003, 51.

[57] An example of the way in which the certification movement might be used to assist indigenous groups is to be found in the forest certification scheme of the Forest Stewardship Council. This certification scheme recognizes the right of indigenous peoples to be compensated for the use of their traditional knowledge. See UNCTAD, 'Background note by the UNCTAD Secretariat', TD/B/COM.1/EM.13/2, 22 August 2000, 23, fn.10.

[58] The European Parliament's resolution is titled 'Fair Trade and Development', 2005/2245(INI), adopted 30 May 2006.

advanced slowly. Moreover, the economic case for developing countries embracing this kind of protection is far from clear. [59]

Part V Disclosure of Origin

The CBD recognizes the sovereign rights of states to exploit their resources, a right that extends to genetic resources.[60] By implication, the CBD recognizes the rights of states to develop property rights regimes for genetic resources. A country can police the exploitation of its minerals or forests far more easily than it can the exploitation of its genetic resources. For example, a biologist can easily take a small soil sample out of a country that contains millions of bacteria. Compounds from the bacteria might eventually find their way into the laboratory of a pharmaceutical multinational where they are tested against thousands of screens that detect things like antibiotic activity. In some cases, interesting activity is found, and in rare cases (and after many years) the compound might end up the subject of a patent that protects a blockbuster drug. Assume for a moment that the biologist obtained the soil sample from an indigenous group who used the soil as part of a traditional treatment for wounds. Is that group entitled to any of the profits that the company has made? Our ethical intuitions and corresponding moral argument will in part be affected by the way this kind of example is framed (for example, did the biologist sneak the soil sample out of the village, or did he ask permission?).

Developing countries, bolstered by real examples of patents over resources such as basmati rice, the Enola bean, and turmeric, have argued that patent law should help to preserve their right of exploitation when it comes to genetic resources.[61] The logic of the argument put forward by developing countries is clear enough. Once the international community recognized in the CBD the sovereign right of states to exploit natural resources, subject to other treaties, all states as a matter of international comity had obligations to respect, and more importantly not to undermine that right. The reform of patent law to include

[59] On this point, see the Commission on Intellectual Property Rights, 'Integrating Intellectual Property Rights and Development Policy' (2002), 90. For a comprehensive discussion see W van Caenegem, 'Registered Geographical Indications: Between Intellectual Property and Rural Policy—Part I', 6 (2003), *J of World Intell Prop*, 699.

[60] See Arts 3 and 15.1 of the CBD.

[61] For a critical discussion of these and other cases of 'biopiracy' see C R McManis, 'Fitting Traditional Knowledge Protection and Biopiracy Claims into the Existing Intellectual Property and Unfair Competition Framework' in Burton Ong (ed.), *Intellectual Property and Biological Resources* (Marshall Cavendish Academic, 2004) 425. See also Chapter 9 above (Hon. Jean R Homere).

a disclosure obligation is seen by developing countries as one comparatively modest regulatory adjustment designed to help them protect and exercise a sovereign right over biological assets. Obviously patent applicants will have better information about how they acquired biological material than anybody else. The TRIPS Agreement has been a target of reform because the insertion of a disclosure requirement in that agreement would be the simplest way to globalize such an obligation. This argument over principle has led to some technical issues and debates. Would a disclosure obligation be consistent with other international treaty obligations such as TRIPS or the Patent Cooperation Treaty?[62] What would have to be disclosed in order for the patent applicant to meet his obligation, what would trigger the obligation to disclose, and what would be the consequences of non-disclosure?[63]

Recently, as part of the WTO Doha Round, a group of developing countries led by India and Brazil tabled a text on disclosure of origin.[64] The issue is no longer one of abstract debate. Opposition to the insertion of a disclosure obligation is likely to be strong in the US.

For the purposes of this chapter, the key question is whether a treaty on TK should itself contain a standard mandating disclosure of origin for patent applications dealing with biological materials. Probably the best chance that developing countries have of obtaining a disclosure standard is in the WTO, where the politics of complex linkages across the many sectors of the Organization might work in their favour. A disclosure standard in a treaty on TK would almost certainly consign that treaty to the waste paper basket.

Even if we conclude that a robust disclosure standard should not be in a treaty on TK, it is still worth asking whether a TK treaty might not achieve something more modest when it comes to disclosure of origin; perhaps something even more practicable than what is currently being proposed at the level of treaty law. One strategy worth considering here is whether patent offices might be encouraged to develop an administrative best practice around disclosure.

62 For a comprehensive analysis, and the view that a disclosure requirement is consistent with existing international agreements, see the Memorandum by J Sarnoff, 'Compatibility with Existing International Intellectual Property Agreements of Requirements for Patent Applicants to Disclose Origins of Genetic Resources and Traditional Knowledge and Evidence of Legal Access and Benefit Sharing', 23 June 2004, available at <http://www.piipa.org>.

63 See 'Draft Technical Study on Disclosure Requirements Related to Genetic Resources and Traditional Knowledge', WIPO/GRTKF/IC/10.

64 See 'Communication from Brazil, India, Pakistan, Peru, Thailand and Tanzania', WT/GC/W564, 31 May 2006. Norway has also submitted a proposal. See 'The Relationship between the TRIPS Agreement, the Convention on Biological Diversity and the protection of traditional knowledge—Amending the TRIPS Agreement to Introduce an Obligation to Disclose the Origin of Genetic Resources and Traditional Knowledge in Patent Applications', IP/C/W/473, 14 June 2006.

It is clear that many patent applications in the biotechnology field already contain information about matters like country of origin.[65] There is no reason why patent offices could not develop guidelines and a systematic practice around patents relating to genetic resources and TK. They routinely develop guidelines on many aspects of patent office practice. The Trilateral Offices, for instance, have a long record of cooperation and recently they have been furthering this cooperation in the biotech field.[66] Guidelines on disclosure could be developed as part of a cooperative exercise initiated by the major patent offices of developed and developing countries (the Trilateral Offices along with, say, China, India and Brazil). Importantly, the consequences of a false, incomplete, or misleading disclosure would be determined by national patent law. Over the decades each major patent jurisdiction has developed a refined body of law relating to who is an inventor, co-inventorship, fraud upon the patent office, and so on. A disclosure requirement should aim to harness this law rather than disturb it.

One important advantage of proceeding down this administrative route is its comparative ease of implementation. Even if the Trilateral Offices refused to participate in developing best practice guidelines on disclosure of origin, the major patent offices of developing countries (China, Brazil and India) could begin the process. These developing countries are important emerging markets and so will continue to attract a significant and growing number of biotechnology applications, especially through the PCT filing route. These offices could also request the patent applicant to provide information about related foreign applications (allowable under Article 29(2) of TRIPS). Furthermore, once information relating to origin and use of any genetic material and/or TK was available and published in some patent jurisdictions, the information would be available for use in other jurisdictions. The Trilateral Offices might well decide to participate in the process of globalizing best practice on this matter. These offices do not especially want to be involved in embarrassing biopiracy episodes. Developing administrative best practice around disclosure would be easier than attempting to insert a disclosure standard into existing patent treaty law, especially if its purpose was to enable the existing web of controls in patent law to work more efficiently.

A treaty on TK might attempt to stimulate this process by creating obligations of cooperation amongst the patent offices of states, especially the lead patent offices from developed and developing countries.

---

65 See 'Draft Technical Study', note 63 above, 42–43.

66 The Trilateral Offices are the European Patent Office, the Japanese Patent Office and the United States Patent and Trademark Office. Examples of their cooperation are to be found on the Trilateral website at <http://www.trilateral.net>.

On a final note, it is worth asking who or what would act on the basis of the information that a disclosure obligation generated as part of the application process? In terms of resources not much can be expected from patent offices. The USPTO's 21st Century Strategic Plan estimates that there are 7 million patent applications waiting to be examined.[67] At the level of organizational culture many patent offices take the view that contests over patents are for the marketplace to sort out. All care and no responsibility is their hidden motto. Patent litigation is complex and expensive. Who exactly, one wonders, would monitor and act on the extra information that would be released by a disclosure obligation? This brings us back to the principal argument of this chapter, that a treaty on TK should aim to contribute towards solving problems of enforcement and capacity. The next part of the chapter outlines one approach to these problems.

Part VI Solving Enforcement and Capacity Issues: Pyramids and Networks

I noted at the beginning of this chapter that there has been a rapid proliferation of legal and non-legal norms for the regulation of TK. TK, however, cannot be said to have evolved into a regulatory regime because processes and strategies for monitoring compliance have been largely neglected, as have mechanisms for the enforcement of norms. Even less attention has been paid to capacity issues. Where a breach of a TK norm is identified and there is an enforcement mechanism (for example, an opposition proceeding in a patent office) TK holders may not have the ability and resources to use the enforcement mechanism. When the creation of regulatory norms races ahead of a supporting institutional infrastructure aimed at securing compliance, the norms run the obvious risk of ineffectiveness. The norms never make the passage from paper statements to daily life and living regulation.[68] In the sections that follow two arguments are elaborated to show how the issues of monitoring, enforcement and capacity might be tackled. Roughly, the first argument is that the monitoring and enforcement of TK norms can best be accomplished by adopting a strategy based on the regulatory pyramid. The capacity issues in TK are especially challenging because the holders of TK often lack resources and the misappropriation of TK may take

67 USPTO, 'The 21st Century Strategic Plan' (2003) available at <http://www.uspto.gov>.

68 The phrase living regulation borrows from Eugen Ehrlich's idea of 'living law', the law that derives from the actual patterns of behaviour in a society.

place outside the country in which the TK holder lives. The solution to this kind of capacity problem lies in TK holders enrolling the capacities of others through networking. Bringing these two ideas together the chapter outlines an approach to the enforcement of TK based on the networked enforcement pyramid.

A. The Enforcement Pyramid

One regulatory tool that is being tried for the protection of TK is the creation of protocols/guidelines or other soft norms setting out the uses to which third parties, wherever located, may put the relevant knowledge.[69] The usual objection to the use of protocols is based on enforceability. Protocols are not laws and therefore adherence to them is a voluntary matter.[70] Their advantage is that they are a less costly form of regulation to produce than formal law. They are also a flexible form of protection that can easily be adapted to changes in circumstances. Moreover, they will work with at least some actors. For much the same reason that it is a mistake to assume that all actors are virtuous, it is a mistake to assume that none are so. There are at least some actors who would welcome the guidance that a protocol can provide, since they wish to do the right thing. Many people that work in museums, scientific organizations, or large corporations see respect for other cultures as an inherent value to be defended and acted upon. For this type of actor, protocols and guidelines are valuable sources of information about appropriate and inappropriate uses of TK.

The weakness of protocols and guidelines is a weakness that only exists if they are not part of a broader and integrated enforcement strategy that recognizes that not all actors will be virtuous. Some actors, for instance, may decide on compliance or non-compliance in terms of probabilities of sanction, and costs and benefits. For these kinds of actor, regulatory tools of deterrence become important along with the strong projection of a commitment to enforcement. The idea is to induce them to calculate in favour of compliance. For reasons of irrationality, incompetence or zealotry some actors may not respond to deterrence, and so tools of incapacitation become important. The theory of the enforcement pyramid proceeds on the assumption that there are differently motivated actors in the world for which different regulatory tools will be needed. It holds that there is a distinctive sequence of responses that the regulator must follow in order to maximize compliance (see Figure 11.1 below). The sequence is always the same irrespective of the subject matter.

---

69 The CBD website lists dozens of these as part of its work programme on Art 8(j) of the Convention on Biological Diversity. See <http://www.biodiv.org/programmes/socio-eco/traditional/default.shtml>.

70 But, as has been pointed out, protocols do establish industry standards that may eventually chart the way for legal rights. See 'Consolidated analysis', note 56 above, 75.

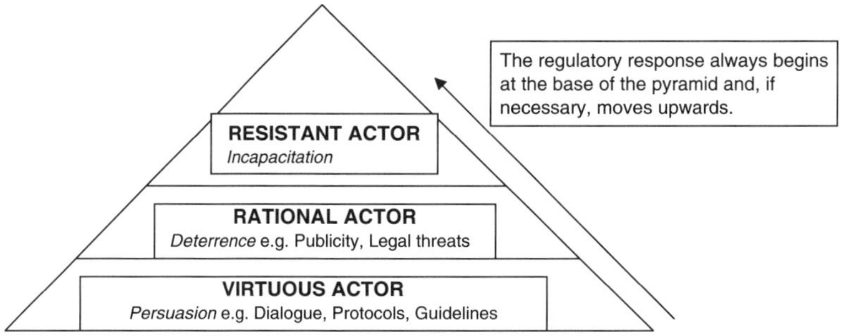

Figure 11.1 Enforcement Pyramid—Actors and Responses[71]

A considerable body of scholarship has shown both theoretically and empirically how enforcement pyramids can increase compliance.[72] At the base of the pyramid are the 'soft' tools of regulation such as guidelines, protocols, and educational strategies. These soft tools assume that actors are disposed to do the 'right thing' and are willing to cooperate. As one moves up the pyramid, the tools of regulation begin to assume a more coercive character until, at the top of the pyramid, there is some form of incapacitation (this depends on the area of regulation but might involve imprisonment, suspension of trade, loss of licence, and so on). Where the regulator is unsuccessful at the bottom of the pyramid he or she can move up the pyramid to deploy the more coercive tools of regulation. An enforcement pyramid gives a regulator a unified set of strategies that can be deployed against all types of actors (virtuous, rationally calculating, resistant, incompetent). As one strategy fails another is wheeled into place. There is an irrevocable presumption in favour of starting at the base of the pyramid with dialogic and information-based strategies.[73] This is less costly, more respectful, and ultimately makes the use of coercion more legitimate, because non-coercive strategies have been given a chance to work. Regulating the use of TK by means of an enforcement pyramid is especially appropriate because, for indigenous groups, respectful engagement with others over the use of their knowledge and resources is the fundamental starting point of any process of regulation.

In its latest manifestation, the enforcement pyramid has been merged with restorative justice approaches.[74] These are approaches that focus on a procedure for bringing together those parties affected by a breach of norms and finding ways

[71] This pyramid draws upon J Braithwaite's pyramid for an integration of restorative, deterrent and incapacitative justice. See ibid, 32.

[72] Ayres and Braithwaite, note 13 above; J Braithwaite, *Restorative Justice and Responsive Regulation* (Oxford University Press, 2002).

[73] See Braithwaite, *Restorative Justice*, ibid 30.

[74] Ibid.

to repair the harm. The emphasis is on a collective process of finding acts that will restore those adversely affected rather than on the procedures that simply aim to punish the wrongdoer. Linking restorative justice approaches to the regulation of TK is appealing because those approaches are most likely to recognize that the misappropriation of TK is a communal harm that needs to be repaired in a communal way. Standard adversarial approaches lack the flexibility to accommodate the communal nature of TK.

Responsive regulation and the enforcement pyramid is an approach conceived of in the context of national business regulation where governments have the powers and resources to adopt responsive regulatory approaches. The regulation of TK poses more complex problems. TK may involve a number of jurisdictions and a number of actors and no agreement as to whether misappropriation has occurred. Even if there is agreement on the facts, there is no single regulator to coordinate an international enforcement strategy, let alone a strategy based on an enforcement pyramid. Capacity issues also loom large. TK holders, for instance, will generally lack the technical expertise to track the use of their knowledge in patent applications. Some idea of the difficulties of using the patent system can be seen from the remarks of the Swedish Patent and Registration Office made in 1999 on the reform of the International Patent Classification system. It observed of the IPC that it 'is too complicated and detailed for the general public or for small offices that only need to search small bodies of patent literature (or do not search at all)' and that the problems with the IPC had grown to a point 'where even experts have trouble making accurate searches'.[75] Another example of the difficulties in using the patent system is to be found in the pharmaceutical sector. Specialist organizations interested in finding out the patent status of HIV/AIDS drugs have reported difficulties in obtaining basic information about patent status in various jurisdictions.[76]

In an area where even well-resourced specialists have problems it seems safe to assume that indigenous groups will experience problems when it comes to tracking the use of their TK through the patent system using the IPC.[77] Unless some

[75] See IPC/R 1/99 Rev. 1 Annex 10, 1–2.

[76] See, for example, P Boulet, C Garrison, E 't Hoen, 'Drug Patents Under the Spotlight', Médecins Sans Frontières (2003), 22; 'Patent Protection and Access to HIV/AIDS Pharmaceuticals in Sub-Saharan Africa', A Report Prepared for the World Intellectual Property Organization by the International Intellectual Property Institute (2000), 37.

[77] A proposal to revise the IPC to accommodate the classification of TK is being worked on by a WIPO Taskforce on Classification of Traditional Knowledge. The Taskforce has prepared a revision proposal in the field of medicinal preparations containing plants. See 'Practical Mechanisms for the Defensive Protection of Traditional Knowledge and Genetic Resources within the Patent System', WIPO/GRTKF/IC/5/6, 19.

way is found to allow indigenous groups to track and monitor the status of patent applications and granted patents, a treaty standard that encouraged the release of more information about a patent application will be of little practical value to indigenous people, or for that matter the understaffed and under-resourced patent offices of many developing countries.[78] It is also worth adding that even before one addresses the capacity problems there is the very basic issue of awareness of one's rights. Ekpere, for example, commenting on the African Union Model Law for the Protection of the Rights of Local Communities Farmers and Breeders and the Regulation of Access to Biological Resources, observes that it is an 'understatement that most Africans are not aware' of the model law or the reasons for its development.[79]

Enough has been said to show that the international regulation of TK faces some very deep and basic problems when it comes to the monitoring and enforcement of norms aimed at protecting the rights of TK holders. As we said at the beginning of this chapter, the danger of symbolic regulation in TK runs high. A treaty on TK may simply end up being a politically convenient piece of regulatory ritualism that delivers no significant benefits to traditional knowledge holders, but allows political elites to claim that the concerns of TK holders have been met and it is time to move on. In order for a TK treaty to avoid the fate of regulatory ritualism, it has to ground the evolution of a regime that ultimately will allow some of the weakest groups in the world to enforce traditional cultural norms across borders against much more powerful actors.

The enforcement pyramid, that we discuss in this section of this Part, provides a strategy for integrating the various regulatory tools that are being developed for the protection of TK. Another virtue of the pyramid is that it maximizes the chance of obtaining compliance with TK norms at the lowest possible cost. It follows that a treaty on TK should contribute to the creation of an international enforcement pyramid for TK. The details of this international pyramid are discussed in the next section of this Part.

78 On the problem of under-resourced patent offices in developing countries see M Leesti and T Pengelly, 'Institutional Issues for Developing Countries in Intellectual Property Policymaking, Administration & Enforcement', Commission on Intellectual Property Rights (2002), Study Paper 9, available at <http://www.iprcommission.org/papers/pdfs/study_papers/sp9_pengelly_study.pdf>.

79 See J A Ekpere, 'The African Union Model Law for the Protection of the Rights of Local Communities Farmers and Breeders and the Regulation of Access to Biological Resources' in Bellman, Dutfield and Meléndez-Ortiz, note 2 above, 232, 237.

B. The GBS and an International Enforcement Pyramid

In the previous section we saw that in the context of national business regulation the enforcement pyramid assumed a single regulator such as a telecoms regulator, a tax regulator, a competition regulator, and so on. Creating a single global TK regulator with coercive powers probably has the same degree of feasibility about it, as does the idea of a single world tax authority. A less ambitious approach might be to use the treaty to commit states to the establishment of a transparent, high profile, multilateral agency that could take on the role of co-ordinating the use of national regulatory tools for TK. The various studies undertaken by the WIPO secretariat show that there are many possible regulatory levers that might be pulled at the national level when it comes to dealing with conduct that harms the interests of TK holders. One critical challenge is to ensure that the first response is not a punitive one, but rather, always begins at the base of the pyramid in the form of dialogue and persuasion. A multilateral agency could take responsibility for collecting and publishing protocols on permissible uses of TK, as well as ensuring that in any dispute over the use of TK, protocol and dialogue between the parties formed the first response.

In terms of organizational structure this multilateral agency could follow the Global Bio-Collecting Society (GBS) model that has been proposed elsewhere and recommended for further exploration.[80] The basic idea behind the GBS is that TK holders, states and business actors would share in its governance. Its primary functions would be technical assistance (e.g. help with drafting laws and protocols) and the coordination of enforcement responses based on the enforcement pyramid. The GBS would basically be a networker of networks at different levels of the pyramid. It would bring in those networks that had the capability to deliver the enforcement response that was required at the level in the pyramid to which the enforcement dispute had escalated. By way of example, indigenous networks would be involved at the dialogic base of the pyramid. If this did not succeed restorative justice approaches could be tried, and if these failed deterrent approaches based on threats of publicity or legal action could be used at the next level of the pyramid. Here the GBS might involve

80 See P Drahos, 'Indigenous Knowledge, Intellectual Property and Biopiracy: Is a Global Bio-Collecting Society the Answer?', [2000] 22 *Euro IP R*, 245–250. The Expert Meeting on Systems and National Experiences for Protecting Traditional Knowledge, Innovations and Practices observed that a 'possible role for the Global Bio-Collecting Society in monitoring access to TK could be explored'. See UNCTAD, 'Outcome of the Expert Meeting' TD/B/COM.1/EM.13/L.1, 9 November 2000, 5. Support for considering the idea was also expressed in Report of the International Seminar on Systems for the Protection and Commercialization of Traditional Knowledge, New Delhi, 3–5 April 2002, 13.

NGO networks expert in campaigning and public shaming, or law firms willing to do *pro bono* work on TK. If there was still no compliance, the GBS would continue to involve other actors capable of delivering more serious sanctions (for example, patent offices, environmental agencies). In effect, the subtlety and strength of this international enforcement pyramid would vary from case to case, as it would depend on the strength and content of the tools of regulation that had been developed at the national level by individual states. But, given the proliferation of TK norms in the last decade, the GBS would always be able to coordinate some sort of response. Moreover, some strong deterrent sanctions would be available in all jurisdictions (e.g. adverse publicity). Figure 11.2 below illustrates this networked enforcement pyramid.

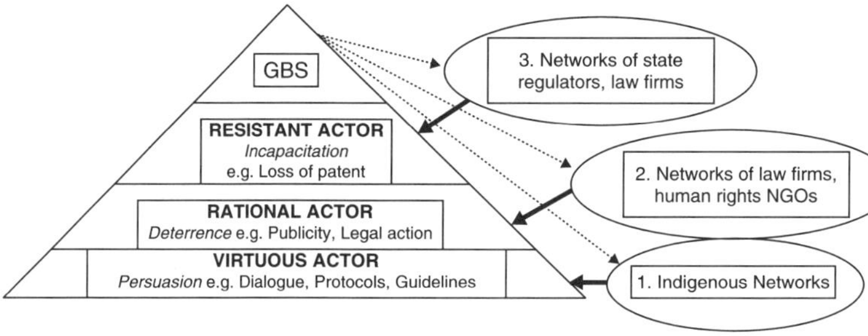

Figure 11.2 Networked International Enforcement Pyramid for TK showing how networks can be coordinated by a multilateral agency to constitute a robust pyramid[81]

This international enforcement pyramid, we have seen, is different from the usual responsive regulatory pyramid, in that such pyramids typically assume a single regulator. Here the GBS is not a regulator in the classical sense, but rather a coordinator of other actors. This pyramid, in keeping with the philosophy of responsive regulation, begins with the presumption that it is best to start at the base of the pyramid. Other actors will often be in a better position to begin the process of engagement than the GBS. If, for example, a museum breaches a protocol of customary use it may change its behaviour once the breach is pointed out to it. In some cases the GBS may cast its shadow over the process, thereby alerting a potential offender to the possibility of an escalation up the pyramid if persuasion and dialogue do not work. The point is that, in a case where enforcement has to work across borders and accommodate a diversity of standards and values,

[81] This pyramid draws upon J Braithwaite's pyramid for an integration of restorative, deterrent and incapacitative justice. See Braithwaite, *Restorative Justice*, note 71 above, 32.

there is no one actor that can manage all the tools of enforcement. But there does have to be an actor that can manage the many information problems that occur in this type of enforcement environment, and that can coordinate a response amongst the actors best placed to utilize the next stage in the enforcement response. It will be this coordination that constitutes the enforcement pyramid and therefore its responsive effects. Without this kind of coordination, enforcement responses will fall to the ad hoc initiatives of different actors. The result will be that sometimes the punishment will be unnecessarily severe because an excessive level of response was the first response, or there will be a failure of punishment because the cooperation of those actors capable of implementing a response at the top of the pyramid (for example, patent offices) has not been obtained. The effect will be to create uncertainty and resentment amongst some actors who believe that they have been unfairly targeted. In such a world trust decreases and defiance may well increase.[82]

C. A Treaty on TK and Existing International Regimes

TK is an issue that cuts across work programmes within fora, as well as the work programmes of different fora. The Commission on Intellectual Property Rights, after noting the large number of international bodies that were working on aspects of TK, observed that '[t]here is much to gain at this early stage by considering the issue in a number of fora'.[83] At some point, however, the question of which forum is appropriate for a treaty will have to be considered. A summary by the WTO Secretariat noted that there are essentially two views on the forum issue.[84] Some states (for example, the EU and US) take the view that WIPO's work programme on the issue should be given priority. Other states (for example, Brazil and India) want an approach that is integrated across the relevant fora such as the CBD, FAO, WTO, and WIPO. One of the real dangers of having so many international organizations work on TK, and adding more and more norms to those that are already being generated at state level, is that the regulation of TK begins to lose coherence. Instead of coherence there is a clash of cultures, legal approaches, and enforcement strategies. Ultimately, the goal and purpose of regulation becomes lost. One reason for supporting a treaty that makes enforcement its priority is that an enforcement perspective is likely to bring with it a more practical monitoring and problem-solving approach to individual cases of TK misuse. In many ways the best thing that could happen to TK is for it

[82] For the reasons as to why defiance might increase see Braithwaite, Restorative Justice, note 71 above, Chapter 4.

[83] Commission on Intellectual Property Rights, note 59 above, 79.

[84] WTO Note to the Secretariat, note 36 above.

to be taken out of the grandstanding geopolitics of interlinked international negotiations, and for it to enter the quiet world of technical problem solving.

One possibility that should be explored is whether key organizations such as the WIPO, the FAO, and the CBD might be able to establish a Global Bio-Collecting Society as a joint initiative. Each of these organizations has important specialist skills and knowledge that the GBS would need to draw on (WIPO, for instance, has matchless expertise in running registration systems). It would be worthwhile, therefore, to explore the role that these international organizations could play in the establishment and governance of the GBS. Involving these organizations in the GBS would also be a practical means of achieving greater coherence and coordination on the issue of TK more generally. A GBS, for example, could pull together the work of different international organizations on the development of protocols, guidelines, and codes of conduct, and issue them as an integrated set. Such a set would be likely to gain a greater *de facto* authority and following, because they would be linked to an agent capable of carrying out or coordinating an enforcement response.

The areas of TK and biodiversity are rife with free-rider and collective action problems. On any realistic assessment, international coordination is going to be painfully slow. One advantage of basing an approach on the creation of a GBS is that it would give priority to the enforcement issue, and encourage states to make more efficient use of existing norms, rather than devoting resources to the creation of new norms that in any case would still have to be enforced.

Conclusion

The central conclusion of this chapter is that a treaty on TK should focus on the enforcement dimension of TK. Specifically, this would involve members in the establishment of a Global Bio-Collecting Society that would coordinate enforcement work so as to constitute an international enforcement pyramid. The treaty should also establish a review mechanism and a set of indicators that could be used to evaluate the progress of states on the regulation of TK. At this stage of the evolution of protection for TK, a treaty should avoid setting detailed substantive international norms of protection. Instead, states should focus on creating a treaty that does not discourage the development of national approaches and norm-creation on TK, but does offer the members of such a treaty a means of cooperating in, and coordinating the enforcement of TK. A treaty that is modest in setting substantive standards, but strong on coordinating national enforcement activities, will be far more likely to avoid becoming a dead letter.

12

INTELLECTUAL PROPERTY INTERSECTIONS WITH TRADE AND LABOUR RULES: RETHINKING DOMESTIC AND INTERNATIONAL STRATEGIES TO PROMOTE BIODIVERSITY FOLLOWING THE 'NAFTA CORN' EXAMPLE

Chantal Thomas

Introduction

Across the Mexico–United States border, international trade rules have interacted with biodiversity norms and labour migration patterns in the context of the 'NAFTA Corn Case',[1] a specific and important example of trade liberalization under the North American Free Trade Agreement (NAFTA). First, corn imports have surged into Mexico from the United States under import policy reforms brought about by NAFTA and related economic liberalizations in Mexico. Second, displaced agricultural labour has migrated out of rural Mexico into Mexican cities, *maquiladoras* (factories that import materials and equipment on a duty- and tariff-free basis for assembly or manufacturing, and then re-export the assembled product, usually back to the originating country), and, not infrequently, the United States. Third, concern has spread throughout Mexico regarding the potential jeopardy posed by imported strains of US (hybridized, monocultured) corn to ancient strains of maize and corn, both among those who see local agriculture as important to the preservation of biodiversity and indigenous genetic resources, and among those who see local agriculture as important to the economy.[2]

'Biodiversity' has important implications for intellectual property law and policy: a rich and diverse supply of biotechnology is the desired result of intellectual property protection, and in particular of patents. In the modern age, genetic variety in plants and animals has been recognized as both critically important and rapidly diminishing. On the one hand, biodiversity has yielded the genetic materials for dramatic advancement in science and medicine. On the other hand, the rise of socio-economic integration and mass-production economies of scale have created a streamlining effect on agricultural variety, with many fewer plants and animals under human cultivation now than past epochs.[3] Thus, economic industrialization and globalization both rely on the technology yielded by biodiversity and threaten the physical environments and social practices that preserve that biodiversity.

---

1 The term 'case' is used in the sense of a case study, rather than a formal legal proceeding.

2 There is currently quite visible debate and concern about declining corn production in Mexico stemming from trade liberalization. See, e.g. J Arvizu, 'Vitral politico: La bomba de tiempo' *El Universal*, 12 February 2007 ('México perdió interés en el campo, en producir suficiente maíz . . . para alimentar a su población'); D Ibarra, 'Agricultura y políticas públicas', *El Universal*, 7 February 2007 ('a los problemas estructurales del viejo cuño del agro mexicano . . . se añaden otros asociados con la apertura comercial y el abandono de las políticas protectoras de los campesinos').

3 K Bosselmann, 'Plants and Politics: The International Legal Regime Concerning Biotechnology and Biodiversity' (1996) 7 *Colorado J of Int'l Env L & Policy* 111, 129 ('ancient cultivators used at least 500 major vegetables, the present varieties have narrowed down to 200 species').

Moreover, a key aspect of the value of genetic variability is that its specific value is unknowable. Its economic potential lies in the idea that, as investors and innovators come into contact with genetic material, they will produce yet-unknown applications. Until particular innovators come around to do so, however, the economic value of biodiversity remains latent. Protecting biodiversity, therefore, means protecting inputs of unspecificied, and yet assured, value.[4] The United Nations Convention on Biological Diversity, established as part of the Rio Summit in 1992, has recognized 'the intrinsic value of biological diversity and of the ecological, genetic, social, economic, scientific, educational, cultural, recreational and aesthetic values of biological diversity and its components'.[5]

Despite the depth and breadth of existing scholarship on intellectual property and biodiversity, the NAFTA Corn Case exposes an under-theorized lacuna within this discourse. Most participants in this aspect of the debate over intellectual property and development assume that traditional strains of biotechnology are of *economic value* to multinational firms and investors. The common fact pattern provides that a sophisticated investor exploits indigenous biotechnology by introducing it into larger markets.

Within this presumed fact pattern, the debated issue concerns whether, following this exploitation, the ownership of and profits from that technology should accrue at least in part to the communities within which it originated.[6] The subject of indigenous rights to traditional knowledge largely addresses this phenomenon.[7] The most specific—and the most disputed—provisions in the Convention on Biological Diversity establish principles relating to the sharing of benefits flowing and technology transferring from such transnationally exploitable genetic resources.[8]

But what if the genetic resources in question—relatively low-yield local grain seeds—appear without immediate economic value to investors? These plant varieties are particularly vulnerable in the wake of trade liberalization where local

---

[4] R Thomas, *The Nature of Open Space Programs: Linking Land Protection and Biodiversity Conservation* (Environmental Law Institute, 2006), 3.

[5] Convention on Biological Diversity (Rio de Janeiro, 5 June 1992), UNTS 30619 (1993) 142, 143).

[6] '*The Mobility of Labour and Capital, a Study in International Investment and Labour Flow* [S Sassen](Cambridge University Press, 1990) stipulates that those who have the ultimate responsibility of carrying the costs of conservation and sustainable use of the resources must also be given fair and equitable share in the benefits derived from this use.' GK Rosendal, 'Impacts of Overlapping International Regimes: The Case of Biodiversity' (2001) 7 *Global Governance* 95, 103.

[7] D Gervais, 'Traditional Knowledge & Intellectual Property: A TRIPS-Compatible Approach' (2005) *Mich State LR* 1, 1–23; SJ Anaya, *Indigenous People in International Law* (Oxford University Press, 2004).

[8] Art 16, Convention on Biological Diversity, note 5 above.

production is displaced by agribusiness imports.[9] The potential dangers posed by such displacement to sustainable development in poor countries pertain, not only to the potential instability of the cost of living and related issues of food security, but also to the potential harms of replacing local genetic varieties with imported genetic varieties.

Such replacement could occur either intentionally, through voluntary adoption by local farmers; or unintentionally, through contamination. With respect to the import of corn under NAFTA, the threat of contamination of local varieties by these genetically engineered imported varieties remains unquantified. Some early data suggest that local landraces are hardy enough to survive contamination,[10] and other reports highlight the positive effects that can come from cross-pollination of maize varieties.[11] Nevertheless, very little information has been gathered regarding this issue, and the specialized benefits of indigenous strains, described below, are significant enough that the overriding goal within biodiversity law and policy, of preserving knowledge of and access to these local genetic varieties, emerges as paramount in this context.

Even if the shift results from voluntary adoption of imported varieties, as opposed to contamination, a variety of associated costs—some relatively hidden—could raise the cost of production for local farmers. The cost of repurchasing seeds, since many hybrid strains do not produce sowable seeds for the season after they have been planted, is one.[12] In addition, these strains have been 'designed for use with other proprietary agricultural inputs such as fertilizers and pesticides' that not only further raise costs of production but potentially also 'have serious social impacts'.[13] Finally, genetically engineered seeds that produce high yields in their original growing context (in this case, the United States) may not transfer well to local growing environments in Mexico. By contrast, local seeds, though lower in yield, may be better adapted to soil and other climate conditions, producing greater security for farmers.[14] These possible effects on farmer income and yield, in addition to secondary social and cultural considerations, are among

---

9 Bosselmann, note 3 above, 131 ('[t]he growth of agribusiness is likely to further accelerate due to the recent promotion of free trade. The US and the UK have been the main advocates for a system of free trade not hindered by protectionism and subsidies').

10 A Nadal, 'Corn in NAFTA: Eight Years After' (2002) (Research Report prepared for the North American Commission for Environmental Cooperation) 1.

11 ML Morris, *Impacts of International Maize Breeding Research in Developing Countries, 1966–1998* (2002) (International Maize and Wheat Improvement Center (CIMMYT)) 4.

12 Ibid.

13 G Dutfield, *Intellectual Property Rights, Trade and Biodiversity* (Earthscan, 2000).

14 Nadal, note 10 above, 1.

those contemplated as the potential dangers of imported corn varieties in the Mexican context.[15]

There are many reasons, then, to stabilize and secure genetic information relating to local corn varieties. Were this case one that attracted bioprospectors, one might rest assured that, at the very least, this information-gathering activity would be under way, driven by market incentives.[16] The difficulty in such circumstances would be in ensuring appropriate transfer of technology and sharing of benefits.

In this case, however, the danger to biodiversity is enhanced by the lack of proprietary interest by those actors—large agribusinesses—who would be willing and able to sustain the patenting process. Moreover, even if such interest existed, the genetic information contained in local traditional seeds might not meet the patentability requirements. In this unpatented and perhaps unpatentable environment, is it appropriate to speak of 'intellectual property'? Is local agriculture a form of public good or commons that should, instead, be protected by the public sector? Or is it, instead, an untapped form of private wealth to which one might exhort the conversion of heretofore undifferentiated assets into private property? Recalling (with some trepidation) Hernando de Soto's theory of capitalism as fundamentally dependent on the creation and protection of property, such a solution would devise and confer individual property rights that would recognize existing, but informal, investments of local farmers and communities in the cultivation of indigenous plant varieties.[17] One can conceptualize the problem, and the accompanying solution, through either a 'public sector, public good' or a 'private sector, property rights' lens. As Part II(B) of this chapter delineates, both approaches are evident in the policies adopted and implemented so far, though the implications remain as yet uncertain. Given the skepticism around the viability of de Soto's approach, particularly in an intellectual property context, a balance of both is likely required.

This chapter begins by recounting the particulars of this case study, delving into not only the specific events of corn imports, but also the broader context

[15] S Brush and M Chauvet, 'Assessment of Social and Cultural Effects Associated with Transgenic Maize Production' in North American Commission for Environmental Cooperation Secretariat Report, *Maize and Biodiversity: The Effects of Transgenic Maize in Mexico: Background Volume* (2004), Chapter 6.

[16] Graham Dutfield has noted research asserting that the patent process might inherently harm biodiversity due to its 'bias towards centralized research', note 13 above, 44 (citing WV Reid, 'Genetic Resources and Sustainable Agriculture: Creating Incentives for Local Innovation and Adaptation' Biopolicy Series No 2, African Centre for Technology Studies).

[17] H de Soto, *The Mystery of Capital: Why Capitalism Triumphs in the West and Fails Everywhere Else* (Basic Books, 2006).

of liberalization. The chapter then relates the NAFTA Corn Case to prevailing discourses on trade, labour and intellectual property, showing that these discourses have not yet satisfactorily incorporated important lessons from each other. The chapter concludes by considering various solutions, both proposed and adopted, to address the harmful effects associated with the NAFTA Corn Case.

Part I The NAFTA Corn Case

Domestic corn or maize in Mexico holds a great deal of significance both economically and environmentally. Economically, corn remains far and away the single most important agricultural crop in Mexico, accounting for over two-thirds of gross value of agricultural production[18] and over half of the total area under cultivation for all crops.[19] Corn tortillas are a basic staple of Mexican consumption, accounting for 59 per cent of total human energy consumption and 36 per cent of total human protein consumption.[20]

Environmentally, domestic corn production in Mexico also features an unusually large degree of genetic diversity. In part this biodiversity stems from Mexico's history as the origin of maize production, with domestic maize cultivation reaching back well over 5,000 years.[21] In addition, the heterogeneity of Mexico's climate, and the ubiquity of maize production throughout its territory, has yielded a wide variety of 'landraces', genetic strains closely adapted to the particulars of local climates.[22] The unforgiving nature of many of these climates, with shallow or poor soil, has produced some notably hardy local varieties.[23]

As the foregoing briefly illustrates, genetic variability in corn production in Mexico has its own clear benefits, in the form of high levels of adaptation to the challenges of agriculture in a wide range of climates, leading to the ability of maize to become the staple food for the population at large. It is this genetic

18 A Nadal and TA Wise, 'The Environmental Costs of Agricultural Trade Liberalization: Mexico–US Maize Trade Under NAFTA' (2004) (Working Group on Development and Environment in the Americas, Discussion Paper Number 4).

19 Nadal, note 10 above, 1.

20 Nadal and Wise, note 18 above.

21 Ibid.

22 Nadal, note 10 above ('[f]or many of Mexico's corn growers, the genetic variability of corn is one of the most important technological assets').

23 Ibid.

diversity that potentially faces jeopardy from surging agricultural imports under trade liberalization.

The threats to biodiversity exemplified by the NAFTA Corn Case can be characterized as both direct and indirect. Direct threats arise out of contamination of indigenous strains by imported strains—so, the physical imports themselves. Indirect threats arise out of a much more complex set of background conditions that reduce agricultural production in Mexico as a consequence both of trade liberalization and of adverse dynamics in labour flows and labour protections. Perhaps counterintuitively, these latter, more indirect phenomena may ultimately pose the more serious threat to indigenous biodiversity in Mexico. Although this chapter discusses both direct and indirect dynamics, its primary objective is to elucidate the background context of trade liberalization and labour relations, particularly under NAFTA, and to consider possible intellectual property mechanisms that might be enlisted to reduce the adverse impact of these background dynamics on indigenous corn production.

A. Macro-economic Reform in Mexico: Trade Liberalization and Labour Policy

The trade liberalization undertaken in the NAFTA era should be viewed against the backdrop of a decade's worth of calls for economic reform in Mexico away from a statist, inward-looking orientation model and towards a marketized, outward-looking growth model.[24]

While liberalization was evident in the rapid removal of barriers to cross-border trade, when it came to the domestic market the government in fact adopted quite *dirigiste*, corporatist, and in that sense illiberal, measures in reducing the ability of labour unions to stand in the way of the larger goal of controlling inflation. Central to the disinflation strategy was the government's 'incomes' policy, which called for the implementation of wage controls. Incomes policy was practiced through *pactos*, whose parties were 'government-friendly unions', 'the business community', and 'the government'.[25] The first *pacto*, the Economic Solidarity Pact (PSE) in December 1987, was renamed the Pact for Stability and Economic Growth in 1988, and was periodically renewed thereafter.

---

[24] For a detailed account of this dynamic, see C Thomas, 'Trade and Labor Flows in Mexico' (manuscript on file with author, 2007).

[25] R Dornbusch, A Warner, G Calvo and S Fischer, 'Mexico: Stabilization, Reform and No Growth' (1994) Brookings Papers on Economic Activity, 253, 271.

The relative decline of both the influence of organized labour and the level of formal labour protections from the era of the first *pactos* through NAFTA can be traced to several factors: the political debate on the possibility of 'flexibilization' of labour regulations; the informalization of employment; and the related increase in employment in the *maquiladoras*.

First, an ongoing debate over the necessity of 'flexibilization' of labour regulations has likely undercut the bargaining power of official unions.[26] In any case, official unions became less assertive than in previous eras, and more and more associated with a posture of complicity towards non-enforcement of the basic labour protections embodied in the Mexican Constitution and the 1970 labour regulation. Second, any effect of the flexibilization reforms, in undermining the position of official unions, would be underscored by their helplessness to protect workers from the impact of macro-economic destabilizations. Third, informalization of employment would necessarily contribute to the relative softness in the bargaining position of organized labour. Rapid urbanization resulting from economic dislocations created an equally rapidly expanded labour force in cities that was most easily absorbed into informal-sector employment. In addition, the shift to the *maquiladora* sector created a dampening effect on labour organization. In part, this was because of the concomitant rise of subcontractor suppliers to *maquiladoras*. In part, the *maquiladoras* themselves appear to have proven relatively resistant to labour organization.[27]

In this sense, NAFTA may have contributed indirectly to relative weakness in labour organizing, by unleashing these dynamics that constrained the ability of workers to organize. On the face of it, NAFTA's direct requirements appear to have had very little effect either way. The NAFTA 'side agreement on labour', the North American Agreement on Labour Cooperation (NAALC),[28] although it calls on governments to 'promote' a wide range of labour principles,[29] establishes a process for examining complaints only with respect to a signatory's

[26] Enrique de la Garza Toledo, *NAFTA, manufactura y trabajo* (CLACSO, 1998), 77, 79 ('desde 1988 se inició un debate que no termina aún acerca de la necesidad de flexibilizar la ley laboural, y que sa intensificado después de la entrada en vigor del NAFTA').

[27] The most straightforward explanation of the lower level of labour organization in the *maquila* sector arises out of the incentives of companies to maximize profits in this sector by discouraging labour organization. Some commentators have speculated that the relatively low levels of labour organization in the *maquila* sector may stem from the fact that the majority of *maquiladora* workers are women, who are subject to a variety of socio-economic and cultural factors that appear to inhibit union organizing.

[28] North American Agreement on Labour Cooperation, opened for signature 8 September 1993, Can.–Mex.–US, 32 ILM 1499 (entered into force 1 January 1994).

[29] Ibid, Art 1(2).

non-enforcement of its own laws.[30] Effectively, therefore, the NAALC does not establish positive obligations but rather addresses signatories' existing labour laws.

Even the obligation to enforce existing labour laws harboured the potential to be transformative in the Mexican context, however, with the long-standing and ever-increasing tolerance by the official unions of non-compliant labour practices. In its application, the NAALC seems to have been unable to gain any momentum in this respect.

From the beginning, it was clear that the primary function of the agreement would lie in its potential for monitoring and building opportunities for exchange and dialogue amongst labour unions. The primary mechanism is an investigation conducted by a NAALC National Administrative Office (NAO), at its own initiative or at the petition of a labour union in a signatory state other than the one in which the alleged violation occurred.[31] Ministerial Consultations occupy the next level up. If such consultations fail, an Evaluation Committee of Experts (ECE) may examine the matter and issue a report.

For a core of labour issues, defined by the NAALC as 'occupational safety and health, child labour or minimum wage technical labour standards', the ECE may recommend further action upon finding a 'persistent pattern of failure'.[32] From there, if the matter cannot be resolved through consultations, a panel may be convened and sanctions recommended.[33] Thus, although a relatively formal dispute settlement process exists, its availability is restricted to limited and attenuated circumstances.

Notwithstanding the relative lack of emphasis on formal enforcement power, one might have hoped that labour unions could use the NAALC's information-gathering capabilities more than they have. Regarding labour practices in Mexico, the first year of the NAALC saw a promising start, with petitions by several US unions (among them the AFL–CIO and the United Electrical, Radio and Machine Workers of America) to the US NAO[34] to investigate labour practices in the Mexican subsidiaries of Honeywell, General Electric and Sony corporations.[35]

---

30 Ibid, Part Four.

31 Ibid, Art 21.

32 Ibid, Art 27.

33 Ibid, Arts 28–41.

34 US NAO Reports 940001, 940002, 940003 & 940004. Report 940004 was withdrawn before completion.

35 US NAO Reports 940001, 940002 & 940003.

The last of these investigations resulted in the NAO's recommendation of Ministerial Consultations. The Ministerial Consultations themselves produced a series of information-gathering activities: three public seminars on union registration and certification; the establishment by the Mexican Secretariat of Labour and Social Welfare of a task force to study labour law and practice related to the registration of unions; and a meeting between the Mexican Secretariat and the company's management and labour representatives.[36]

Tellingly, most of the NAO reports centred precisely around the ability of workers to organize independent unions. The above-mentioned petitions filed against the subsidiaries of Honeywell, General Electric, and Sony, all focused on the right of freedom of association, and the right to organize. The Honeywell and General Electric cases alleged that managers had fired workers for attempting to join independent factory unions, as well as questionable labour practices regarding the influence of the state in the national labour Arbitration and Conciliation Boards.[37] The Sony case also involved attempts by workers to form an independent union. The petitioners alleged, and the NAO found, that management had committed several harmful practices, including threatening organizers with dismissal and demotion and using police to suppress employee demonstrations with violence.[38] In this case, the NAO did recommend consultations, and issued a follow-up report pursuant to then-US Secretary of Labor's directive to continue to observe union registration activities.[39]

This initial enthusiasm for the NAALC process would appear to have faded, however, as in the next eight years, only a total of 12 such reports were filed (an average of 1.5 reports per year).[40] Ministerial Consultations resulted from half of those 12 reports. The next step up the pyramid, formation of an Evaluative Committee of Experts, never occurred. The possible reasons for the relative lack of use of the NAALC mechanism—perhaps including a troubled history of relations between US and Mexican unions, and the perceived unlikeliness of momentum, since the process was unlikely to escalate—would be the

[36] See 940003, Follow-Up Report.

[37] N L Grimm, 'The North American Agreement on Labor Cooperation and Its Effects on Women Working in the *Maquiladoras*' (1998) 48 *American U LR* 179, 212–213. In these cases the NAO did not recommend further action because workers had accepted severance pay packages, which in the view of the NAO Report precluded further action under NAALC. 94003, ibid.

[38] Grimm, ibid, 214.

[39] Ibid.

[40] US NAO Reports 96001, 9702, 9703, 9901, 2000–01, 2001–01, 2003–01. The decrease in anticipated use of the NAO can be implied by the changes in the claim numbering system evident in this list.

basis for a very interesting research project. This is beyond the scope of the current chapter, however. Whatever the reasons, the NAALC mechanism is relatively disused. Thus, although NAFTA and NAALC gestured towards containing or balancing trade liberalization with respect for labour rights, in practice the labour part of this equation appears not to have materialized. As a consequence, NAALC has not been able to diffuse the dislocation resulting from trade liberalization under NAFTA and contemporaneous reforms.

B. Economic Destabilization and Labour Migration

While formal and public sector employment was declining due to fiscal austerity measures, the private sector failed to grow enough to absorb the difference. The sluggishness of domestic private sector growth stemmed at least in part from two other disinflation strategies adopted alongside 'incomes policy'. First, an overvalued currency and associated highs in relative prices, together with high interest rates, contributed to the high real cost of credit, impeding the ability of domestic firms to expand. Second, the rapid introduction of imports effectuated a shift of consumer spending from domestic to imported items, particularly since the overvalued currency meant that prices of Mexican goods were at all-time highs relative to imported and international goods; although exports grew throughout this period, they were dwarfed by imports.

The picture that emerges from this period overall is the combination of relative compliance of official labour unions with liberalizing reforms, declines in formal employment, and increases in the informal sector. All of these changes in turn spurred increases in labour out of rural areas, and therefore out of traditional indigenous agriculture.

Migrant labour streams flowed, in part, into the growing *maquiladora* industry. *Maquiladora* employment quadrupled from 105,000 to approximately 400,000.[41] Dislocations caused by instability in international capital flows and exchange rate policy appear to have been directly linked to surges in *maquiladoras*, with sharp increases in *maquiladora* operations tracking peso devaluations.[42]

Beyond the *maquiladoras*, migrant labour also flowed into the United States. Recorded immigration into the United States had reached an all-time high: 190 million in 2005, with the US share at 20.2 per cent of total worldwide

---

41 US BLS 1994.

42 P Martin, 'Mexico–US Migration,' in *NAFTA Revisited: Achievements and Challenges* (Institute for International Economics, 2005), 56 ('[t]he number of *maquiladoras* and their employment increased sharply after several peso devaluations, and reached a peak of 1.3 million in 2000').

immigration.[43] Mexican immigration accounts for fully one-quarter of immigration into the United States.[44] Mexico accounts for approximately one-third of the 'foreign-born population' in the US.[45] The Department of Homeland Security recently estimated unauthorized migrants from Mexico to be 6 million; other estimates are up to 12 million.[46] Thus, in the NAFTA case, trade and migration turned out not to be substitutes, but rather complements.[47]

Movement across these markets occurs more easily against a background of lowered transaction costs. These efficiencies of the global economy arise both from technological gains in transportation and communication, and from reduced tariff barriers arising out of trade liberalization agreements. Increased legal trade flows across borders beget increased illegal trade flows by creating opportunities to use otherwise legal commercial carriers for smuggling. In addition, increased volume of cross-border traffic translates into decreased effectiveness of border inspection.[48]

Philip Martin has written on how this dynamic occurred in the context of NAFTA:

> Studies on NAFTA's prospective impact agreed that the bulk of the additional jobs due to NAFTA would be created in Mexico. One hoped-for side effect of NAFTA was a reduction in unauthorized migration. This did not happen. Instead, the number of unauthorized Mexicans living in the United States rose from an estimated 2.5 million in 1995 to 4.5 million in 2000, representing an annual increase of 400,000 a year.[49]

C. Background Economic Conditions, Dislocation and Local Maize Production

In the general atmosphere of economic liberalization described above, Mexico undertook a variety of internal reforms to liberalize the economy which affected corn production. For example, in 1992 an amendment to the Mexican Constitution was adopted to allow alienation of rural property (*ejidos*).

---

43 UN Secretary-General, 'Report on Migration and Development', 2006. available at <http://www.un.org/esa/population/hldmigration/index.html>.

44 'World Migration Report', published by the International Organization for Migration.

45 Center for Immigration Studies, 2001.

46 US Department of Homeland Security, 'Report on Unauthorized Migration', 2006.

47 This relationship between trade and immigration belies the standard 'Hecksher–Olin Theory of Factor Complementarity', which holds that trade and immigration are substitutes for each other. Instead, in this situation, trade and immigration actually served as complements to each other. For more on the relationship between illegal migration and international trade, see C Thomas, 'Globalization and the Border' (2007) 38 *McGeorge Law Review* (forthcoming).

48 See C Thomas, 'Illegal Markets and International Trade' (draft forthcoming 2007).

49 Martin, note 42 above, 449.

With specific reference to corn, price supports were removed in 1993. Reductions in public spending, including in government-financed farmer credit, were also important reforms.[50]

Historically, corn in Mexico has been highly protected: a guaranteed price of corn twice the world price has served as the social safety net in rural areas. Mexico had about 3 million corn farmers in the mid-1990s, but during the same period the 75,000 corn farmers in Iowa produced twice as much corn as Mexico, at half the price.

Even in the context of trade liberalization and the negotiation of NAFTA, the Mexican government had recognized the 'delicate' political nature of import competition with domestic corn production. It initially negotiated the placement of corn in the most protected category under NAFTA's trade liberalization framework, providing for a 15-year phase-out of tariffs.[51] After NAFTA was adopted, however, the Mexican government refrained from levying the negotiated tariffs, so that corn products from the United States encountered no barriers to import after the first 30 months. Over the next half-decade, US corn imports increased in market share from 8 per cent to 21 per cent.[52] At the same time, domestic corn producer prices fell by as much as 46 per cent.[53]

The drop in producer prices created an incentive to shift away from corn production. Although this had been one of the intended effects of liberalization, the rapidity with which tariffs were removed led to an equally sudden impact on domestic farmers and farm workers. The share of agriculture in total employment decreased from 36 per cent to 22 per cent.[54] The rural population declined from 31 per cent to 26 per cent.[55]

Unfortunately, the import surge did not succeed in keeping the consumer prices down. In the corn sector specifically, a coincident consolidation of

---

50 Ibid. Rate of growth of government-financed farmer credit decreases from 11 per cent to 20 per cent.

51 Under NAFTA, the government was to replace its previous import quota system with a tariff-rate quota system: that is, rather than imposing an absolute ban on imports above a certain number, the imports above that number would instead be allowed but subject to a tariff.

52 Nadal and Wise, note 18 above.

53 Ibid.

54 Statistical Abstract of Latin America, 2002.

55 Secretaría de Agricultura, Ganadería, Desarrollo Rural, Pesca y Alimentatión (SAGARPA), Antonio Ruiz García, 'Rural Development Undersecretary, Sustainable Development and Rural Poverty: A Mexican Perspective'(Address to the Woodrow Wilson Center, Washington, DC) (2001).

the domestic tortilla industry meant instead that the prices of this basic staple increased five-fold in the same time period.[56]

More generally, the combination of Mexico's trade and monetary policies caused the cost of living not to decrease, but rather to increase substantially. Prior to 1994, this increase was due to the real appreciation of the peso combined with the related shift in consumption over to imported goods, which were relatively inexpensive. When the peso devalued, the constraints on conditions for domestic producer growth meant that imports continued to be a significant source of consumption, except that now the devalued currency meant that they were relatively expensive.[57]

These changes appeared to affect the Mexican countryside particularly. Rural poverty increased from 135 million to 165 million, with 80 per cent of the rural population living in poverty.[58] The increase in rural poverty and unemployment contributed to the increase in informal employment over the same period, with the overall share of waged work falling from approximately 60 per cent to 55 per cent, as agricultural workers left the countryside to seek a living elsewhere.[59]

D. The NAFTA Corn Case—A Summary of General and Specific Dynamics

In sum, Mexico made several changes to its domestic legal and administrative framework that were not captured formally in NAFTA, but that were a central part of its structural economic reform, including: change to its constitutional law allowing for the alienation of rural property; decrease in public spending causing a shrinkage not only of the public sector but also of the formal economy, leading to a rise in both the informal economy and the incidence of poverty; changes in monetary policy, leading to high interest rates that discouraged local firms from investing, contributing to the stagnation of the local economy; and currency devaluations, leading to a greater desire for hard currency, greatly

[56] Nadal and Wise, note 18 above.

[57] Exchange rate: 0.05 pesos/dollar increased to 6.41 pesos/dollar. World Bank, 'World Development Indicators Online Database' (2006).

[58] OECD, 'Placed-Based Policies for Rural Development: The Micro-Regions Strategy, Mexico' (Case Study) (2003).

[59] S Gabbard, R Mines, and B Boccalandro, 'Migrant Farmworkers: Pursuing Security in an Unstable Labor Market'. Based on data from the National Agricultural Workers Survey. Department of Labor, May 1994. (Research report no. 5).

increasing the attractiveness of migration and the possibility of remittances of hard currency.

When coupled with the accelerated liberalization of corn imports into the United States engineered by NAFTA, the result was a collapse in corn imports, a crowding-out of small producers, and a stream of economic migration. As a result, these macro-economic shifts in resources associated with trade liberalization mean that maize might be threatened, both because local production in maize decreased, and because imported strains of corn may have become intermingled with local strains.

Part II Trade, Labour, IP and Biodiversity: Real Connections and Discursive Gaps

In the NAFTA Corn Case, the flux of trade imports under NAFTA, and in particular corn import surges into Mexico from the United States, created implications both for labour and for diverse genetic resources. The implications of the NAFTA Corn Case for the intersecting regimes of trade, labour and intellectual property remain understudied.[60]

A. Labour as a Causal Factor in the Relationship between Trade Flows and Intellectual Property

To the extent that there has been a discourse on the connection between intellectual property (IP) protection and development,[61] it has centred on whether a low-enforcement IP regime is or is not more conducive to promoting economic growth in developing economies.[62] Within this debate, labour flows play a

60 Important research has been completed on this issue by Dan Badelescu and Alejandro Nadal. D Badelescu, 'Global Forces, Local Consequences—Technology, Agriculture & Labor in the Developing World', Presentation at the INTELL 8 Conference in Cuernavaca, 29 June 2006; Nadal and Wise, note 18 above.

61 For an example of a critique of the prevailing debate's polarization of efficiency and distributive justice, see M Chon, 'Intellectual Property and the Development Divide' (2006) 27 *Cardozo LR* 2821, 2831.

62 R G Okediji, 'Copyright and Public Welfare in Global Perspective' (1999) 7 *Indiana J of Global L Studies* 117, 125–135, 147–157 (recounting the tenets and controversies within the debate over whether intellectual property fosters or impedes economic development); K Aoki, 'Neocolonialism, Anticommons Property, and Biopiracy in the (Not-So-Brave) New World Order of International Intellectual Property Protection'(1998) 6 *Indiana J of Global L Studies* 11, 18–28 (discussing the

conceptually tangential role,[63] at most arising as a particular *result* of trade flows and economic growth which, according to one's stance in the familiar debate, either do or do not themselves depend on IP protection.[64] Labour rules and labour flows exert no independent causality in this equation.

As the NAFTA Corn example demonstrates, however, labour flows may actually catalyze a particular interaction between trade policy and biodiversity. Without the traditional stewards of small-holding agriculture to attend to it, as a practical matter, indigenous biotechnologies may suffer the threat of extinction. NAFTA displaced agricultural workers in Mexico and caused flows of surplus labour into Mexican cities, *maquiladoras* and ultimately the United States. This sudden increase in labour supply generated practical implications for labour practices in both Mexico and the US, creating additional supply and vulnerability on the part of workers.

Moreover, the relative weakness in both national and international labour protections, in terms of the enforcement of labour standards and the provision for labour 'adjustment', exacerbated the vulnerability of this excess labour supply. Thus, the practical and legal conditions within which this change took place bode ill for the implementation of labour standards. An obvious recommendation for regulatory reform here would be the enhancement of international and national labour protections—while this recommendation is hardly novel, this chapter hopefully demonstrates how efficacy in labour law generates effects far beyond their immediate context, with implications not only for trade but also for biodiversity.

Labour rules and dynamics play a central part in the equation because the impact of trade liberalization on labour flows facilitates and catalyzes the dynamic whereby import surges displace local farming and therefore jeopardize local agricultural strains. It is hypothesized here that an increase in enforcement of existing labour laws and labour standards in Mexico, enabling an increase in bargaining power of Mexican workers, would have a salutary effect on this

debate over intellectual property and development in the context of the creation of the World Trade Organization and its Agreement on Trade-Related Intellectual Property Rights).

63 The most visible conceptual role of labour within intellectual property discourse has been the Lockean philosophical underpinning of the right to property protection, including intellectual property, as the fruit of one's labour. J Hughes, 'The Philosophy of Intellectual Property'(1988) 77 *Georgetown LJ* 287, 297–300.

64 D Halbert, 'Intellectual Property in the Year 2025'(2001) 49 *J of Copyright Soc* 225, 234–235 (noting that major US technology firms have located research and development facilities in China despite that country's 'poor intellectual property records', thus belying the prevailing US view that IP protection directly influences international investment).

dynamic,[65] potentially stabilizing internal and external migration flows as well as domestic agriculture.

B. Trade, Biodiversity and Intellectual Property

Notwithstanding the uncertain direction of current trade negotiations on agriculture,[66] international law does envisage a range of regulatory mechanisms that might be harnessed to protect indigenous biodiversity from the destabilizing forces of trade liberalization and labour migration, as described in Part I above. At the outset, the relevant regulatory measures can be divided into public sector and private sector categories. This purely heuristic terminology does not refer to the presence or absence of the state or of the law: in both contexts, regulatory enforcement is required. The distinction refers only to the actor who initiates enforcement: in the 'private sector', individual rights generally are enforced by the state only when individual right-holders seek remedies; in the 'public sector', regulatory enforcement and action can be initiated by the state directly.

It is in the domain of the private sector that intellectual property rights may potentially play a role both in protecting local production and, consequently, in conserving biodiversity. Although intellectual property rights have often been conceived as potentially hostile to biodiversity, there may be some potential here for determining synergies between the two, by devising a form of intellectual property right that recognizes the particular needs and context of local farmers.

This section discusses the guidance available under international law with respect to both private sector and public sector mechanisms. In the private sector category, the primary instrument is the International Convention for the Protection of New Varieties of Plants; in the public sector category, it is the Convention on Biological Diversity. This section will address both instruments in the Mexican context, as well as the relationship of these two conventions

65 For an examination of the concept of 'flexibility' as applied in the contexts of labour law and economic law, see A Santos, 'What Kind of 'Flexibility' in Labor and Employment Regulation for Economic Development?' (manuscript on file with author, 2007).

66 The potential effects of trade concessions liberalizing agriculture, while beyond the scope of this chapter, are both crucial and as yet undetermined: ongoing negotiations over the WTO's Doha Development Agenda envisage allowing trade restrictions for developing countries, or to protect food security, the precise contours of which remain undefined. The WTO maintains a helpful and relatively current summary of the state of play in agricultural negotiations, entitled 'WTO Agricultural Backgrounder: The Issues, and Where We Are Now', available at <http://www.wto.org/English/tratop_e/agric_e/negs_bkgrnd00_contents_e.htm>.

to Mexico's primary trade obligations under international law, in the NAFTA and the WTO Agreements.

Private Sector Solutions

Although traditionally patent law has not been hospitable to protecting plant varieties,[67] within international law an alternative framework exists to provide a form of intellectual property protection to breeders: the International Convention ('Union'[68]) for the Protection of New Varieties of Plants, or UPOV Convention.[69] The UPOV Convention establishes plant 'breeders' rights' to prevent production, or reproduction, or sale[70] to a breeder of a plant variety that meets the four conditions of novelty, distinctness, uniformity, and stability.[71] With novelty being defined as existing in the absence of any recent sale or other disposal by the applicant,[72] these requirements typically are easier to meet than those of the patent process.

The IP protection offered by the UPOV Convention contains two regulatory requirements that potentially render it suboptimal for local farmers and traditional local agricultural varieties. In both cases, however, Mexico's law implementing the UPOV (the Federal Law on Plant Varieties ('Federal Law')) has adjusted the terms of the convention to suit the particular challenges described herein.[73] Mexico's adjustment through implementation demonstrates both how

67 JB Bai, 'Protecting Plant Varieties under TRIPS and NAFTA', (1997) 32 *Texas Int'l LJ* 139, 143 (noting the two primary obstacles to be, first, that 'before the advent of recombinant DNA technology, traditional plant breeding methods were perceived to lack an inventive step required for patent protection' and, second, that plant breeders could not meet the disclosure requirement in patent law, which requires the inventor to describe the invention sufficiently to enable a person skilled in the art to reproduce the invention').

68 International Convention for the Protection of New Varieties of Plants, 2 December 1961, 815 UNTS 89, Art 1(x) ('"Union" means the Union for the Protection of New Varieties of Plants founded by the Act of 1961 and further mentioned in the Act of 1972, the Act of 1978 and in this Convention').

69 2 December 1961, as revised at Geneva on 10 November 1972, on 23 October 1978, and on 19 March 1991.

70 Ibid, Art 14. Art 15 (1) allows for exceptions to this general right for 'acts done privately and for non-commercial purposes, acts done for experimental purposes, and acts done for the purpose of breeding other varieties'. Art 15(2), discussed below, establishes additional restrictions.

71 Ibid, Art 5.

72 Ibid, Art 6(1) (i) ('in the territory of the Contracting Party in which the application has been filed earlier than one year before that date'); (ii) ('in a territory other than that of the Contracting Party in which the application has been filed earlier than four years or, in the case of trees or of vines, earlier than six years before the said date').

73 Ley Federal de Variedades Vegetales, published in Diario Oficial de la Federación, Vol DXVII, No 19, 23, 25 October 1996. The Office of the Union has translated the law and accompanying regulations, which translation is available at <http://www.upov.int/en/publications/npvlaws/index.htm>.

international intellectual property law can incorporate development concerns insufficiently, and how those concerns might nevertheless be incorporated at the national, implementation level.

The first potential problem in the UPOV text, for development purposes in general and the Mexico and NAFTA Corn Case in particular, lies in the restrictive nature of the definitional conditions for enjoyment of the rights described above (novelty, distinctness, uniformity, and stability), even though those requirements may be less stringent than patent requirements which might create harmful consequences where the varieties in question are traditional.

The UPOV Convention, however, also contemplates that countries may adjust the contours of this right to reflect local conditions, by providing that signatory states may 'within reasonable limits . . . restrict the breeder's right . . . in order to permit farmers to use for propagating purposes, on their own holdings, the product of the harvest which they have obtained by planting'.[74] Indeed, Mexico's implementing regulation provides that breeder's rights shall not apply to others' 'multiplication of propagating material, in so far as, it is intended for personal use as grain for consumption or seed for sowing'.[75] In this way, Mexico's implementation provides an incentive structure for farmers who wish to record plant varieties, without prohibiting local and traditional cultivation of that variety by others. As such, it seeks a balance between the goal of property protection and that of biodiversity conservation, setting up the possibility for existing traditional and local agricultural strains to be registered.

The second potential problem lies in the UPOV Convention's seeming evidentiary requirement of value added by applicants, so that purely traditional plant varieties would be excluded from registry and protection. Although the formal requirement of novelty itself pertains to a procedural rather than a substantive characteristic, the UPOV Convention defines 'breeder' in its first Article as fundamentally 'the person who bred, or discovered and developed, a variety'.[76] In this way, it would appear that 'the convention limits breeder's rights to those who manipulate the genetic material to some degree . . . . An individual can not gain breeder's rights for a plant variety found in its natural state.'[77]

---

74 UPOV Convention, note 72 above, Art 15(2).

75 Federal Law of Plant Variety, note 76 above, Art 5(II).

76 UPOV Convention, note 72 above, Art 1(iv). Subsidiary definitions include 'the person who is the employer of the aforementioned person or who has commissioned the latter's work' and 'the successor in title of the first or second aforementioned person, as the case may be'.

77 M Hannig, 'An Examination of the Possibility to Secure Intellectual Property Rights for Plant Genetic Resources Developed by Indigenous Peoples of the NAFTA States', (1996) 13 *Arizona J of Int'l and Comp L* 175, 234–235.

This understanding of the law would reduce its utility to the goal of conserving existing biodiversity. In its own national implementing law, however, Mexico has varied the definition of breeder slightly from the treaty text. The Federal Law defines 'breeder' as 'the person . . . who has through an *improvement process* obtained and developed a new plant variety of any genus and species';[78] and 'improvement process' is in turn defined as 'the technique or set of techniques whereby a new plant variety is developed and its protection made possible on account of its novelty, distinctness, stability and uniformity'.[79] The Mexican law's definition of 'breeder' may be argued to do nothing more than restate the four requirements, unlike the UPOV definition of 'breeder' which appears to add additional substantive content. Since the 'novelty' requirement is procedural and not substantive, the Federal Law therefore avoids any question of whether the breeder did or did not 'manipulate' the variety.

Through these adaptations in implementation, Mexican plant variety law incorporates development concerns, and retains its capacity to help conserve biodiversity existing in local and traditional agriculture. The question remains, however, whether such laws are consistent with the stricter intellectual property rights established in Mexico's primary international trade obligations under NAFTA and the WTO.

Relationship to International Trade Law

The WTO Agreement on Trade-Related Intellectual Property Rights (TRIPS)[80] accommodates the possibility of specialized, and less stringent, intellectual property protection for agricultural production in its Article 27.3. This establishes an exception to the general patent requirement for plants and animals, which WTO members may exclude from patentability as long as they establish a system 'for the protection of plant varieties either by patents or by an effective *sui generis* system'. This provision is generally accepted as applying to the UPOV Convention as a possible (though not exclusive) basis for such a system.[81]

In the context of the larger debate around intellectual property and development, however, WTO members have questioned the efficacy of TRIPS Article 27.3's provisions. First, many developing states have expressed concerns around the

78 Federal Law of Plant Variety, note 76 above, Art 2(IV) (emphasis added).

79 Ibid, Art 2(V).

80 Agreement on the Trade-Related Intellectual Property Rights, 15 April 1994, Marrakech WTO Agreement, Annex 1C, Legal Instruments—Results of the Uruguay Round Vol 31; 33 ILM 81.

81 World Trade Organization Council for Trade-Related Aspects of Intellectual Property Rights ('TRIPS Council'), 'Note by the Secretariat: Review of the Provisions of Article 27.3(B)' (2006) (WTO Document No. IP/C/W/369/Rev.1) 14–22.

UPOV as a basis for a *sui generis* system of protection, particularly regarding the more restrictive aspects of the UPOV Convention described above; other states have expressed the view that the UPOV provisions are not sufficiently restrictive to constitute 'effective protection' under Article 27.3.[82] Second, disagreement persists as to whether plants should be patentable at all, given concerns not only related to economic development, but also related to protection of traditional knowledge and biodiversity.[83]

For these reasons, during the Doha Ministerial Conference the WTO membership called for a review of Article 27.3 along multiple dimensions: the question of plant patentability, the relationship between TRIPS and the UPOV Convention, the efficacy of the UPOV Convention and other forms of *sui generis* plant variety protection, and, finally, the relationship between TRIPS and the Convention on Biological Diversity.[84]

NAFTA's provisions on intellectual property mirror those of the WTO in establishing basic patentability requirements, and allowing for exclusion from patentability of plants provided that an effective *sui generis* system of plant variety protection is maintained.[85] Unlike the TRIPS Agreement, however, NAFTA explicitly incorporates the UPOV Convention.[86] Given that NAFTA is deemed to be consistent with the WTO under GATT Article 24 allowing for regional agreements, one might argue that the questions under the WTO regarding the status of the UPOV and plant variety protection would not trouble Mexican plant variety law, at least insofar as its impact on trade between NAFTA signatories is concerned. At the same time, a subsequent agreement in the WTO that generates a substantively different relationship between the UPOV Convention and TRIPS might indeed generate additional legal obligations for Mexico.[87]

With these ongoing negotiations and debates at the international level, it is possible that Mexico's regulatory choices in interpreting and implementing

82 Ibid, 17–19.

83 Ibid, 2–14.

84 World Trade Organization Ministerial Declaration on the TRIPS Agreement and Public Health, 14 November 2001, 41 ILM 755 (Doha Declaration) (WTO Document No. WT/MIN(01)/DEC/1), para (19).

85 Canada–Mexico–United States: North American Free Trade Agreement, 32 ILM 605 (1993), Art 1709, cl 3.

86 Ibid, Art 1701 (providing that 'each Party shall, at a minimum, give effect to . . . the substantive provisions of' the Geneva Convention, the Berne Convention, the Paris Convention, and the UPOV Convention).

87 Vienna Convention on the Law of Treaties (23 May 1969) 1155 UNTS 331, Arts 30–32. For a discussion of the relationship between WTO law and other international law, see J Pauwelyn, *Conflict of Norms in Public International Law: How WTO Law Relates to Other Rules of International Law* (Cambridge University Press, 2003).

the UPOV Convention may themselves be called into review in the future. In sum, the framers of the Mexican plant variety law have attempted to resolve policy questions relating to the appropriate balance between economic development, intellectual property, indigenous farming, and biodiversity at the local level, without waiting for resolution to emerge on the multilateral plane.

Public Sector Solutions

The debate within the WTO described in the foregoing subsection suggests that private sector solutions such as intellectual property rights may not sufficiently address concerns relating to protecting indigenous biodiversity. This can be demonstrated with reference to the UPOV Convention, for example. Even with adjustments such as those embodied in the Mexican plant variety law, plant breeders' rights may not fully provide for the protection of local agriculture. Local strains may not be sufficiently distinct from each other, or sufficiently internally homogenous, to merit recognition under the law's requirements. In addition, incentives and information asymmetries may be such that individual farmers are not induced to avail themselves of the law. These defects become more apparent when one considers that the objective of biodiversity protection extends beyond protecting actual use, to preserving *knowledge* relating to genetic diversity.[88] Where incentives do not exist for registration by individual farmers of plant breeders' rights, local knowledge about indigenous plant varieties might be lost. Under such circumstances, public sector intervention may be appropriate.

The Convention on Biological Diversity (CBD) provides the primary source within international law for a right and responsibility upon signatory states to take affirmative steps towards these ends.[89] Although qualified by the 'sovereign right to exploit their own resources pursuant to their own environmental policies',[90] the CBD requires signatories to develop 'national strategies' for the 'conservation and sustainable use of biological diversity'.[91]

Such strategies are described primarily as *in situ* and *ex situ*. *In situ* strategies seek to preserve 'components of biological diversity' in their natural habitats, through such measures as the establishment of protected geographical areas and the protection of indigenous communities.[92] *Ex situ* strategies refer to measures to preserve biodiversity outside natural habitats, for example through physical

88 Convention on Biological Diversity, note 5 above, Art 7 (describing the importance of, and the obligation to pursue, the identification and monitoring of 'components of biological diversity').

89 Ibid,142.

90 Ibid, Art 3.

91 Ibid, Art 6.

92 Ibid, Arts 2 and 8(a),(j).

gathering and storage of local seeds; or in the form of support for and execution of research and data-gathering for the maintenance of a database of genetic information.[93]

Notwithstanding these general provisions, as well as the scope and importance of the CBD, its text provides relatively little guidance regarding concrete steps to be taken by signatories to preserve biodiversity.[94] Nevertheless, individual signatories have achieved varying degrees of success in devising means of implementation of these broad principles. Of the general measures contemplated by the CBD, the most success appears to have been achieved in physical storage and information gathering. Costa Rica's Instituto Nacional de Biodiversidad is perhaps the best-known example, with public–private partnerships intended to harness the technological capabilities of bioprospectors for purposes of recording genetic information.

In the Mexican context, the leader in public sector research is the non-profit group CIMMYT (International Maize and Wheat Improvement Center). CIMMYT seeks not only to record information related to indigenous genetic strains, but also and primarily to explore ways in which genetic breeding might preserve the benefits of indigenous varieties while reducing the harms arising out of unintentional cross-pollination.[95] Thus, CIMMYT caters both to public research objectives relating to biodiversity, and to economic development objectives arising out of both the public and the private sectors.[96]

While the CIMMYT contributes importantly to biodiversity policy goals in Mexico, it is unclear whether the Mexican government itself has taken sufficient measures to meet its obligations under the CBD. A 2004 study found, for example, that the 'official Mexican government positions' and 'roles and responsibilities of specific government departments' on this issue were 'unknown or not understood by the public'.[97]

At the same time, within international law, Mexico has reaffirmed not only its commitment to biodiversity measures, but also to the 'precautionary approach' to biodiversity, through its adoption not only of the CBD but also of the 2000 Cartagena Protocol on Biosafety. The Cartagena Protocol was adopted under the

93 Ibid, Arts 2, 9.

94 Bosselmann, note 3 above, 136 ('[t]he Convention does call for conservation of biodiversity, mainly *in situ*, but this is qualified by language like "as far as possible" or "in accordance with its particular conditions and capabilities" that weakens a nation's individual commitments').

95 Morris, note 11 above.

96 Ibid, 7–16 (describing CIMMYT's consultation to both public and private research efforts).

97 North American Commission for Environmental Cooperation Secretariat Report, *Maize and Biodiversity: The Effects of Transgenic Maize in Mexico: Key Recommendations and Findings* (2004) 25.

auspices of the CBD to address specifically the potential threats to biodiversity posed by the transboundary movement of genetically modified organisms such as transgenic maize.[98] Recent pledges of assistance by development institutions may result in a better-defined set of public policies and practices by the Mexican government on biodiversity and maize.[99]

Relationship to International Trade Law

The intersections between public sector measures described above and Mexico's primary international trade commitments are multiple. The *in situ* and *ex situ* measures described above might be called 'preservation' strategies. Preservation strategies are relatively uncontroversial from the perspective of international economic law. Additionally, however, intervention might take the form of trade restrictions intended to protect local production from the initial threat of contamination, which might be called a 'preemption' strategy. Preemption strategies, in the form of trade barriers, would be much more controversial under trade laws. To be sure, many would argue that they would violate the general principle that trade barriers should constitute a measure of last resort to achieving social goals. The practice of using tariffs to achieve social and political goals has fallen into deep disfavour in the era of trade liberalization and globalization; yet, for a variety of reasons, when used in moderation it may represent the best way for a government to take immediate steps to stabilize a domestic socio-economic crisis. This subsection will consider first the WTO and then NAFTA.

In the WTO context, constraints on protective measures arise under both the Sanitary and Phytosanitary (SPS)[100] and the Technical Barriers to Trade (TBT)[101] Agreements, each of which imposes obligations of non-discriminatory treatment, encourages harmonization of regulatory measures, and requires transparent assessment and decision-making procedures. With respect to trade barriers imposed for biodiversity purposes, in the *EC Biotech* decisions, the WTO recently found inconsistency between the SPS Agreement, *inter alia*, and trade barriers imposed by the European Community and its member states against genetically modified organisms.[102]

98 Cartagena Protocol on Biosafety to the Convention on Biological Diversity (Cartagena Biosafety Protocol) (Montreal, 29 January 2000), Art 1.

99 NAC EC Secretariat Report, note 100 above, 25 (noting a $1 million grant by the UN Development Program and the Global Environment Facility).

100 Agreement on the Application of Sanitary and Phytosanitary Measures, Final Act Embodying the Results of the Uruguay Round of Multilateral Trade Negotiations (Marrakech, 15 April 1994).

101 Agreement on Technical Barriers to Trade, Final Act Embodying the Results of the Uruguay Round of Multilateral Trade Negotiations (Marrakech, 15 April 1994).

102 World Trade Organization Dispute Settlement Body, *EC – Approval and Marketing of Biotech Products*, Panel Reports WT/DS291 (Complaint by the United States), WT/DS292 (Complaint by Canada), and WT/DS293 (Complaint by Argentina).

On the question of intellectual property rights and the TRIPS Agreement, the CBD says very little about the relationship between biodiversity and intellectual property rights. The primary language on the intersection of biodiversity and intellectual property is in Article 16, which addresses technology transfer.[103] The lack of clarity in terms of the relationship between the public policy of biodiversity, as reaffirmed by the CBD, and the TRIPS Agreement, has become the subject of talks in the WTO's current negotiations on the Doha Development Agenda.[104]

In the context of NAFTA, the reversal of trade liberalization for US corn imports would not necessarily create a violation, as the bound tariff rates have been higher than those applied to corn imports.[105] In addition, if the tariffs satisfy the 'Most-Favoured Nation' principle by being indiscriminately applicable to all like imports, then the government should have some legal flexibility to raise the tariff.

It is auspicious that one of the best studies on the economic and social effects of corn imports under NAFTA arises under the auspices of its sister treaty, the North American Agreement for Environmental Cooperation (NAAEC).[106] Article 13 of the NAAEC provides that the North American Commission for Environmental Cooperation (CEC) Secretariat can prepare a report on a relevant environmental matter, and Article 14 provides that the Secretariat may consider requests by non-governmental organizations to prepare a Report on a particular environmental matter.

Following a 2001 report by the Mexican government of contamination of local genetic varieties by transgenic maize in the states of Oaxaca, Puebla, and Diconsa, the CEC Secretariat was petitioned to prepare a report on the matter by 'members of Mexican civil society, international organizations and, in particular, indigenous and peasant groups from Oaxaca'.[107] The result has been a wide-ranging series of studies commissioned and published by the CEC.[108] The CEC Secretariat itself rejects the notion that genetically modified agriculture

---

103 Convention on Biological Diversity, note 5 above, Art 16.

104 Note 87 above, para (19).

105 In the future, the analysis of bound rates may include concessions under the WTO Agreement on Agriculture as well as NAFTA.

106 North American Agreement on Environmental Cooperation (Washington, 9 and 14 September 1993; Ottawa 12 and 14 September 1993; Mexico City, 8 and 14 September 1993; 32 ILM 1480).

107 North American Commission for Environmental Cooperation Secretariat Report, *Maize and Biodiversity: The Effects of Transgenic Maize in Mexico: Key Recommendations and Findings* (2004).

108 Ibid; North American Commission for Environmental Cooperation Secretariat Report, *Maize and Biodiversity: The Effects of Transgenic Maize in Mexico: Background Volume* (2004).

is inherently harmful,[109] but has observed that the research in this area remains too preliminary to determine the specific impacts of US genetically modified corn imports in Mexico.[110]

Moreover, the CEC recognizes that the economic and social effects of corn imports on local production have often been adverse.[111] While the North American Agreement on Environmental Cooperation does not promise much in the way of specific regulatory sanctions or other enforcement measures, it has been able to contribute meaningfully to the ongoing assessment of this issue, and has demonstrated some responsiveness to local concerns.[112]

Conclusion

The NAFTA Corn Case provides an excellent opportunity to explore connections between trade, labour and intellectual property rules that remain understudied in the literature, but that hold demonstrated and important implications for the policy and political economy of liberalizing states. This connection arises when the following circumstances unfold: when trade liberalization stimulates labour migration out of traditional agricultural production, in the process threatening indigenous strains of agricultural biotechnology.

The focus of this chapter is ultimately to show how underlying economic dynamics of globalization, coupled with law and policy in the domains of trade, labour, and intellectual property, have potentially created deleterious consequences for sustainable economic development. In the Mexican context, the NAFTA Corn Case demonstrates how these dynamics might conspire to create dangerous risks for local agriculture, genetic resources and biodiversity. Thus, this chapter provides an example in which the international order remains unfortunately inadequate to the goals both of economic development and of environmental conservation. At the same time, the chapter shows that there are a variety of potentially useful strategies that have only begun to be implemented, including both tailored and relaxed private intellectual property rights, and enhanced public biodiversity programming, for redressing this complex problem.

---

109 *Recommendations and Findings*, ibid, 17–22.

110 Ibid, 23, 27.

111 Ibid, 31; see also *Background Volume*, note 111 above.

112 HM Osofsky, 'The Geography of the CEC's Citizen Submissions Process Mapping the State–Corporate Regulatory Dynamic' (2006) *Mich State J of Int'l L* 463, 465, 477.

13

HARMONIZATION WITHOUT CONSENSUS: CRITICAL REFLECTIONS ON DRAFTING A SUBSTANTIVE PATENT LAW TREATY

Jerome H Reichman and Rochelle Cooper Dreyfuss

Introduction

One can readily understand why proposals to further harmonize domestic patent laws at the international level[1] have recently attracted considerable attention.[2] As the component of intellectual property in global trade continues to grow, the

[1] See Standing Committee on the Law of Patents, (SCP), Draft Substantive Patent Law Treaty (SPLT), 10th Sess, 10–14 May 2004, WIPO Doc SCP/10/2, 30 September 2003; Standing Committee on the Law of Patents, (SCP), 'Information on Certain Recent Developments in Relation to the Draft Substantive Patent Law Treaty (SPLT)', 10th Sess, 10–14 May 2004, WIPO Doc SCP/10/8, 17 March 2004; Standing Committee on the Law of Patents, (SCP), Report, 10th Sess, 10–14 May 2004, WIPO Doc SCP/10/11, 1 June 2005.

[2] See generally papers presented at the World Intellectual Property Organization's Open Forum on the Draft Substantive Patent Law Treaty (SPLT), International Conference Center (ICC), Geneva, 1–3 March 2006 [hereinafter WIPO Open Forum], available at <http://www.wipo.int/meetings/en/2006/scp_of_ge_06/scp_of_ge_06_inf1.html>.

costs of worldwide protection and enforcement have soared.[3] Patent holders have accordingly begun to search for ways to acquire and maintain their exclusive rights more efficiently in an integrated world marketplace.[4] They are also increasingly frustrated by the need to pursue multiple actions for infringement in cross-border disputes. Under the bedrock principle of territoriality, successive litigations can trigger different applications of domestic and international patent norms to the same set of facts, and lead to conflicting judgments and irreconcilable outcomes.[5]

Governments have responded to the upswing in patent applications by searching for techniques that would allow them to share examination responsibilities and costs.[6] Important procedural advances have been embodied in the Patent Cooperation Treaty[7] and in various regional agreements, such as the European Patent Convention.[8] However, these instruments are seldom the product of true

3 See Erwin F Berrier, 'Global Patent Costs Must be Reduced' (1996) 36 *IDEA* 473; Gretchen Ann Bender, 'Clash of the Titans: The Territoriality of Patent Law *vs*. The European Union' (2000) 40 *IDEA* 49.

4 See below, notes 7–17 and accompanying text.

5 See Rochelle C Dreyfuss and Jane C Ginsburg, 'Draft Convention on Jurisdiction and Recognition of Judgments in Intellectual Property Matters' (2002) 77 *Chi–Kent LR* 1065; Mariano Municoy, Symposium, 'Allocation of Jurisdiction on Patent Disputes in the Models Developed by the Hague Conference in Private International Law: Asymmetric Countries and the Relationship of Private Parties' (2005) 4 *Chi–Kent J IP* 342. In the United States, the Court of Appeals for the Federal Circuit was torn by the tension between territoriality and the global exercise of patent rights. Compare, e.g. *Voda v Cordis Corp*, 476 F3d 887 (Fed Cir 2007) (refusing to consolidate multiple related cases) with *AT&T Corp v Microsoft Corp*, 414 F3d 1366 (Fed Cir 2005) (endorsing *de facto* extraterritorial application of domestic software patents to conduct occurring abroad). The Supreme Court has yet to speak on the *Voda* issue, but in *Microsoft Corp v AT&T Corp*, 127 S. Ct 1746 (2007), it reversed the Federal Circuit's extraterritorial application of US patent law to foreign activity.

6 Bruce A Lehman, Chairman of the Board, International Intellectual Property Institute, 'Addressing the Crises in the Global Patent System', Speech on Behalf of the Singapore Intellectual Property Office (October 2004), available at <http://www.iipi.org/topics/regional_intellectual_property_integration.asp>.

7 Patent Cooperation Treaty, 19 June 1970, 28 UST 7645, 1160 UNTS 231.

8 Convention on the Grant of European Patents (European Patent Convention), 5 October 1973, 1065 UNTS 255, available at <http://www.european-patent-office.org/legal/epc/>. In addition, the EC is considering the development of a region-wide Community Patent. See generally, John H Barton, 'Issues Posed by a World Patent System' (2004) 7 *J Int'l Econ L* 341; Hanns Ullrich, 'National, European and Community Patent Protection: Time for Reconsideration', European University Institute, Department of Law, EUI Working Papers, Law No 2006/41 (December, 2006), available at <http://cadmus.iue.it/dspace/handle/1814/6421>. Other nations are contemplating or have enacted similar measures: see Marcelo J Vernengo, 'Kees de Joncheere & Enrique Fefer, Advances in Pharmaceutical Market Integration in MERCOSUR and Other Latin American Countries' (1998) 32 *Drug Information J* 831; Agreement Revising the Bangui Agreement of 2 March 1977 on the Creation of an African Intellectual Property Organization (OAPI), 24 February 1999, available at <http://www.oapi.wipo.net/doc/en/bangui_agreement.pdf>; see also <http://www.oapi.wipo.net/fr/OAPI/index.htm>; The Protocol on Patents and Industrial Designs within the Framework of the African Regional Intellectual Property Organization (ARIPO), 10 December 1982, amended 13 August 2004, available at <http://www.aripo.org/download.php?lng=en>; see also OAPI site (address above).

harmonization exercises, in part because the outcome of examinations conducted within these frameworks is typically a set of individual national patents that remain separately enforceable under local laws.[9] In 1994, the Agreement on Trade-Related Aspects of Intellectual Property Rights (TRIPS Agreement),[10] which incorporated the 1967 text of the Paris Convention for the Protection of Industrial Property,[11] took a major step toward substantive patent law harmonization. It established a set of minimum international standards of protection for some 150 participating countries.[12] Yet this Agreement, which did not attempt to create a uniform or deeply harmonized global patent regime, left ample room for national variations and approaches that are often collectively deemed the TRIPS flexibilities.[13]

The effort by the World Intellectual Property Organization (WIPO) to organize a thorough exploration of the possibilities for further harmonization is therefore a welcome development to much of the patent community.[14] Under the aegis of WIPO's Standing Committee on the Law of Patents (SCP), the Draft Substantive Patent Law Treaty (SPLT)[15] represents an attempt 'to pursue a "deep harmonization" of both the law and practice' concerning not just the drafting, filing, and examination of patent applications, but also cornerstone requirements of patentability, such as novelty, non-obviousness, sufficiency of description, and drafting and interpretation of claims.[16] Notably, through the efforts of

9 See European Patent Convention, note 8 above. A draft European Patent Litigation Agreement is also under consideration: see, e.g. Draft European Patent Litigation Agreement, available at <http://www.european-patent-office.org/epo/epla/pdf/agreement_draft.pdf>.

10 Agreement on Trade-Related Aspects of Intellectual Property Rights, 15 April 1994, Marrakech Agreement Establishing the WTO, Annex 1C, Legal Instruments—Results of the Uruguay Round, Vol 31, 33 ILM 81 (1994).

11 Paris Convention for the Protection of Industrial Property, 20 March 1883, 21 USUST 1583, 828 UNTS 303, amended 28 September 1979; TRIPS Agreement, ibid, Art 2.1.

12 See TRIPS Agreement, note 10 above, Art 27–34.

13 See ibid, Art 1.1. See generally UNCTAD–ICTSD, *Resource Book on TRIPS and Development* (Cambridge University Press, 2007) [hereafter UNCTAD–ICTSD, Resource Book]; Carlos M Correa, *Trade-Related Aspects Of Intellectual Property Rights: A Commentary On The TRIPS Agreement* (Oxford University Press, 2007); Jerome H Reichman, 'Universal Minimum Standards of Intellectual Property Protection under the TRIPS Component of the WTO Agreement,' in Carlos M Correa and A A Yusuf (eds), *Intellectual Property And International Trade—The TRIPS Agreement* (Kluwer Law International, 1998). See also John Sulston, 'International Patent Law Harmonisation, Development and Policy Space for Flexibility,' Presentation Before the WIPO Open Forum, note 2 above.

14 See, Kenji Kamata, 'The Rationale and Benefits of Patent Law Harmonization', Presentation Before the WIPO Open Forum, note 2 above; Daeshik Jeh, 'International Patent Law Harmonization and Development: The Experience of Korea', ibid.

15 See note 1 above.

16 Karen M Hauda, 'The Role of the United States in World-Wide Protection of Industrial Property', in Frank Gotzen (ed), *The Future Of Intellectual Property In The Global Market Of The Information Society* (Bruylant, 2003) 91, 97 ('[t]his approach was adopted in an attempt to avoid the controversial hurdles to agreement that were found in the past.'); see also Philippe Baechtold, 'The Future Role of WIPO, in the Area of Industrial Property', ibid at 139, 142–43

the so-called Group of Friends of Development,[17] this initiative is also being tested against the drive for a more development-friendly agenda at WIPO, with a view to ensuring consideration of the needs of all nations, whatever their technological capacities may be.

Despite the promise such an effort holds, we believe that it is unwise to move to deep substantive harmonization at this time. Barely ten years have passed since the TRIPS Agreement elevated patent standards universally,[18] challenging the technological catch-up strategies of all the developing countries, and saddling these countries with social costs that they are still struggling to absorb.[19] As the endless controversies surrounding pharmaceutical patents make clear,[20] higher standards of global protection—whatever their incentive effects[21]—also generate severe and unintended distributional consequences for the developing world.[22]

(highlighting the need to cover other topics, such as patentable subject matter, the requirement of technical character of an invention, exceptions from patentability, novelty grace period, and issue of equivalents).

17 On 4 October 2004, the General Assembly of the World Intellectual Property Organization agreed to adopt a proposal presented by the Group of Friends of Development (namely: Argentina and Brazil) for the establishment of a Development Agenda for WIPO, Doc WO/GA/31/11. Since then, many other proposals have been presented and discussed, see e.g. Provisional Committee on Proposals Related to a WIPO Development Agenda, 'Proposal for a Decision of the PCDA on the Establishment of a WIPO Development Agenda', PCDA/2/2 (22 June 2006), available at <http://www.stakeholderforum.org/22june2006.html>. See also James Boyle, 'A Manifesto on WIPO and the Future of Intellectual Property' (2004) *Duke L & Tech R* 9.

18 For developing countries, the patent standards (Arts 27–34) of the TRIPS Agreement became generally operational on 1 January 2000; see TRIPS Agreement, note 10 above, Art 65.2; Jerome H Reichman, 'The TRIPS Agreement Comes of Age: Conflict or Cooperation with the Developing Countries?' (2000) 32 *Case W Res J Int'l L* 441, 445–47. However, developing countries that did not previously allow product patents on pharmaceutical and agricultural chemical products were given another five years to cover them, subject to a 'mailbox' provision for patents arising in the meantime: see TRIPS Agreement, note 10 above, Arts 65.4, 70.8–70.9 (mailbox and minimum exclusive marketing rights).

19 See, e.g. Commission On Intellectual Property Rights, *Integrating Intellectual Property Rights And Development Policy* (2002), available at <http://www.iprcommission.org/papers/pdfs/final_report/CIPRfullfinal.pdf> [hereafter CIPR]; Carlos M Correa, *Intellectual Property Rights, The WTO And Developing Countries: The TRIPS Agreement And Policy Options* (Zed Books, 2000) 5–44; Reichman, 'Universal Minimum Standards', note 13 above.

20 See, e.g. Janis M Mueller, 'Taking TRIPS to India—Novartis, Patent Law, and Access to Medicines' (8 February 2007) 356 *New England J. Medicine* 541; Robert Steinbrook, 'Thailand and the Compulsory Licensing of Efavirenz', ibid 544–46; see generally Frederick M Abbott, 'Managing the Hydra: The Herculean Task of Ensuring Access to Essential Medicines,' in Keith Maskus and Jerome H Reichman (eds), *International Public Goods And Transfer Of Technology Under A Globalized Intellectual Property Regime* (Cambridge University Press, 2005) [hereafter *Globalized IP Regime*].

21 See, e.g. Alan O Sykes, 'TRIPS, Pharmaceuticals, Developing Countries, and the Doha "Solution"' (2002) 3 *Chi J Int'l L* 47; Ashish Arora, Andrea Fosfuri, and Alphonso Gambardella, 'Markets for Technology, Intellectual Property Rights and Development,' in Maskus and Reichman, *Globalized IP Regime*, note 20 above, 367.

22 See, e.g. Joseph Stiglitz, 'The Economic Foundations of Intellectual Property', Frei Lecture, Duke University School of Law, 16 February 2007, available at <http://www.law.duke.edu/webcast/>; Margaret Chon, 'Intellectual Property and the Development Divide' (2006) 27 *Cardozo LR* 2821

A further round of harmonization will likely aggravate these and other unresolved problems without producing any offsetting user rights or concessions for these countries. On the contrary, the dynamics of TRIPS and the post-TRIPS trade agreements teaches that even a development-sensitive negotiation process is likely to produce an instrument that furthers the interests of developed countries at the expense of poorer, less powerful participants.[23]

More controversially, we contend that higher levels of harmonization will harm even the developed countries, including those that are most aggressively pressing for yet another round of multilateral intellectual property negotiations.[24] The domestic patent laws as currently practiced were largely formulated for the inventions of the Industrial Revolution, and they still largely reflect the technological premises and concepts of the creative sectors as they were then structured. Yet, in this post-industrial information age, with knowledge-intensive inventions emerging from new kinds of research institutions, creative entities are organized non-hierarchically and along continuously-changing lines.[25] New players, such as universities and scientific research entities, now routinely patent their output, and whole new sectors have emerged, including biotechnology and information technology.[26] Until the operations of these and other new technical communities are better understood, there is greater need for legal experimentation at the substantive level than for harmonization. In the absence of any international governance infrastructure capable of interpreting and amending the law (rather than freezing it prematurely), the argument for delaying harmonization becomes especially compelling.[27] Deep harmonization is particularly inappropriate until other methods for improving the efficiency of a global patent system have been fully explored.

(2006); Peter M Gerhart, 'Distributive Values and Institutional Design in the Provision of Global Public Goods' in Maskus and Reichman, *Globalized IP Regime*, note 20 above, 69.

23 See, e.g. Peter K Yu, 'Five Disharmonizing Trends in the International Intellectual Property Regime', in Peter K Yu (ed), *Intellectual Property And Information Wealth* (Praeger Perspectives, 2007) 73.

24 Other commentators subscribing to this view include Susan K Sell, *Private Power, Public Law: The Globalization Of Intellectual Property Rights* (Cambridge University Press, 2003); David Vivas Eugui and Johanna von Braun, 'Beyond FTA Negotiations: Implementing the New Generation of Intellectual Property Obligations', in Yu, note 23 above, 113.

25 See Yochai Benkler, 'An Unhurried View of Private Ordering in Information Transactions' (2000) 53 *Vanderbilt LR* 2063; James Boyle, 'The Second Enclosure Movement and the Construction of the Public Domain' (2003) 66 *L & Contemp Probs* 33; Charlotte Hess and Elinor Ostrum, 'Ideas, Artifacts, and Facilities: Information as a Common-Pool Resource' (2003) 66 *L & Contemp Probs* 111.

26 See Graeme B Dinwoodie and Rochelle C Dreyfuss, 'Intellectual Property Law and the Public Domain of Science' (2004) 7 (2) *J Int'l Econ L* 431; Arti K Rai and Rebecca S Eisenberg, 'Bayh–Dole Reform and the Progress of Biomedicine' (2003) 66 *L & Contemp Probs* 289.

27 See, e.g. Keith E Maskus and Jerome H Reichman, 'The Globalization of Private Knowledge Goods and the Privatization of Global Public Goods', in Maskus and Reichman, *Globalized IP Regime*, note 20 above, 17–20.

In what follows, we survey the implications of deep harmonization for developing countries in Part I, and for developed countries in Part II. In Part III, we suggest that the appropriate goal for the progressive development of world intellectual property law after TRIPS is to nurture an 'incipient transnational system of innovation',[28] which can, in turn, provide the appropriate template for validating global patent norms over time. Our final conclusions are summarized at the end of the chapter.

Part I Likely Adverse Impact on Developing Countries

Before moving to the controversial claim concerning the effects of harmonization on the developed world, we note that even a cursory look at the results of the TRIPS Agreement demonstrates the problems harmonization of the type envisioned by the SPLT poses for the developing world. Although TRIPS specifically leaves room for nations to tailor their laws to their internal needs and pace of intellectual advancement,[29] experience shows that emerging economies are, in fact, greatly challenged by the need to adjust their development strategies to new legal realities.[30]

A. The Social Costs of TRIPS Patent Standards

In principle, higher standards of patent protection under the TRIPS Agreement will provide needed incentives to invest in the innovative sectors of some developing economies,[31] make high-technology products available to local industries, and serve to attract new licensing agreements and foreign direct investments.[32]

---

[28] Ibid, 43–45.

[29] TRIPS Agreement, note 10 above, Arts 1.1 (leaving members 'free to determine the appropriate method of implementing the provisions of this Agreement within their own legal system and practice'), 7–8 (stressing objectives of promoting innovation and transfer of technology 'to the mutual advantage of producers and users of technological knowledge' and 'the public interest in sectors of vital importance to . . . [Members'] socio-economic and technological development'). See generally UNCTAD–ICTSD, Resource Book, note 13 above (discussing 'flexibilities' within the TRIPS regime).

[30] See, e.g. CIPR, note 19 above, at 8–9, 21–27; Maskus and Reichman, 'Globalization and Privatization', note 27 above, 4–15 (citing authorities); Ruth L. Okediji, 'Public Welfare and the Role of the WTO: Reconsidering the TRIPS Agreement' (2003) 17 *Emory Int'l LR* 819. For a more optimistic view, see Joseph Straus, 'The Impact of the New World Order on Economic Development: The Role of Intellectual Property Rights System' (2006) 6 *J Marshall Rev IP* 1.

[31] See, Straus, ibid.

[32] See, e.g. Keith E Maskus, Kamal Saggi and Thitima Puttitanun, 'Patent Rights and International Technology Transfer Through Direct Investment and Licensing', in Maskus and Reichman,

In practice, however, their different national and regional capabilities, institutions, and endowments limit the developing countries' absorptive capacities and reduce the potential benefits of open markets for knowledge goods. This 'technology divide' is then widened by the high rents that must be paid to technology exporters.[33]

Whether they fall into the high, medium or low income brackets, all the developing countries (except for a small group of Least-Developed Countries) that seek to become suppliers of knowledge goods must compete on roughly the same normative terms and conditions that govern advanced industrialized countries.[34] While some have demonstrated considerable capacity in certain technological sectors,[35] all are struggling to cope with the limits TRIPS places on their ability to reverse-engineer up-to-date foreign technologies. For example (and especially problematical), the ability to produce generic drugs without regard to pharmaceutical patents was completely eliminated in 2006.[36] For an economy like India's, where the generic drug industry is a significant source of income and a key locus of technological development, 'fair following' had been an important strategic option.[37]

Globalized IP Regime, note 20 above, 265; see generally Keith E Maskus, *Intellectual Property Rights In The Global Economy* (Peter G Peterson Institute for International Economics, 2000) 109–42. But see Daniel C K Chow, 'The Role of Intellectual Property in Promoting International Trade and Foreign Direct Investment', in Yu, note 23 above, 187 (stressing China's ability to attract FDI despite weak IPRs).

33 See, e.g. Carlos M Correa, 'Can the TRIPS Agreement Foster Technology Transfer to Developing Countries?' in Maskus and Reichman, *Globalized IP Regime*, note 20 above, 227, 229–32; Carlos M Correa, 'Trends in Technology Transfer—Implications for Developing Countries' (1994) 21 *Sci & Pub Pol* 369. See also Keith E Maskus, 'Encouraging International Technology Transfer' (Draft Report, UNCTAD/ICTSD 2003).

34 See, e.g. TRIPS Agreement, note 10 above, Art 27.1 (requiring that 'patents shall be available for any inventions, whether produces or processes, in all fields of technology . . .' if they meet specified eligibility criteria); ibid., Arts 65–66. As regards pharmaceutical products in particular, see Doha Declaration on the TRIPS Agreement and Public Health, WTO Doc WT/MIN(01)/DEC/2, 14 November 2001 [hereafter Doha Declaration], A7; Decision by the Council for TRIPS of 27 June 2002, Extension of the Transition Period under Article 66.1 of the TRIPS Agreement for Least-Developed Country Members for Certain Obligations with respect to Pharmaceutical Products, WTO Doc IP/C/25, 1 July 2005.

LDCs may postpone implementation of other TRIPS obligations, including the duty to provide patent protection for products other than pharmaceuticals, until 2013; see Extension of the Transition Period under Article 66.1 for Least-Developed Country Members, Decision of the Council for TRIPS of 29 November 2005, WTO Doc IP/C/40, 30 November 2005. During these transition periods, LDCs must continue to respect national treatment and MFN obligations under Arts 3–4 of the TRIPS Agreement.

35 See, e.g. Janice M Mueller, *The Tiger Awakens: The Tumultuous Transformation of India's Patent System and the Rise of Indian Pharmaceutical Innovation* (U of Pittsburgh, Social Science Electronic Publishing, 2006), available at <http://ssrn.com/abstract=923538>; Straus, note 30 above.

36 See note 34 above.

37 See, e.g. Mueller, note 35 above. See generally J H Reichman, 'From Free Riders to Fair Followers: Global Competition under the TRIPS Agreement' (1997) 29 *NYU J Int'l L & Pol* 11.

Whether they engage in the production of knowledge goods for local consumption or for export purposes, developing countries must internalize the TRIPS-mandated intellectual property standards in ways that stimulate potentially innovative industrial sectors without, however, legally discriminating against foreign competitors.[38] They must also avoid undermining those less-advanced sectors of their own economies that meet local needs for knowledge goods at affordable prices. These tensions are reflected, for example, in India's new patent law, where efforts to stimulate the research-based pharmaceutical sector often collide with efforts to preserve its well-developed capacity to supply low-cost drugs for the needy in both domestic and foreign markets.[39]

At the same time, the foreign technology suppliers' demands for increased rent extraction, coupled with refusals to work, refusals to deal, and various forms of unchecked anticompetitive conduct, hamper the efforts of developing countries to acquire high-technology goods on open markets at prices that preserve their own comparative advantages.[40] These practices also frustrate their governments' ability to attract foreign direct investment and to build the infrastructure needed to move to a more competitive position on the technological frontier.[41] While the full extent of these barriers has been insufficiently studied, it seems that high-tech manufacturers in developed countries prefer selling to wholly-owned foreign subsidiaries rather than to potential competitors in developing countries. When sales are made to third parties, the net welfare gains from technology installation may be offset by the costs of increased rent extraction.[42]

Moreover, all the developing countries, even those not engaged in the production of knowledge goods, must maintain patent offices and create mechanisms that enable foreign patent owners to enforce their rights—a costly and burdensome operation.[43] How they accomplish this task will seriously affect their internal development strategies, along with their ability to supply such essential public goods as education, public health, environmental safety, scientific advance,

---

38 TRIPS Agreement, note 10 above, Arts 3 & 4.

39 See Mueller, notes 20 and 35 above.

40 See John H Barton, 'Integrating IPR Policies in Development,' in Christophe Bellman *et al* (eds), *Trading In Knowledge*, 57, 61 (Earthscan, 2003) (stressing difficulties of entry into markets 'dominated by multinational oligopolies' that are 'compounded by the international IP system'); Paul Champ and Amir Attaran, 'Patent Rights and Local Working under the WTO TRIPS Agreement: An Analysis of the US–Brazil Patent Dispute', (2002) 27 *Yale J Int'l L* 365. See also Ruth L. Okediji, 'Sustainable Access to Copyrighted Digital Information Works in Developing Countries,' in Maskus and Reichman, *Globalized IP Regime*, note 20 above, 142.

41 Barton, ibid.

42 See, e.g. Lee L Branstetter, 'Do Stronger Patents Induce More Local Innovation?' in Maskus and Reichman, *Globalized IP Regime*, note 20 above, 309, 317–20.

43 CIPR, note 19 above.

and a soundly competitive marketplace for goods and services.[44] These tensions are linked with, but not necessarily determined by, problems of wealth distribution. For example, the TRIPS Agreement made assumptions about technological self-sufficiency that proved inaccurate and contributed directly to a health crisis over much of the globe.[45] Although the subsequent Doha Round remedied the problem by permitting countries to issue compulsory licenses to meet the health needs of nations unable to produce locally-needed medicines, the Doha Agreement took several years to negotiate and its efficacy has yet to be demonstrated.[46]

Taken together, TRIPS obligations have required all developing countries to address the so-called 'flexibilities' built into that Agreement, with a view to maximizing the benefits and minimizing the social costs of current international minimum standards of intellectual property protection.[47] Increasingly, these same countries must also deal with pressures to provide the higher, TRIPS-Plus levels of intellectual property protection that are embodied in bilateral or regional trade agreements.[48]

B. Shrinking the TRIPS Flexibilities

Against this background, any form of deep harmonization through the SPLT that is likely to win the support of the developed countries seems certain to erode whatever flexibilities the developing countries still retain under the TRIPS Agreement and under subsequently negotiated TRIPS-Plus Free Trade Agreements (including their implicit most-favoured-nation implications).[49] Consider, for example, the eligibility requirement of an inventive step (non-obviousness),

---

[44] Maskus and Reichman, 'Globalization and Privatization', note 27 above. See also Chon, note 22 above, 28–49; Peter K Yu, 'Reconceptualizing Intellectual Property Interests in a Human Rights Framework' (2007) 40 *UC Davis LR* 1039, available at <http://ssrn.com/abstract=927335>.

[45] See, e.g. TRIPS Agreement, note 10 above, Art 31(f); Doha Declaration, note 34 above, ¶ 6; Abbott, note 20 above.

[46] See, e.g. Frederick M Abbott and Jerome H Reichman, Access to Essential Medicines: Lessons Learned Since the Doha Declaration on the TRIPS Agreement and Public Health, and Policy Options for the European Union, Committee on International Trade, Directorate General External Policies of the Union, European Parliament, EXPO/B/INTA/2007/14 (June 2007), available at <http://www.europar/europa.eu/activities/expert/estudies.do?languageEN>; Frederick M Abbott, 'The WTO Medicines Decision: World Pharmaceutical Trade and the Protection of Public Health' (2005) 99 *Am J Int'l L* 317.

[47] See, e.g. UNCTAD–ICTSD, Resource Book, note 13 above; Sisule F Musungu and Cecilia Oh, 'The Use Of Flexibilities In TRIPS By Developing Countries: Can They Promote Access To Medicines?' (2007), available at <http://www.who.int/intellectualproperty/studies/TRIPS_flexibilities/en/index.html>; Reichman, 'From Free Riders to Fair Followers', note 37 above.

[48] See Frederick M Abbott, 'Intellectual Property Rights in a Global Trade Framework: IP Trends in Developing Countries' (2004) 98 *Proc Am Soc of Int'l L* 95, 97.

[49] See TRIPS Agreement, note 10 above, Art 4.

which the TRIPS Agreement now mandates.[50] The standard of inventiveness is intimately tied to a nation's economic goals, and especially to its citizens' technological potential, and the types of creativity it can hope to foster.[51] Even within one nation, determining the right standard can be difficult. In the United States, for example, the threshold of non-obviousness has varied widely at different periods, and this issue has recently become extremely contentious once again.[52]

Perhaps for these reasons, TRIPS leaves the height of the inventive step to national law. Presumably, however, deep harmonization requires convergence on a single standard: finding one that would suit countries at different levels of technological sophistication and for all kinds of intellectual advances could easily prove impossible.[53] Whatever standard is chosen will represent, at best, a mediate position—one that will differ from the optimum for many developing countries.

More generally, there is a risk that virtually every pro-competitive option still left open to developing countries under their domestic patent laws—from exceptions to patentability, to limitations on exclusive rights, and the possibility of imposing compulsory licenses[54]—would shrink or disappear during the SPLT negotiations. After all, on virtually all of these issues, the advanced industrialized countries tend to demand high standards. The United States, for example, has shown little willingness to limit the scope of patentable subject matter by adopting the 'technical effect' requirement found in other countries' patent statutes. It has also resisted the inclusion of exceptions to patentability for health, the environment, or the protection of genetic resources and traditional knowledge. Indeed, the United States appears to be taking the position that any agreement reached must reflect the standards of protection found in current US law.[55] Such intransigence does not bode well for the kind of compromising required to produce an instrument that truly accommodates diverse needs.

---

50 Ibid. Art 27.1 (requiring patents to be made available for inventions that are 'new, involve an inventive step and are capable of industrial application'). Footnote 5 equates the terms 'inventive step' and 'capable of industrial application' with 'nonobvious' and 'useful'.

51 See, e.g. Rochelle C Dreyfuss and Andreas F Lowenfeld, 'Two Achievements of the Uruguay Round: Putting TRIPS and Dispute Resolution Together' (1997) 37 *Va J Int'l L* 275, 300–01. See also CIPR, note 19 above.

52 See, e.g. Adam B Jaffe and Josh Lerner, *Innovation And Its Discontents* (Princeton University Press, 2004) 35; Rebecca S Eisenberg, 'Obvious to Whom? Evaluating Inventions from the Perspective of PHOSITA' (2004) 19 *Berkeley Tech LJ* 885; John H Barton, 'Non-Obviousness' (2003) 43 *IDEA* 475. Indeed, despite 200-plus years of experience with a patent system, the standard of non-obviousness was recently the subject of a Supreme Court case, *KSR Intern Co v Teleflex, Inc* 127 S.Ct 1727 (2007), and the outcome is sure to affect how US patent rights are awarded in the future.

53 For example, although the standard in the United States is currently low (see note 52 above) the standard in India is high: see, Mueller, notes 20 and 35 above.

54 See generally, UNCTAD–ICTSD, Resource Book, note 13 above.

55 See generally, Hauda, note 16 above; Baechtold, note 16 above.

Of course, some relatively high standards were adopted in TRIPS, and even higher ones are being imposed in various bilateral and regional Free Trade Agreements.[56] But in those negotiations, there is, at least theoretically, the prospect that higher intellectual property standards will be exchanged for trade concessions in other areas, leading to some degree of equity. The rents to be extracted from a highly protectionist intellectual property regime would thus be offset (to some extent) by new market access opportunities. In the context of a free-standing patent agreement, such as the SPLT, no such compensation is possible. There is little in the way of offsetting doctrinal concessions that private stakeholders would permit developed-country negotiators to offer developing countries in return for adopting a patent regime that the latter regard as suboptimal. Such a bargaining stalemate, indeed, is precisely what caused the Diplomatic Conference to Revise the Paris Convention to fail in 1985 and led the technology-exporting countries to bring intellectual property within the Uruguay Round of multilateral trade negotiations in 1986.[57]

Admittedly, one might counter-argue that the benefits of a smoothly working worldwide patent system will ultimately trickle down to developing countries and help them climb the technological innovation ladder. Such a system would, in theory, lower transaction costs, produce greater legal certainty, and permit emerging economies to invest in building the technological skills of their population, secure in the knowledge that technology transfer and foreign direct investment will follow.[58]

One problem with this argument is that no-one knows the exact contours of a system that would produce these results, and a good case can be made for quite divergent approaches. For example, one of us has taken the Indian example to heart and argued that developing countries would benefit from a patent system that makes it easy to acquire protection, on the theory that such a regime would

---

56 See, e.g. Australia–United States Free Trade Agreement, 18 May 2004, 118 Stat 919, Art 17.4.7(e)(i), available at <http://www.dfat.gov.au/trade/negotiations/us_fta/final-text/index.html> (prohibiting parallel importation, even though the issue is left open by the TRIPS Agreement, note 10 above, Art 6). See generally, Carlos M Correa, 'Defeating the WTO System for Access to Medicines' (2004) 36 *Case W Res J Int'l L* 79, 80.

57 See Punta Del Este Declaration, World Trade Organization, Ministerial Declaration of 20 September 1986, MIN(86)/W/19, 25 ILM 1623 (1986), available at <http://www.sice.oas.org/trade/Punta_e.asp>. See generally Sell, note 24 above; Peter K Yu, 'Symposium, Currents and Crosscurrents in the International Intellectual Property Regime' (2004) 38 *Loyola LA LR* 323; Frederick M Abbott, 'First World Assets in the Third World: Intellectual Property Negotiations in the GATT Multilateral Framework' (1989) 22 *Vand J Transnat'l L* 689.

58 Compare Maskus, Saggi and Puttitanun, note 32 above, with John H Barton, 'Issues Posed by a World Patent System,' in Maskus and Reichman, *Globalized IP Regime*, note 20 above, 617, 621–28 (arguing that there is a strong need to accommodate developing countries' problems).

encourage innovation at the level at which it can be realistically elicited, and that the resulting patents would produce 'buy in', in the form of an appreciation for the wealth that intellectual property protection creates.[59] Conversely, the other has suggested exactly the opposite: that the need to build competitive markets mandates that the acquisition of full patent rights should be made relatively difficult. On this view, governments should rely on second-tier regimes, such as utility model laws or 'compensatory liability regimes'—liability rules, to stimulate investment in locally-attainable adaptations or improvements of foreign technology, and in 'cumulative and sequential innovation' generally.[60] In the absence of empirical evidence either way, experimentation makes more sense than freezing the law prematurely.

Trumping all of these substantive and strategic considerations, moreover, is the fact that what developing countries most need is a period of calm and stability in which to devise intellectual property strategies consistent with both the TRIPS Agreement and the needs of their own emerging national and regional systems of innovation. This is a lengthy, arduous, and difficult task in its own right. It is hard for governments and civil society to interact in devising innovation policies that will maximize the use of local assets, minimize the social costs of high international minimum standards of intellectual property protection, and preserve an optimal supply of public goods that are as essential to long-term development prospects as legal incentives to innovate.[61] They cannot succeed if, at the international level, a new round of multilateral intellectual property negotiations threatens to raise the technological ladder once again, before they even get a solid foothold on it.[62]

Part II Likely Adverse Impact on Developed Countries

However cogent the aforementioned concerns of developing countries might be, one must nonetheless weigh them against the supposed benefits of deep harmonization.[63] If lower transaction costs, increased legal certainty, and greater economies

---

59 Dreyfuss and Lowenfeld, note 51 above.

60 Reichman, 'From Free Riders to Fair Followers', note 37 above; Maskus and Reichman, 'Globalization and Privatization', note 27 above; Jerome H Reichman and Tracy Lewis, 'Using Liability Rules to Stimulate Local Innovation in Developing Countries: Application to Traditional Knowledge,' in Maskus and Reichman, *Globalized IP Regime*, note 20 above, 337–66.

61 Margaret Chon, for example, highlights the problem of providing schoolchildren with affordable textbooks: note 22 above.

62 Maskus and Reichman, 'Globalization and Privatization', note 27 above, 35–41.

63 See, e.g. Daeshik Jeh, note 14 above. See also Baechtold, note 16 above; Hauda, note 16 above.

of scale and scope prove as remunerative as the advocates of harmonization contend, one could envisage a compromise scheme that adopts law appropriate for developed economies but permits developing countries to pursue a slower track, further placating them with selected concessions[64] and compensatory side payments.[65]

The sad truth, however, is that no-one has managed to put forward a vision of a properly functioning patent system for the *developed* world that commands even the appearance of a consensus. There are as many different proposals and solutions on the table as there are thinkers and investigators. With its relatively experienced patent office, excellent trial courts, specialized appellate court, and a Supreme Court poised to add a generalist perspective, the United States uniquely possesses the kind of institutional infrastructure needed to build and maintain a strong patent law system.[66] Even so, all that the proponents for change in that country can agree on is that the current patent law badly needs reform. The risk of litigation is rising rapidly, which creates a drag on innovation and imposes disincentives to invest in creative production.[67] Two studies by the National Academies and another by the Federal Trade Commission;[68] numerous legal and economics scholars;[69] along with a variety

---

64 Concessions might include greater harmonization of international patent law with the Convention on Biological Diversity, with imposition of certificates of origin, prior consent for inventions making use of developing country resources, and with some recognition of traditional knowledge in international intellectual property law. See, e.g. Graham Dutfield, 'Legal and Economic Aspects of Traditional Knowledge,' in Maskus and Reichman, *Globalized IP Regime*, note 20 above, 495–520; Thomas Cottier and Marion Panizzon, 'Legal Perspectives on Traditional Knowledge: The Case For Intellectual Property Protection' (2004) 7 *J Int'l Econ L* 371.

65 See, e.g. Robert O Keohane, 'Comment: Norms, Institutions, and Cooperation', in Maskus and Reichman, *Globalized IP Regime*, note 20 above, 65–68.

66 See, e.g. Rochelle C Dreyfuss, 'The Federal Circuit: A Case Study in Specialized Courts' (1989) 64 *NYU LR* 1.

67 See Michael J Meurer and James Bessen, 'The Patent Litigation Explosion' (2005) Am L & Econ Ass'n 15th Annual Meeting, Paper 57, available at <http://law.bepress.com/alea/15th/art57>. See also Scott Stern and Fiona Murray, 'Do Formal Intellectual Property Rights Hinder the Free Flow of Scientific Knowledge? An Empirical Test of the Anti-Commons Hypothesis' (2005) NBER Working Paper No W11465, available at <http://ssrn.com/abstract=755701>.

68 National Research Council, *A Patent System for the 21st Century* (The National Academies, 2004); ibid, *Reaping the Benefits of Genomic and Proteomic Research: Intellectual Property Rights, Innovation, and Public Health* (2006); Federal Trade Commission, 'To Promote Innovation: The Proper Balance of Competition and Patent Law and Policy' (2003), available at <http://www.ftc.gov/os/2003/10/innovationrpt.pdf>.

69 See, e.g. Maskus and Reichman, 'Globalization and Privatization', note 27 above, 24 nn. 85–88 (citing critical articles by Professors Rai, Kesan, Thomas, Leung, Quillen and Ogden, Baird, Merges, Lemley, Heller and Eisenberg, Barton and others); Rochelle C Dreyfuss, 'Pathological Patenting: The PTO as Cause or Cure' (2006) 104 *Mich LR* 1559; Robert P Merges, 'As Many as Six Impossible Patents Before Breakfast: Property Rights for Business Concepts and Patent System Reform' (1999) 14 *Berkeley Tech. LJ* 577; Jaffe and Lerner, note 52 above, 35 (contending that patents are now available 'to pretty much anyone who asked for one, despite the legal tests or novelty and nonobviousness', a trend that 'now undermines rather than fosters the crucial

of judges[70] have offered various diagnoses of the problems and assorted, and often contradictory, prescriptions for change. In Europe, similar uncertainty exists as the EPO's recent publication, entitled 'Scenarios for the Future', frankly acknowledges.[71]

It should surprise no-one that new technologies and new modes of producing them will raise hard questions that cannot be answered by routine tinkering with a patent paradigm launched in Venice in the fifteenth century and refined by the United Kingdom in the seventeenth century.[72] There are major new challenges for which our past experiences give only untested and untrustworthy hypotheses, with no convincing empirical studies on the horizon to resolve the doubts. These problems affect all aspects of patent protection. Not only are there substantial discordant views on how high the inventive step should be, there are also disagreements on virtually every substantive topic under discussion in connection with the SPLT: novelty and utility standards, the research exemption, compulsory licenses—along with standards for analysing infringement and awarding relief.[73]

Furthermore, there are a multitude of open procedural questions, including questions about the level of scrutiny that patent offices give to applications, the standards for re-examining issued patents, as well as the availability of avenues to challenge patents administratively (through opposition procedures) and judicially (through, for instance, declaratory judgment actions).[74] The National Academies' Report criticized the reluctance of the Federal Circuit to defer to the examination guidelines that the US Patent Office applies to new technologies, while

process of innovation'. In reality, Jaffe and Lerner are more optimistic than they sound, because they think the problems stem from how the patent law is applied and not from what it provides).

70 See, e.g. *In re Fisher*, 421 F3d 1365 (Fed Cir, 2005) (disagreement between majority and dissent on the utility standards); *University of Rochester v GD Searle & Co, Inc*, 358 F3d 916 (Fed Cir 2003) (disagreement between majority and dissent on the written description requirement); *Integra Lifesciences v Merck*, 331 F3d 860 (Fed Cir 2003) (disagreement between majority and dissent on the scope of infringement liability), reversed, 545 US 193 (2005).

71 European Patent Office (EPO), 'Scenarios for the Future—How Might IP Regimes Evolve by 2005? What Global Legitimacy Might Such Regimes Have?' (2007).

72 See generally John F Duffy, 'Harmony and Diversity in Global Patent Law' (2002) 17 *Berkeley Tech LJ* 685.

73 See, e.g. US Department of Commerce, 'Request for Comments on the International Effort to Harmonize the Substantive Requirements of Patent Law', 66 Fed Reg 15409 (2001) (listing 17 differences between US patent law and the law of other developed countries). See also James Gleick, 'Patently Absurd' (12 March 2000) *NY Times Magazine*, 44.

74 For US examples, see, e.g. Patent Reform Act of 2005, HR 2795, 109th Cong, 1st Sess (2005) (suggesting institution of an opposition procedure); *MedImmune, Inc v Genentech, Inc*, 127 SC 764 (2007) (standing to challenge patent validity in a declaratory judgment action). See also Mark A Lemley, 'Rational Ignorance at the Patent Office' (2001) 95 *Northwestern U LR* 1495 (discussing appropriate level of scrutiny in the Patent Office).

applying unrealistic standards of its own that ignore what those skilled in the art actually know.[75] Others have questioned vesting powers over patent law in a single specialized court, pointing to the Federal Circuit's penchant for *de novo* review,[76] its apparent lack of interest in economics or patent policy,[77] and its insulation from criticism.[78]

This is not the place to explore all of the problems with which the system is currently grappling. Our purpose is to demonstrate how promulgating substantive law in the absence of either a normative consensus, or an authority competent (in both the cognitive and juridic sense) to administer and revise it, will interfere with the emergence of new industries, with scientific advancement, and with the development of new approaches to encouraging and supporting innovation.

A. Emerging Industries

While it is certainly true that there is broad dissatisfaction with the domestic patent systems, many of the complaints—at least in the United States—are based on law developed for emerging sectors, principally information technology and biotechnology.[79] These issues merit a deeper look.

Information Technologies (IT)

With regard to the IT sector, there is considerable debate over whether exclusive rights are necessary to promote development of software and business methods, and—even if they are—whether patent protection is the appropriate regime to use. Unlike copyrights and contractual rights, patents create claims that are good even against independent inventors. For cumulative technologies or where interoperability is an important goal, the need to sift through prior

75 See 'A Patent System for the 21st Century', note 68 above.

76 See, e.g. Samantha A Jameson, 'The Problems of the Utility Analysis in Fisher and its Associated Policy Implications and Flaws' (2006) 56 *Duke LJ* 311 (questioning whether the PTO is equipped to deal with policy and criticizing the decision in *Fisher*).

77 Compare *In re Fisher*, note 70 above ('we observe that the government and its *amici* express concern that allowing EST patents without proof of utility would discourage research, delay scientific discovery, and thwart progress in the "useful Arts" and "Science." . . . [These] are public policy considerations which are more appropriately directed to Congress as the legislative branch of government, rather than this court as a judicial body responsible simply for interpreting and applying statutory law'). See generally, Rochelle C Dreyfuss, 'The Federal Circuit: A Continuing Experiment in Specialization' (2004) 54 *Case W Res LR* 769.

78 See, e.g. Arti K Rai, 'Engaging Facts and Policy: A Multi-Institutional Approach to Patent System Reform' (2003) 103 *Colum LR* 1035; Arti K Rai, 'Allocating Power over Fact-Finding in the Patent System' (2004) 19 *Berkeley Tech LJ* 907; Dreyfuss,'Pathological Patenting', note 69 above.

79 See, e.g. Dan Burk and Mark A Lemley, 'Is Patent Law Technologically Specific?' (2002) 17 *Berkeley LJ* 1155.

patents and negotiate rights arguably creates a high tax on innovation and a drag on development.[80]

Other untoward consequences may flow from the decision to permit patenting in this sector. For example, the risk of debilitating suits motivates participants to acquire multiple patents, hoping that with enough potential counterclaims, they can fend off or negotiate their way out of difficulty. The result is a vicious cycle: thickets of rights that are expensive (or nearly impossible) to clear, requiring an ever-larger arsenal of defensive protection.[81] Furthermore, many IT products involve multiple inventions and, accordingly, a multiplicity of licences.[82] In that environment, hold-out possibilities are numerous and, as the Blackberry case nearly demonstrated, can potentially undermine the investments of producers, other patentees, and the public.[83]

In addition, some products in this sector are characterized by strong network effects and standard setting, which may make switching costs high and lock consumers into inferior products.[84] Those holding patent rights in the products towards which a market has tipped receive awards out of all proportion to the technical contributions of the inventors. When these patents also dominate their fields, they allow right holders to prevent entry by competitors.[85]

Commentators further criticize the way the law has been administered. To some, the European approach, which looks for a technical effect, is superior because it greatly limits the kinds of information technology that can be protected.[86] Others note that, because courts assume the level of skill in the art to be high, they relieve patentees of the obligation to disclose the underlying code. These patents can be very broad and, because they fail to enable, they deprive the public of one

---

[80] Many of these problems were identified well before patents on software were issued. See Pamela Samuelson, Randall Davis, Mitchell D Kapor and J H Reichman, 'A Manifesto Concerning the Legal Protection of Computer Programs' (1994) 94 *Colum LR* 2308.

[81] Jaffe and Lerner, note 52 above.

[82] See, e.g. Bronwyn H Hall and Rosemarie Ham Ziedonis, 'The Patent Paradox Revisited: An Empirical Study of Patenting in the US Semiconductor Industry, 1979–1995' (2001) 32 *RAND J Econ* 101.

[83] See *NTP, Inc v Research in Motion, Ltd*, 418 F3d 1282 (Fed Cir 2005). See generally Jeremiah Chan and Matthew Fawcett, 'Footsteps of the Patent Troll' (2005) 10 *IP L Bull* 1.

[84] Michael L Katz and Carl Shapiro, 'Network Externalities, Competition, and Compatibility' (1985) 75 *Am Econ R* 424, 424; Christopher R Leslie, 'The Anticompetitive Effects of Unenforced Invalid Patents' (2006) 91 *Minn LR* 101.

[85] See, e.g. Rochelle C Dreyfuss, 'Unique Works/Unique Challenges at the Intellectual Property/Competition Law Interface,' in *European Competition Law Annual 2005*. See also Carl Shapiro, 'Navigating the Patent Thicket: Cross Licenses, Patent Pools, and Standard-Setting,' in Adam Jaffe *et al*, (eds) *Innovation Policy And The Economy* (MIT Press, 2001), Vol 1.

[86] Rochelle Dreyfuss, 'Are Business Method Patents Bad for Business?' (2000) 16 *Santa Clara Computer & High Tech LJ* 264; John R Thomas, 'The Patenting of the Liberal Professions' (1999) 40 *BC LR* 1139.

of the significant benefits of the patent system.[87] Moreover, because monetary damages are based on the value of the product and not of the patent that has been infringed, this sector attracts 'trolls', who are in the business of making money through litigation rather than through product development.[88]

Biotechnology

The burgeoning field of biotechnology is experiencing a different set of problems. Here, the level of skill is considered quite low,[89] which leads to narrow patents and the danger of an 'anticommons effect'.[90] When that occurs, property rights cannot be aggregated efficiently to create, for example, effective methods for assembling and screening new molecules, or to realize the ambitions of personalized medicine, which would require whole-genome sequencing.

Because US courts tend to conceptualize DNA as molecules rather than information products,[91] patent rights in some cases can easily be evaded by—essentially—paraphrasing the information covered by the patent.[92] As a result, the patent may yield insufficient incentives to support research in a given area.[93] Paradoxically, however, there is also a growing number of patents in this field—particularly patents on genes and certain proteins—that, at least for research purposes, is so broad, it is unlikely a patent holder could efficiently exploit the entire breadth of the claims.[94] Meanwhile, the potential blocking effects appear increasingly serious.

Reconciling the Needs of Different Sectors

It is not clear that these problems will be easy to resolve. First, there is disagreement within each sector on the existence, scope, and nature of the problem. For example, despite the strong and persistent complaints about patents in the software industry, there is empirical evidence demonstrating that the patent

87 Dan L Burk and Mark A Lemley, 'Policy Levers in Patent Law' (2003) 89 *Va LR* 1575, 1689.

88 See, e.g. Amy L Landers, 'Let the Games Begin: Incentives to Innovation in the New Economy of Intellectual Property Law' (2006) 46 *Santa Clara LR* 307.

89 See, e.g. *In re Deuel*, 51 F3d 1552 (Fed Cir 1995); *In re Bell*, 991 F2d 781 (Fed Cir 1993).

90 Michael A Heller and Rebecca S Eisenberg, 'Can Patents Deter Innovation? The Anticommons in Biomedical Research' (1 May 1998) 280 *Science* 698.

91 See, e.g. Arti K Rai, 'Intellectual Property Rights in Biotechnology: Addressing New Technology' (1999) 34 Wake Forest LR 827.

92 Helen M Berman and Rochelle C Dreyfuss, 'Reflections on the Science and Law of Structural Biology, Genomics, and Drug Development' (2006) 53 *UCLA LR* 871.

93 Burk and Lemley, 'Policy Levers', note 87 above, 1677–79.

94 See, e.g. Eileen M Kane, 'Splitting the Gene: DNA Patents and the Genetic Code' (2004) 71 *Tenn LR* 707, 710 & n.13. See also Kyle Jensen and Fiona Murray, 'Intellectual Property Landscape of the Human Genome' (October 14, 2005) 310 *Science* (suggesting that sometimes a single gene can be associated with as many as 20 patents).

system is not hurting (and may be helping) the development of this industry.[95] Patent reform is thus stalling, at least in part because domestic stakeholders cannot even agree that reform will be worth the dislocations it will entail.

Second, there are disputes about how the problems should be handled. For example, some economists claim that re-engineering the law is not necessary. They argue that the system could be restored to order by the simple expedient of improving the quality of the patents that are issued (that is, by creating a mechanism for ensuring that patents are issued only for inventions that are truly non-obvious).[96]

Third, it is proving so difficult to find common ground among the various patent industries that suggestions have been made for sector-specific legislation.[97] If heeded, this approach could take patent law down untested pathways culminating in a set of clumsy *sui generis* regimes.[98] Moreover, even if such an approach proved politically feasible in a domestic setting, it could elicit objections grounded in the TRIPS Agreement, which requires that 'patents be available and patent rights enjoyable without discrimination as to . . . the field of technology'.[99] Significantly, TRIPS is only a minimum standard regime. Were the United States bound by an instrument that required complete substantive harmonization, resolving the issues that exist within emerging industries will not be possible without endless rounds of entangling negotiations (and, if the system includes enforceable obligations, unsettling appeals).[100]

95 Robert P. Merges, 'Patents, Entry and Growth in the Software Industry' (Social Science Electronic Publishing, 2006), available at <http://papers.ssrn.com/sol3/papers.cfm?abstract_id=92620>; Ronald J Mann, 'Do Patents Facilitate Financing in the Software Industry?' (2005) 83 *Tex LR* 961.

96 Jaffe and Lerner, note 52 above, 197–205.

97 Burk and Lemley, 'Is Patent Law Technologically Specific?', note 79 above.

98 See Jerome H Reichman, 'Legal Hybrids Between the Patent and Copyright Paradigms' (1994) 94 *Colum LR* 2432.

99 TRIPS Agreement, note 10 above, Art 27(1); *Canada – Patent Protection of Pharmaceutical Products*, WT/DS114/R (Report of WTO Dispute Settlement Panel, 2000)(distinguishing between permissible 'reconcilable differentiation' attributable to the needs of different product sectors and impermissible 'discrimination.'). But see Graeme B Dinwoodie and Rochelle C Dreyfuss, 'Diversifying Without Discriminating: Complying with the Mandates of the TRIPS Agreement' (2007) 13 *Mich Telecom & Tech LR* 445 (suggesting that some types of differentiation should withstand challenge).

100 The TRIPS dispute resolution experience is not an entirely happy one in this respect, because WTO Settlement Panels have been ill-equipped to deal with technical legal issues; see, e.g. Joost Pauwelyn, 'WTO Dispute Settlement: Of Sovereign Interests, Private Rights, and Public Goods,' in Maskus and Reichman, *Globalized IP Regime*, note 20 above, 817; Dinwoodie and Dreyfuss, 'IP Law and Science', note 26 above; Gregory Shaffer, 'Recognizing Public Goods in WTO Dispute Settlement: Who Participates? Who Decides? The Case of TRIPS and Pharmaceutical Patents Protection,' in Maskus and Reichman, *Globalized IP Regime*, note 20 above, 884.

One should also note that the technologies discussed above are hardly the end of the line: science is sure to generate new and equally daunting innovation opportunities in the future. One such development already on the horizon is synthetic biotechnology.[101] Because it utilizes both software and biotechnological advances, this field potentially suffers from the combined impact of patenting problems in both sectors.[102] Were the SPLT to be implemented, signatories would have diminished capacity to adapt the legal order so that such new opportunities could flourish.

B. Scientific Advancement

The prospects for the future could become even more troubling. As patenting moves upstream to cover fundamental advances, existing dysfunctions within the system could impede scientific progress and reduce the chances of generating future opportunities for innovation. Drawing once again on the situation in the United States as an example, a reorganization under way within the scientific community has begun to pose hard and unresolved problems for patent law.

The major development here is undoubtedly the entry of universities into the patent system. Since the passage of the Bayh–Dole Act in 1980,[103] which permits universities to hold patents on the fruits of federally-funded research, patent participation by the university sector has significantly increased.[104] Although the statute aimed mainly to encourage technology transfer, universities increasingly understand it as a funding mechanism, with many untoward consequences for science and education. Most obviously, work that once would have gone into the public domain, where it could have been put to general and free use, is now privatized.[105]

---

101 Synthetic biology is an engineering field that utilizes artificially-constructed DNA to construct/program useful 'machines' (such as plants that produce fuel). See Philip Ball, 'Starting from Scratch' (2004) 431 *Nature* 624.

102 See Arti K Rai and James Boyle, 'Synthetic Biology: Caught between Property Rights, the Public Domain, and the Commons' (2007), available at <http://ssrn.com/abstract=941732>.

103 35 USC §§200–212.

104 The issue of cause and effect is itself a subject of dispute. Some claim that the Bayh–Dole Act created the university patenting phenomenon; others contend that universities' desire to patent gave rise to the Act. See David C Mowery, Richard R Nelson, Bhaven N Sampet, and Arvids A Ziedonis, 'The Growth of Patenting and Licensing by US Universities: An Assessment of the Effects of the Bayh–Dole Act of 1980' (2001) 30 *Research Policy* 99.

105 See, e.g. Rai and Eisenberg, note 26 above; Rebecca S Eisenberg, 'Public Research and Private Development: Patents and Technology Transfer in Government-Sponsored Research' (1998) 82 *Va LR* 1663. See also J H Reichman and Paul F Uhlir, 'A Contractually Reconstructed Research Commons for Scientific Data in a Highly Protectionist Intellectual Property Environment' (2003) 66 *L & Contemp Probs* 315.

Moreover, universities have become advocates for the kind of patent rights that generate the most severe problems. Because academia engages in fundamental research, universities want patents that cover fundamental discoveries. These patents create broad rights over core methodologies and research tools—rights that can dominate diverse research agendas.[106] Although there is some empirical evidence indicating that universities have begun to patent more selectively and license these opportunities more wisely,[107] horror stories abound in which universities reportedly signed over rights without any guarantee that their licensees would bring products to market. Indeed, sometimes universities appear to have licensed rights to institutions that had private reasons to stifle research and access.[108] Perhaps to counter this problem, the courts have begun to deploy various patent law theories to narrow the ambit of broad claims,[109] but overly-narrow rights in 'slivers of innovation' create problems of their own.[110]

Even if the universities' behaviour were to improve, problems with their patenting practices could persist. Courts have decided that since universities are behaving as commercial actors, patent law should treat them that way. As a result, courts do not afford academic researchers special privileges to delay work on patentable subject matter, even when the delay was caused by attempts to preserve pedagogic opportunities for students.[111] This creates one of a series of new conflicts between a university's educational mission and its commercial goals; between a faculty member's research and teaching commitments; and between the academy's duties as honest brokers in science policy debates and its proprietary self-interest.

Far more worrisome is the judicial trend to deny academics engaged in scholarly inquiry any further research exemptions from infringement liability.[112]

---

106 See, e.g. Rebecca S Eisenberg, 'Bargaining Over the Transfer of Proprietary Research Tools: Is the Market Failing or Emerging?' in Rochelle C Dreyfuss *et al* (eds), Expanding The Boundaries Of Intellectual Property (Oxford University Press, 2001) 223. See also Rebecca S Eisenberg, 'Reaching through the Genome', in F. Scott Kieff (ed), Perspectives On Properties Of The Human Genome Project (Elsevier Academic Press, 2003) 209–230 [hereafter *Perspectives*].

107 See David C Mowery, Bhaven N Sampet, and Arvids A Ziedonis, 'Learning to Patent: Institutional Experience, Learning, and the Characteristics of US University Patents After Bayh–Dole, 1980–1994' (2002) 48 *Management Science* 73.

108 See, e.g, Avital Bar-Shalom and Robert Cook-Deegan, 'Patents and Innovation in Cancer Therapeutics: Lessons from CellPro' (2002) 80 The Milbank Quarterly, 637.

109 See, e.g. *Rochester v Searle*, note 70 above.

110 See text at note 90, above. See also J H Reichman, 'Saving the Patent Law from Itself,' in Kieff, *Perspectives*, note 106 above, 289.

111 *Griffith v Kanamaru*, 816 F2d 624 (Fed Cir 1987).

112 *Madey v Duke University*, 307 F3d 1351, 1362 (Fed Cir 2002) ('our precedent does not immunize any conduct that is in keeping with the alleged infringer's legitimate business, regardless of commercial implications. For example, major research universities, such as Duke, often sanction and fund research projects with arguably no commercial application whatsoever. However, these

While few infringement suits have actually been filed against universities to date, if such cases were to proliferate unchecked, the cost of basic science would soar. Even in the absence of suits against scientists, a recent empirical study has uncovered evidence that university research is beginning to suffer from an anticommons effect.[113] Although there are also studies showing that patents have little direct impact on university work, erosion of the Mertonian norms has been documented and there is clearly increased secrecy and reluctance to share research materials.[114] Furthermore, patenting could easily come to affect scholarly agendas, shifting attention from the basic work that opens whole new fields of knowledge, to applied research aimed narrowly at exploiting particular commercial markets. Again, the empirical evidence is mixed, but the effects of an increasing interest in patenting (and commerce) on the part of university faculty is alarming.[115]

In theory of course, legislation might remedy some of these problems. For example a codified research exemption could be enacted.[116] Patent applications from academics could be examined differently, and the scope of patents could be adjusted to deal with the anticommons effect. When necessary, compulsory licenses to unblock dependent patents and enable improvers to reach the market could also be enacted, a solution that remains fully consistent with the TRIPS Agreement.[117]

---

projects unmistakably further the institution's legitimate business objectives, including educating and enlightening students and faculty participating in these projects. These projects also serve, for example, to increase the status of the institution and lure lucrative research grants, students and faculty').

113 Stern and Murray, note 67 above.

114 Timothy Caulfield, Robert M Cook-Deegan, F Scott Kieff, and John P Walsh, 'Evidence and Anecdotes: An Analysis of Human Gene Patenting Controversies' (2006) 24 *Nature Biotechnology* 1091; Wesley M Cohen, John P Walsh and Charlene Cho, 'View from the Bench: Patents and Material Transfers' (2005) 309 *Science* 2002.

115 See, e.g. Mario Calderini, Chiara Fanzoni, and Andrea Vezzulli, 'If Star Scientists do not Patent: The Effect of Productivity, Basicness and Impact on the Decision to Patent in the Academic World' (Social Science Electronic Publishing, 2006), available at <http://ssrn.com/abstract=912525> (suggesting that eminent scientists do not patent); Pierre Azoulay, Waverly Ding, and Toby Stuart, 'The Determinants of Faculty Patenting Behavior: Demographics or Opportunities?' (2005) NBER Working Paper Series, available at <http://ssrn.com/abstract=727128> (suggesting that younger faculty and faculty associated with patent holders tend to patent, irrespective of eminence); Richard R Nelson, 'Observations on the Post Bayh–Dole Rise of Patenting at American Universities' (2001) 26 *J Tech Transfer* 13 (stating that the rising number of patents suggests trouble down the road); Jerry G Thursby and Marie C Thursby, 'Who is Selling the Ivory Tower? Sources of Growth in University Licensing' (2000) NBER Working Paper Series., available at <http://ssrn.com/abstract=232103> (showing that agendas are not changing).

116 See, e.g. Rochelle C Dreyfuss, 'Protecting the Public Domain of Science: Has the Time for an Experimental Use Defense Arrived?' (2004) 46 *Ariz LR* 457.

117 See TRIPS Agreement, note 10 above, Art 31(l); Jerome H Reichman with Catherine Hasenzahl, 'Non-Voluntary Licensing of Patented Inventions: Historical Perspective, Legal Framework

Yet, as we saw earlier, and as the marginal notes attest, there is substantial disagreement on the very existence of the problems and on the wisdom of proposed legislative solutions.[118] Were the laws in question subject to substantive international obligations, these problems would be compounded many times over. Some economies might rely on the spill-over benefits of basic research; others might see commercializing university work as an important source of funding. Another complicating factor is that universities do not participate equally in all commercial sectors. Consequently, arguments about technological neutrality would arise in any attempt to alter the patent system to protect core scientific progress.

C. New Approaches

It bears emphasizing that, when faced with the problems of new technologies and new players, countries have adopted very different strategies. In particular, the US approach outlined above differs significantly from developments in Europe. With regard to patents in biotechnology, for example, the European Patent Office, following the European Directive on Biotechnology,[119] seems to be breaking away from the 'chemical compound' analogy that typifies US law and has begun to treat DNA patents as information products, whose eligibility tests should turn on the quality and industrial applicability of the information revealed.[120]

The EC Biotechnology Directive also added a new compulsory license to facilitate interaction between infringing plant breeders and biotech patents.[121] When implementing the Biotechnology Directive, moreover, a number of European governments have embarked on new directions of their own, at the expense of a uniform law. While some were initially unwilling to fully implement the Biotechnology Directive at all,[122] others, such as Germany, have attempted to limit gene patents to the use or purpose recited in the application.[123]

under TRIPS, and an Overview of the Practice in Canada and the USA' (UNCTAD–ICTSD, September 2003).

118 Compare, e.g. Richard A Epstein, 'Steady the Course: Property Rights in Genetic Material,' in Kieff, *Perspectives*, note 106 above, 168 with Rochelle C Dreyfuss, 'Varying the Course in Patenting Genetic Material: A Counter-Proposal to Richard Epstein's Steady Course,' ibid., at 195.

119 Directive 98/44/EC of the European Parliament and of the Council of 6 July 1998 on the Legal Protection of Biotechnological Inventions, OJ L 213/13, 30 July 1998.

120 See RJ Alerts, 'The Industrial Applicability and Utility Requirements for the Patenting of Genomic Inventions: A Comparison Between European and US Law' (2004) 26 *Eur IP R* 349.

121 Note 119 above, Art 12.

122 The recalcitrant EU Member States all implemented the Directive by the end of 2005; see <http://www.europa.eu.int/comm/internal_market/indprop/docs/invent/state-of-play_en.pdf>.

123 Patentsgesetz (Patent Act) §1a(4).

The European Patent Office also seems to have handled the information technology sector more cautiously than has the United States: it has insisted on a demonstrable 'technical contribution' palpably beyond the state of the art.[124] How the European Patent Office proceeds in this area now that the European Parliament has rejected a proposed Directive on the Patenting of Software deserves careful scrutiny.[125] Furthermore, even if patents on software were eventually to produce the kind of blocking effects being experienced in the United States, many of the European countries formally recognize the possibility of compulsory licenses for dependent patents on improvements.[126] Although these provisions are seldom invoked, they likely exert *in terrorem* effects that lead to efficient licensing practices, and they provide a codified antiblocking measure when needed.

Moreover, the patent system is not the only mechanism for encouraging technological progress. A strong argument can be made for supplementing patents with new kinds of intermediate or second-tier protection systems that are more attuned to present-day technological realities. While robust property-like regimes, such as patent law, presuppose clear boundaries between different rights holders, the actual boundaries between products of the new technologies are often ill-defined. The problem of cumulative innovation is thus aggravated by the ways in which new contributions are dependent on, and intermingled with, earlier innovations. From today's perspective, patents breed high litigation and transaction costs because they artificially divide that which is inherently indivisible, a practice that needlessly decreases the optimum rate of innovation by chilling the ability of second comers to build on earlier contributions for both scientific and commercial purposes.[127]

In sectors where these conditions are prevalent, a different kind of regime might be superior. To give one example, compensatory liability rules may be a good solution for cumulative technologies. They would protect first comers against wholesale duplication while enabling improvers to build on their work, subject

---

[124] E Panagiotidou, 'The Patentability of Computer Programs, According to the Commission's New Proposal for a Directive and to EPO Boards of Appeal Decisions' (2003) 9 *Computer & Telecom LR* 126; Wolfgang Tauchert, 'Patent Protection for Computer Programs—Current Status and New Developments' (2000) 31 *IIC* 812; Thomas Hoeren, 'The European Union Commission and Recent Trends in European Information Law' (2003) 29 *Rutgers Computer & Tech LJ* 1.

[125] See, e.g. Andreas Grosche, 'Software Patents—Boon or Bane for Europe?' (2006) 14 *Int'l J L & Info Tech* 257.

[126] See, e.g. Patents Act 1977, s 48A(1)(1999) (UK); J W Baxter, *World Patent Law and Practice*, §8.02 (Matthew Bender and Co, 2001). See generally Robert Merges, 'Intellectual Property Rights and Bargaining Breakdown: The Case of Blocking Patents' (1994) 62 *Tenn. LR* 75.

[127] See J H Reichman, 'Of Green Tulips and Legal Kudzu; Repackaging Rights in Subpatentable Innovation' (2000) 53 *Vanderbilt LR* 1743.

to an obligation to return a healthy share of the potential gains to the earlier innovator.[128] These entitlements could be voluntarily adopted by industrial sectors or mandated by law or regulation to resolve blocking effects.[129] Other ideas—open source models, collaborative modes of production, clearing house models—have also attracted growing attention,[130] although their dependence on exclusive property rights is often overlooked.[131]

Of course, not all the advocates of deep harmonization claim to know all the answers; rather, some suggest codifying basic aspects of domestic patent law—so-called 'best practices'—that would provide a solid foundation for transnational harmonization.[132] But this approach is based on several fallacies. First, even for countries at similar levels of technological sophistication, 'best practices' are not likely to be the same. Moreover what any given country views as 'best practices' in patent law might reflect other practices in other laws—including copyright, trade secret and above all competition laws—that may diverge widely from one country to another.[133] The advocates of a 'best practices' approach to harmonization do not explain how to identify which practices are generally best or how international lawmakers will keep them responsive to changing needs.

Another more subtle effect of premature legal harmonization is that it could unhelpfully homogenize creative development. The diverging approaches observed in national innovation laws may not solely depend on differing perceptions of how to cure the same set of problems. Some of these differences may

---

128 See e.g. Reichman, ibid; Jerome H Reichman and Tracy Lewis, 'Using Liability Rules to Stimulate Local Innovation in Developing Countries: Application to Traditional Knowledge,' in Maskus and Reichman, *Globalized IP Regime*, note 20 above, 337.

129 See generally Reichman, 'Legal Hybrids', note 98 above.

130 See e.g. Yochai Benkler, *The Wealth Of Networks: How Social Production Transforms Markets And Freedom* (Yale Press, 2006)), available at <http://www.benkler.org/wealth_of_networks/index.php/Download_PDFs_of_the_book>; *Janet Hope*,'Open Source Biotechnology', PhD Thesis, The Australian National University, Canberra, 2004, available at <http://rsss.anu.edu.au/~janeth/home.html>; Ian Ayres and J M Balkin, 'Legal Entitlements as Auctions: Property Rules, Liability Rules, and Beyond' (1996) 106 *Yale LJ* 703.

131 See Boyle, 'The Second Enclosure Movement', note 25 above.

132 See, e.g. Hauda, note 16 above.

133 See Jonathan Zuck, 'Comments Regarding International Antitrust Convergence', WIPO Open Forum, note 2 above (noting the importance of consistent treatment of small businesses in the information technology sector). The debate outlined above suggests that, at a minimum, the level of intellectual property protection in any given country may depend on whether that country has enacted and implemented antitrust law to deal with competitive excesses. Yet the SPLT (like TRIPS) does not mandate protection outside the intellectual property field, and antitrust law is only one of the many related issues that might influence the appropriate level of protection. See, e.g. Maskus and Reichman, 'Globalization and Privatization', note 27 above; Josef Drexl, 'The Critical Role of Competition Law in Preserving Public Goods in Conflict with Intellectual Property Rights', in Maskus and Reichman, *Globalized IP Regime*, note 20 above, 709; Hanns Ullrich, 'Expansionist Intellectual Property Protection and Reductionist Competition Rules: A TRIPS Perspective', ibid, at 726.

emerge from differing problems, differences that arise because each society values its own specific kinds of creativity and prioritizes its technological requirements in its own way. The TRIPS Agreement still leaves countries some room to exclude developments from patentability on such grounds as public policy, or lack of inventiveness, or because the work is not considered in a field of 'technology', and therefore not within the subject matter of patent law.[134] As a result, a country that excels in certain kinds of work has some flexibility to put the tools for accomplishing that work into the public domain; other countries may be good at making the tools and prefer that they be patented.[135]

Because we lack the information necessary to match particular approaches to specific types of innovation opportunities, allowing nations to experiment would be highly beneficial. Some will use legislative solutions; the Supreme Court's recent foray into patent law suggests that the US approach may be judicially based;[136] in some places, voluntary schemes will emerge. Over time, experts can compare and evaluate these experiments and, when one or another solution appears to yield positive results, nations can emulate that approach. In that event, harmonization would be achieved voluntarily and on the basis of actual empirical data and experience, not simply backroom wrangling and special-interest lobbying.[137]

Allowing nations to shape their laws also gives rise to comparative advantages by enabling each nation to foster what its technological community does best. So long as trade is relatively free, the flexibility to experiment enhances social welfare worldwide. Accommodations between national and regional systems of

---

134 See TRIPS Agreement, note 10 above, Art 27.

135 For example, the United States and Canada have taken divergent positions on whether higher-order life forms can be patented, leading to different treatment of mice bred as research tools in the life sciences; compare *Harvard Coll v Canada* (Comm'r of Patents), [2002] 4 SCR 45 (Canada) (holding the oncomouse unpatentable) with US Patent 4,736,866 ('Transgenic non-human mammals') and *Ex p Hibberd*, 227 USPQ (BNA) 443 (Bd of Pat App & Int 1985) (holding living organisms patentable).

136 In the last two years, the Supreme Court has considered seven patent cases: *MedImmune v Genentech*, note 74 above; *eBay, Inc v MercExchange*, LLC, 126 SC 1837 (2006); *Illinois Tool Works, Inc v Independent Ink, Inc*, 547 US 28 (2006); *Laboratory Corp of America v Metabolite Labs, Inc*, 126 SC 2921 (2006) (writ of *certiorari* dismissed as improvidently granted); *Merck KGaA v Integra Lifesciences I, Ltd*, 545 US 193 (2005); *KSR Int'l Co v Teleflex Inc*, note 52 above; *Microsoft Corp v AT&T Corp*, note 5 above.

137 To be sure, special-interest politics will play out in domestic arenas as well. But in the international context, the problems are particularly severe: well-heeled groups may be better at attracting international attention, and differences in the ways in which international and domestic instruments are reviewed tend to systematically unravel carefully negotiated deals in a direction that favours right holders; see Graeme B Dinwoodie and Rochelle C Dreyfuss, 'TRIPS and the Dynamics of International Property Lawmaking' (2004) 36 *Case W Res J Int'l L* 95. See generally Laurence R Helfer, 'Regime Shifting: The TRIPS Agreement and New Dynamics of International Intellectual Property Lawmaking' (2004) 29 *Yale J Int'l L* 1.

innovation can then evolve over time, on the basis of bottom-up preferences. Without an agreed upon legitimate governance process (administrative agencies, courts, and legislature), it is difficult to see how these kinds of continual accommodation can occur. A politically skewed re-regulation of the world market, coupled with excessive privatization of global public goods, could instead make both competition and innovation more difficult.[138]

To put this another way, patent law's *raison d'être* is to encourage the production of novelty and inventiveness. Its success means that there will always be new problems to solve. It makes little sense to preclude the US Supreme Court, the European Court of Justice, and their equivalents elsewhere, along with national agencies and legislatures—all of which have shown themselves capable of creating law responsive to new circumstances—from offering their contributions to the future evolution of the patent system.

Part III Nurturing an Incipient Transnational System of Innovation

Of course, if trade is relatively free and creativity flourishes, some international coordination of the patent system becomes a necessity. But instead of premature harmonization, what an integrated world economy needs is a method for lowering the costs that discrepancies in national laws impose on international actors and a system that will gradually enable innovators in all countries to reach the world market by means that are geared to their different national and regional capabilities and endowments.[139] The trick, then, is to identify the places where some degree of harmonization is necessary and to find a mechanism for revising the law as new coordination problems arise.

Certainly, new measures are needed at the prosecution stage. The priority rules of the Paris Convention, coupled with the PCT and the various procedural advances

138 Maskus and Reichman, 'Globalization and Privatization', note 27 above, 19 (noting the lobbying role of the 'knowledge cartel', which pushes 'governments to regulate the global market in ways that lock in temporary competitive advantages without necessarily advancing the global public interest in innovation, competition or the provision of complementary public goods' and reasoning that 'representatives of the global public interest are unlikely to be seated at the table where hard-law negotiations take place').

139 See Maskus and Reichman, 'Globalization and Privatization', note 27 above, 33–35 (arguing that '[a]ll countries could benefit from a functionally efficient transnational system of innovation if low barriers to entry enabled entrepreneurs everywhere to invest in the production and distribution of knowledge goods').

discussed earlier, move the system in a direction that makes serial applications easier to accomplish.[140] Nonetheless, modest harmonization of the standards of patentability could dramatically lower private costs and make work sharing feasible among national patent offices. It is not, however, necessary to rely on top-down negotiation at WIPO; beneficial moves toward a more unified approach could be made even in the face of a moratorium on new international law making.[141] After all, when the advantages of a particular rule become evident, nations often tend to voluntarily conform their law to that rule. For example, with the exception of the United States, every country has acquiesced in awarding priority on a first-to-file basis; the United States is considering the absolute novelty standard in use elsewhere; and, outside the United States, there is discussion of (and some action towards) introducing a grace period similar to that found in American law.[142]

More important, significant moves towards coordination can be achieved through cooperation at the level of government agencies and courts.[143] These mechanisms are well known in international law generally and are taking hold in transnational patent law as well. For example, at regular meetings of the European, Japanese, and US patent offices, sets of representative cases are discussed and differences in examination practice and procedure are identified. Where law permits, these differences are ironed out, so that the same standards are more likely to be used to examine applications in all participating countries. Further coordination is achieved through examiner exchange programs[144] and regular judicial forums, where patent-law judges can discuss common challenges that arise in their respective national jurisdictions.[145]

---

140 Paris Convention, note 11 above, Art 4; text accompanying notes 6–8, above.

141 See, e.g. Maskus and Reichman, 'Globalization and Privatization', note 27 above, 36–39 (calling for such a moratorium); see also Yu, 'Five Disharmonizing Trends', note 23 above.

142 See US Department of Commerce, note 73 above; for an example of the legislation under consideration in the United States, see Patent Reform Act of 2005, HR 2795, 109th Cong., 1st Sess (2005). For moves in other countries, see Toshiko Takenaka, 'Rethinking the United States First-To-Invent Principle From a Comparative Law Perspective: A Proposal to Restructure §102 Novelty and Priority Provisions' (2002) 39 *Hous LR* 621. See generally John G Mills III, 'A Transnational Patent Convention for the Acquisition and Enforcement of International Patent Rights' (2006) 88 *J Pat. & Trademark Off Soc* 958. See also note 156 below, and accompanying text.

143 See, e.g. Anne-Marie Slaughter, 'Global Government Networks, Global Information Agencies, and Disaggregated Democracy' (2003) 24 *Mich J Int'l L* 1041; ibid, 'A Global Community of Courts' (2003) 44 *Harv Int'l LJ* 191; Robert O Keohane and Joseph S Nye, 'Transgovernmental Relations and International Organizations' (1974) 27 *World Pol* 39, 43; James N Rosenau and Ernst-Otto Czempiel (eds), *Governance Without Government: Order And Change In World Politics* (Cambridge University Press, 1992).

144 See, e.g. The Website of the Trilateral Co-operation at <http://www.trilateral.net/>.

145 See, e.g. Schedule for Fourth International Judges' Conference on Intellectual Property Law, available at <http://www.ipo.org/AM/Template.cfm?Section=Past_Meetings_and_Events&Template=/CM/ContentDisplay.cfm&ContentFileID=6462>.

There are also post-grant issues that could benefit from comprehensive international attention. For example, now that patentees operate globally, infringement suits on parallel patents are becoming more common. These suits are expensive to bring and to defend. Although different results remain technically possible (in that national patents are independent of one another), inconsistent outcomes (in the sense that different parties win in different locations) can complicate global marketing efforts.[146] Some of these transnational cases have provoked courts to give extraterritorial effect to their own laws, a practice that can lead to multiple liabilities for the same harm and damage claims for acts that were legal in the territories where they were performed.[147]

Globalization has also created new opportunities for sharp practices. Examples include harassment of lawful users with successive suits;[148] so-called torpedo actions that prevent the patentee from obtaining timely relief;[149] and because patents are territorial, infringers can spread their activities across several states and leave the patent holder with no one place where the a court can find the patent to have been infringed.[150]

Once again, top-down solutions are not the only conceivable approach. Another less radical response would permit the parties in a transnational case to consolidate all of their claims before a single tribunal, or to coordinate multiple lawsuits through cooperation among the courts where actions are pending. This would reduce costs, conserve court resources, hopefully mitigate the extraterritorial impulse, and reduce opportunities for harassment. In addition, as Graeme Dinwoodie has suggested, courts hearing multijurisdictional cases may be positioned to find middle ground among disparate rules—that is, to further harmonization efforts through common law adjudication.[151] While adjudicators

146 See Paris Convention, note 11 above, Art 4*bis*(1).

147 For example, had the Federal Circuit's decision in *AT & T v Microsoft* stood, see note 5 above, multiple liability for the same assembly of computers could have eventuated. See also *SOCAN v Canadian Assoc'n of Internet Providers*, 2004 SCC 45, 32 CPR (4th) 1, 240 DLR (4th) 193 ¶78 (SC Canada, 30 June 2004) (noting that the decision to find jurisdiction over an internet service provider 'raises the spectre of imposition of copyright duties on a single telecommunication in both the State of transmission and the State of reception', and also noting that 'as with other fields of overlapping liability . . . the answer lies in the making of international or bilateral agreements').

148 See, e.g. *Computer Associates, Inc v Altai, Inc*, 126 F3d 365 (2d Cir 1997) (successive suits for infringing trade secrets brought in the United States and France not barred by *res judicata*).

149 See, e.g. Robin Jacob, 'International Intellectual Property Litigation in the Next Millennium' (1999) 32 *Case W Res J Int'l L* 507; Paul A Coletti, 'No Relief in Sight: Difficulties in Obtaining Judgments in Europe Using EPO Issued Patents' (1999) 81 *J Pat. & Trademark Off Soc* 351.

150 Mark A Lemley, David W O'Brien, Ryan M Kent, Ashok Ramani, and Robert Van Nest, 'Divided Infringement Claims' (2005) 6 *Sedona Conf J* 117.

151 Graeme B Dinwoodie, 'A New Copyright Order: Why National Courts Should Create Global Norms' (2000) 149 *U Pa LR* 469.

have proved reluctant to forge new procedural approaches on their own,[152] several organizations are in the process of proposing guidelines and procedures that courts (or their governments) could adopt. Some apply to transnational litigation generally;[153] others to intellectual property cases specifically.[154] If one of these projects were to succeed, the experience generated would provide future advocates of harmonized patent law with data of extraordinary value.

Even when a more centralized approach becomes propitious, there is always a question as to the level at which harmonization should take place. Thus, a European Community Patent has been under consideration for some time and similar efforts are underway in other regions.[155] The United States, Europe, Japan, and other industrialized countries have entertained the possibility of creating a 'limited package' instrument.[156] These initiatives differ from the SPLT negotiations in a significant way. Because they involve nations that are similar economically and technologically, there is no need to compromise on rules that are, in fact, optimum for no-one. If such arrangements were to move forward, it is conceivable that broader harmonization could eventually trickle down, as nations reaching the technological frontier decided voluntarily to join an existing regime.

---

152 See, e.g. *Voda v Cordis*, note 5 above (rejecting attempt to consolidate US and foreign patent claims); C–4/03, *Gesellschaft für Antriebstechnik mbH & Co KG v Lamellen und Kupplungsbau Beteiligungs KG*, 37 ILC 742 (2006) and C–593/03, *Roche Nederland BV v Primus*, 37 ILC 865 (2006) (prohibiting national courts from aggregating parties or consolidating multiple patent claims).

153 See, e.g. F K Juenger, 'The ILA Principles on Provisional and Protective Measures' (1997) 45 *Am J Comp L* 941; ILA Resolution No 1/2000 on Declining and Referring Jurisdiction in International Litigation (2000), available at <http://www.ila-hq.org/pdf/Civil%20&%20Commercial%20Litigation/RESlitigation.pdf>; Hague Conference on Private International Law, 'Draft Convention on Jurisdiction and Foreign Judgments in Civil and Commercial Matters' (1999), available at <http://hcch.e-vision.nl/index_en.php?act=progress.listing&cat=4> and Convention on Choice of Court Agreements (2005), available at <http://pub.bna.com/eclr/hagueconvention063005.pdf>.

154 The American Law Institute has recently approved a project entitled 'Intellectual Property: Principles Governing Jurisdiction, Choice of Law, and Judgments in Transnational Disputes'; see Dreyfuss and Ginsburg, note 5 above. Similarly, the Max Planck Institute is also working on an International Convention on Jurisdiction and Enforcement of Judgments: see Annette Kur, 'Applicable Law: An Alternative Proposal for International Regulation—The Max-Planck Project on International Jurisdiction and Choice of Law' (2005) 30 *Brook J Int'l L* 951. See also International Association for the Protection of Intellectual Property, 'Jurisdiction and applicable law in the case of cross-border infringement of intellectual property rights' (27 October 2003) at <http://www.aippi.org/>; Yoav Oestreicher, 'Recognition and Enforcement of Foreign Intellectual Property Judgments: Analysis and Guidelines for a New International Convention' (Social Science Electronic Publishing, 2006), available at <http://ssrn.com/abstract=939093>. The European Union has also had a European Patent Litigation Agreement under consideration; see note 9 above.

155 See note 8 above.

156 See, e.g. 'Industrialized Countries to Seek Deal on Global Patent Treaty Outside WIPO,' 72 *Pat, Trademark & Copyright J* 606 (6 October 2006)(naming four 'technical' issues—prior art, grace period, novelty, and inventive step—on which agreement will be sought).

Finally, there are advantages to giving the system established under the TRIPS Agreement more time to evolve, to examine how well emerging economies adapt to the minimum standards it sets out,[157] to scrutinize the decisions of the WTO's dispute settlement apparatus (DSU),[158] and to learn from TRIPS mistakes. As drafted, TRIPS has some of the features that a responsive harmonized law needs: it has a dispute resolution system that could be used to keep the law current and, as the Doha Ministerial Declaration on TRIPS and Public Health demonstrated, a quasi-legislative body able to make larger corrections.[159]

As it stands, however, TRIPS is not a final answer to the problem of harmonizing global patent law. The regime lacks a solid legislative basis for adjusting intellectual property law to changing needs. Further, it focuses solely on the producer end of the equation. Other than precatory statements, it does not establish user rights.[160] Thus, at the international level, it includes no way for the parties to strike the balance between proprietary and access interests that good patent law requires.[161] Although DSU panels have hinted that their charge includes making normative assessments of the legitimate expectations of patentees—a procedure that could, in theory, develop a series of user rights—these panels have looked no farther than a narrow reading of *existing* rules protecting user interests.[162] They articulate nothing like the normative vision required of a dynamic system, capable of responding to new situations.

---

[157] The TRIPS Council bears responsibility for monitoring TRIPS issues; see TRIPS Agreement, note 10 above, Art 68. In addition, there are organizations like Intellectual Property Watch which follow international intellectual property policy making: see <http://ip-watch.org/index.php?res=1024&print=0>.

[158] Understanding on Rules and Procedures Governing the Settlement of Disputes, Art 22, 15 April 1994, Marrakech Agreement Establishing the World Trade Organization, Annex 2, Legal Instruments—Results of the Uruguay Round, 33 ILM 1125 (1994); 1869 UNTS 401.

[159] See, e.g. Doha Declaration, note 34 above. See generally Abbott, 'The WTO Medicines Decision', note 46 above.

[160] See TRIPS Agreement, note 10 above, Preamble and Arts 7 & 8.

[161] See generally, Rochelle Dreyfuss, 'TRIPS—Round II: Should Users Strike Back?' (2004) 71 *U Chi LR* 21. See also Graeme B Dinwoodie, 'The International Intellectual Property Law System: New Actors, New Institutions, New Sources' (2006) 10 *Marq IP LR* 205 (advocating the inclusion of 'substantive maxima' in the TRIPS Agreement).

[162] An example is the *Canada–Pharmaceutical* decision, note 99 above (¶7.56), where the panel was willing to find an exemption permitting the testing of patented pharmaceuticals for regulatory review purposes to be normatively appropriate but only because many members already had experimental use exceptions in their patent laws. See Dinwoodie and Dreyfuss, 'IP Law and Science', note 26 above; Jane C Ginsburg, 'Toward Supranational Copyright Law? The WTO Panel Decision and the "Three Step Test" for Copyright Exemptions' (2001) 187 *Revue Int du Droit d'Auteur* 3, 17 (arguing that the *United States–Section 110(5) of the US Copyright Act*, WTR/DS/160/R (WTO Dispute Settlement Panel 2000) case sought only to 'anticipate what the empirical situation [would] be, [rather] than [provide] an explanation of what the right holder's markets should cover').

Arguably, a properly functioning patent law also requires competition law safeguards. TRIPS permits states to control anticompetitive abuse, but does not mandate such control.[163] If WIPO is to proceed with the SPLT, it would do well to consider what sorts of user safeguards are needed, to determine whether it is viable to separate the regime that creates exclusive rights from the regime that controls monopolies, and to develop experience and consensus regarding this delicate intersection between intellectual property and competition law, with due regard to the needs of countries at different levels of development.[164]

Conclusion

The foregoing survey demonstrates that any attempt to achieve deep harmonization of world patent law at the present time, such as that contemplated by the SPLT, is both premature and counterproductive. The evidence shows, instead, that we have entered a brave new scientific epoch, in which experts have only tentative, divergent ideas about how best to treat a daunting array of emerging new technologies. The current system is dysfunctional because it operates with a set of rudimentary working hypotheses that have not kept pace with technological change. As different countries put these hypotheses to the test, we should be focusing on gaining experience—and data—from living within the parameters set out by TRIPS during a prolonged period of open-minded experimentation.

If we rise above sectarian interests and power politics to focus attention on nurturing the incipient transnational system of innovation that the TRIPS Agreement brought into being, we can stimulate research and innovation on a grander scale than ever before. But let us take the time and invest the effort to get it right. Let us refrain from locking in fleeting, competitive advantages of one group of stakeholders or another, at the expense of real innovators and dynamic entrepreneurs everywhere. Instead of moving forward with harmonization for its own sake, the international intellectual property community must first identify and test trustworthy, empirically supportable solutions that benefit humanity at large.

163 See, e.g. TRIPS Agreement, note 10 above, Arts 8(2) and 31(k).
164 See Drexl, note 133 above; Ullrich, note 133 above.

14

SUBSTANTIVE EQUALITY IN INTERNATIONAL INTELLECTUAL PROPERTY NORM SETTING AND INTERPRETATION

Margaret Chon

Introduction

Recent debates within international intellectual property law reveal a *development divide*—a divide not only between developed and developing countries according to their material well-being, but also a divide in understanding development as growth contrasted with development as freedom. Policy makers from industrialized countries with well-entrenched intellectual property industries tend to view the goal of development through international intellectual property as encouraging economic growth, increasing trade liberalization, promoting foreign direct investment and ultimately enhancing innovation through technology transfer.[1] This approach to innovation relies heavily on a model of development as growth. Conversely, developing countries with less robust or even non-existent intellectual property industries tend to view intellectual property more frequently in relation to pressing domestic social welfare concerns such as access to healthcare. The model of development of freedom centres human capability through the provision of basic needs in the areas of education, health, and nutrition, because these lead to the 'enhancement of human freedom, which is both the main object and the primary means of development'.[2]

Simply put, the growth model of development prioritizes the innovation mandate of intellectual property, while the freedom model of development emphasizes its multi-dimensional aspects. In the latter paradigm, intellectual property not only stimulates innovation but also protects knowledge goods that enhance human capabilities, which in turn build national capacity for innovation. For all countries, the dynamic benefits of intellectual property include the promise of increasing innovation capacity over the long term. But for developed countries, the path

[1] DJ Gervais, 'Intellectual Property, Trade and Development: The State of Play' (2005) 74 *Fordham LR* 505, 516–20; KE Maskus and JH Reichman, 'The Globalization of Private Knowledge Goods and the Privatization of Global Public Goods', in KE Maskus and JH Reichman (eds), *International Public Goods and Transfer of Technology Under a Globalized Intellectual Property Regime* (Cambridge University Press, 2005) 8–11 [hereafter *International Public Goods*].

[2] A Sen, *Development as Freedom* (Knopf, 1999) 53.

to innovation may diverge quite sharply from that for developing countries, and require different kinds of policy and flexibility.

Within trade law as well, one can discern a divide between traditional models and more recently articulated global governance models. In the former, trade liberalization is the *sine qua non* of the trade regime. Wealth maximization without regard to innovation is to be expected; indeed, the innovation mandate of intellectual property may even be irrelevant. By contrast, in the global governance model various social welfare gains, including but not limited to innovation, may be balanced with each other. Trade linkages blur the usual rationales for intellectual property standards, which depart from the typical tariff-reduction trade measures. Furthermore, developing countries experience negative social-welfare consequences of international intellectual property law acutely: for example, the short-term costs of increased prices for intellectual property-protected goods, not to mention compliance and enforcement.[3] Within a trade framework, these costs are often justified by a rationale of greater market access for other goods, and/or the potential of dynamic benefits over the long term in the form of increased innovation. However, regulatory harmonization of intellectual property rules across countries varying widely in their levels of development entails significant implementation costs for developing countries.[4] From the perspective of many of these countries, capacity building has been about building capacity for compliance with top-down intellectual property legal regimes, rather than building capacity from the bottom up, that is, from the local context for innovation based on human development needs.[5] Again, this points out the need for an international intellectual property norm setting and norm interpretation principle that accounts for different social welfare goals.

Thus, international intellectual property laws have vastly different consequences for countries placed along various points of the development and trade spectrum. Simultaneously, international intellectual property law is embedded ever more firmly with formal equality principles. These pose great obstacles to differentiating among the development goals for both industrialized and developing countries. Formal equality is evident in the long-standing principle of national

[3] JE Stiglitz and A Charlton, *Fair Trade for All: How Trade Can Promote Development* (Oxford University Press, 2005) 48 ('many developing countries have been unable to meet their Uruguay Round obligations because of these high costs. By January 2000, up to 90 of the WTO's 109 developing country members were in violation of the SPS, customs valuation, and TRIPS agreements . . . .').

[4] Commission on Intellectual Property Rights, *Integrating Intellectual Property Rights and Development Policy* (2002) Chapter 7.

[5] M Kosteki, 'Intellectual Property and Economic Development: What Technical Assistance to Redress the Balance in Favor of Developing Nations?' (2006) ICTSD Issue Paper No 4.

treatment, present in both major international intellectual property law treaties (the Paris and Berne Conventions) and, more recently, the multilateral trade framework of the WTO TRIPS Agreement.[6] It appears as well in the form of the Most Favoured Nation principle (MFN) of international trade law, which has now been implanted into international intellectual property law through TRIPS Article 4.[7] Non-discrimination forms the bedrock of international trade law. Via TRIPS, these principles combine with increased minimum standards of intellectual property regulation to reduce the ability of individual countries to engage in local norm setting responsive to local conditions that might nonetheless depart from the TRIPS goal of global harmonization of intellectual property standards.[8] Furthermore, the non-discrimination approach of some standards themselves (for example, in TRIPS Article 27.1)[9] makes it difficult for countries to fine-tune their regulation of different industries within a particular sector.[10] More subtly, the formalistic decision-making approach of the WTO dispute settlement body,[11] at least in the several TRIPS decisions it has rendered so far, indicates an indifference to national policies that might distinguish between different industries for different national policy purposes.[12] Combined, these factors permeate the international intellectual property realm with a norm of formal equality. The net result is to decrease national policy space and flexibilities

---

[6] Paris Convention for the Protection of Industrial Property (Paris Convention) (20 March 1883) 21 UST 1583, Art 2; Berne Convention for the Protection of Literary and Artistic Works (Berne Convention) (9 September 1886) 25 UST 1341, 828 UNTS 221, Art 3; Marrakech Agreement Establishing the World Trade Organization, Annex 1C, Legal Instruments—Results of the Uruguay Round, Agreement on Trade-Related Aspects of Intellectual Property Rights (TRIPS) (15 April 1994) 33 ILM 81 [hereinafter TRIPS Agreement or TRIPS], Art 3.

[7] TRIPS, note 6 above, Art 4. The MFN provision of the General Agreement on Tariffs and Trades [hereinafter GATT] (1994) Art I(1) is broader than TRIPS Art 4, but the underlying principles are similar. The TRIPS Art 4 MFN provision has resulted in an increase in overall substantive global minimum intellectual property standards, through its synergy with bilateral agreements.

[8] AA Yusuf, 'TRIPs: Background, Principles and General Provisions', in CM Correa and AA Yusuf (eds), *Intellectual Property and International Trade: the TRIPS Agreement* (Kluwer Law International, 1998) 15–16.

[9] TRIPS, note 6 above, Art 27.1 ('patents shall be available for any inventions . . . in all fields of technology . . . [and] patent rights enjoyable without discrimination as to the place of invention, the field of technology and whether products are imported or locally produced.').

[10] GB Dinwoodie and R Dreyfuss, 'Patenting Science, Protecting the Domain of Accessible Knowledge' (2006) in L Guibault and PB Hugenholtz (2006), *The Future of the Public Domain: Identifying the Commons in Information Law* (Kluwer, 2006) 191, 218–19 (elaborating upon the formalism of Art 27).

[11] JHH Weiler, 'The Rule of Lawyers and the Ethos of Diplomats: Reflections on the Internal and External Legitimacy of WTO Dispute Settlement' (2001) 35(2) *J World Trade* 191, 206 (observing the 'almost obsessive attempts of the Appellate Body to characterize . . . the interpretations of the Agreement as "textual . . . ."').

[12] GB Dinwoodie and R Dreyfuss, 'TRIPS and the Dynamics of Intellectual Property Lawmaking' (2004) 36 *Case W Res J Intl L* 95, 96 (criticizing the formalist interpretation methods of the TRIPS dispute resolution panels, resulting in 'formal equality' among states).

in the application of international intellectual property minimum standards, for both developed and developing countries.

This chapter proposes an alternative to these dominant approaches to international intellectual property. Instead of over-relying on the assumptions of development as growth, it draws also upon the model of development as freedom. Rather than viewing trade primarily as a mechanism for wealth generation, it emphasizes trade as a mechanism to balance various social welfare objectives, including but not limited to innovation. And instead of a formal equality approach to norm setting, it sets forth a substantive equality principle within international intellectual property norm setting and norm interpretation.

This substantive equality principle posits that the goal of a truly inclusive international intellectual property law should be the enhancement of human freedom and capabilities through knowledge goods.[13] Rather than a focus strictly on utilities, income, growth, or even developing innovation capacity (although that is surely important for intellectual property institutions), this approach also considers how intellectual property can play a role in facilitating access to basic education, food security, and healthcare. Ensuring that populations have access to these first-order capabilities then sets the stage for developing innovation capacity in countries without already robust intellectual property industries.

A substantive equality principle should be integrated throughout intellectual property globalization decision making via a legal mechanism akin to the strict scrutiny doctrine in US constitutional law.[14] This doctrine is one of scepticism towards government regulation when certain equality interests are at stake. In the context of international intellectual property norm setting and interpretation, this principle would be triggered where the regulation (in this case, government intervention in the form of the grant of an exclusive right over intellectual property, or the withholding of an exception or limitation of that exclusive right) conflicts with a basic human development need (in this case, the provision of a development-sensitive human capability, as defined in part by the Millennium Development Goals).[15]

---

13 M Chon, 'Intellectual Property and the Development Divide' (2006) 27 *Cardozo LR* 2813, 2828 [hereinafter Chon, 'Development Divide']; F Ismail, 'Mainstreaming Development in the World Trade Organization' (2005) 39(1) *J of World Trade* 11, 12.

14 This generally allows decision makers to review and strike down state-enacted regulation under a non-deferential standard of review (also known as strict scrutiny review), where that regulation will interfere substantially with rights in a listed category such as gender or race.

15 UN Millennium Development Goals (18 September 2000) GA Res 55/2, UN Doc A/RES/55/2, available at <http://www.un.org/millenniumgoals/index.html>.

Part I The Case for a Substantive Equality Principle

This Part explores how the linkages among development, trade, and international intellectual property impact equality between and among developed and developing countries. It raises questions about the universal benefits of formal equality principles within the existing international intellectual property framework, even for industrialized countries. A substantive equality principle is a necessary tool for achieving policy outcomes that balance and differentiate among various domestic and global social welfare goals.

A. The Promise of Development as Freedom

The Current Intellectual Property and Development Framework

Development law traditionally assumes that economic growth is the primary means to development.[16] More recent work, however, highlights that uneven growth coupled with relative inattention to distributional consequences can have enormously destabilizing consequences.[17] As James Thuo Gathii states:

> [D]evelopment specialists often favor a view of development predicated on improved market access and national policy reforms such as deregulation, privatization and liberalization, [while] developing countries favor re-balancing the rights and obligations under existing trade agreements, such as in agriculture and access to essential medicines to arrive at a level playing field that would benefit them as much as developed countries. It is these competing visions of development that are at stake in the Doha [Development] Round . . . . Unless the[y] . . . [are] linked, there is a danger that focusing exclusively on questions of process/transparency will bracket out questions of social justice and equity embedded in the substantive reforms labeled development.[18]

---

16 CM Pereira Neto, 'Development Theory and Foundations of Universal Access Policies' (August 2005) 5–13 (JSD Thesis, Yale Law School, available at <http://lsr.nellco.org/yale/student/papers/12>).

17 C Thomas, 'Poverty Reduction, Trade and Rights' (2003) 18 *American U Intl LR* 1399, 1412–13; K Rittich, 'Transformed Pursuits: The Quest for Equality in Globalized Markets' (2000) 13 *Harvard Human Rights J* 231, 235.

18 JT Gathii, 'Process and Substance in WTO Reform' (2004) 56 *Rutgers LR* 885, 904; see also JE Stiglitz, 'The Ethical Economist', (2005) 84 *Foreign Affairs* 6, 128 (reviewing BM Friedman, *The Moral Consequences of Economic Growth*):

> In short, the debate should not be centered on whether one is in favor of growth or against it. The question should be, are there policies that can promote what might be called moral growth—growth that is sustainable, that increases living standards not just today but for future generations as well, and that leads to a more tolerant, open society? Also, what can be done to ensure that the benefits of growth are shared equitably, creating a society with more social justice and solidarity

The international intellectual property framework accepts many of the assumptions of the development as growth model. The general paradigm is that increasing minimum intellectual property standards leads to both more trade and more growth, promoting greater foreign direct investment in developing countries. Ultimately, innovation occurs through licensing and technology transfer.[19] More generally, Bretton Woods Institutions such as the WTO[20] tend to focus on the private law side of law in development—which

> consists of a core of private law rules supplemented by other laws and regulations that enhance efficiency and secure investment .... These fundamental laws are the protection of property and enforcement of contract rights, augmented by corporations and bankruptcy law, banking and securities regulations, intellectual property protection, and competition laws.[21]

Conversely, certain types of law are not favoured, such as public regulation (as opposed to the 'good law' of private property).[22] The effect of this powerful private/public discursive binary is that 'law is used not just as an aid to development, but also as a mechanism to deny or normalize the distributive implications of market-centered development'.[23] At least three aspects of this over-reliance on the development as growth model are problematic, especially in the context of international intellectual property. These are explored below.

Knowledge Goods are Public Goods

First, intellectual property is simultaneously a form of public regulation and a type of private right; and regardless of whether the label 'right' or 'regulation' is

---

rather than one with deep rifts and cleavages of the kind that became so apparent in New Orleans in the aftermath of Hurricane Katrina?

19 Gervais, 'IP, Trade and Development', note 1 above, 516–20.

20 The three Bretton Woods Institutions (BWIs) are the International Bank for Reconstruction and Development (also known as the World Bank), the International Monetary Fund (IMF), and the World Trade Organization (WTO). The WTO was preceded by the General Agreement on Tariffs and Trade (GATT), formed as an informal alternative because initially the US Congress was opposed to the third leg of the BWI structure. S Ostrey, 'After Doha: Fearful New World?' (2006) 10(5) *Bridges* 3.

21 P Alston, 'Ships Passing in the Night: the Current State of the Human Rights and Development Debate Seen Through the Lens of the Millennium Development Goals' (2005) 27 *Human Rights Q* 755, 784 (noting that development issues covered by the World Bank and IMF Development Committee's Global Monitoring Report 2004 'are pursued in terms of their instrumental value for the promotion of free markets').

22 K Rittich, 'Who's Afraid of the Critique of Adjudication? Tracing the Discourse of Law in Development' (2001) 22 *Cardozo LR* 929, 935.

23 Ibid, 943.

the more apt to apply to the privatization of knowledge goods,[24] knowledge is indisputably an input to the generation of more knowledge.[25] Thus knowledge goods are different from other kinds of goods. Yet even within industrialized countries, a regulatory myopia persists regarding the range of options for stimulating innovation, production, and distribution of knowledge goods. While the intellectual property 'solution' to the public goods market failure 'problem' is an economic policy model that has gained broad consensus,[26] this tends to obscure the full set of policy levers within the patent and copyright systems.[27] Moreover, the full range of *alternatives* to those systems[28] is also under-examined, especially in international intellectual property settings.[29] Options for encouraging innovative activity under diffusion models of information regulation have been characterized as 'piracy', a term that is applied indiscriminately to users in developing countries who resist narrowly framed models of regulating knowledge goods, often for legitimate and rational purposes.[30] If the ultimate goal is to stimulate innovation, both proprietary and non-proprietary models for encouraging the production of knowledge goods have proven track records.[31] This is true historically of what are now deemed industrialized countries.[32] Thus, in the absence of firm empirical data, there is no reason *a priori* persistently to privilege one type of regulation (intellectual property) over another (diffusion or other models).

---

24 For recent incarnations of this debate within the US, contrast S Ghosh, 'Deprivatizing Copyright' (2003) 54 *Case W Res LR* 387 (arguing that Anglo-American copyright involves a 'delegation of the decision-making function historically assigned to a governmental entity to a non-governmental entity') with A Mossoff, 'Is Copyright Property?' (2005) 42 *San Diego LR* 29 (arguing in favour of a natural rights/property rights notion of US copyright).

25 JE Stiglitz, *Globalization and Its Discontents* (WW Norton & Co, 2003) 245 ('in the final stages of the Uruguay negotiations, both the [US] Office of Science and Technology and the Council of Economic Advisors worried that we had not got the balance right—the agreement put producers' interests over users'. We worried that in doing so, the rate of progress and innovation might actually be impeded; after all, knowledge is the most important input into research, and stronger intellectual property rights can increase the price of this input').

26 EW Kitch, 'Elementary and Persistent Errors in the Economic Analysis of Intellectual Property' (2000) 53 *Vand LR* 1727, 1740–41.

27 DL Burk and MA Lemley, 'Policy Levers in Patent Law' (2003) 89 *Virginia LR* 1575; J Cohen, 'Copyright, Commodification, and Culture: Locating the Public Domain', in Guibault and Hugenholtz (eds), *The Future of the Public Domain*, note 10 above, 121–66.

28 HR Varian, 'Copying and Copyright' (2005) 19(2) *J of Econ Perspectives* 121, 134–36 (outlining various business models in a world without copyright).

29 Maskus and Reichman, note 1 above, 3–45; P Drahos, 'The Regulation of Public Goods', in Maskus and Reichman (eds), *Intenational Public Goods*, note 1 above, 46–64.

30 PK Yu, 'Four Common Misconceptions About Copyright Piracy' (2003) 26 *Loyola of LA Intl and Comp LR* 127.

31 Y Benkler, *The Wealth of Networks: How Social Production Transforms Markets and Freedom* (Yale University Press, 2006) 301–55.

32 S Ricketson and JC Ginsburg, *International Copyright and Neighboring Rights: The Berne Convention and Beyond* (Oxford University Press, 2006) 882.

Knowledge Goods Contribute to Public Policy Goals Other Than Innovation

Second, many developing countries did not share this unmitigated view of development as growth, even prior to the WTO.[33] TRIPS itself evidences a counternarrative through its Preamble. This language includes a recognition, not only that intellectual property rights are 'private', but also of 'underlying public policy objectives of national systems for the protection of intellectual property, including development and technological objectives' of all member states.[34] This evinces the traditional intellectual property policy balance between private rights necessary for the stimulation of innovation, on the one hand, and the public interest in access to knowledge goods, on the other.[35] The Preamble also explicitly recognizes 'the special needs of the least-developed country Members in respect of the maximum flexibility in the domestic implementation of laws and regulations in order to enable them to create a sound and viable technological base . . .'.[36]

In addition, TRIPS Articles 7[37] and 8[38] were advanced at the behest of the so-called 'Group of 14' developing countries.[39] The Group of 14 pushed to include language referring to development after it became inevitable that intellectual

33 Ibid, 887–98; RL Okediji, 'The International Copyright System: Limitations, Exceptions and Public Interest Considerations for Developing Countries in the Digital Environment', (2006) 5 (UNCTAD–ICTSD Issue Paper No 15, available at <http://www.iprsonline.org/unctadictsd/docs/ruth%202405.pdf>).

34 TRIPS, note 6 above, Preamble. As Gervais points out, the 'preamble to the TRIPS Agreement is an essential part of it'. Under 'GATT law, preambles are on occasion relied upon to a considerable extent by panels when the wording of a provision is not clear or where it is susceptible to divergent interpretations': D Gervais, *The TRIPS Agreement: Drafting History and Analysis* (2d edn, Sweet & Maxwell, 2003) 80 [hereafter Gervais, *The TRIPS Agreement*].

35 Gervais, ibid, 81 ('several paragraphs of the preamble thus confirm the need for achieving a balance, or, perhaps more accurately, the need to arrive at a series of equilibriums between intellectual property protection and free trade (bearing in mind that, prior to the Uruguay Round, intellectual property was viewed as an exception to free trade in Art XX(d) in GATT); between highly industrialized and developing nations; between the private rights of intellectual property owners and cases where the public interest may trump some aspects of the protection of intellectual property; and more broadly as a reflection of the "contract" that intellectual property represents . . .').

36 TRIPS, note 6 above, Preamble.

37 Ibid, Art 7 (entitled 'Objectives') frames '[t]he protection and enforcement of intellectual property rights' within a framework of 'mutual advantage of producers and users of technological knowledge and in a manner conducive to social and economic welfare, and to a balance of rights and obligations'.

38 Ibid, Art 8 (entitled 'Principles') refers to member states' ability 'to adopt measures necessary to protect public health and nutrition, and to promote the public interest in sectors of vital importance to their socioeconomic and technological development'.

39 These were: Argentina, Brazil, Chile, China, Colombia, Cuba, Egypt, India, Nigeria, Pakistan, Peru, Tanzania, Uruguay, and Zimbabwe. Other Uruguay Round participants that submitted proposed drafts included the European Community, the United States, Switzerland, Japan, and Australia.

property rights were to be included in the global trading framework.[40] By presenting their own text, these countries wanted

> to highlight the importance of public policy objectives underlying national IPR [Intellectual Property Rights] systems, the necessity of recognizing those objectives at the international level and . . . the need to respect and safeguard national legal systems and traditions on IPRs, in view of the diverse needs and levels of development of states participating in the IPR negotiations.[41]

As another commentator put it, '[t]he concerns of developing countries were reflected in large part in two provisions—Articles 7 and 8'.[42]

In contrast to the Preamble, which is a general statement of intent, Articles 7 and 8 should carry more weight in interpretation and implementation of the treaty text.[43] From the perspective of developing countries, the language of 'development' within these Articles was intended to provide them with some leeway to argue in favour of flexibilities in the minimum standards mandated by TRIPS, if these flexibilities served the purposes of development: '[t]he freedom to introduce exceptions or limitations on public ground or to adopt measures to counter abuses on the part of IPRs' rightsholders w[as] partly conceived to attenuate the social costs that developing countries must absorb in order to bring their national IPRs system in line with TRIPS standards'.[44]

Indeed, during the debate in 2001 over the compulsory licensing provisions of TRIPS in the context of the AIDS pandemic, a number of developing countries invoked these references to development to argue before the TRIPS Ministerial

40 Yusuf, note 8 above, 10–14.

41 AO Adede, 'Origins and History of the TRIPS Negotiations', in C Bellmann, G Dutfield and R Meléndez-Ortiz (eds), *Trading in Knowledge: Development Perspectives on TRIPS, Trade and Sustainability* (Earthscan, 2003) 23, 28.

42 Gervais, 'IP, Trade and Development', note 1 above, 508–09:

> ([T]he emerging outline of a possible TRIPS result had essentially been at the level of principles, not legal texts. The draft legal texts, which emanated from the European Community, the United States, Japan, Switzerland, and Australia, foreshadowed a detailed agreement covering all IP rights then in existence. . . . As a reaction, more than a dozen developing countries proposed another 'legal' text, much more limited in scope, with few specific normative aspects. They insisted on the need to maintain flexibility to implement economic and social development objectives. In retrospect, some developing countries may feel that the Uruguay Round Secretariat did them a disservice by preparing a 'composite' text, which melded all industrialized countries' proposals into what became the 'A' proposal, while the developing countries' text became the 'B' text. The final Agreement mirrored the 'A' text. As such, it essentially embodied norms that had been accepted by industrialized countries (footnotes omitted).

43 UNCTAD–ICTSD Project on IPRs and Sustainable Development, *Resource Book on TRIPS and Development* (2005) 123–24.

44 A Moncayo von Hase, 'The Application and Interpretation of the Agreement on Trade-related Aspects of Intellectual Property Rights' in Correa and Yusuf, note 8 above, 137.

in Doha, Qatar ('Doha') that TRIPS should not place limits on public health priorities.[45] The Doha Declaration on TRIPS and Public Health[46] and the subsequent General Council Decision[47] relied heavily on these Articles.[48]

More generally, developing countries have consistently contested the dominant interpretation of development throughout the so-called Doha Development Round.[49] For example, negotiations over the implementation of paragraph 6 of the Doha Declaration have been contentious,[50] recently culminating in proposed TRIPS Article 31*bis*.[51] Also, the current Development Agenda debate at the World Intellectual Property Organization (WIPO) reveals sharply differing conceptions of development, following along the lines of developed and developing countries. Thus, in the intellectual property arena, social concerns inevitably are being weighed against economic considerations in the context of

---

45 Council for Trade-Related Aspects of Intellectual Property Rights, 'Submission on TRIPS and Public Health by the African Group, Barbados, Bolivia, Brazil, Cuba, Dominican Republic, Ecuador, Honduras, India, Indonesia, Jamaica, Pakistan, Paraguay, Philippines, Peru, Sri Lanka, Thailand and Venezuela' IP/C/W/296, ¶18 (20 June 2001). (For example, the argument was advanced that 'Article 7 is a key provision that defines the objectives of the TRIPS Agreement. It clearly establishes that the protection and enforcement of intellectual property rights do not exist in a vacuum. They are supposed to benefit society as a whole and do not aim at the mere protection of private rights.')

46 World Trade Organization, 'Ministerial Declaration on the TRIPS Agreement and Public Health' (2002) WT/MIN(01)/DEC/2, 41 ILM 755 (14 November 2001) [hereafter Doha Declaration] (affirming 'WTO members' *right* to protect public health and, in particular, to promote *access to medicines* for all') (emphases added).

47 World Trade Organization, Decision of the General Council, 'Implementation of Paragraph Six of the Doha Declaration on the TRIPS Agreement and Public Health' (30 August 2003; WT/L/540).

48 Ibid. ('In undertaking this work, the TRIPS Council shall be guided by the objectives and principles set out in Articles 7 and 8 of the TRIPS Agreement and shall take fully into account the development dimension.')

49 JT Gathii, 'The High Stakes of WTO Reform', (2006) 104 *Michigan LR* 1361, 1370 ('[t]he central tension in the mission of the WTO is between its trade liberalization mandate—which is supported by its most powerful members—on the one hand, and ensuring that trade contributes of the development goals of developing countries, such as raising standards of living, on the other. Efforts to mediate the tension between trade liberalization and development are incorporated into the preamble to the 1994 Marrakesh Agreement, which acknowledges that the optimal use of the world's resources must be in accordance with the principle of sustainable development and must be with a view to raising standards of living').

50 D Matthews, 'From the August 3, 2003 WTO decision to the December 6, 2005 agreement on an amendment to TRIPS: improving access to medicines in developing countries?' IPQ No 2 (2006) 91, 94–115; P Roffe with C Spennemann and J von Braun, 'From Paris to Doha: The WTO Doha Declaration on the TRIPS Agreement and Public Health', in P Roffe, G Tansey and D Vivas-Eugui (eds) *Negotiating Health: Intellectual Property and Access to Medicines* (Earthscan/James & James, 2006) 16–26.

51 World Trade Organization, Decision of the General Council, 'Amendment of the TRIPS Agreement' (8 December 2005; WT/L/641).

linkage bargaining. Even within industrialized countries with well-developed intellectual property industries, these two TRIPS Articles represent an important restatement of the foundational balance within many domestic systems of intellectual property.[52]

Knowledge Goods are Inputs to the Production of Other Public Goods

Third, other international organizations offer strong alternative views of development and the ways law can foster it. These views are beginning to impact the view of how intellectual property law should operate in a global policy-making space where the production of multiple public goods must be encouraged.[53] Furthermore, intellectual property law and policy making in the WTO (as well as other norm-setting fora such as the WIPO) are encountering the development as freedom concerns adopted widely in United Nations Millennium Development Goals (UNMDG).[54] No longer is intellectual property just about creation and provision of drugs, entertainment, and food for the richer, industrialized countries. It is now overtly a debate about access to essential healthcare, education, and food for the poor. The human development index (HDI) approach, as opposed to the gross national product (GDP) approach, emphasizes the distribution of human capability opportunities in measuring development.[55] It includes not only the growth measure of per capita GDP, but also literacy and health measures. The United Nations Development Programme (UNDP) has propounded this index, based on the model of development as freedom, since 1991, and it is now widely used as a development metric by other international agencies.[56] Moreover, human rights norms expressed within the context of

> the implementation of article 27 of the UDHR and article 15 of the ICESCR [suggest that b]y striking the right balance in these articles, states may be able to increase the resources that can be used to realize other human rights. After all, a reduction of intellectual property protection that exceeds the core minimum obligations under human rights instruments would provide more access for the public to exercise their rights to cultural participation and development and to the benefits of scientific progress. Such reduction may also further the protection of the right to food

---

52 Dinwoodie and Dreyfuss, 'Patenting Science', note 10 above, 220.

53 I Kaul, I Brunberg and M Stern, *Global Public Goods: International Cooperation in the 21st Century* (Oxford University Press, 1999); I Kaul, P Conceição, KL Goulven and RU Mendoza, *Providing Global Public Goods: Managing Globalization* (Oxford University Press, 2003).

54 Note 15 above. Philip Alston claims that these have arguably attained the status of customary international law: Alston, note 21 above, 771–74.

55 United Nations Development Programme, *Human Development Report* (1991), available at <http://hdr.undp.org/reports/global/1991/en/> (inaugurating a new criterion of development, the Human Development Index (HDI), which measures development through longevity, knowledge, and income sufficiency).

56 M ul Haq, *Reflections on Human Development* (Oxford University Press, 1995).

> (in terms of patented seeds, agrochemicals, and foodstuffs), the right to health (in terms of patented pharmaceuticals), the right to education (in terms of copyrighted textbooks and software), and the right to freedom of expression (in terms of copyrighted works in general).[57]

Even the WTO Appellate Body, in the context of a trade dispute with environmental overtones, recognized that the WTO Agreement should be construed 'in accordance with the objective of sustainable development',[58] which is referenced in the Preamble. It has also looked to sources of law outside the WTO Agreement itself for interpretative guidance on the issue of sustainable development.[59]

These alternative approaches to development must contend with the formal equality rules of intellectual property, which have been forged largely within a model of development as growth. Universal access to primary education, for example, is a goal set by the United Nations as one of the UNMDG. Under the development as growth model, access to education has no particular claim upon the international intellectual property legal framework. Under the development as freedom approach, however, education is arguably a core constituent component of development rather than simply an instrumental aspect of human capital formation to further economic growth. While this is not the first time that the international intellectual property framework has encountered the particular development issue of access to education, the debate is now framed differently.[60] Development now encounters intellectual property consistently on the terrain of trade, which creates linkages to other social welfare goals through TRIPS Articles 7 and 8, as well as through other parts of the WTO Agreements—where questions of sustainable development are squarely part of the trade discourse.[61] Joining the scrutiny of intellectual property's relationship to development are explicit development institutions such as the World Bank and the UNDP,[62] other agencies that have intersecting mandates with intellectual property such

---

57 PK Yu, 'Reconceptualizing IP Interests in a Human Rights Framework', (2007) 40 *U of Cal Davis LR 1039*; LR Helfer, 'Towards a Human Rights Framework for Intellectual Property' (2007) 40 *U of Cal Davis LR* 971 (analysing General Comment 17, which interprets International Covenant on Economic, Social and Cultural Rights (ICESCR) Art 15(1)(c)); RC Dreyfuss, 'Patents and Human Rights: Where is the Paradox?', Molengrafica Series, available at <http://ssrn.com/abstract=929498>.

58 *United States—Import Prohibition on Certain Shrimp and Shrimp Products*, AB–1998–4 (WT/DS58/AB/R, 12 October 1998), para 12.

59 G Marceau, 'A Call for Coherence in International Law: Praises for the Prohibition Against "Clinical Isolation" in WTO Dispute Settlement', (1999) 33 (5) *J World Trade* 87–152.

60 The debate over access to educational materials within the global copyright framework occurred in the 1960s and culminated in the enactment of the Berne Appendix in 1971.

61 UNCTAD–ICTSD, Resource Book, note 43 above, 12 (discussing the WTO Appellate Body's *Shrimp-Turtles* decision).

62 World Bank, *Global Economic Prospects and the Developing Countries 2002: Making Trade Work for the World's Poor* (2002) 133; JE Stiglitz, 'Knowledge as a Global Public Good', in Kaul, Brunberg and Stern, note 53 above, 314–15.

as the World Health Organization,[63] as well as the more traditional international intellectual property norm-setting agencies such as WIPO.

From Growth to Freedom: Reconsidering Intellectual Property's Innovation Mandate

How does the concept of innovation function within this expanding constellation of development concerns and viewpoints? A question that developing countries are asking more insistently is: what exactly is their path to innovation through growth? Development economist Jeffrey Sachs divides the world into three areas: one of endogenous growth in which innovative activity takes place on a significant scale (approximately 1 billion people, including the OECD countries); another area of technological diffusers, absorbing new technology within a span of 5–25 years (approximately 3.5 billion people, including China, India, and Mexico); and a third group, which he calls 'marginalized' (about 2.5 billion people, including the least-developed countries).[64] With respect to the poorest countries, he suggests among other things a rethinking of the intellectual property regime, in particular the need for technology diffusion through copying and reverse engineering.[65]

Historical evidence suggests that the success of national innovation systems based on property rights depends upon freedom of design.[66] In previous eras countries currently heading the intellectual property pack had substantially more room to

63 World Health Assembly Resolution, 'Public health, innovation, essential health research and intellectual property rights: towards a global strategy and plan of action' (27 May 2006, WHA 59.24); World Health Organization, *Commission on Intellectual Property Rights, Innovation and Public Health Report* (2006), available at <http://www.who.int/intellectualproperty>.

64 J Sachs, 'The Global Innovation Divide', in AB Jaffe, J Lerner and S Stern, *Innovation Policy and the Economy* (MIT Press, 2003) 133: ('the top ten innovating countries account for around 94% of all of the patents taken out in the US in the year 2000, yet these countries have a combined population of only around 14% of the world's population. . . . If we look at the bottom 128 countries (with population of at least 1 million). . . each of those countries has fewer than 150 patents. Those countries have 63% of the world's population, but only 1,174 patents in the year 2000, or just 0.75% of all the patents taken out in the US that year').

Sachs serves as the current Director of the UN Millennium Development Project. See UN Millennium Project, *Who We Are*, <http://www.unmillenniumproject.org/who/sachs.htm> (last visited 7 April 2006).

65 Sachs, 'Global Innovation Divide' ibid, 140. His other suggestions include more grants from donor countries (around the order of 0.1 per cent of GNP; a focus by donors on scientific issues, especially those exacerbated by ecological challenges; and a focus on new and dynamic approaches to technology transfer from rich to poor countries).

66 P Drahos, 'An Alternative Framework for the Global Regulation of Intellectual Property Rights' (2005) 21 *Austrian J Development Studies*, available at <http://ssrn.com/abstract=850751>, 44; Ha-Joon Chang, *Kicking Away the Ladder: Development Strategy in Historical Perspective* (Anthem, 2002); RL Ostergard, Jr, *The Development Dilemma: The Political Economy of Intellectual Property Rights in the International System* (LFB Scholarly Publishing, 2003).

design innovation systems suited to their particular economic and cultural needs than developing countries do today.[67] Local flexibilities and policy spaces can and should include strategies to maximize spill-overs (or external benefits) and minimize social costs.[68] Furthermore, if the relatively short history of law and development has taught us anything, it is that a top-down imposition of legal systems without considering either cultural specificity, or the preferences of the society upon which development is being urged, will not result in a happy melding of legal norms.[69] Bottom-up development is defined in part by attention to first-order concerns such as access to food, education, and healthcare, which in turn fosters local capacity for innovation. It should also be guided by local knowledge and local priority setting.[70] From a development as freedom perspective, the innovation mandate of intellectual property is only one of several, equally legitimate priorities for developing countries. This more multi-faceted approach to development is evident as well in the WIPO Development Agenda items, which are discussed below.

The dominant model of development as growth also undervalues the proliferation of insights based on social and cultural theories of creativity, which are as important as economic theories in understanding how states reach a national capacity for innovation measurable and containable by IP.[71] UNESCO's Universal Declaration on Cultural Diversity advocates a model of development that includes cultural diversity and cultural policy.[72] Copyright clearly impacts cultural policy, which in turn affects development from these angles.[73]

---

[67] UNCTAD–ICTSD, Resource Book, note 43 above, 151. An example in the context of US economic development is its late compliance with the Berne Convention, as well as its protective copyright legislation for domestic publishers in the 1891 Chace Act.

[68] Drahos, 'An Alternative Framework', note 66 above, 15.

[69] S Ghosh, 'Modeling Globalization from The Bottom Up: A Review Essay of John Braithwaite and Peter Drahos, *Global Business Regulation*' (2005) 39 *L and Society Rev* 965, 975 (describing the cultural perspective of globalization as 'acknowledg[ing] the reality of markets but recogniz[ing] that the reality . . . often comes into tension with other historical and sociological realities'); DM Trubek and M Galanter, 'Scholars in Self-Estrangement: Some Reflections on the Crisis in Law and Development Studies in the United States' (1974) *Wisconsin LR* 1062, 1071–2 (criticizing legal liberalism in the law and development efforts of the 1960s and 1970s).

[70] O Arewa, 'Piracy, Biopiracy and Borrowing: Culture, Cultural Heritage and the Globalization of Intellectual Property' (2006) Case Legal Studies Research Paper No 04–19, available at <http://ssrn.com/abstract=596921>.

[71] Cohen, note 27 above, 121; M Sunder, 'IP3' (2007) 59 *Stanford LR* 257.

[72] UNESCO, Universal Declaration on Cultural Diversity (2001), available at <http://unesdoc.unesco.org/images/0012/001271/127160m.pdf>.

[73] D Drache and MD Froese, 'The Global Cultural Commons After Cancun: Identity, Diversity and Citizenship' (2006) CLPE Research Paper No 2, available at <http://ssrn.com/abstract=829987>, 35 ('rising literacy and falling fertility rates create[] a scissors effect, in which national culture plays an increasingly central role for the creation of public identity. Few experts have confronted the transformative potential of the rise in literacy worldwide . . . . [T]his may be the most significant trend of our times, transforming the poorest states from "least developed", or even failed

Dilemmas of Intellectual Property Law and Development

When faced with the triple braid of intellectual property, innovation, and development within the international intellectual property framework, developing countries often contend with a lack of policy coordination at the national and international levels, combined with growing complexity and fragmentation of policy-making venues.[74] This is part of what Susan Ostrey has termed a 'knowledge trap' for poorer countries, which are severely and systematically penalized by the knowledge intensity demanded by the deep integration of standards within the world trade system.[75] But arguably all member states, whether developed or developing, are affected negatively by the failure of WIPO and the WTO to embrace a broader development mandate. All states benefit from global communicable disease control and other global public goods such as universal primary education and food security. And all global institutions must coordinate around these areas, if for no other reason than because of the positive spill-over effects on all countries. Yet even when a crisis as urgent as the AIDS pandemic is perceived, there have been enormous institutional barriers to addressing it. The protracted implementation of the General Council Decision with respect to paragraph 6 of the Doha Declaration on TRIPS and Public Health, for example, demonstrates an ongoing structural unwillingness to concede that a broader conception of development is a legitimate aspect of the international intellectual property mandate.[76]

The current *aporias* about the role of intellectual property law in development reflect ongoing perplexities about the overall project of law and development. Debate continues over whether law contributes to development in a positive way, or is neutral or negative with respect to development.[77] Very little explicit reflection takes place within intellectual property about its relationship to development law, much less to development itself. Nonetheless, by virtue of its increasing prominence in trade and innovation sectors, intellectual property will continue to play a primary role in the prioritization of the kinds of knowledge goods relevant to development.

states to developing nations, and at the same time raising social, political and economic expectations in the global south').

74 AA Latif, 'Developing Country Coordination in International Intellectual Property Standard-Setting', (2005) Trade-Related Agenda, Development and Equity (TRADE) Working Papers 24 (South Centre).

75 Ostrey, note 20 above.

76 DW Opderbeck, 'Patents, Essential Medicines and the Innovation Game' (2005) 58 *Vanderbilt LR* 501; C Oh, 'Will the TRIPS Amendment on Compulsory Licensing Work?' (2006) 10(1) *Bridges* 22–23.

77 B Tamanaha, 'The Lessons of Law and Development Studies' (1995) 89 AJIL 470.

The dominant development model upon which international intellectual property norm setting has taken place is predicated on economic growth. This model may obscure other mechanisms for the production and distribution of knowledge goods, which are increasingly being discussed among developing countries, non-governmental organizations and civil society under a rubric of 'access to knowledge' or A2K.[78] In order to be more responsive to the felt needs of developing countries, the international intellectual property framework must begin to incorporate the alternative model of development as freedom.

B. The Promise of Global Governance through Trade

The Current Trade and Development Framework

Certain aspects of liberalizing trade do not bring the same welfare gains for developing countries as for industrialized countries.[79] At the same time, developing countries may bear relatively onerous implementation costs. Intellectual property rules are an example of the very real costs and somewhat dubious benefits of implementation, from the point of view of developing countries.[80] A closer examination of the trade linkage to intellectual property suggests that developing countries may have reason to be sceptical towards international intellectual property as a vehicle for trade-driven growth, despite greater access to developed country markets that may result from such linkage.[81] For example, in the absence

---

78 JM Balkin, 'Presentation at Yale A2K Conference, Balkinization Blog' (Friday, 21 April 2006):

> Access to knowledge can be a confusing term because it actually refers to four different things. Here I borrow Yochai Benkler's typology:
>
> 1. Human knowledge—education, know-how, and the creation of human capital through learning new skills . . .
> 3. Knowledge-embedded goods (KEGs)—goods where the inputs to production involve significant amounts of scientific and technical knowledge, often but not exclusively protected by intellectual property rights. Some key examples are drugs, electronic hardware, and computer software, but in contemporary economic life, information and intellectual property provide an increasingly important share of almost all valuable goods . . .
> 4. Tools for the production of KEGs—examples include scientific and research tools, materials and compounds for experimentation, computer programs and computer hardware.

79 S Polaski, 'The Future of the WTO' (2006) 2, available at <http://www.carnegieendowment.org/files/Polaski_WTO_final_formatted.pdf>; FJ Garcia, *Trade, Inequality, and Justice: Toward a Liberal Theory of Just Trade* (Transnational Publishers, 2003), 8.

80 Stiglitz and Charlton, note 3 above, 48 (reporting that Mexico spent US$30 million to implement an intellectual property enforcement system).

81 D Drache, 'Trade, Development and the Doha Round: A Sure Bet or a Train Wreck?' (2006) CIGI Working Paper No 5, available at <http://ssrn.com/abstract=894943> (questioning overall benefits to developing countries from accepting intellectual property standards in exchange for access to agricultural markets); J Bhagwati, *In Defense of Globalization* (Oxford University Press, 2004) 182–85 (criticizing the insertion of intellectual property rules within the WTO).

of robust domestic competition laws or other preconditions to the development of healthy markets in information goods, excessive rent-seeking behaviour may occur.[82]

As Frank Garcia points out, however, 'linkage issues are seldom approached or even recognized as justice questions within mainstream trade law'.[83] A strong sense of formal equality pervades this area of law: states who participate in global trade negotiations are 'equal players' regardless of their actual negotiating power. Yet systematic asymmetry pervades the structure.[84] As observed by Susan Ostrey,

> [w]hile the idea of equity, insofar as it is included in WTO rules, relates to 'special and differential treatment' (SDT) for developing countries, [and] is both weak and ambiguous, the concept of systemic asymmetry has been completely ignored....
>
> The member countries of the WTO vary widely in power and always will. That was true also under the GATT and the system was in effect managed by a 'club' of like-minded rich countries. The WTO houses a very different system which can be described in many different ways but the word 'complexity' is quite appropriate. The need for knowledge, advanced and sophisticated, is essential. Complexity requires knowledge and knowledge enhances power. The strong are stronger in the WTO because of their store of knowledge and the weak are weaker because of their poverty of knowledge. So the system creates reinforced asymmetry. Maybe the concept of the poverty trap should be replaced by the knowledge trap.[85]

Within this context of asymmetry, international intellectual property is embedded simultaneously within two trade paradigms. One could be characterized as a traditional model, where states vie for maximum advantage in the generation of domestic social welfare. In this model, the goal of innovation might even be irrelevant. As Peter Gerhart describes it:

> [a]dmittedly, if the decision to shift wealth from consumer to producer increases the level of innovation in an efficient direction, then the [international intellectual property] negotiation is not over a zero sum output and the negotiation would increase global welfare. But that is not what negotiators are negotiating about. When the United States goes to the negotiations, it is seeking to increase the wealth *from* its portfolio of knowledge goods, not to increase the portfolio *of* its knowledge goods. It simply wants to capture a larger share of the benefits its innovations create as a goal in itself rather than as the means to increasing investment in innovation.

[82] P Drahos, 'Securing the Future of Intellectual Property: Intellectual Property Owners and Their Nodally Coordinated Enforcement Pyramid' (2004) 36 *Case W Res J Intl L* 3.

[83] Garcia, note 79 above, 9.

[84] RO Keohane, 'Comment: Norms, Institutions, and Cooperation', in Maskus and Reichman, Intenational Public Goods, note 1 above, 65, 65–66.

[85] S Ostrey, 'Who Rules the Future? The Crisis of Governance and Prospects for Global Civil Society' (2006) 6 (paper delivered for the Robarts Centre for Canadian Studies, York University, available at <http://www.utoronto.ca/cis/ostry/>.

> The goal is to induce other countries to pay more for knowledge already generated rather than to pay for investment in new knowledge.[86]

Another trade model could be viewed as an incipient global governance model, where countries cooperate within a legal

> framework capable of reasonably balancing and weighing different, equally legitimate and democratically defined basic values and policy goals of a polity dedicated to promote liberty and welfare in a broad sense.[87]

These multiple policy goals would include stimulating innovation as well as access to the means of basic human flourishing, such as education and healthcare.

At this juncture, it seems clear that the first model operates in practice, and the second operates primarily at the conceptual or discursive level. This ideational nature of the global governance model does not make it any less relevant.[88] Evidence exists of increasing institutional density in the international system after World War Two, although actual global governance structures are still primitive at best.[89] International institutions still function mostly in silo mode, even internally, rather than in cross-agency cooperation.[90] And while scholars debate the wisdom of 'constitutionalization of the WTO',[91] the WTO itself is reticent about its own charge.[92] Yet there are calls from many quarters for a rethinking of how trade should link positively not only to intellectual property but also to poverty reduction and other social questions.[93]

Intellectual Property Distortions Through Trade

Within the traditional trade model, it is common to think of the lack of intellectual property enforcement as inducing trade distortions through under-protection of rights; conversely, however, trade can introduce distortions into intellectual

---

86 P Gerhart, 'The Tragedy of TRIPS' 30 (unpublished manuscript on file with author).

87 T Cottier, 'Limits to International Trade: The Constitutional Challenge' (2000) 94 *Proc American Soc Intll L* 220, 221.

88 JL Dunoff, 'Constitutional Conceits: The WTO's Constitution and the Discipline of International Law' (2006) 17/3 *Eur J of Intl L*.

89 K Raustiala, 'Density and Conflict in International Intellectual Property Law' (2007) 40 *U of Cal Davis LR 1021*; P Yu, 'Intellectual Property and the Information Ecosystem' (2005) 1 *Michigan State LR* 13–18.

90 S Musungu, 'Rethinking innovation, development and intellectual property in the UN: WIPO and Beyond, TRIPS Issues Paper 5' (QUNO, Geneva 2005).

91 M Karjewski, 'Democratic Legitimacy and Constitutional Perspectives of WTO Law' (2001) 35(1) *J of World Trade* 167–81.

92 P Sutherland (Chair), 'The Future of the WTO: Addressing institutional challenges in the new millennium', Report by the Consultative Board to the Director-General Supachai Paitchpakdi (WTO, 2004).

93 JP Trachtman, 'The Missing Link: Coherence and Poverty at the WTO' (2005) 8 *J Intl Econ L* 611 (critiquing the Sutherland Commission report).

property through the over-protection of rights.[94] Even within a domestic regulatory framework, the benefits of positive spill-overs from innovations, once created, are frequently ignored, undervalued or insistently internalized within the intellectual property right holder's private domain rather than the users' or public domain.[95] In a global framework, this effect is exacerbated. Global consumers, whether situated in developed or developing countries, simply do not benefit from the global trade in knowledge goods in the same way that they do from the reduction in tariffs on tangible goods.[96] At the same time, royalties flow lopsidedly from developing countries into industrialized countries, indicating that intellectual property works much better for some than others. This raises the question of whether the advantages from other sectors, stemming from increased market access, will outweigh the clear comparative disadvantages for most countries from including intellectual property in the global trade framework.[97]

---

94 The TRIPS Preamble reflects this duality: ('[d]esiring to reduce distortions and impediments to international trade, taking into account the need to promote effective and adequate protection of intellectual property rights, and to ensure that measures and procedures to enforce intellectual property rights do not themselves become barriers to legitimate trade . . .').

95 MA Lemley and BM Frischmann, 'Spillovers' (2006) (Stanford Law School John M Olin Program in Law and Economics Working Paper, available at <http://ssrn.com/abstract=898881>).

96 Gerhart, note 86 above, 30:

> In tariff negotiations, each country is made better off by the exchange because its export opportunities increase and its consumers benefit from lower import prices. The negotiation is therefore a positive sum game, with net winners on both sides. In intellectual property negotiations, however, an increase in one country's wealth from knowledge goods is a decrease in another country's wealth from knowledge goods. This is because once the knowledge is encapsulated as property it must be rationed through the market system and this makes the decision to create property rights a zero sum game. Producers of knowledge goods win, and consumers of knowledge goods lose.
>
> In other words, the purpose of intellectual property negotiations is to determine how much of the knowledge already generated in the world should be encapsulated in a property regime. That decision is necessarily a decision to shift wealth from consumers to producers without necessarily creating any new knowledge (for the knowledge has already been created), and the negotiation is necessarily over how to split a fixed pie rather than negotiations over how to make the pie bigger.

97 CIPR, note 4 above, 17–18 ('[d]eveloping countries, taken as a whole, are net importers of technology, most of which is supplied by the developed countries . . . . Developing countries, and a few developed ones, would be the net losers [in TRIPS]. The country sustaining the largest loss [from global minimum patent standards] in the study by the World Bank was Korea ($15 billion)' [citing World Bank, *Global Economic Prospects and the Developing Countries 2002: Making Trade Work for the World's Poor*, 133]); JT Gathii, 'Re-Characterizing the Social in the Constitutionalization of the WTO: A Preliminary Analysis', (2001) 7 *SPG Widener L Symposium J* 137, 147 ('[t]he theory of comparative advantage is linear to the extent that it is based on a theory of growth that seeks to enlarge the economic pie, as it were, so that there is more to go around once additional wealth is created. This linear paradigm of growth is not necessarily accurate [even] in the developed world context where innovation constitutes a fixed cost and once it is achieved it can be used over and over again. In the context of developing countries, this linear paradigm of growth does not take into account the adverse distributional consequences of liberalization of trade that go alongside its benefits').

In turn, regional, bilateral or multilateral rules that capture more rent for producers at the expense of consumers globally become a basis for raising standards domestically, under the guise of harmonization.[98] Thus users and consumers in both developed and developing countries lose. For example, the WIPO Copyright Treaty was a means for industrialized (groups of) countries such as the US and the EU to promulgate legal remedies against the circumvention of effective technological measures to protect digital content.[99] This standard in turn was enacted into various domestic laws, including the US,[100] where it still remains controversial as a matter of correct social policy.[101] But intellectual property users in developing countries lose relatively more than those in industrialized countries, because the overall welfare gains realized for them through heightened intellectual property standards are far more questionable. The costs, on the other hand, are readily discernible. These include the rents or transfer payments made from the developing world to the developed world as a result of TRIPS, the onerous costs of compliance and enforcement relative to other pressing development needs, and, especially for the least developed countries, the illusory promise that intellectual property will jump-start innovation resulting in eventual intellectual property comparative advantages.[102] Relentless privatizing of some knowledge goods could have 'large efficiency consequences, with the pace of innovation actually impeded and living standards in less developed countries diminished'.[103]

Intellectual Property Balance in a Global Trade Context

Can the intellectual property policy balance between proprietary rights and public access be replicated in the global trade context? This question does not have a straightforward answer.[104] In addition to the traditional domestic policy balance, which is committed to the sovereign domains of individual states,

98 *Eldred v Ashcroft* 537 US 186, 205–06 (2003) ('[b]y extending the baseline United States copyright term to life plus 70 years, Congress sought to ensure that American authors would receive the same copyright protection in Europe as their European counterparts').

99 WIPO Copyright Treaty (Geneva, 20 December 1996, 36 ILM 65 (1997)), Art 11 ('Obligations concerning Technological Measures').

100 Digital Millennium Copyright Act of 1988, Pub L No 105–304, 112 Stat 2860 (codified in scattered sections of 17 USC, including §§1201–05 (1996) ('Chapter 12—Copyright Protection and Management Systems').

101 J Litman, *Digital Copyright* (Prometheus Books, 2001), 122–150.

102 JM Finger and P Schuler, *Poor People's Knowledge: Promoting Intellectual Property in Developing Countries* (World Bank/Oxford University Press, 2004) 15 ('[a] poor country will not find the development dimension of IP in its TRIPS. All but a dozen or so of Senegal's 30,000 musicians earn a living in the domestic economy').

103 Stiglitz, 'Knowledge as a Global Public Good', note 62 above, 314–15.

104 DB Barbosa, M Chon and A Moncayo von Hase, 'Slouching Towards Development in International Intellectual Property' (forthcoming, 2007) *Michigan State U LR*.

the international intellectual property framework introduces a second balancing act: one between national rules and international minimum standards. Moreover, TRIPS added a third vector, which is 'policy objectives secured by a balance of intellectual property rights and other tools of economic development'.[105] While TRIPS Article 7 was 'intended to strike a balance that more widely promotes social and economic welfare', does this third balance simply mean that any particular developing country may choose to balance apples against oranges: the adoption of greater standards of intellectual property in exchange for greater market access to textiles and food, in the pursuit of overall social welfare?[106] Or is the third vector a balancing of the innovation goal of intellectual property against various other social welfare goals, such as public health? Or is it the first kind of balance (the domestic balance between private rights and public access, in the pursuit of optimal innovation) writ large on a global stage?

Balance of any kind is increasingly elusive, both as an empirical and even a normative matter. This is not only because TRIPS increased the minimum standards of protection while largely leaving unaddressed exceptions and limitations to rights. It is also because intellectual property, as the *de jure* and *de facto* approach to regulation of innovative activity, connects powerfully to rights rhetoric.

In this tripartite balancing act, where is the public interest located, and how is it to be represented in a setting where legal regimes are negotiated primarily through states? Do consumers in rich states have the same interests as consumers in poor states? Do poor consumers in rich states have more in common with poor consumers in poor states than they do with rich consumers in their own states?[107] How might states mediate the typical intellectual property balance when 'no broker makes the law' but rather 'the policy-makers and the interested parties are one and the same'?[108] Does it make a difference that intellectual property in the international context is primarily about wealth generation through trade rather than innovation through incentivization?[109] What do we make of the increasing divide between investment and incentive[110] and the fact

105 GB Dinwoodie, 'The Global Politics of Intellectual Property' (2006) (presentation at the Association of American Law Schools Mid-Year Meeting, unpublished manuscript on file with author).

106 UNCTAD–ICTSD, Resource Book, note 43 above, 126; D Gervais, *The TRIPS Agreement: Drafting History and Analysis* (1st edn, Sweet & Maxwell, 1998), 81. The WIPO Copyright Treaty preamble also contains a paean to balance: '[r]ecognizing the need to maintain a balance between the rights of authors and the larger public interest, particularly education, research and access to information, as reflected in the Berne Convention'.

107 Gerhart, note 86 above, 19.

108 Ibid, 18.

109 Ibid, 17.

110 P Yu, The International Enclosure Movement (forthcoming, 2007) *Indiana LJ*.

that the least-developed countries may be looking at neither—but simply at compliance?[111]

Also, how is intellectual property balance ensured when the major design principles for a global governance system are only vaguely in blueprint? The deep linkage of intellectual property minimum standards with trade in goods raises issues of first impression with respect to linking other non-trade or 'social' issues—such as environmental and labour standards, human rights laws, health-care, education and poverty-reduction goals.[112] In this regard, what difference does it or should it make that there is either a reality[113] or a perception[114] of a democracy deficit and other forms of unfairness within the WTO and other international intellectual property organizations?

While these global governance issues are far beyond the scope of this chapter, they bear on the question of global distributional consequences. The global governance gaps result in glaring omissions in the production and distribution of goods supposedly incentivized by intellectual property, such as goods addressing 'neglected diseases'—neglected precisely because they are concentrated in areas that are poor or non-markets.[115] These second-generation concerns with respect to drugs for the developing world focus attention on the pressing need for knowledge goods generally for development. They raise hard questions about whether the intellectual property link to trade represents the interests of all member states, in a social welfare sense. What do we mean when we speak of intellectual property capacity building for poor countries? Are rich countries producing knowledge goods for poor countries that truly address the needs of poor countries? What if these kinds of knowledge goods are not being produced? How do we or should we incentivize the production of knowledge goods that do meet the needs of the world's poor?[116] Can viable global intellectual property markets be developed by

---

111 Ibid.

112 J Braithwaite and P Drahos, *Global Business Regulation* (Cambridge University Press, 2000) 220; Barbosa, Chon, and Moncayo von Hase, note 104 above.

113 Gathii, 'High Stakes', note 49 above, 1362 (attributing the disruptions and deadlock in multilateral trade negotiations to 'a democratic deficit arising from lack of transparency in the negotiating process and lack of diverse participation of stakeholders within the WTO').

114 FJ Garcia, 'Trade Justice and Security' (2005) Boston College Law School Research Paper No 84, 18, available at <http://ssrn.com/abstract=838285> (arguing that even the perception of unfairness should lead to the conclusion that 'there needs to be genuine, searching dialogue with states and groups claiming that trade/globalization is unjust. Even if it is merely perception, it matters').

115 CIPR, note 4 above, 37–40 (concluding that patent rights will have little impact on stimulating research and development into diseases affecting the very poorest populations).

116 WW Fisher and T Syed, 'Why We Should Reform Developed Nations' Drug Innovation Systems to Address the Health Crisis in the Developing World' (2007) 40 *U of Cal Davis LR 581*; JP Love, 'Measures to Enhance Access to Medical Technologies, and New Methods of Stimulating Medical R&D' (2007) 40 *U of Cal Davis LR* 679; Dreyfuss, 'Patents and HR: Paradox?', note 57

and for poor countries?[117] Or is the entire point of international intellectual property to distribute wealth from poor countries to rich countries, derived from innovation already available in rich countries, and developed primarily for populations in those countries?

From the perspective of many developing countries, capacity building has been about building capacity for compliance with top-down intellectual property legal regimes, not about building capacity from the bottom up, that is, from the local context for innovation.[118] If the indeterminate term 'capacity' normatively refers to the latter, then building it will depend on disaggregation of intellectual property law and policy, despite the non-discrimination norms: taking into consideration the industry (drugs *versus* pesticides *versus* seeds), the country (Canada *versus* India *versus* Senegal), the type of knowledge (easily appropriable or not), etc.[119] While the formalist, industry-neutral character of international intellectual property standards is admirable in some ways, it can be obscene in other contexts. In a global context, a textbook for a suburban New Yorker is not the same textbook as needed by a student in rural Africa. Thus, in addition to disaggregation, more contextualization of intellectual property law and policy is required with respect to the development use to which a particular knowledge good is put.[120]

Development in Trade

The two primary tools for development within the traditional trade framework are special and differential treatment (S&D), endorsed by the industrialized countries, and greater access to technology, typically endorsed by developing countries.[121] Historically, these two tools have neither been sufficient nor sufficiently implemented, for purposes of development. This is true also in the intellectual

above, 17–18 (outlining creative proposals for restructuring global R&D, manufacture, and distribution of drugs for neglected developing countries).

117 Drache and Froese, note 73 above ('[w]hy does not TRIPS benefit southern cultural producers and smaller northern ones as well? The frank answer is that these independent producers are not part of a vertically integrated corporate commodity chain for distribution. And many do not want to be. Furthermore, TRIPS was not drafted with the interests of small, local producers in mind').

118 CIPR, note 4 above, Chapter 7; Kosteki, note 5 above.

119 Drahos, 'The Regulation of Public Goods', note 29 above, 46, 52–55 (analysing knowledge goods as a taxonomy along several different axes: (1) pure *versus* impure; (2) independent of norms, exist as norms, dependent on norms; (3) capability-independent *versus* capability-dependent; (4) information goods: codified *versus* uncodified knowledge; (5) artefact-embodied *versus* skill-embodied).

120 Chon, 'Development Divide', note 13 above, 2902.

121 Okediji, note 33 above, 5 ('the failure to obtain an international agreement on technology transfer in part occasioned acknowledgements within TRIPS of the freedom of countries to interfere with abuses of intellectual property rights that adversely affect, *inter alia*, technology transfer'); DD Bradlow, 'Differing Conceptions of Development and the Content of International

property context.[122] The issue of technology transfer and technical assistance has received very little attention in the literature so far, and has not been operationalized much beyond the exporting of intellectual property norms,[123] although it has been institutionalized within the TRIPS framework.[124]

Current approaches to trade and development, even outside intellectual property, emphasize *balanced* rules. Balance means assessments of costs and benefits, preservation of flexibility, and transparency of development impact.[125] In contrast to what is demanded by these new approaches, however, there seems to be a hardening of the arteries within the international intellectual property framework. Formalistic norm setting and norm interpretation are problems, even for industrialized countries with well established intellectual property industries.[126] Intellectual property is represented as being in the social welfare interests of all countries, in a formal equality sense. As pointed out in the previous section, any robust innovation policy should consider other means and forms of regulation. Developing countries arguably need the most flexibilities in this regard.

Finally, both the rapidity of technological changes and the increased interconnectedness of global knowledge production have altered the economics of global public goods production.[127] The availability of public goods is critical even for developed countries in the global context, e.g. Tamiflu for a potential avian flu outbreak, or Cipro for bioterrorism threats such as anthrax.[128] This has caused even countries advocating the strong development as growth approach to resort to unfavoured tools of access such as threatened compulsory licensing.[129]

Development Law' (2005) 21 *South African J Human Rights* 1 (available at <http://ssrn.com/abstract=788070>).

122 Within TRIPS, note 6 above, Arts 66(2), 67 and 69 address technical assistance and technology transfer. S&D is implemented in TRIPS via the transition periods for the LDCs to implement their obligations under Art 66(2); the TRIPS General Council extended this period to 2016.

123 D Matthews and V Munoz-Tellez, 'Bilateral Technical Assistance and TRIPS: The United States, Japan and European Communities in Comparative Perspective', (2006) 9 *J World IP* 629, 649–50 (analysing Art 67 technical assistance efforts from 1996–2005; concluding that while subtle differences exist among US, EU, and Japanese approaches to technical assistance, relatively few activities focus on Arts 7 and 8, or on flexibilities); KM Koepsel, 'How Do Developed Countries Meet Their Obligations Under Article 67 of the TRIPS Agreement?', (2004) 44 *IDEA* 167 (describing difficulty in meeting reporting requirements of Art 67, as well as technology transfer requirements under Art 66(2)).

124 TRIPS, note 6 above, Arts 66(2) and 67.

125 Ismail, note 13 above, 12.

126 Dinwoodie and Dreyfuss, 'TRIPS and the Dynamics of IP Lawmaking', note 12 above, 96.

127 JP Love and T Hubbard, 'Paying for Public Goods' in RA Ghosh, *Code: Collaborative Ownership and the Digital Economy* (MIT Press, 2005) 207.

128 Matthews, note 50 above, 110, 112.

129 SK Sell, 'Books, Drugs and Seeds: the Politics of Access' TACD, The Politics And Ideology Of Intellectual Property, Brussels, 20–21 March 2006, 53, 59, available at <http://www.tacd.org/events/intellectual-property/index.htm>.

In particular, digital networked technologies have challenged dominant assumptions about knowledge production.[130] Copyright law and policy developed over many years without fully internalizing the user's activities; they were traditionally more concerned about commercial relations among businesses involved in knowledge creation and dissemination.[131] The increasingly visible role of users within digital networks has caused a sea change in dominant business models in this realm.[132] These changes raise the possibility of creative and out-of-the-box approaches towards the generation and distribution of knowledge goods.

Conclusion

An approach towards development as freedom converges with the incipient global governance model of trade. Together, they indicate the need for scepticism towards heightened intellectual property standards as the universal solvent for innovation, especially where human development issues are implicated. The following Part elaborates on the substantive equality principle that embodies this heightened regulatory scepticism.

Part II Application of the Substantive Equality Principle

A. A Definition of Substantive Equality

The Formal Equality Landscape

Formal equality within international intellectual property is shaped at the level of applicable legal principles as well as within dispute resolution mechanisms. MFN, a bedrock principle of the multilateral trading system of GATT, was recently imported into international intellectual property via TRIPS Article 4.[133] Combined with the principle of national treatment,[134] which had already been a long-standing provision of the Berne and Paris Conventions,[135] the TRIPS Agreement then embodies two powerful principles of non-discrimination. Within trade instruments, MFN is a principle of non-discrimination among

130 J Litman, 'Sharing and Stealing' (2004) 37 *Hastings Comm and Ent LJ*.

131 DJ Gervais, 'Towards a New Core International Copyright Norm: The Reverse Three-Step Test' (2005) 9 *Marquette IP R* 1, 7.

132 E Pfanner, 'Universal Music Group and an Online Site Plan a Joint Venture to Challenge iTunes' (*NY Times*, 30 August 2006) C5.

133 TRIPS, note 6 above, Art 4; GATT (1994) Art I(1).

134 Ibid, Art 3.

135 Paris Convention, note 6 above, Art 2; Berne Convention, note 6 above, Art 5.

foreign nationals; within all the international intellectual property instruments, national treatment is a principle of non-discrimination barring internal discrimination in favour of domestic actors over non-nationals. The 'floor' of acceptable conduct is set 'voluntarily' by each member state: in the case of MFN, by any 'advantage, favour, privilege or immunity granted by a Member to the nationals of any other country';[136] in the case of national treatment, by any 'treatment . . . accord[ed]' to its own nationals.[137] These two non-discrimination principles within TRIPS are entrenched within GATT/WTO generally, although MFN status was quite often recognized in the breach.[138] This may continue to be the case under TRIPS.[139] As discussed earlier, these non-discrimination principles have historically impeded efforts to infuse trade with nuanced development efforts because they are relatively hostile to differentiation among states, including by development status. They are the two pillars of 'formal equality' within international intellectual property.[140]

A third aspect of formal equality rests within a specific section of TRIPS. TRIPS modified the global minimum patent standards substantially with its rule that 'patent rights [be] enjoyable without discrimination as to place of invention, the field of technology and whether products are imported or locally produced'.[141] This patent-specific non-discrimination principle radically revised the domestic policy space for all member states, which previously had been allowed, for example, to withhold the granting of patents for pharmaceutical products, or to encourage patent holders to work the patent locally. Article 27(1), in the guise of non-discrimination, raised the minimum standards of protection in the patent domain to a much higher level than existed previously. This represents a type of 'aggregation' or technology-neutrality that is increasingly criticized as a matter of internal US policy.[142]

---

136 TRIPS, note 6 above, Art 4.

137 Ibid, Art 3.

138 T Broude, 'The Rule(s) of Trade and the *Rhetos* of Development: Reflections on the Functional and Aspirational Legitimacy of the WTO', (2006) 27(4) *Columbia J of Transnational L*, 221, 232–3, available at <http://ssrn.com/abstract =902922>, 11–12 ('[t]he non-discriminatory nature of the GATT/WTO should therefore be taken as a relative matter rather than an absolute one. The question has (of course) never been whether non-discrimination should be abolished as a guiding or organizing principle, but rather, under which circumstances should discrimination be condemned and under which should it be absolved. In the main, this has been regarded as a question of trade economics: in blunt lay terms, when does discrimination create more trade than it diverts?')

139 UNCTAD–ICTSD, Resource Book, note 43 above, 79–81.

140 Ibid, 89.

141 TRIPS, note 6 above, Art 27(1).

142 Burk and Lemley, note 27 above.

At the level of dispute resolution, the WTO relies on highly formalistic decision-making processes, which have caused two leading international intellectual property observers to characterize the dispute settlement system as one of formal equality, in the context of analysing industrialized countries' innovation policy.[143] This observation of formalism in norm interpretation, a fourth pillar of formal equality, has parallels in the general trade literature, where the dispute settlement system has been criticized for the same reasons.[144] Moreover, a relatively small percentage of the complaints filed with the WTO have been filed by developing countries so far, and industrialized countries like the US have refused to implement WTO rulings adverse to their domestic interests. These facts suggest that 'after a decade of operation the WTO remains a rich man's club beyond the reach of most developing nations'.[145]

Substantive Equality Defined

By contrast to these formal equality pillars, I propose that a substantive equality principle should inform a development-oriented international intellectual property law. As stated previously, the law maker will be more sceptical of the validity of the regulation (in this case, the government intervention in the form of the grant of an exclusive right over intellectual property or the withholding of an exception or limitation of that exclusive right) where it conflicts with the provision of a development-sensitive human need, as defined in part by the Millennium Development Goals. This principle of equality would be applied both domestically as well as in international decision-making venues.[146]

This substantive equality principle is intended to achieve distributive outcomes. It may allow law makers to distinguish between different technologies, despite the mandate of non-discrimination in Article 27(1). It may allow law makers to distinguish between different industries, countries and levels of development, if necessary. It is a thumb on the scale of scepticism with respect to regulatory intervention generally in the form of intellectual property in all domains (whether patent, copyright, trademark, trade secret, unfair competition, geographical indicators, etc.), when those grants will interfere with a well-defined development goal. It is not intended necessarily to operate at the level of constitutional law,

143 Dinwoodie and Dreyfuss, 'TRIPS and the Dynamics of IP Lawmaking', note 12 above, 96.

144 Broude, note 138 above, 16, 239 ('[t]he other side of this coin, a growth defect in its own right, is the formalistic and legalized nature of the WTO's dispute settlement system. Lashed to an almost static political norm-making system, the judicial branch of the WTO is extremely careful not to stray from the boundaries of political consensus, for fear of damaging its own legitimacy, when faced with sensitive issues').

145 Drache, note 81 above.

146 Chon, 'Development Divide', note 13 above, 2885.

except as the term 'constitutionalization' is used (loosely) in reference to more balance of social policies within all intellectual property norm-setting and norm-interpreting venues more generally. It can be employed both at the international level and the national level; both in public law and private ordering. It is supposed to be decentralized, in order to address the multiple sites of international intellectual property norm setting and norm interpretation.

B. Application of the Substantive Equality Principle to Norm Interpretation: A Case Study

Access to Educational Materials: First and Second Order Strategies

How might a developing country begin to address access to education under the existing international intellectual property framework? While increasing access to education is a specific goal of the UNMDG,[147] and school enrolments indeed are rising, most areas of the world severely lack adequate educational materials.[148] Textbook provision through bulk compensated access—that is, through the purchase of hard copies of protected content at affordable prices—is a first-best strategy from the point of view of both copyright owners and users.[149] As Ruth Okediji has stated,

> [b]ulk access . . . is . . . critical to developing countries where education is a top development priority. For such countries, the freedom to quote from copyrighted material . . . is secondary to the need for affordable access to educational texts, scientific journals and other learning materials. Ironically, however, issues regarding bulk access have not featured prominently in the welfare critique or demands for reform of the international intellectual property system.[150]

Unfortunately, while desirable, bulk access is often unavailable from the perspective of developing country populations. The reasons for this lack of access

147 UN Millennium Development Goals, note 15 above ('[a]chieve universal primary education' as well as '[p]romote gender equality and empower women' by 'eliminate[ing] gender disparity in primary and secondary education preferably by 2005, and at all levels by 2015').

148 M Chon, 'Intellectual Property From Below: Copyright and Capability for Education', (2007) 40 *U of Cal Davis LR 803.*

149 Okediji, note 33 above, 6 (defining bulk access as 'access to sufficient copies of copyrighted works at affordable prices'); RL Okediji, 'Sustainable Access to Copyrighted Digital Information Works in Developing Countries', in Maskus and Reichman (eds), Intenational Public Goods, note 1 above, 148 (defining access in four ways: 'the unencumbered right to utilize a creative work (uncompensated creative access), privately negotiated terms of use between owners and users (negotiated access), qualified opportunities to utilize certain types of works through compulsory licensing (mandatory compensated access); as well as the opportunity to purchase and own the physical embodiment of the protected content (bulk compensated access)').

150 RL Okediji, 'Africa and the Global Intellectual Property System: Beyond the Agency Model' (2006) *African Foundation for International Law* 207, 230.

are complex[151] but the outcome is clear: often textbooks are unaffordable.[152] Even with differential pricing by publishers, for a student in a developing country the price of a textbook can be many times higher, as a percentage of GDP per capita, than the price for a student in a developed country.[153] Although consumers sometimes take advantage of the first sale doctrine and other exhaustion rules to maximize access to educational content,[154] the TRIPS flexibility allowing countries to enact a rule of international exhaustion is an insufficient component in encouraging the movement of copyright-protected content from developed to developing countries.[155]

A next-best strategy from the point of view of publishers might appear to be compulsory licensing. However, the Berne Appendix, hard-fought-for by developing countries and added to the Berne Convention in 1971, has been exceedingly unhelpful as a method of enabling access to educational materials for developing countries.[156] As of 2006, astoundingly few countries have filed a notice with WIPO to invoke the compulsory licensing provisions of the Appendix.[157] Part of the reason for this must be its opacity. The Appendix exceeds the length of the original Berne Convention. Examples of its complexity and the barriers it poses to access include waiting periods from three to seven years to get a license, after which the author can still terminate any time, as well as different provisions for translation and reproduction licenses, which cover the same works. Occasional calls have issued for its revision or even outright revocation.[158]

---

151 Chon, 'Intellectual Property From Below', note 148 above.

152 A Rens, A Prabhala and D Kawooya, 'Intellectual Property, Education and Access to Knowledge in Southern Africa', Paper commissioned by Trade Law Centre for Southern Africa for UNCTAD and ICTSD, available from: <http://www.iprsonline.org/unctadictsd/docs/06%2005%2031%20tralac%20amended-pdf.pdf > (2006) 12 (analysing reasons for excessive pricing of books in the Southern African market).

153 Consumers International, *Copyright and Access to Knowledge: Policy Recommendations on Flexibilities in Copyright Laws* (2006) 41, available at <http://www.consumersinternational.org/Shared_ASP_Files/UploadedFiles/23775AAE-3EE7-4AE2-A730-281DCE859AD4_COPYRIGHT Final16.02.06.pdf> (estimating that asking an Indonesian student $81.70 for a textbook would be equivalent to asking a US student to pay $3,170.97).

154 T Lewin, 'Students Find $100 Textbooks Cost $50, Purchased Overseas' (NY Times, 21 October 2003).

155 TRIPS, note 6 above, Art 6 ('Exhaustion') is agnostic on the question of parallel imports.

156 Berne Convention, note 6 above, Appendix (entitled 'Special Provisions Regarding Developing Countries'); Ricketson and Ginsburg, note 32 above, 957; Okediji, 'Sustainable Access in Developing Countries', note 149 above, 162–66; CIPR, note 4 above, 104.

157 Only 15 countries have filed declarations under Art 1 with respect to the facilities provided by Arts II and III (Notification numbers 79, 91, 109, 110, 232, 233, 234, 235, 236, 237, 238, 239, 240, 245, and 248, available at <http://www.wipo.int/treaties/en/ShowResults.jsp?search_what=N&treaty_id=15>).

158 A Story, 'Burn Berne: Why the Leading International Copyright Convention Must Be Repealed' (2003) 40 *Houston LR* 763.

But mostly it stands as an inscrutable monument to how and why the concept of equitable remuneration may not address the development divide. A substantive equality principle would suggest that WIPO could play a far greater role in revising and facilitating access through the Berne Appendix and other forms of licensing. This is discussed at greater length in Section C below, which addresses norm setting.

Access to Educational Materials: A Third Strategy

Another strategy, considered at length here, might be a more widespread enactment of domestic exceptions to copyright under national laws. Encouragement of educational exceptions by developing countries would be consistent with the general Berne and TRIPS frameworks, which contain a specific and long-standing exception in the form of Berne Article 10(2). However, depending on how aggressive and broad these national exceptions are, they may raise several legal issues under the current international copyright framework. One is the capacity and political will of member states to enact far-reaching exceptions. Another possible question is whether these exceptions would comply with their obligations under Berne and TRIPS respectively? Another issue is the treatment of these exceptions under the so-called three-step tests of TRIPS and Berne. Would the special circumstances and policies of developing countries factor into the application of these tests? And finally, how might these exceptions be treated in the digital realm, and specifically in the context of the WIPO Copyright Treaty (WCT)?[159]

At first glance, educational exceptions appear to be easily consistent with Berne and TRIPS. The so-called illustration for teaching provision of Berne, Article 10(2), states:

> [i]t shall be a matter for legislation in the countries of the Union, and for special agreements existing or to be concluded between them, to permit for the utilization, to the extent justified by the purpose, of literary or artistic works by way of illustration in publications, broadcasts or sound or visual recordings for teaching, provided such utilization is compatible with fair practice.[160]

From its inception at the origin of the Berne Convention, the term 'teaching' in Article 10(2) covered primary to tertiary levels of teaching.[161] This scope of

159 WIPO Copyright Treaty, note 99 above, CRNR/DC/97.

160 Berne Convention, note 6 above, Art 10(2). The exact meaning of 'fair practice' is unclear. Ricketson and Ginsburg document that the programme for the 1967 Stockholm Revision Conference includes a statement that 'the use in question can only be accepted after an objective appreciation': Ricketson and Ginsburg, note 32 above, 786.

161 Ricketson and Ginsburg, ibid, 789.

coverage was affirmed at the 1967 Stockholm Revision Conference.[162] The Stockholm Revision Conference Committee's Report suggests that there is no particular quantitative limitation and that an educational use could include an entire work in appropriate circumstances.[163] Moreover, permissible exceptions under Article 10(2) should be defined in the first instance by national legislation; Article 10 simply sets outer boundaries. As a recent WIPO study on copyright exceptions and limitations indicates, 'fair practice' should be up to the national tribunal to determine in the first instance but also defined in part by Berne Article 9(2), that is, the Berne three-step test.[164] It goes on to suggest that specific educational uses allowed under the Article 10(2) exception would presumably comply with the more general scope of the three-step test.[165] In developing countries where textbooks and other teaching materials are scarce, a substantive equality principle would suggest that national legislatures enact the fullest expansion of this Berne-endorsed exception wherever possible. This would enable countries to engage not just in reproduction, but also in broadcast and public performance of works for teaching purposes.

What about countries that have not enacted educational exceptions (or that even have curtailed the potential policy space for educational exceptions to copyright provided by Article 10(2)?[166] These choices may reflect the lack of domestic institutional capacity to design appropriate policies as much as deliberate social policy.[167] Where the former is the case, encouraging the domestic enactment of the broadest possible educational exceptions, including an illustration for teaching purposes, can begin to create a type of access to works for

[162] Ibid, 792 ('the utilization must be "by way of illustration" for the purposes of "teaching". This scope of the latter expression received considerable attention from the delegates at the Stockholm Conference, and the following exegesis of their views was provided in the Committee's report:

> The wish was expressed that it should be made clear in this Report that the word 'teaching' was to include teaching at all levels—in educational institutions and universities, municipal and State schools, and private schools. Education outside these institutions, for instance general teaching available to the general public but not include [*sic*] in the above categories, should be excluded').

[163] Ibid, 792 ('[t]he words "by way of illustration" impose some limitation, but would not exclude the uses of the whole of a work in appropriate circumstances. For example, in the case of an artistic work or short literary work it might be argued that it is necessary to reproduce the whole work if it is to be properly utilized for teaching purposes'). At least one delegate to the Stockholm Conference took the position that the term 'borrowings' in an earlier translation of the French 'emprunts' indicated that 'the use of an entire work might be allowable within article 10(2), under some circumstances'. Ibid.

[164] WIPO, 'Study on Limitations and Exceptions of Copyright and Related Rights in the Digital Environment' (5 April 2003; SCCR/9/7) 13 (prepared by S Ricketson).

[165] Ibid, 21.

[166] Chon, 'Intellectual Property From Below', note 148 above; Okediji, note 33 above, 32.

[167] Okediji, 'Africa and the Global IP System', note 150 above, 241.

educational purposes that may counterbalance the lack of bulk access to textbooks through market mechanisms or the Berne Appendix. The fact that a country historically may have had a narrower exception previously should not estop it from enacting a broader one. Indeed no provision in Berne or TRIPS prevents a country from utilizing the maximum policy space allowed by Article 10(2).

In tandem, developing countries might set international exhaustion rules that allow parallel importation of copies of educational materials passing muster under the provisions of the US fair use doctrine or other countries' broader educational exceptions.[168] This 'parallel educational use' would be both Berne- and TRIPS-compliant.[169] These various strategies could provide an important point of access to educational materials from industrialized countries without the onerous licensing and equitable remuneration requirements of the Berne Appendix. A substantive equality principle points strongly in the direction of endorsing creative norm interpretation of this sort, so as to increase access by consumers in developing countries.

What are other possible strategies that may push against the permissible boundaries of Article 10(2)? There are slightly more ambiguous areas. A country might decide that its educational exceptions will cover non-face-to-face instruction, including correspondence or online classes.[170] It might decide that instruction may be conducted by lay teachers. These kinds of teaching are not endorsed in the Berne Convention Stockholm Revision Committee Notes. A domestic exception may specifically provide for translations and adaptations into local languages. Translation rights are explicitly covered by Berne Article 8 but not covered by Article 10(2). They are also covered by the Berne Appendix and thus presumably subject to compulsory licensing. Similarly, adaptations are subject to Berne Article 12 but not explicitly mentioned in Article 10(2). While some have suggested that implied exceptions for translations are automatically tagged to educational exceptions as 'minor exceptions', this is not a settled area of law.[171] For each of these grey areas, a substantive equality principle would be sceptical of a strong rights claim (whether in the rights holders' reproduction, broadcast, performance, translation, or adaptation rights). It would support the broadest possible interpretation of an educational exception and/or implied exception, consistent with the development objective of access to education.

168 17 USC §107 ('Limitations on exclusive rights: Fair use').
169 TRIPS, note 6 above, Art 6 (entitled 'Exhaustion').
170 WIPO, 'Study on Limitations and Exceptions', note 164 above, 15.
171 Ibid, 39.

Are there some even more controversial strategies? A country might decide to eschew the reprographic society or collective rights model and permit uncompensated multiple copies of a work for educational use, including large numbers of copies for individual classroom use.[172] It might decide to extend the exception to adult literacy campaigns. Or a country might decide to exempt textbooks entirely from copyright protection. It might decide to enact a broad, US-style fair use exception in addition to specific educational exceptions.[173] These policy choices might be highly controversial, not only as a matter of national policy, but also as a matter of compliance with Berne Article 10(2) and/or the applicable three-step tests. While the ideal solution to lack of textbook access is the provision of textbooks through domestic publisher capacity or affordable imports, these alternative strategies may be necessary for temporary periods in order to facilitate knowledge diffusion for purposes of basic education.

Access to Educational Materials: Strategies Based on Sharing and Leveraging the Non-rivalrous Nature of Knowledge Goods in Digitized Networks

Especially where schools are short on books, libraries have an important role to play in expanding educational access to copyright works through domestic exceptions and limitations.[174] While there is some uncertainty in industrialized countries over whether library exceptions pass the three-step tests of Berne/TRIPS, a domestic court or WTO dispute settlement panel should apply the substantive equality principle to such domestic library exceptions enacted pursuant to Article 10(2) in developing countries.[175] If there is evidence that they were enacted with the development objectives of promoting access to basic education, then there should be more deference with respect to their legitimacy, particularly whether or not they 'conflict with the normal exploitation of a work' under step two. The next section of this Part explores this three-step analysis in more detail.

---

172 In the US, the Supreme Court has not addressed this educational strategy definitively. A Bartow, 'Educational Fair Use in Copyright: Reclaiming the Right to Photocopy Freely' (1998) 60 *U Pitt. LR* 149. In Brazil, the International Trade Law and Development Institute recently initiated a lawsuit against the Brazilian Association of Reprography Rights, to challenge the national law that mandates compensation via a reprographic rights society. A2k weblog, 'NGO Files Lawsuit Against Brazilian Publishers Association' (24 July 2006), available at <http://www.a2kbrasil.org.br/ENG/NGO-Files-Law-Suit-Against>.

173 Consumers International, *Copyright and Access to Knowledge*, note 153 above (advocating the inclusion of broad fair use provisions in national laws to promote access to educational materials).

174 LN Gasaway, 'Values Conflict in the Digital Environment: Librarians *Versus* Copyright Holders' (2000) 24 *Columbia—VLA J of L and the Arts* 115.

175 Compare S Ricketson, 'The Three-Step Test, Deemed Quantities, Libraries and Closed Exceptions' (Centre for Copyright Studies, 2002), 82–83 (examining Australian educational copying provisions) with MJ Tawfik, 'International Copyright Law and "Fair Dealing" as a "User Right"', (UNESCO e-Copyright Bulletin, 2005) (examining Canadian fair dealing doctrine covering scholarship and research).

Digital technology has tremendous potential to leverage information for development. The WCT neither reduced nor extended the scope or applicability of existing Berne exceptions, including the Berne Appendix and Berne Article 10(2).[176] It also does not foreclose the enactment of further domestic exceptions and limitations to digital rights sounding in copyright.[177] Countries should enact digital-specific educational exceptions. Arguably, these exceptions might even exceed the scope of Article 10(2).[178] Open course content initiatives spearheaded by global intergovernmental agencies such as UNESCO[179] and the interventions

[176] WIPO, 'Study on Limitations and Exceptions', note 164 above, 63. Interestingly, however, although

> the intention here was not to alter the status quo under Berne,. . . it is equally clear that it was accepted that some, at least, of the existing limitations and exceptions under national law might not meet the three-step criteria although they fell within the scope of either other express provisions of Berne or the minor exceptions doctrine. While the views expressed in the Basic Proposal indicate that it was intended to modify these existing exceptions, where necessary, so as to conform with the three-step test, this was not accepted by the delegates, and the wording of the second paragraph of the agreed statement confirms this. Accordingly, WCT members are not required to modify limitations and exceptions that are consistent with the present Berne text, even if these would not pass the three-step test in Article 10(2). There will, of course, be room for argument as to whether any of the existing Berne exceptions and limitations, including the minor reservations doctrine, do, in fact, go beyond the limits of the three-step test, but, to the extent that this is so, it seems clear that the three-step test cannot 'trump' these existing limitations and exceptions.

[177] WIPO Copyright Treaty, 'Agreed Statements Concerning the WIPO Copyright Treaty', Statement Concerning Article 10 ('[i]t is understood that the provisions of Article 10 permit Contracting Parties to carry forward and appropriately extend into the digital environment limitations and exceptions in their national laws which have been considered acceptable under the Berne Convention. Similarly, these provisions should be understood to permit Contracting Parties to devise new exceptions and limitations that are appropriate in the digital network environment. It is also understood that Article 10(2) [which is the WCT three-step test] neither reduces nor extends the scope of applicability of the limitations and exceptions permitted by the Berne Convention').

The purpose of the agreed statements 'is to provide guidance in the interpretation of particularly treaty provisions': Ricketson and Ginsburg, note 32 above, 151. Furthermore, '[a]greements of this kind are therefore not part of the "preparatory work" of the treaty, which may only be used as supplementary means of interpretation pursuant to article 32 . . . but will form part of the context of the treaty for the primary task of interpretation under article 31(1)'; ibid, 191.

[178] Ricketson and Ginsburg, ibid, 871–72. In this regard, developing countries should not follow the model of developed countries such as the US, which has tried to rein in the losses associated with digital reproduction of its music and film industries, by enacting domestic legislation that impedes rather than promotes access to education. Digital Media Project, 'Obstacles to Educational Uses of Copyrighted Material in the Digital Age: A Foundational White Paper' (2006), available at <http://cyber.law.harvard.edu/media/files/copyrightandeducation.html>. LN Gasaway, 'Distance Learning and Copyright: An Update' (2001) 49 *J of the Copyright Soc of the USA* 195; KD Crews, 'Distance Education and Copyright Law: The Limits and Meaning of Copyright Policy' (2000) 27 *J College and Univ L* 15.

[179] UNESCO Virtual University, 'Open Educational Resources, Open content for higher education' (available at <http://portal.unesco.org/ci/en/files/21713/11438000259OER_Forum_Final_Report.pdf/OER%2BForum%2BFinal%2BReport.pdf >).

of educational institutions such as the Massachusetts Institute of Technology[180] in the tertiary textbook arena indicate that provision of these types of public goods can take many forms in conjunction with market-based mechanisms for distribution. Large-scale library digitization projects, such as the Google Book project based in the US, are now supplemented by the Google Literacy Project, launched in the fall of 2006 in conjunction with UN agencies.[181] In the Carnegie-Mellon University's Million Book Project, books are being scanned to supplement libraries in developing countries such as China and India.[182] These and other new digital initiatives such as GlobalText and Wikibooks have enormous potential to expand the informational universes of tertiary educational institutions.

Currently, Chile is spearheading an effort in WIPO to study international minimum exceptions and limitations for educational and other uses in the digital context.[183] Simultaneously, however, there are strong efforts within WIPO to expand the reach of digital rights,[184] and by industrialized countries to expand digital rights bilaterally.[185]

A Substantive Equality Interpretation of the Three-step Tests

Recall that under a substantive equality principle, the norm interpretation should be sceptical of the right and deferential to the exception. A substantive equality principle would first lead a norm-interpreting body, such as a national court or WTO dispute settlement panel, first to defer to the legislative intent regarding the 'fair practice' nature of the educational exception, so as to avoid any need to invoke a potential analysis under the three-step tests, either under Berne Article 9(2), which affects the reproduction right only, or TRIPS Article 13, which applies to exceptions to all rights. Indeed, one interpretation is that no conflict exists between the pre-existing targeted teaching exception represented by Berne Article 10(2) and the more general provision of Berne Article 9(2), which was

180 'MIT to make nearly all course materials available free on the World Wide Web' (MIT News Office, 2001) available at <http://web.mit.edu/newsoffice/2001/ocw.html>.

181 For details, see <http://www.google.com/literacy/>.

182 Frequently asked questions about the Million Book Project (available at <http://www.library.cmu.edu/Libraries/MBP_FAQ.html>).

183 WIPO Provisional Committee on Proposals Related to a WIPO Development Agenda, First Session (12 January 2006) PCDA/1/2; WIPO, 'Proposal by Chile on the Analysis of Exceptions and Limitations' (22 November 2005) SCCR/13/5; WIPO, 'Proposal by Chile on the Subject of Exceptions and Limitations to Copyright' (2 November 2004) SCCR12/3.

184 WIPO, 'Revised Draft Basic Proposal for the WIPO Treaty on the Protection of Broadcasting Organizations' (31 July 2006) SCCR/15/20.

185 Electronic Frontier Foundation, 'US–Chile Free Trade Agreement Analysis of Exceptions and Limitations and Technological Protection Measures' (2004) (available at <http://www.eff.org/IP/FTAA/20040830_uschile_fta.pdf>).

intended to cover other types of exceptions. This interpretation, consistent with the drafting history of the Berne Convention, is that the 'operation of the [educational exception] provisions within their specific sphere is unaffected by the more general provision in Article 9(2), and that the uses allowed under them are therefore excluded from its scope'.[186] Indeed, the position that new exceptions under TRIPS would pass muster under TRIPS Article 30's analogous three-step test for patents, pursuant to Article 8's 'public health' principle, gave rise to an Article 30-based proposal for compulsory licensing of patented pharmaceuticals during the negotiations of the implementation of paragraph 6 of the Doha Declaration.[187]

Another possible view, however, is that while Article 10(2)'s requirement of 'fair practice' is 'essentially a question for national tribunals to determine in each particular instance', it is also possibly measured by the three-step test of Article 9(2).[188] To the extent that there is a perceived conflict between an exception enacted under the ambit of Berne Article 10(2) and the flexibility allowed generally under the Berne Article 9(2) and TRIPS Article 13, decision makers should allow the broadest possible exceptions to promote access to educational materials for purposes of development. Thus domestic educational exceptions enacted in developing countries pursuant to Article 10(2) should be read in light of TRIPS Articles 7 and 8, which refer to development.[189]

Without the operation of a substantive equality principle, an educational exception that allowed uncompensated multiple copies, for example, might push the boundaries of acceptability under Berne Article 10(2). As the Committee Report to the Stockholm Conference pointed out with respect to photocopying:

> [i]f it consists of producing a very large number of copies, it may not be permitted, as it conflicts with a normal exploitation of the work. If it implies a rather large number of copies for use in industrial undertakings, it may not unreasonably prejudice

---

186 WIPO, 'Study on Limitations and Exceptions', note 164 above, 21.

187 Matthews, note 50 above, 94–96 (reporting arguments that an Art 30 approach would not require 'authorization from the patent holder, compensation of the patent holder or the issuing of licenses').

188 Ricketson and Ginsburg, note 32 above, 786.

189 Accordingly Moncayo von Hase, note 44 above, 136:

> It is . . . very important for developing countries to be able to shape the exceptions to the exclusive rights . . . in pursuance of any objectives set forth in the Articles 7 and 8 of the Agreement. In such context, a delicate situation would arise if one member would question the scope and extent of an exception to the exclusive right of IPR holders . . . before a WTO panel. Unless the panel confines itself to determine whether such a measure or exception has the effect of abolishing the very existence of the exclusive rights of the right holder or not, such a dispute should not lead to the replacement of the member's legitimate policy views based on the public objectives acknowledged by Article 7 and 8 of TRIPs . . . .

> the legitimate interests of the author, provided that, according to national legislation, an equitable remuneration is paid. If a small number of copies is made, photocopying may be permitted without payment, particularly for individual or scientific use.[190]

The *United States – Section 110(5)* panel stated that an exception would only comport with the first step of the three-step test ('certain special cases') if it is 'clearly defined and narrow in its scope and reach'.[191] It evaluated this criterion by the percentage of businesses that took advantage of the exception. Empirical data was available from both parties, which were both extremely well-resourced. Moreover, the panel assumed that if a majority of businesses made use of the exception, then the exception swallowed the rule and *ergo* did not comply with the first step. Finally, the panel refused to inquire into the public policy purpose of the exception.

Under a substantive equality principle, the analysis of step one would be more sceptical of the rights holder and much more deferential to the national policy underlying the exception. A development divide exists between countries that can participate meaningfully in a collection society model, and those that might not be able to.[192] An analysis of a particular educational exception should push beyond the question whether the exception is clearly defined and narrow.[193] Under a substantive equality principle, a panel should explicitly consider and defer to a developing country's stated policy of promoting education for development. This interpretative approach would contrast, again, with a differently weighted application of the three-step test towards exceptions of industrialized countries and/or disputes between them over the scope of such exceptions.

Under an interpretation influenced by a substantive equality principle, analysis of the second step of Berne Article 9(2) or TRIPS Article 13 is affected as well.

---

190 *United States – Section 110(5) of the US Copyright Act*, Report of the Panel (WTO DS 15 June 2000; WT/S160/R) para 6.73 [hereinafter *Section 110(5)* panel] (quoting Records of the Intellectual Property Conference of Stockholm. 11 June to 14 July 1967, Report on the Work of Main Committee I (Substantive Provisions of the Berne Convention: Articles 1 to 20).

191 *Section 110(5)* panel, ibid, para 6.112 ('[i]n our view, the first condition of Article 13 requires that a limitation or exception in national legislation should be clearly defined and should be narrow in its scope and reach'); see also J Ginsburg, 'Toward Supranational Copyright Law? The WTO Panel Decision and the "Three-Step Test" for Copyright Exceptions', (2001) 187 *Revue Intle du Droit d'Auteur* 3.

192 A Story, C Darch and D Halbert, *The Copy/South Dossier: Issues in the economics, politics and ideology of copyright in the global South* (Copy/South Research Group, 2006) 41–46 (analyzing the viability of reprographic rights societies in the developing world).

193 *Section 110(5)* panel, note 190 above, para 6.111 ('we believe that the term "certain special cases" should not lightly be equated with "special purpose". . . . [However,] public policy purposes stated by law-makers when enacting a limitation or exception may be useful from a factual perspective for making inferences about the scope of a[n] . . . exception').

Multiple copying may not 'conflict with normal exploitation of the work'. As even a WIPO study on exceptions and limitations acknowledged recently,

> [t]he words 'normal exploitation' give no guidance as to the kinds of non-economic normative considerations that may be relevant here, and the extent to which they may limit uses that would otherwise be within the scope of normal exploitation by the copyright owner. Striking this balance is left as a matter for national legislation. Value judgments will need to be made, and these will clearly vary according to the society and culture concerned. In keeping with the first step, however, these non-economic purposes will need to be clearly and specifically articulated, and will need to be set against the stated objective of the Convention, which is the protection of the rights of authors. This indicates that such justifications will need a clear public interest character that goes beyond the purely individual interests of copyright users. In this regard, it can be said that they should be of analogous significance to those already accepted as appropriate under other provisions of the Berne Convention, such as Article 10 . . . .[194]

Indeed, the *Section 110(5)* panel itself acknowledged that

> it should not be forgotten that *domestic laws already contained a series of exceptions in favour of various public and cultural interests* and. . . it would be vain to suppose that countries would be ready at this stage to abolish these exceptions to any appreciable extent.[195]. . . [I]n our view, not every use of a work, which in principle is covered by the scope of exclusive rights and involves commercial gain, necessarily conflicts with a normal exploitation of that work. If this were the case, hardly any exception or limitation could pass the test of the second condition and Article 13 might be left devoid of meaning, because normal exploitation would be equated with full use of exclusive rights.[196]

Again, these interpretations look first to domestic development priorities and policies, rather than to the rights holders' claims, in determining the proper ambit of the treaty interpretation.

Finally, with respect to step three, that is, whether the exception results in 'unreasonable prejudice to the legitimate interests of the rightsholder', the WTO panel interpreted this to cover even a 'potential . . . unreasonable loss of income to the copyright holder'.[197] An educational exception that allows for multiple copying for classroom use would fail on this prong far too easily, even in countries where no collective rights organizations or other market mechanisms currently exist. Of all the interventions discussed so far, this is where a substantive equality principle has the most potentially dramatic impact. A national court or a WTO dispute settlement body employing a substantive equality principle would

194 WIPO, 'Study on Limitations and Exceptions', note 164 above, 26.

195 *Section 110(5)* panel, note 190 above, para 6.181 (original emphasis; quoting Swedish/BIRPI study).

196 Ibid, para 6.182.

197 Ibid, para 6.229.

interpret this step very differently. It would be sceptical towards the claim that the rights holder is entitled to a future income stream, especially in the context of an exception enacted to remedy current shortages of educational materials. Infrastructure might not exist for income collection, either because the textbook market itself is underdeveloped, or because the mechanisms for reprographic rights societies are not yet in place. Thus the 'potential market' test is far too deferential to the rights holder.[198] Along these lines, one commentator suggests that the third step should include a reasonableness criterion, which takes into account the balance of the rights holders, on the one hand, and the needs of users on the other.[199] In any event, a panel should interpret this step quite differently for developing countries with substantial need for access to educational materials and substantial barriers to access.

The Future of Creative Educational Access Models

It is unclear whether, without further treaty revisions, countries may create new limitations or exceptions to rights (beyond those already identified or that fall within so-called minor exceptions). Indeed almost all leading commentators are in agreement that TRIPS Article 13 does not justify the creation of new limitations or compulsory licensing mechanisms, on the rationale that to do so would to violate TRIPS Article 2(2) and Berne Article 20.[200] Thus, in order to create more legal certainty, a multilateral treaty provision should be negotiated to maintain and extend limitations and exceptions for developing countries in order to preserve a local policy space for developing countries, particularly in the face of bilateral efforts by industrialized countries to increase rights. A substantive equality principle would support such a norm-setting endeavour. This is discussed in more depth in the next Part of this chapter.

Since its beginning, Article 10(2) has had the *imprimatur* of consensus by Berne Convention members. As recently observed

> the precise nature of such exceptions and limitations [to copyright] was to be left to the reserved powers of the State to protect the welfare interests of its citizens. As a result, minimum rights were developed internationally through consensus, while specific exceptions and limitations remained the domain of the State. As the Convention matured, it came to reflect and incorporate limitations and exceptions that had evolved over time in [a] large number of States.[201]

198 Indeed, at least one commentator has criticized the panel decision, stating that it 'conflated the second and third steps': Gervais, 'The Reverse Three-Step Test', note 131 above, 19.

199 Ibid, 18–19.

200 Ricketson and Ginsburg, note 32 above, 857; WIPO, 'Study on Limitations and Exceptions', note 164 above, 49; Gervais, *The TRIPS Agreement*, note 34 above, 145; P Goldstein, *International Copyright: Principles, Law, Practice* (Oxford University Press, 2001) 294.

201 Okediji, note 33 above, 10.

The exact parameters of educational exceptions for purposes of development are still not explored fully as of this writing. Pragmatically, however, it would not require much in terms of technical assistance or capacity building to draft and implement model exceptions for educational fair practice. Coupled with a substantive equality principle in norm interpretation, these legal initiatives should easily be Berne- and TRIPS-compliant.

C. Application of the Substantive Equality Principle to Norm Setting: A Case Study

Development Within International Intellectual Property Norm-setting Organizations

Focusing now on the WIPO–WTO institutional division of labour, their roles and competence are in flux post-TRIPS.[202] Arguably TRIPS threw WIPO's hegemony into doubt by allowing industrialized countries with powerful intellectual property interests to shift to a more favourable regime (the trade regime) for norm setting.[203] However, paradoxically TRIPS has increased WIPO's visibility, with respect to norm spreading if not norm setting, through its 1995 technical cooperation agreement with WTO to provide technical assistance to developing countries under Article 67 of the TRIPS Agreement.[204] Moreover, WIPO has far greater financial resources than the WTO to engage in intellectual property norm-setting activities of any stripe, by virtue of its revenue from filing fees from the various treaties it administers. Since the Marrakech meeting, it has successfully concluded several treaties.[205]

It appears that industrialized countries are now shifting regimes back again from WTO to WIPO. The International Bureau of WIPO is moving forward in what could be viewed as TRIPS-Plus norm-setting initiatives, such as the draft substantive patent law treaty through the Standing Committee on the Law

202 J Watal, *Intellectual Property Rights in the WTO and Developing Countries* (Kluwer Law International, 2001) 396–402 (forecasting institutional matters of relevance to implementation of TRIPS, such as division of authority and competence between the WTO and WIPO); S Musungu and G Dutfield, 'Multilateral agreements and a TRIPS-Plus world', WIPO, TRIPS Issues Papers 3 (QUNO, 2003) 16 [hereafter Musungu and Dutfield] (focusing on the role of WIPO post-TRIPS).

203 Raustiala, note 89 above; P Yu, 'Currents and Cross-currents in the International Intellectual Property Regime' (2004) *Loyola of LA LR* 323, 408–17; LR Helfer, 'Regime Shifting: The TRIPS Agreement and the New Dynamic of International Intellectual Property Law-Making' (2004) 29 *Yale J Intl L* 1, 42 n186.

204 Agreement Between the World Intellectual Property Organization and the World Trade Organization (22 December 1995) 35 ILM 754.

205 WIPO Copyright Treaty, note 99 above; WIPO Performances and Phonograms Treaty, 20 December 1996, 36 ILM 76; Patent Law Treaty, 2 June 2000, 39 ILM 1047; The Singapore Treaty on the Law of Trademarks, 28 March 2006, TLT/R/DC/30.

of Patents,[206] the draft broadcasting treaty discussions within its Standing Committee on Copyright and Related Rights (SCCR),[207] as well as soft-law norm-setting activities in the Standing Committee on the Law of Trademarks, Industrial Designs and Geographical Indications.[208] Thus it appears that, if anything, TRIPS has reinforced WIPO's primacy on intellectual property matters, at least *vis-à-vis* any other alternative contender within the international UN agency system.[209]

At the same time, the legitimacy of the current Doha Development Round at the WTO is in question.[210] Given the agreements to disagree so far during the Doha Round, which was supposed to prioritize the needs of developing countries, the US and other intellectual property-rich nations are increasingly looking at bilateral 'solutions' to trade issues, including intellectual property. The multilateral solutions of the WTO, while imperfect, are giving way to Berne-Plus, TRIPS-Plus[211] and even US-Plus[212] standards negotiated via free trade agreements. As Peter Drahos notes, these turn the non-discrimination principle of MFN into a ratchet upwards for rights holders:

> Each new bilateral agreement that sets higher standards of intellectual property is picked up by the MFN principle of TRIPS. The savings of MFN become significant

206 WIPO Draft Substantive Patent Law Treaty [Clean Text] (Geneva, 30 September 2003; SCP/10/4).

207 WIPO 'Revised Draft Proposal, Broadcasting Organizations', note 184 above.

208 These activities have culminated in the adoption by the WIPO General Assembly and the Assembly of the Paris Union of three Joint Recommendations: (1) Concerning Provisions on the Protection of Well-Known Marks in 1999; (2) Concerning Trademark Licenses in 2000; and (3) Concerning Provisions on the Protection of Marks, and Other Industrial Property Rights in Signs, on the Internet in 2001. WIPO Trademark Joint Recommendations are available at <http://www.wipo.int/activities/en/development_iplaw.html>. In addition, WIPO recently successfully concluded a Diplomatic Conference for the Adoption of a Revised Trademark Treaty: The Singapore Treaty on the Law of Trademarks (28 March 2006; TLT/R/DC/30).

209 Musungu, note 90 above.

210 SJ Cho, 'The WTO Doha Round Negotiation: Suspended Indefinitely' (2006) 10(22) *ASIL Insight*.

211 'TRIPS-Plus' refers to bilateral agreements or regional multilateral agreements, often denominated as 'free trade agreements', in which minimum standards are negotiated that exceed the TRIPS minimum standards, which often have the effect of reducing the flexibilities and policy space of developing countries. Examples of this include Art 17(5) of the US–Chile Free Trade Agreement, which sets copyright term at life of the author plus 70 years. This exceeds the requirements of Art 9 of TRIPS, note 6 above, Art 9 (incorporating Berne Convention, note 6 above, Art 7(1)), which establishes a term of life of the author plus 50 years. United States–Chile Free Trade Agreement, Art 17(5) (6 June 2003) available at <http://www.ustr.gov/Trade_Agreements/Bilateral/Chile_FTA/Section_Index.html>; FM Abbott, 'The Cycle of Action and Reaction: Developments and Trends in Intellectual Property and Health' in Roffe, Tansey and Vivas-Eugui (eds), *Negotiating Health*, note 50 above, 31–33 (describing various restrictions in regulatory flexibility resulting from free trade agreements negotiated by the US).

212 FM Abbott, 'Intellectual Property Provisions of Bilateral and Regional Trade Agreements in Light of US Federal Law' (2006) UNCTAD–ICTSD Project on IPRs and Sustainable Development, 1, 9, 11 (describing several examples of US-Plus standards adopted by other countries because the scope of exceptions to the US standard allowed by the bilateral agreement is narrower than would be available under US law).

> as more states enter into agreements with the US. If, for example, 29 states each enter into a bilateral agreement with the US that contains the same provisions on intellectual property, the MFN principle spreads those standards amongst all the states. Without MFN 435 [separate] agreements would be needed.[213]

Moreover, MFN might prevent member states from discriminating between foreign nationals with respect to exceptions and limitations to rights.[214]

The success of industrialized countries in implementing specific intellectual property strategies is not due only to their ability to shift back and forth between the WTO/trade and the WIPO framework. It also depends heavily on the insularity of these norm-setting organizations as regards foundational understandings of development and trade. Developing countries continue to articulate alternative views of development, based loosely on a development as freedom model. UN agencies other than WIPO, such as the World Health Organization, the Food and Agriculture Organization, or the UN High Commission on Human Rights, are more sympathetic to the human capabilities approach, and may view their mandates broadly as intersecting with the intellectual property norm-setting mandates of WIPO.[215] Nonetheless, these other organizations are still ancillary to the intellectual property norm-setting regime, which is currently dominated by the WTO and WIPO. Unless dominant intellectual property agencies begin to mainstream alternative views of development, developing countries will be preaching to the proverbial choir at education, health, and human rights agencies. A substantive equality principle expresses this normative goal of incorporating a development as freedom model within WIPO. It would operate within a norm-setting environment such as WIPO to include social welfare goals other than innovation.

Developing the Development Agenda at WIPO

In this context, WIPO is being asked by some member states to rethink its norm-setting mandate with respect to development. In 2004, developing country member states initiated a proposal called the 'Establishment of a Development Agenda for WIPO'.[216] Among other things, this proposal called for WIPO to implement its functions in the context of various initiatives of the United Nations of which it is an agency. The Development Agenda discussion

---

213 Drahos, 'An Alternative Framework', note 66 above, 7.

214 UNCTAD–ICTSD, Resource Book, note 43 above, 78.

215 Musungu, note 90 above; Helfer, 'Regime Shifting', note 203 above.

216 WIPO, 'Proposal by Argentina and Brazil for the Establishment of a Development Agenda for WIPO' (27 August 2004; WO/GA/31/11) [hereafter AB Proposal]; see also WIPO, 'Report on the Thirty-First (15th Extraordinary) Session' (5 October 2004; WO/GA/31/15) 33–7. This proposal was joined by 12 other member states (Bolivia, Cuba, Dominican Republic, Ecuador, Egypt, Iran, Kenya, Peru, Sierra Leone, South Africa, Tanzania and Venezuela).

has highlighted the significance of WIPO's inclusion as a member of the UN system. Because of its long and somewhat complex history—initially as BIRPI, an administrative bureau for the Paris and Berne Conventions in 1893, then as WIPO, an international intellectual property organization not affiliated with the UN, and in its current incarnation as a specialized agency of the UN as of 1974—WIPO perhaps has multiple and fractured identities.[217] On the one hand, it is an intellectual property maximalist organization, reflecting its origins as a bureau for two treaties that were drafted by and for the rights holders of industrialized countries. This history of promoting intellectual property worldwide on behalf of industrialized countries is reflected in its 1967 WIPO Convention, which states that the organization's purpose is to '*promote the protection of intellectual property throughout the world . . .*'.[218] On the other hand, since 1974, WIPO has another mandate as a UN agency. The 1974 Agreement between the United Nations and WIPO refers to the latter being 'a specialized agency [within the UN] and as being responsible for taking appropriate action in accordance with its basic instrument, treaties and agreements administered by it, *inter alia*, for promoting creative intellectual activity and for facilitating the transfer of technology related to industrial property to the developing countries in order to accelerate *economic, social and cultural development*'.[219]

The initial Development Agenda proposal reiterated the instrumental purpose of intellectual property and called for a contextualized assessment of the impact of intellectual property on development. It alluded several times to WIPO's role as a UN agency.[220] For example, it stated that

> [a]s a United Nations specialized agency, WIPO has an obligation to ensure that its technical cooperation activities are geared towards implementing all relevant UN development objectives, which are not limited to economic development alone. These activities should also be fully consistent with the requirements of UN operational activities in this field—they must be, in particular, neutral, impartial and demand-driven.[221]

---

217 Musungu and Dutfield, note 202 above, 4.

218 Convention Establishing the World Intellectual Property Organization (Stockholm, 14 July 1967) 21 UST 1749, 848 UNTS 3, Art 3 (emphasis added). General information about the Convention is available at <http://www.wipo.int/treaties/en/convention/summary_wipo_convention.html>.

219 Agreement between the United Nations and the World Intellectual Property Organization (17 December 1974) 956 UNTS 405 Art 1 (emphasis added) (available at <http://www.wipo.int/treaties/en/agreement/index.html>); J Boyle, 'A Manifesto on WIPO and the Future of Intellectual Property', (2004) *Duke L and Tech R* 9.

220 WIPO, AB Proposal, note 216 above, 2.

221 Ibid, 4.

It also referred to paragraph 19 of the WTO's Doha Ministerial Declaration, in setting the mandate for the TRIPS Council in the context of the Doha Development Agenda, which refers explicitly to the need to 'take fully into account the development dimension'.[222] Among other specific suggestions, the proposal requested that WIPO adopt a high-level declaration on intellectual property and development, and consider amending its convention to incorporate the development dimension into WIPO's objectives and functions.[223]

From the initial proposal considered by the WIPO General Assembly in the fall of 2004 through June 2007, various member states have made further formal submissions in six subsequent meetings.[224] A clash of perspectives, if not civilizations, is evident over the term 'development'. For example, the US equates development to growth, emphasizing the benefits of intellectual property and the dangers of piracy.[225] On the other hand, the Chilean proposal urged WIPO to study 'the costs [of intellectual property systems] and, in turn, the most . . . appropriate levels of protection of intellectual property rights, taking into account the degree of development and particular social and cultural situation in a country, based on the minimum standard[s] established by the Agreement on Trade-Related Aspects of Intellectual Property (TRIPS)'.[226] Gathering these multiple perspectives under one big tent at the conclusion of the February 2006 meeting of the Provisional Committee for the Development Agenda (PCDA),

---

222 Decision of the General Council, 'Implementation of Doha Paragraph Six', note 47 above.

223 WIPO, AB Proposal, note 216 above. Other specific actions proposed include safeguarding public interest flexibilities such as exceptions for the specific development needs of developing countries. It specifically recommended that the objectives and principles of TRIPS, note 6 above, Arts 7 and 8 be incorporated into WIPO's draft Substantive Patent Law Treaty (SPLT), note 206 above. It proposed that WIPO take up discussions on a draft Treaty on Access to Knowledge and Technology, to be guided by a balanced approach to intellectual property enforcement, and to promote further development-oriented technical cooperation and assistance.

224 These submissions include proposals submitted to the intersessional intergovernmental meeting (IIM) First Session (11–13 April 2005) by the so-called 'Friends of Development' (IIM/1/4), the US (IIM/1/2), Mexico (IIM/1/3) and the UK (IIM/1/5); proposals submitted to the IIM Second Session (20–22 June 2005) by Bahrain and co-sponsors (IIM/2/2), UK (IIM/2/3); a proposal submitted to the IIM Third Session (20–22 July 2005) by Morocco, on behalf of the Africa Group (IIM/3/2); proposals submitted to the Provisional Committee on the Development Agenda (PCDA) First Session (20–24 February 2006) by Chile (PCDA/1/2), Colombia (PCDA/1/3), US (PCDA/1/4), Argentina and others (PCDA/1/5); and proposals submitted to the PCDA Second Session (26–30 June 2006) by Argentina and others (PCDA/2/2) and the Kyrgyz Republic (PCDA/2/3).

225 WIPO, 'Proposal by the United States of America to Establish a Partnership Program in WIPO: An Elaboration of Issues Raised in Document IIM/I/2' (17 February 2006; PCDA/1/4).

226 WIPO, Proposal by Chile (12 January 2006; PCDA/1/2).

the WIPO Secretariat organized the separate proposals (over a hundred) into six clusters.[227] These included:

(a) technical assistance and capacity building;
(b) norm setting, flexibilities, public policy and public domain;
(c) technology transfer, information and communication technology (ICT), and access to knowledge;
(d) assessments, evaluation and impact studies;
(e) institutional matters including mandate and governance; and
(f) other issues.

At the second meeting of the PCDA in June 2006, member states reached an *impasse* with regard to how to proceed on discussing these proposals. The PCDA Chair circulated a draft proposal to the General Assembly, including an annex of items around which 'emerging consensus' was discerned 'without prejudice to any proposals submitted during the IIM/PCDA process'.[228] In his remarks, he suggested that any remaining proposals would be considered later during the process, although not discussed during the present meeting.[229] It is significant, however, that over 70 specific proposals were omitted from the Chair's draft proposal to the General Assembly. About half of the proposals in Clusters A and E, and a majority of proposals in the other Clusters, apparently did not reflect 'consensus'. Many of the proposals that did not make it into the 'Chair's cut' were proposals originally advanced by the group of developing countries that had initiated the Development Agenda discussion. Not surprisingly, these were the proposals that most directly challenged WIPO's existing development model. For example, the original call '[t]o amend [the] WIPO Convention, bringing it in line with WIPO's mandate as a UN-specialized agency' was left out.

The June 2006 PCDA meeting essentially ended with the delegates from Argentina and Brazil (two of the co-sponsors of the original Development Agenda proposal) insisting that each item be discussed on its merits, and all

227 WIPO, 'Report of the First Session of the Provisional Committee on Proposals Related to a WIPO Development Agenda' (20–24 February 2006; PCDA/1/6 Prov 2, including an Annex containing all the proposals).

228 WIPO, untitled document circulated as draft proposal of the Chair of the Provisional Committee on Proposals Related to a WIPO Development Agenda document (26–30 June 2006; on file with author). At the very end of the second PCDA meeting, it was submitted by the Kyrgyz Republic as a document entitled 'Proposal on Recommendation to the General Assembly of WIPO' and resubmitted to the General Assembly in the fall of 2006 in that form (PCDA/2/3).

229 WIPO, 'Report, First Session, on Development Agenda Proposals', note 227 above, 37.

proposals be discussed as a package. They refused to proceed according to the Chair's proposed consensus approach.[230]

> Nonetheless, at the fall 2006 WIPO General Assembly meeting, member states decided to renew the PCDA's mandate for another year. The committee will hold two 5-day sessions to discuss the 111 proposals made thus far on the development agenda. The first will examine the 40 proposals identified by [PCDA Chair] Gauto Vielman's controversial June proposal as enjoying more widespread support; the second will focus on the remaining 71 proposals. WIPO members directed the PCDA to streamline proposals to avoid duplication, and to separate proposals that require action from those that outline general principles. They also empowered the chair of the PCDA to work with member governments, rather than the WIPO Secretariat, to prepare the initial working documents of the committee.[231]

As this book was going to press, the third session of the PCDA, held from 19 to 23 February 2007, has just concluded. This meeting yielded much more concrete agreement and consensus with respect to development goals important to developing countries.[232]

Throughout the procedural manoeuvring over the last three years, which is a proxy for deep disagreement over substantive development approaches, some consensus over the Development Agenda is beginning to emerge. As one WIPO official stated at the conclusion of the second PCDA meeting, 'everyone agrees that there should be a Development Agenda'.[233] This represents a major movement from positions staked out by various member states at the beginning of the process in September 2004. Moreover, even the member states who vehemently objected to the tailoring of proposals at the second PCDA meeting agreed that the overall process should continue in some form.[234] Finally, in the 2006 General Assembly meeting, WIPO endorsed the examination of all 111 proposals, rather than leaving the majority of them in hiatus.

---

230 WIPO, 'Report of the Provisional Committee on Proposals Related to a WIPO Development Agenda' (PCDA) (22 September 2006; WO/GA/33/2 Rev) 2.

231 'WIPO General Assembly Finds Way Forward on Broadcast Treaty, Development Agenda' (4 October 2006) 10(32) *Bridges*, available at <http://www.ictsd.org/weekly/06-10-04/index.htm>).

232 Provisional Committee on Proposals Related to a Development Agenda (PCDA) Third Session, Summary of Chair, available at <http://www.wipo.int/edocs/prdocs/en/2007/wipo_pr_2007_478.html#pcda>.

233 Remarks of P Rai, Acting Director, Intellectual Property and Economic Development Division, WIPO to author (7 July 2006).

234 WIPO, 'Report, First Session, on Development Agenda Proposals', note 227 above, P 54 (Statement of Argentina) ('[i]t supported the Delegation of Brazil and also wished to add that it was indeed interested and keen in the process continuing. It had started a process, which it hoped would remain on the table, until solutions were found, in an inclusive, democratic and transparent manner').

The Agenda of Development as Growth

The Development Agenda debate so far points to the constraints upon WIPO to reflect upon its own changing identity and role *vis-à-vis* development. This is due in part to its historical 'embeddedness' within a development as growth model, and in part to disagreement among member states about what development should mean. The importance of development as a general concept is quite evident at WIPO through the increasing prominence of 'developmentspeak' on its website[235] and by its officials.[236] Many within WIPO believe that the organization is already pursuing the goal of implementing intellectual property in the service of development. However, when the WIPO Secretariat refers to its role in enhancing development, it refers solely to a particular kind of development. This is absolutely clear in the official literature of the organization, where the benefits of intellectual property, especially for the poorest countries, are overstated and the costs minimized.[237] The absence of any perspective of development as freedom comes through most sharply in WIPO's discussion of its development role *vis-à-vis* education. The lament is about the lack of education around intellectual property rather than the lack of access to basic education.[238]

The primary way WIPO currently defines development is to strengthen intellectual property legal infrastructure, offices, capacity building, and human resources to enhance the promotion of intellectual property and economic growth.[239] Its agreement with the WTO reinforces this view of development as being directed towards an improved understanding of intellectual property and greater participation in the global intellectual property system. More recently, its aim is to help build strategic partnerships between businesses in developing and industrialized countries, focusing in part on small and medium enterprises. These efforts are development-friendly but within a particular model of development as growth.

WIPO's development stance is also apparent in the kinds of member-state proposal that WIPO chooses to prioritize in its standing committees. For example, since 1998 and especially in its recent sessions, the Standing Committee on Copyright and Related Rights (SCCR) has focused energy on the protection

235 WIPO, 'Intellectual Property for Development', available at <http://www.wipo.int/ip-development/en/>.

236 K Idris and H Arai, *The Intellectual Property-Conscious Nation: Mapping the Path from Developing to Developed* (World Intellectual Property Association, 2006).

237 K Idris, *Intellectual Property: A Power Tool for Economic Growth* (2003), 44–46.

238 Idris and Arai, note 236 above, 56–57.

239 Idris, note 237 above, 20–29.

of broadcasting organizations.[240] This is viewed as a natural extension of the digital agenda, which began in 1996 with the negotiations over the WIPO Copyright and Performances and Phonograms Treaties. On the other hand, a Chilean proposal to study international minimum exceptions and limitations, proposed to the SCCR's 12th session and discussed at some length during its 13th session, has languished.[241]

A Substantive Equality Principle in the Development Agenda and Other Norm-setting Activities

A substantive equality principle, if implemented within this norm-setting context, would make a difference in the way the WIPO Secretariat exercises its considerable discretion to prioritize and implement its member-driven activities. It would cause the various decision-making processes within the institution to embrace the consideration of various social welfare goals in addition to innovation.

At the end of the PCDA's February 2007 meeting, member states agreed to bring the following two Cluster B items to the General Assembly for approval:

> 10. Norm-setting activities shall:
>
> be inclusive and member driven;
> take into account different levels of development;
> take into consideration a balance between costs and benefits;
> be a participatory process, which takes into consideration the interests and priorities of all WIPO Member States and the viewpoints of other stakeholders, including accredited inter-governmental organizations and non-governmental organizations; and
> be in line with the principle of neutrality of the WIPO Secretariat.
>
> 11. Consider the preservation of the public domain within WIPO's normative processes and deepen the analysis of the implications and benefits of a rich and accessible public domain.[242]

If eventually WIPO were to adopt this particular approach into its norm-setting activities (either by implementing this proposal or otherwise), it might prioritize the Chilean proposal within the SCCR. In addition to the general

240 WIPO 'Revised Draft Proposal, Broadcasting Organizations', note 184 above. At the fall 2006 General Assembly meeting, the GA rejected the Copyright Committee's proposal to send the treaty straight to a conference to be finalized. Instead, the GA said the proposal must be approved by two more meetings before it can be the subject of an approving diplomatic conference. WIPO, 'Protection of Broadcasting Organizations' (22 September 2006; WO/GA/33/4).

241 WIPO, 'Proposal by Chile, Exceptions and Limitations', note 183 above; WIPO, 'Proposal by Chile, Exceptions and Limitations to Copyright', note 183 above.

242 Chair's Summary, note 232 above.

study WIPO already commissioned on exceptions and limitations in the digital environment,[243] it would further investigate the use of flexibilities specifically in the area of development for basic education in developing countries. Combined with a substantive equality approach, WIPO would focus on intellectual property rights and exceptions as policy tools for enhancing access to basic education, and advanced research for developing countries—perhaps even suggesting users' rights or substantive maxima that might override national standards. As outlined earlier, this is necessary because of the rigidity imposed by the various three-step tests within Berne, TRIPS and the WCT. And as illustrated by the earlier analysis, the full range of creative possibilities in this area has not been addressed in WIPO's mainstream development and/or technical assistance efforts. Instead, intellectual property norm-setting suggestions that explore the maximum extent of flexibilities for purposes of educational development are currently relegated to academics, NGOs or self-help efforts on the part of developing countries.

As a corollary to norm setting, a substantive equality principle would cause WIPO to explore the reasons why the Berne Appendix has been under-utilized. In the different context of newly-minted compulsory licensing provisions pursuant to proposed Article 31*bis*, several commentators have suggested that WIPO should play a proactive role in ensuring that developing member states understand and take advantage of these provisions.[244] Compulsory licensing frameworks presuppose a relatively well-developed domestic intellectual property capacity and infrastructure. As anyone who has been involved in negotiating voluntary licences within the US knows, any transaction involves costs. When cross-border transactions are involved, another whole layer of complexity must be mediated. WIPO would seem to be the most obvious institutional player to facilitate these global and hybrid public–private transactions. This might mean implementing technical assistance to enhance domestic capacity, whether in the form of drafting model legislation, or coordinating information related to private publishers whose works are the subject of the licences.[245]

WIPO's role so far with respect to the Berne Appendix, however, has been very much a passive caretaking one, which has led virtually all commentators to find the Appendix to be of little use in remedying the global inequality in access to educational content. Indeed, 35 years ago, an early commentator on the 1967 Stockholm Revision Conference suggested various proactive methods for

243 WIPO, 'Study on Limitations and Exceptions', note 164 above.

244 Matthews, note 50 above, 130; Oh, note 76 above.

245 Indeed, the World Bank has drafted six model documents for assisting countries to implement the 8 December 2005 decision of the WTO General Council on Article 31*bis*. Matthews, note 50 above, 130.

fostering access to educational materials on the part of developing countries.[246] However, WIPO has since engaged in formally equal norm setting and technical assistance.[247] A substantive equality principle, if implemented within WIPO, would result in a different approach.

Conclusion: Matching Development Reality to Rhetoric

Neither the WTO nor WIPO have had core institutional identities as development agencies. Yet they have been embedded within a particular and powerful paradigm of development as growth. Now, increasingly urgent claims are pressed upon the international intellectual property framework to recognize concerns within the model of development as freedom. When 'development' is placed on the agenda, however, it is often used to signify very different approaches to intellectual property. The linkage to trade has exacerbated this tendency, and caused the innovation mandate of domestic intellectual property to appear somewhat quaint and even irrelevant. Moreover, the insistence on formal equality principles makes it difficult to initiate balanced development-oriented approaches, which necessitate dsitinguishing between differently-situated member states.

All this leads to a failure of institutional design, in which the functional aspects of the international intellectual property framework lag behind increasingly explicit aspirations of development voiced both within and outside the system. As recently observed,

> [p]olicy choices of international social redistribution and economic intervention, can rest only with difficulty on a legal mechanism of formal non-discrimination; quite the contrary, they necessitate degrees of 'positive discrimination' or 'affirmative action', not only between the rich and the poor, the developed and the developing, but between different sorts and categories of developing economies.[248]

Yet the rhetoric of development in international law, whether in international development law, trade law, or intellectual property law, is asynchronous with its actual implementation. This substantive equality proposal is an effort to move reality closer to rhetoric.

---

246 AH Lazar, 'Developing Countries and Authors' Rights in International Copyright' (1971) 19 *Copyright L Symp (ASCAP)* 1, 37. These include arrangements for an international copyright clearing house, facilitating co-publishing in developing countries, translation aid, development of regional cooperation, currency conversion guarantees, funds for payments of royalties, and national or regional copyright tribunals.

247 Consumers International, *Copyright and Access to Knowledge*, note 153 above (surveying recent WIPO Draft Laws for Copyright and Related Rights, and noting restrictive provisions for educational exceptions).

248 Broude, note 138 above, 257–8.

Formal equality means that the states are deemed to be equal before the law despite inequalities in actual levels of development. Substantive equality recognizes the differences between states and takes those differences in account. This principle accords more local control over innovation policies and defers to national sovereignty when global minimum standards may threaten domestic social welfare goals. It recognizes substantive differences between types of developing country on the basis of their differing developmental needs, consistent with newer models of development law. It also encourages global governance mechanisms that overtly weigh different factors to reach social welfare maximization. It is a natural outgrowth of the increasing density and recursiveness of the international intellectual property law-making framework, and the need for more inter-agency coordination on a global level. It dovetails with approaches suggested by others to restore balance in international intellectual property.[249] And finally, it accounts for an immense development divide, which can be overcome in part by the fairer distribution of knowledge goods between formally equal nation states.

249 Dinwoodie and Dreyfuss, 'Patenting Science', note 10 above, 220–21 (advocating the use of 'substantive maxima' to preserve an international public domain of knowledge); P Yu, 'TRIPS and its Discontents' (2006) 10 *Marquette IP LR* 371–79 (engaging in the 'constructive ambiguity' of TRIPS so as to maximize the possibility of a 'pro-development' presumption in norm interpretation); Gervais, 'IP, Trade and Development', note 1 above, 528–34 (suggesting that developing countries utilize the 'normative elasticity' of TRIPS to formulate policy responsive to their needs); Maskus and Reichman, 'Globalization of Private Knowledge/Privatization of Global Public Goods', note 1 above, (suggesting a moratorium on stronger intellectual property standards and an institutional infrastructure for reconciling existing standards with national systems of innovation); Okediji, 'Sustainable Access in Developing Countries', note 149 above, 181–86 (suggesting a number of proposals, including an international fair use doctrine); RC Dreyfuss, 'TRIPS-Round II: Should Users Strike Back?' (2004) 71 *U Chicago LR* 21 (calling for the articulation of a user right in the context of TRIPS).

15

EPILOGUE: A TRIPS IMPLEMENTATION TOOLBOX

Daniel J Gervais

This chapter focuses on various aspects of the implementation of the Agreement on the Trade-Related Aspects of Intellectual Property Rights (TRIPS).[1] This chapter is a 'companion' chapter to various chapters of this book, in particular Chapter 1, which deals with various levels of protection and policy equations beyond strict intellectual property norms. A more complete implementation toolset should be based on the theoretical analyses contained in the preceding chapters and the recommendations contained in the following pages. Any detailed legislative measure should also take account of commentaries on each of the TRIPS Articles.[2] Readers are strongly encouraged to read, at a minimum, Chapters 1 and 2 prior to commencing this chapter.

[1] Agreement on Trade-Related Aspects of Intellectual Property Rights, 15 April 1994, Marrakech Agreement Establishing the World Trade Organization, Annex 1C, Legal Instruments—Results of the Uruguay Round, 33 ILM 1197 (1994) [hereafter TRIPS].

[2] This chapter does *not* aim to provide a detailed implementation plan for each provision of the Agreement. See especially Daniel Gervais, *The TRIPS Agreement: Drafting History and Analysis* (2nd edn, Sweet & Maxwell, 2003); and Carlos Correa, *Trade-Related Aspects of Intellectual Property Rights: A Commentary on the TRIPS Agreement* (Oxford University Press, 2007).

Part I Purpose of This Chapter

The proposed recommendations in this chapter are obviously not an exhaustive list. Rather they are a starting point for a national TRIPS implementation strategy and should be adapted to the priorities and goals set by individual countries. Each country has unique characteristics, whether economic, cultural, or both, and the variable geometry of national implementations is, or should be, a reflection of this reality. The following recommendations are based on the author's work on the TRIPS Agreement and experience gained in the training of, and work done with, officials of more than 40 developing countries to design or improve TRIPS implementations. This chapter offers a guide and a starting point to some of the common questions and issues that have arisen during training or implementation of TRIPS.

The history and difficulties associated with the negotiation of the TRIPS Agreement have led many commentators to subscribe to subtraction narratives, suggesting that emerging and developing countries should limit the impact of TRIPS as much as possible by using all available flexibilities.[3]

This chapter, however, takes a somewhat different view. It reflects the analysis in Chapter 1 that, summarized, is as follows: after the initial phase of negotiation based on 'addition narratives' (according to which higher levels of intellectual property were thought to be beneficial both for IPR holders in industrialized nations and for developing nations), and a second phase based on 'subtraction narratives' (suggesting, as just noted, that TRIPS was essentially negative for the developing world and should be 'fought'),[4] we have now entered a third phase,

[3] For example, the South Bulletin, a publication of the South Centre, an intergovernmental organization for developing countries, suggests that developing countries can impose stringent rules on patent disclosure (i.e. disclosure of the intervention which is sufficiently clear and comprehensive for a skilled person in the related activity to reproduce the inventive step), and subsequently grant narrow patents (i.e. patents that protect a very limited range of variations and thus offer no—or little—protection for variations that are not explicitly claimed); or that they can liberally grant improvement patents to local actors and protect their 'minor' innovations, which often refer to incremental innovations which build on more fundamental discoveries, and are thus crucial for tailoring imported technologies to local conditions. Such flexibilities allow local actors to 'invent around' patents without governments risking litigation for infringement. Another example mentioned is the flexible use of compulsory licences that allow a government to authorize itself or third parties to use a patent without the permission of the patent holder. 'Agreements that Curtail Policy Space' South Bulletin 130—September 2006 TRIPS, 410. Maximum use of flexibilities is also the general thrust of several parts of a recent TRIPS Commentary published by UNCTAD–ICTSD. See UNCTAD–ICTSD, *Resource Book on TRIPS and Development* (UNCTAD–ICTSD, 2005).

[4] However, by allowing extremes to be explored, phases one and two were necessary precursors to the current phase.

based on 'calibration narratives', according to which: (a) IPR are not good or bad *per se*; (b) they will work in developing nations above a certain threshold of development to attract foreign investment, foster innovation and growth; but (c) implementation of TRIPS-compatible IPRs and innovation policies requires myriad policy developments and regulatory efforts, and will entail welfare costs which WTO members should aim to minimize.[5]

Against this backdrop, this chapter suggests that developing and emerging economies should (a) know what the available flexibilities are and (b) use them to the extent necessary to enhance domestic innovation and related industrial activities, as well as to preserve their information and biological resources, while minimizing or compensating for welfare costs. For example, India probably should not make use of TRIPS normative flexibility in the same way for copyright and patents, considering its huge film industry but fledgling (by international standards) research-based pharmaceutical industry. A second example for the same country is the novelty and non-obviousness/inventiveness thresholds. If India were to opt for high thresholds (and potentially higher thresholds specific to pharmaceuticals), thereby denying patent protection to certain less innovative products, it might not be able to issue patents on pharmaceuticals derived from traditional medicinal knowledge held in India (e.g. Ayurvedic medicine). The same could be said of traditional medicinal knowledge in other parts of the world. This simply shows that intellectual property and innovation policies are not a simple calculus,[6] and that neither the simplistic addition, nor the subtraction narratives are very useful as guides to optimal policy formulations.

This chapter and Chapter 1 taken together suggest that the TRIPS implementation must form part of a broader policy analysis and strategy informed by priority-setting, innovation incentives, FDI development, and a strong focus on education. Countries should aim to build on, and develop, existing strengths and thus become innovation players on the global stage. At the same time, one

[5] This move, from mere criticism to a more constructive approach, was evident at the third meeting of the Provisional Committee on Proposals Related to a WIPO Development Agenda (PCDA—Geneva, 19–23 February 2007). Several proposals (e.g. Proposal 6 of Cluster A) focus on helping developing countries craft national innovation strategies. See <http://www.wipo.int/meetings/fr/details.jsp?meeting_id=11926>.

[6] As Professor Yoshiyuki Tamura noted, at a symposium on the Pros and Cons of Strong Intellectual Property Protection held in December 2006 at Waseda University, the significance of the patent system relies on promotion of innovation and early publication of innovation, avoidance of overlapping investment by prompt patent prosecution, and an incentive to commercialize an invention by prompt patent prosecution. He pointed out all of these factors are linked to efficiency (as measures against underlying policy objectives). For example, issues such as patentable subject matter, sufficiency of patentability, or the scope of protection, should be determined in the context of efficiency. Available at <http://www.21coe-win-cls.org/rclip/newsletter/e_200702.pdf>.

must also recognize that innovation builds on innovation ('standing on the shoulders of giants')[7] and that patents require worldwide novelty and thus knowledge of the global state of the art in any given field. This is often a big step up for newcomers at the innovation fair. Yet simple ideas often spawn large commercial successes, and global innovation may also be adapted to suit local interests and priorities; and any such improvement on an existing product or process is itself liable to be protected by an intellectual property right.

Against this backdrop, how should individual countries approach their implementation of TRIPS? Many, in fact most, developing countries have already formally implemented TRIPS.[8] Their focus should now be to develop and implement a full innovation policy (as discussed in Chapter 1). In doing so, they should revise their TRIPS implementation as needed. Innovation policy making is an ongoing process. Such revisions may also be necessary for those countries that have agreed to adopt TRIPS-Plus norms in bilateral instruments, since one of the principal effects of the bilateral instruments, especially those signed with the United States government in recent years, has been precisely to curtail the TRIPS 'policy space'.[9] For example, a Memorandum attached to the US–Jordan bilateral ('free') trade agreement[10] states that 'Jordan shall take all steps necessary to ensure that where "use" is defined in certain measures as importation in "large quantities at reasonable prices", such conditions on importation shall be deleted' and further 'Jordan shall take all steps necessary to clarify that the exclusion from patent protection of "mathematical methods" in Article 4(B) of Jordan's Patent Law does not include such "methods" as business methods or computer-related inventions'.

At other times, bilateral agreements restate TRIPS norms but often with a variance. One wonders whether such was intended. It can certainly be argued that the variance in language indicates the negotiators' (or the demanders') perception of how TRIPS should be interpreted. For example, Article 14 of the US–Bahrain FTA provides that '[e]ach Party shall provide that *authors, performers,*

---

7 A phrase frequently but perhaps erroneously attributed to Sir Isaac Newton. See JK Merton, *On the Shoulder of Giants: The Post-Italianate Edition* (Univ Chicago Press, 1993).

8 Developing countries had until 2000 to implement TRIPS (with a possible extension until January 2005 on pharmaceutical patents for those countries—such as India—that did not previously provide such protection). Least-developed countries have now been given an extension until 2013 (under TRIPS (note 1 above) Art 66(1)). See the Decision of the Council for TRIPS of 29 November 2005.

9 See Chapter 4 above (Professor Kamperman Sanders).

10 'Memorandum of Understanding on Issues related to the Protection of Intellectual Property Rights under the Agreement between the United States and Jordan on the Establishment of a Free Trade Area'. See <http://www.ustr.gov/assets/Trade_Agreements/Bilateral/Jordan/Annexes/asset_upload_file120_8462.pdf>.

and producers of phonograms have the *right to authorize or prohibit* all reproductions of their works, performances, and phonograms, *in any manner or form, permanent or temporary*'[11] whereas TRIPS Article 14 provides that '[i]n respect of a fixation of their performance *on a phonogram, performers* shall have the *possibility of preventing* the following acts *when undertaken without their authorization*: the fixation of their unfixed performance and the reproduction of such fixation'; and that *'[p]roducers* of phonograms shall enjoy the right to authorize or prohibit the *direct or indirect* reproduction of their phonograms'. TRIPS also incorporates the right of reproduction of authors contained in Article 9(1) of the Berne Convention.[12] The scope of the FTA provision is interesting because, unlike TRIPS, it melds the three categories of rights holders, thus jettisoning the traditional distinction between authors, on the one hand, and holders of 'neighbouring' or 'related' rights on the other. But more importantly, it provides performers with a much broader right, which is not limited to performances fixed on phonograms. The right is an exclusive one (right to authorize or prohibit) and applies to reproductions 'in any manner or form, permanent or temporary', an expression whose meaning is arguably broader than 'direct or indirect', and certainly less open to diverging interpretations.

A number of FTAs try to influence the future of IP normatively at the international level.[13] They mandate increased IP protection and enforcement, and include stringent limits on the scope of extant exceptions in TRIPS and other multilateral instruments. As a result, countries negotiating FTAs, or bilateral investment treaties containing intellectual property norms, should carefully consider the purpose and effects of each departure from the language of the TRIPS Agreement. Countries that have signed such Agreements must naturally consider the impact of the FTAs when implementing TRIPS or revisions to any such implementations.

We now turn to specific implementation initiatives that could be considered to enhance the chances that TRIPS implementation will generate positive outcomes. The implementation initiatives are presented with respect to each specie of the intellectual property rights.

[11] See: <http://www.ustr.gov/Trade_Agreements/Bilateral/Bahrain_FTA/Section_Index.html> (emphasis added).

[12] Berne Convention for the Protection of Literary and Artistic Works, 9 September 1886, 25 UST 1341, 828 UNTS 221 (emphasis added).

[13] See Chapter 4 above (Professor Kamperman Sanders).

Part II Specific Implementation Tools

A. Copyright

The TRIPS Agreement incorporates the economic rights set forth in the Berne Convention.[14] It adds an obligation to protect computer programs, in source or object code, and compilations. In the latter case, this is only the extrinsic protection under copyright law of the selection or arrangement of the contents (i.e. databases and other compilations that are 'original' from a copyright standpoint). This does not include protection of databases under a *sui generis* regime, like the one in place in the European Union.[15] Because of the uncertain positive effects of the *sui generis* right where such a regime is in place, it may not be necessary to consider such a right at this stage.[16] In order to implement copyright optimally WTO members could provide guidance on some of the definitional *lacunæ* of the TRIPS Agreement. For instance, to limit uncertainty, either under national law or in accompanying publications, the government may provide guidance as to the scope of protection by defining the central concept of originality. Under most copyright regimes, once a literary or artistic creation is deemed original it is protected without formalities.[17] However, the central concept of originality is not explicitly defined in either the Berne Convention or the TRIPS Agreement. National courts asked to apply copyright norms may initially find this normative fuzziness somewhat puzzling, as would potential users or creators of copyright works. A definition based on implicit international standards could thus form part of the domestic implementation or revision of a country's copyright law. The emerging international definition is based on the existence of creative choices made by the author, that is, choices in the creation process that were dictated neither by the function (if any) of the work (in the case of functional

---

[14] An expression which excludes the 'moral right' contained, in particular, in Art 6*bis*(1) of the Berne Convention, note 12 above.

[15] Directive on the Legal Protection of Databases, Council Directive 96/9, 1996 OJ (L 77) 20 (EC). See also Commission of the European Communities, 'First Evaluation of Directive 96/9/EC on the Legal Protection of Databases', COM (2005) (12 December 2005).

[16] See Daniel Gervais, 'The Protection of Databases' (2007) *Chi–Kent LR*; and J Lipton, 'Balancing Private Rights and Public Policies: Reconceptualizing Property in Databases' (2003) 18 *Berkeley Tech LJ* 773.

[17] The Berne Convention, note 12 above, prohibits mandatory formalities as a condition for the existence or exercise of copyright protection. See Daniel Gervais, 'The Purpose of Copyright Law in Canada' (2005) 2 *Univ Ottawa L & Tech J* 315, available at <http://www.uoltj.ca/articles/vol2.2/2005.2.2.uoltj.Gervais.315–356.pdf>, 347–353; and S Ricketson and Jane C Ginsburg, *International Copyright and Neighbouring Rights: The Berne Convention and Beyond* (Oxford University Press, 2006).

objects such as a chair or a computer program), nor industry standards, nor the tools used to create the work.[18] In its simplest expression, a court, having to determine whether a creation is protected by copyright law, would have to decide whether two different authors in similar circumstances would have produced the same or a very similar work, in which case the presumption is that the creation is not original, owing to the absence of a creative space.

If providing guidance on originality is theoretically important, because it is the most fundamental notion in copyright law, there are relatively few practical cases where originality is in doubt. There are, however, at least four other aspects which should be considered when implementing or revising national copyright norms to comply with TRIPS: public lending right, effective collective management system, exceptions in the TRIPS Agreement, and post-TRIPS development.

First, while TRIPS adds to the Berne obligations a right to prohibit rental of computer programs, sound recordings, and (though only if certain conditions are present) audiovisual works (typically VHS tapes or DVDs), it does not expressly prohibit public lending by libraries. In allowing public lending, certain WTO members have opted to provide compensation for the loss of revenue by domestic authors and publishers.[19]

Second, and this may be one of the most important steps in ensuring that copyright works, WTO members should ensure that a functional collective management system is present. Under a collective management regime, rights holders pool their rights, thus allowing users to obtain a license to use an entire repertory of works. The best example is the licensing of music to radio and television broadcasters, but other common examples include reprography (photocopying and certain digital uses) and the cable retransmission of films, and reproduction of works of art and photography.[20] Several models of collective management system already exist, but in most cases the creation of new collectives will require governmental support, though support may be obtained from international NGOs such as the International Confederation of Societies of Authors and Composers (CISAC)[21] and the International Federation of Reprographic and Rights Organizations (IFRRO),[22] and from intergovernmental

18 See Daniel Gervais, 'Feist Goes Global: A Comparative Analysis of the Notion of Originality in Copyright Law' (2002) 49:4 *J of the Copyright Soc of the USA* 949.

19 For example, Canada has such a system. See the Public Lending Rights Commission at <http://www.plr-dpp.ca/>. As noted on the website, 'the Public Lending Right (PLR) Commission distributes annual payments to Canadian authors for the presence of their books in Canadian public libraries'.

20 See Daniel Gervais (ed), *Collective Management of Copyright and Related Rights* (Kluwer, 2006) and <http://www.collectivemanagement.net>.

21 See <http://www.cisac.org>.

22 See <http://www.ifrro.org>.

organizations, in particular the World Intellectual Property Organization (WIPO). Steps may be taken to accelerate the process by which a collective acquires the authority to license, where this is necessary.[23] One solution, which a number of WTO members might consider, is the extended repertoire (ER), a system which has been in use for decades in several countries.[24] Under the ER system, once a collective management organization has obtained a substantial number of mandates from domestic rights holders, it may apply to extend its repertory to include all remaining rights holders (domestic and foreign) except those that do not want to be part of the system. The initial 'opt in' system effectively becomes an 'opt out' regime once the tipping-point of substantiality has been reached.[25] In administering an ER regime or, indeed, the entire collective management infrastructure, WTO members should ensure that proper supervision is in place. An independent (expert) administrative unit with adjudicatory powers is one of the most viable options in that regard.

Collective management is also useful in creating a sound basis to manage internet-based uses. In practice it has proven difficult, and not optimally lucrative, to prevent use of copyright material by internet users. A better option, above certain income levels and minimal thresholds of internet penetration, though one which took too long to emerge, is allowing use of a repertory of works by users who pay to be part of a network or class of users.[26] The best way to implement such a system at this juncture is to use a collective management system.[27]

A third element to consider is the extent of exceptions, including those for education and research. Any exception to copyright must comply with the three-step test, a Berne Convention requirement (Article 9(2) of the Berne Convention) incorporated in Article 13 of the TRIPS Agreement.[28] The test requires that the exceptions to copyright rights must be limited in scope, and should not

---

[23] In cases where compulsory licensing is permitted under international standards and in use, such as cable retransmission or reproduction of sound recordings, a collective mechanism is required to receive the remuneration, but the right to collect may be given directly by law or regulation, i.e. on a involuntary basis. A purely voluntary system (the default rule under copyright treaties and TRIPS) remains possible.

[24] See T Koskinen-Olsson, 'Collective Management in the Nordic Countries' in Gervais, *Collective Management*, note 20 above, 257.

[25] See Daniel Gervais, 'The Changing Role of Copyright Collectives' in ibid.

[26] See Daniel Gervais, 'The Price of Social Norms: Towards a Liability Regime for File-Sharing' (2004) 12:1 *J of Intell Prop L* 39; and WW Fischer, III, *Promises to Keep: Technology, Law and the Future of Entertainment* (Stanford University Press, 2004).

[27] See Gervais, 'The Changing Role of Copyright Collectives', note 25 above, 28.

[28] See M Ficsor, 'How Much of What? The Three-Step Test and Its Application in Two Recent WTO Dispute Settlement Cases' (2002) 192 *Revue Int du Droit d'Auteur* 111, 231–242; Daniel Gervais, 'The Reverse Three-Step Test: Towards a New Core International Norm' (2004) 9 *Marq IP LR* 1, 13–21; M Senftleben, *Copyright, Limitations and the Three-Step Test* (Kluwer, 2004), 226–227.

substantially deprive rights holders of revenues they could legitimately expect as a result of normal commercial exploitation of the work. For example, limited exceptions may thus be made for education (including a limited exception for spontaneous photocopying, though this may also be covered under a general collective management regime), research, criticism, parody and other transformative uses, and some types of private consumption, provided that such exceptions do not interfere significantly with normal commercial exploitation of the work. An educational exception might carve out materials designed specifically for the educational market, otherwise the exception might deprive the author and other rights holders of one of their main sources of income.

Because it may not be easy to formulate an adequate exhaustive list of exceptions, exceptions may instead be formulated as an open-ended set of criteria to be applied by courts.[29] This should eventually generate a body of case law, but by not providing sufficient guidance to courts the boat of copyright equilibrium may be led onto policy shoals. Interestingly, a reverse approach was followed in the United States, where uses which had been allowed by courts were codified as 'fair use' in the Copyright Act of the United States in 1976 as a set of four criteria, namely:

(1) the purpose and character of the use, including whether such use is of a commercial nature or is for non-profit educational purposes;
(2) the nature of the copyrighted work;
(3) the amount and substantiality of the portion used in relation to the copyrighted work as a whole; and
(4) the effect of the use upon the potential market for or value of the copyrighted work.[30]

This approach has the advantage of flexibility but the disadvantage of uncertainty, especially because the fair use exception is an affirmative defence.[31] Another approach is to provide a set of specific exceptions expressed as a combination of

29 The recent debates on the revision of the European Directive 2001/29/EC of the European Parliament and the Council of 22 May 2001 on the harmonization of certain aspects of copyright and related rights in the information society (OJ (L 167) 10) are a case in point. See the Report prepared under the direction of the University of Amsterdam's Institute for Information Law, available at <http://www.ivir.nl/publications/guibault/Infosoc_report_2007.pdf>.

30 17 USC 107.

31 See *Campbell v Acuff-Rose Music*, 510 US 569, 591–2 (US SC, 1994). This explains why (legally, not necessarily in keeping with long-standing equilibriums) the Digital Millennium Copyright Act of 1998, which, in implementing the WIPO Copyright Treaties of December 1996, basically prohibits tampering with or circumventing technological protection measures (including most forms of Digital Rights Management or DRM), did not *have to* allow circumvention for fair use. At the time of this writing, a Bill entitled the Freedom and Innovation Revitalizing US Entrepreneurship Act of 2007 (FAIR USE Act) of 2007 had been introduced in the US Congress which would allow circumvention to perform a fair use of works 'of substantial public interest', as well as acts (arguably fair uses) performed for certain specific purposes (e.g. education).

allowed purposes (non-profit education, criticism, etc). This is the preferred approach in civil (also known as 'Roman' or 'Continental') legal systems. In the legal systems of several Commonwealth members, there is an exigency under the 'fair dealing' regime that the use (reproduction, communication to the public, etc) covered by the exception be limited to the extent required to achieve the purpose. This approach provides greater certainty but may require further legislative intervention to adjust existing exceptions, or create new ones, to reflect changing technological and market conditions.

In formulating exceptions, it may be useful to distinguish transformative uses or other re-uses of material that serve a public interest purpose (such as criticism) from uses for private consumption or the creation of pure derivatives such as translations and adaptations. In other words, the test for copyright exceptions is perhaps better formulated, not in terms of whether the use of the original material is commercial in nature, but rather on whether the use is transformative and unlikely to be voluntarily licensed, and the existence of an exception serves a clear public interest purpose. One way to express this is in allowing uses that do not merely supersede the objects of the original work, but add something new, with a further purpose or different character, altering the first with new expression, meaning, or message.[32]

WTO members may also consider expanding collective licensing. If the educational community in a WTO member (public education generally forms part of state institutions) and copyright holders represented by a collective could not agree, a neutral governmental body, such as a copyright tribunal or board, could be called upon to impose a tariff, thereby allowing the uses required for education while ensuring proper compensation for copyright holders.[33] This is often the most expeditious way out of the copyright licensing labyrinth, and proper and adequate administrative or quasi-judicial supervision ensures that all interests

The enumerative approach chosen in the list of acceptable uses seems closer to the Commonwealth or indeed the Continental systems.

[32] This formulation paraphrases the decision by the US Supreme Court in *Campbell v Acuff–Rose, ibid*, 579.

[33] Such an agreement was reached, e.g. in the United States, where guidelines were agreed upon by representatives of the various stakeholders. See the 'Agreement for Guidelines for Classroom Copying in Not-For-Profit Educational Institutions' worked out between the Ad Hoc Committee of Educational Organizations on Copyright Law Revision and the authors and publishers (reprinted at HR Rep No 1476, 94th Cong, 2d Sess 68–70 (1976)); and the 'Guidelines for Educational Uses of Music' (reprinted at HR Rep No 1476, 94th Cong, 2d Sess 70–71 (1976)) negotiated by the National Music Publishers Association, Inc, the Music Teachers National Association, the Music Educators National Conference, the National Association of Schools of Music, and the abovementioned Ad Hoc Committee.

affected by licensing (authors, other rights holders, distributors, and all categories of user) may be heard, protected, and balanced.[34]

A fourth element to consider is the impact of the post-TRIPS normative framework, in particular the WIPO Copyright Treaty (WCT) [35] and the WIPO Performances and Phonograms Treaty (WPPT).[36] The two treaties, and in particular their anti-circumvention provisions,[37] are often included in recent bilateral treaties.[38] The right in question is provided to allow copyright holders to prohibit the making available and/or use of technologies created to circumvent or defeat technological protection devices (commonly referred to as Digital Rights Management or DRM systems). Such devices may be used to prevent certain uses of copyright material, whether the copying of commercial DVDs or the transfer of music files from a certain format or device to another.[39] Prohibiting circumvention when such circumvention would trigger a copyright violation is what the two treaties require.[40] However, some rights holders believe (and have attempted to convince WTO members) that it is necessary to prohibit *any* circumvention, including circumvention for purposes which would not amount to infringement of the underlying copyright right (for example, circumvention to perform a use covered by an exception, or, to take a more extreme example, circumvention of the protection of a work no longer protected by copyright such as older motion pictures). Their argument is that allowing circumvention for a permitted purpose leads to unprotected copies circulating on the internet and

[34] The Canadian Copyright Board, the operations of which are not limited to a strict adjudicatory function but also encompasses internal research and policy-related functions, is a good example. See Mario Bouchard, 'Collective Management in Commonwealth Jurisdictions: Comparing Canada with Australia', in Gervais, *Collective Management*, note 20 above, 283–310.

[35] WIPO Copyright Treaty, 36 ILM 65 (adopted by the Diplomatic Conference on 20 December 1996), available at <http://www.wipo.int/treaties/en/ip/wct/trtdocs_wo033.html>. It entered into force on 6 May 2002.

[36] WIPO Performances and Phonograms Treaty, 36 ILM 76 (also adopted by the Diplomatic Conference on 20 December 1996), available at <http://www.wipo.int/treaties/en/ip/wppt/trtdocs_wo034.html>. It entered into force on 20 May 2002.

[37] Art 11 WIPO Copyright Treaty and Art 18 WIPO Performances and Phonograms Treaty provide that Contracting Parties 'shall provide adequate legal protection and effective legal remedies against the circumvention of effective technological measures that are used by [rights holders] in connection with the exercise of their rights under this Treaty and that restrict acts, in respect of their [works, performances or phonograms] which are not authorized by [the rights holders] concerned or permitted by law'.

[38] See <http://www.tripsagreement.net>.

[39] The example of iTunes downloads being tied to Apple's iPod devices comes to mind.

[40] See note 37 above; Jane C Ginsburg, 'Legal Protection of Technological Measures Protecting Works of Authorship: International Obligations and the US Experience' (2005) 3 Columbia Law Sch *Columbia Pub L & L Theory Working Papers*, Paper 0593. Available at <http://lsr.nellco.org/columbia/pllt/papers/0593>; and Uwe Gasser, 'Legal Frameworks and Technological Protection of Digital Content: Moving Forward Towards a Best Practice Model' (2006) 17 *Fordham IP Media & Ent LJ* 39.

being used for purposes well beyond the original (intended) use; and, therefore, a protection against circumvention tied to the existence of an underlying copyright violation is not 'effective' protection as is required by Articles 11 WCT and 18 WPPT.[41] This is a careful balancing act. WTO members should carefully consider their options and ensure that legitimate protection does not unduly impede legitimate uses.

Where appropriate, developing and least-developed WTO members should acquaint themselves with the Appendix to the Berne Convention, also incorporated into TRIPS, and, when appropriate, use the exceptions provided therein. In spite of its rather complex set of requirements and conditions, the Appendix allows the issuance of compulsory licenses for the reproduction and translation of certain works (essentially books). Relatively few WTO members have made use of the Appendix.[42]

Finally, as discussed in Chapter 1, WTO members should encourage domestic creativity by providing balanced information about the copyright and its exceptions,[43] and use other non-legal means of supporting local content and encouraging local creative efforts; for example through awards and festivals,[44] offering grants and subsidies, and assisting authors, performers, and other rights holders in setting up trade associations and support groups.

B. Trademarks and Geographical Indications

The TRIPS Agreement requires that WTO members protect both trademarks on goods and service marks, and also that well-known marks be protected at a higher level.[45] As Professor Khoury demonstrates in Chapter 8, the introduction of

41 See M Ficsor, *The Law of Copyright and the Internet* (Oxford University Press, 2002), para 6.01. It is worth noting that a majority of countries that have adopted anticircumvention provisions outlaw both the act of circumvention itself and so-called 'preparatory activities', i.e. the trafficking in circumvention devices and services. This is also the approach favoured in a number of bilateral agreements. See Gasser, ibid, 51–52.

42 A Declaration to the WIPO Secretariat is required. As of January 2007, the following countries had made such a Declaration which was still in effect: Algeria, Bangladesh, Cuba, Jordan, Mongolia, Oman, the Philippines, Sudan, Sri Lanka, Syria, Thailand, and the United Arab Emirates.

43 Such as the information circulars provided by the United States Copyright Office, available at <http://www.copyright.gov/circs/>.

44 A good example is the Panafrican Film and Television Festival of Ouagadougou (FESPACO), held every other year in Burkina Faso. A significant rise in film making is visible in that country. See <http://www.fespaco.bf/index_en.html>.

45 Based on Arts 15 and 16 of TRIPS, note 1 above, a well-known mark is generally known even in markets where goods or services in association with which the mark is used are not available. Marks that are still associated in the mind of the average consumer with such mark, even when used

TRIPS-compatible trademark protection leads to the reduction of trade in counterfeit goods. However, this trade is often associated with illegal international financial flows, and generally produces little if any revenue for the state, or local employment.[46] Moreover, one cannot ignore the added danger when the goods concerned are functional things such as pharmaceutical products or automobile parts.[47] It is also true, however, that when trade in counterfeit luxury goods is stopped, the market for the genuine products may not blossom because the consumer base for both sets of products overlaps only to a small extent. This is not a reason to favour trade in counterfeit goods. That said, it leads to one of the most frequent questions that may arise in this context—the extent to which the state should devote resources to stopping trade in counterfeit goods. When dealing with 'functional goods', there is a clear public safety consideration which trumps the argument based on the text of the TRIPS Preamble, that intellectual property rights are (only) 'private rights'.[48] In other cases, WTO members with limited enforcement resources may legitimately ask for technical and other assistance from rights holder organizations, and intergovernmental organizations such as the World Customs Organization.

In formulating trademark policy and training officials and judges to implement the policies, WTO members should insist on the dual nature of trademarks and geographical indications. While one of the purposes of these is to protect the owner of the mark, and the goodwill and brand loyalty acquired after years of successful marketing of products and services, there is also a strong consumer information and protection component.

That said, there are cases where the state might need to intervene to protect the interests of local distributors. Owners of strong or desirable trademarks may impose anticompetitive conditions on distributors, manufacturers, and/or resellers. Articles 8(2) and 40 of TRIPS allow WTO members to provide remedies against such abusive practices. Whilst the Agreement provides examples of what may constitute anticompetitive measures, it does not provide details of

in association with goods and services substantially different from those in association with which the mark is used, are considered strong and are often well-known internationally.

46 In cases where domestic manufacture of counterfeit goods is a significant commercial activity, the factories may be repurposed; perhaps to produce legitimate goods of a similar nature but not bearing the infringing mark(s).

47 Daniel Gervais, 'The International Legal Framework on Border Measures in the fight against Counterfeiting and Piracy' in O Vrins and M Schneider (eds), *Enforcement of Intellectual Property Rights through Border Measures: Law and Practice in the EU* (Oxford University Press, 2006) 37.

48 Gervais, *The TRIPS Agreement*, note 2 above, 80–82.

the remedies that may be put in place.[49] Competition legislation may be required to deal with cases such as tying arrangements (being contractually obligated to purchase product B when purchasing product A), and companies buying all competitors' patents or other intellectual property to eliminate competition.[50] Experience tends to show that competition legislation may be better viewed as distinct from intellectual property, not only structurally (as a separate piece of legislation), but also in terms of its enforcement. In other words, the authorities tasked with the implementation and enforcement of intellectual property and competition legislation should ideally be distinct. Simply put, intellectual property officials and registry offices often see themselves as acting first and foremost on behalf of rights holders, and may not be the best source for competition analyses of potential abuses of intellectual property rights.

A related issue is that concerning parallel imports (also referred to as 'grey market'). Counterfeit goods are goods manufactured without the authorization of the trademark owner or one of its agents, while parallel import goods are goods manufactured in one country with such an authorization but exported to and sold in a country other than the country for which the goods were manufactured. WTO members may adopt a policy allowing parallel imports, but there are a number of important policy considerations and possible effects of doing so.[51] Parallel imports usually will be allowed to increase the price pressure on domestic goods, if the same goods are available on a different market at a lower price. However, they will reduce the profit margins of local manufacturers and distributors and, in extreme cases, may drive them out of business. In addition, the policy should apply to identical goods in order to avoid consumer confusion.

---

[49] Art 40(2) (note 1 above) provides as follows: '[n]othing in this Agreement shall prevent Members from specifying in their legislation licensing practices or conditions that may in particular cases constitute an abuse of intellectual property rights having an adverse effect on competition in the relevant market. As provided above, a Member may adopt, consistently with the other provisions of this Agreement, appropriate measures to prevent or control such practices, which may include *for example exclusive grant-back conditions, conditions preventing challenges to validity and coercive package licensing*, in the light of the relevant laws and regulations of that Member' (emphasis added).

[50] Other cases that are considered anti-competitive in certain countries include refusals to licence and generally abuse of patent rights. As suggested by Professor John Barton, developing countries should consider codes of good practices, perhaps on a regional basis and/or by sharing national experiences (as exemplified by the International Competition Network. See <http://www.internationalcompetitionnetwork.org/>).

[51] TRIPS (note 1 above) Art 6 provides that '[f]or the purposes of dispute settlement under this Agreement, subject to the provisions of Articles 3 and 4 nothing in this Agreement shall be used to address the issue of the exhaustion of intellectual property rights'. The reference to Arts 3 and 4 is to ensure that the policy is applied to both national and foreign rights holders in the same way, and that any preferential treatment accorded rights holders of another WTO member (for example under a bilateral agreement) are extended under the most-favoured-nation principle, to rights holders of all other WTO members.

Alternatively, a strict labelling policy should be in place for goods that differ, even if only slightly, from those traditionally available in the local market.

Geographical indications are similar to trademarks to the extent that they identify the source of a product, but differ to the extent that the source is not a specific provider/producer but rather providers/producers originating in the territory of a WTO member, or a region or locality in that territory, and where a given quality, reputation or other characteristic of the good is essentially attributable to this geographical origin.[52] As a result of the efforts by the European Commission during the TRIPS negotiations,[53] representing countries such as France, there is a higher level of protection for indications that apply to wines and spirits,[54] and ongoing negotiations to set up an international registry.[55] The fact that wines and spirits are protected at a higher level has been a contentious issue in the Doha Round discussions.[56] Geographical indications perform the same dual function as trademarks (protection of producers and information of consumers). WTO members may opt to protect indications which apply to goods other than wines and spirits that originate in their territory, and seek the recognition of the protection of such indications in bilateral and regional discussions. Local protection is a critical factor also under Article 24(9) of TRIPS.[57] They should also provide assistance to association of producers in adopting the necessary (internal) norms and codes of conducts to ensure that protected indications are properly understood and enforced.

As with other intellectual property rights requiring registration,[58] TRIPS implementation also requires that a professional intellectual property office be set up. It is, generally, better (and more efficient) to set up a single office to perform all

52 TRIPS, note 1 above, Art 22.

53 See Gervais, *The TRIPS Agreement*, note 2 above, 188–209.

54 Under TRIPS (note 1 above) Art 23, WTO members must provide 'legal means' for interested parties to prevent use of a geographical indication identifying wines and spirits for wines and spirits not originating in the place indicated by the geographical indication in question, even where the true origin of the goods is indicated or the geographical indication is used in translation or accompanied by expressions such as 'kind', 'type', 'style', 'imitation' or the like. Under Art 22 (which applies to all geographical indications), the use must be misleading or constitute unfair competition; a higher threshold.

55 A registration system protecting 'appellations of origins', a related but slightly different concept (see Gervais, note 2 above, 188–190), is in place. See the Lisbon Agreement for the Protection of Appellations of Origin and their International Registration (1958). As of January 2007, 26 countries had ratified the Lisbon Agreement.

56 See Gervais, ibid, 51.

57 Which provides as follows: '[t]here shall be no obligation under this Agreement to protect geographical indications which are not or cease to be protected in their country of origin, or which have fallen into disuse in that country'. TRIPS (note 1 above), Art 24(9).

58 Though in common law jurisdictions, trademark protection arises from commercial use, and registration (which may provide additional protection) is mostly seen as a confirmation of the trademark owner's 'title'.

registration functions. More technical functions (such as certain examination functions) may be developed on a regional basis and may rely in part on the work of major intellectual property offices.[59] Those offices should also provide informational tools to facilitate local innovation, in particular patent information.[60]

C. Patents and Designs

The protection of industrial designs applies to the aesthetic (not strictly functional) aspects of useful objects such as automobile parts, furniture and appliances, and clothing. The protection of 'works of applied art' under copyright law may apply in addition to design protection. In a number of countries, the overlapping protections are limited,[61] which is allowed under the Berne Convention[62] and TRIPS.[63] The protection of designs under patent law is also possible, although while TRIPS Article 25 requires designs that are new or original to be protected, patent law traditionally requires both novelty and non-obviousness (known in a number of legal systems as the 'inventive step' criterion).[64] One of the difficulties here is to articulate the proper distinction between copyright and design protection.[65] Unless a WTO member has an existing industry which requires a very high degree of protection and might benefit from formality-free copyright protection, it may be sound policy to limit copyright protection on goods that are produced in large, industrial quantities. However, an argument in favour of design protection with a low novelty/originality threshold is that this allows

59 Especially those whose status is recognized under the Patent Cooperation Treaty as international examination offices. There were 12 as of January 2007: Austria, Australia, Canada, China, European Patent Organization, Finland, Japan, Korea, Russia, Spain, Sweden and the United States PTO.

60 See Chapter 1.

61 For example under Canadian law the protection under copyright no longer applies to useful articles of which more than 50 copies are produced. See Daniel Gervais and E Judge, *Intellectual Property: The Law in Canada* (Carswell, 2005), 575–614.

62 Under Art 2(7) of the Berne Convention (note 12 above), 'it shall be a matter for legislation in the countries of the Union to determine the extent of the application of their laws to works of applied art and industrial designs and models, as well as the conditions under which such works, designs and models shall be protected.' Art 7(4) allows Berne Union members to determine the appropriate term of protection (under copyright) beyond a minimum term of 25 years from the date of the making of the work. The Berne term in most cases is life of the author plus 50 years.

63 TRIPS (note 1 above) Art 9 incorporates Arts 2 and 7 of the Berne Convention (note 12 above) into the Agreement.

64 In addition to utility or industrial applicability, which should not pose major difficulties when dealing with 'useful articles'.

65 See Jerome H Reichman, 'Design Protection and the Legislative Agenda' (1992) 55 *Law & Contemp Probs* 281, 284–290.

localized versions of foreign designs to be protected domestically even if not very different from the foreign design.

The area of patent law is more difficult. The subtraction narratives, alluded to earlier, have tended to converge on the definitional gaps in TRIPS. Indeed, whilst TRIPS defines the three patentability criteria (for the first time at the multilateral level), and establishes functional synonymy between the (essentially) North American notions of non-obviousness and utility, on the one hand, and 'inventive step' and industrial applicability, on the other, the Agreement stops short of defining such notions, an issue which has plagued the Substantive Patent Law Treaty (SPLT) discussions for the past several years.[66]

Subtraction narratives suggest that by defining novelty in very strict terms, and imposing high thresholds of utility/industrial applicability and non-obviousness/inventiveness, WTO members may be able to deny patent protection to several applicants. WTO members should consider the need for a satisfactory level of patent protection to encourage FDI, as is demonstrated in other chapters of this book. A high patentability threshold may prevent local industries from patenting innovations which are derivatives or improvements of existing technologies, including new uses of known compounds. It is suggested that a proper implementation of the TRIPS patent provisions should include internationally recognized patentability criteria (as they would be applied in international examination offices under the Patent Cooperation Treaty (PCT)). Countries rich with traditional knowledge, especially in the medicinal field, should endeavour to apply a novelty criterion that reflects this knowledge. That, however, may require some documentation of the traditional knowledge invoked to deny a claim. There are ways to limit the potentially negative effects of documentation (including (mis-)appropriation) by limiting disclosure to essential elements and to cases where disclosure is necessary.[67] It may also be preferable not to allow a grace period (between disclosure and the application), as any such disclosure may prevent patentability in countries which use the first-to-file system and generally require absolute novelty.

If following international definitional guidelines is preferable, WTO members may also choose to apply a somewhat stricter test of utility than has been applied

66 See Chapter 13 and WIPO, 'Information on Certain Recent Developments in Relation to the Draft Substantive Patent Law Treaty', document SCP/10/8.

67 See Daniel Gervais, 'Traditional Knowledge & Intellectual Property: A TRIPS-Compatible Approach' (2005) *Mich St LR* 137.

in recent years by certain national offices, where mere predictions of utility have been found to be sufficient, especially in the genetic (biotechnological) field.[68]

Exceptions to exclusive rights are also important. The WTO Dispute-Settlement Body adopted a report which recognises the TRIPS legality of an exception allowing the use of a patented invention to obtain marketing approval a few months prior to the expiry of the patent.[69] Limited exceptions for private, non-commercial use and experimental use may also be provided.

Patentability of plants and plant varieties is a controversial topic. WTO members must provide protection for plant varieties but not necessarily under patent law.[70] A *sui generis* regime is possible. There is no explicit reference in the Agreement to the UPOV system,[71] two 'versions' of which exist, namely the 1978 version and the 1991 version.[72] Concerns were expressed by several countries over the impact on biodiversity and potential conflict between TRIPS and the Convention on Biological Diversity (CBD).[73] The issues also extend to patents, and disclosure and benefit-sharing requirements that may be imposed on patent applicants claiming inventions incorporating genetic resources or traditional knowledge. A pragmatic solution might combine a reasonable level of plant variety protection combined with an appropriate degree of protection of biodiversity. It is theoretically possible but may not be easy to create a non-UPOV *sui generis* system that meets the effectiveness test of Article 27(3)(b), but in any event that may the wrong policy goal. Chapter 11 (Professor Drahos) offers several challenging thoughts for WTO members who wish to take proactive steps in this area. However, the issue is not one of incompatibility between intellectual property rights, on the one hand; and biodiversity and protection of traditional knowledge and genetic resources on the other. First, because intellectual

68 A question that has been a source of controversy in the United States (see C D Lopez-Beverage, 'Should Congress Do Something About Upstream Clogging Caused by the Deficient Utility of Expressed Sequence Tag Patents?' (2005) 10 *J Tech L & Policy* 35), especially since the case of *In re Fisher* (421 F3d 1365, 1379 (Fed Cir 2005)). See TT Williams, '*In Re Fisher*: Raising the Utility Hurdle for Express Sequence Tags' (2006) 21 *Berkeley Tech LJ* 123. Certain commentators have suggested that a separate intellectual property right should apply to Expressed Sequence Tags (ESTs), which are short DNA sequences containing the information to code (usually) a portion of a protein. See S A Jameson, 'The Problems of the Utility Analysis in *Fisher* and its Associated Policy Implications and Flaws' (2006) 56 *Duke LJ* 311.

69 See Gervais, *The TRIPS Agreement*, note 2 above, 243.

70 TRIPS (note 1 above) Art 27(3)(b).

71 The French-language acronym of the International Union for the Protection of New Varieties of Plants. See <http://www.upov.int>.

72 See document WIPO–UPOV/SYM/02/2.

73 See 'The Relationship between the Convention on Biological Diversity (CBD) and the Agreement on the Trade-related Aspects of Intellectual Property Rights (TRIPS); with a focus on Article 27.3 (b)' (11 May 2000), WTO document IP/C/W/175; and Gervais, *The TRIPS Agreement*, note 2 above, 232.

property rights are not rights to use, but rather rights to exclude others from using. Second, because full disclosure is a tenet of patent law, and of patent-like *sui generis* systems. Rather, a 'mosaic' approach to policy making in this area would grant appropriate protection but take measures to protect traditional knowledge and genetic resources from misappropriation and unwarranted commercial use. In so doing, however, WTO members should strive to preserve the incentive effect of intellectual property rights and therefore find the proper equilibrium.

Perhaps more importantly, implementing TRIPS-compatible patent protection must be accompanied by efforts to establish a patent office (regionally or nationally) that also functions as a source of information and innovation policies, especially measures aimed at growing small and medium-sized enterprises.[74]

WTO members may wish to implement two sets of provisions to accompany their patent legislation. First, they may wish to emulate most European countries, Canada and several US States and establish price controls on essential pharmaceutical products. However, the purpose should not be to defeat the patents by imposing extremely low prices, but rather to have in place a safety valve to preserve social welfare where this is required, especially in the case of patented pharmaceuticals with no alternatives in contexts where a publicly-funded healthcare system (or publicly funded 'prescription drug plan') is in place.[75] This may prevent normal market mechanisms and fully functional price discrimination from working. It has led certain countries to favour international exhaustion (parallel import) of certain pharmaceutical products. The cost of any such measures on domestic research and development should form part of the policy equation.

Second, as already mentioned, intellectual property implementation should be accompanied by appropriate, TRIPS-compatible competition legislation.

Conclusion

The implementation of the TRIPS Agreement in developing and least-developed countries must form part of a broader policy strategy—a policy matrix that is based on priority-setting, innovation incentives, FDI development, and a strong

---

[74] WIPO has a section devoted to this sector of activity. See <http://www.wipo.int/sme/en/>. See in particular the guide entitled 'Inventing the Future: An Introduction to Patents for Small and Medium-sized Enterprises' (8 July 2005), available at <http://www.wipo.int/sme/en/documents/guides/inventing_future.html>.

[75] In medical emergencies of epidemic proportions, TRIPS (note 1 above) Art 31*bis* and, until this is in force, the 2003 Decision on TRIPS and Public Health, may be used to manufacture or import products under a compulsory license regime. There has been little if any use made of this system since it was established, however.

focus on education on the one side, and the use of existing flexibilities of the TRIPS Agreement. This would help to ensure that the intellectual property rights framework is balanced according to innovation and related industrial activities, and sustainability of information and biological resources, while minimizing (or compensating for) welfare costs. The solutions suggested in this chapter are a starting point for the TRIPS implementation policy and should be used as a starting point for WTO countries in building their implementation framework.

INDEX